2004 Astrological Pocket Planner

ISBN: 0-7387-0132-7

Cover design by Gavin Dayton Duffy
Designed by Susan Van Sant
Edited by K. M. Brielmaier

A special thanks to Aina Allen for astrological proofreading.

Set in Eastern and Pacific Times. Ephemeris and aspect data generated by ACS Publications. Re-use is prohibited.

Published by
LLEWELLYN WORLDWIDE
P.O. Box 64383 Dept. 0-7387-0132-7
St. Paul, MN 55164-0383, U.S.A.

Printed in the United States of America
Typography property of Llewellyn Worldwide, Ltd.

Table of Contents

Mercury Retrograde 2004

	DATE	**ET**	PT			DATE	**ET**	PT
Mercury Retrograde	12/17/03	**11:02 am**	8:02 am	—	Mercury Direct	1/6	**8:44 am**	5:44 am
Mercury Retrograde	4/6	**4:28 pm**	1:28 pm	—	Mercury Direct	4/30	**9:05 am**	6:05 am
Mercury Retrograde	8/9	**8:32 pm**	5:32 pm	—	Mercury Direct	9/2	**9:09 am**	6:09 am
Mercury Retrograde	11/30	**7:17 am**	4:17 am	—	Mercury Direct	12/20	**1:28 am**	10:28 pm (12/19)

Moon Void-of-Course 2004

Times are listed in Eastern Time in this table only. All other information in the *Pocket Planner* is listed in both Eastern Time and Pacific Time. Refer to "Time Zone Conversions" on page 7 for changing to other time zones. Note: All times are corrected for Daylight Saving Time.

Last Aspect		Moon Enters New Sign			Last Aspect		Moon Enters New Sign			Last Aspect		Moon Enters New Sign		
Date	Time	Date	Sign	Time	Date	Time	Date	Sign	Time	Date	Time	Date	Sign	Time
JANUARY					**FEBRUARY**					**MARCH**				
12/31	9:27 pm	1	♉	12:02 am	2	7:56 am	2	♋	9:03 am	2	10:42 pm	3	♌	4:18 am
2	2:21 pm	3	♊	12:58 pm	4	12:52 pm	4	♌	7:50 pm	5	12:13 pm	5	♍	12:18 pm
5	6:14 pm	6	♋	1:38 am	6	12:38 pm	7	♍	4:03 am	7	3:49 am	7	♎	5:31 pm
7	3:00 pm	8	♌	12:38 pm	8	7:23 pm	9	♎	10:12 am	9	7:43 am	9	♏	9:03 pm
10	5:00 pm	10	♍	9:37 pm	11	12:42 am	11	♏	2:58 pm	11	11:11 pm	11	♐	11:57 pm
13	3:01 am	13	♎	4:38 am	13	8:39 am	13	♐	6:35 pm	13	4:01 pm	14	♑	2:51 am
14	11:46 pm	15	♏	9:33 am	15	3:20 pm	15	♑	9:14 pm	16	12:34 am	16	♒	6:10 am
17	6:48 am	17	♐	12:18 pm	17	12:00 am	17	♒	11:27 pm	18	7:15 am	18	♓	10:26 am
18	10:58 pm	19	♑	1:24 pm	19	12:34 pm	20	♓	2:27 am	20	3:57 pm	20	♈	4:29 pm
21	12:34 am	21	♒	2:11 pm	21	5:10 pm	22	♈	7:45 am	22	10:14 am	23	♉	1:10 am
23	4:33 am	23	♓	4:29 pm	24	1:55 pm	24	♉	4:30 pm	24	5:29 pm	25	♊	12:35 pm
25	6:09 am	25	♈	10:06 pm	25	9:55 pm	27	♊	4:22 am	27	5:44 pm	28	♋	1:23 am
27	11:59 pm	28	♉	7:46 am	29	5:08 am	29	♋	5:12 pm	30	11:00 am	30	♌	1:07 pm
29	9:04 pm	30	♊	8:18 pm										

Moon Void-of-Course 2004 (cont.)

APRIL

Last Aspect Date	Time	Moon Enters New Sign Date	Sign	Time
1	6:56 pm	1	♍	9:45 pm
3	1:23 pm	4	♎	3:52 am
5	5:26 pm	6	♏	6:24 am
7	7:06 am	8	♐	7:50 am
9	8:30 pm	10	♑	9:33 am
11	11:46 pm	12	♒	12:33 pm
14	3:27 pm	14	♓	5:24 pm
16	9:43 am	17	♈	12:24 am
19	9:21 am	19	♉	9:43 am
20	3:36 pm	21	♊	9:10 pm
23	7:22 pm	24	♋	9:56 am
26	5:56 am	26	♌	10:14 pm
28	10:08 pm	29	♍	8:00 am

MAY

Last Aspect Date	Time	Moon Enters New Sign Date	Sign	Time
1	7:31 am	1	♎	2:03 pm
3	12:49 pm	3	♏	4:38 pm
4	5:36 pm	5	♐	5:08 pm
7	7:50 am	7	♑	5:17 pm
9	9:03 am	9	♒	6:46 pm
11	3:31 pm	11	♓	10:52 pm
13	10:14 pm	14	♈	6:02 am
16	8:17 am	16	♉	3:57 pm
19	12:52 am	19	♊	3:47 am
21	8:13 am	21	♋	4:35 pm
22	2:58 pm	24	♌	5:07 am
26	5:42 am	26	♍	3:52 pm
28	12:17 pm	28	♎	11:22 pm
30	3:09 pm	31	♏	3:08 am

JUNE

Last Aspect Date	Time	Moon Enters New Sign Date	Sign	Time
1	5:15 pm	2	♐	3:52 am
3	1:12 pm	4	♑	3:12 am
5	8:28 am	6	♒	3:10 am
7	2:09 pm	8	♓	5:38 am
9	7:37 pm	10	♈	11:49 am
12	7:31 am	12	♉	9:37 pm
14	10:34 pm	15	♊	9:44 am
17	4:27 pm	17	♋	10:37 pm
20	6:46 am	20	♌	11:05 am
22	3:54 am	22	♍	10:10 pm
24	1:19 pm	25	♎	6:50 am
26	7:41 pm	27	♏	12:13 pm
28	8:57 pm	29	♐	2:15 pm
30	10:53 pm	7/1	♑	2:01 pm

JULY

Last Aspect Date	Time	Moon Enters New Sign Date	Sign	Time
6/30	10:53 pm	1	♑	2:01 pm
3	10:25 am	3	♒	1:22 pm
4	10:15 pm	5	♓	2:26 pm
7	1:30 am	7	♈	7:03 pm
9	8:52 am	10	♉	3:51 am
11	7:29 pm	12	♊	3:45 pm
14	8:33 am	15	♋	4:40 am
17	7:24 am	17	♌	4:56 pm
19	2:50 pm	20	♍	3:44 am
21	5:48 pm	22	♎	12:39 pm
24	5:54 pm	24	♏	7:08 pm
26	6:48 am	26	♐	10:48 pm
28	11:06 am	28	♑	11:57 pm
30	7:21 am	30	♒	11:54 pm

AUGUST

Last Aspect Date	Time	Moon Enters New Sign Date	Sign	Time
1	4:51 pm	2	♓	12:34 am
3	10:58 pm	4	♈	3:59 am
6	9:59 am	6	♉	11:26 am
8	8:46 pm	8	♊	10:33 pm
10	3:59 pm	11	♋	11:20 am
13	6:17 am	13	♌	11:30 pm
15	9:24 pm	16	♍	9:49 am
18	3:15 am	18	♎	6:09 pm
20	9:39 pm	21	♏	12:37 am
22	4:53 pm	23	♐	5:08 am
25	7:13 am	25	♑	7:46 am
26	10:58 pm	27	♒	9:08 am
29	5:23 am	29	♓	10:33 am
31	4:28 am	31	♈	1:46 pm

SEPTEMBER

Last Aspect Date	Time	Moon Enters New Sign Date	Sign	Time
2	12:17 pm	2	♉	8:16 pm
5	2:56 am	5	♊	6:24 am
7	2:08 pm	7	♋	6:50 pm
10	12:41 am	10	♌	7:06 am
11	9:22 pm	12	♍	5:16 pm
14	8:55 pm	15	♎	12:54 am
16	9:31 pm	17	♏	6:25 am
19	8:24 am	19	♐	10:30 am
21	12:19 pm	21	♑	1:35 pm
23	3:41 pm	23	♒	4:10 pm
25	2:25 am	25	♓	6:55 pm
27	9:12 pm	27	♈	10:57 pm
29	9:53 pm	30	♉	5:24 am

OCTOBER

Last Aspect Date	Time	Moon Enters New Sign Date	Sign	Time
2	12:34 pm	2	♊	2:55 pm
4	6:28 am	5	♋	2:54 am
7	8:13 am	7	♌	3:23 pm
9	6:42 am	10	♍	2:00 am
12	3:32 am	12	♎	9:32 am
14	10:22 am	14	♏	2:10 pm
16	11:43 am	16	♐	4:58 pm
18	11:46 am	18	♑	7:07 pm
20	5:59 pm	20	♒	9:38 pm
22	8:20 am	23	♓	1:13 am
25	1:17 am	25	♈	6:24 am
27	8:24 am	27	♉	1:37 pm
29	5:50 pm	29	♊	11:11 pm
31	8:21 pm	11/1	♋	9:53 am

NOVEMBER

Last Aspect Date	Time	Moon Enters New Sign Date	Sign	Time
10/31	8:21 pm	1	♋	9:53 am
3	9:00 pm	3	♌	10:32 pm
6	3:45 am	6	♍	10:00 am
8	1:32 pm	8	♎	6:23 pm
10	11:02 pm	10	♏	11:05 pm
12	8:34 pm	13	♐	12:56 am
14	10:58 am	15	♑	1:33 am
16	10:07 pm	17	♒	2:39 am
19	12:50 am	19	♓	5:38 am
21	10:35 am	21	♈	11:11 am
23	1:47 pm	23	♉	7:16 pm
25	11:37 pm	26	♊	5:25 am
28	10:04 am	28	♋	5:10 pm
30	11:28 pm	12/1	♌	5:50 am

DECEMBER

Last Aspect Date	Time	Moon Enters New Sign Date	Sign	Time
11/30	11:28 pm	1	♌	5:50 am
3	9:52 am	3	♍	6:00 pm
5	9:28 pm	6	♎	3:46 am
8	3:41 am	8	♏	9:43 am
10	6:03 am	10	♐	11:54 am
11	11:03 pm	12	♑	11:42 am
14	6:43 am	14	♒	11:10 am
16	3:33 am	16	♓	12:24 pm
18	11:40 am	18	♈	4:52 pm
21	12:16 am	21	♉	12:52 am
23	8:41 am	23	♊	11:32 am
25	8:30 am	25	♋	11:38 pm
28	2:34 am	28	♌	12:14 pm
30	9:54 am	31	♍	12:33 am

How to Use the *Pocket Planner*

by Leslie Nielsen

This handy guide contains information that can be most valuable to you as you plan your daily activities. As you read through the first few pages, you can start to get a feel for how well organized this guide is.

Read the Symbol Key on the next page, which is rather like astrological shorthand. The characteristics of the planets can give you direction in planning your strategies. Much like traffic signs that signal "go," "stop," or even "caution," you can determine for yourself the most propitious time to get things done.

You'll find tables that show the dates when Mercury is retrograde (℞) or direct (D). Because Mercury deals with the exchange of information, a retrograde Mercury makes miscommunication more noticeable.

There's also a section dedicated to the times when the Moon is void-of-course (v/c). These are generally poor times to conduct business because activities begun during these times usually end badly or fail to get started. If you make an appointment during a void-of-course, you might save yourself a lot of aggravation by confirming the time and date later. The Moon is only void-of-course for seven percent of the time when business is usually conducted during a normal work day (that is, 8:00 am to 5:00 pm). Sometimes, by waiting a matter of minutes or a few hours until the Moon has left the void-of-course phase, you have a much better chance to make action move more smoothly. Moon voids can also be used successfully to do routine activities or inner work, such as dream therapy or personal contemplation.

You'll find Moon phases, as well as each of the Moon's entries into a new sign. Times are expressed in Eastern time (in bold type) and Pacific time (in medium type). The New Moon time is generally best for beginning new activities, as the Moon is increasing in light and can offer the element of growth to our endeavors. When the Moon is Full, its illumination is greatest and we can see the results of our efforts. When it moves from Full stage back to the New stage, it can best be used to reflect on our projects. If necessary, we can make corrections at the New Moon.

The section of "Planetary Stations" will give you the times when the planets are changing signs or direction, thereby affording us opportunities for new starts.

The ephemeris in the back of your *Pocket Planner* can be very helpful to you. Read the particular sign and degree of planets and asteroids. As you start to work with the ephemeris, you may notice that not all planets seem to be comfortable in every sign. Think of the planets as actors, and the signs as the costumes they wear. Sometimes, costumes just itch. If you find this to be so for a certain time period, you may choose to delay your plans for a time or be more creative with the energies at hand.

As you turn to the daily pages, you'll find information about the Moon's sign, phase, and the time it changes phase. Also, you will find times and dates when the planets and asteroids change sign and go either retrograde or direct, major holidays, a three-month calendar, and room to record your appointments.

This guide is a powerful tool. Make the most of it!

Symbol Key

Planets:	☉ Sun	⚳ Ceres	♄ Saturn
	☽ Moon	⚴ Pallas	⚷ Chiron
	☿ Mercury	⚵ Juno	♅ Uranus
	♀ Venus	⚶ Vesta	♆ Neptune
	♂ Mars	♃ Jupiter	♇ Pluto
Signs:	♈ Aries	♌ Leo	♐ Sagittarius
	♉ Taurus	♍ Virgo	♑ Capricorn
	♊ Gemini	♎ Libra	♒ Aquarius
	♋ Cancer	♏ Scorpio	♓ Pisces
Aspects:	☌ Conjunction (0-8°)	⚺ Semisextile (30°)	⚹ Sextile (60°)
	□ Square (90°)	△ Trine (120°)	
	⚻ Quincunx (150°)	☍ Opposition (180°)	
Motion:	℞ Retrograde	D Direct	

World Map of Time Zones

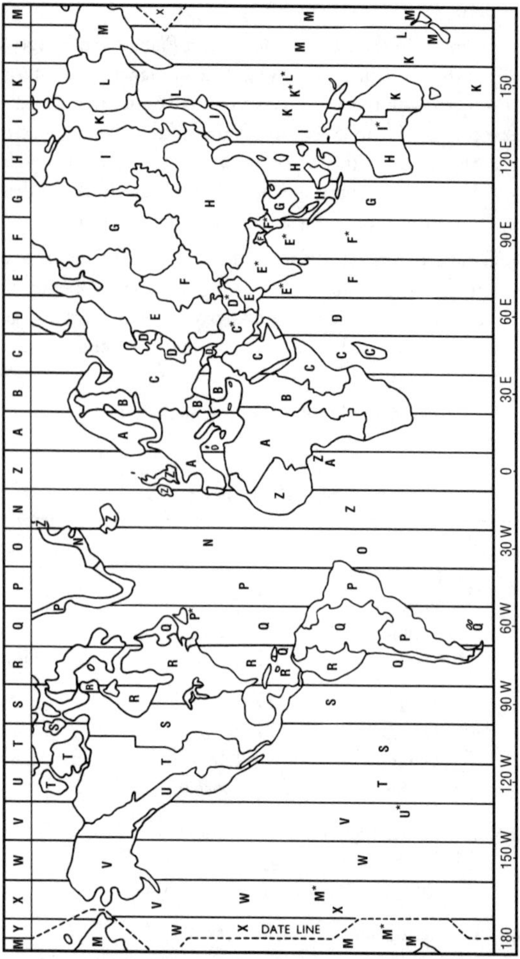

Time Zone Conversions

World Time Zones

Compared to Eastern Standard Time

( )	From Map	(Y)	Subtract 7 hours	(C*)	Add 8.5 hours
(S)	CST/Subtract 1 hour	(A)	Add 6 hours	(D*)	Add 9.5 hours
(R)	EST	(B)	Add 7 hours	(E*)	Add 10.5 hours
(Q)	Add 1 hour	(C)	Add 8 hours	(F*)	Add 11.5 hours
(P)	Add 2 hours	(D)	Add 9 hours	(I*)	Add 14.5 hours
(O)	Add 3 hours	(E)	Add 10 hours	(K*)	Add 15.5 hours
(N)	Add 4 hours	(F)	Add 11 hours	(L*)	Add 16.5 hours
(Z)	Add 5 hours	(G)	Add 12 hours	(M*)	Add 18 hours
(T)	MST/Subtract 2 hours	(H)	Add 13 hours	(P*)	Add 2.5 hours
(U)	PST/Subtract 3 hours	(I)	Add 14 hours	(V*)	Subtract 4.5 hours
(V)	Subtract 4 hours	(K)	Add 15 hours		
(W)	Subtract 5 hours	(L)	Add 16 hours		
(X)	Subtract 6 hours	(M)	Add 17 hours		

Planetary Stations for 2004

	JAN	FEB	MAR	APR	MAY	JUN	JUL	AUG	SEP	OCT	NOV	DEC
☿	12/17 –1/6			4/6– 4/30				8/9– 9/2				11/30 –12/20
♀						5/17–6/29						
♂												
♃			1/3–5/4									
♄		10/25–3/7										11/8–3/21
♅								6/10–11/11				
♆								5/17–10/24				
♇						3/24–8/30						
⚷							5/2–9/26					
⚳	11/23–2/25											
⚴												
⚵							5/17–9/1					
⚶									7/27–10/28			

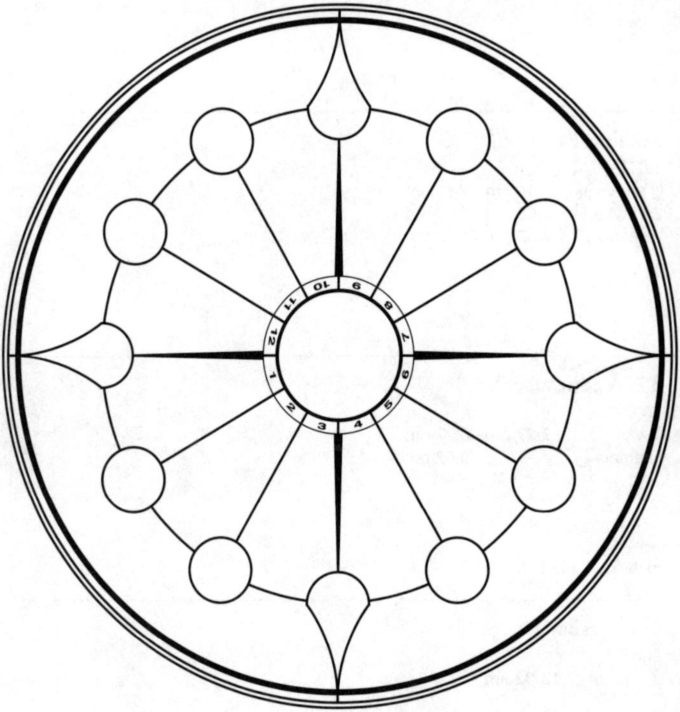

1
2
3
4
5
6
7
8
9
10
11
12

29 Monday

1st ♓
☽ enters ♈ **1:08 pm** 10:08 am

30 Tuesday

1st ♈
♅ enters ♓ **4:14 am** 1:14 am
2nd Quarter **5:03 am** 2:03 am
☿ enters ♐ **2:52 pm** 11:52 am

31 Wednesday

2nd ♈
☽ v/c **9:27 pm** 6:27 pm
☽ enters ♉ 9:02 pm

New Year's Eve

1 Thursday

2nd ♈
☽ enters ♉ **12:02 am**

New Year's Day • Kwanzaa Ends

Eastern time in bold type
Pacific time in medium type

2 Friday

2nd ♉

☽ v/c **2:21 pm** 11:21 am

3 Saturday

2nd ♉

☽ enters ♊ **12:58 pm** 9:58 am

♃ ℞ **6:57 pm** 3:57 pm

4 Sunday

2nd ♊

December 2003

S	M	T	W	T	F	S
	1	2	3	4	5	6
7	8	9	10	11	12	13
14	15	16	17	18	19	20
21	22	23	24	25	26	27
28	29	30	31			

January 2004

S	M	T	W	T	F	S
				1	2	3
4	5	6	7	8	9	10
11	12	13	14	15	16	17
18	19	20	21	22	23	24
25	26	27	28	29	30	31

February 2004

S	M	T	W	T	F	S
1	2	3	4	5	6	7
8	9	10	11	12	13	14
15	16	17	18	19	20	21
22	23	24	25	26	27	28
29						

Eastern time in bold type
Pacific time in medium type

5 Monday

2nd ♊
☽ v/c **6:14 pm** 3:14 pm
☽ enters ♋ 10:38 pm

6 Tuesday

2nd ♊
☽ enters ♋ **1:38 am**
☿ D **8:44 am** 5:44 am

7 Wednesday

2nd ♋
Full Moon **10:40 am** 7:40 am
☽ v/c **3:00 pm** 12:00 pm

8 Thursday

3rd ♋
☽ enters ♌ **12:38 pm** 9:38 am

Eastern time in bold type
Pacific time in medium type

9 Friday
3rd ♌

10 Saturday
3rd ♌

☽ v/c	**5:00 pm**	2:00 pm
☽ enters ♍	**9:37 pm**	6:37 pm

11 Sunday
3rd ♍

December 2003

S	M	T	W	T	F	S
	1	2	3	4	5	6
7	8	9	10	11	12	13
14	15	16	17	18	19	20
21	22	23	24	25	26	27
28	29	30	31			

January 2004

S	M	T	W	T	F	S
				1	2	3
4	5	6	7	8	9	10
11	12	13	14	15	16	17
18	19	20	21	22	23	24
25	26	27	28	29	30	31

February 2004

S	M	T	W	T	F	S
1	2	3	4	5	6	7
8	9	10	11	12	13	14
15	16	17	18	19	20	21
22	23	24	25	26	27	28
29						

Eastern time in bold type
Pacific time in medium type

12 Monday

3rd ♍

13 Tuesday

3rd ♍

☽ v/c	**3:01 am**	12:01 am
☽ enters ♎	**4:38 am**	1:38 am

14 Wednesday

3rd ♎

☿ enters ♑	**6:02 am**	3:02 am
♀ enters ♓	**12:16 pm**	9:16 am
4th Quarter	**11:46 pm**	8:46 pm
☽ v/c	**11:46 pm**	8:46 pm

15 Thursday

4th ♎

☽ enters ♏	**9:33 am**	6:33 am

Eastern time in bold type
Pacific time in medium type

16 Friday

4th ♏

17 Saturday

4th ♏
☽ v/c **6:48 am** 3:48 am
☽ enters ♐ **12:18 pm** 9:18 am

18 Sunday

4th ♐
☽ v/c **10:58 pm** 7:58 pm

December 2003

S	M	T	W	T	F	S
	1	2	3	4	5	6
7	8	9	10	11	12	13
14	15	16	17	18	19	20
21	22	23	24	25	26	27
28	29	30	31			

January 2004

S	M	T	W	T	F	S
				1	2	3
4	5	6	7	8	9	10
11	12	13	14	15	16	17
18	19	20	21	22	23	24
25	26	27	28	29	30	31

February 2004

S	M	T	W	T	F	S
1	2	3	4	5	6	7
8	9	10	11	12	13	14
15	16	17	18	19	20	21
22	23	24	25	26	27	28
29						

Eastern time in bold type
Pacific time in medium type

19 Monday

4th ♐
☽ enters ♑ **1:24 pm** 10:24 am

Birthday of Martin Luther King, Jr. (observed)

20 Tuesday

4th ♑
☉ enters ♒ **12:42 pm** 9:42 am
☽ v/c 9:34 pm

Sun enters Aquarius

21 Wednesday

4th ♑
☽ v/c **12:34 am**
☽ enters ♒ **2:11 pm** 11:11 am
New Moon **4:05 pm** 1:05 pm

22 Thursday

1st ♒

Chinese New Year (monkey)

Eastern time in bold type
Pacific time in medium type

23 Friday

1st ♒

☽ v/c	**4:33 am**	1:33 am
⚵ enters ♑	**5:32 am**	2:32 am
☽ enters ♓	**4:29 pm**	1:29 pm

24 Saturday

1st ♓

25 Sunday

1st ♓

☽ v/c	**6:09 am**	3:09 am
☽ enters ♈	**10:06 pm**	7:06 pm

December 2003

S	M	T	W	T	F	S
	1	2	3	4	5	6
7	8	9	10	11	12	13
14	15	16	17	18	19	20
21	22	23	24	25	26	27
28	29	30	31			

January 2004

S	M	T	W	T	F	S
				1	2	3
4	5	6	7	8	9	10
11	12	13	14	15	16	17
18	19	20	21	22	23	24
25	26	27	28	29	30	31

February 2004

S	M	T	W	T	F	S
1	2	3	4	5	6	7
8	9	10	11	12	13	14
15	16	17	18	19	20	21
22	23	24	25	26	27	28
29						

Eastern time in bold type
Pacific time in medium type

26 Monday

1st ♈

27 Tuesday

1st ♈

☽ v/c **11:59 pm** 8:59 pm

28 Wednesday

1st ♈

☽ enters ♉ **7:46 am** 4:46 am

2nd Quarter 10:03 pm

29 Thursday

1st ♉

2nd Quarter **1:03 am**

☽ v/c **9:04 pm** 6:04 pm

Eastern time in bold type
Pacific time in medium type

30 Friday

2nd ♉
☽ enters ♊ **8:18 pm** 5:18 pm

31 Saturday

2nd ♊

1 Sunday

2nd ♊

January 2004

S	M	T	W	T	F	S
				1	2	3
4	5	6	7	8	9	10
11	12	13	14	15	16	17
18	19	20	21	22	23	24
25	26	27	28	29	30	31

February 2004

S	M	T	W	T	F	S
1	2	3	4	5	6	7
8	9	10	11	12	13	14
15	16	17	18	19	20	21
22	23	24	25	26	27	28
29						

March 2004

S	M	T	W	T	F	S
	1	2	3	4	5	6
7	8	9	10	11	12	13
14	15	16	17	18	19	20
21	22	23	24	25	26	27
28	29	30	31			

2 Monday

2nd ♊
☽ v/c **7:56 am** 4:56 am
☽ enters ♋ **9:03 am** 6:03 am

Imbolc • Groundhog Day

3 Tuesday

2nd ♋
♂ enters ♉ **5:04 am** 2:04 am

4 Wednesday

2nd ♋
☽ v/c **12:52 pm** 9:52 am
☽ enters ♌ **7:50 pm** 4:50 pm

5 Thursday

2nd ♌

Eastern time in bold type
Pacific time in medium type

6 Friday

2nd ♌

Full Moon	**3:47 am**	12:47 am
☽ v/c	**12:38 pm**	9:38 am
☿ enters ♒	**11:20 pm**	8:20 pm

7 Saturday

3rd ♌

☽ enters ♍	**4:03 am**	1:03 am

8 Sunday

3rd ♍

♀ enters ♈	**11:20 am**	8:20 am
☽ v/c	**7:23 pm**	4:23 pm

January 2004

S	M	T	W	T	F	S
				1	2	3
4	5	6	7	8	9	10
11	12	13	14	15	16	17
18	19	20	21	22	23	24
25	26	27	28	29	30	31

February 2004

S	M	T	W	T	F	S
1	2	3	4	5	6	7
8	9	10	11	12	13	14
15	16	17	18	19	20	21
22	23	24	25	26	27	28
29						

March 2004

S	M	T	W	T	F	S
	1	2	3	4	5	6
7	8	9	10	11	12	13
14	15	16	17	18	19	20
21	22	23	24	25	26	27
28	29	30	31			

Eastern time in bold type
Pacific time in medium type

9 Monday

3rd ♍

☽ enters ♎ **10:12 am** 7:12 am

10 Tuesday

3rd ♎

☽ v/c 9:42 pm

11 Wednesday

3rd ♎

☽ v/c **12:42 am**

☽ enters ♏ **2:58 pm** 11:58 am

12 Thursday

3rd ♏

Eastern time in bold type

Pacific time in medium type

13 Friday

3rd ♏
4th Quarter **8:39 am** 5:39 am
☽ v/c **8:39 am** 5:39 am
☽ enters ♐ **6:35 pm** 3:35 pm

14 Saturday

4th ♐
⚵ enters ♒ **2:07 pm** 11:07 am

Valentine's Day

15 Sunday

4th ♐
☽ v/c **3:20 pm** 12:20 pm
☽ enters ♑ **9:14 pm** 6:14 pm

January 2004

S	M	T	W	T	F	S
				1	2	3
4	5	6	7	8	9	10
11	12	13	14	15	16	17
18	19	20	21	22	23	24
25	26	27	28	29	30	31

February 2004

S	M	T	W	T	F	S
1	2	3	4	5	6	7
8	9	10	11	12	13	14
15	16	17	18	19	20	21
22	23	24	25	26	27	28
29						

March 2004

S	M	T	W	T	F	S
	1	2	3	4	5	6
7	8	9	10	11	12	13
14	15	16	17	18	19	20
21	22	23	24	25	26	27
28	29	30	31			

16 Monday

4th ♑
☽ v/c 9:00 pm

Presidents' Day (observed)

17 Tuesday

4th ♑
☽ v/c **12:00 am**
☽ enters ♒ **11:27 pm** 8:27 pm

18 Wednesday

4th ♒
☉ enters ♓ 11:50 pm

Sun enters Pisces

19 Thursday

4th ♒
☉ enters ♓ **2:50 am**
☽ v/c **12:34 pm** 9:34 am
☽ enters ♓ 11:27 pm

Sun enters Pisces

Eastern time in bold type
Pacific time in medium type

20 Friday

4th ≈

☽ enters ♓ **2:27 am**

New Moon **4:18 am** 1:18 am

21 Saturday

1st ♓

☽ v/c **5:10 pm** 2:10 pm

22 Sunday

1st ♓

☽ enters ♈ **7:45 am** 4:45 am

Islamic New Year

January 2004

S	M	T	W	T	F	S
				1	2	3
4	5	6	7	8	9	10
11	12	13	14	15	16	17
18	19	20	21	22	23	24
25	26	27	28	29	30	31

February 2004

S	M	T	W	T	F	S
1	2	3	4	5	6	7
8	9	10	11	12	13	14
15	16	17	18	19	20	21
22	23	24	25	26	27	28
29						

March 2004

S	M	T	W	T	F	S
	1	2	3	4	5	6
7	8	9	10	11	12	13
14	15	16	17	18	19	20
21	22	23	24	25	26	27
28	29	30	31			

Eastern time in bold type
Pacific time in medium type

23 Monday

1st ♈

24 Tuesday

1st ♈

☽ v/c	**1:55 pm**	10:55 am
☽ enters ♉	**4:30 pm**	1:30 pm
♀ enters ♉		10:33 pm

Mardi Gras

25 Wednesday

1st ♉

♀ enters ♉	**1:33 am**	
☿ enters ♓	**7:58 am**	4:58 am
⚳ D	**1:38 pm**	10:38 am
☽ v/c	**9:55 pm**	6:55 pm

Ash Wednesday

26 Thursday

1st ♉

Eastern time in bold type
Pacific time in medium type

27 Friday

1st ♉
☽ enters ♊ **4:22 am** 1:22 am
2nd Quarter **10:24 pm** 7:24 pm

28 Saturday

2nd ♊

29 Sunday

2nd ♊
☽ v/c **5:08 am** 2:08 am
☽ enters ♋ **5:12 pm** 2:12 pm

Leap Day

January 2004

S	M	T	W	T	F	S
				1	2	3
4	5	6	7	8	9	10
11	12	13	14	15	16	17
18	19	20	21	22	23	24
25	26	27	28	29	30	31

February 2004

S	M	T	W	T	F	S
1	2	3	4	5	6	7
8	9	10	11	12	13	14
15	16	17	18	19	20	21
22	23	24	25	26	27	28
29						

March 2004

S	M	T	W	T	F	S
	1	2	3	4	5	6
7	8	9	10	11	12	13
14	15	16	17	18	19	20
21	22	23	24	25	26	27
28	29	30	31			

1 Monday

2nd ♋

2 Tuesday

2nd ♋

☽ v/c **10:42 pm** 7:42 pm

3 Wednesday

2nd ♋

☽ enters ♌ **4:18 am** 1:18 am

4 Thursday

2nd ♌

Eastern time in bold type
Pacific time in medium type

5 Friday

2nd ♌

☽ v/c	**12:13 pm**	9:13 am
☽ enters ♍	**12:18 pm**	9:18 am
♀ enters ♉	**1:12 pm**	10:12 am

6 Saturday

2nd ♍

Full Moon	**6:14 pm**	3:14 pm

7 Sunday

3rd ♍

☽ v/c	**3:49 am**	12:49 am
♄ D	**11:51 am**	8:51 am
☽ enters ♎	**5:31 pm**	2:31 pm

Purim

February 2004

S	M	T	W	T	F	S
1	2	3	4	5	6	7
8	9	10	11	12	13	14
15	16	17	18	19	20	21
22	23	24	25	26	27	28
29						

March 2004

S	M	T	W	T	F	S
	1	2	3	4	5	6
7	8	9	10	11	12	13
14	15	16	17	18	19	20
21	22	23	24	25	26	27
28	29	30	31			

April 2004

S	M	T	W	T	F	S
				1	2	3
4	5	6	7	8	9	10
11	12	13	14	15	16	17
18	19	20	21	22	23	24
25	26	27	28	29	30	

Eastern time in bold type
Pacific time in medium type

8 Monday

3rd ♎

9 Tuesday

3rd ♎

☽ v/c	**7:43 am**	4:43 am
☽ enters ♏	**9:03 pm**	6:03 pm

10 Wednesday

3rd ♏

11 Thursday

3rd ♏

☽ v/c	**11:11 pm**	8:11 pm
☽ enters ♐	**11:57 pm**	8:57 pm

Eastern time in bold type
Pacific time in medium type

12 Friday

3rd ♐
☿ enters ♈ **4:44 am** 1:44 am

13 Saturday

3rd ♐
4th Quarter **4:01 pm** 1:01 pm
☽ v/c **4:01 pm** 1:01 pm
☽ enters ♑ 11:51 pm

14 Sunday

4th ♐
☽ enters ♑ **2:51 am**

February 2004

S	M	T	W	T	F	S
1	2	3	4	5	6	7
8	9	10	11	12	13	14
15	16	17	18	19	20	21
22	23	24	25	26	27	28
29						

March 2004

S	M	T	W	T	F	S
	1	2	3	4	5	6
7	8	9	10	11	12	13
14	15	16	17	18	19	20
21	22	23	24	25	26	27
28	29	30	31			

April 2004

S	M	T	W	T	F	S
				1	2	3
4	5	6	7	8	9	10
11	12	13	14	15	16	17
18	19	20	21	22	23	24
25	26	27	28	29	30	

Eastern time in bold type
Pacific time in medium type

15 Monday

4th ♑
☽ v/c 9:34 pm

16 Tuesday

4th ♑
☽ v/c **12:34 am**
☽ enters ♒ **6:10 am** 3:10 am

17 Wednesday

4th ♒

St. Patrick's Day

18 Thursday

4th ♒
☽ v/c **7:15 am** 4:15 am
☽ enters ♓ **10:26 am** 7:26 am

Eastern time in bold type
Pacific time in medium type

19 Friday

4th ♓
☉ enters ♈ 10:49 pm

Sun enters Aries • Ostara • Spring Equinox • 10:49 pm PST

20 Saturday

4th ♓

☉ enters ♈	**1:49 am**	
☽ v/c	**3:57 pm**	12:57 pm
☽ enters ♈	**4:29 pm**	1:29 pm
New Moon	**5:41 pm**	2:41 pm
♂ enters ♊		11:39 pm

Sun enters Aries • Ostara • Spring Equinox • 1:49 am EST

21 Sunday

1st ♈
♂ enters ♊ **2:39 am**

February 2004

S	M	T	W	T	F	S
1	2	3	4	5	6	7
8	9	10	11	12	13	14
15	16	17	18	19	20	21
22	23	24	25	26	27	28
29						

March 2004

S	M	T	W	T	F	S
	1	2	3	4	5	6
7	8	9	10	11	12	13
14	15	16	17	18	19	20
21	22	23	24	25	26	27
28	29	30	31			

April 2004

S	M	T	W	T	F	S
				1	2	3
4	5	6	7	8	9	10
11	12	13	14	15	16	17
18	19	20	21	22	23	24
25	26	27	28	29	30	

22 Monday

1st ♈︎
☽ v/c **10:14 am** 7:14 am
☽ enters ♉︎ 10:10 pm

23 Tuesday

1st ♈︎
☽ enters ♉︎ **1:10 am**

24 Wednesday

1st ♉︎
♇ ℞ **10:09 am** 7:09 am
☽ v/c **5:29 pm** 2:29 pm

25 Thursday

1st ♉︎
☽ enters ♊︎ **12:35 pm** 9:35 am

Eastern time in bold type
Pacific time in medium type

26 Friday

1st ♊

27 Saturday

1st ♊

☽ v/c	**5:44 pm**	2:44 pm
☽ enters ♋		10:23 pm

28 Sunday

1st ♊

☽ enters ♋	**1:23 am**	
2nd Quarter	**6:48 pm**	3:48 pm

February 2004

S	M	T	W	T	F	S
1	2	3	4	5	6	7
8	9	10	11	12	13	14
15	16	17	18	19	20	21
22	23	24	25	26	27	28
29						

March 2004

S	M	T	W	T	F	S
	1	2	3	4	5	6
7	8	9	10	11	12	13
14	15	16	17	18	19	20
21	22	23	24	25	26	27
28	29	30	31			

April 2004

S	M	T	W	T	F	S
				1	2	3
4	5	6	7	8	9	10
11	12	13	14	15	16	17
18	19	20	21	22	23	24
25	26	27	28	29	30	

Eastern time in bold type
Pacific time in medium type

29 Monday
2nd ♋

30 Tuesday
2nd ♋
☽ v/c **11:00 am** 8:00 am
☽ enters ♌ **1:07 pm** 10:07 am

31 Wednesday
2nd ♌
☿ enters ♉ **9:27 pm** 6:27 pm

1 Thursday
2nd ♌
☽ v/c **6:56 pm** 3:56 pm
☽ enters ♍ **9:45 pm** 6:45 pm

April Fools' Day

Eastern time in bold type
Pacific time in medium type

2 Friday

2nd ♍

3 Saturday

2nd ♍

♀ enters ♊	**9:57 am**	6:57 am
☽ v/c	**1:23 pm**	10:23 am
☽ enters ♎		11:52 pm

4 Sunday

2nd ♍

☽ enters ♎ **3:52 am**

Palm Sunday • Daylight Saving Time begins at 2 am

March 2004

S	M	T	W	T	F	S
	1	2	3	4	5	6
7	8	9	10	11	12	13
14	15	16	17	18	19	20
21	22	23	24	25	26	27
28	29	30	31			

April 2004

S	M	T	W	T	F	S
				1	2	3
4	5	6	7	8	9	10
11	12	13	14	15	16	17
18	19	20	21	22	23	24
25	26	27	28	29	30	

May 2004

S	M	T	W	T	F	S
						1
2	3	4	5	6	7	8
9	10	11	12	13	14	15
16	17	18	19	20	21	22
23	24	25	26	27	28	29
30	31					

5 Monday

2nd ♎
Full Moon	**7:03 am**	4:03 am
☽ v/c	**5:26 pm**	2:26 pm

6 Tuesday

3rd ♎
☽ enters ♏	**6:24 am**	3:24 am
☿ ℞	**4:28 pm**	1:28 pm

Passover begins

7 Wednesday

3rd ♏
☽ v/c	**7:06 am**	4:06 am

8 Thursday

3rd ♏
☽ enters ♐	**7:50 am**	4:50 am

Eastern time in bold type
Pacific time in medium type

9 Friday

3rd ♐

☽ v/c **8:30 pm** 5:30 pm

Good Friday • Orthodox Good Friday

10 Saturday

3rd ♐

☽ enters ♑ **9:33 am** 6:33 am

11 Sunday

3rd ♑

4th Quarter **11:46 pm** 8:46 pm

☽ v/c **11:46 pm** 8:46 pm

Easter • Orthodox Easter

March 2004

S	M	T	W	T	F	S
	1	2	3	4	5	6
7	8	9	10	11	12	13
14	15	16	17	18	19	20
21	22	23	24	25	26	27
28	29	30	31			

April 2004

S	M	T	W	T	F	S
				1	2	3
4	5	6	7	8	9	10
11	12	13	14	15	16	17
18	19	20	21	22	23	24
25	26	27	28	29	30	

May 2004

S	M	T	W	T	F	S
						1
2	3	4	5	6	7	8
9	10	11	12	13	14	15
16	17	18	19	20	21	22
23	24	25	26	27	28	29
30	31					

12 Monday

4th ♑
☽ enters ♒ **12:33 pm** 9:33 am
☿ enters ♈ **9:23 pm** 6:23 pm

Passover ends

13 Tuesday

4th ♒

14 Wednesday

4th ♒
☽ v/c **3:27 pm** 12:27 pm
☽ enters ♓ **5:24 pm** 2:24 pm

15 Thursday

4th ♓

Eastern time in bold type
Pacific time in medium type

16 Friday

4th ♓

⚵ enters ♓ **5:46 am** 2:46 am

☽ v/c **9:43 am** 6:43 am

☽ enters ♈ 9:24 pm

17 Saturday

4th ♈

☽ enters ♈ **12:24 am**

18 Sunday

4th ♈

March 2004

S	M	T	W	T	F	S
	1	2	3	4	5	6
7	8	9	10	11	12	13
14	15	16	17	18	19	20
21	22	23	24	25	26	27
28	29	30	31			

April 2004

S	M	T	W	T	F	S
				1	2	3
4	5	6	7	8	9	10
11	12	13	14	15	16	17
18	19	20	21	22	23	24
25	26	27	28	29	30	

May 2004

S	M	T	W	T	F	S
						1
2	3	4	5	6	7	8
9	10	11	12	13	14	15
16	17	18	19	20	21	22
23	24	25	26	27	28	29
30	31					

Eastern time in bold type
Pacific time in medium type

19 Monday

4th ♈

New Moon	**9:21 am**	6:21 am
☽ v/c	**9:21 am**	6:21 am
☽ enters ♉	**9:43 am**	6:43 am
☉ enters ♉	**1:50 pm**	10:50 am

Sun enters Taurus • Solar Eclipse 29° ♈ 49' • 9:35 am ET/6:35 am PT

20 Tuesday

1st ♉

☽ v/c	**3:36 pm**	12:36 pm

21 Wednesday

1st ♉

☽ enters ♊	**9:10 pm**	6:10 pm

22 Thursday

1st ♊

Earth Day

Eastern time in bold type
Pacific time in medium type

23 Friday

1st ♊
☽ v/c **7:22 pm** 4:22 pm

24 Saturday

1st ♊
☽ enters ♋ **9:56 am** 6:56 am
♀ enters ♊ **12:55 pm** 9:55 am

25 Sunday

1st ♋

March 2004

S	M	T	W	T	F	S
	1	2	3	4	5	6
7	8	9	10	11	12	13
14	15	16	17	18	19	20
21	22	23	24	25	26	27
28	29	30	31			

April 2004

S	M	T	W	T	F	S
				1	2	3
4	5	6	7	8	9	10
11	12	13	14	15	16	17
18	19	20	21	22	23	24
25	26	27	28	29	30	

May 2004

S	M	T	W	T	F	S
						1
2	3	4	5	6	7	8
9	10	11	12	13	14	15
16	17	18	19	20	21	22
23	24	25	26	27	28	29
30	31					

26 Monday

1st ♋

☽ v/c **5:56 am** 2:56 am

☽ enters ♌ **10:14 pm** 7:14 pm

27 Tuesday

1st ♌

2nd Quarter **1:32 pm** 10:32 am

28 Wednesday

2nd ♌

☽ v/c **10:08 pm** 7:08 pm

29 Thursday

2nd ♌

☽ enters ♍ **8:00 am** 5:00 am

Eastern time in bold type
Pacific time in medium type

30 Friday

2nd ♍
☿ D **9:05 am** 6:05 am

1 Saturday

2nd ♍
☽ v/c **7:31 am** 4:31 am
☽ enters ♎ **2:03 pm** 11:03 am
⚷ ℞ 10:12 pm

Beltane

2 Sunday

2nd ♎
⚷ ℞ **1:12 am**

April 2004

S	M	T	W	T	F	S
				1	2	3
4	5	6	7	8	9	10
11	12	13	14	15	16	17
18	19	20	21	22	23	24
25	26	27	28	29	30	

May 2004

S	M	T	W	T	F	S
						1
2	3	4	5	6	7	8
9	10	11	12	13	14	15
16	17	18	19	20	21	22
23	24	25	26	27	28	29
30	31					

June 2004

S	M	T	W	T	F	S
		1	2	3	4	5
6	7	8	9	10	11	12
13	14	15	16	17	18	19
20	21	22	23	24	25	26
27	28	29	30			

Eastern time in bold type
Pacific time in medium type

3 Monday

2nd ♎

☽ v/c	**12:49 pm**	9:49 am
☽ enters ♏	**4:38 pm**	1:38 pm

4 Tuesday

2nd ♏

Full Moon	**4:33 pm**	1:33 pm
☽ v/c	**5:36 pm**	2:36 pm
♃ D	**11:06 pm**	8:06 pm

Lunar Eclipse 14° ♏ 42' • 4:31 pm ET/1:31 pm PT

5 Wednesday

3rd ♏

☽ enters ♐	**5:08 pm**	2:08 pm

Cinco de Mayo

6 Thursday

3rd ♐

Eastern time in bold type
Pacific time in medium type

7 Friday

3rd ♐

♂ enters ♋	**4:45 am**	1:45 am
☽ v/c	**7:50 am**	4:50 am
☽ enters ♑	**5:17 pm**	2:17 pm

8 Saturday

3rd ♑

9 Sunday

3rd ♑

☽ v/c	**9:03 am**	6:03 am
☽ enters ♒	**6:46 pm**	3:46 pm

Mother's Day

April 2004

S	M	T	W	T	F	S
				1	2	3
4	5	6	7	8	9	10
11	12	13	14	15	16	17
18	19	20	21	22	23	24
25	26	27	28	29	30	

May 2004

S	M	T	W	T	F	S
						1
2	3	4	5	6	7	8
9	10	11	12	13	14	15
16	17	18	19	20	21	22
23	24	25	26	27	28	29
30	31					

June 2004

S	M	T	W	T	F	S
		1	2	3	4	5
6	7	8	9	10	11	12
13	14	15	16	17	18	19
20	21	22	23	24	25	26
27	28	29	30			

10 Monday

3rd ≈

11 Tuesday

3rd ≈

4th Quarter	**7:04 am**	4:04 am
☽ v/c	**3:31 pm**	12:31 pm
☽ enters ♓	**10:52 pm**	7:52 pm

12 Wednesday

4th ♓

13 Thursday

4th ♓

☽ v/c	**10:14 pm**	7:14 pm

Eastern time in bold type
Pacific time in medium type

14 Friday

4th ♓
☽ enters ♈ **6:02 am** 3:02 am

15 Saturday

4th ♈
☿ enters ♉ 11:54 pm

16 Sunday

4th ♈
☿ enters ♉ **2:54 am**
☽ v/c **8:17 am** 5:17 am
☽ enters ♉ **3:57 pm** 12:57 pm
⚵ ℞ 11:49 pm

April 2004

S	M	T	W	T	F	S
				1	2	3
4	5	6	7	8	9	10
11	12	13	14	15	16	17
18	19	20	21	22	23	24
25	26	27	28	29	30	

May 2004

S	M	T	W	T	F	S
						1
2	3	4	5	6	7	8
9	10	11	12	13	14	15
16	17	18	19	20	21	22
23	24	25	26	27	28	29
30	31					

June 2004

S	M	T	W	T	F	S
		1	2	3	4	5
6	7	8	9	10	11	12
13	14	15	16	17	18	19
20	21	22	23	24	25	26
27	28	29	30			

Eastern time in bold type
Pacific time in medium type

17 Monday

4th ♉

⚵ ℞	**2:49 am**	
♆ ℞	**8:13 am**	5:13 am
♀ ℞	**6:29 pm**	3:29 pm

18 Tuesday

4th ♉

⚳ enters ♌	**2:00 pm**	11:00 am
New Moon		9:52 pm
☽ v/c		9:52 pm

19 Wednesday

1st ♉

New Moon	**12:52 am**	
☽ v/c	**12:52 am**	
☽ enters ♊	**3:47 am**	12:47 am

20 Thursday

1st ♊

☉ enters ♊	**12:59 pm**	9:59 am

Sun enters Gemini

Eastern time in bold type
Pacific time in medium type

21 Friday

1st ♊
☽ v/c **8:13 am** 5:13 am
☽ enters ♋ **4:35 pm** 1:35 pm

22 Saturday

1st ♋
☽ v/c **2:58 pm** 11:58 am

23 Sunday

1st ♋

April 2004

S	M	T	W	T	F	S
				1	2	3
4	5	6	7	8	9	10
11	12	13	14	15	16	17
18	19	20	21	22	23	24
25	26	27	28	29	30	

May 2004

S	M	T	W	T	F	S
						1
2	3	4	5	6	7	8
9	10	11	12	13	14	15
16	17	18	19	20	21	22
23	24	25	26	27	28	29
30	31					

June 2004

S	M	T	W	T	F	S
		1	2	3	4	5
6	7	8	9	10	11	12
13	14	15	16	17	18	19
20	21	22	23	24	25	26
27	28	29	30			

24 Monday

1st ♋
☽ enters ♌ **5:07 am** 2:07 am

25 Tuesday

1st ♌

26 Wednesday

1st ♌
☽ v/c **5:42 am** 2:42 am
☽ enters ♍ **3:52 pm** 12:52 pm

Shavuot

27 Thursday

1st ♍
2nd Quarter **3:57 am** 12:57 am

Eastern time in bold type
Pacific time in medium type

28 Friday

2nd ♍

☽ v/c **12:17 pm** 9:17 am

☽ enters ♎ **11:22 pm** 8:22 pm

29 Saturday

2nd ♎

30 Sunday

2nd ♎

☽ v/c **3:09 pm** 12:09 pm

Pentecost

April 2004

S	M	T	W	T	F	S
				1	2	3
4	5	6	7	8	9	10
11	12	13	14	15	16	17
18	19	20	21	22	23	24
25	26	27	28	29	30	

May 2004

S	M	T	W	T	F	S
						1
2	3	4	5	6	7	8
9	10	11	12	13	14	15
16	17	18	19	20	21	22
23	24	25	26	27	28	29
30	31					

June 2004

S	M	T	W	T	F	S
		1	2	3	4	5
6	7	8	9	10	11	12
13	14	15	16	17	18	19
20	21	22	23	24	25	26
27	28	29	30			

31 Monday

2nd ♎
☽ enters ♏ **3:08 am** 12:08 am

Memorial Day (observed)

1 Tuesday

2nd ♏
☽ v/c **5:15 pm** 2:15 pm

2 Wednesday

2nd ♏
☽ enters ♐ **3:52 am** 12:52 am
Full Moon 9:20 pm

3 Thursday

3rd ♐
Full Moon **12:20 am**
☽ v/c **1:12 pm** 10:12 am

Eastern time in bold type
Pacific time in medium type

4 Friday

3rd ♐
☽ enters ♑ **3:12 am** 12:12 am

5 Saturday

3rd ♑
☽ v/c **8:28 am** 5:28 am
☿ enters ♊ **8:47 am** 5:47 am

6 Sunday

3rd ♑
☽ enters ♒ **3:10 am** 12:10 am

May 2004

S	M	T	W	T	F	S
						1
2	3	4	5	6	7	8
9	10	11	12	13	14	15
16	17	18	19	20	21	22
23	24	25	26	27	28	29
30	31					

June 2004

S	M	T	W	T	F	S
		1	2	3	4	5
6	7	8	9	10	11	12
13	14	15	16	17	18	19
20	21	22	23	24	25	26
27	28	29	30			

July 2004

S	M	T	W	T	F	S
				1	2	3
4	5	6	7	8	9	10
11	12	13	14	15	16	17
18	19	20	21	22	23	24
25	26	27	28	29	30	31

Eastern time in bold type
Pacific time in medium type

7 Monday

3rd ♒
☽ v/c **2:09 pm** 11:09 am

8 Tuesday

3rd ♒
☽ enters ♓ **5:38 am** 2:38 am

9 Wednesday

3rd ♓
4th Quarter **4:02 pm** 1:02 pm
☽ v/c **7:37 pm** 4:37 pm

10 Thursday

4th ♓
♅ ℞ **11:47 am** 8:47 am
☽ enters ♈ **11:49 am** 8:49 am

Eastern time in bold type
Pacific time in medium type

11 Friday

4th ♈

12 Saturday

4th ♈

☽ v/c	**7:31 am**	4:31 am
☽ enters ♉	**9:37 pm**	6:37 pm

13 Sunday

4th ♉

May 2004

S	M	T	W	T	F	S
						1
2	3	4	5	6	7	8
9	10	11	12	13	14	15
16	17	18	19	20	21	22
23	24	25	26	27	28	29
30	31					

June 2004

S	M	T	W	T	F	S
		1	2	3	4	5
6	7	8	9	10	11	12
13	14	15	16	17	18	19
20	21	22	23	24	25	26
27	28	29	30			

July 2004

S	M	T	W	T	F	S
				1	2	3
4	5	6	7	8	9	10
11	12	13	14	15	16	17
18	19	20	21	22	23	24
25	26	27	28	29	30	31

Eastern time in bold type
Pacific time in medium type

14 Monday

4th ♉
☽ v/c **10:34 pm** 7:34 pm
♀ enters ♋ 10:09 pm

Flag Day

15 Tuesday

4th ♉
♀ enters ♋ **1:09 am**
☽ enters ♊ **9:44 am** 6:44 am

16 Wednesday

4th ♊

17 Thursday

4th ♊
New Moon **4:27 pm** 1:27 pm
☽ v/c **4:27 pm** 1:27 pm
☽ enters ♋ **10:37 pm** 7:37 pm

Eastern time in bold type
Pacific time in medium type

18 Friday
1st ♋

19 Saturday
1st ♋
☿ enters ♋ **3:49 pm** 12:49 pm

20 Sunday
1st ♋
☽ v/c **6:46 am** 3:46 am
☽ enters ♌ **11:05 am** 8:05 am
☉ enters ♋ **8:57 pm** 5:57 pm

Sun enters Cancer • Litha • Summer Solstice • 8:57 pm ET/5:57 pm PT
Father's Day

May 2004

S	M	T	W	T	F	S
						1
2	3	4	5	6	7	8
9	10	11	12	13	14	15
16	17	18	19	20	21	22
23	24	25	26	27	28	29
30	31					

June 2004

S	M	T	W	T	F	S
		1	2	3	4	5
6	7	8	9	10	11	12
13	14	15	16	17	18	19
20	21	22	23	24	25	26
27	28	29	30			

July 2004

S	M	T	W	T	F	S
				1	2	3
4	5	6	7	8	9	10
11	12	13	14	15	16	17
18	19	20	21	22	23	24
25	26	27	28	29	30	31

21 Monday

1st ♌

22 Tuesday

1st ♌
☽ v/c **3:54 am** 12:54 am
☽ enters ♍ **10:10 pm** 7:10 pm

23 Wednesday

1st ♍
♂ enters ♌ **4:50 pm** 1:50 pm

24 Thursday

1st ♍
☽ v/c **1:19 pm** 10:19 am

Eastern time in bold type
Pacific time in medium type

25 Friday

1st ♍
☽ enters ♎ **6:50 am** 3:50 am
2nd Quarter **3:08 pm** 12:08 pm

26 Saturday

2nd ♎
☽ v/c **7:41 pm** 4:41 pm

27 Sunday

2nd ♎
☽ enters ♏ **12:13 pm** 9:13 am

May 2004

S	M	T	W	T	F	S
						1
2	3	4	5	6	7	8
9	10	11	12	13	14	15
16	17	18	19	20	21	22
23	24	25	26	27	28	29
30	31					

June 2004

S	M	T	W	T	F	S
		1	2	3	4	5
6	7	8	9	10	11	12
13	14	15	16	17	18	19
20	21	22	23	24	25	26
27	28	29	30			

July 2004

S	M	T	W	T	F	S
				1	2	3
4	5	6	7	8	9	10
11	12	13	14	15	16	17
18	19	20	21	22	23	24
25	26	27	28	29	30	31

Eastern time in bold type
Pacific time in medium type

28 Monday

2nd ♏

☽ v/c **8:57 pm** 5:57 pm

29 Tuesday

2nd ♏

☽ enters ♐ **2:15 pm** 11:15 am

♀ D **7:16 pm** 4:16 pm

30 Wednesday

2nd ♐

☽ v/c **10:53 pm** 7:53 pm

1 Thursday

2nd ♐

☽ enters ♑ **2:01 pm** 11:01 am

Eastern time in bold type
Pacific time in medium type

2 Friday

2nd ♑

Full Moon	**7:09 am**	4:09 am

3 Saturday

3rd ♑

☽ v/c	**10:25 am**	7:25 am
☽ enters ♒	**1:22 pm**	10:22 am

4 Sunday

3rd ♒

☿ enters ♌	**10:52 am**	7:52 am
☽ v/c	**10:15 pm**	7:15 pm

Independence Day

June 2004

S	M	T	W	T	F	S
		1	2	3	4	5
6	7	8	9	10	11	12
13	14	15	16	17	18	19
20	21	22	23	24	25	26
27	28	29	30			

July 2004

S	M	T	W	T	F	S
				1	2	3
4	5	6	7	8	9	10
11	12	13	14	15	16	17
18	19	20	21	22	23	24
25	26	27	28	29	30	31

August 2004

S	M	T	W	T	F	S
1	2	3	4	5	6	7
8	9	10	11	12	13	14
15	16	17	18	19	20	21
22	23	24	25	26	27	28
29	30	31				

5 Monday

3rd ♒
☽ enters ♓ **2:26 pm** 11:26 am

6 Tuesday

3rd ♓
☽ v/c 10:30 pm

7 Wednesday

3rd ♓
☽ v/c **1:30 am**
☽ enters ♈ **7:03 pm** 4:03 pm

8 Thursday

3rd ♈

Eastern time in bold type
Pacific time in medium type

9 Friday

4th Quarter **3:34 am** 12:34 am
☽ v/c **8:52 am** 5:52 am

10 Saturday

4th ♈
☽ enters ♉ **3:51 am** 12:51 am

11 Sunday

4th ♉
☽ v/c **7:29 pm** 4:29 pm

June 2004

S	M	T	W	T	F	S
		1	2	3	4	5
6	7	8	9	10	11	12
13	14	15	16	17	18	19
20	21	22	23	24	25	26
27	28	29	30			

July 2004

S	M	T	W	T	F	S
				1	2	3
4	5	6	7	8	9	10
11	12	13	14	15	16	17
18	19	20	21	22	23	24
25	26	27	28	29	30	31

August 2004

S	M	T	W	T	F	S
1	2	3	4	5	6	7
8	9	10	11	12	13	14
15	16	17	18	19	20	21
22	23	24	25	26	27	28
29	30	31				

12 Monday

4th ♉
☽ enters ♊ **3:45 pm** 12:45 pm

13 Tuesday

4th ♊

14 Wednesday

4th ♊
☽ v/c **8:33 am** 5:33 am

15 Thursday

4th ♊
☽ enters ♋ **4:40 am** 1:40 am

Eastern time in bold type
Pacific time in medium type

16 Friday

4th ♋

17 Saturday

4th ♋

New Moon	**7:24 am**	4:24 am
☽ v/c	**7:24 am**	4:24 am
☽ enters ♌	**4:56 pm**	1:56 pm

18 Sunday

1st ♌

June 2004

S	M	T	W	T	F	S
		1	2	3	4	5
6	7	8	9	10	11	12
13	14	15	16	17	18	19
20	21	22	23	24	25	26
27	28	29	30			

July 2004

S	M	T	W	T	F	S
				1	2	3
4	5	6	7	8	9	10
11	12	13	14	15	16	17
18	19	20	21	22	23	24
25	26	27	28	29	30	31

August 2004

S	M	T	W	T	F	S
1	2	3	4	5	6	7
8	9	10	11	12	13	14
15	16	17	18	19	20	21
22	23	24	25	26	27	28
29	30	31				

19 Monday

1st ♌
☽ v/c **2:50 pm** 11:50 am

20 Tuesday

1st ♌
☽ enters ♍ **3:44 am** 12:44 am

21 Wednesday

1st ♍
☽ v/c **5:48 pm** 2:48 pm

22 Thursday

1st ♍
☉ enters ♌ **7:50 am** 4:50 am
☽ enters ♎ **12:39 pm** 9:39 am

Sun enters Leo

Eastern time in bold type
Pacific time in medium type

23 Friday

1st ♎

24 Saturday

1st ♎

☽ v/c	**5:54 pm**	2:54 pm
☽ enters ♏	**7:08 pm**	4:08 pm
2nd Quarter	**11:37 pm**	8:37 pm

25 Sunday

2nd ♏

☿ enters ♍	**9:58 am**	6:58 am

June 2004

S	M	T	W	T	F	S
		1	2	3	4	5
6	7	8	9	10	11	12
13	14	15	16	17	18	19
20	21	22	23	24	25	26
27	28	29	30			

July 2004

S	M	T	W	T	F	S
				1	2	3
4	5	6	7	8	9	10
11	12	13	14	15	16	17
18	19	20	21	22	23	24
25	26	27	28	29	30	31

August 2004

S	M	T	W	T	F	S
1	2	3	4	5	6	7
8	9	10	11	12	13	14
15	16	17	18	19	20	21
22	23	24	25	26	27	28
29	30	31				

Eastern time in bold type
Pacific time in medium type

26 Monday

2nd ♏
☽ v/c **6:48 am** 3:48 am
☽ enters ♐ **10:48 pm** 7:48 pm

27 Tuesday

2nd ♐
⚵ ℞ **10:45 pm** 7:45 pm

28 Wednesday

2nd ♐
☽ v/c **11:06 am** 8:06 am
☽ enters ♑ **11:57 pm** 8:57 pm

29 Thursday

2nd ♑
⚳ enters ♍ **2:39 pm** 11:39 am

Eastern time in bold type
Pacific time in medium type

30 Friday

2nd ♑

☽ v/c **7:21 am** 4:21 am

☽ enters ♒ **11:54 pm** 8:54 pm

31 Saturday

2nd ♒

Full Moon **2:05 pm** 11:05 am

1 Sunday

3rd ♒

☽ v/c **4:51 pm** 1:51 pm

☽ enters ♓ 9:34 pm

Lammas

July 2004

S	M	T	W	T	F	S
				1	2	3
4	5	6	7	8	9	10
11	12	13	14	15	16	17
18	19	20	21	22	23	24
25	26	27	28	29	30	31

August 2004

S	M	T	W	T	F	S
1	2	3	4	5	6	7
8	9	10	11	12	13	14
15	16	17	18	19	20	21
22	23	24	25	26	27	28
29	30	31				

September 2004

S	M	T	W	T	F	S
			1	2	3	4
5	6	7	8	9	10	11
12	13	14	15	16	17	18
19	20	21	22	23	24	25
26	27	28	29	30		

Eastern time in bold type
Pacific time in medium type

2 Monday
3rd ♓
☽ enters ♓ **12:34 am**

3 Tuesday
3rd ♓
☽ v/c **10:58 pm** 7:58 pm

4 Wednesday
3rd ♓
☽ enters ♈ **3:59 am** 12:59 am
♀ enters ♌ **11:51 am** 8:51 am

5 Thursday
3rd ♈

Eastern time in bold type
Pacific time in medium type

6 Friday

3rd ♈

☽ v/c	**9:59 am**	6:59 am
☽ enters ♉	**11:26 am**	8:26 am

7 Saturday

3rd ♉

♀ enters ♋	**7:02 am**	4:02 am
4th Quarter	**6:01 pm**	3:01 pm

8 Sunday

4th ♉

☽ v/c	**8:46 pm**	5:46 pm
☽ enters ♊	**10:33 pm**	7:33 pm

July 2004

S	M	T	W	T	F	S
				1	2	3
4	5	6	7	8	9	10
11	12	13	14	15	16	17
18	19	20	21	22	23	24
25	26	27	28	29	30	31

August 2004

S	M	T	W	T	F	S
1	2	3	4	5	6	7
8	9	10	11	12	13	14
15	16	17	18	19	20	21
22	23	24	25	26	27	28
29	30	31				

September 2004

S	M	T	W	T	F	S
			1	2	3	4
5	6	7	8	9	10	11
12	13	14	15	16	17	18
19	20	21	22	23	24	25
26	27	28	29	30		

9 Monday

4th ♊
☿ ℞ **8:32 pm** 5:32 pm

10 Tuesday

4th ♊
♂ enters ♍ **6:14 am** 3:14 am
☽ v/c **3:59 pm** 12:59 pm

11 Wednesday

4th ♊
☽ enters ♋ **11:20 am** 8:20 am

12 Thursday

4th ♋

Eastern time in bold type
Pacific time in medium type

13 Friday

4th ♋
☽ v/c **6:17 am** 3:17 am
☽ enters ♌ **11:30 pm** 8:30 pm

14 Saturday

4th ♌

15 Sunday

4th ♌
New Moon **9:24 pm** 6:24 pm
☽ v/c **9:24 pm** 6:24 pm

July 2004

S	M	T	W	T	F	S
				1	2	3
4	5	6	7	8	9	10
11	12	13	14	15	16	17
18	19	20	21	22	23	24
25	26	27	28	29	30	31

August 2004

S	M	T	W	T	F	S
1	2	3	4	5	6	7
8	9	10	11	12	13	14
15	16	17	18	19	20	21
22	23	24	25	26	27	28
29	30	31				

September 2004

S	M	T	W	T	F	S
			1	2	3	4
5	6	7	8	9	10	11
12	13	14	15	16	17	18
19	20	21	22	23	24	25
26	27	28	29	30		

Eastern time in bold type
Pacific time in medium type

16 Monday

1st ♌
☽ enters ♍ **9:49 am** 6:49 am

17 Tuesday

1st ♍

18 Wednesday

1st ♍
☽ v/c **3:15 am** 12:15 am
☽ enters ♎ **6:09 pm** 3:09 pm

19 Thursday

1st ♎

Eastern time in bold type
Pacific time in medium type

20 Friday

1st ♎

☽ v/c	**9:39 pm**	6:39 pm
☽ enters ♏		9:37 pm

21 Saturday

1st ♏

☽ enters ♏ **12:37 am**

22 Sunday

1st ♏

☉ enters ♍	**2:53 pm**	11:53 am
☽ v/c	**4:53 pm**	1:53 pm

Sun enters Virgo

July 2004

S	M	T	W	T	F	S
				1	2	3
4	5	6	7	8	9	10
11	12	13	14	15	16	17
18	19	20	21	22	23	24
25	26	27	28	29	30	31

August 2004

S	M	T	W	T	F	S
1	2	3	4	5	6	7
8	9	10	11	12	13	14
15	16	17	18	19	20	21
22	23	24	25	26	27	28
29	30	31				

September 2004

S	M	T	W	T	F	S
			1	2	3	4
5	6	7	8	9	10	11
12	13	14	15	16	17	18
19	20	21	22	23	24	25
26	27	28	29	30		

Eastern time in bold type
Pacific time in medium type

23 Monday

1st ♏
☽ enters ♐ **5:08 am** 2:08 am
2nd Quarter **6:12 am** 3:12 am

24 Tuesday

2nd ♐
☿ enters ♌ **9:33 pm** 6:33 pm

25 Wednesday

2nd ♐
☽ v/c **7:13 am** 4:13 am
☽ enters ♑ **7:46 am** 4:46 am

26 Thursday

2nd ♑
☽ v/c **10:58 pm** 7:58 pm

Eastern time in bold type
Pacific time in medium type

27 Friday

2nd ♑
☽ enters ♒ **9:08 am** 6:08 am

28 Saturday

2nd ♒

29 Sunday

2nd ♒
☽ v/c **5:23 am** 2:23 am
☽ enters ♓ **10:33 am** 7:33 am
Full Moon **10:22 pm** 7:22 pm

July 2004

S	M	T	W	T	F	S
				1	2	3
4	5	6	7	8	9	10
11	12	13	14	15	16	17
18	19	20	21	22	23	24
25	26	27	28	29	30	31

August 2004

S	M	T	W	T	F	S
1	2	3	4	5	6	7
8	9	10	11	12	13	14
15	16	17	18	19	20	21
22	23	24	25	26	27	28
29	30	31				

September 2004

S	M	T	W	T	F	S
			1	2	3	4
5	6	7	8	9	10	11
12	13	14	15	16	17	18
19	20	21	22	23	24	25
26	27	28	29	30		

30 Monday

3rd ♓
♇ D **3:38 pm** 12:38 pm

31 Tuesday

3rd ♓
☽ v/c **4:28 am** 1:28 am
☽ enters ♈ **1:46 pm** 10:46 am

1 Wednesday

3rd ♈
⚵ D **11:45 am** 8:45 am

2 Thursday

3rd ♈
☿ D **9:09 am** 6:09 am
☽ v/c **12:17 pm** 9:17 am
☽ enters ♉ **8:16 pm** 5:16 pm

Eastern time in bold type
Pacific time in medium type

3 Friday

3rd ♉

4 Saturday

3rd ♉

☽ v/c 11:56 pm

5 Sunday

3rd ♉

☽ v/c **2:56 am**

☽ enters ♊ **6:24 am** 3:24 am

August 2004

S	M	T	W	T	F	S
1	2	3	4	5	6	7
8	9	10	11	12	13	14
15	16	17	18	19	20	21
22	23	24	25	26	27	28
29	30	31				

September 2004

S	M	T	W	T	F	S
			1	2	3	4
5	6	7	8	9	10	11
12	13	14	15	16	17	18
19	20	21	22	23	24	25
26	27	28	29	30		

October 2004

S	M	T	W	T	F	S
					1	2
3	4	5	6	7	8	9
10	11	12	13	14	15	16
17	18	19	20	21	22	23
24	25	26	27	28	29	30
31						

Eastern time in bold type
Pacific time in medium type

6 Monday

3rd ♊
4th Quarter **11:10 am** 8:10 am
♀ enters ♌ **6:16 pm** 3:16 pm

Labor Day

7 Tuesday

4th ♊
☽ v/c **2:08 pm** 11:08 am
☽ enters ♋ **6:50 pm** 3:50 pm

8 Wednesday

4th ♋

9 Thursday

4th ♋
☽ v/c 9:41 pm

Eastern time in bold type
Pacific time in medium type

10 Friday

4th ♋

☽ v/c **12:41 am**

☿ enters ♍ **3:38 am** 12:38 am

☽ enters ♌ **7:06 am** 4:06 am

11 Saturday

4th ♌

☽ v/c **9:22 pm** 6:22 pm

12 Sunday

4th ♌

☽ enters ♍ **5:16 pm** 2:16 pm

August 2004

S	M	T	W	T	F	S
1	2	3	4	5	6	7
8	9	10	11	12	13	14
15	16	17	18	19	20	21
22	23	24	25	26	27	28
29	30	31				

September 2004

S	M	T	W	T	F	S
			1	2	3	4
5	6	7	8	9	10	11
12	13	14	15	16	17	18
19	20	21	22	23	24	25
26	27	28	29	30		

October 2004

S	M	T	W	T	F	S
					1	2
3	4	5	6	7	8	9
10	11	12	13	14	15	16
17	18	19	20	21	22	23
24	25	26	27	28	29	30
31						

13 Monday

4th ♍

14 Tuesday

4th ♍

New Moon	**10:29 am**	7:29 am
☽ v/c	**8:55 pm**	5:55 pm
☽ enters ♎		9:54 pm

15 Wednesday

1st ♎

☽ enters ♎ **12:54 am**

16 Thursday

1st ♎

☽ v/c	**9:31 pm**	6:31 pm

Rosh Hashanah

Eastern time in bold type
Pacific time in medium type

17 Friday

1st ♎

☽ enters ♏ **6:25 am** 3:25 am

18 Saturday

1st ♏

19 Sunday

1st ♏

☽ v/c **8:24 am** 5:24 am

☽ enters ♐ **10:30 am** 7:30 am

August 2004

S	M	T	W	T	F	S
1	2	3	4	5	6	7
8	9	10	11	12	13	14
15	16	17	18	19	20	21
22	23	24	25	26	27	28
29	30	31				

September 2004

S	M	T	W	T	F	S
			1	2	3	4
5	6	7	8	9	10	11
12	13	14	15	16	17	18
19	20	21	22	23	24	25
26	27	28	29	30		

October 2004

S	M	T	W	T	F	S
					1	2
3	4	5	6	7	8	9
10	11	12	13	14	15	16
17	18	19	20	21	22	23
24	25	26	27	28	29	30
31						

Eastern time in bold type
Pacific time in medium type

20 Monday

1st ♐

21 Tuesday

1st ♐
2nd Quarter **11:54 am** 8:54 am
☽ v/c **12:19 pm** 9:19 am
☽ enters ♑ **1:35 pm** 10:35 am

22 Wednesday

2nd ♑
☉ enters ♎ **12:30 pm** 9:30 am

Sun enters Libra • Mabon • Fall Equinox • 12:30 pm ET/9:30 am PT

23 Thursday

2nd ♑
☽ v/c **3:41 pm** 12:41 pm
☽ enters ♒ **4:10 pm** 1:10 pm

Eastern time in bold type
Pacific time in medium type

24 Friday

2nd ♒
♃ enters ♎ **11:23 pm** 8:23 pm
☽ v/c 11:25 pm

25 Saturday

2nd ♒
☽ v/c **2:25 am**
☽ enters ♓ **6:55 pm** 3:55 pm

Yom Kippur

26 Sunday

2nd ♓
♂ enters ♎ **5:15 am** 2:15 am
⚷ D **1:20 pm** 10:20 am

August 2004

S	M	T	W	T	F	S
1	2	3	4	5	6	7
8	9	10	11	12	13	14
15	16	17	18	19	20	21
22	23	24	25	26	27	28
29	30	31				

September 2004

S	M	T	W	T	F	S
			1	2	3	4
5	6	7	8	9	10	11
12	13	14	15	16	17	18
19	20	21	22	23	24	25
26	27	28	29	30		

October 2004

S	M	T	W	T	F	S
					1	2
3	4	5	6	7	8	9
10	11	12	13	14	15	16
17	18	19	20	21	22	23
24	25	26	27	28	29	30
31						

27 Monday

2nd ♓

⚴ enters ♍	**9:33 am**	6:33 am
☽ v/c	**9:12 pm**	6:12 pm
☽ enters ♈	**10:57 pm**	7:57 pm

28 Tuesday

2nd ♈

Full Moon	**9:09 am**	6:09 am
☿ enters ♎	**10:13 am**	7:13 am

29 Wednesday

3rd ♈

☽ v/c	**9:53 pm**	6:53 pm

30 Thursday

3rd ♈

☽ enters ♉	**5:24 am**	2:24 am

Sukkot begins

Eastern time in bold type
Pacific time in medium type

1 Friday

3rd ♉

2 Saturday

3rd ♉

☽ v/c **12:34 pm** 9:34 am

☽ enters ♊ **2:55 pm** 11:55 am

3 Sunday

3rd ♊

⚳ enters ♎ **4:06 am** 1:06 am

♀ enters ♍ **1:20 pm** 10:20 am

September 2004

S	M	T	W	T	F	S
			1	2	3	4
5	6	7	8	9	10	11
12	13	14	15	16	17	18
19	20	21	22	23	24	25
26	27	28	29	30		

October 2004

S	M	T	W	T	F	S
					1	2
3	4	5	6	7	8	9
10	11	12	13	14	15	16
17	18	19	20	21	22	23
24	25	26	27	28	29	30
31						

November 2004

S	M	T	W	T	F	S
	1	2	3	4	5	6
7	8	9	10	11	12	13
14	15	16	17	18	19	20
21	22	23	24	25	26	27
28	29	30				

4 Monday

3rd ♊
☽ v/c **6:28 am** 3:28 am
☽ enters ♋ 11:54 pm

5 Tuesday

3rd ♊
☽ enters ♋ **2:54 am**

6 Wednesday

3rd ♋
4th Quarter **6:12 am** 3:12 am

Sukkot ends

7 Thursday

4th ♋
☽ v/c **8:13 am** 5:13 am
☽ enters ♌ **3:23 pm** 12:23 pm

Eastern time in bold type
Pacific time in medium type

8 Friday

4th ♌

9 Saturday

4th ♌

☽ v/c **6:42 am** 3:42 am

☽ enters ♍ 11:00 pm

10 Sunday

4th ♌

☽ enters ♍ **2:00 am**

September 2004

S	M	T	W	T	F	S
			1	2	3	4
5	6	7	8	9	10	11
12	13	14	15	16	17	18
19	20	21	22	23	24	25
26	27	28	29	30		

October 2004

S	M	T	W	T	F	S
					1	2
3	4	5	6	7	8	9
10	11	12	13	14	15	16
17	18	19	20	21	22	23
24	25	26	27	28	29	30
31						

November 2004

S	M	T	W	T	F	S
	1	2	3	4	5	6
7	8	9	10	11	12	13
14	15	16	17	18	19	20
21	22	23	24	25	26	27
28	29	30				

Eastern time in bold type
Pacific time in medium type

11 Monday

4th ♍

Columbus Day (observed)

12 Tuesday

4th ♍

☽ v/c **3:32 am** 12:32 am

☽ enters ♎ **9:32 am** 6:32 am

13 Wednesday

4th ♎

New Moon **10:48 pm** 7:48 pm

Solar Eclipse 21° ♎ 06' • 11:00 pm ET/8:00 pm PT

14 Thursday

1st ♎

☽ v/c **10:22 am** 7:22 am

☽ enters ♏ **2:10 pm** 11:10 am

Eastern time in bold type

Pacific time in medium type

15 Friday

1st ♏
☿ enters ♏ **6:57 pm** 3:57 pm

Ramadan begins

16 Saturday

1st ♏
☽ v/c **11:43 am** 8:43 am
☽ enters ♐ **4:58 pm** 1:58 pm

17 Sunday

1st ♐

September 2004

S	M	T	W	T	F	S
			1	2	3	4
5	6	7	8	9	10	11
12	13	14	15	16	17	18
19	20	21	22	23	24	25
26	27	28	29	30		

October 2004

S	M	T	W	T	F	S
					1	2
3	4	5	6	7	8	9
10	11	12	13	14	15	16
17	18	19	20	21	22	23
24	25	26	27	28	29	30
31						

November 2004

S	M	T	W	T	F	S
	1	2	3	4	5	6
7	8	9	10	11	12	13
14	15	16	17	18	19	20
21	22	23	24	25	26	27
28	29	30				

18 Monday

1st ♐

☽ v/c	**11:46 am**	8:46 am
☽ enters ♑	**7:07 pm**	4:07 pm

19 Tuesday

1st ♑

20 Wednesday

1st ♑

2nd Quarter	**5:59 pm**	2:59 pm
☽ v/c	**5:59 pm**	2:59 pm
☽ enters ♒	**9:38 pm**	6:38 pm

21 Thursday

2nd ♒

Eastern time in bold type
Pacific time in medium type

22 Friday

2nd ♒

☽ v/c	**8:20 am**	5:20 am
☉ enters ♏	**9:49 pm**	6:49 pm
☽ enters ♓		10:13 pm

Sun enters Scorpio

23 Saturday

2nd ♒

☽ enters ♓	**1:13 am**	

24 Sunday

2nd ♓

♆ D	**7:56 am**	4:56 am
☽ v/c		10:17 pm

September 2004

S	M	T	W	T	F	S
			1	2	3	4
5	6	7	8	9	10	11
12	13	14	15	16	17	18
19	20	21	22	23	24	25
26	27	28	29	30		

October 2004

S	M	T	W	T	F	S
					1	2
3	4	5	6	7	8	9
10	11	12	13	14	15	16
17	18	19	20	21	22	23
24	25	26	27	28	29	30
31						

November 2004

S	M	T	W	T	F	S
	1	2	3	4	5	6
7	8	9	10	11	12	13
14	15	16	17	18	19	20
21	22	23	24	25	26	27
28	29	30				

Eastern time in bold type
Pacific time in medium type

25 Monday

2nd ♓
☽ v/c **1:17 am**
☽ enters ♈ **6:24 am** 3:24 am

26 Tuesday

2nd ♈

27 Wednesday

2nd ♈
☽ v/c **8:24 am** 5:24 am
☽ enters ♉ **1:37 pm** 10:37 am
Full Moon **11:07 pm** 8:07 pm
⚶ D 10:50 pm

Lunar Eclipse 5° ♉ 02' • 11:05 pm ET/8:05 pm PT

28 Thursday

3rd ♉
⚶ D **1:50 am**
♀ enters ♎ **8:39 pm** 5:39 pm

Eastern time in bold type
Pacific time in medium type

29 Friday

3rd ♉
☽ v/c **5:50 pm** 2:50 pm
☽ enters ♊ **11:11 pm** 8:11 pm

30 Saturday

3rd ♊

31 Sunday

3rd ♊
☽ v/c **8:21 pm** 5:21 pm

Halloween/Samhain • Daylight Saving Time ends at 2 am

September 2004

S	M	T	W	T	F	S
			1	2	3	4
5	6	7	8	9	10	11
12	13	14	15	16	17	18
19	20	21	22	23	24	25
26	27	28	29	30		

October 2004

S	M	T	W	T	F	S
					1	2
3	4	5	6	7	8	9
10	11	12	13	14	15	16
17	18	19	20	21	22	23
24	25	26	27	28	29	30
31						

November 2004

S	M	T	W	T	F	S
	1	2	3	4	5	6
7	8	9	10	11	12	13
14	15	16	17	18	19	20
21	22	23	24	25	26	27
28	29	30				

Eastern time in bold type
Pacific time in medium type

1 Monday

3rd ♊
☽ enters ♋ **9:53 am** 6:53 am

All Saints' Day

2 Tuesday

3rd ♋

Election Day (general)

3 Wednesday

3rd ♋
☽ v/c **9:00 pm** 6:00 pm
☽ enters ♌ **10:32 pm** 7:32 pm

4 Thursday

3rd ♌
☿ enters ♐ **9:40 am** 6:40 am
4th Quarter 9:53 pm

Eastern time in bold type
Pacific time in medium type

5 Friday

3rd ♌
4th Quarter **12:53 am**

6 Saturday

4th ♌

☽ v/c	**3:45 am**	12:45 am
☽ enters ♍	**10:00 am**	7:00 am

7 Sunday

4th ♍

♄ ℞		10:54 pm

October 2004

S	M	T	W	T	F	S
					1	2
3	4	5	6	7	8	9
10	11	12	13	14	15	16
17	18	19	20	21	22	23
24	25	26	27	28	29	30
31						

November 2004

S	M	T	W	T	F	S
	1	2	3	4	5	6
7	8	9	10	11	12	13
14	15	16	17	18	19	20
21	22	23	24	25	26	27
28	29	30				

December 2004

S	M	T	W	T	F	S
			1	2	3	4
5	6	7	8	9	10	11
12	13	14	15	16	17	18
19	20	21	22	23	24	25
26	27	28	29	30	31	

Eastern time in bold type
Pacific time in medium type

8 Monday

4th ♍

♄ ℞ **1:54 am**

☽ v/c **1:32 pm** 10:32 am

☽ enters ♎ **6:23 pm** 3:23 pm

9 Tuesday

4th ♎

10 Wednesday

4th ♎

☽ v/c **11:02 pm** 8:02 pm

☽ enters ♏ **11:05 pm** 8:05 pm

♂ enters ♏ 9:11 pm

11 Thursday

4th ♏

♂ enters ♏ **12:11 am**

♅ D **2:12 pm** 11:12 am

Veterans Day

Eastern time in bold type
Pacific time in medium type

12 Friday

4th ♏

New Moon	**9:27 am**	6:27 am
☽ v/c	**8:34 pm**	5:34 pm
☽ enters ♐		9:56 pm

13 Saturday

1st ♏

☽ enters ♐ **12:56 am**

14 Sunday

1st ♐

☽ v/c	**10:58 am**	7:58 am
☽ enters ♑		10:33 pm

Ramadan ends

October 2004

S	M	T	W	T	F	S
					1	2
3	4	5	6	7	8	9
10	11	12	13	14	15	16
17	18	19	20	21	22	23
24	25	26	27	28	29	30
31						

November 2004

S	M	T	W	T	F	S
	1	2	3	4	5	6
7	8	9	10	11	12	13
14	15	16	17	18	19	20
21	22	23	24	25	26	27
28	29	30				

December 2004

S	M	T	W	T	F	S
			1	2	3	4
5	6	7	8	9	10	11
12	13	14	15	16	17	18
19	20	21	22	23	24	25
26	27	28	29	30	31	

15 Monday

1st ♐
☽ enters ♑ **1:33 am**

16 Tuesday

1st ♑

☽ v/c	**10:07 pm**	7:07 pm
☽ enters ♒		11:39 pm

17 Wednesday

1st ♑
☽ enters ♒ **2:39 am**

18 Thursday

1st ♒

2nd Quarter		9:50 pm
☽ v/c		9:50 pm

Eastern time in bold type
Pacific time in medium type

19 Friday

1st ♒
2nd Quarter **12:50 am**
☽ v/c **12:50 am**
☽ enters ♓ **5:38 am** 2:38 am

20 Saturday

2nd ♓

21 Sunday

2nd ♓
☽ v/c **10:35 am** 7:35 am
☽ enters ♈ **11:11 am** 8:11 am
☉ enters ♐ **6:22 pm** 3:22 pm

Sun enters Sagittarius

October 2004

S	M	T	W	T	F	S
					1	2
3	4	5	6	7	8	9
10	11	12	13	14	15	16
17	18	19	20	21	22	23
24	25	26	27	28	29	30
31						

November 2004

S	M	T	W	T	F	S
	1	2	3	4	5	6
7	8	9	10	11	12	13
14	15	16	17	18	19	20
21	22	23	24	25	26	27
28	29	30				

December 2004

S	M	T	W	T	F	S
			1	2	3	4
5	6	7	8	9	10	11
12	13	14	15	16	17	18
19	20	21	22	23	24	25
26	27	28	29	30	31	

22 Monday

2nd ♈
♀ enters ♏ **8:31 am** 5:31 am

23 Tuesday

2nd ♈
☽ v/c **1:47 pm** 10:47 am
☽ enters ♉ **7:16 pm** 4:16 pm

24 Wednesday

2nd ♉

25 Thursday

2nd ♉
☽ v/c **11:37 pm** 8:37 pm

Thanksgiving Day

Eastern time in bold type
Pacific time in medium type

26 Friday

2nd ♉
☽ enters ♊ **5:25 am** 2:25 am
Full Moon **3:07 pm** 12:07 pm

27 Saturday

3rd ♊

28 Sunday

3rd ♊
☽ v/c **10:04 am** 7:04 am
☽ enters ♋ **5:10 pm** 2:10 pm

October 2004

S	M	T	W	T	F	S
					1	2
3	4	5	6	7	8	9
10	11	12	13	14	15	16
17	18	19	20	21	22	23
24	25	26	27	28	29	30
31						

November 2004

S	M	T	W	T	F	S
	1	2	3	4	5	6
7	8	9	10	11	12	13
14	15	16	17	18	19	20
21	22	23	24	25	26	27
28	29	30				

December 2004

S	M	T	W	T	F	S
			1	2	3	4
5	6	7	8	9	10	11
12	13	14	15	16	17	18
19	20	21	22	23	24	25
26	27	28	29	30	31	

Eastern time in bold type
Pacific time in medium type

29 Monday
3rd ♋

30 Tuesday
3rd ♋

☿ ℞	**7:17 am**	4:17 am
☽ v/c	**11:28 pm**	8:28 pm

1 Wednesday
3rd ♋

☽ enters ♌	**5:50 am**	2:50 am

2 Thursday
3rd ♌

♀ enters ♎	**1:36 pm**	10:36 am

Eastern time in bold type
Pacific time in medium type

3 Friday

3rd ♌

☽ v/c	**9:52 am**	6:52 am
⚵ enters ♒	**4:47 pm**	1:47 pm
☽ enters ♍	**6:00 pm**	3:00 pm

4 Saturday

3rd ♍

4th Quarter	**7:53 pm**	4:53 pm

5 Sunday

4th ♍

☽ v/c	**9:28 pm**	6:28 pm

November 2004

S	M	T	W	T	F	S
	1	2	3	4	5	6
7	8	9	10	11	12	13
14	15	16	17	18	19	20
21	22	23	24	25	26	27
28	29	30				

December 2004

S	M	T	W	T	F	S
			1	2	3	4
5	6	7	8	9	10	11
12	13	14	15	16	17	18
19	20	21	22	23	24	25
26	27	28	29	30	31	

January 2005

S	M	T	W	T	F	S
						1
2	3	4	5	6	7	8
9	10	11	12	13	14	15
16	17	18	19	20	21	22
23	24	25	26	27	28	29
30	31					

Eastern time in bold type
Pacific time in medium type

6 Monday
4th ♍
☽ enters ♎ **3:46 am** 12:46 am

7 Tuesday
4th ♎

8 Wednesday
4th ♎
☽ v/c **3:41 am** 12:41 am
☽ enters ♏ **9:43 am** 6:43 am

Hanukkah begins

9 Thursday
4th ♏

Eastern time in bold type
Pacific time in medium type

10 Friday

4th ♏

☽ v/c	**6:03 am**	3:03 am
☽ enters ♐	**11:54 am**	8:54 am
⚳ enters ♏	**1:51 pm**	10:51 am

11 Saturday

4th ♐

New Moon	**8:29 pm**	5:29 pm
☽ v/c	**11:03 pm**	8:03 pm

12 Sunday

1st ♐

☽ enters ♑	**11:42 am**	8:42 am

November 2004

S	M	T	W	T	F	S
	1	2	3	4	5	6
7	8	9	10	11	12	13
14	15	16	17	18	19	20
21	22	23	24	25	26	27
28	29	30				

December 2004

S	M	T	W	T	F	S
			1	2	3	4
5	6	7	8	9	10	11
12	13	14	15	16	17	18
19	20	21	22	23	24	25
26	27	28	29	30	31	

January 2005

S	M	T	W	T	F	S
						1
2	3	4	5	6	7	8
9	10	11	12	13	14	15
16	17	18	19	20	21	22
23	24	25	26	27	28	29
30	31					

Eastern time in bold type
Pacific time in medium type

13 Monday
1st ♑

14 Tuesday
1st ♑

☽ v/c	**6:43 am**	3:43 am
☽ enters ♒	**11:10 am**	8:10 am

15 Wednesday
1st ♒

Hanukkah ends

16 Thursday
1st ♒

☽ v/c	**3:33 am**	12:33 am
♀ enters ♐	**12:10 pm**	9:10 am
☽ enters ♓	**12:24 pm**	9:24 am

Eastern time in bold type
Pacific time in medium type

17 Friday
1st ♓

18 Saturday
1st ♓

2nd Quarter	**11:40 am**	8:40 am
☽ v/c	**11:40 am**	8:40 am
☽ enters ♈	**4:52 pm**	1:52 pm

19 Sunday
2nd ♈

☿ D		10:28 pm

November 2004

S	M	T	W	T	F	S
	1	2	3	4	5	6
7	8	9	10	11	12	13
14	15	16	17	18	19	20
21	22	23	24	25	26	27
28	29	30				

December 2004

S	M	T	W	T	F	S
			1	2	3	4
5	6	7	8	9	10	11
12	13	14	15	16	17	18
19	20	21	22	23	24	25
26	27	28	29	30	31	

January 2005

S	M	T	W	T	F	S
						1
2	3	4	5	6	7	8
9	10	11	12	13	14	15
16	17	18	19	20	21	22
23	24	25	26	27	28	29
30	31					

20 Monday

2nd ♈
☿ D **1:28 am**
☽ v/c 9:16 pm
☽ enters ♉ 9:52 pm

21 Tuesday

2nd ♈
☽ v/c **12:16 am**
☽ enters ♉ **12:52 am**
☉ enters ♑ **7:42 am** 4:42 am

Sun enters Capricorn • Yule • Winter Solstice • 7:42 am EST/4:42 am PST

22 Wednesday

2nd ♉

23 Thursday

2nd ♉
☽ v/c **8:41 am** 5:41 am
☽ enters ♊ **11:32 am** 8:32 am

Eastern time in bold type
Pacific time in medium type

24 Friday

2nd ♊

Christmas Eve

25 Saturday

2nd ♊

☽ v/c	**8:30 am**	5:30 am
♂ enters ♐	**11:04 am**	8:04 am
☽ enters ♋	**11:38 pm**	8:38 pm

Christmas Day

26 Sunday

2nd ♋

Full Moon	**10:06 am**	7:06 am

Kwanzaa begins

November 2004

S	M	T	W	T	F	S
	1	2	3	4	5	6
7	8	9	10	11	12	13
14	15	16	17	18	19	20
21	22	23	24	25	26	27
28	29	30				

December 2004

S	M	T	W	T	F	S
			1	2	3	4
5	6	7	8	9	10	11
12	13	14	15	16	17	18
19	20	21	22	23	24	25
26	27	28	29	30	31	

January 2005

S	M	T	W	T	F	S
						1
2	3	4	5	6	7	8
9	10	11	12	13	14	15
16	17	18	19	20	21	22
23	24	25	26	27	28	29
30	31					

Eastern time in bold type
Pacific time in medium type

27 Monday

3rd ♋
☽ v/c 11:34 pm

28 Tuesday

3rd ♋
☽ v/c **2:34 am**
☽ enters ♌ **12:14 pm** 9:14 am

29 Wednesday

3rd ♌

30 Thursday

3rd ♌
☽ v/c **9:54 am** 6:54 am
☽ enters ♍ 9:33 pm

Eastern time in bold type
Pacific time in medium type

31 Friday

3rd ♌
☽ enters ♍ **12:33 am**

New Year's Eve

1 Saturday

3rd ♍
☽ v/c 10:23 pm

New Year's Day • Kwanzaa ends

2 Sunday

3rd ♍
☽ v/c **1:23 am**
☽ enters ♎ **11:19 am** 8:19 am

November 2004

S	M	T	W	T	F	S
	1	2	3	4	5	6
7	8	9	10	11	12	13
14	15	16	17	18	19	20
21	22	23	24	25	26	27
28	29	30				

December 2004

S	M	T	W	T	F	S
			1	2	3	4
5	6	7	8	9	10	11
12	13	14	15	16	17	18
19	20	21	22	23	24	25
26	27	28	29	30	31	

January 2005

S	M	T	W	T	F	S
						1
2	3	4	5	6	7	8
9	10	11	12	13	14	15
16	17	18	19	20	21	22
23	24	25	26	27	28	29
30	31					

Eastern time in bold type
Pacific time in medium type

The Year 2005

January

S	M	T	W	T	F	S
						1
2	3	4	5	6	7	8
9	10	11	12	13	14	15
16	17	18	19	20	21	22
23	24	25	26	27	28	29
30	31					

February

S	M	T	W	T	F	S
		1	2	3	4	5
6	7	8	9	10	11	12
13	14	15	16	17	18	19
20	21	22	23	24	25	26
27	28					

March

S	M	T	W	T	F	S
		1	2	3	4	5
6	7	8	9	10	11	12
13	14	15	16	17	18	19
20	21	22	23	24	25	26
27	28	29	30	31		

April

S	M	T	W	T	F	S
					1	2
3	4	5	6	7	8	9
10	11	12	13	14	15	16
17	18	19	20	21	22	23
24	25	26	27	28	29	30

May

S	M	T	W	T	F	S
1	2	3	4	5	6	7
8	9	10	11	12	13	14
15	16	17	18	19	20	21
22	23	24	25	26	27	28
29	30	31				

June

S	M	T	W	T	F	S
			1	2	3	4
5	6	7	8	9	10	11
12	13	14	15	16	17	18
19	20	21	22	23	24	25
26	27	28	29	30		

July

S	M	T	W	T	F	S
					1	2
3	4	5	6	7	8	9
10	11	12	13	14	15	16
17	18	19	20	21	22	23
24	25	26	27	28	29	30
31						

August

S	M	T	W	T	F	S
	1	2	3	4	5	6
7	8	9	10	11	12	13
14	15	16	17	18	19	20
21	22	23	24	25	26	27
28	29	30	31			

September

S	M	T	W	T	F	S
				1	2	3
4	5	6	7	8	9	10
11	12	13	14	15	16	17
18	19	20	21	22	23	24
25	26	27	28	29	30	

October

S	M	T	W	T	F	S
						1
2	3	4	5	6	7	8
9	10	11	12	13	14	15	16
17	18	19	20	21	22	23
24	25	26	27	28	29	30
31						

November

S	M	T	W	T	F	S
	1	2	3	4	5	6
7	8	9	10	11	12	13
14	15	16	17	18	19	20
21	22	23	24	25	26	27
28	29	30				

December

S	M	T	W	T	F	S
				1	2	3	4
5	6	7	8	9	10	11
12	13	14	15	16	17	18
19	20	21	22	23	24	25
26	27	28	29	30	31	

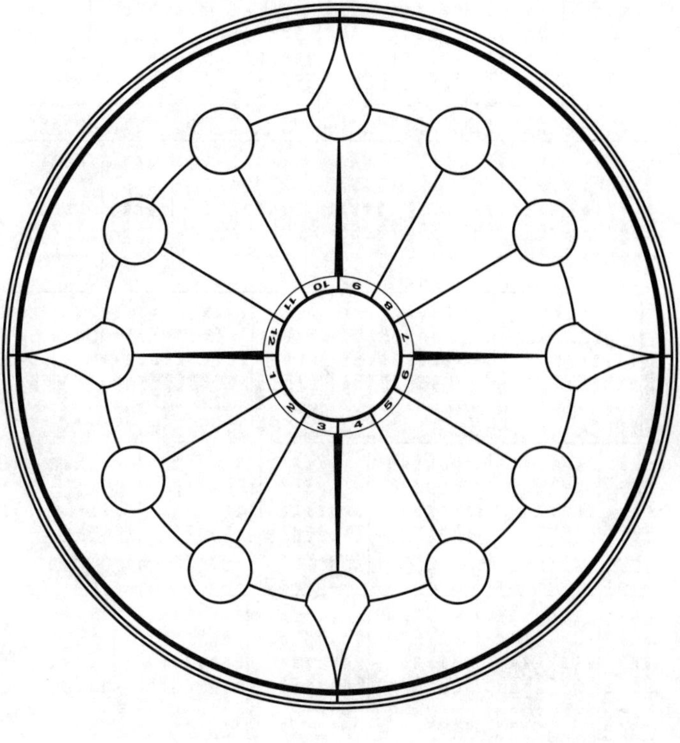

1
2
3
4
5
6
7
8
9
10
11
12

JANUARY 2003

1 WEDNESDAY

☽⚺♂	**1:15 am**	
☽☍♄	**9:10 am**	6:10 am
☽⚹♀	**10:45 am**	7:45 am
☉☌⚷	**11:09 am**	8:09 am
☽⚹♅	**12:23 pm**	9:23 am
♀⚻♄	**1:14 pm**	10:14 am
☽⚺☿	**3:57 pm**	12:57 pm

2 THURSDAY

☽□⚴	**6:31 am**	3:31 am
☽□⚳	**9:01 am**	6:01 am
☽⚺♆	**11:14 am**	8:14 am
☽⚹⚵	**1:14 pm**	10:14 am
☽☌⚷	**1:30 pm**	10:30 am
☽☌☉	**3:23 pm**	12:23 pm
☽⚻♃	**11:30 pm**	8:30 pm
♀□☿		9:28 pm
☽⚺♇		11:25 pm

3 FRIDAY

♀□☿	**12:28 am**	
☽⚺♇	**2:25 am**	
☽⚹♂	**7:22 am**	4:22 am
⚷⚹⚵	**11:41 am**	8:41 am
☽⚻♄	**12:43 pm**	9:43 am
♀□♅	**3:38 pm**	12:38 pm
☽⚺♀	**3:47 pm**	12:47 pm
☽⚺♅	**4:32 pm**	1:32 pm
☽⚹♀	**4:36 pm**	1:36 pm
☽☌☿	**7:56 pm**	4:56 pm

4 SATURDAY

☽△⚴	**12:19 pm**	9:19 am
☽⚹⚳	**2:47 pm**	11:47 am
☽☌♆	**4:22 pm**	1:22 pm
☽⚺⚷	**7:01 pm**	4:01 pm
☽□⚵	**7:25 pm**	4:25 pm
☽⚺☉		10:04 pm

5 SUNDAY

☽⚺☉	**1:04 am**	
☿⚹♀	**3:00 am**	12:00 am
☽☍♃	**4:46 am**	1:46 am
☽⚹♇	**8:22 am**	5:22 am
♅☌♀	**8:44 am**	5:44 am
☽□♂	**4:18 pm**	1:18 pm
☽△♄	**6:48 pm**	3:48 pm
☽☌♅	**11:21 pm**	8:21 pm
☽☌♀	**11:39 pm**	8:39 pm
☽⚺☿		9:50 pm

6 MONDAY

☽⚺☿	**12:50 am**	
☽□♀	**3:44 am**	12:44 am
☿⚺♀	**3:09 pm**	12:09 pm
☉⚻♃	**8:34 pm**	5:34 pm
☽⚻⚴	**9:14 pm**	6:14 pm
☽⚺⚳	**11:47 pm**	8:47 pm
☿⚺♅	**11:50 pm**	8:50 pm
☽⚺♆		9:36 pm

7 TUESDAY

☽⚺♆	**12:36 am**	
☽⚹⚷	**3:43 am**	12:43 am
☽△⚵	**4:51 am**	1:51 am
☽⚻♃	**1:08 pm**	10:08 am
♂⚻♄	**1:36 pm**	10:36 am
☽⚹☉	**2:47 pm**	11:47 am
☽□♇	**5:35 pm**	2:35 pm

8 WEDNESDAY

☽□♄	**4:08 am**	1:08 am
☽△♂	**5:02 am**	2:02 am
☽⚹☿	**6:55 am**	3:55 am
☽⚺♅	**9:31 am**	6:31 am
☽⚺♀	**11:03 am**	8:03 am
☽△♀	**7:09 pm**	4:09 pm
☿⚹♂	**7:18 pm**	4:18 pm
☉⚺♇		10:32 pm

9 THURSDAY

☉⚺♇	**1:32 am**	
♆⚹⚳	**3:05 am**	12:05 am
☽☍⚴	**9:28 am**	6:28 am
☽⚹♆	**12:01 pm**	9:01 am
☽☌⚳	**12:10 pm**	9:10 am
☿⚻♄	**2:30 pm**	11:30 am
☽□⚷	**3:36 pm**	12:36 pm
☽⚻⚵	**5:32 pm**	2:32 pm
☽△♃		9:23 pm

10 FRIDAY

☽△♃	**12:23 am**	
☽△♇	**5:41 am**	2:41 am
☽□☉	**8:15 am**	5:15 am
☽□☿	**1:43 pm**	10:43 am
☽⚹♄	**4:02 pm**	1:02 pm
☽⚻♂	**8:48 pm**	5:48 pm
☽⚹♅	**10:10 pm**	7:10 pm
☽⚹♀		10:04 pm

11 SATURDAY

☽⚹♀	**1:04 am**	
☽⚻♀	**1:26 pm**	10:26 am
☉☌☿	**3:02 pm**	12:02 pm
☽⚻⚴	**11:22 pm**	8:22 pm
♂□♅	**11:47 pm**	8:47 pm
☽□♆		9:59 pm
☽⚺⚳		11:14 pm

12 SUNDAY

☽□♆	**12:59 am**	
☽⚺⚳	**2:14 am**	
☽△⚷	**4:55 am**	1:55 am
☽☍⚵	**7:36 am**	4:36 am
☽□♃	**12:36 pm**	9:36 am
☽⚻♇	**6:36 pm**	3:36 pm
☽△☿	**8:20 pm**	5:20 pm
☽△☉		11:36 pm

13 MONDAY

☽△☉	**2:36 am**	
☽⚺♄	**4:18 am**	1:18 am
☽□♅	**10:54 am**	7:54 am
☿⚺♇	**11:53 am**	8:53 am
☽☍♂	**12:44 pm**	9:44 am
☽□♀	**3:03 pm**	12:03 pm
☉⚻♄	**9:39 pm**	6:39 pm

14 TUESDAY

☽☍♀	**7:02 am**	4:02 am
☽△⚴	**12:06 pm**	9:06 am
☽△♆	**12:51 pm**	9:51 am
☽⚹⚳	**3:06 pm**	12:06 pm
☽⚻⚷	**4:55 pm**	1:55 pm
☽⚻⚵	**8:09 pm**	5:09 pm
☽⚹♃	**11:16 pm**	8:16 pm
☽⚻☿		10:53 pm

15 WEDNESDAY

☽⚻☿	**1:53 am**	
☽☍♇	**5:41 am**	2:41 am
☽☌♄	**2:29 pm**	11:29 am
☽⚻☉	**6:16 pm**	3:16 pm
☽△♅	**9:16 pm**	6:16 pm
☽⚻♂		10:51 pm
☽△♀		11:23 pm

16 THURSDAY

☽⚻♂	**1:51 am**	
☽△♀	**2:23 am**	
☿⚻♃	**1:20 pm**	10:20 am
☽⚻♀	**9:03 pm**	6:03 pm
♂□♀	**9:38 pm**	6:38 pm
☽□⚴	**9:41 pm**	6:41 pm
☽⚻♆	**9:43 pm**	6:43 pm
☽□⚳		9:50 pm
♆△⚴		9:53 pm
☽☍⚷		10:50 pm

17 FRIDAY

☽□⚳	**12:50 am**	
♆△⚴	**12:53 am**	
☽☍⚷	**1:50 am**	
☽△⚵	**5:25 am**	2:25 am
♀⚹♆	**5:35 am**	2:35 am
☽☍☿	**5:54 am**	2:54 am
♀⚹⚴	**6:21 am**	3:21 am
☽⚺♃	**6:52 am**	3:52 am
☉⚺♅	**9:36 am**	6:36 am
☿⚹⚵	**11:49 am**	8:49 am
☽⚻♇	**1:34 pm**	10:34 am
☽⚺♄	**9:28 pm**	6:28 pm

18 SATURDAY

☽⚻♅	**4:21 am**	1:21 am
☽☍☉	**5:48 am**	2:48 am
☽⚻♀	**10:14 am**	7:14 am
☽△♂	**11:11 am**	8:11 am

19 SUNDAY

☽☍♆	**3:26 am**	12:26 am
☽⚹⚴	**3:57 am**	12:57 am
☽△♀	**7:08 am**	4:08 am
☽△⚳	**7:19 am**	4:19 am
☽⚻⚷	**7:35 am**	4:35 am
☽⚻☿	**8:35 am**	5:35 am
♀△⚳	**10:13 am**	7:13 am
☽□⚵	**11:29 am**	8:29 am
☽☌♃	**11:33 am**	8:33 am
♀⚺⚷	**1:33 pm**	10:33 am
♃□⚵	**1:56 pm**	10:56 am
☽△♇	**6:31 pm**	3:31 pm
☿⚺♀	**8:29 pm**	5:29 pm
☽⚹♄		10:45 pm

20 MONDAY

☽⚹♄	**1:45 am**	
⚷□⚳	**4:39 am**	1:39 am
☿□⚳	**8:36 am**	5:36 am
☽☍♅	**8:46 am**	5:46 am
☿☌⚷	**10:09 am**	7:09 am
☽⚻☉	**2:03 pm**	11:03 am
☽☍♀	**3:26 pm**	12:26 pm
☽□♂	**5:40 pm**	2:40 pm

21 TUESDAY

☽⚻♆	**7:04 am**	4:04 am
☽⚺⚴	**8:01 am**	5:01 am
♀△♃	**10:35 am**	7:35 am
☽△☿	**10:40 am**	7:40 am
☽△⚷	**11:19 am**	8:19 am
☽⚻⚳	**11:43 am**	8:43 am
☽⚺♃	**2:23 pm**	11:23 am
☽□♀	**2:44 pm**	11:44 am
☽⚹⚵	**3:33 pm**	12:33 pm
☉⚺♀	**5:09 pm**	2:09 pm
☽□♇	**9:46 pm**	6:46 pm

22 WEDNESDAY

♀⚺⚵	**3:54 am**	12:54 am
☽□♄	**4:34 am**	1:34 am
☽⚻♅	**11:52 am**	8:52 am
☽⚻♀	**7:25 pm**	4:25 pm
☽△☉	**8:49 pm**	5:49 pm
☽⚹♂	**10:53 pm**	7:53 pm

23 THURSDAY

☽△♆	**9:55 am**	6:55 am
☽☌⚴	**11:16 am**	8:16 am
☽□☿	**1:12 pm**	10:12 am
☽□⚷	**2:22 pm**	11:22 am
☽☍⚳	**3:26 pm**	12:26 pm
☽⚹♃	**4:38 pm**	1:38 pm
☽⚺⚵	**6:59 pm**	3:59 pm
☽⚹♀	**9:37 pm**	6:37 pm
☽⚹♇		9:34 pm

24 FRIDAY

☽⚹♇	**12:34 am**	
☽△♄	**7:05 am**	4:05 am
☽△♅	**2:48 pm**	11:48 am
☽△♀	**11:22 pm**	8:22 pm

25 SATURDAY

☽□☉	**3:33 am**	12:33 am
☽⚺♂	**4:08 am**	1:08 am
♃△⚳	**8:19 am**	5:19 am
☽□♆	**12:57 pm**	9:57 am
♀☌♇	**12:59 pm**	9:59 am
☽⚺⚴	**2:41 pm**	11:41 am
☽⚹☿	**4:58 pm**	1:58 pm
☽⚹⚷	**5:40 pm**	2:40 pm
☽□♃	**7:08 pm**	4:08 pm
☽⚻⚳	**7:28 pm**	4:28 pm
☽☌⚵	**10:43 pm**	7:43 pm
☉⚹♂		9:26 pm

26 SUNDAY

☉⚹♂	**12:26 am**	
☽⚺♇	**3:44 am**	12:44 am
☽⚺♀	**4:57 am**	1:57 am
☽⚻♄	**10:02 am**	7:02 am
☽□♅	**6:14 pm**	3:14 pm
☿☌⚷	**11:18 pm**	8:18 pm

27 MONDAY

☽□♀	**3:54 am**	12:54 am
☽☌♂	**10:02 am**	7:02 am
☽⚹☉	**11:00 am**	8:00 am
☽⚹♆	**4:38 pm**	1:38 pm
☽⚹⚴	**6:41 pm**	3:41 pm
☿⚻♃	**8:51 pm**	5:51 pm
☽⚺⚷	**9:37 pm**	6:37 pm
☽△♃	**10:16 pm**	7:16 pm
☽⚺☿	**10:20 pm**	7:20 pm
☽△⚳		9:12 pm

28 TUESDAY

☽△⚳	**12:12 am**	
☽⚺⚵	**3:06 am**	12:06 am
☽☌♇	**7:36 am**	4:36 am
☽☌♀	**1:13 pm**	10:13 am
☽☍♄	**1:43 pm**	10:43 am
♀☍♄	**7:13 pm**	4:13 pm
☽⚹♅	**10:26 pm**	7:26 pm

29 WEDNESDAY

☽⚹♀	**9:19 am**	6:19 am
♃⚻⚷	**1:26 pm**	10:26 am
☽⚺♂	**4:55 pm**	1:55 pm
☽⚺☉	**7:32 pm**	4:32 pm
☽⚺♆	**9:12 pm**	6:12 pm
☽□⚴	**11:33 pm**	8:33 pm
☽⚻♃		11:17 pm
☽☌⚷		11:30 pm

30 THURSDAY

☽⚻♃	**2:17 am**	
☽☌⚷	**2:30 am**	
☽☌☿	**5:34 am**	2:34 am
☽□⚳	**5:58 am**	2:58 am
☽⚹⚵	**8:28 am**	5:28 am
☽⚺♇	**12:27 pm**	9:27 am
☿□⚳	**4:55 pm**	1:55 pm
☽⚻♄	**6:27 pm**	3:27 pm
☉☌♆	**6:32 pm**	3:32 pm
☽⚺♀	**10:53 pm**	7:53 pm

31 FRIDAY

☽⚺♅	**3:47 am**	12:47 am
☽⚺♀	**4:06 pm**	1:06 pm
☽⚹♂		10:21 pm

Eastern time in bold type
Pacific time in medium type

JANUARY 2003

☽ Last Aspect day	EST / hr:mn / PST	asp	☽ Ingress sign day	EST / hr:mn / PST
1	**12:23 pm** 9:23 am	⚹ ♅	♑ 1	**6:42 pm** 3:42 pm
3	**7:56 pm** 4:56 pm	☌ ☿	♒ 3	**10:56 pm** 7:56 pm
6	**3:44 am** 12:44 am	□ ♀	♓ 6	**5:57 am** 2:57 am
8	**6:55 am** 3:55 am	⚹ ☿	♈ 8	**4:15 pm** 1:15 pm
10	**10:10 pm** 7:10 pm	⚹ ♅	♉ 11	**4:48 am** 1:48 am
13	**12:44 pm** 9:44 am	☍ ♂	♊ 13	**5:08 pm** 2:08 pm
15	**9:16 pm** 6:16 pm	△ ♅	♋ 15	11:56 pm
15	**9:16 pm** 6:16 pm	△ ♅	♋ 16	**2:56 am**
18	**5:48 am** 2:48 am	☍ ☉	♌ 18	**9:29 am** 6:29 am
20	**8:46 am** 5:46 am	☍ ♅	♍ 20	**1:32 pm** 10:32 am
22	**4:34 am** 1:34 am	□ ♄	♎ 22	**4:23 pm** 1:23 pm
24	**2:48 pm** 11:48 am	△ ♅	♏ 24	**7:09 pm** 4:09 pm
26	**6:14 pm** 3:14 pm	□ ♅	♐ 26	**10:26 pm** 7:26 pm
28	**10:26 pm** 7:26 pm	⚹ ♅	♑ 28	11:30 pm
28	**10:26 pm** 7:26 pm	⚹ ♅	♑ 29	**2:30 am**
30	**5:34 am** 2:34 am	☌ ☿	♒ 31	**7:44 am** 4:44 am

☽ Phases & Eclipses phase	day	EST / hr:mn / PST
New Moon	2	**3:23 pm** 12:23 pm
2nd Quarter	10	**8:15 am** 5:15 am
Full Moon	18	**5:48 am** 2:48 am
4th Quarter	25	**3:33 am** 12:33 am

Planet Ingress	day	EST / hr:mn / PST
♀ ♐	7	**8:07 am** 5:07 am
♂ ♐	16	**11:22 pm** 8:22 pm
⚴ ♓	16	10:15 pm
⚴ ♓	17	**1:15 am**
☉ ♒	20	**6:53 am** 3:53 am

Planetary Motion	day	EST / hr:mn / PST
☿ ℞	2	**1:21 pm** 10:21 am
☿ D	22	**8:08 pm** 5:08 pm

DATE		SID.TIME	SUN	MOON	NODE	MERCURY	VENUS	MARS	JUPITER	SATURN	URANUS	NEPTUNE	PLUTO	CERES	PALLAS	JUNO	VESTA	CHIRON
1	W	6:40:56	10 ♑ 08 13	16 ♐ 02	08 ♊ ℞ 29	28 ♑ 11	23 ♏ 40	19 ♏ 34	16 ♌ ℞ 53	24 ♊ ℞ 27	26 ♒ 16	09 ♒ 34	18 ♐ 17	08 ♈ 01	25 ♒ 08	10 ♏ 19	06 ♎ 30	10 ♑ 45
2	Th	6:44:52	11 09 23	00 ♑ 10	08 27	28 ℞ 25	24 37	20 13	16 48	24 22	26 18	09 36	18 19	08 13	25 26	10 35	06 46	10 51
3	F	6:48:49	12 10 34	14 07	08 23	28 27	25 34	20 51	16 43	24 17	26 21	09 38	18 21	08 26	25 43	10 51	07 01	10 57
4	Sa	6:52:46	13 11 45	27 47	08 18	28 19	26 32	21 30	16 37	24 13	26 24	09 40	18 23	08 39	26 01	11 06	07 17	11 03
5	Su	6:56:42	14 12 56	11 ♒ 09	08 12	27 59	27 30	22 09	16 31	24 08	26 27	09 42	18 25	08 52	26 18	11 22	07 31	11 10
6	M	7:00:39	15 14 07	24 10	08 06	27 27	28 28	22 48	16 26	24 04	26 29	09 44	18 27	09 05	26 36	11 37	07 46	11 16
7	T	7:04:35	16 15 17	06 ♓ 52	07 59	26 43	29 27	23 26	16 20	24 00	26 32	09 46	18 30	09 19	26 53	11 53	08 00	11 22
8	W	7:08:32	17 16 27	19 15	07 54	25 49	00 ♐ 27	24 05	16 14	23 55	26 35	09 48	18 32	09 33	27 11	12 08	08 14	11 28
9	Th	7:12:28	18 17 37	01 ♈ 23	07 51	24 45	01 27	24 44	16 07	23 51	26 38	09 51	18 34	09 47	27 29	12 23	08 28	11 34
10	F	7:16:25	19 18 46	13 20	07 D 49	23 34	02 27	25 22	16 01	23 47	26 41	09 53	18 36	10 01	27 47	12 37	08 41	11 40
11	Sa	7:20:22	20 19 55	25 11	07 49	22 17	03 28	26 01	15 54	23 43	26 44	09 55	18 38	10 15	28 05	12 52	08 54	11 46
12	Su	7:24:18	21 21 03	07 ♉ 00	07 50	20 58	04 30	26 40	15 48	23 38	26 47	09 57	18 40	10 30	28 23	13 06	09 07	11 52
13	M	7:28:15	22 22 10	18 54	07 52	19 38	05 31	27 18	15 41	23 34	26 50	09 59	18 42	10 45	28 42	13 21	09 20	11 58
14	T	7:32:11	23 23 17	00 ♊ 57	07 ℞ 53	18 21	06 33	27 57	15 34	23 30	26 53	10 02	18 44	11 00	29 00	13 35	09 32	12 04
15	W	7:36:08	24 24 24	13 13	07 53	17 07	07 36	28 36	15 27	23 27	26 56	10 04	18 46	11 15	29 18	13 49	09 43	12 10
16	Th	7:40:04	25 25 30	25 47	07 51	16 01	08 38	29 14	15 20	23 23	26 59	10 06	18 48	11 31	29 37	14 02	09 55	12 15
17	F	7:44:01	26 26 35	08 ♋ 40	07 47	15 01	09 41	29 53	15 13	23 19	27 02	10 08	18 50	11 47	29 55	14 16	10 06	12 21
18	Sa	7:47:57	27 27 40	21 52	07 41	14 11	10 45	00 ♐ 32	15 06	23 15	27 05	10 10	18 51	12 02	00 ♓ 14	14 29	10 17	12 27
19	Su	7:51:54	28 28 44	05 ♌ 24	07 33	13 30	11 48	01 10	14 58	23 12	27 08	10 13	18 53	12 19	00 32	14 42	10 27	12 33
20	M	7:55:51	29 29 47	19 12	07 24	12 58	12 52	01 49	14 51	23 08	27 11	10 15	18 55	12 35	00 51	14 55	10 37	12 39
21	T	7:59:47	00 ♒ 30 50	03 ♍ 12	07 15	12 36	13 57	02 28	14 43	23 05	27 14	10 17	18 57	12 51	01 10	15 08	10 47	12 45
22	W	8:03:44	01 31 53	17 21	07 07	12 22	15 01	03 06	14 36	23 02	27 18	10 19	18 59	13 08	01 29	15 20	10 56	12 51
23	Th	8:07:40	02 32 55	01 ♎ 33	07 01	12 D 18	16 06	03 45	14 28	22 58	27 21	10 22	19 01	13 25	01 47	15 33	11 05	12 56
24	F	8:11:37	03 33 56	15 45	06 57	12 21	17 11	04 24	14 20	22 55	27 24	10 24	19 02	13 42	02 06	15 45	11 14	13 02
25	Sa	8:15:33	04 34 57	29 55	06 D 55	12 33	18 16	05 02	14 13	22 52	27 27	10 26	19 04	13 59	02 25	15 57	11 22	13 08
26	Su	8:19:30	05 35 58	14 ♏ 00	06 55	12 51	19 22	05 41	14 05	22 49	27 31	10 28	19 06	14 16	02 44	16 09	11 30	13 14
27	M	8:23:26	06 36 58	28 00	06 ℞ 56	13 15	20 28	06 20	13 57	22 46	27 34	10 31	19 08	14 33	03 04	16 20	11 37	13 19
28	T	8:27:23	07 37 58	11 ♐ 55	06 56	13 46	21 34	06 58	13 49	22 44	27 37	10 33	19 09	14 51	03 23	16 32	11 44	13 25
29	W	8:31:20	08 38 57	25 43	06 55	14 22	22 40	07 37	13 41	22 41	27 40	10 35	19 11	15 09	03 42	16 43	11 50	13 31
30	Th	8:35:16	09 39 56	09 ♑ 23	06 51	15 02	23 47	08 16	13 33	22 38	27 44	10 38	19 13	15 27	04 01	16 54	11 57	13 36
31	F	8:39:13	10 40 53	22 54	06 44	15 47	24 53	08 54	13 25	22 36	27 47	10 40	19 14	15 45	04 21	17 04	12 02	13 42

EPHEMERIS CALCULATED FOR 12 MIDNIGHT GREENWICH MEAN TIME. ALL OTHER DATA AND FACING ASPECTARIAN PAGE IN **EASTERN TIME (BOLD)** AND PACIFIC TIME (REGULAR).

FEBRUARY 2003

1 SATURDAY

☽✶♂	**1:21 am**	
☽☌♆	**3:10 am**	12:10 am
☽☌☉	**5:48 am**	2:48 am
☽△⚶	**5:49 am**	2:49 am
☉△⚶	**6:00 am**	3:00 am
☽☍♃	**7:45 am**	4:45 am
☽⚺⚷	**8:54 am**	5:54 am
☽✶⚳	**1:24 pm**	10:24 am
☽⚺☿	**3:21 pm**	12:21 pm
☽□⚵	**3:25 pm**	12:25 pm
☿✶⚵	**4:34 pm**	1:34 pm
☽✶♇	**6:56 pm**	3:56 pm
☽△♄		9:54 pm

2 SUNDAY

☽△♄	**12:54 am**	
☉☍♃	**4:12 am**	1:12 am
☽✶♀	**10:54 am**	7:54 am
☽☌♅	**11:02 am**	8:02 am
♀✶♅	**12:27 pm**	9:27 am
♂✶♆	**4:39 pm**	1:39 pm
☽☌♀		10:06 pm
☉⚺⚷		10:22 pm

3 MONDAY

☽☌♀	**1:06 am**	
☉⚺⚷	**1:22 am**	
☽⚺♆	**11:25 am**	8:25 am
☽□♂	**12:22 pm**	9:22 am
☽⚻⚶	**2:20 pm**	11:20 am
☽⚻♃	**3:26 pm**	12:26 pm
☿⚺♇	**5:27 pm**	2:27 pm
☽✶⚷	**5:39 pm**	2:39 pm
☽⚺☉	**6:58 pm**	3:58 pm
☽⚺⚳	**11:24 pm**	8:24 pm
☽△⚵		9:50 pm

4 TUESDAY

☽△⚵	**12:50 am**	
☽□♇	**3:53 am**	12:53 am
☽✶☿	**4:48 am**	1:48 am
☽□♄	**9:53 am**	6:53 am
☽⚺♅	**8:56 pm**	5:56 pm
☽□♀		11:24 pm

5 WEDNESDAY

☽□♀	**2:24 am**	
♂✶⚶	**6:12 am**	3:12 am
☽⚺♀	**1:03 pm**	10:03 am
♂△♃	**2:25 pm**	11:25 am
☽✶♆	**10:24 pm**	7:24 pm
☽☍⚶		10:33 pm
☽△♃		10:47 pm
☽△♂		11:34 pm

6 THURSDAY

☽☍⚶	**1:33 am**	
☽△♃	**1:47 am**	
☽△♂	**2:34 am**	
☽□⚷	**5:12 am**	2:12 am
☽✶☉	**11:37 am**	8:37 am
☽☌⚳	**12:22 pm**	9:22 am
☽⚻⚵	**1:01 pm**	10:01 am
☿⚻♄	**1:31 pm**	10:31 am
☽△♇	**3:32 pm**	12:32 pm
♃✶⚶	**6:12 pm**	3:12 pm
☽✶♄	**9:28 pm**	6:28 pm
☽□☿	**10:20 pm**	7:20 pm
☉✶⚳	**11:57 pm**	8:57 pm

7 FRIDAY

☉□⚵	**6:29 am**	3:29 am
☽✶♅	**9:22 am**	6:22 am
☽△♀	**9:06 pm**	6:06 pm

8 SATURDAY

☽✶♀	**3:20 am**	12:20 am
⚳⚻⚵	**7:49 am**	4:49 am
☉✶♇	**10:31 am**	7:31 am
♂⚺⚷	**10:48 am**	7:48 am
☽□♆	**11:20 am**	8:20 am
☽□♃	**1:54 pm**	10:54 am
☽⚻⚶	**2:30 pm**	11:30 am
☽△⚷	**6:28 pm**	3:28 pm
☽⚻♂	**6:51 pm**	3:51 pm
☽☍⚵		11:38 pm
☽⚺⚳		11:56 pm

9 SUNDAY

☽☍⚵	**2:38 am**	
☽⚺⚳	**2:56 am**	
☽⚻♇	**4:32 am**	1:32 am
☽□☉	**6:11 am**	3:11 am
☽⚺♄	**10:14 am**	7:14 am
☽△☿	**5:55 pm**	2:55 pm
☽□♅	**10:28 pm**	7:28 pm

10 MONDAY

☽⚻♀	**4:03 pm**	1:03 pm
☽□♀	**5:31 pm**	2:31 pm
☽△♆	**11:47 pm**	8:47 pm
☽✶♃		10:26 pm
☽△⚶		11:44 pm

11 TUESDAY

☽✶♃	**1:26 am**	
☽△⚶	**2:44 am**	
☉△♄	**4:45 am**	1:45 am
☽⚻⚷	**6:55 am**	3:55 am
☽☍♂	**10:10 am**	7:10 am
♀✶♀	**1:17 pm**	10:17 am
☽⚻⚵	**2:58 pm**	11:58 am
☿⚺♅	**3:18 pm**	12:18 pm
☽✶⚳	**4:14 pm**	1:14 pm
☽☍♇	**4:15 pm**	1:15 pm
♇△⚳	**5:04 pm**	2:04 pm
☽☌♄	**9:29 pm**	6:29 pm
☽△☉	**11:00 pm**	8:00 pm

12 WEDNESDAY

☽△♅	**9:29 am**	6:29 am
☽⚻☿	**11:26 am**	8:26 am

13 THURSDAY

☽△♀	**4:39 am**	1:39 am
☽☍♀	**7:22 am**	4:22 am
☽⚻♆	**9:11 am**	6:11 am
☽⚺♃	**10:00 am**	7:00 am
☽□⚶	**11:45 am**	8:45 am
☽☍⚷	**4:03 pm**	1:03 pm
☽⚻♂	**9:36 pm**	6:36 pm
☽△⚵	**11:43 pm**	8:43 pm
☽⚻♇		9:29 pm
☽□⚳		10:49 pm

14 FRIDAY

☽⚻♇	**12:29 am**	
☽□⚳	**1:49 am**	
♀⚺♆	**4:31 am**	1:31 am
☽⚺♄	**5:12 am**	2:12 am
♀⚻♃	**10:34 am**	7:34 am
☽⚻☉	**11:12 am**	8:12 am
☽⚻♅	**4:40 pm**	1:40 pm
☽☍☿		9:08 pm

15 SATURDAY

☽☍☿	**12:08 am**	
♀□⚶	**8:11 am**	5:11 am
☽⚻♀	**11:36 am**	8:36 am
☽☍♆	**2:40 pm**	11:40 am
☽☌♃	**2:49 pm**	11:49 am
☽✶⚶	**4:50 pm**	1:50 pm
☽⚻♀	**5:38 pm**	2:38 pm
☽⚻⚷	**9:15 pm**	6:15 pm
♂⚺⚵		10:55 pm

16 SUNDAY

♂⚺⚵	**1:55 am**	
♃☍♆	**4:12 am**	1:12 am
☽□⚵	**4:32 am**	1:32 am
☽△♂	**4:38 am**	1:38 am
☽△♇	**4:55 am**	1:55 am
☽△⚳	**7:22 am**	4:22 am
☽✶♄	**9:14 am**	6:14 am
♂☌♇	**11:00 am**	8:00 am
☽☍☉	**6:51 pm**	3:51 pm
☽☍♅	**8:18 pm**	5:18 pm

17 MONDAY

☽⚻☿	**8:33 am**	5:33 am
☽☍♀	**3:18 pm**	12:18 pm
☉☌♅	**4:38 pm**	1:38 pm
♀☌⚷	**4:39 pm**	1:39 pm
☽⚺♃	**4:46 pm**	1:46 pm
☽⚻♆	**5:10 pm**	2:10 pm
☽⚺⚶	**6:59 pm**	3:59 pm
☽△⚷	**11:39 pm**	8:39 pm
☽△♀		9:13 pm

18 TUESDAY

☽△♀	**12:13 am**	
☽✶⚵	**6:45 am**	3:45 am
☽□♇	**6:51 am**	3:51 am
☽□♂	**8:48 am**	5:48 am
☽⚻⚳	**10:20 am**	7:20 am
☽□♄	**10:56 am**	7:56 am
☽⚻♅	**9:58 pm**	6:58 pm
☽⚻☉		9:00 pm
♇⚺⚵		9:21 pm

19 WEDNESDAY

☽⚻☉	**12:00 am**	
♇⚺⚵	**12:21 am**	
♄✶⚳	**11:26 am**	8:26 am
♃⚻♀	**2:56 pm**	11:56 am
☽△☿	**3:07 pm**	12:07 pm
☽✶♃	**5:34 pm**	2:34 pm
☽⚻♀	**5:39 pm**	2:39 pm
☽△♆	**6:30 pm**	3:30 pm
☽☌⚶	**7:59 pm**	4:59 pm
☽□⚷		10:06 pm

20 THURSDAY

☽□⚷	**1:06 am**	
☽□♀	**5:39 am**	2:39 am
☽✶♇	**8:06 am**	5:06 am
☽⚺⚵	**8:16 am**	5:16 am
♂☍♄	**9:14 am**	6:14 am
☽△♄	**12:08 pm**	9:08 am
☽✶♂	**12:16 pm**	9:16 am
☽☍⚳	**12:45 pm**	9:45 am
☿☍♃	**2:12 pm**	11:12 am
☽△♅	**11:29 pm**	8:29 pm
☿⚺♀	**11:31 pm**	8:31 pm
☿☌♆		10:50 pm

21 FRIDAY

☿☌♆	**1:50 am**	
☽△☉	**5:04 am**	2:04 am
♆⚺♀	**10:41 am**	7:41 am
♂△⚳	**11:02 am**	8:02 am
♀⚺♇	**12:47 pm**	9:47 am
☿△⚶	**1:49 pm**	10:49 am
♀✶⚵	**4:36 pm**	1:36 pm
☽□♃	**6:52 pm**	3:52 pm
☽□♆	**8:20 pm**	5:20 pm
☽△♀	**8:33 pm**	5:33 pm
☽⚺⚶	**9:29 pm**	6:29 pm
☽□☿	**10:25 pm**	7:25 pm

22 SATURDAY

☽✶⚷	**3:16 am**	12:16 am
☽⚺♇	**10:14 am**	7:14 am
☽☌⚵	**10:37 am**	7:37 am
☽✶♀	**12:08 pm**	9:08 am
☽⚻♄	**2:20 pm**	11:20 am
☽⚻⚳	**4:14 pm**	1:14 pm
☽⚺♂	**4:52 pm**	1:52 pm
☽□♅		11:15 pm

23 SUNDAY

☽□♅	**2:15 am**	
♀⚻⚶	**4:25 am**	1:25 am
☽□☉	**11:46 am**	8:46 am
♀⚻♄	**2:45 pm**	11:45 am
☽△♃	**9:40 pm**	6:40 pm
☿⚺⚷	**10:33 pm**	7:33 pm
☽✶♆	**11:45 pm**	8:45 pm
☽✶⚶		9:28 pm
☽□♀		10:06 pm

24 MONDAY

☽✶⚶	**12:28 am**	
☽□♀	**1:06 am**	
☽⚺⚷	**7:04 am**	4:04 am
☽✶☿	**8:05 am**	5:05 am
☽☌♇	**2:05 pm**	11:05 am
☽⚺⚵	**2:41 pm**	11:41 am
☽☍♄	**6:16 pm**	3:16 pm
☽⚺♀	**8:51 pm**	5:51 pm
☽△⚳	**9:36 pm**	6:36 pm
☽☌♂	**11:28 pm**	8:28 pm

25 TUESDAY

☽✶♅	**6:50 am**	3:50 am
♀□⚳	**9:08 am**	6:08 am
☽✶☉	**8:45 pm**	5:45 pm
☽⚻♃		11:18 pm

26 WEDNESDAY

☽⚻♃	**2:18 am**	
☽⚺♆	**5:01 am**	2:01 am
☽□⚶	**5:11 am**	2:11 am
☽✶♀	**7:40 am**	4:40 am
☽☌⚷	**12:45 pm**	9:45 am
☿✶♇	**1:34 pm**	10:34 am
☽⚺♇	**7:45 pm**	4:45 pm
♆△⚶	**7:49 pm**	4:49 pm
☿□⚵	**8:25 pm**	5:25 pm
☽✶⚵	**8:34 pm**	5:34 pm
☽⚺☿	**8:35 pm**	5:35 pm
☽⚻♄		9:04 pm

27 THURSDAY

☽⚻♄	**12:04 am**	
☽□⚳	**4:59 am**	1:59 am
☽☌♀	**7:58 am**	4:58 am
☽⚺♂	**8:09 am**	5:09 am
♀⚺♂	**12:20 pm**	9:20 am
☽⚺♅	**1:16 pm**	10:16 am
☿△♄		10:51 pm

28 FRIDAY

☿△♄	**1:51 am**	
☽⚺☉	**7:59 am**	4:59 am
☽☍♃	**8:41 am**	5:41 am
☽△⚶	**11:34 am**	8:34 am
☽☌♆	**12:04 pm**	9:04 am
☽⚺♀	**4:08 pm**	1:08 pm
☉⚻♃	**4:16 pm**	1:16 pm
☽⚺⚷	**8:13 pm**	5:13 pm

Eastern time in bold type
Pacific time in medium type

FEBRUARY 2003

☽ Last Aspect day	EST / hr:mn / PST	asp	☽ Ingress sign	day	EST / hr:mn / PST
2	**11:02 am** 8:02 am	☌ ♅	♓	2	**2:55 pm** 11:55 am
4	**9:53 am** 6:53 am	□ ♄	♈	4	9:44 pm
4	**9:53 am** 6:53 am	□ ♄	♈	5	**12:44 am**
7	**9:22 am** 6:22 am	⚹ ♅	♉	7	**12:59 pm** 9:59 pm
9	**10:28 pm** 7:28 pm	□ ♅	♊	9	10:45 pm
9	**10:28 pm** 7:28 pm	□ ♅	♊	10	**1:45 am**
12	**9:29 am** 6:29 am	△ ♅	♋	12	**12:19 pm** 9:19 am
13	**7:22 am** 4:22 am	☍ ♀	♌	14	**7:04 pm** 4:04 pm
16	**8:18 pm** 5:18 pm	☍ ♅	♍	16	**10:22 pm** 7:22 pm
18	**10:56 am** 7:56 am	□ ♄	♎	18	**11:48 pm** 8:48 pm
20	**11:29 pm** 8:29 pm	△ ♅	♏	20	10:09 pm
20	**11:29 pm** 8:29 pm	△ ♅	♏	21	**1:09 am**
22	11:15 pm	□ ♅	♐	23	**3:46 am** 12:46 am
23	**2:15 am**	□ ♅	♐	23	**3:46 am** 12:46 am
25	**6:50 am** 3:50 am	⚹ ♅	♑	25	**8:11 am** 5:11 am
27	**7:58 am** 4:58 am	☌ ♀	♒	27	**2:24 pm** 11:24 am

☽ Phases & Eclipses phase	day	EST / hr:mn / PST
New Moon	1	**5:48 am** 2:48 am
2nd Quarter	9	**6:11 am** 3:11 am
Full Moon	16	**6:51 pm** 3:51 pm
4th Quarter	23	**11:46 am** 8:46 am

Planet Ingress	day	EST / hr:mn / PST
♀ ♑	4	**8:27 am** 5:27 am
☿ ♒	12	**8:00 pm** 5:00 pm
☉ ♓	18	**9:00 pm** 6:00 pm

Planetary Motion	day	EST / hr:mn / PST
⚶ ℞	11	**4:36 pm** 1:36 pm
♄ D	21	11:41 pm
♄ D	22	**2:41 am**

DATE		SID.TIME	SUN	MOON	NODE	MERCURY	VENUS	MARS	JUPITER	SATURN	URANUS	NEPTUNE	PLUTO	CERES	PALLAS	JUNO	VESTA	CHIRON
1	Sa	8:43:09	11 ♒ 41 50	06 ♒ 14	06 ♊ ℞ 34	16 ♑ 37	26 ♐ 00	09 ♐ 33	13 ♌ ℞ 17	22 ♊ ℞ 33	27 ♒ 50	10 ♒ 42	19 ♐ 16	16 ♈ 03	04 ♓ 40	17 ♏ 15	12 ♎ 08	13 ♑ 47
2	Su	8:47:06	12 42 46	19 20	06 22	17 29	27 07	10 12	13 09	22 31	27 54	10 44	19 17	16 22	04 59	17 25	12 12	13 53
3	M	8:51:02	13 43 40	02 ♓ 10	06 10	18 25	28 15	10 50	13 01	22 29	27 57	10 47	19 19	16 40	05 19	17 35	12 17	13 58
4	T	8:54:59	14 44 33	14 45	05 57	19 24	29 22	11 29	12 53	22 27	28 01	10 49	19 21	16 59	05 38	17 44	12 21	14 04
5	W	8:58:55	15 45 25	27 05	05 46	20 26	00 ♑ 30	12 07	12 45	22 25	28 04	10 51	19 22	17 18	05 58	17 54	12 24	14 09
6	Th	9:02:52	16 46 16	09 ♈ 12	05 38	21 30	01 38	12 46	12 37	22 23	28 07	10 54	19 23	17 37	06 17	18 03	12 27	14 15
7	F	9:06:49	17 47 05	21 08	05 32	22 37	02 45	13 25	12 29	22 21	28 11	10 56	19 25	17 56	06 37	18 12	12 30	14 20
8	Sa	9:10:45	18 47 53	02 ♉ 57	05 29	23 46	03 54	14 03	12 21	22 20	28 14	10 58	19 26	18 15	06 57	18 21	12 32	14 25
9	Su	9:14:42	19 48 39	14 46	05 D 27	24 57	05 02	14 42	12 13	22 18	28 18	11 00	19 28	18 34	07 16	18 29	12 33	14 30
10	M	9:18:38	20 49 24	26 38	05 ℞ 27	26 09	06 10	15 20	12 06	22 17	28 21	11 03	19 29	18 54	07 36	18 37	12 34	14 36
11	T	9:22:35	21 50 08	08 ♊ 40	05 27	27 23	07 19	15 59	11 58	22 15	28 25	11 05	19 30	19 13	07 56	18 45	12 ℞ 35	14 41
12	W	9:26:31	22 50 49	20 57	05 26	28 39	08 27	16 37	11 50	22 14	28 28	11 07	19 32	19 33	08 16	18 53	12 35	14 46
13	Th	9:30:28	23 51 30	03 ♋ 33	05 24	29 57	09 36	17 16	11 42	22 13	28 31	11 09	19 33	19 53	08 36	19 00	12 35	14 51
14	F	9:34:24	24 52 08	16 33	05 18	01 ♒ 16	10 45	17 55	11 35	22 12	28 35	11 12	19 34	20 13	08 55	19 07	12 34	14 56
15	Sa	9:38:21	25 52 45	29 58	05 10	02 36	11 54	18 33	11 27	22 11	28 38	11 14	19 35	20 33	09 15	19 14	12 33	15 01
16	Su	9:42:18	26 53 20	13 ♌ 47	04 59	03 57	13 03	19 12	11 20	22 10	28 42	11 16	19 36	20 53	09 35	19 21	12 31	15 06
17	M	9:46:14	27 53 54	27 59	04 47	05 20	14 13	19 50	11 12	22 10	28 45	11 18	19 38	21 13	09 55	19 27	12 29	15 11
18	T	9:50:11	28 54 26	12 ♍ 27	04 35	06 44	15 22	20 29	11 05	22 09	28 49	11 20	19 39	21 34	10 15	19 33	12 26	15 16
19	W	9:54:07	29 54 57	27 04	04 24	08 09	16 31	21 07	10 58	22 09	28 52	11 23	19 40	21 54	10 35	19 39	12 23	15 20
20	Th	9:58:04	00 ♓ 55 26	11 ♎ 43	04 15	09 35	17 41	21 45	10 51	22 08	28 56	11 25	19 41	22 15	10 55	19 44	12 19	15 25
21	F	10:02:00	01 55 54	26 17	04 09	11 02	18 51	22 24	10 44	22 08	28 59	11 27	19 42	22 36	11 15	19 49	12 15	15 30
22	Sa	10:05:57	02 56 21	10 ♏ 41	04 06	12 31	20 01	23 02	10 37	22 D 08	29 03	11 29	19 43	22 57	11 35	19 54	12 11	15 34
23	Su	10:09:53	03 56 46	24 53	04 05	14 00	21 11	23 41	10 30	22 08	29 06	11 31	19 44	23 17	11 55	19 59	12 05	15 39
24	M	10:13:50	04 57 11	08 ♐ 50	04 05	15 31	22 21	24 19	10 23	22 08	29 10	11 33	19 45	23 39	12 16	20 03	12 00	15 44
25	T	10:17:47	05 57 33	22 33	04 04	17 02	23 31	24 58	10 16	22 09	29 13	11 35	19 46	24 00	12 36	20 07	11 54	15 48
26	W	10:21:43	06 57 55	06 ♑ 04	04 02	18 35	24 41	25 36	10 10	22 09	29 16	11 38	19 46	24 21	12 56	20 10	11 47	15 52
27	Th	10:25:40	07 58 15	19 22	03 57	20 08	25 51	26 14	10 04	22 09	29 20	11 40	19 47	24 42	13 16	20 14	11 40	15 57
28	F	10:29:36	08 58 33	02 ♒ 30	03 49	21 43	27 02	26 53	09 57	22 10	29 23	11 42	19 48	25 04	13 36	20 17	11 32	16 01

EPHEMERIS CALCULATED FOR 12 MIDNIGHT GREENWICH MEAN TIME. ALL OTHER DATA AND FACING ASPECTARIAN PAGE IN **EASTERN TIME (BOLD)** AND PACIFIC TIME (REGULAR).

MARCH 2003

1 SATURDAY

	Eastern	Pacific
☽ ⚹ ♇	**3:12 am**	12:12 am
☽ □ ⚵	**4:11 am**	1:11 am
☽ △ ♄	**7:39 am**	4:39 am
☽ ☌ ☿	**11:54 am**	8:54 am
☽ ⚹ ⚳	**2:18 pm**	11:18 am
☽ ⚹ ♂	**6:56 pm**	3:56 pm
☽ ⚺ ♀	**9:29 pm**	6:29 pm
☽ ☌ ♅	**9:30 pm**	6:30 pm
♀ ⚺ ♅	**9:39 pm**	6:39 pm
☉ ⚻ ⚶		9:54 pm

2 SUNDAY

	Eastern	Pacific
☉ ⚻ ⚶	**12:54 am**	
☿ ⚹ ⚳	**11:16 am**	8:16 am
☉ ⚺ ♆	**2:19 pm**	11:19 am
☽ ⚻ ♃	**4:54 pm**	1:54 pm
☽ ⚻ ⚶	**7:41 pm**	4:41 pm
☽ ⚺ ♆	**9:01 pm**	6:01 pm
☽ ☌ ☉	**9:35 pm**	6:35 pm
☽ ☌ ♀		11:39 pm

3 MONDAY

	Eastern	Pacific
☽ ☌ ♀	**2:39 am**	
☽ ⚹ ⚷	**5:38 am**	2:38 am
☽ □ ♇	**12:36 pm**	9:36 am
☽ △ ⚵	**1:43 pm**	10:43 am
☽ □ ♄	**5:14 pm**	2:14 pm
☽ ⚺ ⚳		10:49 pm
♂ ⚹ ♅		11:30 pm

4 TUESDAY

	Eastern	Pacific
☽ ⚺ ⚳	**1:49 am**	
♂ ⚹ ♅	**2:30 am**	
☽ ⚺ ☿	**6:30 am**	3:30 am
☽ ⚺ ♅	**7:48 am**	4:48 am
☽ □ ♂	**8:04 am**	5:04 am
☽ ⚹ ♀	**1:44 pm**	10:44 am
☿ ☌ ♅	**4:16 pm**	1:16 pm
☿ ⚹ ♂		9:01 pm

5 WEDNESDAY

	Eastern	Pacific
☿ ⚹ ♂	**12:01 am**	
☽ △ ♃	**3:13 am**	12:13 am
☽ ☍ ⚶	**5:46 am**	2:46 am
☽ ⚹ ♆	**8:06 am**	5:06 am
☽ ⚺ ☉	**1:54 pm**	10:54 am
☽ ⚺ ♀	**3:29 pm**	12:29 pm
☽ □ ⚷	**5:11 pm**	2:11 pm
☽ △ ♇		9:07 pm
☽ ⚻ ⚵		10:19 pm

6 THURSDAY

	Eastern	Pacific
☽ △ ♇	**12:07 am**	
☽ ⚻ ⚵	**1:19 am**	
☽ ⚹ ♄	**4:58 am**	1:58 am
☽ ☌ ⚳	**3:37 pm**	12:37 pm
☉ ☌ ♀	**5:52 pm**	2:52 pm
☽ ⚹ ♅	**8:10 pm**	5:10 pm
☽ △ ♂	**11:35 pm**	8:35 pm

7 FRIDAY

	Eastern	Pacific
☽ ⚹ ☿	**4:34 am**	1:34 am
☉ ⚹ ⚷	**7:38 am**	4:38 am
☽ □ ♀	**8:42 am**	5:42 am
☽ □ ♃	**3:22 pm**	12:22 pm
☽ ⚻ ⚶	**5:31 pm**	2:31 pm
☽ □ ♆	**8:57 pm**	5:57 pm

8 SATURDAY

	Eastern	Pacific
☽ ⚹ ♀	**6:06 am**	3:06 am
☽ △ ⚷	**6:21 am**	3:21 am
☽ ⚹ ☉	**8:20 am**	5:20 am
☽ ⚻ ♇	**1:06 pm**	10:06 am
☽ ☍ ⚵	**2:17 pm**	11:17 am
⚷ ⚹ ♀	**4:42 pm**	1:42 pm
☽ ⚺ ♄	**6:04 pm**	3:04 pm

9 SUNDAY

	Eastern	Pacific
☽ ⚺ ⚳	**6:37 am**	3:37 am
☽ □ ♅	**9:29 am**	6:29 am
☽ ⚻ ♂	**4:03 pm**	1:03 pm
♀ ☍ ♃	**11:18 pm**	8:18 pm
☿ ⚻ ♃		11:57 pm

10 MONDAY

	Eastern	Pacific
☿ ⚻ ♃	**2:57 am**	
☽ ⚹ ♃	**3:49 am**	12:49 am
☽ □ ☿	**3:58 am**	12:58 am
☽ △ ♀	**4:21 am**	1:21 am
☽ △ ⚶	**5:22 am**	2:22 am
☽ △ ♆	**9:53 am**	6:53 am
☿ ⚺ ♀	**10:50 am**	7:50 am
☿ ⚻ ⚶	**12:34 pm**	9:34 am
♀ △ ⚶	**1:18 pm**	10:18 am
☉ □ ♇	**4:51 pm**	1:51 pm
☽ ⚻ ⚷	**7:13 pm**	4:13 pm
☽ □ ♀	**8:24 pm**	5:24 pm
☽ ☍ ♇		10:29 pm
☽ □ ☉		11:15 pm
☽ ⚻ ⚵		11:34 pm

11 TUESDAY

	Eastern	Pacific
☽ ☍ ♇	**1:29 am**	
☽ □ ☉	**2:15 am**	
☽ ⚻ ⚵	**2:34 am**	
☉ △ ⚵	**5:55 am**	2:55 am
☽ ☌ ♄	**6:24 am**	3:24 am
☽ ⚹ ⚳	**8:10 pm**	5:10 pm
☿ ⚺ ♆	**8:11 pm**	5:11 pm
☽ △ ♅	**9:19 pm**	6:19 pm

12 WEDNESDAY

	Eastern	Pacific
☽ ☍ ♂	**6:28 am**	3:28 am
♀ ☌ ♆	**1:35 pm**	10:35 am
☽ ⚺ ♃	**2:07 pm**	11:07 am
☽ □ ⚶	**2:58 pm**	11:58 am
☽ ⚻ ♆	**8:18 pm**	5:18 pm
☽ ⚻ ♀	**8:59 pm**	5:59 pm
☽ △ ☿		9:13 pm

13 THURSDAY

	Eastern	Pacific
☽ △ ☿	**12:13 am**	
☽ ☍ ⚷	**5:11 am**	2:11 am
☉ □ ♄	**6:38 am**	3:38 am
☽ △ ♀	**7:35 am**	4:35 am
☽ ⚻ ♇	**10:49 am**	7:49 am
☽ △ ⚵	**11:41 am**	8:41 am
☽ ⚺ ♄	**3:31 pm**	12:31 pm
☽ △ ☉	**4:13 pm**	1:13 pm
♅ ⚹ ⚳	**5:07 pm**	2:07 pm

14 FRIDAY

	Eastern	Pacific
☽ ⚻ ♅	**5:27 am**	2:27 am
☽ □ ⚳	**5:45 am**	2:45 am
☿ ⚹ ⚷	**11:58 am**	8:58 am
☽ ⚻ ♂	**4:24 pm**	1:24 pm
☽ ☌ ♃	**8:31 pm**	5:31 pm
☽ ⚹ ⚶	**8:42 pm**	5:42 pm
☽ ☍ ♆		11:36 pm

15 SATURDAY

	Eastern	Pacific
☽ ☍ ♆	**2:36 am**	
☽ ☍ ♀	**8:10 am**	5:10 am
☽ ⚻ ⚷	**10:54 am**	7:54 am
♃ ⚹ ⚶	**12:07 pm**	9:07 am
☿ ☌ ♀	**1:32 pm**	10:32 am
☽ ⚻ ♀	**2:14 pm**	11:14 am
☽ ⚻ ☿	**2:19 pm**	11:19 am
☽ △ ♇	**3:55 pm**	12:55 pm
☽ □ ⚵	**4:35 pm**	1:35 pm
☽ ⚹ ♄	**8:24 pm**	5:24 pm
☽ ⚻ ☉		9:53 pm
☿ □ ♇		11:19 pm

16 SUNDAY

	Eastern	Pacific
☽ ⚻ ☉	**12:53 am**	
☿ □ ♇	**2:19 am**	
☿ △ ⚵	**6:53 am**	3:53 am
☽ ☍ ♅	**9:23 am**	6:23 am
☽ △ ⚳	**10:52 am**	7:52 am
♀ ⚺ ⚷	**5:36 pm**	2:36 pm
☽ △ ♂	**9:43 pm**	6:43 pm
☽ ⚺ ⚶	**10:38 pm**	7:38 pm
☽ ⚺ ♃	**11:03 pm**	8:03 pm

17 MONDAY

	Eastern	Pacific
☽ ⚻ ♆	**5:04 am**	2:04 am
☿ □ ♄	**12:34 pm**	9:34 am
☽ △ ⚷	**12:58 pm**	9:58 am
♂ □ ⚶	**1:28 pm**	10:28 am
☽ ⚻ ♀	**2:36 pm**	11:36 am
☽ ☍ ♀	**5:06 pm**	2:06 pm
☽ □ ♇	**5:33 pm**	2:33 pm
☽ ⚹ ⚵	**6:00 pm**	3:00 pm
☽ □ ♄	**9:56 pm**	6:56 pm
☽ ☍ ☿	**11:17 pm**	8:17 pm
♂ ⚻ ♃		11:05 pm

18 TUESDAY

	Eastern	Pacific
♂ ⚻ ♃	**2:05 am**	
☽ ☍ ☉	**5:35 am**	2:35 am
☽ ⚻ ♅	**10:23 am**	7:23 am
☽ ⚻ ⚳	**12:54 pm**	9:54 am
♇ □ ♀	**12:58 pm**	9:58 am
☽ ☌ ⚶	**10:16 pm**	7:16 pm
☽ ⚹ ♃	**11:14 pm**	8:14 pm
☽ □ ♂		9:15 pm

19 WEDNESDAY

	Eastern	Pacific
☽ □ ♂	**12:15 am**	
♀ △ ⚵	**3:07 am**	12:07 am
♀ ⚹ ♇	**3:29 am**	12:29 am
☽ △ ♆	**5:23 am**	2:23 am
♀ □ ⚵	**7:16 am**	4:16 am
♀ ⚺ ♀	**9:12 am**	6:12 am
☽ □ ⚷	**1:12 pm**	10:12 am
☽ ⚹ ♇	**5:33 pm**	2:33 pm
☽ ⚺ ⚵	**5:48 pm**	2:48 pm
☽ ⚻ ♀	**6:12 pm**	3:12 pm
☽ △ ♀	**6:46 pm**	3:46 pm
☽ △ ♄	**10:02 pm**	7:02 pm

20 THURSDAY

	Eastern	Pacific
☽ ⚻ ☿	**6:21 am**	3:21 am
☽ ⚻ ☉	**8:54 am**	5:54 am
☽ △ ♅	**10:28 am**	7:28 am
☽ ☍ ⚳	**2:05 pm**	11:05 am
☽ ⚺ ⚶	**9:29 pm**	6:29 pm
☽ □ ♃	**11:07 pm**	8:07 pm
☽ ⚹ ♂		11:25 pm

21 FRIDAY

	Eastern	Pacific
☽ ⚹ ♂	**2:25 am**	
☽ □ ♆	**5:35 am**	2:35 am
☉ ⚺ ♅	**9:55 am**	6:55 am
♀ △ ♄	**1:31 pm**	10:31 am
☽ ⚹ ⚷	**1:38 pm**	10:38 am
☿ ⚺ ♅	**2:21 pm**	11:21 am
☽ ⚺ ♇	**5:57 pm**	2:57 pm
☽ ☌ ⚵	**5:58 pm**	2:58 pm
☉ ☌ ☿	**6:34 pm**	3:34 pm
☽ △ ♀	**7:46 pm**	4:46 pm
♇ ⚺ ⚵	**10:18 pm**	7:18 pm
☽ ⚻ ♄	**10:43 pm**	7:43 pm
☽ □ ♀	**11:30 pm**	8:30 pm

22 SATURDAY

	Eastern	Pacific
☽ □ ♅	**11:36 am**	8:36 am
☽ △ ☉	**1:24 pm**	10:24 am
☽ △ ☿	**2:55 pm**	11:55 am
☽ ⚻ ⚳	**4:31 pm**	1:31 pm
☽ ⚹ ⚶	**10:02 pm**	7:02 pm
☽ △ ♃		9:26 pm

23 SUNDAY

	Eastern	Pacific
☽ △ ♃	**12:26 am**	
☿ ⚺ ⚳	**4:43 am**	1:43 am
☽ ⚺ ♂	**6:21 am**	3:21 am
☽ ⚹ ♆	**7:27 am**	4:27 am
☽ ⚺ ⚷	**3:57 pm**	12:57 pm
☽ ⚺ ⚵	**8:03 pm**	5:03 pm
☽ ☌ ♇	**8:20 pm**	5:20 pm
☽ □ ♀	**11:30 pm**	8:30 pm
☽ ☍ ♄		10:32 pm

24 MONDAY

	Eastern	Pacific
☽ ☍ ♄	**1:32 am**	
☽ ⚹ ♀	**6:58 am**	3:58 am
♂ ⚺ ♆	**8:20 am**	5:20 am
☿ ☍ ⚶	**12:40 pm**	9:40 am
☽ ⚹ ♅	**3:06 pm**	12:06 pm
☽ □ ☉	**8:51 pm**	5:51 pm
☽ △ ⚳	**9:36 pm**	6:36 pm
☽ □ ⚶		9:58 pm

25 TUESDAY

	Eastern	Pacific
☽ □ ⚶	**12:58 am**	
☽ □ ☿	**3:24 am**	12:24 am
☽ ⚻ ♃	**4:19 am**	1:19 am
☿ △ ♃	**9:27 am**	6:27 am
☽ ⚺ ♆	**11:58 am**	8:58 am
☉ ⚺ ⚳	**1:16 pm**	10:16 am
☽ ☌ ♂	**1:16 pm**	10:16 am
☽ ☌ ⚷	**9:00 pm**	6:00 pm
☽ ⚹ ⚵		9:46 pm
☽ ⚺ ♇		10:26 pm

26 WEDNESDAY

	Eastern	Pacific
☽ ⚹ ⚵	**12:46 am**	
☽ ⚺ ♇	**1:26 am**	
☽ ⚹ ♀	**6:11 am**	3:11 am
☽ ⚻ ♄	**7:09 am**	4:09 am
☽ ⚺ ♀	**6:05 pm**	3:05 pm
☉ ☍ ⚶	**6:18 pm**	3:18 pm
☽ ⚺ ♅	**9:25 pm**	6:25 pm

27 THURSDAY

	Eastern	Pacific
☽ □ ⚳	**5:44 am**	2:44 am
☽ △ ⚶	**6:30 am**	3:30 am
☽ ⚹ ☉	**7:47 am**	4:47 am
☽ ☍ ♃	**10:59 am**	7:59 am
☿ ⚹ ♆	**12:36 pm**	9:36 am
☽ ☌ ♆	**7:14 pm**	4:14 pm
☽ ⚹ ☿	**8:28 pm**	5:28 pm
⚳ ⚻ ⚶	**9:23 pm**	6:23 pm
☽ ⚺ ♂	**11:21 pm**	8:21 pm

28 FRIDAY

	Eastern	Pacific
♄ □ ♀	**3:37 am**	12:37 am
☽ ⚺ ⚷	**4:45 am**	1:45 am
♀ ☌ ♅	**7:44 am**	4:44 am
☽ □ ⚵	**8:04 am**	5:04 am
☽ ⚹ ♇	**9:12 am**	6:12 am
☽ △ ♄	**3:27 pm**	12:27 pm
☽ ⚺ ♀	**3:43 pm**	12:43 pm
☿ □ ♂	**9:12 pm**	6:12 pm
☉ △ ♃		9:31 pm

29 SATURDAY

	Eastern	Pacific
☉ △ ♃	**12:31 am**	
☽ ☌ ♅	**6:18 am**	3:18 am
☽ ☌ ♀	**8:36 am**	5:36 am
☽ ⚻ ⚶	**2:21 pm**	11:21 am
☽ ⚹ ⚳	**4:34 pm**	1:34 pm
☽ ⚻ ♃	**8:05 pm**	5:05 pm
☽ ⚺ ☉	**9:49 pm**	6:49 pm
☿ □ ⚷		10:11 pm

30 SUNDAY

	Eastern	Pacific
☿ □ ⚷	**1:11 am**	
☽ ⚺ ♆	**4:51 am**	1:51 am
☽ ⚹ ♂	**12:06 pm**	9:06 am
☽ ⚹ ⚷	**2:47 pm**	11:47 am
☽ ⚺ ☿	**5:25 pm**	2:25 pm
☽ △ ⚵	**5:28 pm**	2:28 pm
☿ ⚻ ⚵	**5:42 pm**	2:42 pm
☽ □ ♇	**7:12 pm**	4:12 pm
☽ □ ♄		10:59 pm

31 MONDAY

	Eastern	Pacific
☽ □ ♄	**1:59 am**	
☽ ☌ ♀	**3:37 am**	12:37 am
☿ △ ♇	**4:13 am**	1:13 am
♀ ⚻ ⚶	**10:44 am**	7:44 am
☽ ⚺ ♅	**5:14 pm**	2:14 pm
☽ ☍ ⚶		9:05 pm
☽ ⚺ ♀		10:53 pm

Eastern time in bold type
Pacific time in medium type

MARCH 2003

☽ Last Aspect day	EST / hr:mn / PST	asp	☽ Ingress sign day	EST / hr:mn / PST
1	**9:30 pm** 6:30 pm	☌ ♅	♓ 1	**10:26 pm** 7:26 pm
4	**8:04 am** 5:04 am	□ ♂	♈ 4	**8:30 am** 5:30 am
6	**8:10 pm** 5:10 pm	⚹ ♅	♉ 6	**8:36 pm** 5:36 pm
9	**9:29 am** 6:29 am	□ ♅	♊ 9	**9:38 am** 6:38 am
11	**6:24 am** 3:24 am	☌ ♄	♋ 11	**9:12 pm** 6:12 pm
13	**4:13 pm** 1:13 pm	△ ☉	♌ 14	**5:06 am** 2:06 am
15	**8:24 pm** 5:24 pm	⚹ ♄	♍ 16	**8:52 am** 5:52 am
18	**5:35 am** 2:35 am	☍ ☉	♎ 18	**9:43 am** 6:43 am
19	**10:02 pm** 7:02 am	△ ♄	♏ 20	**9:38 am** 6:38 am
21	**11:30 pm** 8:30 pm	□ ♀	♐ 22	**10:33 am** 7:33 am
24	**6:58 am** 3:58 am	⚹ ♀	♑ 24	**1:48 pm** 10:48 am
25	**1:16 pm** 10:16 am	☌ ♂	♒ 26	**7:51 pm** 4:51 pm
28	**3:27 pm** 12:27 pm	△ ♄	♓ 29	**4:26 am** 1:26 am
30	10:59 pm	□ ♄	♈ 31	**3:04 pm** 12:04 pm
31	**1:59 am**	□ ♄	♈ 31	**3:04 pm** 12:04 pm

☽ Phases & Eclipses phase	day	EST / hr:mn / PST
New Moon	2	**9:35 pm** 6:35 pm
2nd Quarter	10	11:15 pm
2nd Quarter	11	**2:15 am**
Full Moon	18	**5:35 am** 2:35 am
4th Quarter	24	**8:51 pm** 5:51 pm

Planet Ingress	day	EST / hr:mn / PST
♀ ♒	2	**7:40 am** 4:40 am
♂ ♑	4	**4:17 pm** 1:17 pm
☿ ♓	4	**9:04 pm** 6:04 pm
♅ ♓	10	**3:53 pm** 12:53 pm
⚳ ♉	13	**6:26 am** 3:26 am
☉ ♈	20	**8:00 pm** 5:00 am
☿ ♈	21	**7:16 am** 4:16 am
♀ ♓	27	**1:14 pm** 10:14 am

Planetary Motion	day	EST / hr:mn / PST
⚵ ℞	8	**7:01 am** 4:01 am
♇ ℞	22	9:13 pm
♇ ℞	23	**12:13 am**

DATE		SID.TIME	SUN	MOON	NODE	MERCURY	VENUS	MARS	JUPITER	SATURN	URANUS	NEPTUNE	PLUTO	CERES	PALLAS	JUNO	VESTA	CHIRON
1	Sa	10:33:33	09 ♓ 58 50	15 ♒ 26	03 ♊ ℞ 38	23 ♒ 19	28 ♑ 12	27 ♐ 31	09 ♌ ℞ 51	22 ♊ 11	29 ♒ 27	11 ♒ 44	19 ♐ 49	25 ♈ 25	13 ♓ 56	20 ♏ 19	11 ♎ ℞ 24	16 ♑ 05
2	Su	10:37:29	10 59 05	28 12	03 25	24 55	29 23	28 09	09 45	22 11	29 30	11 46	19 50	25 47	14 17	20 22	11 16	16 10
3	M	10:41:26	11 59 19	10 ♓ 45	03 11	26 33	00 ♒ 33	28 48	09 40	22 12	29 34	11 48	19 50	26 08	14 37	20 24	11 07	16 14
4	T	10:45:22	12 59 30	23 08	02 57	28 12	01 44	29 26	09 34	22 13	29 37	11 50	19 51	26 30	14 57	20 25	10 58	16 18
5	W	10:49:19	13 59 40	05 ♈ 19	02 45	29 51	02 55	00 ♑ 04	09 28	22 15	29 40	11 52	19 52	26 52	15 17	20 27	10 48	16 22
6	Th	10:53:16	14 59 48	17 20	02 35	01 ♓ 32	04 06	00 43	09 23	22 16	29 44	11 54	19 52	27 14	15 38	20 28	10 38	16 26
7	F	10:57:12	15 59 54	29 13	02 27	03 14	05 17	01 21	09 18	22 17	29 47	11 56	19 53	27 36	15 58	20 28	10 27	16 29
8	Sa	11:01:09	16 59 57	11 ♉ 01	02 23	04 57	06 27	01 59	09 13	22 19	29 50	11 58	19 53	27 58	16 18	20 ℞ 29	10 16	16 33
9	Su	11:05:05	17 59 59	22 48	02 D 21	06 41	07 39	02 37	09 08	22 20	29 54	12 00	19 54	28 20	16 39	20 29	10 05	16 37
10	M	11:09:02	18 59 59	04 ♊ 38	02 20	08 26	08 50	03 15	09 03	22 22	29 57	12 02	19 54	28 42	16 59	20 28	09 53	16 41
11	T	11:12:58	19 59 56	16 38	02 ℞ 21	10 13	10 01	03 53	08 59	22 24	00 ♓ 00	12 04	19 55	29 05	17 19	20 28	09 41	16 44
12	W	11:16:55	20 59 52	28 52	02 20	12 00	11 12	04 31	08 54	22 26	00 04	12 06	19 55	29 27	17 40	20 27	09 28	16 48
13	Th	11:20:51	21 59 45	11 ♋ 26	02 19	13 49	12 23	05 10	08 50	22 28	00 07	12 07	19 55	29 49	18 00	20 25	09 16	16 51
14	F	11:24:48	22 59 36	24 24	02 15	15 39	13 34	05 48	08 46	22 30	00 10	12 09	19 56	00 ♉ 12	18 20	20 24	09 03	16 55
15	Sa	11:28:45	23 59 24	07 ♌ 50	02 08	17 30	14 46	06 26	08 42	22 32	00 14	12 11	19 56	00 34	18 41	20 22	08 49	16 58
16	Su	11:32:41	24 59 11	21 45	02 00	19 22	15 57	07 04	08 38	22 34	00 17	12 13	19 56	00 57	19 01	20 19	08 36	17 01
17	M	11:36:38	25 58 55	06 ♍ 07	01 50	21 15	17 09	07 42	08 35	22 37	00 20	12 15	19 56	01 20	19 21	20 16	08 22	17 05
18	T	11:40:34	26 58 37	20 50	01 39	23 10	18 20	08 19	08 32	22 39	00 23	12 16	19 57	01 42	19 42	20 13	08 07	17 08
19	W	11:44:31	27 58 17	05 ♎ 48	01 30	25 05	19 32	08 57	08 28	22 42	00 26	12 18	19 57	02 05	20 02	20 10	07 53	17 11
20	Th	11:48:27	28 57 55	20 51	01 22	27 02	20 43	09 35	08 25	22 45	00 29	12 20	19 57	02 28	20 22	20 06	07 38	17 14
21	F	11:52:24	29 57 32	05 ♏ 50	01 17	28 59	21 55	10 13	08 23	22 48	00 33	12 22	19 57	02 51	20 42	20 02	07 24	17 17
22	Sa	11:56:20	00 ♈ 57 06	20 35	01 D 15	00 ♈ 58	23 06	10 51	08 20	22 51	00 36	12 23	19 57	03 14	21 03	19 58	07 09	17 19
23	Su	12:00:17	01 56 39	05 ♐ 03	01 15	02 58	24 18	11 29	08 18	22 54	00 39	12 25	19 ℞ 57	03 37	21 23	19 53	06 54	17 22
24	M	12:04:13	02 56 10	19 11	01 15	04 58	25 30	12 06	08 15	22 57	00 42	12 27	19 57	04 00	21 43	19 48	06 38	17 25
25	T	12:08:10	03 55 40	02 ♑ 57	01 ℞ 16	06 59	26 42	12 44	08 13	23 00	00 45	12 28	19 57	04 23	22 04	19 42	06 23	17 27
26	W	12:12:07	04 55 07	16 24	01 15	09 01	27 54	13 22	08 12	23 04	00 48	12 30	19 57	04 46	22 24	19 37	06 08	17 30
27	Th	12:16:03	05 54 33	29 33	01 12	11 03	29 05	14 00	08 10	23 07	00 51	12 31	19 57	05 10	22 44	19 30	05 52	17 32
28	F	12:20:00	06 53 57	12 ♒ 26	01 08	13 05	00 ♓ 17	14 37	08 09	23 11	00 54	12 33	19 57	05 33	23 05	19 24	05 37	17 35
29	Sa	12:23:56	07 53 19	25 05	01 00	15 07	01 29	15 15	08 07	23 14	00 57	12 34	19 57	05 56	23 25	19 17	05 21	17 37
30	Su	12:27:53	08 52 40	07 ♓ 33	00 51	17 09	02 41	15 52	08 06	23 18	01 00	12 36	19 56	06 20	23 45	19 10	05 06	17 39
31	M	12:31:49	09 51 58	19 50	00 42	19 10	03 53	16 30	08 05	23 22	01 03	12 37	19 56	06 43	24 05	19 03	04 51	17 42

EPHEMERIS CALCULATED FOR 12 MIDNIGHT GREENWICH MEAN TIME. ALL OTHER DATA AND FACING ASPECTARIAN PAGE IN **EASTERN TIME (BOLD)** AND PACIFIC TIME (REGULAR).

APRIL 2003

1 TUESDAY
☽ ☍ ⚶ **12:05 am**
☽ ⚺ ♀ **1:53 am**
☽ ⚺ ⚳ **5:35 am** 2:35 am
☽ △ ♃ **7:09 am** 4:09 am
☽ ☌ ☉ **2:19 pm** 11:19 am
☽ ⚹ ♆ **4:21 pm** 1:21 pm
♂ ☌ ⚷ **7:44 pm** 4:44 pm
☿ ⚹ ♄ **11:29 pm** 8:29 pm
☽ □ ⚷ 11:37 pm
☽ □ ♂ 11:58 pm

2 WEDNESDAY
☽ □ ⚷ **2:37 am**
☽ □ ♂ **2:58 am**
☽ ⚻ ⚵ **4:32 am** 1:32 am
☽ △ ♇ **6:57 am** 3:57 am
☽ ⚹ ♄ **2:16 pm** 11:16 am
☉ ⚹ ♆ **3:32 pm** 12:32 pm
☽ ☌ ☿ **5:05 pm** 2:05 pm
☽ ⚺ ⚴ **5:22 pm** 2:22 pm
☿ ⚺ ⚴ **7:07 pm** 4:07 pm

3 THURSDAY
♂ ⚹ ⚵ **3:44 am** 12:44 am
♃ □ ⚳ **4:57 am** 1:57 am
☽ ⚹ ♅ **5:47 am** 2:47 am
♀ ⚻ ♃ **6:24 am** 3:24 am
♀ ⚹ ⚳ **7:07 am** 4:07 am
☽ ⚻ ⚶ **11:16 am** 8:16 am
☽ □ ♃ **7:43 pm** 4:43 pm
☽ ☌ ⚳ **8:14 pm** 5:14 pm
☽ ⚹ ♀ **9:14 pm** 6:14 pm

4 FRIDAY
☽ □ ♆ **5:12 am** 2:12 am
☽ ⚺ ☉ **8:34 am** 5:34 am
☽ △ ⚷ **3:39 pm** 12:39 pm
☽ ☍ ⚵ **4:42 pm** 1:42 pm
☽ △ ♂ **7:15 pm** 4:15 pm
☽ ⚻ ♇ **7:51 pm** 4:51 pm

5 SATURDAY
☽ ⚺ ♄ **3:38 am** 12:38 am
♂ ⚺ ♇ **6:29 am** 3:29 am
☽ ⚹ ⚴ **8:10 am** 5:10 am
☽ ⚺ ☿ **5:38 pm** 2:38 pm
☽ □ ♅ **7:05 pm** 4:05 pm
☽ △ ⚶ **11:05 pm** 8:05 pm

6 SUNDAY
☿ ⚹ ♅ **4:27 am** 12:27 am
☽ ⚹ ♃ **9:46 am** 6:46 am
☽ ⚺ ⚳ **12:21 pm** 9:21 am
☽ □ ♀ **6:07 pm** 3:07 pm
☽ △ ♆ **7:16 pm** 4:16 pm

7 MONDAY
☿ ⚻ ⚶ **3:25 am** 12:25 am
☽ ⚹ ☉ **3:57 am** 12:57 am
☽ ⚻ ⚷ **5:35 am** 2:35 am
♀ ⚺ ♆ **5:38 am** 2:38 am
☽ ⚻ ⚵ **5:42 am** 2:42 am
☽ ☍ ♇ **9:32 am** 6:32 am
☽ ⚻ ♂ **12:17 pm** 9:17 am
⚷ ⚹ ⚵ **12:36 pm** 9:36 am
☽ ☌ ♄ **5:34 pm** 2:34 pm
☉ ⚻ ⚵ **10:29 pm** 7:29 pm
☽ □ ⚴ **11:20 pm** 8:20 pm
☉ □ ⚷ 9:26 pm

8 TUESDAY
☉ □ ⚷ **12:26 am**
☽ △ ♅ **8:25 am** 5:25 am
☽ □ ⚶ **10:55 am** 7:55 am
☽ ⚹ ☿ **4:36 pm** 1:36 pm
☽ ⚺ ♃ **9:26 pm** 6:26 pm
☽ ⚹ ⚳ 10:49 pm

9 WEDNESDAY
☽ ⚹ ⚳ **1:49 am**
☽ ⚻ ♆ **6:33 am** 3:33 am
☽ △ ♀ **11:40 am** 8:40 am
☽ △ ⚵ **3:37 pm** 12:37 pm
☽ ☍ ⚷ **4:23 pm** 1:23 pm
☽ □ ☉ **7:40 pm** 4:40 pm
☽ ⚻ ♇ **7:58 pm** 4:58 pm
☉ △ ♇ **11:32 pm** 8:32 pm
☽ ☍ ♂ 10:34 pm

10 THURSDAY
☽ ☍ ♂ **1:34 am**
☽ ⚺ ♄ **3:57 am** 12:57 am
☿ □ ♃ **7:08 am** 4:08 am
☽ △ ⚴ **10:33 am** 7:33 am
☽ ⚻ ♅ **5:44 pm** 2:44 pm
☽ ⚹ ⚶ **6:53 pm** 3:53 pm
♀ △ ⚵ 9:08 pm

11 FRIDAY
♀ △ ⚵ **12:08 am**
☽ ☌ ♃ **5:45 am** 2:45 am
☽ □ ☿ **8:31 am** 5:31 am
☽ □ ⚳ **11:28 am** 8:28 am
♀ ⚹ ⚷ **1:50 pm** 10:50 am
☽ ☍ ♆ **2:14 pm** 11:14 am
☽ □ ⚵ **9:51 pm** 6:51 pm
☽ ⚻ ⚷ **11:21 pm** 8:21 pm
☽ ⚻ ♀ 9:16 pm
☽ △ ♇ 11:33 pm

12 SATURDAY
☽ ⚻ ♀ **12:16 am**
☽ △ ♇ **2:33 am**
☽ △ ☉ **6:31 am** 3:31 am
☽ ⚻ ♂ **10:18 am** 7:18 am
☽ ⚹ ♄ **10:18 am** 7:18 am
♂ ⚻ ♄ **10:30 am** 7:30 am
☽ ⚻ ⚴ **5:24 pm** 2:24 pm
☽ ☍ ♅ **10:53 pm** 7:53 pm
☽ ⚺ ⚶ **11:00 pm** 8:00 pm
☿ ☌ ⚳ 9:58 pm
♀ □ ♇ 11:03 pm

13 SUNDAY
☿ ☌ ⚳ **12:58 am**
♀ □ ♇ **2:03 am**
♅ ⚻ ⚶ **5:36 am** 2:36 am
☽ ⚺ ♃ **9:58 am** 6:58 am
☽ △ ⚳ **4:39 pm** 1:39 pm
☽ △ ☿ **5:40 pm** 2:40 pm
☽ ⚻ ♆ **5:49 pm** 2:49 pm
☿ □ ♆ **7:27 pm** 4:27 pm
☽ ⚹ ⚵ 9:11 pm
☽ △ ⚷ 11:18 pm

14 MONDAY
☽ ⚹ ⚵ **12:11 am**
☽ △ ⚷ **2:18 am**
☽ □ ♇ **5:11 am** 2:11 am
☽ ☍ ♀ **7:38 am** 4:38 am
☽ ⚻ ☉ **12:31 pm** 9:31 am
☽ □ ♄ **12:46 pm** 9:46 am
☽ △ ♂ **2:38 pm** 11:38 am
☉ ⚹ ♄ **4:38 pm** 1:38 pm
☽ ☍ ⚴ **8:16 pm** 5:16 pm
☽ ☌ ⚶ **11:45 pm** 8:45 pm
☽ ⚻ ♅ 9:27 pm

15 TUESDAY
☽ ⚻ ♅ **12:27 am**
☽ ⚹ ♃ **10:55 am** 7:55 am
♆ □ ⚳ **12:09 pm** 9:09 am
☽ △ ♆ **6:21 pm** 3:21 pm
☽ ⚻ ⚳ **6:30 pm** 3:30 pm
☽ ⚻ ☿ **10:01 pm** 7:01 pm
☽ ⚺ ⚵ **11:48 pm** 8:48 pm
☽ □ ⚷ 11:29 pm

16 WEDNESDAY
☽ □ ⚷ **2:29 am**
☽ ⚹ ♇ **5:11 am** 2:11 am
☽ ⚻ ♀ **11:43 am** 8:43 am
☽ △ ♄ **12:50 pm** 9:50 am
☽ ☍ ☉ **3:36 pm** 12:36 pm
☽ □ ♂ **4:22 pm** 1:22 pm
☽ ⚻ ⚴ **8:56 pm** 5:56 pm
☿ ☍ ⚵ **9:25 pm** 6:25 pm
☽ ⚺ ⚶ **10:41 pm** 7:41 pm
☽ △ ♅ 9:05 pm
♀ □ ♄ 11:52 pm

17 THURSDAY
☽ △ ♅ **12:05 am**
♀ □ ♄ **2:52 am**
☽ □ ♃ **10:25 am** 7:25 am
☽ □ ♆ **5:43 pm** 2:43 pm
☽ ☍ ⚳ **7:07 pm** 4:07 pm
☉ □ ♂ **9:55 pm** 6:55 pm
☽ ☌ ⚵ **10:30 pm** 7:30 pm
☽ ☍ ☿ 9:24 pm
☽ ⚹ ⚷ 10:52 pm

18 FRIDAY
☽ ☍ ☿ **12:24 am**
☽ ⚹ ⚷ **1:52 am**
☽ ⚺ ♇ **4:30 am** 1:30 am
☽ ⚻ ♄ **12:33 pm** 9:33 am
☽ △ ♀ **3:17 pm** 12:17 pm
☽ ⚹ ♂ **5:52 pm** 2:52 pm
☽ ⚻ ☉ **6:24 pm** 3:24 pm
☽ △ ⚴ **9:36 pm** 6:36 pm
☽ ⚹ ⚶ **9:44 pm** 6:44 pm
☽ □ ♅ **11:52 pm** 8:52 pm
⚴ ☍ ⚶ 10:36 pm

19 SATURDAY
⚴ ☍ ⚶ **1:36 am**
☿ △ ⚷ **6:10 am** 3:10 am
☽ △ ♃ **10:31 am** 7:31 am
☽ ⚹ ♆ **5:59 pm** 2:59 pm
☽ ⚻ ⚳ **8:45 pm** 5:45 pm
☽ ⚺ ⚵ **10:13 pm** 7:13 pm
☽ ⚺ ⚷ 11:26 pm

20 SUNDAY
☽ ⚺ ⚷ **2:26 am**
☽ ⚻ ☿ **3:22 am** 12:22 am
☽ ☌ ♇ **5:06 am** 2:06 am
☽ ☍ ♄ **1:55 pm** 10:55 am
☉ ⚻ ⚶ **2:15 pm** 11:15 am
☽ □ ♀ **9:02 pm** 6:02 pm
☽ ⚺ ♂ **9:23 pm** 6:23 pm
☽ □ ⚶ **10:40 pm** 7:40 pm
☽ △ ☉ **11:24 pm** 8:24 pm
☽ □ ⚴ 9:18 pm
☽ ⚹ ♅ 10:38 pm

21 MONDAY
☽ □ ⚴ **12:18 am**
☽ ⚹ ♅ **1:38 am**
♀ ⚹ ♂ **4:50 am** 1:50 am
⚳ ☍ ⚵ **8:07 am** 5:07 am
☽ ⚻ ♃ **12:58 pm** 9:58 am
♀ ☍ ⚶ **2:08 pm** 11:08 am
☉ ⚺ ⚴ **6:30 pm** 3:30 pm
☽ ⚺ ♆ **8:46 pm** 5:46 pm
♂ △ ⚶ **9:33 pm** 6:33 pm
☽ ⚹ ⚵ 9:27 pm
☽ △ ⚳ 10:13 pm

22 TUESDAY
☽ ⚹ ⚵ **12:27 am**
☽ △ ⚳ **1:13 am**
☿ ⚻ ♇ **3:28 am** 12:28 am
☽ ☌ ⚷ **5:44 am** 2:44 am
☽ ⚺ ♇ **8:31 am** 5:31 am
☽ △ ☿ **8:40 am** 5:40 am
☉ ⚹ ♅ **8:57 am** 5:57 am
☽ ⚻ ♄ **6:20 pm** 3:20 pm
♀ ☌ ⚴ 9:11 pm
☽ △ ⚶ 11:43 pm

23 WEDNESDAY
♀ ☌ ⚴ **12:11 am**
☽ △ ⚶ **2:43 am**
♀ ⚺ ♅ **4:21 am** 1:21 am
☽ ☌ ♂ **4:27 am** 1:27 am
☽ ⚹ ⚴ **6:24 am** 3:24 am
☽ ⚺ ♅ **6:38 am** 3:38 am
☽ ⚹ ♀ **6:52 am** 3:52 am
☽ □ ☉ **8:18 am** 5:18 am
♅ ⚺ ⚴ **4:52 pm** 1:52 pm
☽ ☍ ♃ **6:50 pm** 3:50 pm
☽ ☌ ♆ 11:58 pm

24 THURSDAY
☽ ☌ ♆ **2:58 am**
☽ □ ⚵ **5:57 am** 2:57 am
☽ □ ⚳ **9:26 am** 6:26 am
☽ ⚺ ⚷ **12:30 pm** 9:30 am
☽ ⚹ ♇ **3:22 pm** 12:22 pm
☽ □ ☿ **4:48 pm** 1:48 pm
☽ △ ♄ 11:19 pm

25 FRIDAY
☽ △ ♄ **2:19 am**
♂ ⚺ ♅ **7:21 am** 4:21 am
☽ ⚻ ⚶ **10:10 am** 7:10 am
☽ ☌ ♅ **3:05 pm** 12:05 pm
☽ ⚺ ♂ **3:27 pm** 12:27 pm
☽ ⚺ ⚴ **4:12 pm** 1:12 pm
☽ ⚺ ♀ **9:14 pm** 6:14 pm
☽ ⚹ ☉ **9:30 pm** 6:30 pm

26 SATURDAY
☽ ⚻ ♃ **4:06 am** 1:06 am
☉ ⚺ ♀ **9:58 am** 6:58 am
☽ ⚺ ♆ **12:26 pm** 9:26 am
☽ △ ⚵ **2:29 pm** 11:29 am
☽ ⚹ ⚳ **9:09 pm** 6:09 pm
☽ ⚹ ⚷ **10:23 pm** 7:23 pm
♂ ⚹ ⚴ 10:01 pm
☽ □ ♇ 10:18 pm

27 SUNDAY
♂ ⚹ ⚴ **1:01 am**
☽ □ ♇ **1:18 am**
☽ ⚹ ☿ **3:04 am** 12:04 am
☽ □ ♄ **1:18 pm** 10:18 am
☽ ☍ ⚶ **8:25 pm** 5:25 pm
☽ ⚺ ♅ 11:16 pm

28 MONDAY
☽ ⚺ ♅ **2:16 am**
☽ ☌ ⚴ **4:54 am** 1:54 am
☽ ⚹ ♂ **5:34 am** 2:34 am
⚷ △ ⚳ **9:30 am** 6:30 am
☽ ⚺ ☉ **2:01 pm** 11:01 am
☽ ☌ ♀ **3:09 pm** 12:09 pm
☽ △ ♃ **3:56 pm** 12:56 pm
♀ △ ♃ **11:19 pm** 8:19 pm
☽ ⚹ ♆ 9:13 pm
☽ ⚻ ⚵ 10:11 pm

29 TUESDAY
☽ ⚹ ♆ **12:13 am**
☽ ⚻ ⚵ **1:11 am**
☽ □ ⚷ **10:23 am** 7:23 am
☽ ⚺ ⚳ **11:16 am** 8:16 am
☽ △ ♇ **1:19 pm** 10:19 am
☽ ⚺ ☿ **2:19 pm** 11:19 am
☉ □ ♃ **3:32 pm** 12:32 pm
☽ ⚹ ♄ 11:12 pm

30 WEDNESDAY
☽ ⚹ ♄ **2:12 am**
☽ ⚻ ⚶ **8:25 am** 5:25 am
☽ ⚹ ♅ **3:01 pm** 12:01 pm
☽ ⚺ ⚴ **7:16 pm** 4:16 pm
☽ □ ♂ **9:25 pm** 6:25 pm
♆ □ ⚵ 10:21 pm

Eastern time in bold type
Pacific time in medium type

APRIL 2003

☽ Last Aspect day	EST / hr:mn / PST		asp	☽ Ingress sign day	EST / hr:mn / PST	
2	**5:05 pm**	2:05 pm	☌ ☿	♉ 3	**3:20 am**	12:20 am
4	**7:15 pm**	4:15 pm	△ ♂	♊ 5	**4:24 pm**	1:24 pm
7	**5:34 pm**	2:34 pm	☌ ♄	♋ 8	**5:36 am**	2:36 am
9		10:34 pm	☍ ♂	♌ 10	**2:54 pm**	11:54 am
10	**1:34 am**		☍ ♂	♌ 10	**2:54 pm**	11:54 am
12	**10:18 am**	7:18 am	⚹ ♄	♍ 12	**8:07 pm**	5:07 pm
14	**2:38 pm**	11:38 am	△ ♂	♎ 14	**9:42 pm**	6:42 pm
16	**4:22 pm**	1:22 pm	□ ♂	♏ 16	**9:16 pm**	6:16 pm
18	**5:52 pm**	2:52 pm	⚹ ♂	♐ 18	**8:51 pm**	5:51 pm
20	**9:02 pm**	6:02 pm	□ ♀	♑ 20	**10:20 pm**	7:20 pm
22	**8:40 am**	5:40 am	△ ☿	♒ 22		11:58 pm
22	**8:40 am**	5:40 am	△ ☿	♒ 23	**2:58 am**	
24		11:19 pm	△ ♄	♓ 25	**11:02 am**	8:02 am
25	**2:19 am**		△ ♄	♓ 25	**11:02 am**	8:02 am
27	**1:18 pm**	10:18 am	□ ♄	♈ 27	**9:54 pm**	6:54 pm
29		11:12 pm	⚹ ♄	♉ 30	**10:26 am**	7:26 am
30	**2:12 am**		⚹ ♄	♉ 30	**10:26 am**	7:26 am

☽ Phases & Eclipses phase	day	EST / hr:mn / PST	
New Moon	1	**2:19 pm**	11:19 am
2nd Quarter	9	**7:40 pm**	4:40 pm
Full Moon	16	**3:36 pm**	12:36 pm
4th Quarter	23	**8:18 am**	5:18 am

Planet Ingress	day	EST / hr:mn / PST	
☿ ♉	5	**9:37 am**	6:37 am
♀ ♈	17	**12:26 pm**	9:26 am
☉ ♉	20	**8:03 am**	5:03 am
♀ ♈	21	**12:18 pm**	9:18 am
♂ ♒	21	**7:48 pm**	4:48 pm
⚶ ♍	22	**4:23 am**	1:23 am

Planetary Motion	day	EST / hr:mn / PST	
♃ D	3	**10:04 pm**	7:04 pm
⚷ ℞	25	**1:12 pm**	10:12 am
☿ ℞	26	**7:59 am**	4:59 am

DATE		SID.TIME	SUN	MOON	NODE	MERCURY	VENUS	MARS	JUPITER	SATURN	URANUS	NEPTUNE	PLUTO	CERES	PALLAS	JUNO	VESTA	CHIRON
1	T	12:35:46	10 ♈ 51 15	01 ♈ 59	00 ♊ ℞ 32	21 ♈ 10	05 ♓ 05	17 ♑ 07	08 ♌ ℞ 05	23 ♊ 26	01 ♓ 06	12 ♒ 39	19 ♐ ℞ 56	07 ♉ 07	24 ♓ 26	18 ♏ ℞ 55	04 ♎ ℞ 35	17 ♑ 44
2	W	12:39:42	11 50 29	13 59	00 23	23 08	06 17	17 45	08 04	23 30	01 08	12 40	19 55	07 30	24 46	18 47	04 20	17 46
3	Th	12:43:39	12 48 41	25 53	00 16	25 05	07 29	18 22	08 04	23 34	01 11	12 41	19 55	07 54	25 06	18 39	04 05	17 47
4	F	12:47:36	13 48 51	07 ♉ 42	00 11	27 00	08 42	18 59	08 D 04	23 38	01 14	12 43	19 55	08 18	25 26	18 30	03 50	17 49
5	Sa	12:51:32	14 48 00	19 29	00 D 08	28 53	09 54	19 36	08 04	23 42	01 17	12 44	19 54	08 41	25 46	18 21	03 35	17 51
6	Su	12:55:29	15 47 06	01 ♊ 17	00 08	00 ♉ 42	11 06	20 14	08 04	23 47	01 19	12 45	19 54	09 05	26 06	18 12	03 20	17 53
7	M	12:59:25	16 46 09	13 08	00 09	02 29	12 18	20 51	08 04	23 51	01 22	12 47	19 53	09 29	26 27	18 02	03 05	17 54
8	T	13:03:22	17 45 11	25 08	00 10	04 12	13 30	21 28	08 05	23 56	01 25	12 48	19 53	09 52	26 47	17 52	02 51	17 56
9	W	13:07:18	18 44 10	07 ♋ 22	00 ℞ 11	05 50	14 42	22 05	08 06	24 00	01 27	12 49	19 52	10 16	27 07	17 42	02 37	17 57
10	Th	13:11:15	19 43 07	19 53	00 12	07 25	15 55	22 42	08 07	24 05	01 30	12 50	19 52	10 40	27 27	17 32	02 23	17 59
11	F	13:15:11	20 42 02	02 ♌ 47	00 11	08 55	17 07	23 19	08 08	24 10	01 32	12 51	19 51	11 04	27 47	17 21	02 10	18 00
12	Sa	13:19:08	21 40 55	16 07	00 09	10 21	18 19	23 55	08 10	24 15	01 35	12 52	19 51	11 28	28 07	17 10	01 56	18 01
13	Su	13:23:05	22 39 45	29 56	00 05	11 41	19 32	24 32	08 11	24 20	01 37	12 53	19 50	11 52	28 27	16 59	01 44	18 02
14	M	13:27:01	23 38 32	14 ♍ 14	00 00	12 56	20 44	25 09	08 13	24 25	01 40	12 54	19 49	12 16	28 47	16 48	01 31	18 03
15	T	13:30:58	24 37 18	28 57	29 ♉ 55	14 06	21 56	25 46	08 15	24 30	01 42	12 55	19 49	12 40	29 07	16 37	01 19	18 04
16	W	13:34:54	25 36 01	13 ♎ 59	29 50	15 10	23 09	26 22	08 17	24 35	01 45	12 56	19 48	13 04	29 27	16 25	01 07	18 05
17	Th	13:38:51	26 34 43	29 12	29 46	16 09	24 21	26 59	08 19	24 40	01 47	12 57	19 47	13 28	29 46	16 13	00 55	18 06
18	F	13:42:47	27 33 22	14 ♏ 25	29 43	17 02	25 33	27 35	08 22	24 46	01 49	12 58	19 46	13 52	00 ♈ 06	16 01	00 44	18 06
19	Sa	13:46:44	28 32 00	29 28	29 D 43	17 49	26 46	28 12	08 24	24 51	01 52	12 59	19 46	14 16	00 26	15 48	00 33	18 07
20	Su	13:50:40	29 30 36	14 ♐ 14	29 43	18 30	27 58	28 48	08 27	24 56	01 54	13 00	19 45	14 41	00 46	15 36	00 23	18 07
21	M	13:54:37	00 ♉ 29 10	28 37	29 45	19 05	29 11	29 24	08 30	25 02	01 56	13 01	19 44	15 05	01 06	15 23	00 13	18 08
22	T	13:58:34	01 27 43	12 ♑ 35	29 46	19 35	00 ♈ 23	00 ♒ 00	08 33	25 08	01 58	13 02	19 43	15 29	01 25	15 11	00 03	18 08
23	W	14:02:30	02 26 14	26 09	29 ℞ 47	19 58	01 36	00 36	08 37	25 13	02 00	13 03	19 42	15 53	01 45	14 58	29 ♍ 54	18 09
24	Th	14:06:27	03 24 43	09 ♒ 18	29 47	20 15	02 48	01 12	08 40	25 19	02 02	13 03	19 41	16 17	02 05	14 45	29 45	18 09
25	F	14:10:23	04 23 11	22 07	29 46	20 27	04 01	01 48	08 44	25 25	02 04	13 04	19 40	16 42	02 24	14 31	29 37	18 ℞ 09
26	Sa	14:14:20	05 21 37	04 ♓ 39	29 44	20 ℞ 33	05 13	02 24	08 48	25 31	02 06	13 05	19 39	17 06	02 44	14 18	29 29	18 09
27	Su	14:18:16	06 20 02	16 56	29 40	20 33	06 26	03 00	08 52	25 37	02 08	13 05	19 38	17 30	03 03	14 05	29 22	18 09
28	M	14:22:13	07 18 25	29 03	29 37	20 27	07 39	03 36	08 56	25 43	02 10	13 06	19 37	17 55	03 23	13 51	29 15	18 09
29	T	14:26:09	08 16 46	11 ♈ 01	29 33	20 16	08 51	04 11	09 01	25 49	02 12	13 06	19 36	18 19	03 42	13 38	29 09	18 08
30	W	14:30:06	09 15 05	22 53	29 30	20 01	10 04	04 47	09 05	25 55	02 14	13 07	19 35	18 44	04 02	13 24	29 03	18 08

EPHEMERIS CALCULATED FOR 12 MIDNIGHT GREENWICH MEAN TIME. ALL OTHER DATA AND FACING ASPECTARIAN PAGE IN **EASTERN TIME (BOLD)** AND PACIFIC TIME (REGULAR).

MAY 2003

1 THURSDAY
♆ □ ⚵ **1:21 am**
☿ ⊼ ♇ **3:38 am** 12:38 am
☽ □ ♃ **5:09 am** 2:09 am
☽ ☌ ☉ **8:15 am** 5:15 am
☽ ⊻ ♀ **10:54 am** 7:54 am
☿ ☌ ⚳ **12:18 pm** 9:18 am
☽ ☍ ⚵ **12:55 pm** 9:55 am
☽ □ ♆ **1:09 pm** 10:09 am
♇ ⊼ ⚳ **8:07 pm** 5:07 pm
☽ △ ⚷ **11:19 pm** 8:19 pm
☽ ☌ ☿ 10:27 pm
☽ ⊼ ♇ 11:12 pm
☽ ☌ ⚳ 11:25 pm

2 FRIDAY
☽ ☌ ☿ **1:27 am**
☽ ⊼ ♇ **2:12 am**
☽ ☌ ⚳ **2:25 am**
♀ ⊼ ⚵ **3:47 am** 12:47 am
♀ ⚹ ♆ **8:57 am** 5:57 am
☽ ⊻ ♄ **3:46 pm** 12:46 pm
☽ △ ⚶ **9:02 pm** 6:02 pm

3 SATURDAY
☽ □ ♅ **4:11 am** 1:11 am
☉ ☍ ⚵ **7:10 am** 4:10 am
☽ ⚹ ⚴ **9:57 am** 6:57 am
☽ △ ♂ **1:34 pm** 10:34 am
☽ ⚹ ♃ **6:30 pm** 3:30 pm
☉ □ ♆ **8:18 pm** 5:18 pm
☽ ⊼ ⚵ 9:38 pm
☽ △ ♆ 11:02 pm
☽ ⊻ ☉ 11:33 pm

4 SUNDAY
☽ ⊼ ⚵ **12:38 am**
☽ △ ♆ **2:02 am**
☽ ⊻ ☉ **2:33 am**
☿ △ ⚷ **4:31 am** 1:31 am
☽ ⚹ ♀ **6:39 am** 3:39 am
☽ ⊻ ☿ **11:39 am** 8:39 am
☽ ⊼ ⚷ **11:58 am** 8:58 am
☽ ☍ ♇ **2:46 pm** 11:46 am
☽ ⊻ ⚳ **5:14 pm** 2:14 pm

5 MONDAY
☽ ☌ ♄ **4:43 am** 1:43 am
☽ □ ⚶ **9:03 am** 6:03 am
☽ △ ♅ **4:26 pm** 1:26 pm
☿ ⊻ ♀ **5:31 pm** 2:31 pm
☽ □ ⚴ **11:32 pm** 8:32 pm

6 TUESDAY
☽ ⊼ ♂ **4:25 am** 1:25 am
☽ ⊻ ♃ **6:40 am** 3:40 am
♀ □ ⚷ **10:39 am** 7:39 am
☽ △ ⚵ **11:04 am** 8:04 am
☽ ⊼ ♆ **1:32 pm** 10:32 am
☽ ⚹ ☉ **7:02 pm** 4:02 pm
☽ ⚹ ☿ **8:03 pm** 5:03 pm
☽ ☍ ⚷ **11:00 pm** 8:00 pm
☽ □ ♀ 9:21 pm
☽ ⊼ ♇ 10:40 pm

7 WEDNESDAY
☽ □ ♀ **12:21 am**
☽ ⊼ ♇ **1:40 am**
☉ ☌ ☿ **3:21 am** 12:21 am
☽ ⚹ ⚳ **6:06 am** 3:06 am
♀ △ ♇ **1:36 pm** 10:36 am
☽ ⊻ ♄ **3:37 pm** 12:37 pm
☽ ⚹ ⚶ **7:05 pm** 4:05 pm
☽ ⊼ ♅ 11:23 pm

8 THURSDAY
☽ ⊼ ♅ **2:23 am**
☽ △ ⚴ **10:27 am** 7:27 am
♂ ☍ ♃ **1:36 pm** 10:36 am
☽ ☌ ♃ **4:11 pm** 1:11 pm
☽ ☍ ♂ **4:17 pm** 1:17 pm
☽ □ ⚵ **6:57 pm** 3:57 pm
☉ △ ⚷ **9:12 pm** 6:12 pm
☽ ☍ ♆ **10:16 pm** 7:16 pm
☽ □ ☿ 10:51 pm

9 FRIDAY
☽ □ ☿ **1:51 am**
☽ ⊼ ⚷ **7:05 am** 4:05 am
☽ □ ☉ **7:53 am** 4:53 am
☽ △ ♇ **9:34 am** 6:34 am
☽ △ ♀ **2:03 pm** 11:03 am
☽ □ ⚳ **3:35 pm** 12:35 pm
☽ ⚹ ♄ **11:13 pm** 8:13 pm
☽ ⊻ ⚶ 10:55 pm

10 SATURDAY
☽ ⊻ ⚶ **1:55 am**
☉ ⊼ ♇ **6:30 am** 3:30 am
☽ ☍ ♅ **8:55 am** 5:55 am
♂ □ ⚵ **12:55 pm** 9:55 am
♀ ⊻ ⚳ **2:59 pm** 11:59 am
☽ ⊼ ⚴ **5:38 pm** 2:38 pm
☽ ⊻ ♃ **10:07 pm** 7:07 pm
☽ ⚹ ⚵ **11:29 pm** 8:29 pm
☽ ⊼ ♂ 9:06 pm

11 SUNDAY
☽ ⊼ ♂ **12:06 am**
☽ ⊼ ♆ **3:25 am** 12:25 am
☽ △ ☿ **4:38 am** 1:38 am
☽ △ ⚷ **11:35 am** 8:35 am
☽ □ ♇ **1:53 pm** 10:53 am
☽ △ ☉ **4:13 pm** 1:13 pm
☽ △ ⚳ **9:08 pm** 6:08 pm
☽ ⊼ ♀ **10:58 pm** 7:58 pm

12 MONDAY
☽ □ ♄ **3:09 am** 12:09 am
☽ ☌ ⚶ **5:16 am** 2:16 am
☽ ⊼ ♅ **11:55 am** 8:55 am
☿ □ ♆ **12:30 pm** 9:30 am
☽ ☍ ⚴ **9:08 pm** 6:08 pm
☽ ⚹ ♃ 9:38 pm
☽ ⊻ ⚵ 9:49 pm

13 TUESDAY
☽ ⚹ ♃ **12:38 am**
☽ ⊻ ⚵ **12:49 am**
☽ △ ♂ **4:07 am** 1:07 am
☽ ⊼ ☿ **4:44 am** 1:44 am
☽ △ ♆ **5:16 am** 2:16 am
♃ □ ⚵ **8:48 am** 5:48 am
☽ □ ⚷ **12:56 pm** 9:56 am
☿ □ ♂ **1:19 pm** 10:19 am
☽ ⚹ ♇ **3:07 pm** 12:07 pm
☽ ⊼ ☉ **8:49 pm** 5:49 pm
☽ ⊼ ⚳ **11:28 pm** 8:28 pm

14 WEDNESDAY
☽ ☍ ♀ **4:08 am** 1:08 am
☽ △ ♄ **4:13 am** 1:13 am
♀ ⚹ ♄ **5:15 am** 2:15 am
☽ ⊻ ⚶ **5:57 am** 2:57 am
♂ ☌ ♆ **10:35 am** 7:35 am
☽ △ ♅ **12:21 pm** 9:21 am
☽ ⊼ ⚴ **10:12 pm** 7:12 pm
☽ ☌ ⚵ 9:06 pm
☽ □ ♃ 9:57 pm

15 THURSDAY
☽ ☌ ⚵ **12:06 am**
☽ □ ♃ **12:57 am**
♀ ⊼ ⚶ **3:08 am** 12:08 am
☽ ☍ ☿ **3:19 am** 12:19 am
☽ □ ♆ **5:07 am** 2:07 am
☽ □ ♂ **5:49 am** 2:49 am
☽ ⚹ ⚷ **12:32 pm** 9:32 am
☽ ⊻ ♇ **2:41 pm** 11:41 am
☽ ☍ ☉ **11:36 pm** 8:36 pm
☽ ☍ ⚳ 9:20 pm

16 FRIDAY
☽ ☍ ⚳ **12:20 am**
☽ ⊼ ♄ **4:05 am** 1:05 am
☽ ⚹ ⚶ **5:33 am** 2:33 am
☽ ⊼ ♀ **7:47 am** 4:47 am
☽ □ ♅ **11:53 am** 8:53 am
☉ ☌ ⚳ **6:57 pm** 3:57 pm
☽ △ ⚴ **10:44 pm** 7:44 pm
☽ ⊻ ⚵ **11:00 pm** 8:00 pm
☽ △ ♃ 9:54 pm
☽ ⊼ ☿ 11:00 pm

17 SATURDAY
☽ △ ♃ **12:54 am**
☽ ⊼ ☿ **2:00 am**
☽ ⚹ ♆ **4:45 am** 1:45 am
⚴ ⊼ ⚵ **6:43 am** 3:43 am
☽ ⚹ ♂ **7:18 am** 4:18 am
☽ ⊻ ⚷ **12:13 pm** 9:13 am
☽ ☌ ♇ **2:26 pm** 11:26 am
☽ ⊼ ⚳ 10:48 pm

18 SUNDAY
☽ ⊼ ⚳ **1:48 am**
☽ ⊼ ☉ **3:02 am** 12:02 am
☽ ☍ ♄ **4:41 am** 1:41 am
☽ □ ⚶ **5:59 am** 2:59 am
♀ ⚹ ♅ **11:39 am** 8:39 am
☽ ⚹ ♅ **12:27 pm** 9:27 am
☽ △ ♀ **12:31 pm** 9:31 am
☽ ⚹ ⚵ **11:19 pm** 8:19 pm
☽ □ ⚴ 9:48 pm
☽ ⊼ ♃ 11:25 pm
☽ △ ☿ 11:38 pm

19 MONDAY
☽ □ ⚴ **12:48 am**
☽ ⊼ ♃ **2:25 am**
☽ △ ☿ **2:38 am**
☽ ⊻ ♆ **6:03 am** 3:03 am
☉ ⊻ ♄ **7:25 am** 4:25 am
☽ ⊻ ♂ **10:45 am** 7:45 am
☽ ☌ ⚷ **1:49 pm** 10:49 am
☽ ⊻ ♇ **4:11 pm** 1:11 pm
☿ □ ♃ **7:47 pm** 4:47 pm
☉ △ ⚶ 11:39 pm

20 TUESDAY
☉ △ ⚶ **2:39 am**
☽ △ ⚳ **5:54 am** 2:54 am
☽ ⊼ ♄ **7:52 am** 4:52 am
☽ △ ⚶ **9:02 am** 6:02 am
☽ △ ☉ **9:29 am** 6:29 am
☽ ⊻ ♅ **3:46 pm** 12:46 pm
☽ □ ♀ **8:50 pm** 5:50 pm
☽ □ ⚵ 11:35 pm

21 WEDNESDAY
☽ □ ⚵ **2:35 am**
☽ ⚹ ⚴ **6:09 am** 3:09 am
☽ □ ☿ **6:55 am** 3:55 am
☽ ☍ ♃ **7:10 am** 4:10 am
☽ ☌ ♆ **10:33 am** 7:33 am
☽ ☌ ♂ **5:53 pm** 2:53 pm
☽ ⊻ ⚷ **6:47 pm** 3:47 pm
☽ ⚹ ♇ **9:21 pm** 6:21 pm

22 THURSDAY
☽ □ ⚳ **1:59 pm** 10:59 am
♂ ⊻ ⚷ **2:16 pm** 11:16 am
☽ △ ♄ **2:49 pm** 11:49 am
☽ ⊼ ⚶ **3:55 pm** 12:55 pm
☽ □ ☉ **8:31 pm** 5:31 pm
☽ ☌ ♅ **10:51 pm** 7:51 pm

23 FRIDAY
♀ ☍ ⚵ **4:28 am** 1:28 am
☽ △ ⚵ **9:33 am** 6:33 am
☽ ⚹ ♀ **10:10 am** 7:10 am
☽ ⊻ ⚴ **3:36 pm** 12:36 pm
☽ ⚹ ☿ **3:50 pm** 12:50 pm
☽ ⊼ ♃ **3:54 pm** 12:54 pm
☽ ⊻ ♆ **6:53 pm** 3:53 pm
☿ □ ♃ **9:25 pm** 6:25 pm
♄ ⊻ ⚳ 11:29 pm

24 SATURDAY
♄ ⊻ ⚳ **2:29 am**
☽ ⚹ ⚷ **3:31 am** 12:31 am
☉ □ ♅ **3:37 am** 12:37 am
☽ ⊻ ♂ **5:20 am** 2:20 am
☽ □ ♇ **6:19 am** 3:19 am
♃ △ ⚴ **1:45 pm** 10:45 am
☽ □ ♄ 10:33 pm
☽ ⚹ ⚳ 11:07 pm
☽ ☍ ⚶ 11:36 pm
♂ ⚹ ♇ 11:58 pm

25 SUNDAY
☽ □ ♄ **1:33 am**
☽ ⚹ ⚳ **2:07 am**
☽ ☍ ⚶ **2:36 am**
♂ ⚹ ♇ **2:58 am**
☽ ⊻ ♅ **9:28 am** 6:28 am
☽ ⚹ ☉ **12:02 pm** 9:02 am
☽ ⊼ ⚵ **7:45 pm** 4:45 pm
⚳ △ ⚶ **9:31 pm** 6:31 pm

26 MONDAY
♀ □ ♃ **3:29 am** 12:29 am
☽ △ ♃ **3:58 am** 12:58 am
☽ ⊻ ♀ **4:01 am** 1:01 am
☽ ☌ ⚴ **4:29 am** 1:29 am
☽ ⊻ ☿ **5:03 am** 2:03 am
☽ ⚹ ♆ **6:22 am** 3:22 am
♀ ⊻ ⚴ **10:06 am** 7:06 am
☽ □ ⚷ **3:11 pm** 12:11 pm
☽ △ ♇ **6:08 pm** 3:08 pm
☽ ⚹ ♂ **8:02 pm** 5:02 pm
☿ ☌ ♀ **8:04 pm** 5:04 pm

27 TUESDAY
♀ □ ♆ **3:01 am** 12:01 am
☿ □ ♆ **12:16 pm** 9:16 am
☽ ⚹ ♄ **2:41 pm** 11:41 am
☽ ⊼ ⚶ **3:45 pm** 12:45 pm
☽ ⊻ ⚳ **4:49 pm** 1:49 pm
☽ ⚹ ♅ **10:12 pm** 7:12 pm

28 WEDNESDAY
☽ ⊻ ☉ **6:09 am** 3:09 am
☽ ☍ ⚵ **7:43 am** 4:43 am
☽ □ ♃ **5:39 pm** 2:39 pm
☽ ⊻ ⚴ **7:00 pm** 4:00 pm
☽ □ ♆ **7:18 pm** 4:18 pm
☽ ☌ ☿ **8:57 pm** 5:57 pm
☉ ⊼ ⚵ **10:49 pm** 7:49 pm
☽ ☌ ♀ **11:57 pm** 8:57 pm

29 THURSDAY
☽ △ ⚷ **4:00 am** 1:00 am
♆ ⚹ ⚴ **6:40 am** 3:40 am
☽ ⊼ ♇ **7:02 am** 4:02 am
☽ □ ♂ **11:53 am** 8:53 am

30 FRIDAY
☽ ⊻ ♄ **4:20 am** 1:20 am
☽ △ ⚶ **5:27 am** 2:27 am
☽ ☌ ⚳ **7:59 am** 4:59 am
☽ □ ♅ **11:10 am** 8:10 am
♀ △ ⚷ **1:58 pm** 10:58 am
☽ ⊼ ⚵ **7:45 pm** 4:45 pm
☽ ☌ ☉ 9:20 pm

31 SATURDAY
☽ ☌ ☉ **12:20 am**
☽ ⚹ ♃ **7:05 am** 4:05 am
☽ △ ♆ **7:56 am** 4:56 am
☽ ⚹ ⚴ **9:12 am** 6:12 am
☽ ⊻ ☿ **1:27 pm** 10:27 am
☽ ⊼ ⚷ **4:18 pm** 1:18 pm
♀ ⊼ ♇ **7:20 pm** 4:20 pm
☽ ⊻ ♀ **7:21 pm** 4:21 pm
☽ ☍ ♇ **7:21 pm** 4:21 pm
☽ △ ♂ 11:53 pm

Eastern time in bold type
Pacific time in medium type

MAY 2003

☽ Last Aspect day	EST / hr:mn / PST	asp	☽ Ingress sign day	EST / hr:mn / PST
1	10:27 pm	☌ ☿	♊ 2	**11:27 pm** 8:27 pm
2	**1:27 am**	☌ ☿	♊ 2	**11:27 pm** 8:27 pm
5	**4:43 am** 1:43 am	☌ ♄	♋ 5	**11:42 am** 8:42 am
6	9:21 pm	□ ♀	♌ 7	**9:46 pm** 6:46 pm
7	**12:21 am**	□ ♀	♌ 7	**9:46 pm** 6:46 pm
9	**11:13 pm** 8:13 pm	✶ ♄	♍ 10	**4:31 am** 1:31 am
12	**3:09 am** 12:09 am	□ ♄	♎ 12	**7:42 am** 4:42 am
14	**4:13 am** 1:13 am	△ ♄	♏ 14	**8:14 am** 5:14 am
15	**11:36 pm** 8:36 pm	☍ ☉	♐ 16	**7:43 am** 4:43 am
18	**4:41 am** 1:41 am	☍ ♄	♑ 18	**8:03 am** 5:03 am
20	**9:29 am** 6:29 am	△ ☉	♒ 20	**11:01 am** 8:01 am
22	**2:49 pm** 11:49 am	△ ♄	♓ 22	**5:41 pm** 2:41 pm
24	10:33 pm	□ ♄	♈ 25	**3:59 am** 12:59 am
25	**1:33 am**	□ ♄	♈ 25	**3:59 am** 12:59 am
27	**2:41 pm** 11:41 am	✶ ♄	♉ 27	**4:32 pm** 1:32 pm
29	**11:53 am** 8:53 am	□ ♂	♊ 30	**5:32 am** 2:32 am

☽ Phases & Eclipses phase	day	EST / hr:mn / PST
New Moon	1	**8:15 am** 5:15 am
2nd Quarter	9	**7:53 am** 4:53 am
Full Moon	15	**11:36 pm** 8:36 pm
●	15	24° ♏ 53'
4th Quarter	22	**8:31 pm** 5:31 pm
New Moon	30	9:20 pm
New Moon	31	**12:20 am**
●	30	9° ♊ 20'

Planet Ingress	day	EST / hr:mn / PST
♀ ♉	16	**6:58 am** 3:58 am
☉ ♊	21	**7:12 am** 4:12 am
⚳ ♊	27	**8:48 am** 5:48 am
⚶ ♎	30	**12:06 pm** 9:06 am

Planetary Motion	day	EST / hr:mn / PST
⚶ D	10	10:43 pm
⚶ D	11	**1:43 am**
♆ R	15	**8:48 pm** 5:48 pm
☿ D	20	**3:32 am** 12:32 am

DATE		SID.TIME	SUN	MOON	NODE	MERCURY	VENUS	MARS	JUPITER	SATURN	URANUS	NEPTUNE	PLUTO	CERES	PALLAS	JUNO	VESTA	CHIRON
1	Th	14:34:03	10 ♉ 13 23	04 ♉ 42	29 ♉R 28	19 ♉R 41	11 ♈ 16	05 ♒ 22	09 ♌ 10	26 ♊ 01	02 ♓ 16	13 ♒ 07	19 ♐R 34	19 ♉ 08	04 ♈ 21	13 ♏R 11	28 ♍R 58	18 ♑R 08
2	F	14:37:59	11 11 39	16 30	29 26	19 16	12 29	05 57	09 15	26 07	02 17	13 08	19 33	19 32	04 40	12 57	28 53	18 07
3	Sa	14:41:56	12 09 53	28 18	29 D 25	18 48	13 42	06 32	09 20	26 14	02 19	13 08	19 31	19 57	05 00	12 43	28 49	18 07
4	Su	14:45:52	13 08 06	10 ♊ 09	29 26	18 17	14 54	07 07	09 25	26 20	02 21	13 09	19 30	20 21	05 19	12 30	28 45	18 06
5	M	14:49:49	14 06 16	22 06	29 27	17 44	16 07	07 42	09 30	26 26	02 22	13 09	19 29	20 46	05 38	12 16	28 41	18 05
6	T	14:53:45	15 04 25	04 ♋ 12	29 28	17 08	17 20	08 17	09 36	26 33	02 24	13 10	19 28	21 10	05 57	12 02	28 38	18 04
7	W	14:57:42	16 02 32	16 30	29 29	16 32	18 32	08 52	09 41	26 40	02 25	13 10	19 27	21 35	06 16	11 49	28 36	18 04
8	Th	15:01:38	17 00 37	29 04	29 30	15 54	19 45	09 26	09 47	26 46	02 27	13 10	19 25	21 59	06 35	11 35	28 34	18 03
9	F	15:05:35	17 58 41	11 ♌ 56	29 R 31	15 17	20 58	10 01	09 53	26 53	02 28	13 10	19 24	22 24	06 54	11 22	28 33	18 02
10	Sa	15:09:32	18 56 42	25 12	29 31	14 41	22 10	10 35	09 59	26 59	02 30	13 11	19 23	22 48	07 13	11 08	28 32	18 01
11	Su	15:13:28	19 54 41	08 ♍ 52	29 30	14 06	23 23	11 09	10 05	27 06	02 31	13 11	19 21	23 13	07 32	10 55	28 D 32	17 59
12	M	15:17:25	20 52 38	22 58	29 29	13 32	24 36	11 43	10 12	27 13	02 32	13 11	19 20	23 38	07 51	10 42	28 32	17 58
13	T	15:21:21	21 50 34	07 ♎ 29	29 29	13 02	25 49	12 17	10 18	27 20	02 34	13 11	19 19	24 02	08 10	10 29	28 32	17 57
14	W	15:25:18	22 48 27	22 20	29 28	12 34	27 01	12 51	10 25	27 27	02 35	13 11	19 17	24 27	08 28	10 16	28 33	17 55
15	Th	15:29:14	23 46 19	07 ♏ 25	29 27	12 09	28 14	13 24	10 32	27 34	02 36	13 11	19 16	24 51	08 47	10 03	28 35	17 54
16	F	15:33:11	24 44 10	22 36	29 D 27	11 49	29 27	13 58	10 39	27 41	02 37	13 R 11	19 14	25 16	09 05	09 50	28 37	17 52
17	Sa	15:37:07	25 41 59	07 ♐ 43	29 27	11 32	00 ♉ 40	14 31	10 46	27 48	02 38	13 11	19 13	25 41	09 24	09 38	28 40	17 51
18	Su	15:41:04	26 39 47	22 38	29 27	11 19	01 52	15 04	10 53	27 55	02 39	13 11	19 12	26 05	09 42	09 25	28 43	17 49
19	M	15:45:01	27 37 33	07 ♑ 12	29 27	11 11	03 05	15 37	11 00	28 02	02 40	13 11	19 10	26 30	10 01	09 13	28 46	17 47
20	T	15:48:57	28 35 19	21 22	29 R 28	11 D 08	04 18	16 10	11 08	28 09	02 41	13 11	19 09	26 54	10 19	09 01	28 50	17 45
21	W	15:52:54	29 33 03	05 ♒ 05	29 28	11 08	05 31	16 43	11 15	28 16	02 42	13 11	19 07	27 19	10 37	08 49	28 55	17 43
22	Th	15:56:50	00 ♊ 30 46	18 21	29 28	11 14	06 44	17 15	11 23	28 23	02 43	13 11	19 06	27 44	10 55	08 37	28 59	17 41
23	F	16:00:47	01 28 28	01 ♓ 13	29 D 28	11 24	07 56	17 48	11 31	28 30	02 43	13 10	19 04	28 08	11 13	08 26	29 05	17 39
24	Sa	16:04:43	02 26 09	13 45	29 28	11 38	09 09	18 20	11 39	28 38	02 44	13 10	19 03	28 33	11 31	08 15	29 10	17 37
25	Su	16:08:40	03 23 48	25 59	29 28	11 57	10 22	18 52	11 47	28 45	02 45	13 10	19 01	28 58	11 49	08 04	29 17	17 35
26	M	16:12:36	04 21 27	08 ♈ 01	29 28	12 20	11 35	19 23	11 55	28 52	02 46	13 10	19 00	29 22	12 07	07 53	29 23	17 33
27	T	16:16:33	05 19 05	19 54	29 29	12 48	12 48	19 55	12 03	29 00	02 46	13 09	18 58	29 47	12 25	07 43	29 30	17 30
28	W	16:20:30	06 16 42	01 ♉ 42	29 29	13 20	14 01	20 26	12 12	29 07	02 47	13 09	18 57	00 ♊ 12	12 43	07 32	29 38	17 28
29	Th	16:24:26	07 14 18	13 29	29 30	13 55	15 14	20 57	12 20	29 14	02 47	13 08	18 55	00 36	13 00	07 22	29 46	17 26
30	F	16:28:23	08 11 52	25 18	29 R 30	14 35	16 27	21 28	12 29	29 22	02 48	13 08	18 53	01 01	13 18	07 12	29 54	17 23
31	Sa	16:32:19	09 09 26	07 ♊ 11	29 30	15 19	17 39	21 59	12 38	29 29	02 48	13 08	18 52	01 25	13 35	07 03	00 ♎ 03	17 21

EPHEMERIS CALCULATED FOR 12 MIDNIGHT GREENWICH MEAN TIME. ALL OTHER DATA AND FACING ASPECTARIAN PAGE IN **EASTERN TIME (BOLD)** AND PACIFIC TIME (REGULAR).

JUNE 2003

1 SUNDAY

☽ △ ♂	**2:53 am**	
☽ ☌ ♄	**4:55 pm**	1:55 pm
☽ □ ⚶	**6:09 pm**	3:09 pm
☽ ⚺ ⚳	**9:56 pm**	6:56 pm
☽ △ ♅	**10:59 pm**	7:59 pm

2 MONDAY

☿ △ ⚷	**3:54 am**	12:54 am
☽ △ ⚵	**6:34 am**	3:34 am
☽ ⚺ ☉	**4:44 pm**	1:44 pm
☽ ⚺ ♃	**7:00 pm**	4:00 pm
☽ ⚻ ♆	**7:03 pm**	4:03 pm
☽ □ ♀	**9:43 pm**	6:43 pm
♃ ☍ ♆	**10:55 pm**	7:55 pm
☽ ☍ ⚷		11:58 pm

3 TUESDAY

☽ ☍ ⚷	**2:58 am**	
☽ ⚹ ☿	**4:54 am**	1:54 am
♅ □ ⚳	**5:17 am**	2:17 am
☽ ⚻ ♇	**6:00 am**	3:00 am
☽ ⚹ ♀	**12:27 pm**	9:27 am
☽ ⚻ ♂	**3:48 pm**	12:48 pm
☿ ⚻ ♇	**6:37 pm**	3:37 pm
☉ △ ♆	**10:27 pm**	7:27 pm

4 WEDNESDAY

☉ ⚹ ♃	**3:14 am**	12:14 am
☽ ⚺ ♄	**3:29 am**	12:29 am
☽ ⚹ ⚶	**4:52 am**	1:52 am
☽ ⚻ ♅	**8:44 am**	5:44 am
☽ ⚹ ⚳	**9:39 am**	6:39 am
☽ □ ⚵	**3:23 pm**	12:23 pm

5 THURSDAY

☽ ☍ ♆	**3:55 am**	12:55 am
☽ ☌ ♃	**4:36 am**	1:36 am
☽ ⚹ ☉	**6:17 am**	3:17 am
☽ △ ♀	**7:46 am**	4:46 am
☽ ⚻ ⚷	**11:19 am**	8:19 am
☽ △ ♇	**2:19 pm**	11:19 am
☽ □ ☿	**6:12 pm**	3:12 pm
♀ □ ♂	**7:53 pm**	4:53 pm
☽ ☍ ♂		10:55 pm
☽ □ ♀		11:18 pm

Eastern time in bold type
Pacific time in medium type

6 FRIDAY

☽ ☍ ♂	**1:55 am**	
☽ □ ♀	**2:18 am**	
☉ ⚹ ♀	**10:11 am**	7:11 am
☽ ⚹ ♄	**11:26 am**	8:26 am
☽ ⚺ ⚶	**1:00 pm**	10:00 am
☽ ☍ ♅	**3:55 pm**	12:55 pm
☽ □ ⚳	**6:31 pm**	3:31 pm
☽ ⚹ ⚵	**9:43 pm**	6:43 pm

7 SATURDAY

☽ ⚻ ♆	**10:05 am**	7:05 am
☽ ⚺ ♃	**11:25 am**	8:25 am
☽ ⚻ ♀	**2:56 pm**	11:56 am
☽ □ ☉	**4:28 pm**	1:28 pm
☽ △ ⚷	**4:58 pm**	1:58 pm
☽ □ ♇	**7:54 pm**	4:54 pm
☉ ⚻ ⚷	**11:27 pm**	8:27 pm

8 SUNDAY

☽ △ ☿	**4:36 am**	1:36 am
☽ ⚻ ♂	**8:55 am**	5:55 am
☽ △ ♀	**12:27 pm**	9:27 am
☽ □ ♄	**4:32 pm**	1:32 pm
☽ ☌ ⚶	**6:18 pm**	3:18 pm
☽ ⚻ ♅	**8:19 pm**	5:19 pm
☽ △ ⚳		9:20 pm
☽ ⚺ ⚵		10:25 pm

9 MONDAY

☽ △ ⚳	**12:20 am**	
☽ ⚺ ⚵	**1:25 am**	
☽ △ ♆	**1:32 pm**	10:32 am
☽ ⚹ ♃	**3:26 pm**	12:26 pm
☉ ☍ ♇	**4:44 pm**	1:44 pm
☽ ☍ ♀	**7:12 pm**	4:12 pm
☽ □ ⚷	**7:57 pm**	4:57 pm
☽ ⚹ ♇	**10:50 pm**	7:50 pm
☽ △ ☉	**11:17 pm**	8:17 pm

10 TUESDAY

⚳ ⚻ ⚵	**6:03 am**	3:03 am
☽ ⚻ ☿	**12:08 pm**	9:08 am
☽ △ ♂	**1:00 pm**	10:00 am
♀ ⚺ ♄	**4:38 pm**	1:38 pm
☽ △ ♄	**7:05 pm**	4:05 pm
☽ ⚻ ♀	**7:17 pm**	4:17 pm
☽ ⚺ ⚶	**9:04 pm**	6:04 pm
☽ △ ♅	**10:15 pm**	7:15 pm
☿ □ ♂		10:48 pm
☽ ☌ ⚵		11:49 pm

11 WEDNESDAY

☿ □ ♂	**1:48 am**	
☽ ☌ ⚵	**2:49 am**	
☽ ⚻ ⚳	**3:33 am**	12:33 am
⚷ □ ♀	**4:48 am**	1:48 am
☽ □ ♆	**2:48 pm**	11:48 am
☽ □ ♃	**5:14 pm**	2:14 pm
☽ ⚹ ⚷	**8:53 pm**	5:53 pm
♀ △ ⚶	**9:08 pm**	6:08 pm
☽ ⚻ ♀	**9:14 pm**	6:14 pm
☽ ⚺ ♇	**11:46 pm**	8:46 pm

12 THURSDAY

☽ ⚻ ☉	**3:39 am**	12:39 am
♀ □ ♅	**6:56 am**	3:56 am
☽ □ ♂	**3:11 pm**	12:11 pm
☽ ☍ ☿	**5:51 pm**	2:51 pm
☽ ⚻ ♄	**8:03 pm**	5:03 pm
☽ ⚹ ⚶	**10:18 pm**	7:18 pm
☽ □ ♅	**10:43 pm**	7:43 pm
☽ ☍ ♀		9:07 pm
☽ ⚺ ⚵		11:55 pm

13 FRIDAY

☽ ☍ ♀	**12:07 am**	
☽ ⚺ ⚵	**2:55 am**	
☽ ☍ ⚳	**5:19 am**	2:19 am
☽ ⚹ ♆	**3:04 pm**	12:04 pm
☿ ⚺ ♄	**5:57 pm**	2:57 pm
☽ △ ♃	**6:05 pm**	3:05 pm
☽ ⚺ ⚷	**8:59 pm**	5:59 pm
☽ △ ♀	**10:25 pm**	7:25 pm
☽ ☌ ♇	**11:58 pm**	8:58 pm
♅ ⚻ ⚶		9:09 pm

14 SATURDAY

♅ ⚻ ⚶	**12:09 am**	
☽ ☍ ☉	**7:16 am**	4:16 am
♀ ⚻ ⚵	**8:23 am**	5:23 am
☽ ⚹ ♂	**5:05 pm**	2:05 pm
☿ □ ♅	**6:04 pm**	3:04 pm
☽ ☍ ♄	**8:56 pm**	5:56 pm
☿ △ ⚶	**9:23 pm**	6:23 pm
☽ ⚹ ♅	**11:12 pm**	8:12 pm
☽ □ ⚶	**11:36 pm**	8:36 pm
☽ ⚻ ☿	**11:49 pm**	8:49 pm

15 SUNDAY

☽ ⚹ ⚵	**3:15 am**	12:15 am
☽ ⚻ ♀	**5:04 am**	2:04 am
☽ ⚻ ⚳	**7:22 am**	4:22 am
☽ ⚺ ♆	**3:56 pm**	12:56 pm
☽ ⚻ ♃	**7:41 pm**	4:41 pm
☽ ☌ ⚷	**9:55 pm**	6:55 pm
☽ □ ♀		9:30 pm
☽ ⚺ ♇		10:06 pm

16 MONDAY

☽ □ ♀	**12:30 am**	
☽ ⚺ ♇	**1:06 am**	
☿ ⚻ ⚵	**5:58 am**	2:58 am
☽ ⚻ ☉	**12:22 pm**	9:22 am
☽ ⚺ ♂	**8:38 pm**	5:38 pm
♀ ☌ ⚳	**9:13 pm**	6:13 pm
☽ ⚻ ♄	**11:34 pm**	8:34 pm
☽ ⚺ ♅		10:28 pm
☽ △ ⚶		11:49 pm

17 TUESDAY

☽ ⚺ ♅	**1:28 am**	
☽ △ ⚶	**2:49 am**	
☽ □ ⚵	**5:30 am**	2:30 am
♇ △ ♀	**5:55 am**	2:55 am
☽ △ ☿	**8:50 am**	5:50 am
☽ △ ⚳	**11:40 am**	8:40 am
☽ △ ♀	**12:36 pm**	9:36 am
☽ ☌ ♆	**7:08 pm**	4:08 pm
☽ ☍ ♃	**11:52 pm**	8:52 pm
☽ ⚺ ⚷		10:21 pm

18 WEDNESDAY

☽ ⚺ ⚷	**1:21 am**	
☽ ⚹ ♇	**4:52 am**	1:52 am
☽ ⚹ ♀	**5:22 am**	2:22 am
☿ ☌ ⚳	**2:01 pm**	11:01 am
☽ △ ☉	**9:08 pm**	6:08 pm

19 THURSDAY

☽ ☌ ♂	**3:39 am**	12:39 am
☽ △ ♄	**5:35 am**	2:35 am
☽ ☌ ♅	**7:03 am**	4:03 am
☽ ⚻ ⚶	**9:37 am**	6:37 am
☽ △ ⚵	**11:09 am**	8:09 am
☽ □ ⚳	**7:50 pm**	4:50 pm
☽ □ ☿	**11:32 pm**	8:32 pm
☽ □ ♀		9:49 pm
☽ ⚺ ♆		10:59 pm

20 FRIDAY

☽ □ ♀	**12:49 am**	
☽ ⚺ ♆	**1:59 am**	
☽ ⚻ ♃	**7:57 am**	4:57 am
☽ ⚹ ⚷	**8:30 am**	5:30 am
☽ □ ♇	**12:24 pm**	9:24 am
♀ △ ♆	**12:52 pm**	9:52 am
☽ ⚺ ♀	**2:13 pm**	11:13 am
☿ △ ♆	**4:32 pm**	1:32 pm
☿ ☌ ♀	**11:53 pm**	8:53 pm

21 SATURDAY

☽ □ ☉	**10:45 am**	7:45 am
♃ ⚻ ⚷	**1:02 pm**	10:02 am
☽ ⚺ ♂	**2:52 pm**	11:52 am
☽ □ ♄	**3:36 pm**	12:36 pm
☽ ⚺ ♅	**4:29 pm**	1:29 pm
☽ ☍ ⚶	**8:35 pm**	5:35 pm
☽ ⚻ ⚵	**8:41 pm**	5:41 pm
⚵ ⚺ ⚶		9:29 pm

22 SUNDAY

⚵ ⚺ ⚶	**12:29 am**	
☽ ⚹ ⚳	**8:10 am**	5:10 am
☿ ⚻ ⚷	**10:53 am**	7:53 am
☽ ⚹ ♆	**12:33 pm**	9:33 am
☿ ⚹ ♃	**1:55 pm**	10:55 am
☽ ⚹ ♀	**6:03 pm**	3:03 pm
☽ □ ⚷	**7:12 pm**	4:12 pm
☽ △ ♃	**7:49 pm**	4:49 pm
☽ ⚹ ☿	**8:51 pm**	5:51 pm
☽ △ ♇	**11:28 pm**	8:28 pm
♂ △ ♄		9:21 pm
☽ ☌ ♀		11:47 pm

23 MONDAY

♂ △ ♄	**12:21 am**	
☽ ☌ ♀	**2:47 am**	
♀ ⚻ ⚷	**4:52 am**	1:52 am
☿ ☍ ♇	**12:46 pm**	9:46 am
♀ ⚹ ♃	**2:07 pm**	11:07 am
♂ ☌ ♅	**4:02 pm**	1:02 pm

24 TUESDAY

☽ ⚹ ☉	**4:11 am**	1:11 am
☽ ⚹ ♄	**4:34 am**	1:34 am
☽ ⚹ ♅	**4:45 am**	1:45 am
☽ ⚹ ♂	**5:11 am**	2:11 am
☽ ☍ ⚵	**8:58 am**	5:58 am
☉ ☌ ♄	**9:39 am**	6:39 am
☽ ⚻ ⚶	**10:31 am**	7:31 am
☉ △ ♅	**11:08 am**	8:08 am
☿ ⚹ ♀	**1:15 pm**	10:15 am
♄ △ ♅	**7:34 pm**	4:34 pm
♀ ☍ ♇	**10:00 pm**	7:00 pm
☽ ⚺ ⚳	**11:03 pm**	8:03 pm
☉ △ ♂	**11:54 pm**	8:54 pm
☽ □ ♆		10:15 pm

25 WEDNESDAY

☽ □ ♆	**1:15 am**	
☽ △ ⚷	**7:47 am**	4:47 am
☽ □ ♃	**9:41 am**	6:41 am
☽ ⚻ ♇	**12:16 pm**	9:16 am
☽ ⚺ ♀	**1:57 pm**	10:57 am
☽ ⚺ ♀	**5:02 pm**	2:02 pm
☽ ⚺ ☿	**10:04 pm**	7:04 pm

26 THURSDAY

☉ △ ⚵	**2:10 pm**	11:10 am
☽ □ ♅	**5:36 pm**	2:36 pm
☽ ⚺ ♄	**6:10 pm**	3:10 pm
☽ □ ♂	**8:02 pm**	5:02 pm
☽ ⚻ ⚵	**9:44 pm**	6:44 pm
☽ ⚺ ☉	**10:24 pm**	7:24 pm
☽ △ ⚶		9:54 pm
♀ ⚹ ♀		11:23 pm

27 FRIDAY

☽ △ ⚶	**12:54 am**	
♀ ⚹ ♀	**2:23 am**	
♆ △ ⚳	**12:19 pm**	9:19 am
☽ △ ♆	**1:46 pm**	10:46 am
☽ ☌ ⚳	**1:49 pm**	10:49 am
☽ ⚻ ⚷	**7:57 pm**	4:57 pm
☽ ⚹ ♃	**11:03 pm**	8:03 pm
☽ ☍ ♇		9:30 pm

28 SATURDAY

☽ ☍ ♇	**12:30 am**	
☽ ⚹ ☿	**6:29 am**	3:29 am
☽ ☌ ♀	**9:00 am**	6:00 am
☉ □ ⚶	**6:59 pm**	3:59 pm
☽ ☌ ☿	**10:31 pm**	7:31 pm

29 SUNDAY

☽ △ ♅	**4:59 am**	1:59 am
♂ △ ⚵	**5:58 am**	2:58 am
☽ ☌ ♄	**6:14 am**	3:14 am
☽ △ ⚵	**9:02 am**	6:02 am
☽ △ ♂	**9:07 am**	6:07 am
☽ □ ⚶	**1:36 pm**	10:36 am
☽ ☌ ☉	**2:39 pm**	11:39 am
☽ ⚻ ♆		9:24 pm
☽ ⚺ ⚳		11:30 pm

30 MONDAY

☽ ⚻ ♆	**12:24 am**	
☽ ⚺ ⚳	**2:30 am**	
☽ ☍ ⚷	**6:09 am**	3:09 am
☽ ⚺ ♃	**10:18 am**	7:18 am
☽ ⚻ ♇	**10:41 am**	7:41 am
☿ △ ♅	**11:27 am**	8:27 am
☽ □ ♀	**5:38 pm**	2:38 pm
☿ ☌ ♄	**9:14 pm**	6:14 pm
☽ ⚺ ♀		10:08 pm

JUNE 2003

☽ Last Aspect				☽ Ingress			
day	EST / hr:mn / PST		asp	sign day	EST / hr:mn / PST		
1	**4:55 pm**	1:55 pm	☌ ♄	♋ 1	**5:27 pm**	2:27 pm	
3	**12:27 pm**	9:27 am	⚹ ♀	♌ 4	**3:25 am**	12:25 am	
5		11:18 pm	□ ♀	♍ 6	**10:51 am**	7:51 am	
6	**2:18 am**		□ ♀	♍ 6	**10:51 am**	7:51 am	
8	**12:27 pm**	9:27 am	△ ♀	♎ 8	**3:30 pm**	12:30 pm	
10	**1:00 pm**	10:00 am	△ ♂	♏ 10	**5:39 pm**	2:39 pm	
12	**5:51 pm**	2:51 pm	☍ ☿	♐ 12	**6:12 pm**	3:12 pm	
14	**5:05 pm**	2:05 pm	⚹ ♂	♑ 14	**6:38 pm**	3:38 pm	
14	**11:12 pm**	8:12 pm	⚹ ♅	♒ 16	**8:41 pm**	5:41 pm	

☽ Last Aspect				☽ Ingress		
day	EST / hr:mn / PST		asp	sign day	EST / hr:mn / PST	
18	**9:08 pm**	6:08 pm	△ ☉	♓ 18		10:57 pm
18	**9:08 pm**	6:08 pm	△ ☉	♓ 19	**1:57 am**	
21	**10:45 am**	7:45 am	□ ☉	♈ 21	**11:06 am**	8:06 am
22	**11:28 pm**	8:28 pm	△ ♇	♉ 23	**11:15 pm**	8:15 pm
25	**9:41 am**	6:41 am	□ ♃	♊ 26	**12:13 pm**	9:13 am
28	**10:31 pm**	7:31 pm	☌ ☿	♋ 28		8:52 pm
28	**10:31 pm**	7:31 pm	☌ ☿	♋ 29	**12:52 am**	
29	**2:39 pm**	11:39 am	☌ ☉	♌ 7/1	**9:13 am**	6:13 am

☽ Phases & Eclipses			
phase	day	EST / hr:mn / PST	
2nd Quarter	7	**4:28 pm**	1:28 pm
Full Moon	14	**7:16 am**	4:16 am
4th Quarter	21	**10:45 am**	7:45 am
New Moon	29	**2:39 pm**	11:39 am

Planet Ingress			
	day	EST / hr:mn / PST	
♄ ♋	3	**9:28 pm**	6:28 pm
♀ ♊	9	**11:32 pm**	8:32 pm
☿ ♊	12	**9:34 pm**	6:34 pm
♂ ♓	16	**10:25 pm**	7:25 pm
☉ ♋	21	**3:10 pm**	12:10 pm
☿ ♋	29	**6:17 am**	3:17 am

Planetary Motion			
	day	EST / hr:mn / PST	
♅ ℞	6		11:58 pm
♅ ℞	7	**2:58 am**	
⚵ D	29	**9:46 am**	6:46 am

DATE		SID.TIME	SUN	MOON	NODE	MERCURY	VENUS	MARS	JUPITER	SATURN	URANUS	NEPTUNE	PLUTO	CERES	PALLAS	JUNO	VESTA	CHIRON
1	Su	16:36:16	10 ♊ 06 59	19 ♊ 10	29 ♉ ℞ 30	16 ♉ 06	18 ♉ 52	22 ♒ 29	12 ♌ 47	29 ♊ 37	02 ♓ 48	13 ♒ ℞ 07	18 ♐ ℞ 50	01 ♊ 50	13 ♈ 53	06 ♏ ℞ 54	00 ♎ 12	17 ♑ ℞ 18
2	M	16:40:12	11 04 31	01 ♋ 18	29 29	16 57	20 05	22 59	12 56	29 44	02 49	13 07	18 49	02 15	14 10	06 45	00 22	17 15
3	T	16:44:09	12 02 01	13 36	29 27	17 51	21 18	23 29	13 05	29 52	02 49	13 06	18 47	02 39	14 27	06 36	00 32	17 12
4	W	16:48:05	12 59 31	26 06	29 25	18 49	22 31	23 59	13 14	00 ♋ 00	02 49	13 05	18 46	03 04	14 44	06 28	00 42	17 10
5	Th	16:52:02	13 56 59	08 ♌ 49	29 23	19 50	23 44	24 28	13 23	00 07	02 49	13 05	18 44	03 29	15 02	06 20	00 53	17 07
6	F	16:55:59	14 54 26	21 49	29 22	20 55	24 57	24 57	13 33	00 15	02 49	13 04	18 42	03 53	15 18	06 12	01 04	17 04
7	Sa	16:59:55	15 51 51	05 ♍ 06	29 D 21	22 03	26 10	25 26	13 42	00 22	02 ℞ 49	13 03	18 41	04 18	15 35	06 05	01 15	17 01
8	Su	17:03:52	16 49 16	18 42	29 21	23 14	27 23	25 54	13 52	00 30	02 49	13 03	18 39	04 42	15 52	05 58	01 27	16 58
9	M	17:07:48	17 46 39	02 ♎ 38	29 21	24 28	28 36	26 23	14 02	00 38	02 49	13 02	18 38	05 07	16 09	05 51	01 39	16 55
10	T	17:11:45	18 44 01	16 54	29 22	25 45	29 49	26 51	14 11	00 45	02 49	13 01	18 36	05 32	16 25	05 44	01 52	16 52
11	W	17:15:41	19 41 23	01 ♏ 26	29 23	27 05	01 ♊ 02	27 18	14 21	00 53	02 49	13 01	18 34	05 56	16 42	05 38	02 05	16 49
12	Th	17:19:38	20 38 43	16 13	29 ℞ 24	28 28	02 15	27 46	14 31	01 01	02 49	13 00	18 33	06 21	16 58	05 32	02 18	16 45
13	F	17:23:34	21 36 02	01 ♐ 07	29 25	29 54	03 28	28 13	14 41	01 09	02 48	12 59	18 31	06 45	17 14	05 27	02 32	16 42
14	Sa	17:27:31	22 33 21	16 02	29 24	01 ♊ 23	04 41	28 39	14 51	01 16	02 48	12 58	18 30	07 10	17 30	05 22	02 46	16 39
15	Su	17:31:28	23 30 39	00 ♑ 50	29 22	02 55	05 55	29 06	15 02	01 24	02 48	12 57	18 28	07 34	17 46	05 17	03 00	16 36
16	M	17:35:24	24 27 56	15 23	29 19	04 30	07 08	29 32	15 12	01 32	02 47	12 56	18 26	07 59	18 02	05 12	03 14	16 32
17	T	17:39:21	25 25 13	29 36	29 16	06 08	08 21	29 57	15 23	01 40	02 47	12 55	18 25	08 23	18 18	05 08	03 29	16 29
18	W	17:43:17	26 22 29	13 ♒ 24	29 12	07 49	09 34	00 ♓ 23	15 33	01 47	02 46	12 54	18 23	08 48	18 33	05 04	03 45	16 26
19	Th	17:47:14	27 19 45	26 45	29 09	09 32	10 47	00 48	15 44	01 55	02 46	12 53	18 22	09 12	18 49	05 01	04 00	16 22
20	F	17:51:10	28 17 00	09 ♓ 42	29 06	11 18	12 00	01 12	15 54	02 03	02 45	12 52	18 20	09 37	19 04	04 57	04 16	16 19
21	Sa	17:55:07	29 14 16	22 16	29 D 05	13 07	13 13	01 36	16 05	02 11	02 45	12 51	18 19	10 01	19 20	04 54	04 32	16 15
22	Su	17:59:04	00 ♋ 11 31	04 ♈ 31	29 05	14 59	14 26	02 00	16 16	02 19	02 44	12 50	18 17	10 25	19 35	04 52	04 48	16 12
23	M	18:03:00	01 08 46	16 32	29 05	16 53	15 40	02 24	16 27	02 26	02 43	12 49	18 15	10 50	19 50	04 50	05 05	16 08
24	T	18:06:57	02 06 00	28 24	29 07	18 50	16 53	02 46	16 38	02 34	02 43	12 48	18 14	11 14	20 05	04 48	05 22	16 04
25	W	18:10:53	03 03 15	10 ♉ 12	29 09	20 49	18 06	03 09	16 49	02 42	02 42	12 47	18 12	11 38	20 19	04 46	05 39	16 01
26	Th	18:14:50	04 00 30	22 00	29 ℞ 10	22 50	19 19	03 31	17 00	02 50	02 41	12 46	18 11	12 03	20 34	04 45	05 57	15 57
27	F	18:18:46	04 57 44	03 ♊ 52	29 10	24 53	20 33	03 53	17 11	02 58	02 40	12 44	18 09	12 27	20 48	04 44	06 14	15 54
28	Sa	18:22:43	05 54 59	15 51	29 09	26 59	21 46	04 14	17 22	03 05	02 39	12 43	18 08	12 51	21 03	04 43	06 32	15 50
29	Su	18:26:39	06 52 13	28 01	29 06	29 05	22 59	04 34	17 34	03 13	02 38	12 42	18 06	13 16	21 17	04 D 43	06 51	15 46
30	M	18:30:36	07 49 27	10 ♋ 23	29 01	01 ♋ 13	24 13	04 54	17 45	03 21	02 37	12 41	18 05	13 40	21 31	04 43	07 09	15 43

EPHEMERIS CALCULATED FOR 12 MIDNIGHT GREENWICH MEAN TIME. ALL OTHER DATA AND FACING ASPECTARIAN PAGE IN **EASTERN TIME (BOLD)** AND PACIFIC TIME (REGULAR).

JULY 2003

1 TUESDAY

☽ ⊻ ♀	**1:08 am**	
♃ △ ♇	**8:47 am**	5:47 am
☿ △ ⚵	**10:56 am**	7:56 am
☽ ⊼ ♅	**2:03 pm**	11:03 am
☽ ⊻ ♄	**3:55 pm**	12:55 pm
☽ □ ⚵	**6:02 pm**	3:02 pm
☽ ⊻ ☿	**7:27 pm**	4:27 pm
☽ ⊼ ♂	**7:33 pm**	4:33 pm
☿ △ ♂	**8:06 pm**	5:06 pm
☽ ✶ ⚶	**11:48 pm**	8:48 pm

2 WEDNESDAY

☽ ⊻ ☉	**3:53 am**	12:53 am
☽ ☍ ♆	**8:39 am**	5:39 am
☽ ✶ ⚳	**12:33 pm**	9:33 am
☽ ⊼ ⚷	**2:00 pm**	11:00 am
☽ △ ♇	**6:31 pm**	3:31 pm
☽ ☌ ♃	**7:05 pm**	4:05 pm
☿ □ ⚶		10:03 pm
☽ △ ⚴		11:16 pm

3 THURSDAY

☿ □ ⚶	**1:03 am**	
☽ △ ⚴	**2:16 am**	
☽ ✶ ♀	**2:06 pm**	11:06 am
☽ ☍ ♅	**8:50 pm**	5:50 pm
☽ ✶ ♄	**11:15 pm**	8:15 pm
☽ ✶ ⚵		9:49 pm

4 FRIDAY

☽ ✶ ⚵	**12:49 am**	
☽ ☍ ♂	**3:28 am**	12:28 am
⚷ ⊼ ⚳	**5:27 am**	2:27 am
☽ ⊻ ⚶	**7:39 am**	4:39 am
☽ ✶ ☿	**12:39 pm**	9:39 am
☽ ✶ ☉	**2:22 pm**	11:22 am
☽ ⊼ ♆	**2:44 pm**	11:44 am
☉ ⊼ ♆	**7:28 pm**	4:28 pm
☽ △ ⚷	**7:44 pm**	4:44 pm
☽ □ ⚳	**8:14 pm**	5:14 pm
☽ □ ♇		9:15 pm
☿ ⊼ ♆		10:30 pm
☽ ⊻ ♃		10:40 pm

5 SATURDAY

☽ □ ♇	**12:15 am**	
☿ ⊼ ♆	**1:30 am**	
☽ ⊻ ♃	**1:40 am**	
☉ ☌ ☿	**6:20 am**	3:20 am
☽ ⊼ ⚴	**8:41 am**	5:41 am
☽ □ ♀		9:25 pm
☽ ⊼ ♅		10:40 pm

6 SUNDAY

☽ □ ♀	**12:25 am**	
☽ ⊼ ♅	**1:40 am**	
☽ □ ♄	**4:35 am**	1:35 am
☽ ⊻ ⚵	**5:43 am**	2:43 am
☿ ☍ ⚷	**7:50 am**	4:50 am
☽ ⊼ ♂	**9:15 am**	6:15 am
☽ ☌ ⚶	**1:30 pm**	10:30 am
♀ △ ♅	**2:21 pm**	11:21 am
☽ △ ♆	**6:59 pm**	3:59 pm
☿ ⊻ ⚳	**9:08 pm**	6:08 pm
☽ □ ☉	**10:32 pm**	7:32 pm
☽ □ ⚷	**11:40 pm**	8:40 pm
☽ △ ⚳		10:56 pm
☽ □ ☿		11:38 pm

7 MONDAY

☽ △ ⚳	**1:56 am**	
☽ □ ☿	**2:38 am**	
☽ ✶ ♇	**4:11 am**	1:11 am
☽ ✶ ♃	**6:23 am**	3:23 am
☿ ⊼ ♇	**12:44 pm**	9:44 am
☽ ☍ ⚴	**1:15 pm**	10:15 am
☉ ☍ ⚷	**2:17 pm**	11:17 am

8 TUESDAY

♀ ☌ ♄	**4:30 am**	1:30 am
☽ △ ♅	**4:51 am**	1:51 am
☿ ⊻ ♃	**5:24 am**	2:24 am
☽ △ ♄	**8:13 am**	5:13 am
☽ △ ♀	**8:32 am**	5:32 am
☽ ☌ ⚵	**9:00 am**	6:00 am
☽ △ ♂	**1:15 pm**	10:15 am
♀ △ ⚵	**2:17 pm**	11:17 am
☽ ⊻ ⚶	**5:40 pm**	2:40 pm
☽ □ ♆	**9:41 pm**	6:41 pm
☽ ✶ ⚷		11:07 pm

9 WEDNESDAY

☽ ✶ ⚷	**2:07 am**	
☽ △ ☉	**4:49 am**	1:49 am
☽ ⊼ ⚳	**5:58 am**	2:58 am
☽ ⊻ ♇	**6:39 am**	3:39 am
☽ □ ♃	**9:35 am**	6:35 am
☽ △ ☿	**1:58 pm**	10:58 am
☽ ⊼ ⚴	**4:19 pm**	1:19 pm

10 THURSDAY

♇ ☍ ⚳	**5:19 am**	2:19 am
☽ □ ♅	**6:46 am**	3:46 am
☿ □ ⚴	**7:34 am**	4:34 am
☉ ⊼ ♇	**7:57 am**	4:57 am
☉ ⊻ ⚳	**9:57 am**	6:57 am
☽ ⊼ ♄	**10:36 am**	7:36 am
☽ ⊻ ⚵	**11:07 am**	8:07 am
☽ ⊼ ♀	**3:04 pm**	12:04 pm
☽ □ ♂	**3:56 pm**	12:56 pm
☽ ✶ ⚶	**8:41 pm**	5:41 pm
☽ ✶ ♆	**11:20 pm**	8:20 pm

11 FRIDAY

♀ △ ♂	**3:28 am**	12:28 am
☽ ⊻ ⚷	**3:35 am**	12:35 am
☽ ☌ ♇	**8:13 am**	5:13 am
☽ ☍ ⚳	**9:01 am**	6:01 am
☽ ⊼ ☉	**9:57 am**	6:57 am
☽ △ ♃	**11:53 am**	8:53 am
☽ △ ⚴	**6:34 pm**	3:34 pm
☽ ⊼ ☿	**11:49 pm**	8:49 pm

12 SATURDAY

☽ ✶ ♅	**8:14 am**	5:14 am
☽ ☍ ♄	**12:37 pm**	9:37 am
☽ ✶ ⚵	**12:53 pm**	9:53 am
☽ ✶ ♂	**6:17 pm**	3:17 pm
☽ ☍ ♀	**9:15 pm**	6:15 pm
☉ ⊻ ♃	**10:49 pm**	7:49 pm
☽ □ ⚶	**11:35 pm**	8:35 pm
☽ ⊻ ♆		9:55 pm

13 SUNDAY

☽ ⊻ ♆	**12:55 am**	
☽ ☌ ⚷	**5:06 am**	2:06 am
☽ ⊻ ♇	**9:56 am**	6:56 am
☽ ⊼ ⚳	**12:15 pm**	9:15 am
☽ ⊼ ♃	**2:28 pm**	11:28 am
☽ ☍ ☉	**3:21 pm**	12:21 pm
☽ □ ⚴	**9:17 pm**	6:17 pm

14 MONDAY

☽ ☍ ☿	**10:21 am**	7:21 am
☽ ⊻ ♅	**10:33 am**	7:33 am
♀ □ ⚶	**10:58 am**	7:58 am
☿ ⊼ ♅	**11:42 am**	8:42 am
♀ ⊼ ♆	**3:25 pm**	12:25 pm
☽ ⊼ ♄	**3:38 pm**	12:38 pm
☽ □ ⚵	**3:43 pm**	12:43 pm
☽ ⊻ ♂	**9:46 pm**	6:46 pm
♆ △ ⚶		10:14 pm

15 TUESDAY

♆ △ ⚶	**1:14 am**	
☽ ☌ ♆	**3:52 am**	12:52 am
☽ △ ⚶	**3:57 am**	12:57 am
☽ ⊼ ♀	**5:07 am**	2:07 am
☽ ⊻ ⚷	**8:06 am**	5:06 am
☽ ✶ ♇	**1:20 pm**	10:20 am
♄ △ ⚵	**3:01 pm**	12:01 pm
☽ △ ⚳	**5:23 pm**	2:23 pm
☽ ☍ ♃	**6:57 pm**	3:57 pm
☽ ⊼ ☉	**11:02 pm**	8:02 pm
☽ ✶ ⚴		11:05 pm
☿ □ ⚵		11:05 pm
☿ ⊻ ♄		11:21 pm

16 WEDNESDAY

☽ ✶ ⚴	**2:05 am**	
☿ □ ⚵	**2:05 am**	
☿ ⊻ ♄	**2:21 am**	
♀ ☍ ⚷	**1:05 pm**	10:05 am
☽ ☌ ♅	**3:16 pm**	12:16 pm
☽ △ ⚵	**9:12 pm**	6:12 pm
☽ △ ♄	**9:18 pm**	6:18 pm
☽ ⊼ ☿		9:20 pm

17 THURSDAY

☽ ⊼ ☿	**12:20 am**	
☽ ☌ ♂	**4:01 am**	1:01 am
☽ ⊻ ♆	**9:43 am**	6:43 am
☽ ⊼ ⚶	**11:30 am**	8:30 am
☽ ✶ ⚷	**2:04 pm**	11:04 am
☽ △ ♀	**4:51 pm**	1:51 pm
☽ □ ♇	**7:50 pm**	4:50 pm
☽ □ ⚳		11:01 pm
☽ ⊼ ♃		11:50 pm

18 FRIDAY

☽ □ ⚳	**2:01 am**	
☽ ⊼ ♃	**2:50 am**	
☉ □ ⚴	**3:24 am**	12:24 am
☿ ⊼ ♂	**3:36 am**	12:36 am
☽ ⊻ ⚴	**10:21 am**	7:21 am
☽ △ ☉	**10:49 am**	7:49 am
♀ ⊼ ♇	**11:26 pm**	8:26 pm
☽ ⊻ ♅	**11:31 pm**	8:31 pm

19 SATURDAY

☽ ⊼ ⚵	**6:24 am**	3:24 am
☽ □ ♄	**6:40 am**	3:40 am
☽ ⊻ ♂	**1:54 pm**	10:54 am
☿ ☍ ♆	**4:58 pm**	1:58 pm
☽ ✶ ♆	**7:11 pm**	4:11 pm
☽ △ ☿	**7:35 pm**	4:35 pm
☽ ☍ ⚶	**11:04 pm**	8:04 pm
☽ □ ⚷	**11:40 pm**	8:40 pm

20 SUNDAY

☽ △ ♇	**5:58 am**	2:58 am
♃ ✶ ⚳	**8:52 am**	5:52 am
☽ □ ♀	**9:29 am**	6:29 am
☽ △ ♃	**2:30 pm**	11:30 am
☽ ✶ ⚳	**2:35 pm**	11:35 am
⚷ □ ⚶	**3:25 pm**	12:25 pm
☿ ⊼ ⚷	**10:14 pm**	7:14 pm
☽ ☌ ⚴	**10:15 pm**	7:15 pm
☿ ✶ ⚶		9:23 pm

21 MONDAY

☿ ✶ ⚶	**12:23 am**	
☽ □ ☉	**3:01 am**	12:01 am
☽ ✶ ♅	**11:01 am**	8:01 am
☽ ☍ ⚵	**6:52 pm**	3:52 pm
☽ ✶ ♄	**7:15 pm**	4:15 pm
☽ ✶ ♂		11:41 pm

22 TUESDAY

☽ ✶ ♂	**2:41 am**	
☽ □ ♆	**7:26 am**	4:26 am
☽ △ ⚷	**11:51 am**	8:51 am
☽ ⊼ ⚶	**1:35 pm**	10:35 am
☿ △ ♇	**5:38 pm**	2:38 pm
☽ ⊼ ♇	**6:30 pm**	3:30 pm
☽ □ ☿	**6:39 pm**	3:39 pm
♀ ⊻ ♃	**7:25 pm**	4:25 pm

23 WEDNESDAY

☽ □ ♃	**4:22 am**	1:22 am
☽ ✶ ♀	**5:14 am**	2:14 am
☽ ⊻ ⚳	**5:27 am**	2:27 am
♀ ⊻ ⚳	**8:12 am**	5:12 am
☽ ⊻ ⚴	**11:57 am**	8:57 am
☽ ✶ ☉	**9:15 pm**	6:15 pm
☽ □ ♅	**11:45 pm**	8:45 pm

24 THURSDAY

☽ ⊼ ⚵	**8:18 am**	5:18 am
☽ ⊻ ♄	**8:45 am**	5:45 am
☽ □ ♂	**3:51 pm**	11:51 am
☽ △ ♆	**8:00 pm**	5:00 pm
☽ ⊼ ⚷		9:10 pm

25 FRIDAY

☽ ⊼ ⚷	**12:10 am**	
☉ ⊼ ♅	**3:31 am**	12:31 am
☽ △ ⚶	**4:12 am**	1:12 am
☽ ☍ ♇	**6:53 am**	3:53 am
☽ ✶ ☿	**4:52 pm**	1:52 pm
☽ ✶ ♃	**5:38 pm**	2:38 pm
☽ ☌ ⚳	**7:37 pm**	4:37 pm
☿ ☌ ♃	**11:17 pm**	8:17 pm
☽ ⊻ ♀		9:09 pm
☽ ✶ ⚴		9:39 pm

26 SATURDAY

☽ ⊻ ♀	**12:09 am**	
☽ ✶ ⚴	**12:39 am**	
♀ □ ⚴	**5:51 am**	2:51 am
☽ △ ♅	**11:07 am**	8:07 am
☽ ⊻ ☉	**1:51 pm**	10:51 am
☿ ✶ ⚳	**7:02 pm**	4:02 pm
☽ △ ⚵	**8:04 pm**	5:04 pm
☽ ☌ ♄	**8:29 pm**	5:29 pm
☽ △ ♂		11:53 pm

27 SUNDAY

☽ △ ♂	**2:53 am**	
☽ ⊼ ♆	**6:31 am**	3:31 am
☽ ☍ ⚷	**10:22 am**	7:22 am
☽ □ ⚶	**4:21 pm**	1:21 pm
☽ ⊼ ♇	**4:56 pm**	1:56 pm

28 MONDAY

☽ ⊻ ♃	**4:11 am**	1:11 am
☽ ⊻ ⚳	**6:53 am**	3:53 am
☿ △ ⚴	**9:17 am**	6:17 am
♇ ✶ ⚶	**10:05 am**	7:05 am
☽ □ ⚴	**10:31 am**	7:31 am
☽ ⊻ ☿	**10:41 am**	7:41 am
☽ ☌ ♀	**3:25 pm**	12:25 pm
☽ ⊼ ♅	**7:41 pm**	4:41 pm
☽ ☌ ☉		11:53 pm

29 TUESDAY

☽ ☌ ☉	**2:53 am**	
☽ □ ⚵	**4:53 am**	1:53 am
☽ ⊻ ♄	**5:14 am**	2:14 am
☽ ⊼ ♂	**10:50 am**	7:50 am
☽ ☍ ♆	**2:08 pm**	11:08 am
☽ ⊼ ⚷	**5:40 pm**	2:40 pm
☽ △ ♇		9:06 pm
☽ ✶ ⚶		10:20 pm

30 WEDNESDAY

☽ △ ♇	**12:06 am**	
☽ ✶ ⚶	**1:20 am**	
☉ □ ⚵	**10:49 am**	7:49 am
♀ ⊼ ♅	**11:16 am**	8:16 am
☽ ☌ ♃	**11:46 am**	8:46 am
☽ ✶ ⚳	**3:04 pm**	12:04 pm
☉ ⊻ ♄	**3:23 pm**	12:23 pm
☽ △ ⚴	**5:28 pm**	2:28 pm
☽ ☌ ☿	**11:58 pm**	8:58 pm
☽ ☍ ♅		10:34 pm

31 THURSDAY

☽ ☍ ♅	**1:34 am**	
☽ ⊻ ♀	**3:02 am**	12:02 am
☽ ✶ ⚵	**11:07 am**	8:07 am
☽ ✶ ♄	**11:21 am**	8:21 am
☽ ⊻ ☉	**12:40 pm**	9:40 am
☿ ☍ ♅	**2:24 pm**	11:24 am
☽ ☍ ♂	**4:13 pm**	1:13 pm
☽ ⊼ ♆	**7:21 pm**	4:21 pm
☽ △ ⚷	**10:40 pm**	7:40 pm

Eastern time in bold type
Pacific time in medium type

JULY 2003

☽ Last Aspect day	EST / hr:mn / PST	asp	☽ Ingress sign day	EST / hr:mn / PST
6/29	**2:39 pm** 11:39 am	☌ ☉	♌ 1	**9:13 am** 6:13 am
3	**2:06 pm** 11:06 am	⚹ ♀	♍ 3	**4:16 pm** 1:16 pm
4	9:15 pm	□ ♇	♎ 5	**9:20 pm** 6:20 pm
5	**12:15 am**	□ ♇	♎ 5	**9:20 pm** 6:20 pm
7	**6:23 am** 3:23 am	⚹ ♃	♏ 7	9:43 pm
7	**6:23 am** 3:23 am	⚹ ♃	♏ 8	**12:43 am**
9	**1:58 pm** 10:58 am	△ ☿	♐ 9	11:48 pm
9	**1:58 pm** 10:58 am	△ ☿	♐ 10	**2:48 am**
11	**11:53 am** 8:53 am	△ ♃	♑ 12	**4:21 am** 1:21 am
13	**3:21 pm** 12:21 pm	☍ ☉	♒ 14	**6:38 am** 3:38 am
15	**6:57 pm** 3:57 pm	☍ ♃	♓ 16	**11:14 am** 8:14 am
18	**10:49 am** 7:49 am	△ ☉	♈ 18	**7:20 pm** 4:20 pm
21	**3:01 am** 12:01 am	□ ☉	♉ 21	**6:48 am** 3:48 am
23	**5:14 am** 2:14 am	⚹ ♀	♊ 23	**7:42 pm** 4:42 pm
25	**5:38 pm** 2:38 pm	⚹ ♃	♋ 26	**7:23 am** 4:23 am
28	**3:25 pm** 12:25 pm	☌ ♀	♌ 28	**4:17 pm** 1:17 pm
30	**11:46 am** 8:46 am	☌ ♃	♍ 30	**10:27 pm** 7:27 pm

☽ Phases & Eclipses phase	day	EST / hr:mn / PST
2nd Quarter	6	**10:32 pm** 7:32 pm
Full Moon	13	**3:21 pm** 12:21 pm
4th Quarter	21	**3:01 am** 12:01 am
New Moon	28	11:53 pm
New Moon	29	**2:53 am**

Planet Ingress	day	EST / hr:mn / PST
♀ ♋	4	**1:39 pm** 10:39 am
☿ ♌	13	**8:10 am** 5:10 am
☉ ♌	22	11:04 pm
☉ ♌	23	**2:04 am**
♀ ♌	28	9:25 pm
♀ ♌	29	**12:25 am**
☿ ♍	30	**10:05 am** 7:05 am

Planetary Motion	day	EST / hr:mn / PST
♂ R	29	**3:36 am** 12:36 am

DATE		SID.TIME	SUN	MOON	NODE	MERCURY	VENUS	MARS	JUPITER	SATURN	URANUS	NEPTUNE	PLUTO	CERES	PALLAS	JUNO	VESTA	CHIRON
1	T	18:34:33	08 ♋ 46 41	22 ♋ 58	28 ♉ R 55	03 ♋ 22	25 ♊ 26	05 ♓ 14	17 ♌ 56	03 ♋ 29	02 ♓ R 36	12 ♒ R 40	18 ♐ R 03	14 ♊ 04	21 ♈ 45	04 ♏ 43	07 ♎ 28	15 ♑ R 39
2	W	18:38:29	09 43 55	05 ♌ 47	28 48	05 32	26 39	05 33	18 08	03 37	02 35	12 38	18 02	14 28	21 58	04 43	07 47	15 35
3	Th	18:42:26	10 41 08	18 49	28 41	07 43	27 53	05 51	18 20	03 44	02 34	12 37	18 00	14 53	22 12	04 44	08 06	15 31
4	F	18:46:22	11 38 21	02 ♍ 05	28 35	09 53	29 06	06 09	18 31	03 52	02 33	12 36	17 59	15 17	22 25	04 46	08 26	15 28
5	Sa	18:50:19	12 35 34	15 33	28 30	12 04	00 ♋ 19	06 27	18 43	04 00	02 31	12 34	17 58	15 41	22 38	04 47	08 45	15 24
6	Su	18:54:15	13 32 47	29 14	28 27	14 14	01 33	06 44	18 55	04 08	02 30	12 33	17 56	16 05	22 52	04 49	09 05	15 20
7	M	18:58:12	14 29 59	13 ♎ 07	28 D 27	16 24	02 46	07 00	19 06	04 15	02 29	12 32	17 55	16 29	23 04	04 51	09 26	15 16
8	T	19:02:08	15 27 11	27 12	28 27	18 33	04 00	07 15	19 18	04 23	02 27	12 30	17 53	16 53	23 17	04 54	09 46	15 13
9	W	19:06:05	16 24 23	11 ♏ 28	28 28	20 41	05 13	07 31	19 30	04 31	02 26	12 29	17 52	17 17	23 30	04 56	10 07	15 09
10	Th	19:10:02	17 21 35	25 53	28 R 29	22 47	06 27	07 45	19 42	04 38	02 24	12 27	17 51	17 41	23 42	04 59	10 28	15 05
11	F	19:13:58	18 18 46	10 ♐ 25	28 28	24 53	07 40	07 59	19 54	04 46	02 23	12 26	17 49	18 05	23 54	05 03	10 49	15 01
12	Sa	19:17:55	19 15 58	24 57	28 26	26 56	08 54	08 12	20 06	04 54	02 21	12 24	17 48	18 29	24 06	05 06	11 10	14 58
13	Su	19:21:51	20 13 10	09 ♑ 26	28 21	28 59	10 07	08 25	20 18	05 01	02 20	12 23	17 47	18 53	24 18	05 10	11 31	14 54
14	M	19:25:48	21 10 22	23 44	28 14	00 ♌ 59	11 21	08 37	20 31	05 09	02 18	12 21	17 46	19 16	24 29	05 14	11 53	14 50
15	T	19:29:44	22 07 34	07 ♒ 47	28 06	02 58	12 34	08 48	20 43	05 17	02 17	12 20	17 44	19 40	24 41	05 19	12 15	14 47
16	W	19:33:41	23 04 47	21 30	27 57	04 55	13 48	08 58	20 55	05 24	02 15	12 18	17 43	20 04	24 52	05 24	12 37	14 43
17	Th	19:37:37	24 02 00	04 ♓ 50	27 49	06 51	15 01	09 08	21 07	05 32	02 13	12 17	17 42	20 28	25 03	05 29	12 59	14 39
18	F	19:41:34	24 59 13	17 46	27 42	08 44	16 15	09 17	21 20	05 39	02 12	12 15	17 41	20 51	25 14	05 34	13 22	14 36
19	Sa	19:45:31	25 56 27	00 ♈ 21	27 36	10 36	17 29	09 26	21 32	05 47	02 10	12 14	17 39	21 15	25 24	05 39	13 44	14 32
20	Su	19:49:27	26 53 42	12 37	27 33	12 26	18 42	09 34	21 45	05 54	02 08	12 12	17 38	21 39	25 34	05 45	14 07	14 28
21	M	19:53:24	27 50 57	24 39	27 D 32	14 14	19 56	09 40	21 57	06 02	02 06	12 11	17 37	22 02	25 45	05 51	14 30	14 25
22	T	19:57:20	28 48 14	06 ♉ 31	27 32	16 01	21 10	09 47	22 10	06 09	02 04	12 09	17 36	22 26	25 54	05 58	14 53	14 21
23	W	20:01:17	29 45 31	18 19	27 R 33	17 45	22 24	09 52	22 22	06 17	02 03	12 08	17 35	22 49	26 04	06 04	15 16	14 18
24	Th	20:05:13	00 ♌ 42 49	00 ♊ 09	27 33	19 28	23 37	09 57	22 35	06 24	02 01	12 06	17 34	23 13	26 13	06 11	15 40	14 14
25	F	20:09:10	01 40 08	12 05	27 32	21 09	24 51	10 01	22 47	06 31	01 59	12 04	17 33	23 36	26 23	06 18	16 03	14 11
26	Sa	20:13:06	02 37 27	24 11	27 29	22 48	26 05	10 04	23 00	06 39	01 57	12 03	17 32	23 59	26 32	06 25	16 27	14 07
27	Su	20:17:03	03 34 48	06 ♋ 31	27 23	24 26	27 19	10 06	23 13	06 46	01 55	12 01	17 31	24 23	26 40	06 33	16 51	14 04
28	M	20:21:00	04 32 09	19 08	27 15	26 01	28 33	10 07	23 25	06 53	01 53	12 00	17 30	24 46	26 49	06 41	17 15	14 00
29	T	20:24:56	05 29 31	02 ♌ 01	27 05	27 35	29 46	10 R 08	23 38	07 00	01 51	11 58	17 29	25 09	26 57	06 49	17 39	13 57
30	W	20:28:53	06 26 54	15 11	26 54	29 07	01 ♌ 00	10 08	23 51	07 07	01 49	11 56	17 28	25 32	27 05	06 57	18 04	13 54
31	Th	20:32:49	07 24 18	28 37	26 43	00 ♍ 37	02 14	10 07	24 04	07 15	01 46	11 55	17 27	25 55	27 12	07 06	18 28	13 50

EPHEMERIS CALCULATED FOR 12 MIDNIGHT GREENWICH MEAN TIME. ALL OTHER DATA AND FACING ASPECTARIAN PAGE IN **EASTERN TIME (BOLD)** AND PACIFIC TIME (REGULAR).

AUGUST 2003

1 FRIDAY
☽ □ ♇ **5:02 am** 2:02 am
☽ ⚺ ⚶ **7:55 am** 4:55 am
☽ ⚺ ♃ **5:14 pm** 2:14 pm
☽ □ ⚳ **9:06 pm** 6:06 pm
☽ ⚻ ♀ **10:24 pm** 7:24 pm

2 SATURDAY
☽ ⚻ ♅ **5:43 am** 2:43 am
☽ ⚺ ☿ **10:20 am** 7:20 am
☽ ⚹ ♀ **12:20 pm** 9:20 am
☉ ⚻ ♂ **1:13 pm** 10:13 am
☽ ⚺ ⚵ **3:44 pm** 12:44 pm
☽ □ ♄ **3:50 pm** 12:50 pm
☽ ⚻ ♂ **7:59 pm** 4:59 pm
☽ ⚹ ☉ **8:31 pm** 5:31 pm
☽ △ ♆ **11:08 pm** 8:08 pm
☽ □ ⚷ 11:18 pm

3 SUNDAY
☽ □ ⚷ **2:18 am**
☽ ⚹ ♇ **8:42 am** 5:42 am
☽ ☌ ⚶ **1:10 pm** 10:10 am
☽ ⚹ ♃ **9:33 pm** 6:33 pm
☽ △ ⚳ 11:01 pm
☽ ☍ ♀ 11:17 pm

4 MONDAY
☽ △ ⚳ **2:01 am**
☽ ☍ ♀ **2:17 am**
♄ △ ⚵ **3:42 am** 12:42 am
♀ ⚺ ♄ **7:45 am** 4:45 am
♀ □ ⚵ **7:55 am** 4:55 am
☽ △ ♅ **8:57 am** 5:57 am
☉ ☍ ♆ **9:54 am** 6:54 am
⚳ ⚹ ♀ **2:49 pm** 11:49 am
☽ ⚹ ☿ **7:11 pm** 4:11 pm
☽ △ ♄ **7:32 pm** 4:32 pm
☽ ☌ ⚵ **7:35 pm** 4:35 pm
☽ □ ♀ **8:33 pm** 5:33 pm
☽ △ ♂ **10:56 pm** 7:56 pm
☿ ⚹ ♄ **11:12 pm** 8:12 pm
☿ ⚹ ⚵ **11:58 pm** 8:58 pm
☽ □ ♆ 11:14 pm

5 TUESDAY
☽ □ ♆ **2:14 am**
☽ □ ☉ **3:28 am** 12:28 am
☽ ⚹ ⚷ **5:17 am** 2:17 am
☽ ⚺ ♇ **11:46 am** 8:46 am
☽ ⚺ ⚶ **5:49 pm** 2:49 pm
♀ ⚻ ♂ **10:02 pm** 7:02 pm
☽ □ ♃ 10:22 pm

6 WEDNESDAY
☽ □ ♃ **1:22 am**
☉ ⚻ ⚷ **5:03 am** 2:03 am
☽ ⚻ ♀ **5:38 am** 2:38 am
☽ ⚻ ⚳ **6:25 am** 3:25 am
☿ ☍ ♂ **9:12 am** 6:12 am
☽ □ ♅ **11:47 am** 8:47 am
☽ ⚻ ♄ **10:51 pm** 7:51 pm
☽ ⚺ ⚵ **11:06 pm** 8:06 pm
☽ □ ♂ 10:28 pm

7 THURSDAY
☽ □ ♂ **1:28 am**
☽ □ ☿ **3:12 am** 12:12 am
☽ △ ♀ **4:19 am** 1:19 am
☽ ⚹ ♆ **5:01 am** 2:01 am
☽ ⚺ ⚷ **7:59 am** 4:59 am
☽ △ ☉ **10:02 am** 7:02 am
♀ ☍ ♆ **12:18 pm** 9:18 am
☽ ☌ ♇ **2:35 pm** 11:35 am
☽ ⚹ ⚶ **10:15 pm** 7:15 pm
☿ ⚻ ♆ **11:37 pm** 8:37 pm

8 FRIDAY
☽ △ ♃ **5:01 am** 2:01 am
☽ △ ♀ **8:48 am** 5:48 am
☽ ☍ ⚳ **10:40 am** 7:40 am
☽ ⚹ ♅ **2:31 pm** 11:31 am
♀ ⚻ ⚷ **8:55 pm** 5:55 pm
☽ ☍ ♄ 11:11 pm
☽ ⚹ ⚵ 11:39 pm

9 SATURDAY
☽ ☍ ♄ **2:11 am**
☽ ⚹ ⚵ **2:39 am**
☽ ⚹ ♂ **3:56 am** 12:56 am
☽ ⚺ ♆ **7:53 am** 4:53 am
☿ △ ⚷ **9:01 am** 6:01 am
☽ ☌ ⚷ **10:47 am** 7:47 am
☽ △ ☿ **10:57 am** 7:57 am
☽ ⚻ ♀ **12:10 pm** 9:10 am
☽ ⚻ ☉ **4:46 pm** 1:46 pm
☽ ⚺ ♇ **5:35 pm** 2:35 pm

10 SUNDAY
☽ □ ⚶ **3:01 am** 12:01 am
☉ △ ♇ **4:42 am** 1:42 am
☽ ⚻ ♃ **9:03 am** 6:03 am
☽ □ ♀ **12:23 pm** 9:23 am
☽ ⚻ ⚳ **3:25 pm** 12:25 pm
☽ ⚺ ♅ **5:46 pm** 2:46 pm

11 MONDAY
☽ ⚻ ♄ **6:16 am** 3:16 am
☽ □ ⚵ **7:00 am** 4:00 am
☽ ⚺ ♂ **7:05 am** 4:05 am
♂ △ ⚵ **10:11 am** 7:11 am
☽ ☌ ♆ **11:35 am** 8:35 am
☽ ⚺ ⚷ **2:30 pm** 11:30 am
☽ ⚻ ☿ **7:31 pm** 4:31 pm
☽ ☍ ♀ **9:17 pm** 6:17 pm
☽ ⚹ ♇ **9:39 pm** 6:39 pm
☽ ☍ ☉ 9:48 pm
♀ △ ♇ 10:19 pm

12 TUESDAY
☽ ☍ ☉ **12:48 am**
♀ △ ♇ **1:19 am**
☽ △ ⚶ **9:12 am** 6:12 am
☽ ☍ ♃ **2:35 pm** 11:35 am
☽ ⚹ ♀ **5:27 pm** 2:27 pm
☽ △ ⚳ **9:52 pm** 6:52 pm
☽ ☌ ♅ **10:38 pm** 7:38 pm
♂ △ ♄ **10:55 pm** 7:55 pm
☿ □ ♇ **11:01 pm** 8:01 pm

13 WEDNESDAY
☽ ☌ ♂ **12:01 pm** 9:01 am
☽ △ ♄ **12:19 pm** 9:19 am
☽ △ ⚵ **1:25 pm** 10:25 am
☽ ⚺ ♆ **5:21 pm** 2:21 pm
☽ ⚹ ⚷ **8:20 pm** 5:20 pm
♅ △ ⚳ **10:51 pm** 7:51 pm

14 THURSDAY
☽ □ ♇ **4:01 am** 1:01 am
☽ ☍ ☿ **6:29 am** 3:29 am
☽ ⚻ ♀ **9:27 am** 6:27 am
☽ ⚻ ☉ **11:48 am** 8:48 am
☽ ⚻ ⚶ **6:13 pm** 3:13 pm
☽ ⚻ ♃ **10:54 pm** 7:54 pm
☽ ⚺ ♀ 10:12 pm

15 FRIDAY
☽ ⚺ ♀ **1:12 am**
☽ ⚺ ♅ **6:17 am** 3:17 am
☽ □ ⚳ **7:20 am** 4:20 am
☽ ⚺ ♂ **7:45 pm** 4:45 pm
☽ □ ♄ **9:27 pm** 6:27 pm
☽ ⚻ ⚵ **11:02 pm** 8:02 pm
☽ ⚹ ♆ 11:10 pm

16 SATURDAY
☽ ⚹ ♆ **2:10 am**
☽ □ ⚷ **5:16 am** 2:16 am
☽ △ ♇ **1:33 pm** 10:33 am
☽ ⚻ ☿ **8:51 pm** 5:51 pm
☽ △ ♀ 10:55 pm
☽ △ ☉ 11:49 pm

17 SUNDAY
☽ △ ♀ **1:55 am**
☽ △ ☉ **2:49 am**
☽ ☍ ⚶ **6:50 am** 3:50 am
☽ △ ♃ **10:36 am** 7:36 am
☽ ☌ ♀ **12:08 pm** 9:08 am
☽ ⚹ ♅ **5:05 pm** 2:05 pm
☽ ⚹ ⚳ **8:15 pm** 5:15 pm

18 MONDAY
☽ ⚹ ♂ **6:17 am** 3:17 am
☽ ⚹ ♄ **9:40 am** 6:40 am
☽ ☍ ⚵ **11:49 am** 8:49 am
☽ □ ♆ **1:54 pm** 10:54 am
☉ ☌ ♀ **2:05 pm** 11:05 am
☽ △ ⚷ **5:03 pm** 2:03 pm
☽ ⚻ ♇ 10:47 pm

19 TUESDAY
☽ ⚻ ♇ **1:47 am**
☽ △ ☿ **1:32 pm** 10:32 am
☽ □ ☉ **8:48 pm** 5:48 pm
☽ □ ♀ **9:36 pm** 6:36 pm
☽ ⚻ ⚶ **9:55 pm** 6:55 pm
☽ □ ♃ 9:29 pm
☽ ⚺ ♀ 10:01 pm
♀ ⚹ ⚶ 11:13 pm

20 WEDNESDAY
☽ □ ♃ **12:29 am**
☽ ⚺ ♀ **1:01 am**
♀ ⚹ ⚶ **2:13 am**
☽ □ ♅ **5:43 am** 2:43 am
☽ ⚺ ⚳ **11:02 am** 8:02 am
☽ □ ♂ **5:59 pm** 2:59 pm
☉ ⚹ ⚶ **9:45 pm** 6:45 pm
☽ ⚺ ♄ **11:04 pm** 8:04 pm
☽ ⚻ ⚵ 10:47 pm
☽ △ ♆ 11:37 pm

21 THURSDAY
☽ ⚻ ⚵ **1:47 am**
☽ △ ♆ **2:37 am**
☽ ⚻ ⚷ **5:42 am** 2:42 am
♀ ☌ ♃ **6:23 am** 3:23 am
♀ △ ♀ **6:33 am** 3:33 am
♃ △ ♀ **7:20 am** 4:20 am
☽ ☍ ♇ **2:29 pm** 11:29 am
☉ △ ♀ 10:05 pm

22 FRIDAY
☉ △ ♀ **1:05 am**
☽ □ ☿ **5:11 am** 2:11 am
☉ ☌ ♃ **6:08 am** 3:08 am
☽ △ ⚶ **12:30 pm** 9:30 am
☽ ⚹ ♀ **1:13 pm** 10:13 am
☽ ⚹ ♃ **1:45 pm** 10:45 am
☽ ⚹ ☉ **2:15 pm** 11:15 am
☽ ⚹ ♀ **4:39 pm** 1:39 pm
☽ △ ♅ **5:30 pm** 2:30 pm
♆ □ ⚵ **7:29 pm** 4:29 pm
☽ ☌ ⚳ 9:37 pm
♀ ☍ ♅ 9:49 pm

23 SATURDAY
☽ ☌ ⚳ **12:37 am**
♀ ☍ ♅ **12:49 am**
☽ △ ♂ **4:18 am** 1:18 am
♀ ☍ ⚶ **7:27 am** 4:27 am
☽ ☌ ♄ **10:49 am** 7:49 am
☽ ⚻ ♆ **1:37 pm** 10:37 am
☽ △ ⚵ **1:58 pm** 10:58 am
☽ ☍ ⚷ **4:30 pm** 1:30 pm
☽ ⚻ ♇ 9:58 pm

24 SUNDAY
☽ ⚻ ♇ **12:58 am**
☉ ☍ ♅ **6:02 am** 3:02 am
☽ ⚹ ☿ **4:51 pm** 1:51 pm
☽ □ ♀ **10:24 pm** 7:24 pm
☽ □ ⚶ **11:52 pm** 8:52 pm
☽ ⚺ ♃ **11:55 pm** 8:55 pm
☽ ⚻ ♅ 11:17 pm
♃ ⚹ ⚶ 11:21 pm

25 MONDAY
☽ ⚻ ♅ **2:17 am**
♃ ⚹ ⚶ **2:21 am**
☽ ⚺ ☉ **3:58 am** 12:58 am
☽ ⚺ ♀ **7:38 am** 4:38 am
☽ ⚺ ⚳ **10:43 am** 7:43 am
☽ ⚻ ♂ **11:31 am** 8:31 am
☽ ⚺ ♄ **7:08 pm** 4:08 pm
☽ ☍ ♆ **9:14 pm** 6:14 pm
☽ □ ⚵ **10:37 pm** 7:37 pm
☽ ⚻ ⚷ **11:55 pm** 8:55 pm

26 TUESDAY
♂ △ ⚳ **4:00 am** 1:00 am
☽ △ ♇ **8:00 am** 5:00 am
♀ ☍ ♂ **6:17 pm** 3:17 pm
☽ ⚺ ☿ **11:52 pm** 8:52 pm

27 WEDNESDAY
☽ △ ♀ **4:05 am** 1:05 am
♀ ⚹ ⚳ **4:15 am** 1:15 am
☽ ☌ ♃ **6:28 am** 3:28 am
☽ ⚹ ⚶ **7:25 am** 4:25 am
☽ ☍ ♅ **7:41 am** 4:41 am
☽ ☌ ☉ **1:26 pm** 10:26 am
♅ △ ⚶ **2:54 pm** 11:54 am
☽ ☍ ♂ **3:35 pm** 12:35 pm
☽ ⚹ ⚳ **5:12 pm** 2:12 pm
☽ ☌ ♀ **6:06 pm** 3:06 pm
☽ ⚹ ♄ 9:10 pm
☽ ⚻ ♆ 10:43 pm

28 THURSDAY
☽ ⚹ ♄ **12:10 am**
☽ ⚻ ♆ **1:43 am**
☽ ⚹ ⚵ **4:00 am** 1:00 am
☽ △ ⚷ **4:16 am** 1:16 am
☽ □ ♇ **12:05 pm** 9:05 am
☉ ☍ ♂ **1:59 pm** 10:59 am
⚷ ⚹ ⚵ **6:00 pm** 3:00 pm

29 FRIDAY
☽ ☌ ☿ **3:26 am** 12:26 am
☽ ⚻ ♀ **7:17 am** 4:17 am
☽ ⚺ ♃ **10:30 am** 7:30 am
☽ ⚻ ♅ **10:45 am** 7:45 am
☽ ⚺ ⚶ **12:22 pm** 9:22 am
☽ ⚻ ♂ **5:37 pm** 2:37 pm
☽ ⚺ ☉ **8:11 pm** 5:11 pm
☽ □ ⚳ **9:24 pm** 6:24 pm
♃ ☍ ♅ 9:37 pm
☽ ⚺ ♀ 10:51 pm

30 SATURDAY
♃ ☍ ♅ **12:37 am**
☽ ⚺ ♀ **1:51 am**
☽ □ ♄ **3:16 am** 12:16 am
☽ △ ♆ **4:22 am** 1:22 am
☽ □ ⚷ **6:51 am** 3:51 am
☽ ⚺ ⚵ **7:32 am** 4:32 am
☽ ⚹ ♇ **2:37 pm** 11:37 am
♀ ⚹ ♄ **7:23 pm** 4:23 pm
☉ ⚹ ⚳ **11:49 pm** 8:49 pm

31 SUNDAY
☽ ⚺ ☿ **5:11 am** 2:11 am
♀ ⚻ ♆ **6:21 am** 3:21 am
☽ ☍ ♀ **9:26 am** 6:26 am
☽ △ ♅ **12:55 pm** 9:55 am
☽ ⚹ ♃ **1:35 pm** 10:35 am
☽ ☌ ⚶ **4:22 pm** 1:22 pm
☽ △ ♂ **6:59 pm** 3:59 pm
☽ △ ⚳ 9:56 pm
☽ ⚹ ☉ 11:06 pm

Eastern time in bold type
Pacific time in medium type

AUGUST 2003

☽ Last Aspect day	EST / hr:mn / PST	asp	☽ Ingress sign day	EST / hr:mn / PST
1	**5:02 am** 2:02 am	□ ♇	♎ 1	11:48 pm
1	**5:02 am** 2:02 am	□ ♇	♎ 2	**2:48 am**
3	**9:33 pm** 6:33 pm	✶ ♃	♏ 4	**6:12 am** 3:12 am
5	10:22 pm	□ ♃	♐ 6	**9:11 am** 6:11 am
6	**1:22 am**	□ ♃	♐ 6	**9:11 am** 6:11 am
8	**5:01 am** 2:01 am	△ ♃	♑ 8	**12:02 pm** 9:02 am
9	**10:57 am** 7:57 am	△ ☿	♒ 10	**3:23 pm** 12:23 pm
12	**2:35 pm** 11:35 am	☍ ♃	♓ 12	**8:19 pm** 5:19 pm
14	**6:29 am** 3:29 am	☍ ☿	♈ 15	**4:00 am** 1:00 am
17	**10:36 am** 7:36 am	△ ♃	♉ 17	**2:52 pm** 11:52 am
19	9:29 pm	□ ♃	♊ 20	**3:41 am** 12:41 am
20	**12:29 am**	□ ♃	♊ 20	**3:41 am** 12:41 am
22	**2:15 pm** 11:15 am	✶ ☉	♋ 22	**3:44 pm** 12:44 pm
24	**4:51 pm** 1:51 pm	✶ ☿	♌ 24	9:48 pm
24	**4:51 pm** 1:51 pm	✶ ☿	♌ 25	**12:48 am**
26	**8:00 am** 5:00 am	△ ♇	♍ 27	**6:27 am** 3:27 am
29	**3:26 am** 12:26 am	☌ ☿	♎ 29	**9:41 am** 6:41 am
30	**2:37 pm** 11:37 am	✶ ♇	♏ 31	**12:00 pm** 9:00 am

☽ Phases & Eclipses phase	day	EST / hr:mn / PST
2nd Quarter	5	**3:28 am** 12:28 am
Full Moon	11	9:48 pm
Full Moon	12	**12:48 am**
4th Quarter	19	**8:48 pm** 5:48 pm
New Moon	27	**1:26 pm** 10:26 am

Planet Ingress	day	EST / hr:mn / PST
⚳ ♋	10	**2:15 pm** 11:15 am
♀ ♍	22	**7:35 am** 4:35 am
☉ ♍	23	**9:08 am** 6:08 am
⚶ ♏	25	11:27 pm
⚶ ♏	26	**2:27 am**
♃ ♍	27	**5:26 am** 2:26 am

Planetary Motion	day	EST / hr:mn / PST
♀ ℞	22	**4:56 pm** 1:56 pm
☿ ℞	28	**9:41 am** 6:41 am
♇ D	28	**11:34 pm** 8:34 pm

DATE		SID.TIME	SUN	MOON	NODE	MERCURY	VENUS	MARS	JUPITER	SATURN	URANUS	NEPTUNE	PLUTO	CERES	PALLAS	JUNO	VESTA	CHIRON
1	F	20:36:46	08 ♌ 21 42	12 ♍ 15	26 ♉ ℞ 33	02 ♍ 05	03 ♌ 28	10 ♓ ℞ 05	24 ♌ 16	07 ♋ 22	01 ♓ ℞ 44	11 ♒ ℞ 53	17 ♐ ℞ 26	26 ♊ 18	27 ♈ 20	07 ♏ 14	18 ♎ 53	13 ♑ ℞ 47
2	Sa	20:40:42	09 19 07	26 04	26 24	03 32	04 42	10 03	24 29	07 29	01 42	11 51	17 26	26 41	27 27	07 23	19 18	13 44
3	Su	20:44:39	10 16 32	10 ♎ 00	26 19	04 56	05 56	09 59	24 42	07 36	01 40	11 50	17 25	27 04	27 34	07 33	19 43	13 41
4	M	20:48:35	11 13 58	24 01	26 16	06 19	07 10	09 55	24 55	07 43	01 38	11 48	17 24	27 27	27 40	07 42	20 08	13 38
5	T	20:52:32	12 11 25	08 ♏ 06	26 D 15	07 40	08 24	09 50	25 08	07 50	01 36	11 47	17 23	27 50	27 46	07 52	20 34	13 35
6	W	20:56:29	13 08 52	22 14	26 ℞ 15	08 59	09 38	09 45	25 21	07 57	01 33	11 45	17 22	28 13	27 52	08 01	20 59	13 32
7	Th	21:00:25	14 06 20	06 ♐ 23	26 15	10 16	10 52	09 38	25 34	08 03	01 31	11 43	17 22	28 35	27 58	08 11	21 25	13 29
8	F	21:04:22	15 03 49	20 33	26 13	11 30	12 06	09 31	25 47	08 10	01 29	11 42	17 21	28 58	28 03	08 22	21 50	13 26
9	Sa	21:08:18	16 01 19	04 ♑ 41	26 09	12 43	13 20	09 23	26 00	08 17	01 27	11 40	17 20	29 20	28 08	08 32	22 16	13 23
10	Su	21:12:15	16 58 50	18 44	26 02	13 53	14 34	09 15	26 13	08 24	01 24	11 38	17 20	29 43	28 13	08 43	22 42	13 20
11	M	21:16:11	17 56 21	02 ♒ 40	25 53	15 01	15 48	09 06	26 26	08 30	01 22	11 37	17 19	00 ♋ 05	28 17	08 54	23 08	13 17
12	T	21:20:08	18 53 54	16 23	25 41	16 07	17 02	08 56	26 39	08 37	01 20	11 35	17 19	00 28	28 21	09 05	23 34	13 15
13	W	21:24:05	19 51 27	29 50	25 29	17 10	18 16	08 46	26 52	08 43	01 17	11 34	17 18	00 50	28 25	09 16	24 00	13 12
14	Th	21:28:01	20 49 02	12 ♓ 58	25 17	18 11	19 30	08 35	27 05	08 50	01 15	11 32	17 18	01 12	28 28	09 27	24 27	13 09
15	F	21:31:58	21 46 38	25 48	25 07	19 09	20 45	08 23	27 18	08 56	01 13	11 30	17 17	01 34	28 31	09 39	24 53	13 07
16	Sa	21:35:54	22 44 15	08 ♈ 18	24 58	20 04	21 59	08 11	27 31	09 03	01 10	11 29	17 17	01 56	28 34	09 51	25 20	13 04
17	Su	21:39:51	23 41 54	20 32	24 53	20 56	23 13	07 58	27 44	09 09	01 08	11 27	17 16	02 18	28 36	10 03	25 47	13 02
18	M	21:43:47	24 39 35	02 ♉ 33	24 50	21 45	24 27	07 45	27 57	09 15	01 06	11 26	17 16	02 40	28 38	10 15	26 14	13 00
19	T	21:47:44	25 37 17	14 25	24 49	22 31	25 41	07 31	28 10	09 22	01 03	11 24	17 16	03 02	28 40	10 27	26 41	12 57
20	W	21:51:40	26 35 00	26 13	24 D 48	23 13	26 56	07 17	28 23	09 28	01 01	11 22	17 15	03 24	28 41	10 40	27 08	12 55
21	Th	21:55:37	27 32 45	08 ♊ 03	24 ℞ 48	23 52	28 10	07 02	28 36	09 34	00 59	11 21	17 15	03 46	28 42	10 52	27 35	12 53
22	F	21:59:33	28 30 32	20 01	24 47	24 26	29 24	06 47	28 49	09 40	00 56	11 19	17 15	04 07	28 ℞ 43	11 05	28 02	12 51
23	Sa	22:03:30	29 28 21	02 ♋ 11	24 44	24 57	00 ♍ 38	06 32	29 03	09 46	00 54	11 18	17 15	04 29	28 43	11 18	28 30	12 49
24	Su	22:07:27	00 ♍ 26 11	14 37	24 38	25 23	01 53	06 17	29 16	09 52	00 51	11 16	17 15	04 50	28 43	11 31	28 57	12 47
25	M	22:11:23	01 24 03	27 24	24 29	25 44	03 07	06 01	29 29	09 58	00 49	11 15	17 14	05 12	28 42	11 45	29 25	12 45
26	T	22:15:20	02 21 57	10 ♌ 32	24 19	26 01	04 21	05 45	29 42	10 04	00 47	11 13	17 14	05 33	28 41	11 58	29 53	12 43
27	W	22:19:16	03 19 52	24 02	24 07	26 12	05 36	05 29	29 55	10 09	00 44	11 12	17 14	05 54	28 40	12 12	00 ♏ 20	12 41
28	Th	22:23:13	04 17 48	07 ♍ 50	23 55	26 ℞ 18	06 50	05 13	00 ♍ 08	10 15	00 42	11 10	17 14	06 15	28 38	12 26	00 48	12 40
29	F	22:27:09	05 15 46	21 54	23 44	26 19	08 04	04 57	00 21	10 21	00 39	11 09	17 D 14	06 36	28 35	12 40	01 16	12 38
30	Sa	22:31:06	06 13 46	06 ♎ 08	23 35	26 13	09 19	04 41	00 34	10 26	00 37	11 07	17 14	06 57	28 33	12 54	01 44	12 37
31	Su	22:35:02	07 11 47	20 27	23 29	26 02	10 33	04 25	00 47	10 32	00 35	11 06	17 14	07 18	28 30	13 08	02 13	12 35

EPHEMERIS CALCULATED FOR 12 MIDNIGHT GREENWICH MEAN TIME. ALL OTHER DATA AND FACING ASPECTARIAN PAGE IN **EASTERN TIME (BOLD)** AND PACIFIC TIME (REGULAR).

SEPTEMBER 2003

1 MONDAY
☽△⚳	**12:56 am**	
☽⚹☉	**2:06 am**	
☽△♄	**5:52 am**	2:52 am
☽□♆	**6:34 am**	3:34 am
☽⚹♀	**8:55 am**	5:55 am
☽⚹⚷	**9:04 am**	6:04 am
♀△⚷	**10:37 am**	7:37 am
☽☌⚵	**10:42 am**	7:42 am
☽⊻♇	**4:58 pm**	1:58 pm

2 TUESDAY
☽⚹☿	**6:18 am**	3:18 am
♀⚹⚵	**9:55 am**	6:55 am
☽⊼♀	**11:42 am**	8:42 am
☽□♅	**3:19 pm**	12:19 pm
☽□♃	**4:55 pm**	1:55 pm
♂△⚶	**8:28 pm**	5:28 pm
☽□♂	**8:42 pm**	5:42 pm
☽⊻⚶	**8:43 pm**	5:43 pm

3 WEDNESDAY
☽⊼⚳	**4:53 am**	1:53 am
☽□☉	**8:34 am**	5:34 am
☽⊼♄	**8:58 am**	5:58 am
☽⚹♆	**9:16 am**	6:16 am
☽⊻⚷	**11:49 am**	8:49 am
☽⊻⚵	**2:27 pm**	11:27 am
☉⚹♄	**2:48 pm**	11:48 am
☽□♀	**4:40 pm**	1:40 pm
☉⊼♆	**6:31 pm**	3:31 pm
☽☌♇	**7:55 pm**	4:55 pm

4 THURSDAY
☽□☿	**7:23 am**	4:23 am
☽△♀	**2:40 pm**	11:40 am
☽⚹♅	**6:31 pm**	3:31 pm
☽△♃	**9:06 pm**	6:06 pm
☽⚹♂	**11:14 pm**	8:14 pm
♄⊼♆		10:09 pm
☽⚹⚶		10:59 pm

5 FRIDAY
♄⊼♆	**1:09 am**	
☽⚹⚶	**1:59 am**	
♀□♇	**5:31 am**	2:31 am
☉△⚷	**6:53 am**	3:53 am
☽☍⚳	**9:47 am**	6:47 am
☽⊻♆	**12:52 pm**	9:52 am
☽☍♄	**12:58 pm**	9:58 am
☽☌⚷	**3:29 pm**	12:29 pm
☽△☉	**4:09 pm**	1:09 pm
☽⚹⚵	**7:12 pm**	4:12 pm
☽⊻♇	**11:50 pm**	8:50 pm
☽△♀		10:39 pm

6 SATURDAY
☽△♀	**1:39 am**	
☽△☿	**8:43 am**	5:43 am
☽□♀	**6:37 pm**	3:37 pm
☽⊻♅	**10:46 pm**	7:46 pm
☽⊼♃		11:25 pm
☽⊻♂		11:51 pm

7 SUNDAY
☽⊼♃	**2:25 am**	
☽⊻♂	**2:51 am**	
☽□⚶	**8:30 am**	5:30 am
☽⊼⚳	**3:54 pm**	12:54 pm
♂☍♃	**4:00 pm**	1:00 pm
☽☌♆	**5:39 pm**	2:39 pm
☽⊼♄	**6:09 pm**	3:09 pm
☽⊻⚷	**8:22 pm**	5:22 pm
☽⊼☉		10:14 pm
☽□⚵		10:16 pm
☿☌♀		10:35 pm
☉⚹⚵		10:41 pm

8 MONDAY
☽⊼☉	**1:14 am**	
☽□⚵	**1:16 am**	
☿☌♀	**1:35 am**	
☉⚹⚵	**1:41 am**	
☽⚹♇	**5:01 am**	2:01 am
☽⊼☿	**10:41 am**	7:41 am
☽⊼♀	**12:21 pm**	9:21 am
☽⚹♀	**11:55 pm**	8:55 pm

9 TUESDAY
☽☌♅	**4:30 am**	1:30 am
☽☌♂	**8:00 am**	5:00 am
☽☍♃	**9:20 am**	6:20 am
☽△⚶	**4:49 pm**	1:49 pm
☽△⚳	**11:50 pm**	8:50 pm
☽⊻♆		9:08 pm
☽△♄		10:05 pm
☽⚹⚷		11:59 pm

10 WEDNESDAY
☽⊻♆	**12:08 pm**	
☽△♄	**1:05 am**	
☽⚹⚷	**2:59 am**	
☉□♇	**5:37 am**	2:37 am
☽△⚵	**9:16 am**	6:16 am
♆⊼⚳	**11:13 am**	8:13 am
☽□♇	**12:05 pm**	9:05 am
☽☍☉	**12:36 pm**	9:36 am
☽☍☿	**1:56 pm**	10:56 am
☉☌☿	**9:57 pm**	6:57 pm
☽☍♀		10:41 pm

11 THURSDAY
☽☍♀	**1:41 am**	
☽⊻♀	**7:12 am**	4:12 am
☽⊻♅	**12:24 pm**	9:24 am
☿□♇	**1:42 pm**	10:42 am
☽⊻♂	**3:20 pm**	12:20 pm
☽⊼♃	**6:36 pm**	3:36 pm

12 FRIDAY
☽⊼⚶	**3:45 am**	12:45 am
☽⚹♆	**9:01 am**	6:01 am
☽□⚳	**10:20 am**	7:20 am
☽□♄	**10:27 am**	7:27 am
☽□⚷	**12:04 pm**	9:04 am
☿⚹⚵	**1:03 pm**	10:03 am
♄☌⚳	**4:31 pm**	1:31 pm
☽⊼☿	**7:19 pm**	4:19 pm
☽⊼⚵	**7:57 pm**	4:57 pm
☽△♇	**9:40 pm**	6:40 pm

13 SATURDAY
☽⊼☉	**3:10 am**	12:10 am
♀⊼♀	**4:41 am**	1:41 am
☽☌♀	**4:58 pm**	1:58 pm
☽⊼♀	**6:33 pm**	3:33 pm
☽⚹♅	**10:54 pm**	7:54 pm
☽⚹♂		10:18 pm

14 SUNDAY
☽⚹♂	**1:18 am**	
☽△♃	**6:38 am**	3:38 am
☽☍⚶	**5:39 pm**	2:39 pm
☽□♆	**8:29 pm**	5:29 pm
☽⚹♄	**10:26 pm**	7:26 pm
☽⚹⚳	**11:35 pm**	8:35 pm
☽△⚷	**11:43 pm**	8:43 pm

15 MONDAY
☽△☿	**3:19 am**	12:19 am
⚷☍⚳	**4:24 am**	1:24 am
☽☍⚵	**9:19 am**	6:19 am
☽⊼♇	**9:44 am**	6:44 am
♀⊼♅	**11:37 am**	8:37 am
☽△☉	**8:47 pm**	5:47 pm

16 TUESDAY
♇⊻⚵	**4:07 am**	1:07 am
☽⊻♀	**4:44 am**	1:44 am
♀⊼♂	**5:25 am**	2:25 am
☽□♅	**11:25 am**	8:25 am
☽□♂	**1:17 pm**	10:17 am
☽△♀	**2:19 pm**	11:19 am
☽□♃	**8:35 pm**	5:35 pm
☿⚹⚳		11:05 pm

17 WEDNESDAY
☿⚹⚳	**2:05 am**	
☽⊼⚶	**9:15 am**	6:15 am
☽△♆	**9:22 am**	6:22 am
☽⊻♄	**11:46 am**	8:46 am
♆□⚶	**11:50 am**	8:50 am
☽⊼⚷	**12:41 pm**	9:41 am
☽□☿	**1:28 pm**	10:28 am
☽⊻⚳	**2:13 pm**	11:13 am
☽☍♇	**10:45 pm**	7:45 pm
☽⊼⚵	**11:43 pm**	8:43 pm

18 THURSDAY
☽□☉	**3:03 pm**	12:03 pm
☽⚹♀	**4:35 pm**	1:35 pm
☿△⚷	**6:32 pm**	3:32 pm
☽△♅	**11:50 pm**	8:50 pm
☽△♂		10:14 pm

19 FRIDAY
☽△♂	**1:14 am**	
☉⊼♀	**7:02 am**	4:02 am
☽□♀	**9:44 am**	6:44 am
☽⚹♃	**9:59 am**	6:59 am
♀⊻♃	**12:41 pm**	9:41 am
☽⊼♆	**9:10 pm**	6:10 pm
☽△⚶	**11:39 pm**	8:39 pm
☽☌♄	**11:53 pm**	8:53 pm
☽⚹☿		9:08 pm
☽☍⚷		9:27 pm

20 SATURDAY
☽⚹☿	**12:08 am**	
☽☍⚷	**12:27 am**	
☽☌⚳	**3:25 am**	12:25 am
♄△⚶	**6:03 am**	3:03 am
☽⊼♇	**10:07 am**	7:07 am
☿⚹⚶	**11:37 am**	8:37 am
☽△⚵	**12:20 pm**	9:20 am
⚷⚹⚶	**7:29 pm**	4:29 pm
☽□♀		11:03 pm

21 SUNDAY
☽□♀	**2:03 am**	
☽⚹☉	**6:21 am**	3:21 am
☽⊼♅	**9:37 am**	6:37 am
☽⊼♂	**10:40 am**	7:40 am
☿△⚷	**3:52 pm**	12:52 pm
☽⊻♃	**8:14 pm**	5:14 pm
☽⚹♀		10:05 pm

22 MONDAY
☽⚹♀	**1:05 am**	
☽☍♆	**5:40 am**	2:40 am
☽⊻♄	**8:32 am**	5:32 am
☽⊼⚷	**8:49 am**	5:49 am
☽⊻☿	**9:11 am**	6:11 am
☽□⚶	**10:15 am**	7:15 am
☽⊻⚳	**12:52 pm**	9:52 am
☽△♇	**5:51 pm**	2:51 pm
☽□⚵	**9:04 pm**	6:04 pm
☉⊼♅		9:00 pm

23 TUESDAY
☉⊼♅	**12:00 am**	
☽△♀	**7:49 am**	4:49 am
☉⊼♂	**11:54 am**	8:54 am
☽☍♅	**3:33 pm**	12:33 pm
☽☍♂	**4:25 pm**	1:25 pm
☽⊻☉	**4:47 pm**	1:47 pm
♀△♆		10:03 pm
☽☌♃		11:23 pm

24 WEDNESDAY
♀△♆	**1:03 am**	
☽☌♃	**2:23 am**	
☽⊼♆	**10:20 am**	7:20 am
☽⊻♀	**11:15 am**	8:15 am
☽⚹♄	**1:17 pm**	10:17 am
☽△⚷	**1:22 pm**	10:22 am
☽☌☿	**3:44 pm**	12:44 pm
☽⚹⚶	**4:36 pm**	1:36 pm
☽⚹⚳	**6:14 pm**	3:14 pm
☽□♇	**9:52 pm**	6:52 pm
☽⚹⚵		10:54 pm

25 THURSDAY
☽⚹⚵	**1:54 am**	
☽⊼♀	**10:12 am**	7:12 am
♀□♄	**11:21 am**	8:21 am
♀□⚷	**11:27 am**	8:27 am
♄☍⚷	**2:28 pm**	11:28 am
☽⊼♅	**6:13 pm**	3:13 pm
☽⊼♂	**7:02 pm**	4:02 pm
☽☌☉	**11:09 pm**	8:09 pm

26 FRIDAY
☽⊻♃	**5:22 am**	2:22 am
☿⚹⚶	**6:18 am**	3:18 am
☽△♆	**12:13 pm**	9:13 am
☽□⚷	**3:13 pm**	12:13 pm
☽□♄	**3:17 pm**	12:17 pm
☽☌♀	**5:46 pm**	2:46 pm
☽⊻⚶	**8:04 pm**	5:04 pm
☽⊻☿	**8:32 pm**	5:32 pm
☽□⚳	**8:53 pm**	5:53 pm
☽⚹♇	**11:28 pm**	8:28 pm

27 SATURDAY
☿⚹⚳	**3:35 am**	12:35 am
☽⊻⚵	**4:19 am**	1:19 am
☽☍♀	**10:38 am**	7:38 am
☽△♅	**7:10 pm**	4:10 pm
☽△♂	**8:04 pm**	5:04 pm

28 SUNDAY
☽⊻☉	**3:38 am**	12:38 am
☽⚹♃	**6:59 am**	3:59 am
☿□♇	**12:31 pm**	9:31 am
☽□♆	**1:04 pm**	10:04 am
♀⊻⚶	**2:00 pm**	11:00 am
☽⚹⚷	**4:08 pm**	1:08 pm
☽△♄	**4:20 pm**	1:20 pm
♀□⚳	**4:31 pm**	1:31 pm
☽☌⚶	**10:41 pm**	7:41 pm
☽△⚳	**10:43 pm**	7:43 pm
☽⊻♀	**11:10 pm**	8:10 pm
☽⊻♇		9:24 pm
⚳△⚶		9:43 pm
☽⚹☿		10:27 pm

29 MONDAY
☽⊻♇	**12:24 am**	
⚳△⚶	**12:43 am**	
☽⚹☿	**1:27 am**	
☽☌⚵	**6:13 am**	3:13 am
☽⊼♀	**10:46 am**	7:46 am
♀⚹♇	**1:53 pm**	10:53 am
☽□♅	**8:09 pm**	5:09 pm
☽□♂	**9:14 pm**	6:14 pm

30 TUESDAY
☽⚹☉	**8:27 am**	5:27 am
☽□♃	**8:58 am**	5:58 am
☽⚹♆	**2:27 pm**	11:27 am
☽⊻⚷	**5:42 pm**	2:42 pm
☉⊻♃	**5:57 pm**	2:57 pm
☽⊼♄	**6:01 pm**	3:01 pm
☽⊼⚳		10:23 pm
♇⊻⚶		10:54 pm
☽☌♇		11:11 pm
☽⊻⚶		11:12 pm

Eastern time in bold type
Pacific time in medium type

SEPTEMBER 2003

☽ Last Aspect day	EST / hr:mn / PST	asp	☽ Ingress sign day	EST / hr:mn / PST
2	**6:18 am** 3:18 am	⚹ ☿	♐ 2	**2:32 pm** 11:32 am
4	**7:23 am** 4:23 am	□ ☿	♑ 4	**5:51 pm** 2:51 pm
6	**8:43 am** 5:43 am	△ ☿	♒ 6	**10:15 pm** 7:15 pm
8	**5:01 am** 2:01 am	⚹ ♇	♓ 9	**4:07 am** 1:07 am
10	10:41 pm	☍ ♀	♈ 11	**12:09 pm** 9:09 am
11	**1:41 am**	☍ ♀	♈ 11	**12:09 pm** 9:09 am
12	**9:40 pm** 6:40 pm	△ ♇	♉ 13	**10:50 pm** 7:50 pm
16	**11:25 am** 8:25 am	□ ♅	♊ 16	**11:32 am** 8:32 am
18	**11:50 pm** 8:50 pm	△ ♅	♋ 18	9:07 pm
18	**11:50 pm** 8:50 pm	△ ♅	♋ 19	**12:07 am**
21	**6:21 am** 3:21 am	⚹ ☉	♌ 21	**10:02 am** 7:02 am
23	**3:33 pm** 12:33 pm	☍ ♅	♍ 23	**4:04 pm** 1:04 pm
24	**9:52 pm** 6:52 pm	□ ♇	♎ 25	**6:49 pm** 3:49 pm
27	**7:10 pm** 4:10 pm	△ ♅	♏ 27	**7:52 pm** 4:52 pm
29	**8:09 pm** 5:09 pm	□ ♅	♐ 29	**8:57 pm** 5:57 pm

☽ Phases & Eclipses phase	day	EST / hr:mn / PST
2nd Quarter	3	**8:34 am** 5:34 am
Full Moon	10	**12:36 pm** 9:36 am
4th Quarter	18	**3:03 pm** 12:03 pm
New Moon	25	**11:09 pm** 8:09 pm

Planet Ingress	day	EST / hr:mn / PST
♅ ♒	14	**11:47 pm** 8:47 pm
♀ ♎	15	**11:58 am** 8:58 am
☉ ♎	23	**6:47 am** 3:47 am

Planetary Motion	day	EST / hr:mn / PST
⚷ D	17	10:33 pm
⚷ D	18	**1:33 am**
☿ D	20	**4:51 am** 1:51 am
♂ D	27	**3:52 am** 12:52 am

DATE		SID.TIME	SUN	MOON	NODE	MERCURY	VENUS	MARS	JUPITER	SATURN	URANUS	NEPTUNE	PLUTO	CERES	PALLAS	JUNO	VESTA	CHIRON
1	M	22:38:59	08 ♍ 09 49	04 ♏ 46	23 ♉ ℞ 26	25 ♍ ℞ 44	11 ♍ 48	04 ♓ ℞ 09	01 ♍ 00	10 ♋ 37	00 ♓ ℞ 32	11 ♒ ℞ 05	17 ♐ 14	07 ♋ 38	28 ♈ ℞ 26	13 ♏ 22	02 ♏ 41	12 ♑ ℞ 34
2	T	22:42:56	09 07 53	19 03	23 D 25	25 21	13 02	03 54	01 13	10 42	00 30	11 03	17 14	07 59	28 22	13 37	03 09	12 33
3	W	22:46:52	10 05 58	03 ♐ 13	23 ℞ 25	24 51	14 17	03 38	01 26	10 47	00 28	11 02	17 15	08 19	28 18	13 51	03 38	12 31
4	Th	22:50:49	11 04 05	17 18	23 25	24 15	15 31	03 23	01 39	10 53	00 25	11 00	17 15	08 40	28 13	14 06	04 06	12 30
5	F	22:54:45	12 02 13	01 ♑ 15	23 24	23 33	16 45	03 09	01 52	10 58	00 23	10 59	17 15	09 00	28 08	14 21	04 35	12 29
6	Sa	22:58:42	13 00 22	15 04	23 20	22 46	18 00	02 54	02 05	11 03	00 21	10 58	17 15	09 20	28 03	14 36	05 04	12 28
7	Su	23:02:38	13 58 33	28 44	23 14	21 55	19 14	02 40	02 18	11 08	00 18	10 56	17 15	09 40	27 57	14 52	05 32	12 27
8	M	23:06:35	14 56 45	12 ♒ 14	23 05	20 59	20 29	02 27	02 31	11 12	00 16	10 55	17 16	10 00	27 50	15 07	06 01	12 26
9	T	23:10:31	15 54 59	25 33	22 55	20 01	21 43	02 14	02 44	11 17	00 14	10 54	17 16	10 20	27 43	15 22	06 30	12 26
10	W	23:14:28	16 53 15	08 ♓ 38	22 43	19 01	22 58	02 01	02 57	11 22	00 11	10 53	17 16	10 39	27 36	15 38	06 59	12 25
11	Th	23:18:25	17 51 32	21 30	22 32	18 01	24 12	01 49	03 10	11 27	00 09	10 51	17 17	10 59	27 28	15 54	07 28	12 24
12	F	23:22:21	18 49 51	04 ♈ 06	22 22	17 02	25 27	01 37	03 23	11 31	00 07	10 50	17 17	11 18	27 20	16 09	07 57	12 24
13	Sa	23:26:18	19 48 12	16 27	22 15	16 05	26 41	01 26	03 35	11 35	00 05	10 49	17 18	11 38	27 12	16 25	08 27	12 23
14	Su	23:30:14	20 46 35	28 35	22 10	15 11	27 56	01 16	03 48	11 40	00 03	10 48	17 18	11 57	27 03	16 42	08 56	12 23
15	M	23:34:11	21 45 00	10 ♉ 32	22 D 07	14 23	29 10	01 07	04 01	11 44	00 00	10 47	17 19	12 16	26 53	16 58	09 25	12 23
16	T	23:38:07	22 43 27	22 22	22 06	13 41	00 ♎ 25	00 58	04 14	11 48	29 ♒ 58	10 46	17 19	12 35	26 43	17 14	09 55	12 22
17	W	23:42:04	23 41 56	04 ♊ 10	22 07	13 06	01 40	00 49	04 26	11 52	29 56	10 44	17 20	12 53	26 33	17 30	10 24	12 22
18	Th	23:46:00	24 40 28	15 59	22 ℞ 07	12 39	02 54	00 42	04 39	11 56	29 54	10 43	17 21	13 12	26 22	17 47	10 54	12 D 22
19	F	23:49:57	25 39 01	27 56	22 08	12 21	04 09	00 35	04 52	12 00	29 52	10 42	17 21	13 30	26 11	18 04	11 24	12 22
20	Sa	23:53:54	26 37 37	10 ♋ 05	22 07	12 D 13	05 23	00 29	05 04	12 04	29 50	10 41	17 22	13 49	26 00	18 20	11 53	12 22
21	Su	23:57:50	27 36 15	22 33	22 04	12 14	06 38	00 23	05 17	12 08	29 48	10 40	17 23	14 07	25 48	18 37	12 23	12 22
22	M	0:01:47	28 34 55	05 ♌ 22	21 59	12 25	07 52	00 19	05 29	12 12	29 46	10 39	17 23	14 25	25 35	18 54	12 53	12 23
23	T	0:05:43	29 33 37	18 36	21 52	12 46	09 07	00 15	05 42	12 15	29 44	10 38	17 24	14 43	25 23	19 11	13 23	12 23
24	W	0:09:40	00 ♎ 32 22	02 ♍ 16	21 43	13 16	10 22	00 12	05 54	12 19	29 42	10 38	17 25	15 00	25 10	19 28	13 53	12 23
25	Th	0:13:36	01 31 08	16 19	21 35	13 55	11 36	00 09	06 07	12 22	29 40	10 37	17 26	15 18	24 56	19 46	14 23	12 24
26	F	0:17:33	02 29 57	00 ♎ 43	21 27	14 43	12 51	00 08	06 19	12 25	29 38	10 36	17 27	15 35	24 42	20 03	14 53	12 25
27	Sa	0:21:29	03 28 47	15 21	21 21	15 39	14 05	00 D 07	06 32	12 28	29 36	10 35	17 28	15 53	24 28	20 20	15 23	12 25
28	Su	0:25:26	04 27 40	00 ♏ 05	21 17	16 42	15 20	00 07	06 44	12 31	29 34	10 34	17 29	16 10	24 14	20 38	15 53	12 26
29	M	0:29:23	05 26 34	14 49	21 D 16	17 52	16 35	00 08	06 56	12 34	29 32	10 33	17 30	16 26	23 59	20 56	16 24	12 27
30	T	0:33:19	06 25 30	29 25	21 16	19 08	17 49	00 10	07 08	12 37	29 31	10 33	17 31	16 43	23 44	21 13	16 54	12 28

EPHEMERIS CALCULATED FOR 12 MIDNIGHT GREENWICH MEAN TIME. ALL OTHER DATA AND FACING ASPECTARIAN PAGE IN **EASTERN TIME (BOLD)** AND PACIFIC TIME (REGULAR).

OCTOBER 2003

1 WEDNESDAY

☽ ⚻ ⚳	**1:23 am**	
♇ ⚺ ⚶	**1:54 am**	
☽ ☌ ♇	**2:11 am**	
☽ ⚺ ⚶	**2:12 am**	
☽ ⚹ ♀	**5:37 am**	2:37 am
☽ □ ☿	**8:24 am**	5:24 am
☽ ⚺ ⚵	**9:12 am**	6:12 am
☽ △ ⚴	**11:56 am**	8:56 am
☿ ⚹ ⚵	**5:59 pm**	2:59 pm
☽ ⚹ ♅	**10:25 pm**	7:25 pm
☽ ⚹ ♂	**11:50 pm**	8:50 pm

2 THURSDAY

☽ △ ♃	**12:34 pm**	9:34 am
☿ ⚻ ⚴	**1:36 pm**	10:36 am
☽ □ ☉	**3:09 pm**	12:09 pm
☽ ⚺ ♆	**5:28 pm**	2:28 pm
☽ ☌ ⚷	**8:57 pm**	5:57 pm
☽ ☍ ♄	**9:22 pm**	6:22 pm
♇ ⚻ ⚳	**11:14 pm**	8:14 pm

3 FRIDAY

☽ ⚺ ♇	**5:47 am**	2:47 am
☽ ☍ ⚳	**5:54 am**	2:54 am
☽ ⚹ ⚶	**7:43 am**	4:43 am
♀ ⚺ ⚵	**10:19 am**	7:19 am
☽ ⚹ ⚵	**2:11 pm**	11:11 am
☽ □ ♀	**2:28 pm**	11:28 am
☽ □ ⚴	**2:51 pm**	11:51 am
♀ ☍ ⚴	**5:53 pm**	2:53 pm
☽ △ ☿	**6:40 pm**	3:40 pm
☉ △ ♆	**11:22 pm**	8:22 pm
☽ ⚺ ♅		11:40 pm

4 SATURDAY

☽ ⚺ ♅	**2:40 am**	
☽ ⚺ ♂	**4:33 am**	1:33 am
⚴ ⚻ ⚵	**6:14 am**	3:14 am
☽ ⚻ ♃	**6:20 pm**	3:20 pm
☽ ☌ ♆	**10:35 pm**	7:35 pm
☽ △ ☉		9:28 pm
☽ ⚺ ⚷		11:21 pm
☽ ⚻ ♄		11:51 pm

5 SUNDAY

☽ △ ☉	**12:28 am**	
☽ ⚺ ⚷	**2:21 am**	
☽ ⚻ ♄	**2:51 am**	
☽ ⚹ ♇	**11:32 am**	8:32 am
☽ ⚻ ⚳	**12:40 pm**	9:40 am
☽ □ ⚶	**3:39 pm**	12:39 pm
☽ ⚹ ⚴	**7:46 pm**	4:46 pm
☽ □ ⚵	**9:29 pm**	6:29 pm
☽ △ ♀		11:12 pm
☉ □ ⚷		11:17 pm

Eastern time in bold type
Pacific time in medium type

6 MONDAY

☽ △ ♀	**2:12 am**	
☉ □ ⚷	**2:17 am**	
☽ ⚻ ☿	**8:40 am**	5:40 am
☽ ☌ ♅	**9:06 am**	6:06 am
☉ □ ♄	**9:40 am**	6:40 am
☽ ☌ ♂	**11:38 am**	8:38 am
☿ ⚻ ♅	**11:55 am**	8:55 am
☽ ☍ ♃		11:22 pm

7 TUESDAY

☽ ☍ ♃	**2:22 am**	
☽ ⚺ ♆	**5:54 am**	2:54 am
☿ ⚻ ♂	**9:01 am**	6:01 am
☽ ⚹ ⚷	**9:57 am**	6:57 am
☽ △ ♄	**10:32 am**	7:32 am
☽ ⚻ ☉	**12:33 pm**	9:33 am
☽ □ ♇	**7:30 pm**	4:30 pm
☽ △ ⚳	**9:44 pm**	6:44 pm
☽ △ ⚶		11:04 pm
☽ ⚺ ⚴		11:44 pm

8 WEDNESDAY

☽ △ ⚶	**2:04 am**	
☽ ⚺ ⚴	**2:44 am**	
☽ △ ⚵	**7:10 am**	4:10 am
⚴ ⚻ ⚶	**12:42 pm**	9:42 am
☽ ⚻ ♀	**4:56 pm**	1:56 pm
☽ ⚺ ♅	**5:44 pm**	2:44 pm
☽ ⚺ ♂	**9:07 pm**	6:07 pm
♀ △ ♅	**12:48 am**	9:48 pm
☽ ☍ ☿		11:26 pm

9 THURSDAY

☽ ☍ ☿	**2:26 am**	
☽ ⚻ ♃	**12:43 pm**	9:43 am
☽ ⚹ ♆	**3:25 pm**	12:25 pm
☽ □ ⚷	**7:48 pm**	4:48 pm
☽ □ ♄	**8:25 pm**	5:25 pm

10 FRIDAY

☽ ☍ ☉	**3:27 am**	12:27 am
☽ △ ♇	**5:41 am**	2:41 am
☽ □ ⚳	**9:06 am**	6:06 am
☽ ☌ ⚴	**11:43 am**	8:43 am
☽ ⚻ ⚶	**2:59 pm**	11:59 am
♀ △ ♂	**4:32 pm**	1:32 pm
☽ ⚻ ⚵	**7:14 pm**	4:14 pm

11 SATURDAY

☽ ⚹ ♅	**4:31 am**	1:31 am
☉ ⚹ ♇	**7:33 am**	4:33 am
☽ ⚹ ♂	**8:59 am**	5:59 am
☽ ☍ ♀	**10:37 am**	7:37 am
☽ ⚻ ☿	**11:46 pm**	8:46 pm
☽ △ ♃		10:15 pm

12 SUNDAY

☽ △ ♃	**1:15 am**	
☽ □ ♆	**3:02 am**	12:02 am
☽ △ ⚷	**7:44 am**	4:44 am
☽ ⚹ ♄	**8:22 am**	5:22 am
☿ ⚺ ♃	**10:55 am**	7:55 am
☽ ⚻ ♇	**5:53 pm**	2:53 pm
☽ ⚻ ☉	**8:56 pm**	5:56 pm
⚳ □ ⚴	**9:41 pm**	6:41 pm
☿ △ ♆	**9:53 pm**	6:53 pm
☽ ⚺ ⚴	**10:28 pm**	7:28 pm
☽ ⚹ ⚳	**10:30 pm**	7:30 pm

13 MONDAY

☽ ☍ ⚶	**6:04 am**	3:04 am
☽ ☍ ⚵	**9:18 am**	6:18 am
☉ ☍ ⚴	**11:16 am**	8:16 am
☽ □ ♅	**5:02 pm**	2:02 pm
☉ □ ⚳	**8:44 pm**	5:44 pm
☽ □ ♂	**10:44 pm**	7:44 pm

14 TUESDAY

☽ ⚻ ♀	**6:32 am**	3:32 am
☿ □ ⚷	**6:49 am**	3:49 am
☿ □ ♄	**10:49 am**	7:49 am
☽ □ ♃	**3:12 pm**	12:12 pm
☽ △ ♆	**3:59 pm**	12:59 pm
☽ ⚻ ⚷	**8:56 pm**	5:56 pm
☽ ⚺ ♄	**9:30 pm**	6:30 pm
☽ △ ☿	**11:20 pm**	8:20 pm

15 WEDNESDAY

☽ ☍ ♇	**7:04 am**	4:04 am
☽ ⚹ ⚴	**10:00 am**	7:00 am
☽ ⚺ ⚳	**12:45 pm**	9:45 am
☽ △ ☉	**3:35 pm**	12:35 pm
☽ ⚻ ⚶	**9:54 pm**	6:54 pm
☽ ⚻ ⚵		9:00 pm

16 THURSDAY

☽ ⚻ ⚵	**12:00 am**	
☽ △ ♅	**5:54 am**	2:54 am
☽ △ ♂	**12:46 pm**	9:46 am
♃ ⚻ ♆	**2:48 pm**	11:48 am
☽ △ ♀		11:16 pm

17 FRIDAY

☽ △ ♀	**2:16 am**	
☿ ⚹ ♇	**4:27 am**	1:27 am
☽ ⚻ ♆	**4:29 am**	1:29 am
☽ ⚹ ♃	**4:42 am**	1:42 am
☽ ☍ ⚷	**9:30 am**	6:30 am
☽ ☌ ♄	**9:58 am**	6:58 am
☿ ☍ ⚴	**2:38 pm**	11:38 am
☽ ⚻ ♇	**7:15 pm**	4:15 pm
☽ □ ⚴	**8:31 pm**	5:31 pm
☽ □ ☿	**9:39 pm**	6:39 pm
♀ □ ♆	**11:42 pm**	8:42 pm
☽ ☌ ⚳		10:40 pm

18 SATURDAY

☽ ☌ ⚳	**1:40 am**	
♀ ⚹ ♃	**5:33 am**	2:33 am
☽ □ ☉	**8:31 am**	5:31 am
☽ △ ⚶	**11:57 am**	8:57 am
☽ △ ⚵	**12:56 pm**	9:56 am
☽ ⚻ ♅	**4:55 pm**	1:55 pm
☽ ⚻ ♂	**12:43 am**	9:43 pm

19 SUNDAY

☿ □ ⚳	**5:46 am**	2:46 am
☽ ☍ ♆	**2:20 pm**	11:20 am
☽ ⚺ ♃	**3:23 pm**	12:23 pm
☽ □ ♀	**6:28 pm**	3:28 pm
☽ ⚻ ⚷	**7:14 pm**	4:14 pm
♇ △ ⚴	**7:17 pm**	4:17 pm
☽ ⚺ ♄	**7:33 pm**	4:33 pm
♀ ⚹ ⚷		11:43 pm

20 MONDAY

♀ ⚹ ⚷	**2:43 am**	
☽ △ ⚴	**4:05 am**	1:05 am
☽ △ ♇	**4:18 am**	1:18 am
♀ △ ♄	**5:48 am**	2:48 am
☽ ⚺ ⚳	**11:04 am**	8:04 am
☽ ⚹ ☿	**2:54 pm**	11:54 am
☽ ⚹ ☉	**9:04 pm**	6:04 pm
☽ □ ⚶	**10:01 pm**	7:01 pm
☽ □ ⚵	**10:02 pm**	7:02 pm
⚵ ☌ ⚶	**10:34 pm**	7:34 pm
☽ ☍ ♅		9:18 pm

21 TUESDAY

☽ ☍ ♅	**12:18 am**	
☽ ☍ ♂	**8:45 am**	5:45 am
☉ ⚺ ⚵	**3:56 pm**	12:56 pm
☽ ⚻ ♆	**8:15 pm**	5:15 pm
☽ ☌ ♃	**9:57 pm**	6:57 pm
☉ ⚺ ⚶	**11:19 pm**	8:19 pm
☽ △ ⚷		9:58 pm
☽ ⚹ ♄		10:08 pm

22 WEDNESDAY

☽ △ ⚷	**12:58 am**	
☽ ⚹ ♄	**1:08 am**	
☽ ⚹ ♀	**5:20 am**	2:20 am
☽ ⚻ ⚴	**7:54 am**	4:54 am
☽ □ ♇	**9:19 am**	6:19 am
☽ ⚹ ⚳	**4:14 pm**	1:14 pm
☉ △ ♅	**4:18 pm**	1:18 pm
☽ ⚺ ☿		11:03 pm
☽ ⚹ ⚵		11:55 pm

23 THURSDAY

☽ ⚺ ☿	**2:03 am**	
☽ ⚹ ⚵	**2:55 am**	
☽ ⚹ ⚶	**3:40 am**	12:40 am
☽ ⚻ ♅	**3:48 am**	12:48 am
☽ ⚺ ☉	**4:39 am**	1:39 am
♀ ⚻ ⚴	**5:17 am**	2:17 am
♅ □ ⚶	**7:13 am**	4:13 am
☿ ⚺ ⚵	**11:00 am**	8:00 am
☽ ⚻ ♂	**12:48 pm**	9:48 am
☿ △ ♅	**4:57 pm**	1:57 pm
☿ ⚺ ⚶	**9:29 pm**	6:29 pm
☽ △ ♆	**10:33 pm**	7:33 pm
☽ ⚺ ♃		9:45 pm

24 FRIDAY

☽ ⚺ ♃	**12:45 am**	
☽ □ ⚷	**3:09 am**	12:09 am
☽ □ ♄	**3:10 am**	12:10 am
♀ ⚺ ♇	**3:25 am**	12:25 am
♄ ☍ ⚷	**8:03 am**	5:03 am
☽ ☍ ⚴	**8:35 am**	5:35 am
☽ ⚹ ♇	**11:00 am**	8:00 am
☽ ⚺ ♀	**11:40 am**	8:40 am
♅ □ ⚵	**4:42 pm**	1:42 pm
☽ □ ⚳	**6:06 pm**	3:06 pm

25 SATURDAY

☽ △ ♅	**4:31 am**	1:31 am
☽ ⚺ ⚵	**4:47 am**	1:47 am
☉ ☌ ☿	**5:58 am**	2:58 am
☽ ⚺ ⚶	**6:11 am**	3:11 am
☽ ☌ ☉	**8:50 am**	5:50 am
☽ ☌ ☿	**8:59 am**	5:59 am
☽ △ ♂	**2:17 pm**	11:17 am
☽ □ ♆	**10:43 pm**	7:43 pm
☽ ⚹ ♃		10:25 pm
☽ △ ♄		11:13 pm
☽ ⚹ ⚷		11:21 pm

26 SUNDAY

☽ ⚹ ♃	**1:25 am**	
☽ △ ♄	**2:13 am**	
☽ ⚹ ⚷	**2:21 am**	
☽ ⚻ ⚴	**6:37 am**	3:37 am
☽ ⚺ ♇	**10:00 am**	7:00 am
☽ ☌ ♀	**2:53 pm**	11:53 am
☽ △ ⚳	**5:29 pm**	2:29 pm

27 MONDAY

☽ □ ♅	**3:15 am**	12:15 am
☽ ☌ ⚵	**4:37 am**	1:37 am
☽ ☌ ⚶	**6:42 am**	3:42 am
☽ ⚺ ☉	**11:02 am**	8:02 am
☽ ⚺ ☿	**1:41 pm**	10:41 am
☽ □ ♂	**2:11 pm**	11:11 am
☿ △ ♂	**7:29 pm**	4:29 pm
☽ ⚹ ♆	**9:37 pm**	6:37 pm
☽ □ ♃		9:55 pm
☽ ⚻ ♄		11:11 pm
☽ ⚺ ⚷		11:30 pm
♀ △ ⚳		11:57 pm

28 TUESDAY

☽ □ ♃	**12:55 am**	
☽ ⚻ ♄	**2:11 am**	
☽ ⚺ ⚷	**2:30 am**	
♀ △ ⚳	**2:57 am**	
☽ △ ⚴	**5:45 am**	2:45 am
☽ ☌ ♇	**10:14 am**	7:14 am
☽ ⚻ ⚳	**6:22 pm**	3:22 pm
☽ ⚺ ♀	**7:37 pm**	4:37 pm

29 WEDNESDAY

☽ ⚹ ♅	**3:51 am**	12:51 am
☽ ⚺ ⚵	**6:26 am**	3:26 am
☽ ⚺ ⚶	**9:19 am**	6:19 am
☽ ⚹ ☉	**3:37 pm**	12:37 pm
☽ ⚹ ♂	**4:29 pm**	1:29 pm
☽ ⚹ ☿	**9:01 pm**	6:01 pm
☽ ⚺ ♆	**11:01 pm**	8:01 pm

30 THURSDAY

☽ △ ♃	**3:04 am**	12:04 am
☽ ☍ ♄	**3:46 am**	12:46 am
☽ ☌ ⚷	**4:18 am**	1:18 am
☽ □ ⚴	**6:34 am**	3:34 am
☉ △ ♂	**10:55 am**	7:55 am
☽ ⚺ ♇	**12:20 pm**	9:20 am
☿ □ ♆	**2:41 pm**	11:41 am
☽ ☍ ⚳	**9:22 pm**	6:22 pm

31 FRIDAY

☽ ⚹ ♀	**3:07 am**	12:07 am
☽ ⚺ ♅	**6:48 am**	3:48 am
☽ ⚹ ⚵	**10:50 am**	7:50 am
☽ ⚹ ⚶	**2:40 pm**	11:40 am
☽ ⚺ ♂	**9:40 pm**	6:40 pm
☽ □ ☉	**11:25 pm**	8:25 pm

OCTOBER 2003

☽ Last Aspect day	EST / hr:mn / PST		asp	☽ Ingress sign	day	EST / hr:mn / PST	
1	**10:25 pm**	7:25 pm	⚹ ♅	♑	1	**11:21 pm**	8:21 pm
3	**6:40 pm**	3:40 pm	△ ☿	♒	4	**3:45 am**	12:45 am
6	**9:06 am**	6:06 am	☌ ♅	♓	6	**10:20 am**	7:20 am
7	**7:30 pm**	4:30 pm	□ ♇	♈	8	**7:07 pm**	4:07 pm
11	**4:31 am**	1:31 am	⚹ ♅	♉	11	**6:05 am**	3:05 am
13	**5:02 pm**	2:02 pm	□ ♅	♊	13	**6:45 pm**	3:45 pm
16	**5:54 am**	2:54 am	△ ♅	♋	16	**7:41 am**	4:41 am
18	**8:31 am**	5:31 am	□ ☉	♌	18	**6:41 pm**	3:41 pm
20		9:18 pm	☍ ♅	♍	20		11:01 pm
21	**12:18 am**		☍ ♅	♍	21	**2:01 am**	
22	**9:19 am**	6:19 am	□ ♇	♎	23	**5:27 am**	2:27 am
25	**4:31 am**	1:31 am	△ ♅	♏	25	**6:08 am**	3:08 am
27	**3:15 am**	12:15 am	□ ♅	♐	27	**4:55 am**	1:55 am
29	**3:51 am**	12:51 am	⚹ ♅	♑	29	**5:37 am**	2:37 am
31	**3:07 am**	12:07 am	⚹ ♀	♒	31	**8:41 am**	5:41 am

☽ Phases & Eclipses phase	day	EST / hr:mn / PST	
2nd Quarter	2	**3:09 pm**	12:09 pm
Full Moon	10	**3:27 am**	12:27 am
4th Quarter	18	**8:31 am**	5:31 am
New Moon	25	**8:50 am**	5:50 am
2nd Quarter	31	**11:25 pm**	8:25 pm

Planet Ingress		day	EST / hr:mn / PST	
☿	♎	6	**9:28 pm**	6:28 pm
♀	♏	9	**2:56 pm**	11:56 am
☉	♏	23	**4:08 pm**	1:08 pm
☿	♏	24	**7:20 am**	4:20 am
⚶	♐	25	**4:51 am**	1:51 am
⚵	♐	27	**6:07 pm**	3:07 pm

Planetary Motion		day	EST / hr:mn / PST	
♆	D	22	**9:54 pm**	6:54 pm
♄	℞	25	**7:42 pm**	4:42 pm

DATE		SID.TIME	SUN	MOON	NODE	MERCURY	VENUS	MARS	JUPITER	SATURN	URANUS	NEPTUNE	PLUTO	CERES	PALLAS	JUNO	VESTA	CHIRON
1	W	0:37:16	07 ♎ 24 28	13 ♐ 51	21 ♉ 17	20 ♍ 29	19 ♎ 04	00 ♓ 13	07 ♍ 20	12 ♋ 40	29 ♒ ℞ 29	10 ♒ ℞ 32	17 ♐ 32	16 ♋ 59	23 ♈ ℞ 28	21 ♏ 31	17 ♏ 24	12 ♑ 29
2	Th	0:41:12	08 23 28	28 02	21 ℞ 18	21 55	20 19	00 16	07 33	12 43	29 27	10 31	17 33	17 16	23 12	21 49	17 55	12 30
3	F	0:45:09	09 22 29	11 ♑ 58	21 18	23 25	21 33	00 20	07 45	12 45	29 26	10 31	17 34	17 32	22 56	22 07	18 25	12 31
4	Sa	0:49:05	10 21 33	25 38	21 17	24 58	22 48	00 25	07 57	12 48	29 24	10 30	17 35	17 48	22 40	22 25	18 56	12 32
5	Su	0:53:02	11 20 38	09 ♒ 03	21 14	26 35	24 03	00 31	08 09	12 50	29 22	10 29	17 36	18 03	22 23	22 43	19 27	12 33
6	M	0:56:58	12 19 44	22 14	21 10	28 13	25 17	00 37	08 20	12 52	29 21	10 29	17 37	18 19	22 07	23 02	19 57	12 35
7	T	1:00:55	13 18 53	05 ♓ 11	21 04	29 54	26 32	00 45	08 32	12 54	29 19	10 28	17 39	18 34	21 50	23 20	20 28	12 36
8	W	1:04:52	14 18 03	17 55	20 57	01 ♎ 36	27 46	00 53	08 44	12 56	29 18	10 28	17 40	18 49	21 32	23 38	20 59	12 38
9	Th	1:08:48	15 17 15	00 ♈ 27	20 51	03 19	29 01	01 01	08 56	12 58	29 16	10 27	17 41	19 04	21 15	23 57	21 30	12 39
10	F	1:12:45	16 16 29	12 47	20 45	05 03	00 ♏ 16	01 11	09 07	13 00	29 15	10 27	17 42	19 19	20 57	24 15	22 00	12 41
11	Sa	1:16:41	17 15 45	24 56	20 41	06 47	01 30	01 21	09 19	13 02	29 14	10 26	17 44	19 33	20 40	24 34	22 31	12 43
12	Su	1:20:38	18 15 03	06 ♉ 56	20 38	08 32	02 45	01 32	09 30	13 03	29 12	10 26	17 45	19 47	20 22	24 53	23 02	12 45
13	M	1:24:34	19 14 24	18 49	20 D 37	10 17	04 00	01 44	09 42	13 05	29 11	10 26	17 46	20 01	20 04	25 11	23 33	12 47
14	T	1:28:31	20 13 46	00 ♊ 37	20 38	12 02	05 14	01 56	09 53	13 06	29 10	10 25	17 48	20 15	19 46	25 30	24 04	12 49
15	W	1:32:27	21 13 11	12 24	20 39	13 47	06 29	02 09	10 05	13 08	29 09	10 25	17 49	20 29	19 27	25 49	24 35	12 51
16	Th	1:36:24	22 12 38	24 13	20 41	15 32	07 44	02 22	10 16	13 09	29 07	10 25	17 51	20 42	19 09	26 08	25 06	12 53
17	F	1:40:20	23 12 08	06 ♋ 09	20 43	17 16	08 58	02 36	10 27	13 10	29 06	10 25	17 52	20 55	18 51	26 27	25 38	12 55
18	Sa	1:44:17	24 11 40	18 17	20 ℞ 44	19 00	10 13	02 51	10 38	13 11	29 05	10 24	17 54	21 08	18 33	26 46	26 09	12 58
19	Su	1:48:14	25 11 13	00 ♌ 41	20 44	20 43	11 27	03 07	10 49	13 12	29 04	10 24	17 55	21 20	18 14	27 05	26 40	13 00
20	M	1:52:10	26 10 50	13 27	20 43	22 26	12 42	03 23	11 00	13 12	29 03	10 24	17 57	21 33	17 56	27 25	27 11	13 02
21	T	1:56:07	27 10 28	26 37	20 40	24 09	13 57	03 39	11 11	13 13	29 02	10 24	17 58	21 45	17 38	27 44	27 43	13 05
22	W	2:00:03	28 10 09	10 ♍ 15	20 38	25 51	15 11	03 57	11 22	13 14	29 01	10 24	18 00	21 56	17 20	28 03	28 14	13 07
23	Th	2:04:00	29 09 52	24 20	20 34	27 32	16 26	04 14	11 32	13 14	29 01	10 D 24	18 02	22 08	17 02	28 23	28 45	13 10
24	F	2:07:56	00 ♏ 09 37	08 ♎ 50	20 32	29 13	17 41	04 33	11 43	13 14	29 00	10 24	18 03	22 19	16 44	28 42	29 17	13 13
25	Sa	2:11:53	01 09 24	23 40	20 29	00 ♏ 53	18 55	04 52	11 54	13 ℞ 14	28 59	10 24	18 05	22 30	16 26	29 02	29 48	13 16
26	Su	2:15:49	02 09 13	08 ♏ 42	20 D 28	02 32	20 10	05 11	12 04	13 14	28 58	10 24	18 07	22 40	16 09	29 21	00 ♐ 20	13 19
27	M	2:19:46	03 09 04	23 47	20 28	04 11	21 25	05 31	12 14	13 14	28 58	10 24	18 08	22 51	15 51	29 41	00 51	13 22
28	T	2:23:43	04 08 57	08 ♐ 47	20 28	05 50	22 39	05 52	12 25	13 14	28 57	10 24	18 10	23 01	15 34	00 ♐ 01	01 23	13 25
29	W	2:27:39	05 08 52	23 34	20 29	07 28	23 54	06 13	12 35	13 14	28 56	10 25	18 12	23 11	15 17	00 20	01 55	13 28
30	Th	2:31:36	06 08 49	08 ♑ 02	20 31	09 05	25 09	06 34	12 45	13 13	28 56	10 25	18 14	23 20	15 00	00 40	02 26	13 31
31	F	2:35:32	07 08 47	22 08	20 31	10 42	26 23	06 56	12 55	13 13	28 56	10 25	18 16	23 29	14 43	01 00	02 58	13 34

EPHEMERIS CALCULATED FOR 12 MIDNIGHT GREENWICH MEAN TIME. ALL OTHER DATA AND FACING ASPECTARIAN PAGE IN **EASTERN TIME (BOLD)** AND PACIFIC TIME (REGULAR).

NOVEMBER 2003

1 SATURDAY

☽ ☌ ♆	**3:09 am**	12:09 am
☿ ⚹ ♃	**7:48 am**	4:48 am
☽ ⚻ ♃	**8:05 am**	5:05 am
☽ □ ☿	**8:07 am**	5:07 am
☽ ⚻ ♄	**8:08 am**	5:08 am
☿ △ ♄	**8:17 am**	5:17 am
☽ ⚺ ⚷	**8:57 am**	5:57 am
☽ ⚹ ♀	**10:05 am**	7:05 am
♃ ⚹ ♄	**12:13 pm**	9:13 am
☿ ⚹ ⚷	**3:19 pm**	12:19 pm
☽ ⚹ ♇	**5:24 pm**	2:24 pm
♀ □ ♅	**7:43 pm**	4:43 pm
☿ ⚻ ♀	**10:31 pm**	7:31 pm

2 SUNDAY

☽ ⚻ ⚳	**3:27 am**	12:27 am
☽ ☌ ♅	**12:51 pm**	9:51 am
☽ □ ♀	**2:40 pm**	11:40 am
☽ □ ⚵	**6:35 pm**	3:35 pm
☽ □ ⚶	**11:33 pm**	8:33 pm
☉ □ ♆		10:54 pm

3 MONDAY

☉ □ ♆	**1:54 am**	
☽ ☌ ♂	**6:21 am**	3:21 am
⚷ □ ♀	**9:30 am**	6:30 am
☽ ⚺ ♆	**10:27 am**	7:27 am
☽ △ ☉	**11:11 am**	8:11 am
☽ △ ♄	**3:37 pm**	12:37 pm
☽ ☍ ♃	**4:21 pm**	1:21 pm
☽ ⚺ ♀	**4:38 pm**	1:38 pm
☽ ⚹ ⚷	**4:48 pm**	1:48 pm
☽ △ ☿	**11:42 pm**	8:42 pm
♃ ⚻ ♀		10:04 pm
☽ □ ♇		10:36 pm

4 TUESDAY

♃ ⚻ ♀	**1:04 am**	
☽ □ ♇	**1:36 am**	
☽ △ ⚳	**12:39 pm**	9:39 am
☿ ⚺ ♇	**3:05 pm**	12:05 pm
♀ ☌ ⚵	**8:39 pm**	5:39 pm
☽ ⚺ ♅	**9:54 pm**	6:54 pm

5 WEDNESDAY

☽ △ ⚵	**5:32 am**	2:32 am
☽ △ ♀	**6:16 am**	3:16 am
☽ △ ⚶	**11:45 am**	8:45 am
☽ ⚺ ♂	**6:13 pm**	3:13 pm
☉ △ ♄	**6:24 pm**	3:24 pm
☉ ⚻ ♀	**7:24 pm**	4:24 pm
☽ ⚹ ♆	**8:33 pm**	5:33 pm
♄ □ ♀		9:03 pm
☽ ☌ ♀		10:47 pm
☽ □ ♄		10:49 pm
☽ ⚻ ☉		11:30 pm

6 THURSDAY

♄ □ ♀	**12:03 am**	
☽ ☌ ♀	**1:47 am**	
☽ □ ♄	**1:49 am**	
☽ ⚻ ☉	**2:30 am**	
♃ △ ⚷	**3:19 am**	12:19 am
☽ ⚻ ♃	**3:25 am**	12:25 am
☽ □ ⚷	**3:25 am**	12:25 am
☽ △ ♇	**12:26 pm**	9:26 am
☉ ⚹ ⚷	**2:21 pm**	11:21 am
☉ ⚹ ♃	**3:33 pm**	12:33 pm
☽ ⚻ ☿	**7:05 pm**	4:05 pm
☽ □ ⚳		9:18 pm

7 FRIDAY

☽ □ ⚳	**12:18 am**	
☽ ⚹ ♅	**9:16 am**	6:16 am
☽ ⚻ ⚵	**6:53 pm**	3:53 pm
☽ ⚻ ♀		9:51 pm
☽ ⚻ ⚶		11:20 pm

8 SATURDAY

☽ ⚻ ♀	**12:51 am**	
☽ ⚻ ⚶	**2:20 am**	
☽ ⚹ ♂	**8:23 am**	5:23 am
☽ □ ♆	**8:36 am**	5:36 am
☽ ⚺ ♀	**12:46 pm**	9:46 am
☽ ⚹ ♄	**1:50 pm**	10:50 am
☿ △ ⚳	**1:51 pm**	10:51 am
♂ ⚺ ♆	**2:36 pm**	11:36 am
☽ △ ⚷	**3:55 pm**	12:55 pm
☽ △ ♃	**4:23 pm**	1:23 pm
☽ ☍ ☉	**8:13 pm**	5:13 pm
♀ ☌ ⚶		9:26 pm
☽ ⚻ ♇		9:58 pm

9 SUNDAY

♀ ☌ ⚶	**12:26 am**	
☽ ⚻ ♇	**12:58 am**	
☽ ⚹ ⚳	**1:24 pm**	10:24 am
☽ ☍ ☿	**4:44 pm**	1:44 pm
☽ □ ♅	**10:00 pm**	7:00 pm

10 MONDAY

☽ ☍ ⚵	**9:31 am**	6:31 am
☽ ☍ ⚶	**6:07 pm**	3:07 pm
☽ ☍ ♀	**8:56 pm**	5:56 pm
☽ △ ♆	**9:37 pm**	6:37 pm
☽ □ ♂	**11:42 pm**	8:42 pm
☽ ⚹ ♀		9:39 pm
☽ ⚺ ♄		11:41 pm

11 TUESDAY

☽ ⚹ ♀	**12:39 am**	
☽ ⚺ ♄	**2:41 am**	
♀ ⚹ ♆	**3:30 am**	12:30 am
☽ ⚻ ⚷	**5:15 am**	2:15 am
☉ ⚺ ♇	**5:58 am**	2:58 am
☽ □ ♃	**6:09 am**	3:09 am
☿ □ ♅	**9:05 am**	6:05 am
☽ ☍ ♇	**2:10 pm**	11:10 am
☽ ⚻ ☉	**2:54 pm**	11:54 am
♂ ⚺ ♀	**5:25 pm**	2:25 pm
☽ ⚺ ⚳		11:51 pm

12 WEDNESDAY

☽ ⚺ ⚳	**2:51 am**	
♀ △ ♀	**3:51 am**	12:51 am
☽ △ ♅	**10:57 am**	7:57 am
♀ □ ♂	**12:27 pm**	9:27 am
☽ ⚻ ☿	**2:46 pm**	11:46 am
☽ ⚻ ⚵		9:08 pm
♀ ⚻ ♄		11:20 pm

13 THURSDAY

☽ ⚻ ⚵	**12:08 am**	
♀ ⚻ ♄	**2:20 am**	
☽ ⚻ ⚶	**9:40 am**	6:40 am
☽ ⚻ ♆	**10:20 am**	7:20 am
☽ □ ♀	**12:17 pm**	9:17 am
☽ △ ♂	**2:41 pm**	11:41 am
☽ ☌ ♄	**3:05 pm**	12:05 pm
☽ ⚻ ♀	**4:36 pm**	1:36 pm
☽ ☍ ⚷	**6:06 pm**	3:06 pm
☽ ⚹ ♃	**7:22 pm**	4:22 pm
♂ △ ♄		9:27 pm
♆ ⚹ ⚶		9:59 pm
☽ ⚻ ♇		11:39 pm

14 FRIDAY

♂ △ ♄	**12:27 am**	
♆ ⚹ ⚶	**12:59 am**	
☽ ⚻ ♇	**2:39 am**	
♀ ⚺ ⚷	**7:58 am**	4:58 am
☽ △ ☉	**8:39 am**	5:39 am
☽ ☌ ⚳	**3:10 pm**	12:10 pm
♀ □ ♃	**10:34 pm**	7:34 pm
☽ ⚻ ♅	**10:41 pm**	7:41 pm

15 SATURDAY

♀ △ ⚶	**6:01 am**	3:01 am
☽ △ ☿	**10:41 am**	7:41 am
☽ △ ⚵	**1:01 pm**	10:01 am
☽ ☍ ♆	**9:12 pm**	6:12 pm
☽ △ ♀	**10:10 pm**	7:10 pm
☽ △ ⚶	**11:07 pm**	8:07 pm
☽ ⚺ ♄		10:30 pm

16 SUNDAY

☽ ⚺ ♄	**1:30 am**	
☽ ⚻ ♂	**3:32 am**	12:32 am
☽ ⚻ ⚷	**4:52 am**	1:52 am
☽ ⚺ ♃	**6:24 am**	3:24 am
☽ △ ♀	**9:28 am**	6:28 am
☿ ☌ ⚵	**10:53 am**	7:53 am
☽ △ ♇	**12:50 pm**	9:50 am
☽ □ ☉	**11:15 pm**	8:15 pm
☽ ⚺ ⚳		9:46 pm

17 MONDAY

☽ ⚺ ⚳	**12:46 am**	
☽ ☍ ♅	**7:38 am**	4:38 am
☉ △ ⚳	**7:30 pm**	4:30 pm
♂ ⚹ ⚷	**8:42 pm**	5:42 pm
♀ ☌ ♇	**8:51 pm**	5:51 pm
☽ □ ⚵	**10:34 pm**	7:34 pm
☽ □ ☿		11:04 pm

18 TUESDAY

☽ □ ☿	**2:04 am**	
♄ ⚻ ⚶	**3:41 am**	12:41 am
☽ ⚻ ♆	**4:47 am**	1:47 am
☽ ⚻ ♀	**4:59 am**	1:59 am
☽ ⚹ ♄	**8:36 am**	5:36 am
☽ □ ⚶	**8:49 am**	5:49 am
☽ △ ⚷	**12:12 pm**	9:12 am
☽ ☍ ♂	**12:41 pm**	9:41 am
☽ ☌ ♃	**1:52 pm**	10:52 am
☽ □ ♇	**7:29 pm**	4:29 pm
♆ ⚹ ♀	**8:06 pm**	5:06 pm
☽ □ ♀	**9:40 pm**	6:40 pm
☿ △ ♀		11:04 pm
☿ ⚹ ♆		11:43 pm

19 WEDNESDAY

☿ △ ♀	**2:04 am**	
☿ ⚹ ♆	**2:43 am**	
☽ ⚹ ⚳	**6:36 am**	3:36 am
☽ ⚹ ☉	**9:15 am**	6:15 am
☽ ⚻ ♅	**12:54 pm**	9:54 am

20 THURSDAY

☽ ⚹ ⚵	**4:03 am**	1:03 am
☽ ☍ ♀	**8:15 am**	5:15 am
☽ △ ♆	**8:38 am**	5:38 am
♂ ☍ ♃	**8:59 am**	5:59 am
☿ ⚻ ♄	**11:24 am**	8:24 am
☽ □ ♄	**11:59 am**	8:59 am
☽ ⚹ ☿	**12:03 pm**	9:03 am
☽ ⚹ ⚶	**2:20 pm**	11:20 am
☽ □ ⚷	**3:46 pm**	12:46 pm
☽ ⚺ ♃	**5:32 pm**	2:32 pm
☽ ⚻ ♂	**5:45 pm**	2:45 pm
☽ ⚹ ♇	**10:27 pm**	7:27 pm

21 FRIDAY

☽ ⚹ ♀	**5:03 am**	2:03 am
☽ □ ⚳	**8:51 am**	5:51 am
☉ □ ♅	**12:14 pm**	9:14 am
☽ △ ♅	**2:44 pm**	11:44 am
☽ ⚺ ☉	**2:55 pm**	11:55 am
☿ ☌ ⚶	**9:40 pm**	6:40 pm
☿ ⚺ ⚷		11:08 pm

22 SATURDAY

☿ ⚺ ⚷	**2:08 am**	
☽ ⚺ ⚵	**6:12 am**	3:12 am
☽ ⚻ ♀	**8:38 am**	5:38 am
☽ □ ♆	**9:28 am**	6:28 am
⚷ ⚺ ⚶	**11:12 am**	8:12 am
☽ △ ♄	**12:27 pm**	9:27 am
☽ ⚹ ⚷	**4:28 pm**	1:28 pm
☽ ⚺ ⚶	**4:38 pm**	1:38 pm
☽ ⚺ ☿	**5:56 pm**	2:56 pm
☽ ⚹ ♃	**6:19 pm**	3:19 pm
☽ △ ♂	**7:47 pm**	4:47 pm
☿ □ ♃	**10:09 pm**	7:09 pm
☽ ⚺ ♇	**10:46 pm**	7:46 pm
♀ ⚻ ⚳		11:30 pm

23 SUNDAY

♀ ⚻ ⚳	**2:30 am**	
☽ △ ⚳	**8:44 am**	5:44 am
☽ ⚺ ♀	**9:17 am**	6:17 am
☽ □ ♅	**2:28 pm**	11:28 am
☽ ☌ ☉	**5:59 pm**	2:59 pm
☿ □ ♂	**10:13 pm**	7:13 pm

24 MONDAY

☽ ☌ ⚵	**6:42 am**	3:42 am
☽ △ ♀	**7:40 am**	4:40 am
☽ ⚹ ♆	**8:53 am**	5:53 am
☽ ⚻ ♄	**11:38 am**	8:38 am
☽ ⚺ ⚷	**4:02 pm**	1:02 pm
☽ ☌ ⚶	**5:41 pm**	2:41 pm
☽ □ ♃	**6:00 pm**	3:00 pm
☽ □ ♂	**8:44 pm**	5:44 pm
☿ ☌ ♇	**9:13 pm**	6:13 pm
☽ ☌ ♇	**10:11 pm**	7:11 pm
☽ ☌ ☿	**10:17 pm**	7:17 pm

25 TUESDAY

♃ □ ⚶	**4:39 am**	1:39 am
☽ ⚻ ⚳	**8:06 am**	5:06 am
☽ ☌ ♀	**12:57 pm**	9:57 am
☽ ⚹ ♅	**1:57 pm**	10:57 am
♀ △ ⚵	**4:12 pm**	1:12 pm
☽ ⚺ ☉	**8:57 pm**	5:57 pm
♀ ⚹ ♅		10:22 pm

26 WEDNESDAY

♀ ⚹ ♅	**1:22 am**	
☽ □ ♀	**7:14 am**	4:14 am
☽ ⚺ ⚵	**7:41 am**	4:41 am
☽ ⚺ ♆	**8:51 am**	5:51 am
☽ ☍ ♄	**11:28 am**	8:28 am
☽ ☌ ⚷	**4:27 pm**	1:27 pm
♂ □ ♇	**6:24 pm**	3:24 pm
☽ △ ♃	**6:37 pm**	3:37 pm
☽ ⚺ ⚶	**7:46 pm**	4:46 pm
☽ ⚺ ♇	**10:43 pm**	7:43 pm
☽ ⚹ ♂	**10:52 pm**	7:52 pm

27 THURSDAY

☽ ⚺ ☿	**4:03 am**	1:03 am
☽ ☍ ⚳	**8:56 am**	5:56 am
☽ ⚺ ♅	**3:12 pm**	12:12 pm
☽ ⚺ ♀	**6:47 pm**	3:47 pm
☽ ⚹ ☉		11:24 pm

28 FRIDAY

☽ ⚹ ☉	**2:24 am**	
☽ ⚹ ♀	**9:11 am**	6:11 am
☽ ⚹ ⚵	**11:14 am**	8:14 am
☽ ☌ ♆	**11:16 am**	8:16 am
♆ ⚹ ⚵	**12:25 pm**	9:25 am
☽ ⚻ ♄	**1:46 pm**	10:46 am
☽ ⚺ ⚷	**7:35 pm**	4:35 pm
☽ ⚻ ♃	**10:01 pm**	7:01 pm
☽ ⚹ ⚶		9:57 pm
☽ ⚹ ♇		11:09 pm

29 SATURDAY

☽ ⚹ ⚶	**12:57 am**	
☽ ⚹ ♇	**2:09 am**	
☽ ⚺ ♂	**4:15 am**	1:15 am
☿ ⚻ ⚳	**4:54 am**	1:54 am
☽ ⚻ ⚳	**12:50 pm**	9:50 am
☽ ⚹ ☿	**1:47 pm**	10:47 am
☽ ☌ ♅	**7:46 pm**	4:46 pm

30 SUNDAY

☽ ⚹ ♀	**5:05 am**	2:05 am
♇ ☌ ⚶	**9:29 am**	6:29 am
☽ □ ☉	**12:16 pm**	9:16 am
☽ ⚺ ♀	**2:49 pm**	11:49 am
☽ ⚺ ♆	**5:22 pm**	2:22 pm
☽ □ ⚵	**6:45 pm**	3:45 pm
☽ △ ♄	**7:44 pm**	4:44 pm
☽ ⚹ ⚷		11:36 pm

Eastern time in bold type
Pacific time in medium type

NOVEMBER 2003

☽ Last Aspect day	EST / hr:mn / PST	asp	☽ Ingress sign day	EST / hr:mn / PST
2	**2:40 pm** 11:40 am	□ ♀	♓ 2	**2:52 pm** 11:52 am
3	10:36 pm	□ ♇	♈ 4	9:02 pm
4	**1:36 am**	□ ♇	♈ 5	**12:02 am**
7	**9:16 am** 6:16 am	⚹ ♅	♉ 7	**11:29 am** 8:29 am
9	**10:00 pm** 7:00 pm	□ ♅	♊ 9	9:14 pm
9	**10:00 pm** 7:00 pm	□ ♅	♊ 10	**12:14 am**
12	**10:57 am** 7:57 am	△ ♅	♋ 12	**1:10 pm** 10:10 am
14	**8:39 am** 5:39 am	△ ☉	♌ 14	9:48 pm
14	**8:39 am** 5:39 am	△ ☉	♌ 15	**12:48 am**
17	**7:38 am** 4:38 am	☍ ♅	♍ 17	**9:36 am** 6:36 am
19	**9:15 am** 6:15 am	⚹ ☉	♎ 19	**2:42 pm** 11:42 am
21	**2:44 pm** 11:44 am	△ ♅	♏ 21	**4:24 pm** 1:24 pm
23	**2:28 pm** 11:28 am	□ ♅	♐ 23	**4:02 pm** 1:02 pm
25	**1:57 pm** 10:57 am	⚹ ♅	♑ 25	**3:31 pm** 12:31 pm
26	**10:52 pm** 7:52 pm	⚹ ♂	♒ 27	**4:48 pm** 1:48 pm
29	**7:46 pm** 4:46 pm	☌ ♅	♓ 29	**9:25 pm** 6:25 pm

☽ Phases & Eclipses phase	day	EST / hr:mn / PST
Full Moon	8	**8:13 pm** 5:13 pm
●	8	16° ♉ 13'
4th Quarter	16	**11:15 pm** 8:15 pm
New Moon	23	**5:59 pm** 2:59 pm
●	23	1° ♐ 14'
2nd Quarter	30	**12:16 pm** 9:16 am

Planet Ingress	day	EST / hr:mn / PST
♀ ♐	2	**4:42 pm** 1:42 pm
☿ ♐	11	11:19 pm
☿ ♐	12	**2:19 am**
☉ ♐	22	**12:43 pm** 9:43 am
♀ ♑	26	**8:07 pm** 5:07 pm

Planetary Motion	day	EST / hr:mn / PST
♅ D	8	**7:44 am** 4:44 am
⚷ ℞	23	**9:32 pm** 6:32 pm

DATE		SID. TIME	SUN	MOON	NODE	MERCURY	VENUS	MARS	JUPITER	SATURN	URANUS	NEPTUNE	PLUTO	CERES	PALLAS	JUNO	VESTA	CHIRON
1	Sa	2:39:29	08 ♏ 08 47	05 ♒ 51	20 ♉ ℞ 32	12 ♏ 19	27 ♏ 38	07 ♓ 18	13 ♍ 05	13 ♋ ℞ 12	28 ♒ ℞ 55	10 ♒ 25	18 ♐ 17	23 ♋ 38	14 ♈ ℞ 27	01 ♐ 20	03 ♐ 30	13 ♑ 37
2	Su	2:43:25	09 08 48	19 12	20 32	13 55	28 53	07 41	13 15	13 12	28 55	10 26	18 19	23 46	14 11	01 40	04 01	13 41
3	M	2:47:22	10 08 51	02 ♓ 13	20 31	15 30	00 ♐ 07	08 05	13 24	13 11	28 54	10 26	18 21	23 54	13 55	02 00	04 33	13 44
4	T	2:51:18	11 08 55	14 56	20 30	17 05	01 22	08 29	13 34	13 10	28 54	10 26	18 23	24 02	13 40	02 20	05 05	13 48
5	W	2:55:15	12 09 01	27 25	20 29	18 40	02 36	08 53	13 43	13 09	28 54	10 27	18 25	24 10	13 25	02 40	05 37	13 51
6	Th	2:59:12	13 09 09	09 ♈ 40	20 28	20 14	03 51	09 17	13 53	13 08	28 54	10 27	18 27	24 17	13 10	03 00	06 09	13 55
7	F	3:03:08	14 09 18	21 46	20 27	21 48	05 06	09 42	14 02	13 06	28 54	10 28	18 29	24 24	12 56	03 20	06 41	13 58
8	Sa	3:07:05	15 09 29	03 ♉ 44	20 26	23 22	06 20	10 08	14 11	13 05	28 D 54	10 28	18 31	24 30	12 42	03 41	07 12	14 02
9	Su	3:11:01	16 09 42	15 37	20 D 26	24 55	07 35	10 34	14 20	13 03	28 54	10 29	18 33	24 36	12 29	04 01	07 44	14 06
10	M	3:14:58	17 09 56	27 25	20 26	26 27	08 49	11 00	14 29	13 02	28 54	10 29	18 35	24 42	12 15	04 21	08 16	14 10
11	T	3:18:54	18 10 13	09 ♊ 13	20 26	28 00	10 04	11 26	14 38	13 00	28 54	10 30	18 37	24 47	12 03	04 41	08 48	14 14
12	W	3:22:51	19 10 31	21 01	20 26	29 32	11 18	11 53	14 47	12 58	28 54	10 31	18 39	24 52	11 50	05 02	09 20	14 18
13	Th	3:26:47	20 10 51	02 ♋ 54	20 ℞ 26	01 ♐ 04	12 33	12 20	14 55	12 56	28 54	10 31	18 41	24 57	11 38	05 22	09 52	14 22
14	F	3:30:44	21 11 13	14 53	20 26	02 35	13 48	12 48	15 04	12 54	28 54	10 32	18 43	25 01	11 27	05 43	10 24	14 26
15	Sa	3:34:41	22 11 36	27 02	20 26	04 06	15 02	13 15	15 12	12 52	28 55	10 33	18 45	25 05	11 16	06 03	10 56	14 30
16	Su	3:38:37	23 12 02	09 ♌ 25	20 26	05 37	16 17	13 44	15 20	12 50	28 55	10 34	18 47	25 08	11 06	06 24	11 29	14 34
17	M	3:42:34	24 12 29	22 06	20 D 26	07 08	17 31	14 12	15 28	12 48	28 56	10 35	18 49	25 11	10 55	06 44	12 01	14 38
18	T	3:46:30	25 12 59	05 ♍ 09	20 26	08 38	18 46	14 41	15 36	12 45	28 56	10 35	18 51	25 14	10 46	07 05	12 33	14 42
19	W	3:50:27	26 13 30	18 37	20 26	10 08	20 00	15 10	15 44	12 43	28 57	10 36	18 54	25 16	10 37	07 25	13 05	14 47
20	Th	3:54:23	27 14 03	02 ♎ 32	20 27	11 37	21 15	15 39	15 52	12 40	28 57	10 37	18 56	25 18	10 28	07 46	13 37	14 51
21	F	3:58:20	28 14 37	16 52	20 28	13 06	22 29	16 09	15 59	12 37	28 58	10 38	18 58	25 20	10 20	08 06	14 09	14 56
22	Sa	4:02:16	29 15 14	01 ♏ 37	20 28	14 35	23 44	16 38	16 07	12 35	28 58	10 39	19 00	25 21	10 12	08 27	14 41	15 00
23	Su	4:06:13	00 ♐ 15 52	16 40	20 ℞ 29	16 03	24 58	17 09	16 14	12 32	28 59	10 40	19 02	25 22	10 05	08 48	15 14	15 05
24	M	4:10:10	01 16 32	01 ♐ 53	20 28	17 31	26 13	17 39	16 21	12 29	29 00	10 41	19 04	25 ℞ 22	09 59	09 08	15 46	15 09
25	T	4:14:06	02 17 13	17 06	20 28	18 59	27 28	18 10	16 28	12 25	29 01	10 42	19 07	25 22	09 52	09 29	16 18	15 14
26	W	4:18:03	03 17 55	02 ♑ 10	20 26	20 25	28 42	18 41	16 35	12 22	29 02	10 43	19 09	25 21	09 47	09 50	16 50	15 19
27	Th	4:21:59	04 18 39	16 56	20 25	21 52	29 57	19 12	16 42	12 19	29 02	10 45	19 11	25 20	09 42	10 11	17 23	15 23
28	F	4:25:56	05 19 24	01 ♒ 18	20 23	23 17	01 ♑ 11	19 43	16 48	12 16	29 03	10 46	19 13	25 19	09 37	10 31	17 55	15 28
29	Sa	4:29:52	06 20 09	15 13	20 21	24 41	02 25	20 15	16 55	12 12	29 04	10 47	19 15	25 17	09 33	10 52	18 27	15 33
30	Su	4:33:49	07 20 56	28 40	20 D 20	26 05	03 40	20 47	17 01	12 09	29 05	10 48	19 18	25 15	09 30	11 13	19 00	15 38

EPHEMERIS CALCULATED FOR 12 MIDNIGHT GREENWICH MEAN TIME. ALL OTHER DATA AND FACING ASPECTARIAN PAGE IN **EASTERN TIME (BOLD)** AND PACIFIC TIME (REGULAR).

DECEMBER 2003

1 MONDAY

☽ ⚹ ⚷	**2:36 am**	
☽ ☍ ♃	**5:18 am**	2:18 am
☽ □ ♇	**9:27 am**	6:27 am
☽ □ ⚶	**10:27 am**	7:27 am
☽ ☌ ♂	**2:00 pm**	11:00 am
☉ △ ♀	**7:35 pm**	4:35 pm
☽ △ ⚳	**8:32 pm**	5:32 pm
☿ ⚹ ♅		9:53 pm
♄ ⚻ ⚵		10:23 pm

2 TUESDAY

☿ ⚹ ♅	**12:53 am**	
♄ ⚻ ⚵	**1:23 am**	
☽ ⚺ ♅	**4:15 am**	1:15 am
☽ □ ☿	**4:39 am**	1:39 am
☽ □ ♀	**8:32 pm**	5:32 pm
☽ ☌ ♀		9:16 pm
☽ △ ☉		11:57 pm

3 WEDNESDAY

☽ ☌ ♀	**12:16 am**	
☽ △ ☉	**2:57 am**	
☽ ⚹ ♆	**3:15 am**	12:15 am
☽ □ ♄	**5:20 am**	2:20 am
☽ △ ⚵	**6:19 am**	3:19 am
☉ ⚹ ♆	**6:34 am**	3:34 am
☽ □ ⚷	**1:18 pm**	10:18 am
☽ ⚻ ♃	**4:13 pm**	1:13 pm
☽ △ ♇	**8:18 pm**	5:18 pm
☽ △ ⚶	**11:55 pm**	8:55 pm

4 THURSDAY

☽ ⚺ ♂	**3:40 am**	12:40 am
☉ ⚻ ♄	**5:56 am**	2:56 am
☽ □ ⚳	**7:24 am**	4:24 am
♀ □ ☿	**8:39 am**	5:39 am
☽ ⚹ ♅	**3:52 pm**	12:52 pm
☽ △ ☿	**11:25 pm**	8:25 pm

5 FRIDAY

☽ ⚺ ♀	**12:22 pm**	9:22 am
☉ ☌ ⚵	**2:25 pm**	11:25 am
☽ △ ♀	**3:38 pm**	12:38 pm
☽ □ ♆	**3:38 pm**	12:38 pm
♀ ⚺ ♆	**3:38 pm**	12:38 pm
☽ ⚹ ♄	**5:20 pm**	2:20 pm
☽ ⚻ ⚵	**8:30 pm**	5:30 pm
☽ ⚻ ☉	**8:53 pm**	5:53 pm
☽ △ ⚷		11:15 pm

6 SATURDAY

☽ △ ⚷	**2:15 am**	
☽ △ ♃	**5:15 am**	2:15 am
♀ ☍ ♄	**7:04 am**	4:04 am
☽ ⚻ ♇	**9:09 am**	6:09 am
☽ ⚻ ⚶	**3:33 pm**	12:33 pm
☽ ⚹ ♂	**7:26 pm**	4:26 pm
☽ ⚹ ⚳	**7:48 pm**	4:48 pm
♂ △ ⚳		11:25 pm

7 SUNDAY

♂ △ ⚳	**2:25 am**	
☽ □ ♅	**4:54 am**	1:54 am
☽ ⚻ ☿	**7:09 pm**	4:09 pm
☽ ⚹ ♀		10:24 pm

8 MONDAY

☽ ⚹ ♀	**1:24 am**	
☽ △ ♆	**4:47 am**	1:47 am
☽ ⚺ ♄	**6:00 am**	3:00 am
♀ ⚺ ⚵	**6:14 am**	3:14 am
☽ ☍ ⚵	**11:22 am**	8:22 am
☽ ⚻ ♀	**11:48 am**	8:48 am
☽ ☍ ☉	**3:37 pm**	12:37 pm
☽ ⚻ ⚷	**3:41 pm**	12:41 pm
☉ ⚺ ⚷	**4:31 pm**	1:31 pm
☽ □ ♃	**6:40 pm**	3:40 pm
☽ ☍ ♇	**10:18 pm**	7:18 pm

9 TUESDAY

☽ ☍ ⚶	**7:21 am**	4:21 am
☽ ⚺ ⚳	**8:10 am**	5:10 am
☽ □ ♂	**11:17 am**	8:17 am
☽ △ ♅	**5:48 pm**	2:48 pm
⚳ ⚻ ⚶	**10:37 pm**	7:37 pm

10 WEDNESDAY

♀ ☌ ⚷	**3:28 am**	12:28 am
☉ □ ♃	**5:58 am**	2:58 am
☽ ☍ ☿	**1:17 pm**	10:17 am
☽ □ ♀	**1:59 pm**	10:59 am
☽ ⚻ ♆	**5:18 pm**	2:18 pm
☽ ☌ ♄	**6:01 pm**	3:01 pm
☿ □ ♀	**11:11 pm**	8:11 pm
☽ ⚻ ⚵		10:25 pm

11 THURSDAY

☽ ⚻ ⚵	**1:25 am**	
☽ ☍ ⚷	**4:17 am**	1:17 am
☽ ☍ ♀	**6:55 am**	3:55 am
☽ ⚹ ♃	**7:09 am**	4:09 am
☽ ⚻ ☉	**9:17 am**	6:17 am
♀ △ ♃	**9:22 am**	6:22 am
☽ ⚻ ♇	**10:30 am**	7:30 am
☽ ☌ ⚳	**7:23 pm**	4:23 pm
☽ ⚻ ⚶	**9:55 pm**	6:55 pm
☉ ☌ ♇		9:28 pm
☽ △ ♂		10:53 pm

12 FRIDAY

☉ ☌ ♇	**12:28 am**	
☽ △ ♂	**1:53 am**	
☽ ⚻ ♅	**5:28 am**	2:28 am
♀ ⚺ ♇	**7:12 pm**	4:12 pm
☽ △ ♀		10:08 pm

13 SATURDAY

☽ △ ♀	**1:08 am**	
☽ ⚻ ☿	**4:11 am**	1:11 am
☽ ☍ ♆	**4:15 am**	1:15 am
☽ ⚺ ♄	**4:28 am**	1:28 am
☿ ⚺ ♆	**5:22 am**	2:22 am
☿ ☍ ♄	**9:13 am**	6:13 am
☽ △ ⚵	**1:39 pm**	10:39 am
☽ ⚻ ⚷	**3:09 pm**	12:09 pm
☽ ⚺ ♃	**5:49 pm**	2:49 pm
☽ △ ♇	**8:55 pm**	5:55 pm
☽ ⚻ ♀	**11:37 pm**	8:37 pm
☽ △ ☉		9:39 pm

14 SUNDAY

☽ △ ☉	**12:39 am**	
☽ ⚺ ⚳	**4:41 am**	1:41 am
♄ ⚻ ♆	**7:48 am**	4:48 am
☽ △ ⚶	**10:16 am**	7:16 am
☽ ⚻ ♂	**2:13 pm**	11:13 am
☽ ☍ ♅	**3:05 pm**	12:05 pm

15 MONDAY

☽ ⚻ ♀	**10:02 am**	7:02 am
♂ ⚺ ♅	**10:33 am**	7:33 am
☽ ⚹ ♄	**12:37 pm**	9:37 am
☽ ⚻ ♆	**12:51 pm**	9:51 am
☽ △ ☿	**2:50 pm**	11:50 am
☉ ⚻ ⚳	**9:10 pm**	6:10 pm
♀ ☍ ⚳	**10:40 pm**	7:40 pm
☽ □ ⚵	**11:12 pm**	8:12 pm
☽ △ ⚷	**11:29 pm**	8:29 pm
☽ ☌ ♃		10:55 pm

16 TUESDAY

☽ ☌ ♃	**1:55 am**	
☽ □ ♇	**4:45 am**	1:45 am
☉ ⚺ ♀	**6:35 am**	3:35 am
☽ ⚹ ⚳	**11:22 am**	8:22 am
☽ □ ☉	**12:42 pm**	9:42 am
☽ △ ♀	**12:49 pm**	9:49 am
⚷ ⚺ ⚵	**2:05 pm**	11:05 am
☽ □ ⚶	**7:32 pm**	4:32 pm
☽ ⚻ ♅	**9:55 pm**	6:55 pm
☽ ☍ ♂	**11:25 pm**	8:25 pm

17 WEDNESDAY

☽ ☍ ♀	**4:01 pm**	1:01 pm
☽ □ ♄	**5:51 pm**	2:51 pm
☽ △ ♆	**6:28 pm**	3:28 pm
☽ □ ☿	**8:43 pm**	5:43 pm

18 THURSDAY

☽ □ ⚷	**4:44 am**	1:44 am
☽ ⚹ ⚵	**5:27 am**	2:27 am
☽ ⚺ ♃	**6:52 am**	3:52 am
☽ ⚹ ♇	**9:28 am**	6:28 am
☽ □ ⚳	**2:59 pm**	11:59 am
☽ ⚹ ☉	**8:50 pm**	5:50 pm
☽ □ ♀	**9:53 pm**	6:53 pm
☽ ⚹ ⚶		10:18 pm
☽ △ ♅		10:39 pm

19 FRIDAY

☽ ⚹ ⚶	**1:18 am**	
☽ △ ♅	**1:39 am**	
☽ ⚻ ♂	**5:06 am**	2:06 am
♅ ⚹ ⚶	**11:14 am**	8:14 am
☽ ⚻ ♀	**6:58 pm**	3:58 pm
☽ △ ♄	**8:04 pm**	5:04 pm
☽ □ ♆	**9:02 pm**	6:02 pm
☽ ⚹ ☿	**10:09 pm**	7:09 pm

20 SATURDAY

☽ ⚹ ⚷	**6:58 am**	3:58 am
☽ ⚺ ⚵	**8:33 am**	5:33 am
☽ ⚹ ♃	**8:52 am**	5:52 am
☽ ⚺ ♇	**11:18 am**	8:18 am
☽ △ ⚳	**3:51 pm**	12:51 pm
♀ ⚺ ♅	**6:41 pm**	3:41 pm
♃ □ ⚵	**11:24 pm**	8:24 pm
☿ ⚺ ♆		10:07 pm
☽ ⚺ ☉		10:36 pm
☽ □ ♅		11:43 pm

21 SUNDAY

☿ ⚺ ♆	**1:07 am**	
☽ ⚺ ☉	**1:36 am**	
☽ □ ♅	**2:43 am**	
☽ ⚹ ♀	**3:25 am**	12:25 am
☽ ⚺ ⚶	**4:06 am**	1:06 am
☽ △ ♂	**7:54 am**	4:54 am
♀ ⚺ ⚶	**5:35 pm**	2:35 pm
☉ ⚹ ♅	**6:34 pm**	3:34 pm
☽ △ ♀	**7:39 pm**	4:39 pm
☽ ⚻ ♄	**8:06 pm**	5:06 pm
☽ ⚺ ☿	**8:22 pm**	5:22 pm
☽ ⚹ ♆	**9:23 pm**	6:23 pm
☿ ☍ ♄		10:35 pm

22 MONDAY

☿ ☍ ♄	**1:35 am**	
☿ □ ♀	**7:08 am**	4:08 am
☽ ⚺ ⚷	**7:15 am**	4:15 am
☽ □ ♃	**8:56 am**	5:56 am
☽ ☌ ⚵	**9:38 am**	6:38 am
☽ ☌ ♇	**11:18 am**	8:18 am
☽ ⚻ ⚳	**3:05 pm**	12:05 pm
☽ ⚹ ♅		11:29 pm

23 TUESDAY

☽ ⚹ ♅	**2:29 am**	
☽ ☌ ☉	**4:43 am**	1:43 am
♄ □ ♀	**4:43 am**	1:43 am
☽ ☌ ⚶	**5:31 am**	2:31 am
☽ ⚺ ♀	**7:19 am**	4:19 am
☽ □ ♂	**9:29 am**	6:29 am
☽ ☌ ☿	**5:04 pm**	2:04 pm
☽ ☍ ♄	**7:30 pm**	4:30 pm
☽ □ ♀	**7:43 pm**	4:43 pm
☽ ⚺ ♆	**9:08 pm**	6:08 pm

24 WEDNESDAY

☉ ☌ ⚶	**4:55 am**	1:55 am
☽ ☌ ⚷	**7:19 am**	4:19 am
☽ △ ♃	**8:52 am**	5:52 am
☽ ⚺ ⚵	**10:36 am**	7:36 am
☽ ⚺ ♇	**11:17 am**	8:17 am
☽ ☍ ⚳	**2:25 pm**	11:25 am
☽ ⚺ ♅		11:54 pm

25 THURSDAY

☽ ⚺ ♅	**2:54 am**	
☽ ⚺ ⚶	**7:46 am**	4:46 am
♀ ⚹ ♂	**8:29 am**	5:29 am
☽ ⚺ ☉	**8:43 am**	5:43 am
☽ ⚹ ♂	**12:06 pm**	9:06 am
☽ ☌ ♀	**12:17 pm**	9:17 am
☽ ⚺ ☿	**2:03 pm**	11:03 am
♇ ☌ ⚵	**6:57 pm**	3:57 pm
☽ ⚻ ♄	**8:13 pm**	5:13 pm
☽ ⚹ ♀	**9:13 pm**	6:13 pm
☽ ☌ ♆	**10:20 pm**	7:20 pm
☿ ⚺ ♀	**11:07 pm**	8:07 pm

26 FRIDAY

☿ □ ♂	**3:53 am**	12:53 am
☽ ⚺ ⚷	**9:18 am**	6:18 am
☽ ⚻ ♃	**10:43 am**	7:43 am
☽ ⚹ ♇	**1:18 pm**	10:18 am
☽ ⚹ ⚵	**1:43 pm**	10:43 am
☽ ⚻ ⚳	**3:46 pm**	12:46 pm
☉ ☌ ☿	**8:11 pm**	5:11 pm

27 SATURDAY

☽ ☌ ♅	**5:58 am**	2:58 am
☿ ☌ ⚶	**12:04 pm**	9:04 am
☽ ⚹ ☿	**1:02 pm**	10:02 am
☽ ⚹ ⚶	**1:11 pm**	10:11 am
☽ ⚹ ☉	**4:16 pm**	1:16 pm
☽ ⚺ ♂	**6:07 pm**	3:07 pm
☽ ⚺ ♀	**9:08 pm**	6:08 pm
☽ △ ♄		9:07 pm
☽ ⚺ ☿		11:09 pm
☽ ⚺ ♆		11:51 pm

28 SUNDAY

☽ △ ♄	**12:07 am**	
☽ ⚺ ☿	**2:09 am**	
☽ ⚺ ♆	**2:51 am**	
☽ ⚹ ⚷	**2:57 pm**	11:57 am
☽ ☍ ♃	**4:11 pm**	1:11 pm
⚳ ⚻ ⚵	**5:44 pm**	2:44 pm
☽ □ ♇	**7:03 pm**	4:03 pm
☽ △ ⚳	**8:42 pm**	5:42 pm
☽ □ ⚵	**8:50 pm**	5:50 pm

29 MONDAY

♀ ⚻ ♄	**3:38 am**	12:38 am
☽ ⚺ ♅	**1:06 pm**	10:06 am
☽ □ ☿	**3:19 pm**	12:19 pm
☽ □ ⚶	**11:14 pm**	8:14 pm
☉ □ ♂		9:55 pm

30 TUESDAY

☉ □ ♂	**12:55 am**	
☽ ☌ ♂	**4:55 am**	1:55 am
☽ □ ☉	**5:03 am**	2:03 am
☽ □ ♄	**8:09 am**	5:09 am
♀ ⚹ ☿	**11:27 am**	8:27 am
☽ ⚹ ♀	**11:31 am**	8:31 am
☽ ☌ ☿	**11:31 am**	8:31 am
☽ ⚹ ♆	**11:36 am**	8:36 am
♀ ☌ ♆	**12:19 pm**	9:19 am
☿ ⚹ ♅	**2:30 pm**	11:30 am
♆ ⚹ ☿	**6:21 pm**	3:21 pm
☽ □ ⚷		9:53 pm
☽ ⚻ ♃		10:50 pm

31 WEDNESDAY

☽ □ ⚷	**12:53 am**	
☽ ⚻ ♃	**1:50 am**	
☽ △ ♇	**5:00 am**	2:00 am
☽ □ ⚳	**5:33 am**	2:33 am
☽ △ ⚵	**8:26 am**	5:26 am
☉ ☍ ♄	**3:57 pm**	12:57 pm
☽ △ ☿	**9:27 pm**	6:27 pm
☽ ⚹ ♅		9:11 pm

Eastern time in bold type
Pacific time in medium type

DECEMBER 2003

☽ Last Aspect day	EST / hr:mn / PST	asp	☽ Ingress sign day	EST / hr:mn / PST
2	**4:39 am** 1:39 am	□ ☿	♈ 2	**5:56 am** 2:56 am
4	**3:52 pm** 12:52 pm	✱ ♅	♉ 4	**5:30 pm** 2:30 pm
7	**4:54 am** 1:54 am	□ ♅	♊ 7	**6:26 am** 3:26 am
9	**5:48 pm** 2:48 pm	△ ♅	♋ 9	**7:11 pm** 4:11 pm
11	10:53 pm	△ ♂	♌ 12	**6:40 am** 3:40 am
12	**1:53 am**	△ ♂	♌ 12	**6:40 am** 3:40 am
14	**3:05 pm** 12:05 pm	☍ ♅	♍ 14	**4:07 pm** 1:07 pm
16	**12:49 pm** 9:49 am	△ ♀	♎ 16	**10:46 pm** 7:46 pm
18	10:39 pm	△ ♅	♏ 18	11:20 pm
19	**1:39 am**	△ ♅	♏ 19	**2:20 am**
20	11:43 pm	□ ♅	♐ 21	**3:16 am** 12:16 am
21	**2:43 am**	□ ♅	♐ 21	**3:16 am** 12:16 am
22	11:29 pm	✱ ♅	♑ 22	11:55 pm
23	**2:29 am**	✱ ♅	♑ 23	**2:55 am**
24	**8:52 am** 5:52 am	△ ♃	♒ 25	**3:13 am** 12:13 am
27	**5:58 am** 2:58 am	☌ ♅	♓ 27	**6:10 am** 3:10 am
28	**7:03 pm** 4:03 pm	□ ♇	♈ 29	**1:08 pm** 10:08 am
31	**9:27 pm** 6:27 pm	△ ☿	♉ 31	9:02 pm
31	**9:27 pm** 6:27 pm	△ ☿	♉ 1/1	**12:02 am**

☽ Phases & Eclipses phase	day	EST / hr:mn / PST
Full Moon	8	**3:37 pm** 12:37 pm
4th Quarter	16	**12:42 pm** 9:42 am
New Moon	23	**4:43 am** 1:43 am
2nd Quarter	30	**5:03 am** 2:03 am

Planet Ingress	day	EST / hr:mn / PST
☿ ♑	2	**4:34 pm** 1:34 pm
♂ ♈	16	**8:24 am** 5:24 am
⚶ ♑	20	**4:53 am** 1:53 am
♀ ♒	20	10:32 pm
♀ ♒	21	**1:32 am**
☉ ♑	21	11:04 pm
☉ ♑	22	**2:04 am**
♅ ♓	30	**4:14 am** 1:14 am
☿ ♐	30	**2:52 pm** 11:52 am

Planetary Motion	day	EST / hr:mn / PST
♀ D	6	**6:35 am** 3:35 am
☿ ℞	17	**11:02 am** 8:02 am

DATE		SID.TIME	SUN	MOON	NODE	MERCURY	VENUS	MARS	JUPITER	SATURN	URANUS	NEPTUNE	PLUTO	CERES	PALLAS	JUNO	VESTA	CHIRON
1	M	4:37:46	08 ♐ 21 44	11 ♓ 42	20 ♉ 20	27 ♐ 27	04 ♑ 54	21 ♓ 19	17 ♍ 07	12 ♋℞ 05	29 ♒ 07	10 ♒ 49	19 ♐ 20	25 ♋℞ 12	09 ♈℞ 27	11 ♐ 34	19 ♐ 32	15 ♑ 43
2	T	4:41:42	09 22 32	24 21	20 21	28 48	06 09	21 51	17 13	12 01	29 08	10 51	19 22	25 09	09 24	11 55	20 04	15 47
3	W	4:45:39	10 23 21	06 ♈ 41	20 22	00 ♑ 08	07 23	22 23	17 19	11 58	29 09	10 52	19 24	25 05	09 22	12 16	20 36	15 52
4	Th	4:49:35	11 24 12	18 48	20 24	01 26	08 38	22 56	17 25	11 54	29 10	10 53	19 27	25 01	09 21	12 37	21 09	15 57
5	F	4:53:32	12 25 03	00 ♉ 45	20 25	02 42	09 52	23 29	17 30	11 50	29 12	10 55	19 29	24 57	09 20	12 57	21 41	16 02
6	Sa	4:57:28	13 25 55	12 35	20 ℞ 26	03 56	11 06	24 02	17 36	11 46	29 13	10 56	19 31	24 52	09 D 19	13 18	22 13	16 07
7	Su	5:01:25	14 26 48	24 23	20 27	05 07	12 21	24 35	17 41	11 42	29 14	10 58	19 33	24 47	09 19	13 39	22 46	16 13
8	M	5:05:21	15 27 42	06 ♊ 11	20 26	06 14	13 35	25 08	17 46	11 38	29 16	10 59	19 36	24 41	09 20	14 00	23 18	16 18
9	T	5:09:18	16 28 37	18 00	20 23	07 19	14 49	25 42	17 51	11 33	29 17	11 01	19 38	24 35	09 21	14 21	23 51	16 23
10	W	5:13:15	17 29 33	29 55	20 19	08 19	16 04	26 15	17 55	11 29	29 19	11 02	19 40	24 29	09 22	14 42	24 23	16 28
11	Th	5:17:11	18 30 30	11 ♋ 55	20 15	09 15	17 18	26 49	18 00	11 25	29 20	11 04	19 43	24 22	09 24	15 03	24 55	16 33
12	F	5:21:08	19 31 28	24 03	20 09	10 06	18 32	27 23	18 04	11 21	29 22	11 05	19 45	24 15	09 27	15 24	25 28	16 39
13	Sa	5:25:04	20 32 27	06 ♌ 20	20 04	10 50	19 47	27 57	18 08	11 16	29 24	11 07	19 47	24 07	09 29	15 45	26 00	16 44
14	Su	5:29:01	21 33 27	18 49	19 59	11 28	21 01	28 32	18 12	11 12	29 26	11 08	19 49	23 59	09 33	16 06	26 32	16 49
15	M	5:32:57	22 34 28	01 ♍ 33	19 56	11 58	22 15	29 06	18 16	11 07	29 27	11 10	19 52	23 51	09 37	16 27	27 05	16 54
16	T	5:36:54	23 35 29	14 33	19 D 54	12 19	23 29	29 41	18 20	11 03	29 29	11 12	19 54	23 42	09 41	16 47	27 37	17 00
17	W	5:40:50	24 36 32	27 52	19 54	12 ℞ 31	24 43	00 ♈ 15	18 23	10 58	29 31	11 13	19 56	23 33	09 46	17 08	28 10	17 05
18	Th	5:44:47	25 37 36	11 ♎ 34	19 55	12 33	25 57	00 50	18 27	10 53	29 33	11 15	19 59	23 23	09 51	17 29	28 42	17 11
19	F	5:48:44	26 38 41	25 38	19 56	12 24	27 12	01 25	18 30	10 49	29 35	11 17	20 01	23 13	09 57	17 50	29 14	17 16
20	Sa	5:52:40	27 39 47	10 ♏ 04	19 ℞ 57	12 03	28 26	02 00	18 33	10 44	29 37	11 19	20 03	23 03	10 03	18 11	29 47	17 22
21	Su	5:56:37	28 40 53	24 51	19 58	11 31	29 40	02 35	18 35	10 39	29 39	11 20	20 05	22 52	10 10	18 32	00 ♑ 19	17 27
22	M	6:00:33	29 42 01	09 ♐ 52	19 56	10 47	00 ♒ 54	03 11	18 38	10 34	29 41	11 22	20 08	22 42	10 17	18 53	00 51	17 33
23	T	6:04:30	00 ♑ 43 09	25 00	19 52	09 52	02 08	03 46	18 40	10 29	29 43	11 24	20 10	22 30	10 24	19 14	01 24	17 38
24	W	6:08:26	01 44 17	10 ♑ 06	19 47	08 48	03 22	04 22	18 43	10 25	29 45	11 26	20 12	22 19	10 32	19 35	01 56	17 44
25	Th	6:12:23	02 45 26	24 59	19 40	07 35	04 36	04 57	18 45	10 20	29 47	11 28	20 14	22 07	10 41	19 56	02 29	17 49
26	F	6:16:20	03 46 35	09 ♒ 31	19 33	06 16	05 50	05 33	18 46	10 15	29 50	11 30	20 17	21 55	10 49	20 17	03 01	17 55
27	Sa	6:20:16	04 47 45	23 37	19 26	04 55	07 04	06 09	18 48	10 10	29 52	11 31	20 19	21 43	10 59	20 37	03 33	18 00
28	Su	6:24:13	05 48 54	07 ♓ 13	19 21	03 33	08 18	06 45	18 50	10 05	29 54	11 33	20 21	21 30	11 08	20 58	04 06	18 06
29	M	6:28:09	06 50 03	20 22	19 17	02 13	09 32	07 21	18 51	10 00	29 57	11 35	20 23	21 17	11 18	21 19	04 38	18 11
30	T	6:32:06	07 51 12	03 ♈ 04	19 D 16	00 57	10 45	07 57	18 52	09 55	29 59	11 37	20 25	21 04	11 29	21 40	05 10	18 17
31	W	6:36:02	08 52 21	15 25	19 16	29 ♐ 49	11 59	08 34	18 53	09 50	00 ♓ 02	11 39	20 28	20 51	11 39	22 01	05 43	18 23

EPHEMERIS CALCULATED FOR 12 MIDNIGHT GREENWICH MEAN TIME. ALL OTHER DATA AND FACING ASPECTARIAN PAGE IN **EASTERN TIME (BOLD)** AND PACIFIC TIME (REGULAR).

JANUARY 2004

1 THURSDAY

☽ ⚹ ♅	**12:11 am**	
♇ ⚻ ⚳	**7:09 am**	4:09 am
☽ △ ⚴	**1:28 pm**	10:28 am
♂ □ ♄	**3:22 pm**	12:22 pm
☽ ⚹ ♄	**7:34 pm**	4:34 pm
☽ ⚺ ♂	**7:49 pm**	4:49 pm
☽ △ ☉	**10:22 pm**	7:22 pm
☽ □ ♆	**11:44 pm**	8:44 pm
☽ ⚺ ♀		9:28 pm

2 FRIDAY

☽ ⚺ ♀	**12:28 am**	
☽ □ ♀	**6:28 am**	3:28 am
☽ △ ⚷	**1:49 pm**	10:49 am
☽ △ ♃	**2:21 pm**	11:21 am
☉ ⚺ ♆	**2:43 pm**	11:43 am
☽ ⚹ ⚳	**4:59 pm**	1:59 pm
☽ ⚻ ♇	**5:44 pm**	2:44 pm
☽ ⚻ ⚵	**10:55 pm**	7:55 pm

3 SATURDAY

☉ □ ♀	**4:02 am**	1:02 am
☽ ⚻ ☿	**6:54 am**	3:54 am
☽ □ ♅	**1:21 pm**	10:21 am

4 SUNDAY

☽ ⚻ ⚴	**5:27 am**	2:27 am
☽ ⚺ ♄	**8:13 am**	5:13 am
☽ ⚹ ♂	**12:14 pm**	9:14 am
☽ △ ♆	**1:00 pm**	10:00 am
☽ ⚹ ♀	**2:38 pm**	11:38 am
☽ ⚻ ☉	**5:13 pm**	2:13 pm
☽ △ ♀		11:33 pm

5 MONDAY

☽ △ ♀	**2:33 am**	
☽ ⚻ ⚷	**3:18 am**	12:18 am
☽ □ ♃	**3:21 am**	12:21 am
♂ ⚹ ♆	**4:05 am**	1:05 am
☽ ⚺ ⚳	**4:47 am**	1:47 am
☽ ☍ ♇	**6:53 am**	3:53 am
♃ △ ⚷	**7:48 am**	4:48 am
♀ ⚻ ♃	**10:09 am**	7:09 am
♀ ⚺ ⚷	**10:22 am**	7:22 am
☽ ☍ ⚵	**1:38 pm**	10:38 am
☽ ☍ ☿	**6:14 pm**	3:14 pm
♀ ⚻ ⚳	**9:05 pm**	6:05 pm
☽ △ ♅		11:14 pm

6 TUESDAY

☽ △ ♅	**2:14 am**	
♄ ☍ ⚴	**10:42 am**	7:42 am
☽ ☌ ♄	**8:03 pm**	5:03 pm
☽ ☍ ⚴	**8:33 pm**	5:33 pm
♀ ⚹ ♇	**9:44 pm**	6:44 pm
☽ ⚻ ♆		10:17 pm

7 WEDNESDAY

☽ ⚻ ♆	**1:17 am**	
☽ □ ♂	**3:33 am**	12:33 am
☽ □ ♀	**3:48 am**	12:48 am
⚷ ☍ ⚳	**9:49 am**	6:49 am
☽ ☍ ☉	**10:40 am**	7:40 am
♂ ☌ ♀	**11:33 am**	8:33 am
☽ ⚹ ♃	**3:00 pm**	12:00 pm
☽ ☌ ⚳	**3:19 pm**	12:19 pm
☽ ☍ ⚷	**3:28 pm**	12:28 pm
☽ ⚻ ♇	**6:39 pm**	3:39 pm
☽ ⚻ ♀	**8:54 pm**	5:54 pm
☽ ⚻ ⚵		11:42 pm

8 THURSDAY

☽ ⚻ ⚵	**2:42 am**	
☽ ⚻ ☿	**5:54 am**	2:54 am
♃ ⚹ ⚳	**8:48 am**	5:48 am
☽ ⚻ ♅	**1:25 pm**	10:25 am

9 FRIDAY

☽ ⚺ ♄	**6:03 am**	3:03 am
☉ ☍ ⚳	**8:52 am**	5:52 am
☽ ⚻ ⚴	**9:31 am**	6:31 am
☽ ☍ ♆	**11:39 am**	8:39 am
☉ △ ♃	**1:59 pm**	10:59 am
☽ △ ♀	**3:01 pm**	12:01 pm
☽ △ ♂	**4:39 pm**	1:39 pm
☽ ⚺ ⚳	**11:59 pm**	8:59 pm
☽ ⚺ ♃		9:39 pm
☽ ⚻ ☉		10:36 pm
☽ ⚻ ⚷		10:37 pm
☉ ☌ ⚷		10:44 pm

10 SATURDAY

☽ ⚺ ♃	**12:39 am**	
☽ ⚻ ☉	**1:36 am**	
☽ ⚻ ⚷	**1:37 am**	
☉ ☌ ⚷	**1:44 am**	
☽ △ ♇	**4:25 am**	1:25 am
☽ ☍ ♀	**12:31 pm**	9:31 am
☽ △ ⚵	**1:37 pm**	10:37 am
☽ △ ☿	**5:00 pm**	2:00 pm
☽ ☍ ♅	**10:35 pm**	7:35 pm

11 SUNDAY

♀ ⚹ ⚵	**4:03 am**	1:03 am
☉ ⚺ ♇	**1:44 pm**	10:44 am
☽ ⚹ ♄	**2:06 pm**	11:06 am
♆ ⚺ ⚴	**2:59 pm**	11:59 am
☽ ⚻ ♆	**8:00 pm**	5:00 pm
☽ △ ⚴	**8:12 pm**	5:12 pm
☽ ⚻ ♀		9:12 pm

12 MONDAY

☽ ⚻ ♀	**12:12 am**	
☽ ⚻ ♂	**3:27 am**	12:27 am
☽ ⚹ ⚳	**6:46 am**	3:46 am
☽ ☌ ♃	**8:18 am**	5:18 am
☽ △ ⚷	**9:44 am**	6:44 am
☽ □ ♇	**12:10 pm**	9:10 am
☽ △ ☉	**1:59 pm**	10:59 am
☽ □ ⚵	**10:22 pm**	7:22 pm
☽ ⚻ ♀		10:27 pm

13 TUESDAY

☽ ⚻ ♀	**1:27 am**	
☽ □ ☿	**3:01 am**	12:01 am
☽ ⚻ ♅	**5:46 am**	2:46 am
☽ □ ♄	**8:11 pm**	5:11 pm
☽ △ ♆		11:20 pm

14 WEDNESDAY

☽ △ ♆	**2:20 am**	
☽ □ ⚴	**4:36 am**	1:36 am
♂ □ ⚳	**7:03 am**	4:03 am
☽ ☍ ♀	**7:17 am**	4:17 am
☽ □ ⚳	**11:37 am**	8:37 am
☽ ☍ ♂	**11:55 am**	8:55 am
☽ ⚺ ♃	**1:54 pm**	10:54 am
☽ □ ⚷	**3:46 pm**	12:46 pm
☽ ⚹ ♇	**5:52 pm**	2:52 pm
☽ □ ☉	**11:46 pm**	8:46 pm
☿ ⚹ ♅		10:53 pm
♀ ☌ ♅		11:23 pm

15 THURSDAY

☿ ⚹ ♅	**1:53 am**	
♀ ☌ ♅	**2:23 am**	
☿ ⚹ ♀	**3:42 am**	12:42 am
☽ ⚹ ⚵	**4:52 am**	1:52 am
☽ △ ♅	**10:48 am**	7:48 am
☽ ⚹ ☿	**11:24 am**	8:24 am
☽ △ ♀	**11:35 am**	8:35 am
☽ △ ♄		9:10 pm

16 FRIDAY

☽ △ ♄	**12:10 am**	
♂ ⚻ ♃	**4:56 am**	1:56 am
☽ □ ♆	**6:29 am**	3:29 am
☽ ⚹ ⚴	**10:34 am**	7:34 am
☽ ⚻ ♀	**12:07 pm**	9:07 am
☽ △ ⚳	**2:26 pm**	11:26 am
☽ ⚹ ♃	**5:18 pm**	2:18 pm
☽ ⚻ ♂	**5:55 pm**	2:55 pm
☽ ⚹ ⚷	**7:34 pm**	4:34 pm
☽ ⚺ ♇	**9:22 pm**	6:22 pm

17 SATURDAY

☽ ⚹ ☉	**6:48 am**	3:48 am
☽ ⚺ ⚵	**9:02 am**	6:02 am
☽ □ ♅	**1:41 pm**	10:41 am
☽ ⚺ ☿	**5:45 pm**	2:45 pm
☽ □ ♀	**6:53 pm**	3:53 pm
☽ ⚻ ♄		11:07 pm

18 SUNDAY

☽ ⚻ ♄	**2:07 am**	
☽ ⚹ ♆	**8:35 am**	5:35 am
☽ ⚺ ⚴	**2:17 pm**	11:17 am
♂ □ ⚷	**2:26 pm**	11:26 am
☽ △ ♀	**2:54 pm**	11:54 am
☽ ⚻ ⚳	**3:22 pm**	12:22 pm
☽ □ ♃	**6:46 pm**	3:46 pm
☽ ⚺ ⚷	**9:26 pm**	6:26 pm
☽ △ ♂	**9:42 pm**	6:42 pm
☽ ☌ ♇	**10:58 pm**	7:58 pm

19 MONDAY

⚳ □ ♀	**4:44 am**	1:44 am
☉ ⚺ ⚵	**4:55 am**	1:55 am
☽ ☌ ⚵	**11:22 am**	8:22 am
☽ ⚺ ☉	**11:41 am**	8:41 am
⚳ ☍ ⚴	**11:50 am**	8:50 am
☽ ⚹ ♅	**2:56 pm**	11:56 am
☽ ☌ ☿	**10:36 pm**	7:36 pm
☽ ⚹ ♀		9:14 pm
☽ ☍ ♄		11:43 pm

20 TUESDAY

☽ ⚹ ♀	**12:14 am**	
☽ ☍ ♄	**2:43 am**	
♀ □ ⚴	**3:28 am**	12:28 am
♂ △ ♇	**5:02 am**	2:02 am
☽ ⚺ ♆	**9:29 am**	6:29 am
☽ ☍ ⚳	**3:22 pm**	12:22 pm
☽ □ ♀	**4:36 pm**	1:36 pm
☽ ☌ ⚴	**4:49 pm**	1:49 pm
☽ △ ♃	**7:19 pm**	4:19 pm
☽ ☌ ⚷	**10:27 pm**	7:27 pm
☽ ⚺ ♇	**11:46 pm**	8:46 pm
☽ □ ♂		9:34 pm

21 WEDNESDAY

☽ □ ♂	**12:34 am**	
♀ △ ♄	**5:04 am**	2:04 am
☉ ⚺ ♅	**1:15 pm**	10:15 am
☽ ⚺ ⚵	**1:15 pm**	10:15 am
☽ ⚺ ♅	**3:54 pm**	12:54 pm
☽ ☌ ☉	**4:05 pm**	1:05 pm
☿ ☍ ♄	**11:59 pm**	8:59 pm

22 THURSDAY

☽ ⚻ ♄	**3:28 am**	12:28 am
☽ ⚺ ☿	**3:48 am**	12:48 am
☽ ⚺ ♀	**5:38 am**	2:38 am
☽ ☌ ♆	**10:46 am**	7:46 am
☽ ⚻ ⚳	**3:58 pm**	12:58 pm
☽ ⚹ ♀	**7:04 pm**	4:04 pm
☽ ⚺ ⚴	**8:08 pm**	5:08 pm
☽ ⚻ ♃	**8:35 pm**	5:35 pm
☽ ⚺ ⚷		9:22 pm
☽ ⚹ ♇		10:32 pm

23 FRIDAY

☽ ⚺ ⚷	**12:22 am**	
☽ ⚹ ♇	**1:32 am**	
☽ ⚹ ♂	**4:33 am**	1:33 am
♃ △ ⚴	**7:19 am**	4:19 am
☽ ⚹ ⚵	**4:45 pm**	1:45 pm
☽ ☌ ♅	**6:28 pm**	3:28 pm
☽ ⚺ ☉	**10:29 pm**	7:29 pm

24 SATURDAY

☽ △ ♄	**6:15 am**	3:15 am
☽ ⚹ ☿	**11:58 am**	8:58 am
☽ ☌ ♀	**1:48 pm**	10:48 am
☽ ⚺ ♆	**2:25 pm**	11:25 am
☽ △ ⚳	**7:01 pm**	4:01 pm
♀ ⚺ ♆	**8:49 pm**	5:49 pm
☽ ⚺ ♀		9:23 pm
☽ ☍ ♃		9:30 pm
☽ ⚹ ⚴		11:25 pm

25 SUNDAY

☽ ⚺ ♀	**12:23 am**	
☽ ☍ ♃	**12:30 am**	
☽ ⚹ ⚴	**2:25 am**	
♃ ⚻ ♀	**4:11 am**	1:11 am
☽ ⚹ ⚷	**5:10 am**	2:10 am
☽ □ ♇	**6:09 am**	3:09 am
☽ ⚺ ♂	**11:56 am**	8:56 am
☿ ⚺ ♆	**2:27 pm**	11:27 am
☽ □ ⚵	**11:48 pm**	8:48 pm
☽ ⚺ ♅		9:28 pm

26 MONDAY

☽ ⚺ ♅	**12:28 am**	
☽ ⚹ ☉	**9:14 am**	6:14 am
☽ □ ♄	**12:38 pm**	9:38 am
♀ △ ⚳	**4:28 pm**	1:28 pm
☽ ⚹ ♆	**9:54 pm**	6:54 pm
☽ □ ☿		10:29 pm
☽ □ ⚳		10:48 pm
☽ ⚺ ♀		11:58 pm

27 TUESDAY

☽ □ ☿	**1:29 am**	
☽ □ ⚳	**1:48 am**	
☽ ⚺ ♀	**2:58 am**	
☿ ☍ ⚳	**4:14 am**	1:14 am
♅ ⚹ ⚵	**6:45 am**	3:45 am
☽ ⚻ ♃	**8:17 am**	5:17 am
☽ ☌ ♀	**10:00 am**	7:00 am
☽ □ ⚴	**1:11 pm**	10:11 am
☽ □ ⚷	**2:02 pm**	11:02 am
☽ △ ♇	**2:49 pm**	11:49 am
☽ ☌ ♂	**11:59 pm**	8:59 pm
☉ ⚻ ♄		10:25 pm

28 WEDNESDAY

☉ ⚻ ♄	**1:25 am**	
☽ ⚹ ♅	**10:33 am**	7:33 am
☽ △ ⚵	**11:13 am**	8:13 am
⚷ ☌ ⚴	**1:02 pm**	10:02 am
☽ ⚹ ♄	**10:56 pm**	7:56 pm
☽ □ ☉		10:03 pm

29 THURSDAY

☽ □ ☉	**1:03 am**	
♇ ⚺ ⚴	**5:10 am**	2:10 am
♀ ☍ ♃	**7:01 am**	4:01 am
☽ □ ♆	**9:14 am**	6:14 am
☽ ⚹ ⚳	**12:13 pm**	9:13 am
☿ △ ♃	**1:09 pm**	10:09 am
☽ △ ♃	**7:34 pm**	4:34 pm
☽ △ ☿	**8:27 pm**	5:27 pm
☽ ⚹ ♀	**9:04 pm**	6:04 pm
☽ ⚺ ♀	**11:30 pm**	8:30 pm
☽ △ ⚷		11:25 pm
☽ ⚻ ♇		11:54 pm

30 FRIDAY

☽ △ ⚷	**2:25 am**	
☽ ⚻ ♇	**2:54 am**	
☽ △ ⚴	**3:52 am**	12:52 am
☽ ⚺ ♂	**3:42 pm**	12:42 pm
☽ □ ♅	**11:27 pm**	8:27 pm
☽ ⚻ ⚵		10:34 pm

31 SATURDAY

☽ ⚻ ⚵	**1:34 am**	
♀ ⚺ ♀	**5:48 am**	2:48 am
☿ □ ♀	**5:52 am**	2:52 am
☿ ⚹ ♀	**6:08 am**	3:08 am
☽ ⚺ ♄	**11:28 am**	8:28 am
☽ △ ☉	**7:40 pm**	4:40 pm
☽ △ ♆	**10:24 pm**	7:24 pm
☽ ⚺ ⚳		9:19 pm
☿ ☌ ⚷		10:57 pm

Eastern time in bold type
Pacific time in medium type

JANUARY 2004

☽ Last Aspect day	EST / hr:mn / PST		asp	☽ Ingress sign	day	EST / hr:mn / PST	
12/31	**9:27 pm**	6:27 pm	△☿	♉	12/31		9:02 pm
12/31	**9:27 pm**	6:27 pm	△☿	♉	1	**12:02 am**	
2	**2:21 pm**	11:21 am	△♃	♊	3	**12:58 pm**	9:58 am
5	**6:14 pm**	3:14 pm	☍☿	♋	5		10:38 pm
5	**6:14 pm**	3:14 pm	☍☿	♋	6	**1:38 am**	
7	**3:00 pm**	12:00 pm	⚹♃	♌	8	**12:38 pm**	9:38 am
10	**5:00 pm**	2:00 pm	△☿	♍	10	**9:37 pm**	6:37 pm
13	**3:01 am**	12:01 am	□☿	♎	13	**4:38 am**	1:38 am
14	**11:46 pm**	8:46 pm	□☉	♏	15	**9:33 am**	6:33 am
17	**6:48 am**	3:48 am	⚹☉	♐	17	**12:18 pm**	9:18 am
18	**10:58 pm**	7:58 pm	☌♇	♑	19	**1:24 pm**	10:24 am
20		9:34 pm	□♂	♒	21	**2:11 pm**	11:11 am
21	**12:34 am**		□♂	♒	21	**2:11 pm**	11:11 am
23	**4:33 am**	1:33 am	⚹♂	♓	23	**4:29 pm**	1:29 pm
25	**6:09 am**	3:09 am	□♇	♈	25	**10:06 pm**	7:06 pm
27	**11:59 pm**	8:59 pm	☌♂	♉	28	**7:46 am**	4:46 am
29	**9:04 pm**	6:04 pm	⚹♀	♊	30	**8:18 pm**	5:18 pm

☽ Phases & Eclipses

phase	day	EST / hr:mn / PST	
Full Moon	7	**10:40 am**	7:40 am
4th Quarter	14	**11:46 pm**	8:46 pm
New Moon	21	**4:05 pm**	1:05 pm
2nd Quarter	28		10:03 pm
2nd Quarter	29	**1:03 am**	

Planet Ingress

		day	EST / hr:mn / PST	
☿	♑	14	**6:02 am**	3:02 am
♀	♓	14	**12:16 pm**	9:16 am
☉	♒	20	**12:42 pm**	9:42 am
⚵	♑	23	**5:32 am**	2:32 am

Planetary Motion

		day	EST / hr:mn / PST	
♃	℞	3	**6:57 pm**	3:57 pm
☿	D	6	**8:44 am**	5:44 am

DATE		SID.TIME	SUN	MOON	NODE	MERCURY	VENUS	MARS	JUPITER	SATURN	URANUS	NEPTUNE	PLUTO	CERES	PALLAS	JUNO	VESTA	CHIRON
1	Th	6:39:59	09 ♑ 53 30	27 ♈ 30	19 ♉ 17	28 ♐ ℞ 49	13 ♒ 13	09 ♈ 10	18 ♍ 53	09 ♋ ℞ 45	00 ♓ 04	11 ♒ 41	20 ♐ 30	20 ♋ ℞ 38	11 ♈ 51	22 ♐ 21	06 ♑ 15	18 ♑ 28
2	F	6:43:55	10 54 39	09 ♉ 23	19 ℞ 18	27 58	14 27	09 46	18 54	09 40	00 06	11 43	20 32	20 24	12 02	22 42	06 47	18 34
3	Sa	6:47:52	11 55 48	21 11	19 19	27 18	15 40	10 23	18 ℞ 54	09 35	00 09	11 45	20 34	20 10	12 14	23 03	07 19	18 40
4	Su	6:51:49	12 56 56	02 ♊ 58	19 17	26 48	16 54	11 00	18 54	09 30	00 12	11 47	20 36	19 57	12 27	23 24	07 52	18 45
5	M	6:55:45	13 58 05	14 46	19 14	26 28	18 08	11 36	18 54	09 25	00 14	11 49	20 38	19 43	12 39	23 44	08 24	18 51
6	T	6:59:42	14 59 13	26 41	19 08	26 D 18	19 21	12 13	18 54	09 20	00 17	11 51	20 41	19 29	12 52	24 05	08 56	18 57
7	W	7:03:38	16 00 21	08 ♋ 43	18 59	26 17	20 35	12 50	18 53	09 16	00 20	11 54	20 43	19 15	13 06	24 26	09 28	19 02
8	Th	7:07:35	17 01 29	20 56	18 49	26 25	21 48	13 27	18 53	09 11	00 22	11 56	20 45	19 00	13 20	24 46	10 01	19 08
9	F	7:11:31	18 02 37	03 ♌ 18	18 37	26 41	23 01	14 04	18 52	09 06	00 25	11 58	20 47	18 46	13 34	25 07	10 33	19 14
10	Sa	7:15:28	19 03 45	15 51	18 26	27 04	24 15	14 41	18 51	09 01	00 28	12 00	20 49	18 32	13 48	25 27	11 05	19 19
11	Su	7:19:24	20 04 52	28 36	18 15	27 34	25 28	15 18	18 49	08 56	00 31	12 02	20 51	18 18	14 03	25 48	11 37	19 25
12	M	7:23:21	21 06 00	11 ♍ 32	18 07	28 10	26 41	15 55	18 48	08 51	00 33	12 04	20 53	18 03	14 18	26 08	12 09	19 31
13	T	7:27:18	22 07 07	24 40	18 01	28 51	27 54	16 32	18 46	08 47	00 36	12 06	20 55	17 49	14 34	26 29	12 41	19 36
14	W	7:31:14	23 08 14	08 ♎ 02	17 57	29 37	29 07	17 09	18 45	08 42	00 39	12 08	20 57	17 35	14 49	26 49	13 13	19 42
15	Th	7:35:11	24 09 21	21 38	17 D 56	00 ♑ 28	00 ♓ 21	17 47	18 43	08 37	00 42	12 11	20 59	17 21	15 05	27 10	13 45	19 48
16	F	7:39:07	25 10 28	05 ♏ 30	17 ℞ 56	01 22	01 34	18 24	18 40	08 32	00 45	12 13	21 01	17 07	15 22	27 30	14 18	19 53
17	Sa	7:43:04	26 11 35	19 39	17 57	02 20	02 46	19 01	18 38	08 28	00 48	12 15	21 03	16 53	15 39	27 50	14 50	19 59
18	Su	7:47:00	27 12 42	04 ♐ 03	17 56	03 21	03 59	19 39	18 35	08 23	00 51	12 17	21 05	16 39	15 56	28 10	15 22	20 05
19	M	7:50:57	28 13 49	18 41	17 53	04 24	05 12	20 16	18 33	08 19	00 54	12 19	21 07	16 26	16 13	28 31	15 54	20 10
20	T	7:54:53	29 14 55	03 ♑ 27	17 46	05 31	06 25	20 54	18 30	08 14	00 57	12 22	21 09	16 12	16 31	28 51	16 26	20 16
21	W	7:58:50	00 ♒ 16 01	18 15	17 37	06 39	07 38	21 31	18 26	08 10	01 00	12 24	21 11	15 59	16 49	29 11	16 58	20 21
22	Th	8:02:47	01 17 07	02 ♒ 56	17 26	07 50	08 50	22 09	18 23	08 06	01 03	12 26	21 12	15 46	17 07	29 31	17 29	20 27
23	F	8:06:43	02 18 11	17 23	17 14	09 02	10 03	22 47	18 20	08 01	01 06	12 28	21 14	15 33	17 25	29 51	18 01	20 33
24	Sa	8:10:40	03 19 15	01 ♓ 28	17 03	10 16	11 15	23 25	18 16	07 57	01 09	12 31	21 16	15 20	17 44	00 ♑ 11	18 33	20 38
25	Su	8:14:36	04 20 18	15 07	16 53	11 32	12 28	24 02	18 12	07 53	01 13	12 33	21 18	15 07	18 03	00 31	19 05	20 44
26	M	8:18:33	05 21 20	28 20	16 45	12 50	13 40	24 40	18 08	07 49	01 16	12 35	21 20	14 55	18 22	00 51	19 37	20 49
27	T	8:22:29	06 22 20	11 ♈ 07	16 40	14 08	14 52	25 18	18 04	07 45	01 19	12 38	21 21	14 43	18 42	01 11	20 09	20 55
28	W	8:26:26	07 23 20	23 31	16 38	15 28	16 04	25 56	17 59	07 41	01 22	12 40	21 23	14 32	19 02	01 31	20 40	21 00
29	Th	8:30:22	08 24 18	05 ♉ 38	16 37	16 49	17 16	26 34	17 55	07 37	01 25	12 42	21 25	14 20	19 22	01 50	21 12	21 06
30	F	8:34:19	09 25 16	17 33	16 37	18 11	18 28	27 12	17 50	07 33	01 29	12 44	21 27	14 09	19 43	02 10	21 44	21 11
31	Sa	8:38:16	10 26 12	29 22	16 37	19 35	19 40	27 50	17 45	07 29	01 32	12 47	21 28	13 59	20 03	02 30	22 16	21 17

EPHEMERIS CALCULATED FOR 12 MIDNIGHT GREENWICH MEAN TIME. ALL OTHER DATA AND FACING ASPECTARIAN PAGE IN **EASTERN TIME (BOLD)** AND PACIFIC TIME (REGULAR).

FEBRUARY 2004

1 SUNDAY

☽ ⚺ ⚳	**12:19 am**	
☿ ☌ ⚷	**1:57 am**	
☿ ⚺ ♇	**3:56 am**	12:56 am
♀ ⚹ ⚷	**5:48 am**	2:48 am
♀ □ ♇	**7:57 am**	4:57 am
☽ □ ♃	**8:08 am**	5:08 am
☽ ⚹ ♀	**2:20 pm**	11:20 am
☽ ⚻ ⚷	**3:52 pm**	12:52 pm
☽ ☍ ♇	**4:01 pm**	1:01 pm
☽ □ ♀	**4:54 pm**	1:54 pm
☽ ⚻ ☿	**5:38 pm**	2:38 pm
☽ ⚻ ⚶	**7:39 pm**	4:39 pm

2 MONDAY

☉ ☌ ♆	**4:29 am**	1:29 am
☽ ⚹ ♂	**7:56 am**	4:56 am
☽ △ ♅	**12:25 pm**	9:25 am
☽ ☍ ⚵	**3:54 pm**	12:54 pm
☉ ⚻ ⚳	**6:52 pm**	3:52 pm
☿ ☌ ⚶	**7:01 pm**	4:01 pm
♇ ⚺ ⚷	**9:38 pm**	6:38 pm
☽ ☌ ♄	**11:35 pm**	8:35 pm

3 TUESDAY

☽ ⚻ ♆	**10:40 am**	7:40 am
☽ ☌ ⚳	**11:33 am**	8:33 am
☽ ⚻ ☉	**1:18 pm**	10:18 am
♀ ⚹ ⚶	**4:01 pm**	1:01 pm
☽ ⚹ ♃	**7:28 pm**	4:28 pm
♇ △ ♀		11:29 pm

4 WEDNESDAY

♇ △ ♀	**2:29 am**	
☽ ⚻ ♇	**3:37 am**	12:37 am
☽ □ ♀	**3:38 am**	12:38 am
☽ ☍ ⚷	**3:46 am**	12:46 am
⚷ □ ♀	**9:03 am**	6:03 am
☽ ☍ ⚶	**9:36 am**	6:36 am
☽ △ ♀	**10:39 am**	7:39 am
☽ ☍ ☿	**12:52 pm**	9:52 am
☽ □ ♂	**9:54 pm**	6:54 pm
☽ ⚻ ♅	**11:19 pm**	8:19 pm

5 THURSDAY

☽ ⚻ ⚵	**3:55 am**	12:55 am
☽ ⚺ ♄	**9:28 am**	6:28 am
☽ ☍ ♆	**8:30 pm**	5:30 pm
☽ ⚺ ⚳	**8:31 pm**	5:31 pm
♆ ⚻ ⚳	**10:08 pm**	7:08 pm

6 FRIDAY

☽ ☍ ☉	**3:47 am**	12:47 am
☽ ⚺ ♃	**4:18 am**	1:18 am
♂ ⚹ ♅	**4:22 am**	1:22 am
☉ ⚻ ♃	**9:54 am**	6:54 am
☽ △ ♇	**12:38 pm**	9:38 am
☽ ⚻ ⚷	**1:03 pm**	10:03 am
☽ △ ♀	**2:13 pm**	11:13 am
☽ ⚻ ⚶	**8:38 pm**	5:38 pm
☽ ⚻ ♀		9:56 pm

7 SATURDAY

☽ ⚻ ♀	**12:56 am**	
☽ ⚻ ☿	**4:39 am**	1:39 am
☽ ☍ ♅	**7:37 am**	4:37 am
☽ △ ♂	**8:53 am**	5:53 am
☽ △ ⚵	**1:11 pm**	10:11 am
☽ ⚹ ♄	**4:55 pm**	1:55 pm

8 SUNDAY

☽ ⚹ ⚳	**3:13 am**	12:13 am
☽ ⚻ ♆	**3:54 am**	12:54 am
☿ ⚺ ♅	**7:11 am**	4:11 am
☽ ☌ ♃	**10:51 am**	7:51 am
☽ ⚻ ☉	**3:16 pm**	12:16 pm
☽ □ ♇	**7:23 pm**	4:23 pm
☽ △ ⚷	**8:03 pm**	5:03 pm
☽ ⚻ ♀	**10:25 pm**	7:25 pm

9 MONDAY

☽ △ ⚶	**5:14 am**	2:14 am
☽ ☍ ♀	**12:24 pm**	9:24 am
☽ ⚻ ♅	**1:54 pm**	10:54 am
☿ □ ♂	**4:08 pm**	1:08 pm
☽ ⚻ ♂	**5:35 pm**	2:35 pm
☽ △ ☿	**5:41 pm**	2:41 pm
☽ □ ⚵	**8:22 pm**	5:22 pm
☽ □ ♄	**10:30 pm**	7:30 pm

10 TUESDAY

♀ ⚺ ♅	**6:26 am**	3:26 am
☽ □ ⚳	**8:16 am**	5:16 am
☽ △ ♆	**9:32 am**	6:32 am
☽ ⚺ ♃	**3:45 pm**	12:45 pm
☿ ⚺ ⚵	**10:28 pm**	7:28 pm
☉ ⚹ ♇	**10:56 pm**	7:56 pm
☽ ⚹ ♇		9:35 pm
☽ △ ☉		9:42 pm
☽ □ ⚷		10:28 pm

11 WEDNESDAY

☽ ⚹ ♇	**12:35 am**	
☽ △ ☉	**12:42 am**	
☽ □ ⚷	**1:28 am**	
☽ ☍ ♀	**4:58 am**	1:58 am
☿ ⚻ ♄	**10:40 am**	7:40 am
☉ ⚺ ⚷	**12:00 pm**	9:00 am
☽ □ ⚶	**12:10 pm**	9:10 am
☽ △ ♅	**6:47 pm**	3:47 pm
☽ ⚻ ♀	**10:00 pm**	7:00 pm
☽ ☍ ♂		9:42 pm
☽ ⚹ ⚵		11:07 pm
☽ △ ♄		11:49 pm

12 THURSDAY

☽ ☍ ♂	**12:42 am**	
☽ ⚹ ⚵	**2:07 am**	
☽ △ ♄	**2:49 am**	
☽ □ ☿	**4:56 am**	1:56 am
☽ △ ⚳	**12:09 pm**	9:09 am
☽ □ ♆	**1:55 pm**	10:55 am
☽ ⚹ ♃	**7:27 pm**	4:27 pm

13 FRIDAY

☽ ⚺ ♇	**4:35 am**	1:35 am
♄ ☍ ⚵	**5:25 am**	2:25 am
☽ ⚹ ⚷	**5:41 am**	2:41 am
☽ □ ☉	**8:39 am**	5:39 am
☽ ⚻ ♀	**10:18 am**	7:18 am
☽ ⚹ ⚶	**5:50 pm**	2:50 pm
♂ ⚹ ♄	**7:50 pm**	4:50 pm
☽ □ ♅	**10:33 pm**	7:33 pm

14 SATURDAY

♀ □ ♄	**4:58 am**	1:58 am
☽ ⚻ ♄	**6:02 am**	3:02 am
☽ △ ♀	**6:08 am**	3:08 am
☽ ⚻ ♂	**6:33 am**	3:33 am
☽ ⚺ ⚵	**6:40 am**	3:40 am
♂ △ ⚵	**11:17 am**	8:17 am
♀ □ ⚵	**2:36 pm**	11:36 am
☽ ⚹ ☿	**2:46 pm**	11:46 am
☽ ⚻ ⚳	**3:02 pm**	12:02 pm
♀ ⚺ ♂	**4:39 pm**	1:39 pm
☿ ⚻ ⚳	**5:04 pm**	2:04 pm
☽ ⚹ ♆	**5:12 pm**	2:12 pm
☉ ⚹ ♀	**9:16 pm**	6:16 pm
☽ □ ♃	**10:06 pm**	7:06 pm

15 SUNDAY

☽ ☌ ♇	**7:32 am**	4:32 am
☽ ⚺ ⚷	**8:51 am**	5:51 am
☿ ☌ ♆	**12:43 pm**	9:43 am
☽ △ ♀	**2:33 pm**	11:33 am
☽ ⚹ ☉	**3:20 pm**	12:20 pm
☽ ⚺ ⚶	**10:24 pm**	7:24 pm
☽ ⚹ ♅		10:20 pm

16 MONDAY

☽ ⚹ ♅	**1:20 am**	
☽ ☍ ♄	**8:23 am**	5:23 am
☽ ☌ ⚵	**10:15 am**	7:15 am
☽ △ ♂	**11:23 am**	8:23 am
☽ □ ♀	**1:05 pm**	10:05 am
☽ ☍ ⚳	**5:09 pm**	2:09 pm
☽ ⚺ ♆	**7:41 pm**	4:41 pm
☽ ⚺ ☿	**11:35 pm**	8:35 pm
☽ △ ♃		9:00 pm

17 TUESDAY

☽ △ ♃	**12:00 am**	
☿ ⚻ ♃	**3:00 am**	12:00 am
☽ ⚺ ♇	**9:51 am**	6:51 am
☽ ☌ ⚷	**11:23 am**	8:23 am
☽ □ ♀	**6:15 pm**	3:15 pm
☽ ⚺ ☉	**9:22 pm**	6:22 pm
☽ ☌ ⚶		11:30 pm

18 WEDNESDAY

☽ ☌ ⚶	**2:30 am**	
☽ ⚺ ♅	**3:46 am**	12:46 am
☽ ⚻ ♄	**10:32 am**	7:32 am
♀ □ ⚳	**1:06 pm**	10:06 am
☽ ⚺ ⚵	**1:38 pm**	10:38 am
☽ □ ♂	**4:02 pm**	1:02 pm
☽ ⚻ ⚳	**7:18 pm**	4:18 pm
☽ ⚹ ♀	**7:53 pm**	4:53 pm
☽ ☌ ♆	**10:12 pm**	7:12 pm
☽ ⚻ ♃		11:01 pm

19 THURSDAY

☽ ⚻ ♃	**2:01 am**	
☽ ☌ ☿	**8:45 am**	5:45 am
☽ ⚹ ♇	**12:34 pm**	9:34 am
☽ ⚺ ⚷	**2:21 pm**	11:21 am
♅ ⚺ ⚶	**5:46 pm**	2:46 pm
☽ ⚹ ♀	**10:39 pm**	7:39 pm
♀ ⚹ ♆		10:09 pm

20 FRIDAY

♀ ⚹ ♆	**1:09 am**	
☽ ☌ ☉	**4:18 am**	1:18 am
☽ ☌ ♅	**7:07 am**	4:07 am
☽ ⚺ ⚶	**7:34 am**	4:34 am
☽ △ ♄	**1:47 pm**	10:47 am
☿ ⚹ ♇	**4:42 pm**	1:42 pm
☽ ⚹ ⚵	**6:17 pm**	3:17 pm
☽ ⚹ ♂	**10:10 pm**	7:10 pm
☽ △ ⚳	**10:52 pm**	7:52 pm
☽ ⚺ ♆		11:11 pm

21 SATURDAY

☽ ⚺ ♆	**2:11 am**	
☽ ⚺ ♀	**4:27 am**	1:27 am
☽ ☍ ♃	**5:34 am**	2:34 am
☿ ⚺ ⚷	**9:02 am**	6:02 am
♂ ⚹ ⚳	**12:32 pm**	9:32 am
♀ ⚻ ♃	**4:19 pm**	1:19 pm
☽ □ ♇	**5:10 pm**	2:10 pm
☽ ⚹ ⚷	**7:17 pm**	4:17 pm
☽ ⚺ ☿	**8:44 pm**	5:44 pm
☉ ☌ ♅	**9:07 pm**	6:07 pm

22 SUNDAY

☽ ⚺ ♀	**5:31 am**	2:31 am
☽ ⚺ ♅	**12:56 pm**	9:56 am
☽ ⚺ ☉	**2:11 pm**	11:11 am
☽ ⚹ ⚶	**3:23 pm**	12:23 pm
☽ □ ♄	**7:40 pm**	4:40 pm
☽ □ ⚵		10:51 pm

23 MONDAY

☽ □ ⚵	**1:51 am**	
☽ □ ⚳	**5:20 am**	2:20 am
☽ ⚺ ♂	**7:34 am**	4:34 am
☽ ⚹ ♆	**9:08 am**	6:08 am
☽ ⚻ ♃	**12:02 pm**	9:02 am
☽ ☌ ♀	**4:53 pm**	1:53 pm
☉ ⚺ ⚶	**8:24 pm**	5:24 pm
☽ △ ♇		10:02 pm

24 TUESDAY

☽ △ ♇	**1:02 am**	
☽ □ ⚷	**3:34 am**	12:34 am
☽ ⚹ ☿	**1:55 pm**	10:55 am
☽ ☌ ♀	**4:10 pm**	1:10 pm
♂ □ ♆	**4:32 pm**	1:32 pm
☽ ⚹ ♅	**10:18 pm**	7:18 pm

25 WEDNESDAY

☽ □ ⚶	**3:08 am**	12:08 am
☽ ⚹ ☉	**4:30 am**	1:30 am
☽ ⚹ ♄	**5:04 am**	2:04 am
☿ ⚹ ♀	**10:04 am**	7:04 am
☉ △ ♄	**11:15 am**	8:15 am
☽ △ ⚵	**1:11 pm**	10:11 am
☽ ⚹ ⚳	**3:24 pm**	12:24 pm
☽ □ ♆	**7:39 pm**	4:39 pm
☽ ☌ ♂	**9:05 pm**	6:05 pm
☽ △ ♃	**9:55 pm**	6:55 pm

26 THURSDAY

☽ ⚺ ♀	**9:52 am**	6:52 am
♂ △ ♃	**10:12 am**	7:12 am
☽ ⚻ ♇	**12:17 pm**	9:17 am
☽ △ ⚷	**3:15 pm**	12:15 pm
♄ ⚻ ⚶	**11:44 pm**	8:44 pm
☿ ☌ ♅		10:21 pm

27 FRIDAY

☿ ☌ ♅	**1:21 am**	
☽ ⚺ ♀	**6:20 am**	3:20 am
☽ □ ♅	**10:40 am**	7:40 am
♀ △ ♇	**11:34 am**	8:34 am
☽ □ ☿	**12:18 pm**	9:18 am
☽ ⚺ ♄	**5:17 pm**	2:17 pm
☽ △ ⚶	**6:06 pm**	3:06 pm
☽ □ ☉	**10:24 pm**	7:24 pm

28 SATURDAY

☽ ⚻ ⚵	**3:14 am**	12:14 am
☽ ⚺ ⚳	**4:02 am**	1:02 am
☽ △ ♆	**8:29 am**	5:29 am
☽ □ ♃	**9:57 am**	6:57 am
☽ ⚺ ♂	**1:15 pm**	10:15 am
☿ △ ♄	**8:23 pm**	5:23 pm
♀ □ ⚷	**9:53 pm**	6:53 pm
☽ ☍ ♇		10:13 pm

29 SUNDAY

☽ ☍ ♇	**1:13 am**	
☽ ⚻ ⚷	**4:29 am**	1:29 am
☽ ⚹ ♀	**5:08 am**	2:08 am
☿ ⚺ ⚶	**1:56 pm**	10:56 am
⚳ ☍ ⚵	**2:37 pm**	11:37 am
☽ ⚹ ♀	**9:30 pm**	6:30 pm
☽ △ ♅	**11:44 pm**	8:44 pm

Eastern time in bold type
Pacific time in medium type

FEBRUARY 2004

☽ Last Aspect day	EST / hr:mn / PST	asp	☽ Ingress sign day	EST / hr:mn / PST
2	**7:56 am** 4:56 am	✶♂	♋ 2	**9:03 am** 6:03 am
4	**12:52 pm** 9:52 am	☍☿	♌ 4	**7:50 pm** 4:50 pm
6	**12:38 pm** 9:38 am	△♇	♍ 7	**4:03 am** 1:03 am
8	**7:23 pm** 4:23 pm	□♇	♎ 9	**10:12 am** 7:12 am
10	9:42 pm	△⊙	♏ 11	**2:58 pm** 11:58 am
11	**12:42 am**	△⊙	♏ 11	**2:58 pm** 11:58 am
13	**8:39 am** 5:39 am	□⊙	♐ 13	**6:35 pm** 3:35 pm
15	**3:20 pm** 12:20 pm	✶⊙	♑ 15	**9:14 pm** 6:14 pm
16	9:00 pm	△♃	♒ 17	**11:27 pm** 8:27 pm
17	**12:00 am**	△♃	♒ 17	**11:27 pm** 8:27 pm

☽ Last Aspect day	EST / hr:mn / PST	asp	☽ Ingress sign day	EST / hr:mn / PST
19	**12:34 pm** 9:34 am	✶♇	♓ 19	11:27 pm
19	**12:34 pm** 9:34 am	✶♇	♓ 20	**2:27 am**
21	**5:10 pm** 2:10 pm	□♇	♈ 22	**7:45 am** 4:45 am
24	**1:55 pm** 10:55 am	✶☿	♉ 24	**4:30 pm** 1:30 pm
25	**9:55 pm** 6:55 pm	△♃	♊ 27	**4:22 am** 1:22 am
29	**5:08 am** 2:08 am	✶♀	♋ 29	**5:12 pm** 2:12 pm

☽ Phases & Eclipses phase	day	EST / hr:mn / PST
Full Moon	6	**3:47 am** 12:47 am
4th Quarter	13	**8:39 am** 5:39 am
New Moon	20	**4:18 am** 1:18 am
2nd Quarter	27	**10:24 pm** 7:24 pm

Planet Ingress	day	EST / hr:mn / PST
♂ ♉	3	**5:04 am** 2:04 am
☿ ♒	6	**11:20 pm** 8:20 pm
♀ ♈	8	**11:20 am** 8:20 am
⚶ ♒	14	**2:07 pm** 11:07 am
⊙ ♓	18	11:50 pm
⊙ ♓	19	**2:50 am**
⚴ ♉	24	10:33 pm
⚴ ♉	25	**1:33 am**
☿ ♓	25	**7:58 am** 4:58 am

Planetary Motion	day	EST / hr:mn / PST
⚳ D	25	**1:38 pm** 10:38 am

DATE		SID.TIME	SUN	MOON	NODE	MERCURY	VENUS	MARS	JUPITER	SATURN	URANUS	NEPTUNE	PLUTO	CERES	PALLAS	JUNO	VESTA	CHIRON
1	Su	8:42:12	11 ♒ 27 07	11 ♊ 09	16 ♉℞ 35	20 ♑ 59	20 ♓ 52	28 ♈ 28	17 ♍℞ 40	07 ♋℞ 26	01 ♓ 35	12 ♒ 49	21 ♐ 30	13 ♋℞ 48	20 ♈ 24	02 ♑ 49	22 ♑ 47	21 ♑ 22
2	M	8:46:09	12 28 01	23 00	16 30	22 24	22 04	29 06	17 35	07 22	01 39	12 51	21 32	13 38	20 45	03 09	23 19	21 27
3	T	8:50:05	13 28 53	04 ♋ 59	16 23	23 50	23 15	29 44	17 30	07 18	01 42	12 53	21 33	13 29	21 07	03 28	23 50	21 33
4	W	8:54:02	14 29 45	17 10	16 13	25 17	24 27	00 ♉ 22	17 24	07 15	01 45	12 56	21 35	13 19	21 28	03 48	24 22	21 38
5	Th	8:57:58	15 30 35	29 34	16 00	26 45	25 38	01 00	17 19	07 12	01 49	12 58	21 36	13 10	21 50	04 07	24 53	21 43
6	F	9:01:55	16 31 23	12 ♌ 13	15 46	28 14	26 50	01 38	17 13	07 08	01 52	13 00	21 38	13 02	22 12	04 26	25 25	21 49
7	Sa	9:05:51	17 32 11	25 05	15 32	29 44	28 01	02 17	17 07	07 05	01 55	13 03	21 39	12 53	22 35	04 45	25 56	21 54
8	Su	9:09:48	18 32 57	08 ♍ 11	15 19	01 ♒ 14	29 12	02 55	17 01	07 02	01 59	13 05	21 41	12 46	22 57	05 04	26 28	21 59
9	M	9:13:45	19 33 42	21 29	15 09	02 45	00 ♈ 23	03 33	16 55	06 59	02 02	13 07	21 42	12 38	23 20	05 23	26 59	22 04
10	T	9:17:41	20 34 26	04 ♎ 57	15 01	04 18	01 33	04 11	16 48	06 56	02 06	13 09	21 44	12 31	23 43	05 42	27 30	22 09
11	W	9:21:38	21 35 09	18 34	14 56	05 51	02 44	04 49	16 42	06 53	02 09	13 12	21 45	12 25	24 06	06 01	28 02	22 15
12	Th	9:25:34	22 35 51	02 ♏ 20	14 D 54	07 24	03 55	05 28	16 35	06 51	02 12	13 14	21 46	12 19	24 30	06 20	28 33	22 20
13	F	9:29:31	23 36 32	16 13	14 ℞ 54	08 59	05 05	06 06	16 29	06 48	02 16	13 16	21 48	12 13	24 53	06 39	29 04	22 25
14	Sa	9:33:27	24 37 12	00 ♐ 15	14 54	10 34	06 15	06 44	16 22	06 46	02 19	13 18	21 49	12 07	25 17	06 58	29 35	22 30
15	Su	9:37:24	25 37 51	14 24	14 53	12 11	07 26	07 23	16 15	06 43	02 23	13 21	21 50	12 03	25 41	07 16	00 ♒ 06	22 35
16	M	9:41:20	26 38 29	28 40	14 50	13 48	08 36	08 01	16 08	06 41	02 26	13 23	21 51	11 58	26 06	07 35	00 37	22 40
17	T	9:45:17	27 39 05	13 ♑ 00	14 44	15 26	09 46	08 39	16 01	06 39	02 30	13 25	21 53	11 54	26 30	07 53	01 08	22 45
18	W	9:49:14	28 39 40	27 21	14 35	17 05	10 55	09 18	15 54	06 37	02 33	13 27	21 54	11 50	26 55	08 11	01 39	22 49
19	Th	9:53:10	29 40 14	11 ♒ 36	14 24	18 45	12 05	09 56	15 47	06 35	02 36	13 30	21 55	11 47	27 20	08 30	02 10	22 54
20	F	9:57:07	00 ♓ 40 47	25 41	14 12	20 25	13 15	10 34	15 39	06 33	02 40	13 32	21 56	11 44	27 45	08 48	02 41	22 59
21	Sa	10:01:03	01 41 18	09 ♓ 30	14 00	22 07	14 24	11 13	15 32	06 31	02 43	13 34	21 57	11 42	28 10	09 06	03 12	23 04
22	Su	10:05:00	02 41 47	22 59	13 50	23 49	15 33	11 51	15 24	06 29	02 47	13 36	21 58	11 40	28 35	09 24	03 43	23 09
23	M	10:08:56	03 42 14	06 ♈ 06	13 41	25 33	16 42	12 29	15 17	06 28	02 50	13 38	21 59	11 39	29 01	09 42	04 14	23 13
24	T	10:12:53	04 42 40	18 51	13 36	27 17	17 51	13 08	15 09	06 26	02 54	13 40	22 00	11 38	29 27	09 59	04 44	23 18
25	W	10:16:49	05 43 04	01 ♉ 17	13 33	29 03	19 00	13 46	15 02	06 25	02 57	13 43	22 01	11 D 37	29 53	10 17	05 15	23 22
26	Th	10:20:46	06 43 25	13 26	13 D 32	00 ♓ 49	20 08	14 25	14 54	06 24	03 01	13 45	22 02	11 37	00 ♉ 19	10 35	05 46	23 27
27	F	10:24:43	07 43 45	25 22	13 33	02 36	21 16	15 03	14 46	06 22	03 04	13 47	22 03	11 37	00 45	10 52	06 16	23 31
28	Sa	10:28:39	08 44 04	07 ♊ 12	13 ℞ 33	04 25	22 25	15 42	14 39	06 21	03 08	13 49	22 04	11 38	01 12	11 09	06 47	23 36
29	Su	10:32:36	09 44 20	19 01	13 33	06 14	23 33	16 20	14 31	06 20	03 11	13 51	22 05	11 39	01 39	11 27	07 17	23 40

EPHEMERIS CALCULATED FOR 12 MIDNIGHT GREENWICH MEAN TIME. ALL OTHER DATA AND FACING ASPECTARIAN PAGE IN **EASTERN TIME (BOLD)** AND PACIFIC TIME (REGULAR).

MARCH 2004

1 MONDAY
☽ ☌ ♄ **5:52 am** 2:52 am
☽ ⚻ ⚶ **9:24 am** 6:24 am
☽ △ ☿ **11:58 am** 8:58 am
☽ △ ☉ **4:27 pm** 1:27 pm
☽ ☌ ⚳ **4:36 pm** 1:36 pm
☽ ☍ ⚵ **5:09 pm** 2:09 pm
☉ △ ⚳ **6:17 pm** 3:17 pm
☽ ⚻ ♆ **8:58 pm** 5:58 pm
☽ ✶ ♃ **9:35 pm** 6:35 pm

2 TUESDAY
☉ ✶ ⚵ **3:55 am** 12:55 am
☽ ✶ ♂ **4:45 am** 1:45 am
☽ ⚻ ♇ **1:02 pm** 10:02 am
☽ ☍ ⚷ **4:28 pm** 1:28 pm
☿ △ ⚳ **6:26 pm** 3:26 pm
☽ ☐ ♀ **10:42 pm** 7:42 pm
☿ ✶ ⚵ 11:25 pm

3 WEDNESDAY
☿ ✶ ⚵ **2:25 am**
☽ ☐ ⚴ **10:36 am** 7:36 am
☽ ⚻ ♅ **10:47 am** 7:47 am
☽ ⚺ ♄ **4:19 pm** 1:19 pm
♅ ✶ ⚴ **4:32 pm** 1:32 pm
♃ ⚻ ♆ **7:12 pm** 4:12 pm
☉ ☌ ☿ **8:43 pm** 5:43 pm
☽ ☍ ⚶ **10:08 pm** 7:08 pm
☿ ☍ ♃ **10:36 pm** 7:36 pm
☿ ⚺ ♆ **10:54 pm** 7:54 pm
☉ ☍ ♃ 9:05 pm
☉ ⚺ ♆ 9:55 pm
☽ ⚺ ⚳ 11:45 pm

4 THURSDAY
☉ ☍ ♃ **12:05 am**
☉ ⚺ ♆ **12:55 am**
☽ ⚺ ⚳ **2:45 am**
☽ ⚻ ⚵ **4:22 am** 1:22 am
☽ ⚺ ♃ **6:41 am** 3:41 am
☽ ☍ ♆ **6:50 am** 3:50 am
☽ ⚻ ☉ **7:19 am** 4:19 am
☽ ⚻ ☿ **8:11 am** 5:11 am
☽ ☐ ♂ **5:02 pm** 2:02 pm
☽ △ ♇ **9:56 pm** 6:56 pm
☽ ⚻ ⚷ 10:25 pm

Eastern time in bold type
Pacific time in medium type

5 FRIDAY
☽ ⚻ ⚷ **1:25 am**
☽ △ ♀ **12:13 pm** 9:13 am
☽ ☍ ♅ **6:40 pm** 3:40 pm
☽ △ ⚴ **8:15 pm** 5:15 pm
☽ ✶ ♄ **11:39 pm** 8:39 pm

6 SATURDAY
☽ ⚻ ⚶ **7:18 am** 4:18 am
☽ ✶ ⚳ **9:47 am** 6:47 am
☽ △ ⚵ **12:13 pm** 9:13 am
☽ ☌ ♃ **12:46 pm** 9:46 am
☽ ⚻ ♆ **1:34 pm** 10:34 am
☽ ☍ ☉ **6:14 pm** 3:14 pm
☽ ☍ ☿ **11:41 pm** 8:41 pm
☽ △ ♂ 10:47 pm

7 SUNDAY
☽ △ ♂ **1:47 am**
☽ ☐ ♇ **3:49 am** 12:49 am
♃ △ ⚵ **6:43 am** 3:43 am
☽ △ ⚷ **7:23 am** 4:23 am
☿ ✶ ♂ **8:41 pm** 5:41 pm
☽ ⚻ ♀ **10:04 pm** 7:04 pm
☽ ⚻ ♅ **11:51 pm** 8:51 pm
☽ ⚻ ⚴ 11:59 pm

8 MONDAY
☽ ⚻ ⚴ **2:59 am**
☽ ☐ ♄ **4:25 am** 1:25 am
☿ ☐ ♇ **4:52 am** 1:52 am
☽ △ ⚶ **1:44 pm** 10:44 am
☽ ☐ ⚳ **2:29 pm** 11:29 am
☽ ⚺ ♃ **4:35 pm** 1:35 pm
☽ ☐ ⚵ **5:34 pm** 2:34 pm
☽ △ ♆ **5:58 pm** 2:58 pm
♀ ✶ ♅ **9:37 pm** 6:37 pm
♂ ⚻ ♇ **9:46 pm** 6:46 pm
☽ ⚻ ☉ 11:23 pm

9 TUESDAY
☽ ⚻ ☉ **2:23 am**
☿ ✶ ⚷ **7:17 am** 4:17 am
☽ ✶ ♇ **7:43 am** 4:43 am
☽ ⚻ ♂ **8:11 am** 5:11 am
☽ ☐ ⚷ **11:23 am** 8:23 am
☽ ⚻ ☿ **12:02 pm** 9:02 am
⚳ ⚻ ⚶ **2:38 pm** 11:38 am
♆ ⚺ ⚵ **4:40 pm** 1:40 pm
♄ ✶ ⚴ **9:28 pm** 6:28 pm

10 WEDNESDAY
☽ △ ♅ **3:28 am** 12:28 am
☽ ☍ ♀ **5:50 am** 2:50 am
☽ △ ♄ **7:45 am** 4:45 am
☽ ☍ ⚴ **8:06 am** 5:06 am
☽ △ ⚳ **5:59 pm** 2:59 pm
☽ ☐ ⚶ **6:47 pm** 3:47 pm
☽ ✶ ♃ **7:16 pm** 4:16 pm
☽ ☐ ♆ **9:13 pm** 6:13 pm
☽ ✶ ⚵ **9:41 pm** 6:41 pm

11 THURSDAY
♃ ⚻ ⚶ **5:45 am** 2:45 am
♀ ✶ ♄ **6:44 am** 3:44 am
☽ △ ☉ **9:17 am** 6:17 am
☽ ⚺ ♇ **10:44 am** 7:44 am
☽ ☍ ♂ **1:35 pm** 10:35 am
☽ ✶ ⚷ **2:35 pm** 11:35 am
☽ △ ☿ **11:11 pm** 8:11 pm

12 FRIDAY
☉ ☐ ♇ **5:57 am** 2:57 am
☽ ☐ ♅ **6:32 am** 3:32 am
♀ ☌ ⚴ **8:24 am** 5:24 am
☽ ⚻ ♄ **10:38 am** 7:38 am
☽ ⚻ ⚴ **12:44 pm** 9:44 am
☽ ⚻ ♀ **12:56 pm** 9:56 am
♂ △ ⚷ **1:41 pm** 10:41 am
☽ ⚻ ⚳ **9:12 pm** 6:12 pm
☽ ☐ ♃ **9:40 pm** 6:40 pm
☽ ✶ ⚶ **11:29 pm** 8:29 pm
☽ ✶ ♆ 9:10 pm
☽ ⚺ ⚵ 10:30 pm

13 SATURDAY
☽ ✶ ♆ **12:10 am**
☽ ⚺ ⚵ **1:30 am**
☽ ☌ ♇ **1:37 pm** 10:37 am
☽ ☐ ☉ **4:01 pm** 1:01 pm
☽ ⚺ ⚷ **5:40 pm** 2:40 pm
☽ ⚻ ♂ **6:53 pm** 3:53 pm
♆ ☌ ⚶ **8:39 pm** 5:39 pm
♃ ✶ ⚳ 9:24 pm

14 SUNDAY
♃ ✶ ⚳ **12:24 am**
☿ ⚺ ♅ **5:49 am** 2:49 am
☽ ✶ ♅ **9:41 am** 6:41 am
☽ ☐ ☿ **10:17 am** 7:17 am
☽ ☍ ♄ **1:39 pm** 10:39 am
☉ ✶ ⚷ **4:55 pm** 1:55 pm
☽ △ ⚴ **5:31 pm** 2:31 pm
☽ △ ♀ **8:08 pm** 5:08 pm
☽ △ ♃ 9:14 pm
☽ ☍ ⚳ 9:40 pm

15 MONDAY
☽ △ ♃ **12:14 am**
☽ ☍ ⚳ **12:40 am**
☽ ⚺ ♆ **3:20 am** 12:20 am
☽ ⚺ ⚶ **4:23 am** 1:23 am
☽ ☌ ⚵ **5:31 am** 2:31 am
☿ ☐ ♄ **10:57 am** 7:57 am
☽ ⚺ ♇ **4:49 pm** 1:49 pm
☽ ☌ ⚷ **9:06 pm** 6:06 pm
☽ ✶ ☉ **11:08 pm** 8:08 pm
☽ △ ♂ 9:34 pm

16 TUESDAY
☽ △ ♂ **12:34 am**
☽ ⚺ ♅ **1:17 pm** 10:17 am
☽ ⚻ ♄ **5:09 pm** 2:09 pm
♀ △ ♃ **9:00 pm** 6:00 pm
☽ ✶ ☿ **9:56 pm** 6:56 pm
☽ ☐ ⚴ **10:55 pm** 7:55 pm

17 WEDNESDAY
☽ ⚻ ♃ **3:24 am** 12:24 am
☽ ☐ ♀ **4:00 am** 1:00 am
☽ ⚻ ⚳ **4:47 am** 1:47 am
☽ ☌ ♆ **7:08 am** 4:08 am
☿ ⚺ ⚴ **7:24 am** 4:24 am
☽ ☌ ⚶ **9:59 am** 6:59 am
☽ ⚺ ⚵ **10:11 am** 7:11 am
♀ ✶ ⚳ **3:37 pm** 12:37 pm
☽ ✶ ♇ **8:46 pm** 5:46 pm
⚵ ⚺ ⚶ **9:27 pm** 6:27 pm
☽ ⚺ ⚷ 10:21 pm

18 THURSDAY
☽ ⚺ ⚷ **1:21 am**
☉ ✶ ♂ **4:47 am** 1:47 am
☽ ☐ ♂ **7:15 am** 4:15 am
☽ ⚺ ☉ **7:19 am** 4:19 am
☿ ⚻ ♃ **12:31 pm** 9:31 am
☽ ☌ ♅ **5:56 pm** 2:56 pm
☽ △ ♄ **9:47 pm** 6:47 pm
♀ ☐ ♆ **10:02 pm** 7:02 pm

19 FRIDAY
☿ ☐ ⚳ **5:01 am** 2:01 am
☽ ✶ ⚴ **5:39 am** 2:39 am
☽ ☍ ♃ **7:48 am** 4:48 am
☽ △ ⚳ **10:17 am** 7:17 am
☽ ⚺ ☿ **11:01 am** 8:01 am
☽ ⚺ ♆ **12:15 pm** 9:15 am
☽ ✶ ♀ **1:26 pm** 10:26 am
☽ ✶ ⚵ **4:18 pm** 1:18 pm
☽ ⚺ ⚶ **5:06 pm** 2:06 pm
☿ ✶ ♆ **8:22 pm** 5:22 pm
☽ ☐ ♇ 11:17 pm

20 SATURDAY
☽ ☐ ♇ **2:17 am**
☽ ✶ ⚷ **7:15 am** 4:15 am
☽ ✶ ♂ **3:57 pm** 12:57 pm
☽ ☌ ☉ **5:41 pm** 2:41 pm
☽ ⚺ ♅ 9:33 pm

21 SUNDAY
☽ ⚺ ♅ **12:33 am**
☽ ☐ ♄ **4:26 am** 1:26 am
♃ △ ⚴ **4:50 am** 1:50 am
☿ ⚺ ♀ **5:35 am** 2:35 am
☿ ☐ ⚵ **9:13 am** 6:13 am
♀ △ ⚵ **12:08 pm** 9:08 am
☽ ⚻ ♃ **2:19 pm** 11:19 am
☽ ⚺ ⚴ **2:48 pm** 11:48 am
☽ ☐ ⚳ **6:06 pm** 3:06 pm
☽ ✶ ♆ **7:37 pm** 4:37 pm
☽ ☐ ⚵ 9:48 pm
☽ ⚺ ♀ 10:40 pm
☿ ✶ ⚶ 11:36 pm
☽ ✶ ⚶ 11:48 pm
☽ ☌ ☿ 11:49 pm

22 MONDAY
☽ ☐ ⚵ **12:48 am**
☽ ⚺ ♀ **1:40 am**
☿ ✶ ⚶ **2:36 am**
☽ ✶ ⚶ **2:48 am**
☽ ☌ ☿ **2:49 am**
☽ △ ♇ **10:14 am** 7:14 am
☽ ☐ ⚷ **3:41 pm** 12:41 pm
♀ ☐ ⚶ 11:29 pm

23 TUESDAY
♀ ☐ ⚶ **2:29 am**
☽ ⚺ ♂ **3:42 am** 12:42 am
☽ ⚺ ☉ **7:24 am** 4:24 am
☽ ✶ ♅ **9:53 am** 6:53 am
☽ ✶ ♄ **1:52 pm** 10:52 am
☽ △ ♃ **11:35 pm** 8:35 pm

24 WEDNESDAY
☽ ☌ ⚴ **3:08 am** 12:08 am
☽ ✶ ⚳ **4:55 am** 1:55 am
☽ ☐ ♆ **5:49 am** 2:49 am
☽ △ ⚵ **12:17 pm** 9:17 am
☽ ☐ ⚶ **3:39 pm** 12:39 pm
☿ △ ♇ **3:41 pm** 12:41 pm
☉ ⚺ ♅ **3:54 pm** 12:54 pm
☽ ☌ ♀ **5:29 pm** 2:29 pm
☽ ⚻ ♇ **9:00 pm** 6:00 pm
☽ ⚺ ☿ **9:43 pm** 6:43 pm
☽ △ ⚷ 11:57 pm

25 THURSDAY
☽ △ ⚷ **2:57 am**
☽ ☌ ♂ **6:36 pm** 3:36 pm
☽ ☐ ♅ **9:54 pm** 6:54 pm
☽ ✶ ☉ 9:29 pm
☽ ⚺ ♄ 10:56 pm

26 FRIDAY
☽ ✶ ☉ **12:29 am**
☽ ⚺ ♄ **1:56 am**
☽ ☐ ♃ **11:14 am** 8:14 am
♀ ⚻ ♇ **11:19 am** 8:19 am
☽ ⚺ ⚴ **6:08 pm** 3:08 pm
☽ ⚺ ⚳ **6:12 pm** 3:12 pm
☉ ☐ ♄ **6:15 pm** 3:15 pm
☽ △ ♆ **6:19 pm** 3:19 pm
⚳ ✶ ⚴ **8:42 pm** 5:42 pm
♆ ☐ ⚴ **10:40 pm** 7:40 pm
☿ ☐ ⚷ **10:52 pm** 7:52 pm
☽ ⚻ ⚵ 10:58 pm
♆ ⚻ ⚳ 11:30 pm

27 SATURDAY
☽ ⚻ ⚵ **1:58 am**
♆ ⚻ ⚳ **2:30 am**
☽ △ ⚶ **6:46 am** 3:46 am
☽ ☍ ♇ **9:40 am** 6:40 am
☽ ⚺ ♀ **11:44 am** 8:44 am
☽ ⚻ ⚷ **3:55 pm** 12:55 pm
☽ ✶ ☿ **5:44 pm** 2:44 pm

28 SUNDAY
☽ ⚺ ♂ **10:53 am** 7:53 am
☽ △ ♅ **10:59 am** 7:59 am
♂ ☐ ♅ **12:40 pm** 9:40 am
☽ ☌ ♄ **2:55 pm** 11:55 am
☽ ☐ ☉ **6:48 pm** 3:48 pm
☽ ✶ ♃ **11:25 pm** 8:25 pm

29 MONDAY
☽ ⚻ ♆ **7:03 am** 4:03 am
☽ ☌ ⚳ **7:49 am** 4:49 am
☽ ✶ ⚴ **9:26 am** 6:26 am
☽ ☍ ⚵ **3:32 pm** 12:32 pm
♀ △ ⚷ **3:47 pm** 12:47 pm
☽ ⚻ ⚶ **9:33 pm** 6:33 pm
☽ ⚻ ♇ **9:54 pm** 6:54 pm

30 TUESDAY
☽ ☍ ⚷ **4:12 am** 1:12 am
☽ ✶ ♀ **5:14 am** 2:14 am
♇ ✶ ⚶ **6:31 am** 3:31 am
☽ ☐ ☿ **11:00 am** 8:00 am
☉ ⚻ ♃ **9:53 pm** 6:53 pm
☽ ⚻ ♅ **10:34 pm** 7:34 pm
☽ ✶ ♂ 10:27 pm
☽ ⚺ ♄ 11:17 pm

31 WEDNESDAY
☽ ✶ ♂ **1:27 am**
☽ ⚺ ♄ **2:17 am**
☽ ⚺ ♃ **9:43 am** 6:43 am
☽ △ ☉ **10:49 am** 7:49 am
☽ ☍ ♆ **5:33 pm** 2:33 pm
♂ ⚺ ♄ **6:42 pm** 3:42 pm
☽ ⚺ ⚳ **7:07 pm** 4:07 pm
☽ ☐ ⚴ **10:09 pm** 7:09 pm
☽ ⚻ ⚵ 11:25 pm

MARCH 2004

☽ Last Aspect day	EST / hr:mn / PST		asp	☽ Ingress sign	day	EST / hr:mn / PST	
2	**10:42 pm**	7:42 pm	□ ♀	♌	3	**4:18 am**	1:18 am
5	**12:13 pm**	9:13 am	△ ♀	♍	5	**12:18 pm**	9:18 am
7	**3:49 am**	12:49 am	□ ♇	♎	7	**5:31 pm**	2:31 pm
9	**7:43 am**	4:43 am	⚹ ♇	♏	9	**9:03 pm**	6:03 pm
11	**11:11 pm**	8:11 pm	△ ☿	♐	11	**11:57 pm**	8:57 pm
13	**4:01 pm**	1:01 pm	□ ☉	♑	13		11:51 pm
13	**4:01 pm**	1:01 pm	□ ☉	♑	14	**2:51 am**	
15		9:34 pm	△ ♂	♒	16	**6:10 am**	3:10 am
16	**12:34 am**		△ ♂	♒	16	**6:10 am**	3:10 am
18	**7:15 am**	4:15 am	□ ♂	♓	18	**10:26 am**	7:26 am
20	**3:57 pm**	12:57 pm	⚹ ♂	♈	20	**4:29 pm**	1:29 pm
22	**10:14 am**	7:14 am	△ ♇	♉	22		10:10 pm
22	**10:14 am**	7:14 am	△ ♇	♉	23	**1:10 am**	
24	**5:29 pm**	2:29 pm	☌ ♀	♊	25	**12:35 pm**	9:35 am
27	**5:44 pm**	2:44 pm	⚹ ☿	♋	27		10:23 pm
27	**5:44 pm**	2:44 pm	⚹ ☿	♋	28	**1:23 am**	
30	**11:00 am**	8:00 am	□ ☿	♌	30	**1:07 pm**	10:07 am

☽ Phases & Eclipses phase	day	EST / hr:mn / PST	
Full Moon	6	**6:14 pm**	3:14 pm
4th Quarter	13	**4:01 pm**	1:01 pm
New Moon	20	**5:41 pm**	2:41 pm
2nd Quarter	28	**6:48 pm**	3:48 pm

Planet Ingress		day	EST / hr:mn / PST	
♀	♉	5	**1:12 pm**	10:12 am
☿	♈	12	**4:44 am**	1:44 am
☉	♈	19		10:49 pm
☉	♈	20	**1:49 am**	
♂	♊	20		11:39 pm
♂	♊	21	**2:39 am**	
☿	♉	31	**9:27 pm**	6:27 pm

Planetary Motion		day	EST / hr:mn / PST	
♄	D	7	**11:51 am**	8:51 am
♇	℞	24	**10:09 am**	7:09 am

DATE		SID.TIME	SUN	MOON	NODE	MERCURY	VENUS	MARS	JUPITER	SATURN	URANUS	NEPTUNE	PLUTO	CERES	PALLAS	JUNO	VESTA	CHIRON
1	M	10:36:32	10 ♓ 44 34	00 ♋ 54	13 ♉ ℞ 31	08 ♓ 04	24 ♈ 40	16 ♉ 59	14 ♍ ℞ 23	06 ♋ ℞ 20	03 ♓ 14	13 ♒ 53	22 ♐ 05	11 ♋ 41	02 ♉ 06	11 ♑ 44	07 ♒ 47	23 ♑ 45
2	T	10:40:29	11 44 46	12 56	13 26	09 56	25 48	17 37	14 15	06 19	03 18	13 55	22 06	11 43	02 33	12 01	08 18	23 49
3	W	10:44:25	12 44 56	25 11	13 19	11 48	26 55	18 16	14 07	06 18	03 21	13 57	22 07	11 45	03 00	12 18	08 48	23 53
4	Th	10:48:22	13 45 04	07 ♌ 43	13 10	13 41	28 02	18 54	13 59	06 18	03 25	13 59	22 08	11 48	03 27	12 35	09 18	23 57
5	F	10:52:18	14 45 10	20 33	13 00	15 35	29 09	19 32	13 52	06 18	03 28	14 01	22 08	11 52	03 55	12 51	09 48	24 01
6	Sa	10:56:15	15 45 14	03 ♍ 42	12 49	17 30	00 ♉ 16	20 11	13 44	06 17	03 31	14 03	22 09	11 55	04 22	13 08	10 19	24 05
7	Su	11:00:12	16 45 16	17 09	12 40	19 26	01 23	20 49	13 36	06 D 17	03 35	14 05	22 10	11 59	04 50	13 24	10 49	24 10
8	M	11:04:08	17 45 16	00 ♎ 51	12 32	21 22	02 29	21 28	13 28	06 17	03 38	14 07	22 10	12 04	05 18	13 40	11 19	24 13
9	T	11:08:05	18 45 14	14 45	12 26	23 19	03 35	22 06	13 20	06 17	03 42	14 09	22 11	12 09	05 46	13 57	11 48	24 17
10	W	11:12:01	19 45 11	28 48	12 D 23	25 17	04 41	22 45	13 13	06 17	03 45	14 11	22 11	12 14	06 15	14 13	12 18	24 21
11	Th	11:15:58	20 45 06	12 ♏ 55	12 22	27 14	05 46	23 23	13 05	06 18	03 48	14 13	22 12	12 19	06 43	14 29	12 48	24 25
12	F	11:19:54	21 44 59	27 05	12 23	29 12	06 51	24 02	12 57	06 18	03 52	14 15	22 12	12 25	07 12	14 44	13 18	24 29
13	Sa	11:23:51	22 44 51	11 ♐ 14	12 ℞ 24	01 ♈ 10	07 56	24 40	12 49	06 19	03 55	14 17	22 13	12 32	07 40	15 00	13 47	24 32
14	Su	11:27:47	23 44 41	25 23	12 24	03 07	09 01	25 19	12 42	06 19	03 58	14 19	22 13	12 39	08 09	15 16	14 17	24 36
15	M	11:31:44	24 44 29	09 ♑ 28	12 23	05 04	10 05	25 57	12 34	06 20	04 02	14 21	22 13	12 46	08 38	15 31	14 47	24 40
16	T	11:35:41	25 44 16	23 30	12 20	06 59	11 10	26 36	12 27	06 21	04 05	14 23	22 14	12 53	09 07	15 46	15 16	24 43
17	W	11:39:37	26 44 01	07 ♒ 26	12 15	08 54	12 13	27 14	12 19	06 22	04 08	14 24	22 14	13 01	09 37	16 01	15 45	24 47
18	Th	11:43:34	27 43 44	21 13	12 09	10 46	13 17	27 52	12 12	06 23	04 11	14 26	22 14	13 09	10 06	16 16	16 15	24 50
19	F	11:47:30	28 43 25	04 ♓ 50	12 01	12 36	14 20	28 31	12 05	06 24	04 15	14 28	22 14	13 18	10 36	16 31	16 44	24 53
20	Sa	11:51:27	29 43 05	18 14	11 54	14 24	15 23	29 09	11 57	06 26	04 18	14 30	22 14	13 27	11 05	16 46	17 13	24 56
21	Su	11:55:23	00 ♈ 42 42	01 ♈ 22	11 47	16 08	16 26	29 48	11 50	06 27	04 21	14 31	22 15	13 36	11 35	17 00	17 42	25 00
22	M	11:59:20	01 42 17	14 14	11 42	17 49	17 28	00 ♊ 26	11 43	06 29	04 24	14 33	22 15	13 45	12 05	17 14	18 11	25 03
23	T	12:03:16	02 41 51	26 49	11 39	19 26	18 30	01 05	11 36	06 30	04 27	14 35	22 15	13 55	12 35	17 29	18 40	25 06
24	W	12:07:13	03 41 22	09 ♉ 08	11 D 38	20 59	19 32	01 43	11 30	06 32	04 30	14 37	22 ℞ 15	14 06	13 05	17 43	19 09	25 09
25	Th	12:11:10	04 40 51	21 15	11 38	22 27	20 33	02 21	11 23	06 34	04 34	14 38	22 15	14 16	13 36	17 56	19 38	25 12
26	F	12:15:06	05 40 18	03 ♊ 11	11 40	23 49	21 34	03 00	11 16	06 36	04 37	14 40	22 15	14 27	14 06	18 10	20 07	25 15
27	Sa	12:19:03	06 39 43	15 02	11 42	25 06	22 34	03 38	11 10	06 38	04 40	14 41	22 15	14 38	14 37	18 23	20 35	25 17
28	Su	12:22:59	07 39 05	26 51	11 43	26 17	23 34	04 17	11 03	06 40	04 43	14 43	22 15	14 50	15 08	18 37	21 04	25 20
29	M	12:26:56	08 38 25	08 ♋ 44	11 ℞ 44	27 21	24 34	04 55	10 57	06 42	04 46	14 44	22 14	15 02	15 38	18 50	21 32	25 23
30	T	12:30:52	09 37 43	20 46	11 43	28 20	25 33	05 34	10 51	06 45	04 49	14 46	22 14	15 14	16 09	19 03	22 01	25 25
31	W	12:34:49	10 36 58	03 ♌ 02	11 41	29 11	26 31	06 12	10 45	06 47	04 52	14 47	22 14	15 26	16 40	19 16	22 29	25 D 28

EPHEMERIS CALCULATED FOR 12 MIDNIGHT GREENWICH MEAN TIME. ALL OTHER DATA AND FACING ASPECTARIAN PAGE IN **EASTERN TIME (BOLD)** AND PACIFIC TIME (REGULAR).

APRIL 2004

1 THURSDAY

☽ ⚻ ⚵	**2:25 am**	
☽ △ ♇	**7:26 am**	4:26 am
☽ ☍ ⚶	**9:18 am**	6:18 am
☽ ⚻ ⚷	**1:33 pm**	10:33 am
☽ □ ♀	**6:56 pm**	3:56 pm
☽ △ ☿	**10:56 pm**	7:56 pm

2 FRIDAY

☽ ☍ ♅	**6:49 am**	3:49 am
☽ ⚹ ♄	**10:16 am**	7:16 am
☽ □ ♂	**12:07 pm**	9:07 am
☽ ☌ ♃	**4:40 pm**	1:40 pm
☽ ⚻ ☉	**10:26 pm**	7:26 pm
☽ ⚻ ♆		9:29 pm
☽ ⚹ ⚳		11:45 pm

3 SATURDAY

☽ ⚻ ♆	**12:29 am**	
☽ ⚹ ⚳	**2:45 am**	
☽ △ ⚴	**6:53 am**	3:53 am
☽ △ ⚵	**9:31 am**	6:31 am
☽ □ ♇	**1:23 pm**	10:23 am
☽ ⚻ ⚶	**5:03 pm**	2:03 pm
☽ △ ⚷	**7:18 pm**	4:18 pm

4 SUNDAY

☉ ⚹ ♆	**4:06 am**	12:06 am
☽ △ ♀	**5:05 am**	1:05 am
☽ ⚻ ☿	**6:36 am**	3:36 am
☽ ⚻ ♅	**12:35 pm**	9:35 am
☽ □ ♄	**3:51 pm**	12:51 pm
☽ △ ♂	**7:54 pm**	4:54 pm
☽ ⚺ ♃	**9:24 pm**	6:24 pm

5 MONDAY

☽ △ ♆	**5:14 am**	2:14 am
☽ ☍ ☉	**7:03 am**	4:03 am
☽ □ ⚳	**8:09 am**	5:09 am
☿ ⚺ ♀	**10:01 am**	7:01 am
☽ ⚻ ♀	**1:12 pm**	10:12 am
☽ □ ⚵	**2:28 pm**	11:28 am
☽ ⚹ ♇	**5:26 pm**	2:26 pm
☽ △ ⚶	**10:39 pm**	7:39 pm
☽ □ ⚷	**11:15 pm**	8:15 pm
♂ □ ♃		10:16 pm

6 TUESDAY

♂ □ ♃	**1:16 am**	
☉ □ ⚳	**3:47 am**	12:47 am
☽ ☍ ☿	**9:35 am**	6:35 am
☽ ⚻ ♀	**11:02 am**	8:02 am
☽ △ ♅	**2:59 pm**	11:59 am
☽ △ ♄	**6:11 pm**	3:11 pm
⚷ ⚺ ⚶	**6:44 pm**	3:44 pm
☽ ⚹ ♃	**11:06 pm**	8:06 pm
☽ ⚻ ♂		9:13 pm

7 WEDNESDAY

☽ ⚻ ♂	**12:13 am**	
☽ □ ♆	**7:06 am**	4:06 am
☽ △ ⚳	**10:43 am**	7:43 am
☽ ⚻ ☉	**12:24 pm**	9:24 am
☽ ☍ ♀	**4:43 pm**	1:43 pm
☽ ⚹ ⚵	**4:44 pm**	1:44 pm
♀ △ ⚵	**5:21 pm**	2:21 pm
☽ ⚺ ♇	**7:00 pm**	4:00 pm
☽ ⚹ ⚷		9:52 pm
☽ □ ⚶		10:46 pm

8 THURSDAY

☽ ⚹ ⚷	**12:52 am**	
☽ □ ⚶	**1:46 am**	
☽ ⚻ ☿	**10:44 am**	7:44 am
☽ ☍ ♀	**3:43 pm**	12:43 pm
☽ □ ♅	**4:32 pm**	1:32 pm
☽ ⚻ ♄	**7:46 pm**	4:46 pm
☽ □ ♃		9:13 pm

9 FRIDAY

☽ □ ♃	**12:13 am**	
☽ ☍ ♂	**3:53 am**	12:53 am
♀ □ ♅	**5:51 am**	2:51 am
☽ ⚹ ♆	**8:36 am**	5:36 am
☽ ⚻ ⚳	**1:01 pm**	10:01 am
☽ △ ☉	**5:28 pm**	2:28 pm
☽ ⚺ ⚵	**6:52 pm**	3:52 pm
☽ ⚻ ♀	**8:07 pm**	5:07 pm
☽ ☌ ♇	**8:30 pm**	5:30 pm
☽ ⚺ ⚷		11:34 pm

10 SATURDAY

☽ ⚺ ⚷	**2:34 am**	
☽ ⚹ ⚶	**5:01 am**	2:01 am
♇ ⚻ ♀	**5:57 am**	2:57 am

11 SUNDAY

☽ △ ☿	**11:30 am**	8:30 am
☉ □ ⚵	**6:08 pm**	3:08 pm
☽ ⚹ ♅	**6:34 pm**	3:34 pm
☽ ⚻ ♀	**8:52 pm**	5:52 pm
☽ ☍ ♄	**9:55 pm**	6:55 pm
☽ △ ♃		11:00 pm
☽ △ ♃	**2:00 am**	
☽ ⚻ ♂	**8:23 am**	5:23 am
☽ ⚺ ♆	**10:55 am**	7:55 am
☉ △ ♇	**1:35 pm**	10:35 am
♀ ⚺ ♄	**3:27 pm**	12:27 pm
☽ ☍ ⚳	**4:20 pm**	1:20 pm
☽ ☌ ⚵	**10:02 pm**	7:02 pm
☽ ⚺ ♇	**11:03 pm**	8:03 pm
☽ □ ☉	**11:46 pm**	8:46 pm
☽ △ ♀		9:43 pm

12 MONDAY

☽ △ ♀	**12:43 am**	
☽ ☌ ⚷	**5:26 am**	2:26 am
☽ ⚺ ⚶	**9:34 am**	6:34 am
☽ □ ☿	**12:53 pm**	9:53 am
☽ ⚺ ♅	**10:02 pm**	7:02 pm
☽ ⚻ ♄		10:33 pm

13 TUESDAY

☽ ⚻ ♄	**1:33 am**	
☽ △ ♀	**3:39 am**	12:39 am
☉ ⚺ ♀	**4:53 am**	1:53 am
☽ ⚻ ♃	**5:18 am**	2:18 am
☽ △ ♂	**2:43 pm**	11:43 am
☽ ☌ ♆	**2:52 pm**	11:52 am
♂ △ ♆	**6:02 pm**	3:02 pm
☽ ⚻ ⚳	**9:26 pm**	6:26 pm
☽ ⚺ ⚵		11:58 pm

14 WEDNESDAY

☽ ⚺ ⚵	**2:58 am**	
☽ ⚹ ♇	**3:20 am**	12:20 am
♀ □ ♃	**4:57 am**	1:57 am
☽ □ ♀	**7:18 am**	4:18 am
☿ ⚹ ⚶	**7:21 am**	4:21 am
☽ ⚹ ☉	**8:14 am**	5:14 am
☽ ⚺ ⚷	**10:06 am**	7:06 am
☽ ⚹ ☿	**3:27 pm**	12:27 pm
☽ ☌ ⚶	**4:09 pm**	1:09 pm

15 THURSDAY

☽ ☌ ♅	**3:25 am**	12:25 am
☽ △ ♄	**7:12 am**	4:12 am

♇ ⚺ ⚵	**7:58 am**	4:58 am
☉ □ ⚷	**10:30 am**	7:30 am
☽ ☍ ♃	**10:34 am**	7:34 am
☽ □ ♀	**12:41 pm**	9:41 am
☽ ⚺ ♆	**8:51 pm**	5:51 pm
☽ □ ♂	**11:23 pm**	8:23 pm

16 FRIDAY

☽ △ ⚳	**4:47 am**	1:47 am
☽ □ ♇	**9:43 am**	6:43 am
☽ ⚹ ⚵	**10:03 am**	7:03 am
☽ ⚹ ♀	**4:18 pm**	1:18 pm
☽ ⚹ ⚷	**4:54 pm**	1:54 pm
☽ ⚺ ☉	**7:21 pm**	4:21 pm
☽ ⚺ ☿	**7:34 pm**	4:34 pm
☉ ☌ ☿	**9:05 pm**	6:05 pm
☽ ⚺ ⚶		10:04 pm

17 SATURDAY

☽ ⚺ ⚶	**1:04 am**	
⚷ △ ♀	**6:57 am**	3:57 am
☽ ⚺ ♅	**11:02 am**	8:02 am
☽ □ ♄	**3:05 pm**	12:05 pm
☽ ⚻ ♃	**6:03 pm**	3:03 pm
☽ ⚹ ♀		9:16 pm

18 SUNDAY

☽ ⚹ ♀	**12:16 am**	
☿ ⚺ ♀	**3:16 am**	12:16 am
☽ ⚹ ♆	**5:05 am**	2:05 am
☽ ⚹ ♂	**10:40 am**	7:40 am
☽ □ ⚳	**2:34 pm**	11:34 am
☿ □ ⚷	**5:53 pm**	2:53 pm
☽ △ ♇	**6:21 pm**	3:21 pm
☽ □ ⚵	**7:26 pm**	4:26 pm
☽ ☌ ☿		10:32 pm
☽ □ ⚷		10:59 pm

19 MONDAY

☽ ☌ ☿	**1:32 am**	
☽ □ ⚷	**1:59 am**	
☽ ⚺ ♀	**3:55 am**	12:55 am
☽ ☌ ☉	**9:21 am**	6:21 am
☽ ⚹ ⚶	**12:32 pm**	9:32 am
☽ ⚹ ♅	**8:57 pm**	5:57 pm
☽ ⚹ ♄		10:20 pm

20 TUESDAY

☽ ⚹ ♄	**1:20 am**	
☽ △ ♃	**3:50 am**	12:50 am
☽ ⚺ ♀	**2:25 pm**	11:25 am
☽ □ ♆	**3:36 pm**	12:36 pm

☽ ⚺ ♂		9:35 pm
☽ ⚹ ⚳		11:49 pm

21 WEDNESDAY

☽ ⚺ ♂	**12:35 am**	
☽ ⚹ ⚳	**2:49 am**	
☽ ⚻ ♇	**5:13 am**	2:13 am
☽ △ ⚵	**7:05 am**	4:05 am
☽ ⚺ ☿	**9:33 am**	6:33 am
♀ △ ♆	**10:17 am**	7:17 am
☽ △ ⚷	**1:15 pm**	10:15 am
☽ ☌ ♀	**6:03 pm**	3:03 pm
☽ ⚺ ☉		11:06 pm
☽ □ ⚶		11:20 pm

22 THURSDAY

☽ ⚺ ☉	**2:06 am**	
☽ □ ⚶	**2:20 am**	
☉ ⚹ ⚶	**7:15 am**	4:15 am
☽ □ ♅	**8:57 am**	5:57 am
☽ ⚺ ♄	**1:38 pm**	10:38 am
☽ □ ♃	**3:37 pm**	12:37 pm
☿ □ ⚵		11:09 pm

23 FRIDAY

☿ □ ⚵	**2:09 am**	
☽ △ ♆	**3:57 am**	12:57 am
☽ ☌ ♀	**6:34 am**	3:34 am
☽ ☌ ♂	**4:30 pm**	1:30 pm
☽ ⚺ ⚳	**4:54 pm**	1:54 pm
☽ ☍ ♇	**5:42 pm**	2:42 pm
☽ ⚹ ☿	**7:22 pm**	4:22 pm
☽ ⚻ ⚵	**8:19 pm**	5:19 pm
☽ ⚻ ⚷		11:00 pm

24 SATURDAY

☽ ⚻ ⚷	**2:00 am**	
♂ ⚺ ⚳	**6:24 am**	3:24 am
☽ ⚺ ♀	**9:47 am**	6:47 am
♂ ☍ ♇	**2:13 pm**	11:13 am
☽ △ ⚶	**5:27 pm**	2:27 pm
☽ ⚹ ☉	**8:21 pm**	5:21 pm
☽ △ ♅	**9:58 pm**	6:58 pm
♇ ⚻ ⚳	**10:16 pm**	7:16 pm
☿ ⚹ ♂		9:30 pm
☽ ☌ ♄		11:54 pm

25 SUNDAY

☿ ⚹ ♂	**12:30 am**	
☽ ☌ ♄	**2:54 am**	
☽ ⚹ ♃	**4:18 am**	1:18 am
☿ □ ⚳	**8:51 am**	5:51 am

☉ ⚹ ♅	**4:40 pm**	1:40 pm
☽ ⚻ ♆	**4:49 pm**	1:49 pm
☿ △ ♇	**6:13 pm**	3:13 pm
☽ ⚺ ♀	**10:57 pm**	7:57 pm

26 MONDAY

☽ □ ☿	**5:56 am**	2:56 am
☽ ⚻ ♇	**6:15 am**	3:15 am
☽ ☌ ⚳	**7:09 am**	4:09 am
☽ ⚺ ♂	**8:33 am**	5:33 am
☽ ☍ ⚵	**9:29 am**	6:29 am
☽ ☍ ⚷	**2:32 pm**	11:32 am
☽ ⚹ ♀		10:00 pm

27 TUESDAY

☽ ⚹ ♀	**1:00 am**	
♂ ⚻ ⚵	**5:42 am**	2:42 am
☽ ⚻ ⚶	**7:43 am**	4:43 am
☽ ⚻ ♅	**10:06 am**	7:06 am
☽ □ ☉	**1:32 pm**	10:32 am
☽ ⚺ ♄	**3:05 pm**	12:05 pm
☽ ⚺ ♃	**3:54 pm**	12:54 pm

28 WEDNESDAY

☽ ☍ ♆	**4:06 am**	1:06 am
☉ ⚹ ♄	**10:52 am**	7:52 am
☽ ⚹ ♀	**12:58 pm**	9:58 am
☽ △ ☿	**3:29 pm**	12:29 pm
☽ △ ♇	**4:48 pm**	1:48 pm
☉ △ ♃	**6:54 pm**	3:54 pm
☽ ⚺ ⚳	**7:13 pm**	4:13 pm
☽ ⚻ ⚵	**8:25 pm**	5:25 pm
☽ ⚹ ♂	**10:08 pm**	7:08 pm
☽ ⚻ ⚷		9:44 pm

29 THURSDAY

☽ ⚻ ⚷	**12:44 am**	
☽ □ ♀	**1:14 pm**	10:14 am
☽ ☍ ⚶	**6:50 pm**	3:50 pm
☽ ☍ ♅	**7:19 pm**	4:19 pm
☽ ⚹ ♄		9:13 pm
☽ ☌ ♃		9:32 pm
☽ △ ☉		11:56 pm

30 FRIDAY

☽ ⚹ ♄	**12:13 am**	
☽ ☌ ♃	**12:32 am**	
☽ △ ☉	**2:56 am**	
♅ ☌ ⚶	**11:11 am**	8:11 am
☽ ⚻ ♆	**12:04 pm**	9:04 am
☿ ⚹ ♀	**4:02 pm**	1:02 pm
☽ ⚻ ☿	**10:28 pm**	7:28 pm
☽ □ ♀	**10:43 pm**	7:43 pm
☽ □ ♇	**11:48 pm**	8:48 pm
♂ ⚻ ⚷		11:28 pm

Eastern time in bold type
Pacific time in medium type

APRIL 2004

☽ Last Aspect				☽ Ingress			
day	EST	hr:mn / PST	asp	sign	day	EST	hr:mn / PST
1	**6:56 pm**	3:56 pm	□ ♀	♍	1	**9:45 pm**	6:45 pm
3	**1:23 pm**	10:23 am	□ ♇	♎	3		11:52 pm
3	**1:23 pm**	10:23 am	□ ♇	♎	4	**3:52 am**	
5	**5:26 pm**	2:26 pm	✶ ♇	♏	6	**6:24 am**	3:24 am
7	**7:06 am**	4:06 am	□ ♆	♐	8	**7:50 am**	4:50 am
9	**8:30 pm**	5:30 pm	☌ ♇	♑	10	**9:33 am**	6:33 am
11	**11:46 pm**	8:46 pm	□ ☉	♒	12	**12:33 pm**	9:33 am
14	**3:27 pm**	12:27 pm	✶ ☿	♓	14	**5:24 pm**	2:24 pm
16	**9:43 am**	6:43 am	□ ♇	♈	16		9:24 pm
16	**9:43 am**	6:43 am	□ ♇	♈	17	**12:24 am**	

☽ Last Aspect				☽ Ingress			
day	EST	hr:mn / PST	asp	sign	day	EST	hr:mn / PST
19	**9:21 am**	6:21 am	☌ ☉	♉	19	**9:43 am**	6:43 am
20	**3:36 pm**	12:36 pm	□ ♆	♊	21	**9:10 pm**	6:10 pm
23	**7:22 pm**	4:22 pm	✶ ☿	♋	24	**9:56 am**	6:56 am
26	**5:56 am**	2:56 am	□ ☿	♌	26	**10:14 pm**	7:14 pm
28	**10:08 pm**	7:08 pm	✶ ♂	♍	29	**8:00 am**	5:00 am

☽ Phases & Eclipses			
phase	day	EST	hr:mn / PST
Full Moon	5	**7:03 am**	4:03 am
4th Quarter	11	**11:46 pm**	8:46 pm
New Moon	19	**9:21 am**	6:21 am
●	19	29° ♈ 49'	
2nd Quarter	27	**1:32 pm**	10:32 am

Planet Ingress				
		day	EST	hr:mn / PST
♀	♊	3	**9:57 am**	6:57 am
☿	♈	12	**9:23 pm**	6:23 pm
⚳	♓	16	**5:46 am**	2:46 am
☉	♉	19	**1:50 pm**	10:50 pm
♀	♊	24	**12:56 pm**	9:56 am

Planetary Motion				
		day	EST	hr:mn / PST
☿	℞	6	**4:28 pm**	1:28 pm
☿	D	30	**9:05 am**	6:05 am

DATE		SID.TIME	SUN	MOON	NODE	MERCURY	VENUS	MARS	JUPITER	SATURN	URANUS	NEPTUNE	PLUTO	CERES	PALLAS	JUNO	VESTA	CHIRON
1	Th	12:38:45	11 ♈ 36 11	15 ♌ 35	11 ♉ ℞ 37	29 ♈ 56	27 ♉ 30	06 ♊ 50	10 ♍ ℞ 39	06 ♋ 50	04 ♓ 55	14 ♒ 49	22 ♐ ℞ 14	15 ♋ 39	17 ♉ 12	19 ♑ 28	22 ♒ 57	25 ♑ 30
2	F	12:42:42	12 35 22	28 30	11 33	00 ♉ 33	28 27	07 29	10 33	06 53	04 58	14 50	22 14	15 52	17 43	19 40	23 25	25 32
3	Sa	12:46:39	13 34 30	11 ♍ 47	11 29	01 04	29 25	08 07	10 28	06 55	05 01	14 52	22 13	16 05	18 14	19 53	23 53	25 35
4	Su	12:50:35	14 33 37	25 27	11 25	01 27	00 ♊ 21	08 45	10 22	06 58	05 03	14 53	22 13	16 18	18 46	20 05	24 21	25 37
5	M	12:54:32	15 32 41	09 ♎ 27	11 21	01 44	01 17	09 24	10 17	07 01	05 06	14 54	22 13	16 32	19 17	20 16	24 49	25 39
6	T	12:58:28	16 31 43	23 44	11 19	01 ℞ 53	02 13	10 02	10 12	07 04	05 09	14 56	22 12	16 46	19 49	20 28	25 17	25 41
7	W	13:02:25	17 30 43	08 ♏ 13	11 D 18	01 55	03 08	10 40	10 07	07 08	05 12	14 57	22 12	17 01	20 21	20 39	25 45	25 43
8	Th	13:06:21	18 29 41	22 48	11 18	01 51	04 03	11 19	10 02	07 11	05 15	14 58	22 11	17 15	20 53	20 50	26 12	25 45
9	F	13:10:18	19 28 37	07 ♐ 23	11 20	01 40	04 56	11 57	09 57	07 14	05 17	15 00	22 11	17 30	21 25	21 01	26 40	25 47
10	Sa	13:14:14	20 27 32	21 53	11 21	01 24	05 50	12 35	09 52	07 18	05 20	15 01	22 10	17 45	21 57	21 12	27 07	25 49
11	Su	13:18:11	21 26 25	06 ♑ 13	11 22	01 01	06 42	13 14	09 48	07 21	05 23	15 02	22 10	18 00	22 29	21 23	27 34	25 50
12	M	13:22:07	22 25 16	20 22	11 ℞ 23	00 34	07 34	13 52	09 44	07 25	05 25	15 03	22 09	18 16	23 01	21 33	28 01	25 52
13	T	13:26:04	23 24 06	04 ♒ 18	11 22	00 02	08 25	14 30	09 40	07 29	05 28	15 04	22 09	18 31	23 34	21 43	28 29	25 54
14	W	13:30:01	24 22 54	18 00	11 21	29 ♈ 26	09 16	15 08	09 36	07 33	05 30	15 05	22 08	18 47	24 06	21 53	28 55	25 55
15	Th	13:33:57	25 21 40	01 ♓ 27	11 19	28 47	10 05	15 47	09 32	07 37	05 33	15 06	22 07	19 04	24 39	22 02	29 22	25 56
16	F	13:37:54	26 20 24	14 40	11 17	28 06	10 54	16 25	09 28	07 41	05 35	15 07	22 07	19 20	25 12	22 12	29 49	25 58
17	Sa	13:41:50	27 19 06	27 39	11 15	27 24	11 43	17 03	09 25	07 45	05 38	15 08	22 06	19 37	25 44	22 21	00 ♓ 16	25 59
18	Su	13:45:47	28 17 47	10 ♈ 24	11 14	26 40	12 30	17 41	09 22	07 49	05 40	15 09	22 05	19 54	26 17	22 30	00 42	26 00
19	M	13:49:43	29 16 26	22 56	11 12	25 57	13 16	18 20	09 19	07 53	05 43	15 10	22 05	20 11	26 50	22 38	01 09	26 01
20	T	13:53:40	00 ♉ 15 03	05 ♉ 16	11 D 12	25 15	14 02	18 58	09 16	07 58	05 45	15 11	22 04	20 28	27 23	22 47	01 35	26 02
21	W	13:57:36	01 13 38	17 25	11 12	24 34	14 47	19 36	09 13	08 02	05 47	15 12	22 03	20 46	27 56	22 55	02 01	26 03
22	Th	14:01:33	02 12 11	29 25	11 12	23 56	15 30	20 14	09 11	08 07	05 50	15 13	22 02	21 03	28 30	23 03	02 27	26 04
23	F	14:05:30	03 10 42	11 ♊ 19	11 13	23 21	16 13	20 52	09 08	08 11	05 52	15 14	22 01	21 21	29 03	23 10	02 53	26 05
24	Sa	14:09:26	04 09 11	23 08	11 14	22 49	16 54	21 31	09 06	08 16	05 54	15 15	22 00	21 39	29 36	23 18	03 19	26 05
25	Su	14:13:23	05 07 38	04 ♋ 58	11 14	22 21	17 35	22 09	09 04	08 21	05 56	15 15	21 59	21 58	00 ♊ 10	23 25	03 45	26 06
26	M	14:17:19	06 06 02	16 51	11 15	21 57	18 14	22 47	09 03	08 26	05 58	15 16	21 58	22 16	00 43	23 32	04 11	26 06
27	T	14:21:16	07 04 25	28 52	11 ℞ 15	21 37	18 53	23 25	09 01	08 31	06 00	15 17	21 57	22 35	01 17	23 38	04 36	26 07
28	W	14:25:12	08 02 46	11 ♌ 06	11 15	21 23	19 29	24 03	09 00	08 36	06 02	15 17	21 56	22 54	01 51	23 44	05 01	26 07
29	Th	14:29:09	09 01 04	23 37	11 15	21 13	20 05	24 41	08 58	08 41	06 04	15 18	21 55	23 13	02 25	23 50	05 27	26 08
30	F	14:33:05	09 59 21	06 ♍ 29	11 15	21 D 08	20 40	25 20	08 57	08 46	06 06	15 19	21 54	23 32	02 58	23 56	05 52	26 08

EPHEMERIS CALCULATED FOR 12 MIDNIGHT GREENWICH MEAN TIME. ALL OTHER DATA AND FACING ASPECTARIAN PAGE IN **EASTERN TIME (BOLD)** AND PACIFIC TIME (REGULAR).

MAY 2004

1 SATURDAY
♂⊼⚷ **2:28 am**
☽⚹⚳ **3:27 am** 12:27 am
☽△⚵ **3:37 am** 12:37 am
☽△⚷ **7:17 am** 4:17 am
☽□♂ **7:31 am** 4:31 am
⚳☍⚵ **12:46 pm** 9:46 am
♃⚹♄ **4:31 pm** 1:31 pm
☽△♀ **9:12 pm** 6:12 pm
☽⊼♅ 9:42 pm
☽⊼⚴ 10:46 pm
♀☍♇ 11:07 pm

2 SUNDAY
☽⊼♅ **12:42 am**
☽⊼⚴ **1:46 am**
♀☍♇ **2:07 am**
☽⊻♃ **5:25 am** 2:25 am
☽□♄ **5:30 am** 2:30 am
☽⊼☉ **11:35 am** 8:35 am
☽△♆ **4:16 pm** 1:16 pm
☽☍☿ 11:27 pm

3 MONDAY
☽☍☿ **2:27 am**
☽⚹♇ **3:10 am** 12:10 am
☽△♀ **4:05 am** 1:05 am
☽□⚵ **7:06 am** 4:06 am
☽□⚳ **7:51 am** 4:51 am
☽□⚷ **10:16 am** 7:16 am
☽△♂ **12:49 pm** 9:49 am
☽⊼♀ 10:26 pm
☽△♅ 11:50 pm

4 TUESDAY
☽⊼♀ **1:26 am**
☽△♅ **2:50 am**
☽△⚴ **5:10 am** 2:10 am
☽⚹♃ **7:12 am** 4:12 am
☽△♄ **7:37 am** 4:37 am
☿△♇ **1:51 pm** 10:51 am
☽☍☉ **4:33 pm** 1:33 pm
☽□♆ **5:36 pm** 2:36 pm

5 WEDNESDAY
☽⊻♇ **4:00 am** 1:00 am
☽⊼☿ **4:21 am** 1:21 am
☽⊼♀ **6:28 am** 3:28 am
☽⚹⚵ **8:06 am** 5:06 am
☉□♆ **8:49 am** 5:49 am
☽△⚳ **9:42 am** 6:42 am
☽⚹⚷ **10:56 am** 7:56 am
☽⊼♂ **3:34 pm** 12:34 pm
♅□♀ **3:48 pm** 12:48 pm

6 THURSDAY
☽□♅ **3:12 am** 12:12 am
☽☍♀ **3:38 am** 12:38 am
☽□⚴ **6:44 am** 3:44 am
☽□♃ **7:24 am** 4:24 am
☽⊼♄ **8:06 am** 5:06 am
☽⚹♆ **5:43 pm** 2:43 pm
☽⊼☉ **7:58 pm** 4:58 pm

7 FRIDAY
☽☌♇ **4:00 am** 1:00 am
☽△☿ **5:54 am** 2:54 am
☽☍♀ **7:50 am** 4:50 am
♃☍⚴ **7:52 am** 4:52 am
☽⊻⚵ **8:22 am** 5:22 am
☽⊼⚳ **10:54 am** 7:54 am
☽⊻⚷ **11:00 am** 8:00 am
⚷☍⚳ **2:54 pm** 11:54 am
☽☍♂ **5:50 pm** 2:50 pm

8 SATURDAY
☽⚹♅ **3:35 am** 12:35 am
☽⊼♀ **5:54 am** 2:54 am
☽△♃ **7:48 am** 4:48 am
☽⚹⚴ **8:27 am** 5:27 am
☽☍♄ **8:49 am** 5:49 am
♀⊼⚵ **10:03 am** 7:03 am
☽⊻♆ **6:23 pm** 3:23 pm
☽△☉ 9:10 pm
♄△⚴ 11:14 pm

9 SUNDAY
☽△☉ **12:10 am**
♄△⚴ **2:14 am**
☽⊻♇ **4:54 am** 1:54 am
☽□☿ **9:03 am** 6:03 am
☽☌⚵ **9:40 am** 6:40 am
☽⊼♀ **10:07 am** 7:07 am
☽☌⚷ **12:12 pm** 9:12 am
☽☍⚳ **1:21 pm** 10:21 am
☽⊼♂ **9:40 pm** 6:40 pm
☿□⚵ **10:44 pm** 7:44 pm

10 MONDAY
☽⊻♅ **5:38 am** 2:38 am
♃□♀ **7:49 am** 4:49 am
☽⊼♃ **10:01 am** 7:01 am
☽△♀ **10:07 am** 7:07 am
☽⊼♄ **11:24 am** 8:24 am
☽⊻⚴ **12:07 pm** 9:07 am
☿⚹♀ **7:47 pm** 4:47 pm
☽☌♆ **9:06 pm** 6:06 pm

11 TUESDAY
☽□☉ **7:04 am** 4:04 am
☽⚹♇ **8:07 am** 5:07 am
☽⊻⚵ **1:22 pm** 10:22 am
☽△♀ **2:44 pm** 11:44 am
☽⚹☿ **3:31 pm** 12:31 pm
☽⊻⚷ **3:52 pm** 12:52 pm
☽⊼⚳ **6:30 pm** 3:30 pm
☿□⚷ **9:23 pm** 6:23 pm
☉⊼♇ **9:29 pm** 6:29 pm
♄⊻♀ **11:29 pm** 8:29 pm

12 WEDNESDAY
☽△♂ **4:32 am** 1:32 am
☽☌♅ **10:29 am** 7:29 am
☽☍♃ **3:06 pm** 12:06 pm
☽△♄ **4:53 pm** 1:53 pm
☽□♀ **5:33 pm** 2:33 pm
☽☌⚴ **6:52 pm** 3:52 pm
☽⊻♆ 11:47 pm

13 THURSDAY
☽⊻♆ **2:47 am**
☽□♇ **2:20 pm** 11:20 am
☽⚹☉ **5:44 pm** 2:44 pm
☽⚹⚵ **8:06 pm** 5:06 pm
☽□♀ **10:14 pm** 7:14 pm
☽⚹⚷ **10:35 pm** 7:35 pm
☽⊻☿ 11:16 pm

14 FRIDAY
☽⊻☿ **2:16 am**
☽△⚳ **3:00 am** 12:00 am
☽□♂ **2:57 pm** 11:57 am
☿□⚳ **5:31 pm** 2:31 pm
☽⊻♅ **6:23 pm** 3:23 pm
☽⊼♃ **11:17 pm** 8:17 pm
☽□♄ 10:30 pm
☉△⚵ 10:51 pm

15 SATURDAY
☽□♄ **1:30 am**
☉△⚵ **1:51 am**
☽⚹♀ **4:28 am** 1:28 am
☽⊻⚴ **4:54 am** 1:54 am
♀⊼⚷ **7:15 am** 4:15 am
☽⚹♆ **11:27 am** 8:27 am
☽△♇ **11:27 pm** 8:27 pm

16 SUNDAY
☽□⚵ **5:38 am** 2:38 am
♀□⚴ **5:57 am** 2:57 am
☽⊻☉ **7:59 am** 4:59 am
☽□⚷ **8:06 am** 5:06 am
☽⚹♀ **8:17 am** 5:17 am
☉△⚷ **9:22 am** 6:22 am
☉⊻♀ **11:59 am** 8:59 am
☽□⚳ **2:32 pm** 11:32 am
☽☌☿ **5:11 pm** 2:11 pm

17 MONDAY
☽⚹♂ **4:26 am** 1:26 am
☽⚹♅ **4:54 am** 1:54 am
☽△♃ **10:02 am** 7:02 am
☽⚹♄ **12:42 pm** 9:42 am
♂△♅ **1:28 pm** 10:28 am
☽⚹⚴ **5:35 pm** 2:35 pm
☽⊻♀ **6:14 pm** 3:14 pm
☽□♆ **10:28 pm** 7:28 pm

18 TUESDAY
☽⊼♇ **10:43 am** 7:43 am
☽△⚵ **5:12 pm** 2:12 pm
☽△⚷ **7:38 pm** 4:38 pm
☽⊻♀ **7:58 pm** 4:58 pm
☽☌☉ 9:52 pm

19 WEDNESDAY
☽☌☉ **12:52 am**
☽⚹⚳ **4:13 am** 1:13 am
☽⊻☿ **11:22 am** 8:22 am
☽□♅ **5:07 pm** 2:07 pm
☽⊻♂ **7:57 pm** 4:57 pm
☽□♃ **10:29 pm** 7:29 pm
☽⊻♄ 10:32 pm

20 THURSDAY
☽⊻♄ **1:32 am**
☽□⚴ **7:54 am** 4:54 am
☽☌♀ **9:45 am** 6:45 am
☽△♆ **10:55 am** 7:55 am
☽☍♇ **11:14 pm** 8:14 pm

21 FRIDAY
♀⊼⚷ **5:37 am** 2:37 am
☽⊼⚵ **5:49 am** 2:49 am
☽☌♀ **8:13 am** 5:13 am
☽⊼⚷ **8:15 am** 5:15 am
♆△♀ **9:25 am** 6:25 am
☉⚹⚳ **6:20 pm** 3:20 pm
☿⚹♅ **6:43 pm** 3:43 pm
☽⊻⚳ **6:59 pm** 3:59 pm
☽⊻☉ **7:01 pm** 4:01 pm
♂⚹♃ **11:05 pm** 8:05 pm

22 SATURDAY
☽△♅ **6:04 am** 3:04 am
☽⚹☿ **7:28 am** 4:28 am
☽⚹♃ **11:36 am** 8:36 am
☽☌♂ **12:14 pm** 9:14 am
☽☌♄ **2:58 pm** 11:58 am
☽△⚴ **10:39 pm** 7:39 pm
☽⊼♆ **11:45 pm** 8:45 pm
☽⊻♀ 10:45 pm

23 SUNDAY
☽⊻♀ **1:45 am**
☽⊼♇ **11:52 am** 8:52 am
☽☍⚵ **6:21 pm** 3:21 pm
☽⊻♀ **7:55 pm** 4:55 pm
☽☍⚷ **8:47 pm** 5:47 pm
☿△♃ **8:51 pm** 5:51 pm

24 MONDAY
☽☌⚳ **9:26 am** 6:26 am
♆⊻⚴ **11:23 am** 8:23 am
☽⚹☉ **12:46 pm** 9:46 am
☽⊼♅ **6:25 pm** 3:25 pm
☽⊻♃ 9:02 pm
♂☌♄ 10:39 pm

25 TUESDAY
☽⊻♃ **12:02 am**
♂☌♄ **1:39 am**
☽□☿ **3:28 am** 12:28 am
☽⊻♄ **3:35 am** 12:35 am
☽⊻♂ **3:41 am** 12:41 am
☿⚹♄ **4:39 am** 1:39 am
☿⚹♂ **6:33 am** 3:33 am
☽☍♆ **11:33 am** 8:33 am
☽⊼⚴ **12:16 pm** 9:16 am
☽⚹♀ **4:31 pm** 1:31 pm
☽△♇ **11:10 pm** 8:10 pm

26 WEDNESDAY
☽⊼⚵ **5:19 am** 2:19 am
☽⚹♀ **5:42 am** 2:42 am
☽⊼⚷ **7:44 am** 4:44 am
☽⊻⚳ **9:48 pm** 6:48 pm
♀⊼⚵ **9:55 pm** 6:55 pm

27 THURSDAY
☽□☉ **3:57 am** 12:57 am
☽☍♅ **4:36 am** 1:36 am
☽☌♃ **10:09 am** 7:09 am
☉□♅ **12:43 pm** 9:43 am
☽⚹♄ **1:46 pm** 10:46 am
☽⚹♂ **4:18 pm** 1:18 pm
☽△☿ **8:42 pm** 5:42 pm
☽⊼♆ **8:45 pm** 5:45 pm
☿□♆ **9:14 pm** 6:14 pm
☽☍⚴ **11:01 pm** 8:01 pm

28 FRIDAY
☽□♀ **4:09 am** 1:09 am
☽□♇ **7:37 am** 4:37 am
☽□♀ **12:17 pm** 9:17 am
☽△⚵ **1:14 pm** 10:14 am
☽△⚷ **3:38 pm** 12:38 pm
☿⚹⚴ **8:24 pm** 5:24 pm

29 SATURDAY
☽⚹⚳ **6:32 am** 3:32 am
☽⊼♅ **11:19 am** 8:19 am
☽△☉ **2:47 pm** 11:47 am
☽⊻♃ **4:43 pm** 1:43 pm
☽□♄ **8:16 pm** 5:16 pm
☽□♂ 9:45 pm
☽△♆ 11:18 pm

30 SUNDAY
☽□♂ **12:45 am**
☽△♆ **2:18 am**
☽⊼⚴ **5:44 am** 2:44 am
☽⊼☿ **9:13 am** 6:13 am
☽△♀ **11:32 am** 8:32 am
☽⚹♇ **12:21 pm** 9:21 am
☽△♀ **3:09 pm** 12:09 pm
☽□⚵ **5:25 pm** 2:25 pm
☽□⚷ **7:48 pm** 4:48 pm
☉□♃ **8:34 pm** 5:34 pm

31 MONDAY
♇☍♀ **6:04 am** 3:04 am
♂⊼♆ **10:42 am** 7:42 am
☿⊼♇ **11:10 am** 8:10 am
☽□⚳ **11:14 am** 8:14 am
☿⊻♀ **2:00 pm** 11:00 am
☽△♅ **2:19 pm** 11:19 am
☽⚹♃ **7:37 pm** 4:37 pm
☽⊼☉ **9:06 pm** 6:06 pm
☽△♄ **11:05 pm** 8:05 pm
☿⊻♀ 9:43 pm

Eastern time in bold type
Pacific time in medium type

MAY 2004

☽ Last Aspect				☽ Ingress			
day	EST	hr:mn / PST	asp	sign	day	EST	hr:mn / PST
1	**7:31 am**	4:31 am	□ ♂	♎	1	**2:03 pm**	11:03 am
3	**12:49 pm**	9:49 am	△ ♂	♏	3	**4:38 pm**	1:38 pm
4	**5:36 pm**	2:36 pm	□ ♆	♐	5	**5:08 pm**	2:08 pm
7	**7:50 am**	4:50 am	☍ ♀	♑	7	**5:17 pm**	2:17 pm
9	**9:03 am**	6:03 am	□ ☿	♒	9	**6:46 pm**	3:46 pm
11	**3:31 pm**	12:31 pm	⚹ ☿	♓	11	**10:52 pm**	7:52 pm
13	**10:14 pm**	7:14 pm	□ ♀	♈	14	**6:02 am**	3:02 am
16	**8:17 am**	5:17 am	⚹ ♀	♉	16	**3:57 pm**	12:57 pm
18		9:52 pm	☌ ☉	♊	19	**3:47 am**	12:47 am
19	**12:52 am**		☌ ☉	♊	19	**3:47 am**	12:47 am
21	**8:13 am**	5:13 am	☌ ♀	♋	21	**4:35 pm**	1:35 pm
22	**2:58 pm**	11:58 am	☌ ♄	♌	24	**5:07 am**	2:07 am
26	**5:42 am**	2:42 am	⚹ ♀	♍	26	**3:52 pm**	12:52 pm
28	**12:17 pm**	9:17 am	□ ♀	♎	28	**11:22 pm**	8:22 pm
30	**3:09 pm**	12:09 pm	△ ♀	♏	31	**3:08 am**	12:08 am

☽ Phases & Eclipses			
phase	day	EST	hr:mn / PST
Full Moon	4	**4:33 pm**	1:33 pm
☊	4	14° ♏ 42'	
4th Quarter	11	**7:04 am**	4:04 am
New Moon	18		9:52 pm
New Moon	19	**12:52 am**	
2nd Quarter	27	**3:57 am**	12:57 am

Planet Ingress				
		day	EST	hr:mn / PST
♂	♋	7	**4:45 am**	1:45 am
☿	♉	15		11:54 pm
☿	♉	16	**2:54 am**	
⚳	♌	18	**2:00 pm**	11:00 am
☉	♊	20	**12:59 pm**	9:59 am

Planetary Motion				
		day	EST	hr:mn / PST
⚷	℞	1		10:12 pm
⚷	℞	2	**1:12 am**	
♃	D	4	**11:06 pm**	8:06 pm
⚵	℞	16		11:49 pm
⚵	℞	17	**2:49 am**	
♆	℞	17	**8:13 am**	5:13 am
♀	℞	17	**6:29 pm**	3:29 pm

DATE		SID.TIME	SUN	MOON	NODE	MERCURY	VENUS	MARS	JUPITER	SATURN	URANUS	NEPTUNE	PLUTO	CERES	PALLAS	JUNO	VESTA	CHIRON
1	Sa	14:37:02	10 ♉ 57 35	19 ♍ 45	11 ♉ 15	21 ♈ 07	21 ♊ 13	25 ♊ 58	08 ♍ ℞ 56	08 ♋ 51	06 ♓ 08	15 ♒ 19	21 ♐ ℞ 53	23 ♋ 51	03 ♊ 32	24 ♑ 01	06 ♓ 17	26 ♑ 08
2	Su	14:40:59	11 55 47	03 ♎ 26	11 15	21 12	21 44	26 36	08 56	08 57	06 10	15 20	21 52	24 11	04 06	24 06	06 41	26 ℞ 08
3	M	14:44:55	12 53 58	17 33	11 15	21 21	22 14	27 14	08 55	09 02	06 12	15 20	21 51	24 30	04 40	24 11	07 06	26 08
4	T	14:48:52	13 52 06	02 ♏ 03	11 ℞ 15	21 36	22 43	27 52	08 55	09 08	06 14	15 21	21 50	24 50	05 14	24 15	07 31	26 08
5	W	14:52:48	14 50 13	16 50	11 15	21 54	23 10	28 30	08 D 55	09 13	06 15	15 21	21 49	25 10	05 49	24 20	07 55	26 08
6	Th	14:56:45	15 48 18	01 ♐ 48	11 15	22 17	23 35	29 08	08 55	09 19	06 17	15 21	21 48	25 30	06 23	24 24	08 19	26 07
7	F	15:00:41	16 46 22	16 47	11 15	22 45	23 58	29 46	08 55	09 24	06 19	15 22	21 46	25 51	06 57	24 27	08 44	26 07
8	Sa	15:04:38	17 44 24	01 ♑ 41	11 14	23 16	24 20	00 ♋ 24	08 56	09 30	06 20	15 22	21 45	26 11	07 32	24 30	09 07	26 07
9	Su	15:08:34	18 42 25	16 21	11 13	23 52	24 40	01 02	08 56	09 36	06 22	15 22	21 44	26 32	08 06	24 33	09 31	26 06
10	M	15:12:31	19 40 25	00 ♒ 44	11 13	24 31	24 58	01 40	08 57	09 42	06 24	15 23	21 43	26 53	08 40	24 36	09 55	26 06
11	T	15:16:28	20 38 23	14 45	11 D 12	25 15	25 14	02 18	08 58	09 48	06 25	15 23	21 41	27 13	09 15	24 38	10 19	26 05
12	W	15:20:24	21 36 20	28 24	11 12	26 01	25 28	02 56	08 59	09 54	06 26	15 23	21 40	27 34	09 50	24 40	10 42	26 04
13	Th	15:24:21	22 34 15	11 ♓ 41	11 13	26 52	25 41	03 34	09 01	10 00	06 28	15 23	21 39	27 56	10 24	24 42	11 05	26 04
14	F	15:28:17	23 32 09	24 40	11 14	27 45	25 51	04 12	09 02	10 06	06 29	15 23	21 37	28 17	10 59	24 43	11 28	26 03
15	Sa	15:32:14	24 30 02	07 ♈ 21	11 15	28 42	25 58	04 50	09 04	10 12	06 31	15 24	21 36	28 38	11 34	24 44	11 51	26 02
16	Su	15:36:10	25 27 54	19 48	11 16	29 42	26 04	05 28	09 06	10 18	06 32	15 24	21 35	29 00	12 09	24 45	12 14	26 01
17	M	15:40:07	26 25 44	02 ♉ 03	11 ℞ 17	00 ♉ 45	26 ℞ 07	06 06	09 08	10 25	06 33	15 ℞ 24	21 33	29 22	12 44	24 ℞ 45	12 36	26 00
18	T	15:44:03	27 23 33	14 09	11 17	01 51	26 08	06 44	09 10	10 31	06 34	15 24	21 32	29 44	13 19	24 45	12 59	25 58
19	W	15:48:00	28 21 21	26 08	11 16	03 00	26 07	07 22	09 12	10 38	06 35	15 24	21 30	00 ♌ 06	13 54	24 44	13 21	25 57
20	Th	15:51:57	29 19 07	08 ♊ 02	11 15	04 11	26 03	08 00	09 15	10 44	06 36	15 24	21 29	00 28	14 29	24 44	13 43	25 56
21	F	15:55:53	00 ♊ 16 53	19 52	11 12	05 26	25 57	08 38	09 18	10 51	06 37	15 23	21 28	00 50	15 04	24 42	14 05	25 55
22	Sa	15:59:50	01 14 36	01 ♋ 41	11 09	06 42	25 49	09 16	09 20	10 57	06 38	15 23	21 26	01 12	15 39	24 41	14 26	25 53
23	Su	16:03:46	02 12 18	13 32	11 06	08 02	25 38	09 54	09 24	11 04	06 39	15 23	21 25	01 35	16 14	24 39	14 48	25 52
24	M	16:07:43	03 09 59	25 27	11 03	09 24	25 24	10 32	09 27	11 10	06 40	15 23	21 23	01 57	16 49	24 37	15 09	25 50
25	T	16:11:39	04 07 38	07 ♌ 29	11 00	10 49	25 08	11 10	09 30	11 17	06 41	15 23	21 22	02 20	17 25	24 34	15 30	25 48
26	W	16:15:36	05 05 16	19 42	10 58	12 16	24 50	11 48	09 34	11 24	06 42	15 22	21 20	02 43	18 00	24 32	15 51	25 47
27	Th	16:19:33	06 02 52	02 ♍ 10	10 D 57	13 45	24 30	12 26	09 38	11 31	06 43	15 22	21 19	03 06	18 35	24 28	16 12	25 45
28	F	16:23:29	07 00 27	14 57	10 57	15 17	24 07	13 04	09 42	11 38	06 43	15 22	21 17	03 28	19 11	24 25	16 32	25 43
29	Sa	16:27:26	07 58 00	28 07	10 58	16 51	23 42	13 41	09 46	11 45	06 44	15 21	21 16	03 52	19 46	24 21	16 53	25 41
30	Su	16:31:22	08 55 32	11 ♎ 42	11 00	18 28	23 15	14 19	09 50	11 51	06 44	15 21	21 14	04 15	20 21	24 17	17 13	25 39
31	M	16:35:19	09 53 03	25 45	11 01	20 08	22 46	14 57	09 54	11 58	06 45	15 21	21 12	04 38	20 57	24 12	17 33	25 37

EPHEMERIS CALCULATED FOR 12 MIDNIGHT GREENWICH MEAN TIME. ALL OTHER DATA AND FACING ASPECTARIAN PAGE IN **EASTERN TIME (BOLD)** AND PACIFIC TIME (REGULAR).

JUNE 2004

1 TUESDAY

☿ ⚺ ♀	**12:43 am**	
☽ □ ♆	**4:20 am**	1:20 am
☽ △ ♂	**5:08 am**	2:08 am
☽ △ ⚶	**8:43 am**	5:43 am
♀ ☌ ⚴	**11:23 am**	8:23 am
☽ ⚺ ♇	**1:44 pm**	10:44 am
☽ ⚻ ♀	**2:50 pm**	11:50 am
☽ ⚻ ⚴	**3:06 pm**	12:06 pm
☽ ☍ ☿	**5:15 pm**	2:15 pm
☽ ⚹ ⚵	**6:21 pm**	3:21 pm
☽ ⚹ ⚷	**8:46 pm**	5:46 pm
☿ △ ⚵		11:06 pm

2 WEDNESDAY

☿ △ ⚵	**2:06 am**	
☉ ⚺ ♄	**7:42 am**	4:42 am
☽ △ ⚳	**12:54 pm**	9:54 am
☽ □ ♅	**2:36 pm**	11:36 am
☽ □ ♃	**7:56 pm**	4:56 pm
♀ ☍ ♇	**9:24 pm**	6:24 pm
☿ △ ⚷	**10:22 pm**	7:22 pm
☽ ⚻ ♄	**11:24 pm**	8:24 pm
☽ ☍ ☉		9:20 pm

3 THURSDAY

☽ ☍ ☉	**12:20 am**	
☽ ⚹ ♆	**4:05 am**	1:05 am
☽ ⚻ ♂	**6:57 am**	3:57 am
☽ □ ⚶	**9:24 am**	6:24 am
☽ ☍ ♀	**12:39 pm**	9:39 am
☽ ☌ ♇	**1:12 pm**	10:12 am
☽ ☍ ⚴	**4:33 pm**	1:33 pm
☽ ⚺ ⚵	**5:30 pm**	2:30 pm
☽ ⚺ ⚷	**8:04 pm**	5:04 pm
☽ ⚻ ☿	**11:04 pm**	8:04 pm

4 FRIDAY

☽ ⚻ ⚳	**1:27 pm**	10:27 am
⚴ ⚻ ⚵	**1:33 pm**	10:33 am
☽ ⚹ ♅	**1:55 pm**	10:55 am
☽ △ ♃	**7:30 pm**	4:30 pm
☽ ☍ ♄	**11:07 pm**	8:07 pm
☽ ⚻ ☉		11:53 pm

5 SATURDAY

☽ ⚻ ☉	**2:53 am**	
☽ ⚺ ♆	**3:27 am**	12:27 am
♅ ⚻ ⚳	**7:13 am**	4:13 am
☽ ☍ ♂	**8:28 am**	5:28 am
☽ ⚹ ⚶	**9:54 am**	6:54 am
☽ ⚻ ♀	**10:22 am**	7:22 am
☉ △ ♆	**11:40 am**	8:40 am
☽ ⚺ ♇	**12:41 pm**	9:41 am
☽ ☌ ⚵	**4:49 pm**	1:49 pm
♀ □ ⚶	**5:41 pm**	2:41 pm
☽ ⚻ ⚴	**6:10 pm**	3:10 pm
☽ ☌ ⚷	**7:40 pm**	4:40 pm

6 SUNDAY

☽ △ ☿	**5:54 am**	2:54 am
♀ ⚺ ♂	**8:03 am**	5:03 am
☽ ⚺ ♅	**2:18 pm**	11:18 am
☽ ☍ ⚳	**3:10 pm**	12:10 pm
☽ ⚻ ♃	**8:27 pm**	5:27 pm
☽ ⚻ ♄		9:21 pm

7 MONDAY

☽ ⚻ ♄	**12:21 am**	
☽ ☌ ♆	**4:27 am**	1:27 am
⚷ ⚻ ⚴	**5:28 am**	2:28 am
☽ △ ☉	**7:25 am**	4:25 am
☽ △ ♀	**9:42 am**	6:42 am
☽ ⚻ ♂	**12:05 pm**	9:05 am
☽ ⚺ ⚶	**12:23 pm**	9:23 am
☽ ⚹ ♇	**2:09 pm**	11:09 am
☽ ⚺ ⚵	**6:12 pm**	3:12 pm
☽ ⚺ ⚷	**9:31 pm**	6:31 pm
☽ △ ⚴	**10:17 pm**	7:17 pm
♂ △ ⚶		9:31 pm

8 TUESDAY

♂ △ ⚶	**12:31 am**	
☉ ☌ ♀	**4:43 am**	1:43 am
☽ □ ☿	**5:08 pm**	2:08 pm
☽ ☌ ♅	**5:34 pm**	2:34 pm
☽ ⚻ ⚳	**8:03 pm**	5:03 pm
☿ □ ♅	**8:05 pm**	5:05 pm
☽ ☍ ♃		9:31 pm

9 WEDNESDAY

☽ ☍ ♃	**12:31 am**	
☽ △ ♄	**4:48 am**	1:48 am
♂ ⚻ ♇	**8:29 am**	5:29 am
☽ ⚺ ♆	**8:42 am**	5:42 am
☽ □ ♀	**11:59 am**	8:59 am
☽ □ ☉	**4:02 pm**	1:02 pm
☿ ⚹ ⚳	**4:45 pm**	1:45 pm
☽ ☌ ⚶	**6:29 pm**	3:29 pm
☽ □ ♇	**7:03 pm**	4:03 pm
☽ △ ♂	**7:37 pm**	4:37 pm
☽ ⚹ ⚵	**11:00 pm**	8:00 pm
☽ ⚹ ⚷		11:55 pm

10 THURSDAY

☽ ⚹ ⚷	**2:55 am**	
☽ □ ⚴	**6:30 am**	3:30 am
♇ □ ⚶	**6:14 pm**	3:14 pm
☿ □ ♃	**7:51 pm**	4:51 pm
☽ ⚺ ♅		9:38 pm

11 FRIDAY

☽ ⚺ ♅	**12:38 am**	
☽ △ ⚳	**5:08 am**	2:08 am
☉ ☍ ♇	**8:26 am**	5:26 am
☽ ⚻ ♃	**8:31 am**	5:31 am
☽ ⚹ ☿	**10:56 am**	7:56 am
☽ □ ♄	**1:13 pm**	10:13 am
☉ □ ⚶	**3:02 pm**	12:02 pm
☽ ⚹ ♆	**4:45 pm**	1:45 pm
☽ ⚹ ♀	**5:40 pm**	2:40 pm
☿ ⚺ ♄		10:12 pm

12 SATURDAY

☿ ⚺ ♄	**1:12 am**	
☽ △ ♇	**3:44 am**	12:44 am
☽ ⚺ ⚶	**4:36 am**	1:36 am
♂ ☍ ⚵	**5:13 am**	2:13 am
☽ ⚹ ☉	**5:24 am**	2:24 am
☽ □ ⚵	**7:22 am**	4:22 am
☽ □ ♂	**7:31 am**	4:31 am
☽ □ ⚷	**11:59 am**	8:59 am
♀ △ ♆	**1:08 pm**	10:08 am
☽ ⚹ ⚴	**6:57 pm**	3:57 pm
☿ ☌ ♀	**7:24 pm**	4:24 pm
☿ △ ♆	**9:05 pm**	6:05 pm

13 SUNDAY

☉ ⚻ ⚵	**3:32 am**	12:32 am
☽ ⚹ ♅	**11:05 am**	8:05 am
☽ □ ⚳	**5:51 pm**	2:51 pm
☽ △ ♃	**7:52 pm**	4:52 pm
☽ ⚹ ♄		9:52 pm
☽ ⚺ ♀		11:08 pm

14 MONDAY

☽ ⚹ ♄	**12:52 am**	
☽ ⚺ ♀	**2:08 am**	
☽ □ ♆	**3:52 am**	12:52 am
☽ ⚺ ☿	**10:41 am**	7:41 am
☽ ⚻ ♇	**3:11 pm**	12:11 pm
☽ ⚹ ⚶	**5:37 pm**	2:37 pm
☽ △ ⚵	**6:18 pm**	3:18 pm
☽ ⚺ ☉	**10:15 pm**	7:15 pm
☽ ⚹ ♂	**10:34 pm**	7:34 pm
☽ △ ⚷	**11:35 pm**	8:35 pm
♀ ⚺ ♄		9:32 pm

15 TUESDAY

♀ ⚺ ♄	**12:32 am**	
☉ ⚺ ♂	**9:15 am**	6:15 am
☽ ⚺ ⚴	**10:11 am**	7:11 am
☿ ☍ ♇	**11:07 am**	8:07 am
⚵ ⚹ ⚶	**12:30 pm**	9:30 am
☉ ⚻ ⚷	**2:11 pm**	11:11 am
♂ ☍ ⚷	**4:32 pm**	1:32 pm
☽ □ ♅	**11:29 pm**	8:29 pm
☿ ⚻ ⚵		10:56 pm

16 WEDNESDAY

☿ ⚻ ⚵	**1:56 am**	
☿ □ ⚶	**4:57 am**	1:57 am
☽ ⚹ ⚳	**8:35 am**	5:35 am
☽ □ ♃	**9:01 am**	6:01 am
☽ ☌ ♀	**12:12 pm**	9:12 am
☽ ⚺ ♄	**2:10 pm**	11:10 am
☽ △ ♆	**4:29 pm**	1:29 pm
♃ ⚺ ⚳		10:44 pm

17 THURSDAY

♃ ⚺ ⚳	**1:44 am**	
☽ ☍ ♇	**3:51 am**	12:51 am
☽ ⚻ ⚵	**6:16 am**	3:16 am
☿ ⚻ ⚷	**7:46 am**	4:46 am
☽ □ ⚶	**7:50 am**	4:50 am
☽ ⚻ ⚷	**12:12 pm**	9:12 am
☽ ☌ ☿	**1:14 pm**	10:14 am
☽ ⚺ ♂	**2:51 pm**	11:51 am
☽ ☌ ☉	**4:27 pm**	1:27 pm
☿ ⚺ ♂		9:47 pm
☽ ☌ ⚴		11:19 pm

18 FRIDAY

☿ ⚺ ♂	**12:47 am**	
☽ ☌ ⚴	**2:19 am**	
♀ ⚹ ⚳	**11:10 am**	8:10 am
☽ △ ♅	**12:20 pm**	9:20 am
☉ ☌ ☿	**5:24 pm**	2:24 pm
☽ ⚹ ♃	**10:28 pm**	7:28 pm
☽ ⚺ ♀	**10:46 pm**	7:46 pm
☽ ⚺ ⚳	**11:37 pm**	8:37 pm

19 SATURDAY

☽ ☌ ♄	**3:37 am**	12:37 am
☽ ⚻ ♆	**5:12 am**	2:12 am
♀ □ ♃	**5:29 am**	2:29 am
☽ ⚻ ♇	**4:25 pm**	1:25 pm
☽ ☍ ⚵	**6:01 pm**	3:01 pm
☽ △ ⚶	**9:47 pm**	6:47 pm
☽ ☍ ⚷		9:32 pm

20 SUNDAY

☽ ☍ ⚷	**12:32 am**	
☽ ☌ ♂	**6:46 am**	3:46 am
☽ ⚺ ☉	**10:14 am**	7:14 am
☽ ⚺ ☿	**3:22 pm**	12:22 pm
☽ ⚺ ⚴	**5:53 pm**	2:53 pm
☽ ⚻ ♅		9:32 pm

21 MONDAY

☽ ⚻ ♅	**12:32 am**	
☽ ⚹ ♀	**9:00 am**	6:00 am
☿ ☌ ♀	**9:35 am**	6:35 am
☽ ⚺ ♃	**11:07 am**	8:07 am
☽ ☌ ⚳	**1:46 pm**	10:46 am
☽ ⚺ ♄	**4:11 pm**	1:11 pm
☽ ☍ ♆	**5:00 pm**	2:00 pm

22 TUESDAY

☽ △ ♇	**3:54 am**	12:54 am
☽ ⚻ ⚵	**4:41 am**	1:41 am
☽ ⚻ ⚶	**10:26 am**	7:26 am
☽ ⚻ ⚷	**11:41 am**	8:41 am
☿ △ ♅	**6:11 pm**	3:11 pm
☽ ⚺ ♂	**9:10 pm**	6:10 pm
☽ ⚹ ☉		11:16 pm

23 WEDNESDAY

☽ ⚹ ☉	**2:16 am**	
☽ ⚹ ⚴	**7:43 am**	4:43 am
☽ ☍ ♅	**11:07 am**	8:07 am
☽ ⚹ ☿	**2:38 pm**	11:38 am
☽ □ ♀	**6:02 pm**	3:02 pm
☽ ☌ ♃	**9:57 pm**	6:57 pm
☽ ⚺ ⚳		10:54 pm
☽ ⚹ ♄		11:48 pm
☽ ⚻ ♆		11:55 pm

24 THURSDAY

☽ ⚺ ⚳	**1:54 am**	
☽ ⚹ ♄	**2:48 am**	
☽ ⚻ ♆	**2:55 am**	
☿ ⚺ ♀	**9:11 am**	6:11 am
♇ ⚺ ⚵	**11:22 am**	8:22 am
♄ ⚻ ♆	**12:40 pm**	9:40 am
☽ △ ⚵	**1:18 pm**	10:18 am
☽ □ ♇	**1:19 pm**	10:19 am
⚷ ⚹ ⚶	**5:23 pm**	2:23 pm
☽ △ ⚷	**8:37 pm**	5:37 pm
☽ ☍ ⚶	**8:42 pm**	5:42 pm

25 FRIDAY

♆ ☍ ⚳	**7:31 am**	4:31 am
☽ ⚹ ♂	**8:45 am**	5:45 am
☿ ⚹ ♃	**12:48 pm**	9:48 am
☽ □ ☉	**3:08 pm**	12:08 pm
♄ ⚺ ⚳	**4:56 pm**	1:56 pm
☽ □ ⚴	**6:33 pm**	3:33 pm
☽ ⚻ ♅	**7:04 pm**	4:04 pm
☽ △ ♀		9:50 pm

26 SATURDAY

☽ △ ♀	**12:50 am**	
♅ △ ♀	**5:45 am**	2:45 am
☽ ⚺ ♃	**5:53 am**	2:53 am
☽ □ ☿	**8:48 am**	5:48 am
☽ △ ♆	**9:56 am**	6:56 am
☽ □ ♄	**10:26 am**	7:26 am
☽ ⚹ ⚳	**10:50 am**	7:50 am
☿ ⚻ ♆	**4:11 pm**	1:11 pm
☽ □ ⚵	**6:56 pm**	3:56 pm
☽ ⚹ ♇	**7:41 pm**	4:41 pm
☿ ☌ ♄	**8:07 pm**	5:07 pm
☿ ⚺ ⚳		10:04 pm
☽ □ ⚷		11:26 pm

27 SUNDAY

☿ ⚺ ⚳	**1:04 am**	
☽ □ ⚷	**2:26 am**	
☽ ⚻ ⚶	**3:33 am**	12:33 am
☽ □ ♂	**4:31 pm**	1:31 pm
☉ △ ♅	**8:55 pm**	5:55 pm
☽ △ ♅	**11:37 pm**	8:37 pm
☽ △ ☉	**11:49 pm**	8:49 pm
☽ △ ⚴		10:30 pm

28 MONDAY

☽ △ ⚴	**1:30 am**	
☽ ⚻ ♀	**4:41 am**	1:41 am
☽ ⚹ ♃	**10:18 am**	7:18 am
☽ □ ♆	**1:31 pm**	10:31 am
☽ △ ♄	**2:31 pm**	11:31 am
☽ □ ⚳	**3:59 pm**	12:59 pm
☽ △ ☿	**8:57 pm**	5:57 pm
☽ ⚹ ⚵	**9:17 pm**	6:17 pm
☽ ⚺ ♇	**10:38 pm**	7:38 pm
☿ ☍ ⚵	**11:07 pm**	8:07 pm

29 TUESDAY

☽ ⚹ ⚷	**4:51 am**	1:51 am
☽ △ ⚶	**6:49 am**	3:49 am
☿ ⚻ ♇	**9:12 am**	6:12 am
☽ △ ♂	**8:31 pm**	5:31 pm
☽ □ ♅		9:59 pm

30 WEDNESDAY

☽ □ ♅	**12:59 am**	
☽ ⚻ ☉	**4:34 am**	1:34 am
☽ ⚻ ⚴	**4:52 am**	1:52 am
☽ ☍ ♀	**5:45 am**	2:45 am
☽ □ ♃	**11:37 am**	8:37 am
☽ ⚹ ♆	**2:10 pm**	11:10 am
☽ ⚻ ♄	**3:36 pm**	12:36 pm
☉ ☌ ⚴	**4:27 pm**	1:27 pm
☽ △ ⚳	**6:00 pm**	3:00 pm
☽ ⚺ ⚵	**8:57 pm**	5:57 pm
☽ ☌ ♇	**10:53 pm**	7:53 pm
☉ ⚺ ♀	**11:52 pm**	8:52 pm

Eastern time in bold type
Pacific time in medium type

JUNE 2004

☽ Last Aspect				☽ Ingress			
day	EST / hr:mn / PST		asp	sign day	EST / hr:mn / PST		
1	**5:15 pm**	2:15 pm	☍ ☿	♐ 2	**3:52 am**	12:52 am	
3	**1:12 pm**	10:12 am	☌ ♇	♑ 4	**3:12 am**	12:12 am	
5	**8:28 am**	5:28 am	☍ ♂	♒ 6	**3:10 am**	12:10 am	
7	**2:09 pm**	11:09 am	✶ ♇	♓ 8	**5:38 am**	2:38 am	
9	**7:37 pm**	4:37 pm	△ ♂	♈ 10	**11:49 am**	8:49 am	
12	**7:31 am**	4:31 am	□ ♂	♉ 12	**9:37 pm**	6:37 pm	
14	**10:34 pm**	7:34 pm	✶ ♂	♊ 15	**9:44 am**	6:44 am	
17	**4:27 pm**	1:27 pm	☌ ⊙	♋ 17	**10:37 pm**	7:37 pm	
20	**6:46 am**	3:46 am	☌ ♂	♌ 20	**11:05 am**	8:05 am	
22	**3:54 am**	12:54 am	△ ♇	♍ 22	**10:10 pm**	7:10 pm	

☽ Last Aspect				☽ Ingress		
day	EST / hr:mn / PST		asp	sign day	EST / hr:mn / PST	
24	**1:19 pm**	10:19 am	□ ♇	♎ 25	**6:50 am**	3:50 am
26	**7:41 pm**	4:41 pm	✶ ♇	♏ 27	**12:13 pm**	9:13 am
28	**8:57 pm**	5:57 pm	△ ☿	♐ 29	**2:15 pm**	11:15 am
30	**10:53 pm**	7:53 pm	☌ ♇	♑ 7/1	**2:01 pm**	11:01 am

☽ Phases & Eclipses			
phase	day	EST / hr:mn / PST	
Full Moon	2		9:20 pm
Full Moon	3	**12:20 am**	
4th Quarter	9	**4:02 pm**	1:02 pm
New Moon	17	**4:27 pm**	1:27 pm
2nd Quarter	25	**3:08 pm**	12:08 pm

Planet Ingress			
	day	EST / hr:mn / PST	
☿ ♊	5	**8:47 am**	5:47 am
♀ ♋	14		10:09 pm
♀ ♋	15	**1:09 am**	
☿ ♋	19	**3:49 pm**	12:49 pm
⊙ ♋	20	**8:57 pm**	5:57 pm
♂ ♌	23	**4:50 pm**	1:50 pm

Planetary Motion			
	day	EST / hr:mn / PST	
♅ ℞	10	**11:47 am**	8:47 am
♀ D	29	**7:16 pm**	4:16 pm

DATE		SID.TIME	SUN	MOON	NODE	MERCURY	VENUS	MARS	JUPITER	SATURN	URANUS	NEPTUNE	PLUTO	CERES	PALLAS	JUNO	VESTA	CHIRON
1	T	16:39:15	10 ♊ 50 32	10 ♏ 13	11 ♉ ℞ 02	21 ♉ 49	22 ♊ ℞ 16	15 ♋ 35	09 ♍ 59	12 ♋ 05	06 ♓ 45	15 ♒ ℞ 20	21 ♐ ℞ 11	05 ♌ 01	21 ♊ 32	24 ♑ ℞ 07	17 ♓ 52	25 ♑ ℞ 35
2	W	16:43:12	11 48 00	25 04	11 01	23 33	21 43	16 13	10 04	12 13	06 46	15 20	21 09	05 25	22 08	24 02	18 12	25 33
3	Th	16:47:08	12 45 27	10 ♐ 11	10 59	25 20	21 10	16 51	10 08	12 20	06 46	15 19	21 08	05 49	22 44	23 56	18 31	25 31
4	F	16:51:05	13 42 54	25 26	10 55	27 09	20 35	17 29	10 13	12 27	06 47	15 19	21 06	06 12	23 19	23 50	18 50	25 28
5	Sa	16:55:02	14 40 19	10 ♑ 37	10 51	29 00	19 59	18 06	10 19	12 34	06 47	15 18	21 05	06 36	23 55	23 43	19 09	25 26
6	Su	16:58:58	15 37 43	25 36	10 46	00 ♊ 53	19 22	18 44	10 24	12 41	06 47	15 18	21 03	07 00	24 30	23 37	19 27	25 24
7	M	17:02:55	16 35 07	10 ♒ 14	10 42	02 49	18 45	19 22	10 29	12 48	06 47	15 17	21 01	07 24	25 06	23 30	19 46	25 21
8	T	17:06:51	17 32 30	24 26	10 38	04 47	18 07	20 00	10 35	12 56	06 48	15 16	21 00	07 48	25 42	23 22	20 04	25 19
9	W	17:10:48	18 29 53	08 ♓ 10	10 D 36	06 47	17 29	20 38	10 41	13 03	06 48	15 16	20 58	08 12	26 18	23 14	20 22	25 16
10	Th	17:14:44	19 27 15	21 28	10 36	08 49	16 52	21 16	10 47	13 10	06 ℞ 48	15 15	20 57	08 36	26 53	23 06	20 39	25 13
11	F	17:18:41	20 24 36	04 ♈ 21	10 37	10 54	16 15	21 53	10 53	13 18	06 48	15 14	20 55	09 00	27 29	22 58	20 57	25 11
12	Sa	17:22:37	21 21 57	16 54	10 38	12 59	15 38	22 31	10 59	13 25	06 48	15 13	20 54	09 25	28 05	22 49	21 14	25 08
13	Su	17:26:34	22 19 17	29 11	10 ℞ 39	15 07	15 03	23 09	11 05	13 33	06 48	15 13	20 52	09 49	28 41	22 40	21 30	25 05
14	M	17:30:31	23 16 38	11 ♉ 16	10 40	17 16	14 28	23 47	11 12	13 40	06 47	15 12	20 50	10 14	29 16	22 31	21 47	25 02
15	T	17:34:27	24 13 57	23 12	10 39	19 25	13 55	24 25	11 18	13 48	06 47	15 11	20 49	10 38	29 52	22 21	22 03	25 00
16	W	17:38:24	25 11 16	05 ♊ 04	10 36	21 36	13 23	25 03	11 25	13 55	06 47	15 10	20 47	11 03	00 ♋ 28	22 11	22 19	24 57
17	Th	17:42:20	26 08 35	16 53	10 31	23 48	12 53	25 40	11 32	14 03	06 47	15 09	20 46	11 28	01 04	22 01	22 35	24 54
18	F	17:46:17	27 05 53	28 43	10 24	25 59	12 25	26 18	11 39	14 10	06 46	15 08	20 44	11 53	01 40	21 50	22 50	24 51
19	Sa	17:50:13	28 03 11	10 ♋ 34	10 16	28 11	11 59	26 56	11 46	14 18	06 46	15 07	20 42	12 17	02 16	21 40	23 06	24 48
20	Su	17:54:10	29 00 28	22 28	10 07	00 ♋ 23	11 35	27 34	11 53	14 25	06 46	15 06	20 41	12 42	02 52	21 28	23 21	24 45
21	M	17:58:06	29 57 44	04 ♌ 28	09 58	02 34	11 12	28 12	12 01	14 33	06 45	15 05	20 39	13 07	03 28	21 17	23 35	24 41
22	T	18:02:03	00 ♋ 55 00	16 36	09 50	04 44	10 53	28 49	12 08	14 41	06 45	15 04	20 38	13 33	04 04	21 05	23 49	24 38
23	W	18:06:00	01 52 16	28 53	09 43	06 54	10 35	29 27	12 16	14 48	06 44	15 03	20 36	13 58	04 39	20 54	24 03	24 35
24	Th	18:09:56	02 49 30	11 ♍ 23	09 39	09 02	10 20	00 ♌ 05	12 24	14 56	06 43	15 02	20 35	14 23	05 15	20 41	24 17	24 32
25	F	18:13:53	03 46 44	24 08	09 D 37	11 09	10 07	00 43	12 32	15 04	06 43	15 01	20 33	14 48	05 51	20 29	24 30	24 29
26	Sa	18:17:49	04 43 57	07 ♎ 13	09 36	13 15	09 56	01 21	12 40	15 11	06 42	15 00	20 32	15 14	06 27	20 17	24 43	24 25
27	Su	18:21:46	05 41 10	20 41	09 37	15 18	09 48	01 58	12 48	15 19	06 41	14 59	20 30	15 39	07 03	20 04	24 56	24 22
28	M	18:25:42	06 38 23	04 ♏ 33	09 ℞ 38	17 21	09 42	02 36	12 56	15 27	06 41	14 58	20 29	16 05	07 39	19 51	25 08	24 19
29	T	18:29:39	07 35 34	18 51	09 37	19 21	09 D 39	03 14	13 04	15 35	06 40	14 56	20 27	16 30	08 15	19 38	25 21	24 15
30	W	18:33:35	08 32 46	03 ♐ 33	09 35	21 19	09 38	03 52	13 13	15 42	06 39	14 55	20 26	16 56	08 51	19 25	25 32	24 12

EPHEMERIS CALCULATED FOR 12 MIDNIGHT GREENWICH MEAN TIME. ALL OTHER DATA AND FACING ASPECTARIAN PAGE IN **EASTERN TIME (BOLD)** AND PACIFIC TIME (REGULAR).

JULY 2004

1 THURSDAY

☽ ⚻ ☿	**4:28 am**	1:28 am
♀ ⚺ ⚴	**4:40 am**	1:40 am
☽ ⚺ ⚷	**4:45 am**	1:45 am
☿ ☍ ⚷	**6:42 am**	3:42 am
☽ □ ⚶	**7:26 am**	4:26 am
☽ ⚻ ♂	**10:10 pm**	7:10 pm
☽ ⚹ ♅		9:25 pm

2 FRIDAY

☽ ⚹ ♅	**12:25 am**	
☽ ⚻ ♀	**5:20 am**	2:20 am
☽ ☍ ⚴	**6:13 am**	3:13 am
☿ △ ⚶	**6:30 am**	3:30 am
☽ ☍ ☉	**7:09 am**	4:09 am
☽ △ ♃	**11:24 am**	8:24 am
☽ ⚺ ♆	**1:23 pm**	10:23 am
☽ ☍ ♄	**3:17 pm**	12:17 pm
☽ ⚻ ⚳	**6:38 pm**	3:38 pm
☽ ☌ ⚵	**7:30 pm**	4:30 pm
☽ ⚺ ♇	**10:03 pm**	7:03 pm

3 SATURDAY

☽ ☌ ⚷	**3:50 am**	12:50 am
☽ ⚹ ⚶	**7:16 am**	4:16 am
☽ ☍ ☿	**10:25 am**	7:25 am
⚳ ⚻ ⚵	**3:05 pm**	12:05 pm
☽ ☍ ♂	**11:44 pm**	8:44 pm
☽ ⚺ ♅	**11:54 pm**	8:54 pm

4 SUNDAY

♂ ⚻ ♅	**3:27 am**	12:27 am
☽ △ ♀	**5:25 am**	2:25 am
☽ ⚻ ⚴	**7:55 am**	4:55 am
☽ ⚻ ☉	**10:10 am**	7:10 am
☽ ⚻ ♃	**11:45 am**	8:45 am
☽ ☌ ♆	**1:15 pm**	10:15 am
☽ ⚻ ♄	**3:43 pm**	12:43 pm
☽ ⚺ ⚵	**6:56 pm**	3:56 pm
☽ ☍ ⚳	**8:14 pm**	5:14 pm
☽ ⚹ ♇	**10:15 pm**	7:15 pm

5 MONDAY

☽ ⚺ ⚷	**4:12 am**	1:12 am
☽ ⚺ ⚶	**8:35 am**	5:35 am
☉ ⚹ ♃	**2:59 pm**	11:59 am
☽ ⚻ ☿	**6:23 pm**	3:23 pm
☽ ☌ ♅		10:33 pm

6 TUESDAY

☽ ☌ ♅	**1:33 am**	
☽ ⚻ ♂	**3:48 am**	12:48 am
☽ □ ♀	**8:15 am**	5:15 am
☉ ⚻ ♆	**8:56 am**	5:56 am
☽ △ ⚴	**12:28 pm**	9:28 am
☽ ☍ ♃	**2:51 pm**	11:51 am
☽ ⚺ ♆	**3:49 pm**	12:49 pm
☽ △ ☉	**4:21 pm**	1:21 pm
☽ △ ♄	**7:03 pm**	4:03 pm
☽ ⚹ ⚵	**9:09 pm**	6:09 pm
☽ ⚻ ⚳		10:06 pm
☽ □ ♇		10:30 pm

7 WEDNESDAY

☽ ⚻ ⚳	**1:06 am**	
☽ □ ♇	**1:30 am**	
☽ ⚹ ⚷	**7:46 am**	4:46 am
♇ △ ⚳	**12:40 pm**	9:40 am
☽ ☌ ⚶	**1:19 pm**	10:19 am

8 THURSDAY

☿ ⚻ ♅	**4:37 am**	1:37 am
☽ ⚺ ♅	**7:00 am**	4:00 am
☽ △ ☿	**7:22 am**	4:22 am
☽ △ ♂	**12:17 pm**	9:17 am
☉ ☌ ♄	**12:38 pm**	9:38 am
☽ ⚹ ♀	**3:30 pm**	12:30 pm
☽ □ ⚴	**9:34 pm**	6:34 pm
☽ ⚻ ♃	**10:09 pm**	7:09 pm
☽ ⚹ ♆	**10:25 pm**	7:25 pm
☉ ☍ ⚵		9:23 pm
☽ □ ♄		11:34 pm

9 FRIDAY

☉ ☍ ⚵	**12:23 am**	
☽ □ ♄	**2:34 am**	
☽ □ ⚵	**3:16 am**	12:16 am
☽ □ ☉	**3:34 am**	12:34 am
☽ △ ♇	**8:52 am**	5:52 am
☽ △ ⚳	**10:32 am**	7:32 am
♃ ⚹ ♀	**2:11 pm**	11:11 am
♆ ⚻ ⚴	**3:04 pm**	12:04 pm
☽ □ ⚷	**3:27 pm**	12:27 pm
♃ ⚻ ♆	**5:10 pm**	2:10 pm
☽ ⚺ ⚶	**10:20 pm**	7:20 pm
♄ ☍ ⚵		11:50 pm

10 SATURDAY

♄ ☍ ⚵	**2:50 am**	
☽ ⚹ ♅	**4:30 pm**	1:30 pm
☿ ☌ ♂	**7:50 pm**	4:50 pm
☽ □ ♂		10:25 pm
☽ □ ☿		10:55 pm

11 SUNDAY

☽ □ ♂	**1:25 am**	
☽ □ ☿	**1:55 am**	
☽ ⚺ ♀	**3:23 am**	12:23 am
☽ □ ♆	**8:51 am**	5:51 am
☽ △ ♃	**9:28 am**	6:28 am
☽ ⚹ ⚴	**11:08 am**	8:08 am
☽ △ ⚵	**12:56 pm**	9:56 am
☽ ⚹ ♄	**1:59 pm**	10:59 am
☿ ⚹ ♀	**4:30 pm**	1:30 pm
☽ ⚹ ☉	**7:29 pm**	4:29 pm
☽ ⚻ ♇	**7:51 pm**	4:51 pm
☉ ⚻ ♇	**11:53 pm**	8:53 pm
☽ □ ⚳	**11:58 pm**	8:58 pm
☽ △ ⚷		11:33 pm

12 MONDAY

☽ △ ⚷	**2:33 am**	
☽ ⚹ ⚶	**10:39 am**	7:39 am
⚴ ☍ ⚵	**1:41 pm**	10:41 am

13 TUESDAY

☽ □ ♅	**4:42 am**	1:42 am
☿ ☍ ♆	**7:31 am**	4:31 am
☽ ⚹ ♂	**5:21 pm**	2:21 pm
☽ ☌ ♀	**6:11 pm**	3:11 pm
☿ ⚺ ♃	**7:38 pm**	4:38 pm
☽ △ ♆	**9:24 pm**	6:24 pm
☽ □ ♃	**11:00 pm**	8:00 pm
☽ ⚹ ☿	**11:26 pm**	8:26 pm
☽ ⚻ ⚵		9:29 pm

14 WEDNESDAY

☽ ⚻ ⚵	**12:29 am**	
☽ ⚺ ⚴	**3:04 am**	12:04 am
☽ ⚺ ♄	**3:25 am**	12:25 am
☿ ⚻ ⚵	**6:52 am**	3:52 am
☽ ☍ ♇	**8:33 am**	5:33 am
♄ ☌ ⚴	**11:54 am**	8:54 am
☽ ⚺ ☉	**1:39 pm**	10:39 am
⚷ ⚻ ⚳	**2:11 pm**	11:11 am
☽ ⚻ ⚷	**3:07 pm**	12:07 pm
☽ ⚹ ⚳	**3:10 pm**	12:10 pm
☽ □ ⚶		9:07 pm

15 THURSDAY

☽ □ ⚶	**12:07 am**	
☉ ☍ ⚷	**6:59 am**	3:59 am
☿ ⚺ ♄	**10:44 am**	7:44 am
☽ △ ♅	**5:28 pm**	2:28 pm
♃ △ ⚵	**7:20 pm**	4:20 pm
☉ ⚺ ⚳	**11:18 pm**	8:18 pm
☿ ⚺ ⚴	**11:45 pm**	8:45 pm

16 FRIDAY

☽ ⚺ ♂	**9:32 am**	6:32 am
☽ ⚺ ♀	**9:34 am**	6:34 am
☽ ⚻ ♆	**10:02 am**	7:02 am
☽ ☍ ⚵	**12:02 pm**	9:02 am
☽ ⚹ ♃	**12:36 pm**	9:36 am
♀ ⚹ ♂	**12:45 pm**	9:45 am
☽ ☌ ♄	**4:46 pm**	1:46 pm
♂ ☍ ♆	**6:26 pm**	3:26 pm
☽ ☌ ⚴	**6:55 pm**	3:55 pm
♀ △ ♆	**7:30 pm**	4:30 pm
☽ ⚺ ☿	**8:21 pm**	5:21 pm
☽ ⚻ ♇	**9:03 pm**	6:03 pm
☿ △ ♇		11:26 pm

17 SATURDAY

☿ △ ♇	**2:26 am**	
☽ ☍ ⚷	**3:20 am**	12:20 am
☽ ⚺ ⚳	**5:58 am**	2:58 am
☽ ☌ ☉	**7:24 am**	4:24 am
☽ △ ⚶	**12:54 pm**	9:54 am
♂ ⚻ ⚵	**8:42 pm**	5:42 pm
♀ ⚻ ⚵		9:28 pm

18 SUNDAY

♀ ⚻ ⚵	**12:28 am**	
☽ ⚻ ♅	**5:19 am**	2:19 am
♇ ⚻ ⚴	**12:37 pm**	9:37 am
☽ ☍ ♆	**9:31 pm**	6:31 pm
☽ ⚻ ⚵	**10:29 pm**	7:29 pm
☽ ⚹ ♀	**11:59 pm**	8:59 pm
☽ ☌ ♂		9:24 pm
☽ ⚺ ♃		9:59 pm

19 MONDAY

☽ ☌ ♂	**12:24 am**	
☽ ⚺ ♃	**12:59 am**	
☽ ⚺ ♄	**4:50 am**	1:50 am
☽ △ ♇	**8:18 am**	5:18 am
☿ ⚻ ⚷	**9:08 am**	6:08 am
☽ ⚺ ⚴	**9:19 am**	6:19 am
☽ ⚻ ⚷	**2:13 pm**	11:13 am
☽ ☌ ☿	**2:50 pm**	11:50 am
♂ ⚺ ♃	**4:00 pm**	1:00 pm
☽ ☌ ⚳	**7:16 pm**	4:16 pm
☽ ⚺ ☉	**11:23 pm**	8:23 pm
☽ ⚻ ⚶		9:08 pm

20 TUESDAY

☽ ⚻ ⚶	**12:08 am**	
♀ □ ♃	**4:57 am**	1:57 am
☉ △ ⚶	**9:45 am**	6:45 am
☽ ☍ ♅	**3:38 pm**	12:38 pm

21 WEDNESDAY

☽ ⚻ ♆	**7:20 am**	4:20 am
☽ △ ⚵	**7:23 am**	4:23 am
♆ ⚺ ⚵	**10:12 am**	7:12 am
☽ ☌ ♃	**11:38 am**	8:38 am
☽ □ ♀	**12:45 pm**	9:45 am
☽ ⚺ ♂	**1:17 pm**	10:17 am
☽ ⚹ ♄	**3:08 pm**	12:08 pm
☽ □ ♇	**5:48 pm**	2:48 pm
☽ ⚹ ⚴	**9:41 pm**	6:41 pm
☽ △ ⚷	**11:20 pm**	8:20 pm

22 THURSDAY

☽ ⚺ ☿	**6:13 am**	3:13 am
☽ ⚺ ⚳	**6:32 am**	3:32 am
☽ ☍ ⚶	**9:25 am**	6:25 am
☿ ☌ ⚳	**11:50 am**	8:50 am
☽ ⚹ ☉	**1:02 pm**	10:02 am
☽ ⚻ ♅	**11:58 pm**	8:58 pm

23 FRIDAY

⚷ ☍ ⚴	**6:12 am**	3:12 am
♂ ⚺ ♄	**11:32 am**	8:32 am
☽ □ ⚵	**2:17 pm**	11:17 am
☽ △ ♆	**3:03 pm**	12:03 pm
☿ ⚻ ⚶	**7:50 pm**	4:50 pm
☽ ⚺ ♃	**8:02 pm**	5:02 pm
♀ ⚺ ♄	**10:05 pm**	7:05 pm
☽ □ ♄	**11:09 pm**	8:09 pm
☽ △ ♀	**11:12 pm**	8:12 pm
☽ ⚹ ♂	**11:37 pm**	8:37 pm
☽ ⚹ ♇		10:06 pm

24 SATURDAY

☽ ⚹ ♇	**1:06 am**	
☽ □ ⚷	**6:13 am**	3:13 am
☽ □ ⚴	**7:26 am**	4:26 am
☽ ⚹ ⚳	**3:11 pm**	12:11 pm
☽ ⚻ ⚶	**4:12 pm**	1:12 pm
☽ ⚹ ☿	**5:54 pm**	2:54 pm
☽ □ ☉	**11:37 pm**	8:37 pm

25 SUNDAY

☽ △ ♅	**5:47 am**	2:47 am
♂ △ ♇	**5:52 am**	2:52 am
♀ ☍ ♇	**11:00 am**	8:00 am
☽ ⚹ ⚵	**6:41 pm**	3:41 pm
☽ □ ♆	**8:06 pm**	5:06 pm
⚳ ⚻ ⚶	**11:09 pm**	8:09 pm
☽ ⚹ ♃		10:37 pm

26 MONDAY

☽ ⚹ ♃	**1:37 am**	
☽ △ ♄	**4:22 am**	1:22 am
☽ ⚺ ♇	**5:39 am**	2:39 am
☽ ⚻ ♀	**6:40 am**	3:40 am
☽ □ ♂	**6:48 am**	3:48 am
☽ ⚹ ⚷	**10:21 am**	7:21 am
☽ △ ⚴	**2:00 pm**	11:00 am
☽ △ ⚶	**8:05 pm**	5:05 pm
☽ □ ⚳	**8:44 pm**	5:44 pm
☽ □ ☿		10:31 pm

27 TUESDAY

☽ □ ☿	**1:31 am**	
♀ ⚹ ♂	**4:30 am**	1:30 am
☽ △ ☉	**6:42 am**	3:42 am
☽ □ ♅	**8:46 am**	5:46 am
☽ ⚺ ⚵	**8:25 pm**	5:25 pm
☽ ⚹ ♆	**10:23 pm**	7:23 pm

28 WEDNESDAY

☽ □ ♃	**4:20 am**	1:20 am
☽ ⚻ ♄	**6:46 am**	3:46 am
☽ ☌ ♇	**7:30 am**	4:30 am
☽ △ ♂	**10:53 am**	7:53 am
☽ ☍ ♀	**11:06 am**	8:06 am
☽ ⚺ ⚷	**11:51 am**	8:51 am
☉ ⚻ ♅	**1:07 pm**	10:07 am
☽ ⚻ ⚴	**5:34 pm**	2:34 pm
☽ □ ⚶	**9:21 pm**	6:21 pm
☽ △ ⚳	**11:30 pm**	8:30 pm
♀ ⚻ ⚷		9:54 pm

29 THURSDAY

♀ ⚻ ⚷	**12:54 am**	
☽ △ ☿	**5:40 am**	2:40 am
♂ ⚻ ⚷	**7:52 am**	4:52 am
☽ ⚹ ♅	**9:27 am**	6:27 am
☽ ⚻ ☉	**10:53 am**	7:53 am
☽ ☌ ⚵	**8:12 pm**	5:12 pm
☽ ⚺ ♆	**10:40 pm**	7:40 pm

30 FRIDAY

☽ △ ♃	**5:10 am**	2:10 am
☽ ☍ ♄	**7:21 am**	4:21 am
☽ ⚺ ♇	**7:37 am**	4:37 am
☽ ☌ ⚷	**11:45 am**	8:45 am
☽ ⚻ ♂	**1:05 pm**	10:05 am
☽ ⚻ ♀	**1:45 pm**	10:45 am
☽ ☍ ⚴	**7:31 pm**	4:31 pm
☽ ⚹ ⚶	**9:16 pm**	6:16 pm
☽ ⚻ ⚳		9:56 pm

31 SATURDAY

☽ ⚻ ⚳	**12:56 am**	
☽ ⚻ ☿	**8:11 am**	5:11 am
☽ ⚺ ♅	**9:16 am**	6:16 am
♄ ⚻ ♇	**11:20 am**	8:20 am
☽ ☍ ☉	**2:05 pm**	11:05 am
☽ ⚺ ⚵	**7:35 pm**	4:35 pm
☽ ☌ ♆	**10:36 pm**	7:36 pm

Eastern time in bold type
Pacific time in medium type

JULY 2004

☽ Last Aspect day	EST / hr:mn / PST	asp	☽ Ingress sign day	EST / hr:mn / PST
6/30	**10:53 pm** 7:53 pm	☌ ♇	♑ 1	**2:01 pm** 11:01 am
3	**10:25 am** 7:25 am	☍ ☿	♒ 3	**1:22 pm** 10:22 am
4	**10:15 pm** 7:15 pm	⚹ ♇	♓ 5	**2:26 pm** 11:26 am
6	10:30 pm	□ ♇	♈ 7	**7:03 pm** 4:03 pm
7	**1:30 am**	□ ♇	♈ 7	**7:03 pm** 4:03 pm
9	**8:52 am** 5:52 am	△ ♇	♉ 10	**3:51 am** 12:51 am
11	**7:29 pm** 4:29 pm	⚹ ☉	♊ 12	**3:45 pm** 12:45 pm
14	**8:33 am** 5:33 am	☍ ♇	♋ 15	**4:40 am** 1:40 am
17	**7:24 am** 4:24 am	☌ ☉	♌ 17	**4:56 pm** 1:56 pm
19	**2:50 pm** 11:50 am	☌ ☿	♍ 20	**3:44 am** 12:44 am
21	**5:48 pm** 2:48 pm	□ ♇	♎ 22	**12:39 pm** 9:39 am
24	**5:54 pm** 2:54 pm	⚹ ☿	♏ 24	**7:08 pm** 4:08 pm
26	**6:48 am** 3:48 am	□ ♂	♐ 26	**10:48 pm** 7:48 pm
28	**11:06 am** 8:06 am	☍ ♀	♑ 28	**11:57 pm** 8:57 pm
30	**7:21 am** 4:21 am	☍ ♄	♒ 30	**11:54 pm** 8:54 pm

☽ Phases & Eclipses phase	day	EST / hr:mn / PST
Full Moon	2	**7:09 am** 4:09 am
4th Quarter	9	**3:34 am** 12:34 am
New Moon	17	**7:24 am** 4:24 am
2nd Quarter	24	**11:37 pm** 8:37 pm
Full Moon	31	**2:05 pm** 11:05 am

Planet Ingress	day	EST / hr:mn / PST
☿ ♌	4	**10:52 am** 7:52 am
☉ ♌	22	**7:50 am** 4:50 am
☿ ♍	25	**9:58 am** 6:58 am
⚳ ♍	29	**2:39 pm** 11:39 am

Planetary Motion	day	EST / hr:mn / PST
⚶ R	27	**10:45 pm** 7:45 pm

DATE		SID.TIME	SUN	MOON	NODE	MERCURY	VENUS	MARS	JUPITER	SATURN	URANUS	NEPTUNE	PLUTO	CERES	PALLAS	JUNO	VESTA	CHIRON
1	Th	18:37:32	09 ♋ 29 57	18 ♐ 35	09 ♉ R 31	23 ♋ 16	09 ♊ 39	04 ♌ 29	13 ♍ 21	15 ♋ 50	06 ♓ R 38	14 ♒ R 54	20 ♐ R 24	17 ♌ 21	09 ♋ 27	19 ♑ R 11	25 ♓ 44	24 ♑ R 08
2	F	18:41:29	10 27 08	03 ♑ 48	09 24	25 10	09 42	05 07	13 30	15 58	06 37	14 53	20 23	17 47	10 03	18 58	25 55	24 05
3	Sa	18:45:25	11 24 19	19 03	09 16	27 02	09 48	05 45	13 39	16 06	06 36	14 51	20 21	18 13	10 39	18 44	26 05	24 01
4	Su	18:49:22	12 21 30	04 ♒ 09	09 07	28 53	09 56	06 23	13 48	16 13	06 35	14 50	20 20	18 39	11 14	18 31	26 16	23 58
5	M	18:53:18	13 18 41	18 56	08 58	00 ♌ 41	10 06	07 01	13 57	16 21	06 34	14 49	20 18	19 04	11 50	18 17	26 26	23 54
6	T	18:57:15	14 15 52	03 ♓ 17	08 51	02 27	10 18	07 38	14 06	16 29	06 33	14 47	20 17	19 30	12 26	18 03	26 35	23 51
7	W	19:01:11	15 13 03	17 09	08 45	04 11	10 32	08 16	14 15	16 37	06 31	14 46	20 15	19 56	13 02	17 49	26 44	23 47
8	Th	19:05:08	16 10 15	00 ♈ 31	08 42	05 54	10 49	08 54	14 24	16 44	06 30	14 45	20 14	20 22	13 38	17 35	26 53	23 44
9	F	19:09:05	17 07 27	13 26	08 D 41	07 34	11 07	09 32	14 34	16 52	06 29	14 43	20 13	20 48	14 14	17 20	27 02	23 40
10	Sa	19:13:01	18 04 39	25 58	08 41	09 12	11 27	10 10	14 43	17 00	06 28	14 42	20 11	21 15	14 50	17 06	27 10	23 37
11	Su	19:16:58	19 01 52	08 ♉ 12	08 R 42	10 48	11 48	10 47	14 53	17 08	06 26	14 40	20 10	21 41	15 25	16 52	27 17	23 33
12	M	19:20:54	19 59 06	20 13	08 41	12 22	12 12	11 25	15 02	17 16	06 25	14 39	20 09	22 07	16 01	16 38	27 25	23 29
13	T	19:24:51	20 56 20	02 ♊ 06	08 39	13 54	12 37	12 03	15 12	17 23	06 24	14 38	20 07	22 33	16 37	16 24	27 32	23 26
14	W	19:28:47	21 53 34	13 55	08 34	15 23	13 03	12 41	15 22	17 31	06 22	14 36	20 06	23 00	17 13	16 10	27 38	23 22
15	Th	19:32:44	22 50 49	25 43	08 26	16 51	13 32	13 19	15 32	17 39	06 21	14 35	20 05	23 26	17 48	15 56	27 44	23 19
16	F	19:36:40	23 48 04	07 ♋ 35	08 16	18 17	14 01	13 56	15 42	17 47	06 19	14 33	20 03	23 52	18 24	15 41	27 50	23 15
17	Sa	19:40:37	24 45 20	19 30	08 04	19 40	14 32	14 34	15 52	17 55	06 17	14 32	20 02	24 19	19 00	15 28	27 55	23 11
18	Su	19:44:34	25 42 36	01 ♌ 33	07 51	21 01	15 05	15 12	16 03	18 02	06 16	14 30	20 01	24 45	19 35	15 14	28 00	23 08
19	M	19:48:30	26 39 53	13 42	07 38	22 20	15 39	15 50	16 13	18 10	06 14	14 29	20 00	25 12	20 11	15 00	28 04	23 04
20	T	19:52:27	27 37 10	26 00	07 26	23 37	16 14	16 28	16 23	18 18	06 13	14 27	19 59	25 38	20 47	14 46	28 08	23 01
21	W	19:56:23	28 34 27	08 ♍ 28	07 16	24 51	16 50	17 06	16 34	18 25	06 11	14 26	19 57	26 05	21 22	14 33	28 11	22 57
22	Th	20:00:20	29 31 45	21 06	07 09	26 03	17 27	17 43	16 44	18 33	06 09	14 24	19 56	26 32	21 58	14 19	28 14	22 54
23	F	20:04:16	00 ♌ 29 03	03 ♎ 58	07 04	27 13	18 06	18 21	16 55	18 41	06 07	14 22	19 55	26 58	22 33	14 06	28 17	22 50
24	Sa	20:08:13	01 26 21	17 05	07 02	28 19	18 46	18 59	17 06	18 49	06 05	14 21	19 54	27 25	23 09	13 53	28 19	22 46
25	Su	20:12:09	02 23 39	00 ♏ 29	07 02	29 24	19 26	19 37	17 16	18 56	06 04	14 19	19 53	27 52	23 44	13 40	28 21	22 43
26	M	20:16:06	03 20 58	14 14	07 02	00 ♍ 25	20 08	20 15	17 27	19 04	06 02	14 18	19 52	28 19	24 20	13 27	28 22	22 39
27	T	20:20:03	04 18 18	28 20	07 01	01 24	20 51	20 53	17 38	19 11	06 00	14 16	19 51	28 45	24 55	13 15	28 23	22 36
28	W	20:23:59	05 15 38	12 ♐ 47	06 58	02 20	21 35	21 31	17 49	19 19	05 58	14 14	19 50	29 12	25 30	13 02	28 R 23	22 32
29	Th	20:27:56	06 12 58	27 33	06 52	03 13	22 19	22 09	18 00	19 27	05 56	14 13	19 49	29 39	26 06	12 50	28 23	22 29
30	F	20:31:52	07 10 19	12 ♑ 31	06 44	04 02	23 04	22 46	18 11	19 34	05 54	14 11	19 48	00 ♍ 06	26 41	12 39	28 22	22 26
31	Sa	20:35:49	08 07 41	27 34	06 34	04 48	23 51	23 24	18 23	19 42	05 52	14 10	19 47	00 33	27 16	12 27	28 21	22 22

EPHEMERIS CALCULATED FOR 12 MIDNIGHT GREENWICH MEAN TIME. ALL OTHER DATA AND FACING ASPECTARIAN PAGE IN **EASTERN TIME (BOLD)** AND PACIFIC TIME (REGULAR).

AUGUST 2004

1 SUNDAY

☽ ⚻ ♃	**5:56 am**	2:56 am
☿ ☍ ♅	**6:50 am**	3:50 am
☽ ⚹ ♇	**7:45 am**	4:45 am
☽ ⚻ ♄	**7:57 am**	4:57 am
☽ ⚺ ⚷	**11:51 am**	8:51 am
♀ △ ⚶	**2:03 pm**	11:03 am
☽ ☍ ♂	**3:35 pm**	12:35 pm
☽ △ ♀	**4:51 pm**	1:51 pm
☽ ⚺ ⚶	**9:44 pm**	6:44 pm
☽ ⚻ ⚴	**10:05 pm**	7:05 pm

2 MONDAY

☽ ☍ ⚳	**3:12 am**	12:12 am
☽ ☌ ♅	**10:12 am**	7:12 am
☽ ☍ ☿	**11:30 am**	8:30 am
☽ ⚻ ☉	**6:56 pm**	3:56 pm
☽ ⚹ ⚵	**8:32 pm**	5:32 pm
☽ ⚺ ♆		9:15 pm

3 TUESDAY

☽ ⚺ ♆	**12:15 am**	
☽ ☍ ♃	**8:47 am**	5:47 am
☽ □ ♇	**9:59 am**	6:59 am
☽ △ ♄	**10:42 am**	7:42 am
☽ ⚹ ⚷	**2:12 pm**	11:12 am
☉ ⚻ ⚵	**3:05 pm**	12:05 pm
☽ ⚻ ♂	**8:50 pm**	5:50 pm
☽ □ ♀	**10:58 pm**	7:58 pm
☽ ☌ ⚶		9:47 pm

4 WEDNESDAY

☽ ☌ ⚶	**12:47 am**	
☽ △ ⚴	**3:38 am**	12:38 am
☽ ⚻ ⚳	**8:36 am**	5:36 am
☽ ⚺ ♅	**2:12 pm**	11:12 am
☽ ⚻ ☿	**5:46 pm**	2:46 pm
☽ □ ⚵		9:47 pm
♀ □ ⚶		11:26 pm

5 THURSDAY

☽ □ ⚵	**12:47 am**	
♀ □ ⚶	**2:26 am**	
☽ △ ☉	**3:55 am**	12:55 am
☽ ⚹ ♆	**5:22 am**	2:22 am
☽ ⚻ ♃	**3:31 pm**	12:31 pm
☽ △ ♇	**3:56 pm**	12:56 pm
☽ □ ♄	**5:17 pm**	2:17 pm
☽ □ ⚷	**8:18 pm**	5:18 pm
☉ ☍ ♆	**11:07 pm**	8:07 pm

6 FRIDAY

☽ △ ♂	**6:36 am**	3:36 am
☽ ⚺ ⚶	**7:41 am**	4:41 am
☽ ⚹ ♀	**9:59 am**	6:59 am
☽ □ ⚴	**1:45 pm**	10:45 am
♃ □ ♇	**5:31 pm**	2:31 pm
☽ △ ⚳	**6:30 pm**	3:30 pm
☽ ⚹ ♅	**10:15 pm**	7:15 pm
♂ ⚻ ⚶		10:47 pm

7 SATURDAY

♂ ⚻ ⚶	**1:47 am**	
☽ △ ☿	**3:47 am**	12:47 am
☽ △ ⚵	**9:02 am**	6:02 am
☽ □ ♆	**2:33 pm**	11:33 am
☽ □ ☉	**6:01 pm**	3:01 pm
☽ ⚻ ♇		10:53 pm
☽ △ ♃		11:27 pm

8 SUNDAY

☽ ⚻ ♇	**1:53 am**	
☽ △ ♃	**2:27 am**	
☽ ⚹ ♄	**3:59 am**	12:59 am
☽ △ ⚷	**6:20 am**	3:20 am
☽ ⚹ ⚶	**6:12 pm**	3:12 pm
☽ □ ♂	**8:46 pm**	5:46 pm
☽ ⚺ ♀		10:41 pm

9 MONDAY

☽ ⚺ ♀	**1:41 am**	
☽ ⚹ ⚴	**4:02 am**	1:02 am
☽ □ ⚳	**8:19 am**	5:19 am
☽ □ ♅	**9:42 am**	6:42 am
☽ □ ☿	**4:16 pm**	1:16 pm
☽ ⚻ ⚵	**8:20 pm**	5:20 pm
☽ △ ♆		11:37 pm

10 TUESDAY

☽ △ ♆	**2:37 am**	
☽ ⚹ ☉	**11:39 am**	8:39 am
☽ ☍ ♇	**2:20 pm**	11:20 am
☽ □ ♃	**3:59 pm**	12:59 pm
☽ ⚺ ♄	**5:09 pm**	2:09 pm
♅ ☍ ⚳	**5:42 pm**	2:42 pm
☽ ⚻ ⚷	**6:40 pm**	3:40 pm

11 WEDNESDAY

☽ □ ⚶	**6:26 am**	3:26 am
☽ ⚹ ♂	**12:59 pm**	9:59 am
☽ ☌ ♀	**7:29 pm**	4:29 pm
☽ ⚺ ♀	**7:58 pm**	4:58 pm
☉ △ ♇	**8:19 pm**	5:19 pm
☽ △ ♅	**10:19 pm**	7:19 pm
☽ ⚹ ⚳	**11:33 pm**	8:33 pm

12 THURSDAY

☽ ⚹ ☿	**4:35 am**	1:35 am
☽ ☍ ⚵	**8:26 am**	5:26 am
♀ ⚺ ⚴	**11:53 am**	8:53 am
☽ ⚻ ♆	**3:13 pm**	12:13 pm
☽ ⚻ ♇		11:52 pm

13 FRIDAY

☽ ⚻ ♇	**2:52 am**	
☽ ⚺ ☉	**5:32 am**	2:32 am
☽ ⚹ ♃	**5:33 am**	2:33 am
☉ ⚺ ♃	**5:49 am**	2:49 am
☽ ☌ ♄	**6:17 am**	3:17 am
☽ ☍ ⚷	**6:56 am**	3:56 am
♀ △ ♅	**6:57 am**	3:57 am
☉ ⚺ ♄	**4:07 pm**	1:07 pm
♅ ⚻ ⚴	**5:36 pm**	2:36 pm
☽ △ ⚶	**6:07 pm**	3:07 pm
☉ ⚻ ⚷	**10:07 pm**	7:07 pm

14 SATURDAY

☽ ⚺ ♂	**4:24 am**	1:24 am
☽ ⚻ ♅	**10:01 am**	7:01 am
☽ ☌ ⚴	**10:53 am**	7:53 am
☽ ⚺ ♀	**12:20 pm**	9:20 am
☽ ⚺ ⚳	**1:43 pm**	10:43 am
☽ ⚺ ☿	**2:45 pm**	11:45 am
☽ ⚻ ⚵	**7:28 pm**	4:28 pm
☽ ☍ ♆		11:28 pm

15 SUNDAY

☽ ☍ ♆	**2:28 am**	
☿ ☌ ⚳	**4:08 am**	1:08 am
♄ ☍ ⚷	**4:42 am**	1:42 am
☿ ⚹ ♀	**10:10 am**	7:10 am
☽ △ ♇	**1:50 pm**	10:50 am
☽ ⚺ ♃	**5:27 pm**	2:27 pm
☽ ⚻ ⚷	**5:35 pm**	2:35 pm
☽ ⚺ ♄	**5:45 pm**	2:45 pm
☽ ☌ ☉	**9:24 pm**	6:24 pm
♀ ⚹ ⚳	**9:54 pm**	6:54 pm
♃ △ ⚷	**11:59 pm**	8:59 pm

16 MONDAY

☽ ⚻ ⚶	**3:59 am**	12:59 am
☿ ⚺ ⚴	**8:25 am**	5:25 am
☽ ☌ ♂	**5:39 pm**	2:39 pm
☽ ☍ ♅	**7:48 pm**	4:48 pm
☽ ☌ ☿	**10:14 pm**	7:14 pm
☽ ⚺ ⚴	**11:34 pm**	8:34 pm
☽ ☌ ⚳		10:43 pm
☽ ⚹ ♀		11:53 pm

17 TUESDAY

☽ ☌ ⚳	**1:43 am**	
☽ ⚹ ♀	**2:53 am**	
☽ △ ⚵	**4:38 am**	1:38 am
☽ ⚻ ♆	**11:45 am**	8:45 am
♃ ⚹ ♄	**12:33 pm**	9:33 am
☽ □ ♇	**10:49 pm**	7:49 pm
♀ ☍ ⚵		9:09 pm
☽ △ ⚷		11:16 pm

18 WEDNESDAY

♀ ☍ ⚵	**12:09 am**	
☽ △ ⚷	**2:16 am**	
☽ ⚹ ♄	**3:09 am**	12:09 am
☽ ☌ ♃	**3:15 am**	12:15 am
♂ ☍ ♅	**10:14 am**	7:14 am
☽ ⚺ ☉	**10:43 am**	7:43 am
☽ ☍ ⚶	**11:50 am**	8:50 am
☿ ☌ ♂	**3:47 pm**	11:47 am
☿ ☍ ♅	**9:00 pm**	6:00 pm
☉ ⚻ ⚶	**11:45 pm**	8:45 pm

19 THURSDAY

☽ ⚺ ☿	**3:17 am**	12:17 am
☽ ⚻ ♅	**3:38 am**	12:38 am
☽ ⚺ ♂	**4:35 am**	1:35 am
☽ ⚹ ♀	**10:00 am**	7:00 am
☽ ⚺ ⚳	**11:32 am**	8:32 am
☽ □ ⚵	**11:58 am**	8:58 am
☽ □ ♀	**3:03 pm**	12:03 pm
☽ △ ♆	**7:07 pm**	4:07 pm
⚳ △ ⚵	**10:09 pm**	7:09 pm

20 FRIDAY

☽ ⚹ ♇	**5:54 am**	2:54 am
☽ □ ⚷	**9:05 am**	6:05 am
☽ □ ♄	**10:35 am**	7:35 am
☽ ⚺ ♃	**11:04 am**	8:04 am
☽ ⚻ ⚶	**5:49 pm**	2:49 pm
☽ ⚹ ☉	**9:39 pm**	6:39 pm
⚴ ⚻ ⚵		10:59 pm

21 SATURDAY

⚴ ⚻ ⚵	**1:59 am**	
☽ ⚹ ☿	**6:19 am**	3:19 am
☽ △ ♅	**9:37 am**	6:37 am
☽ ⚹ ♂	**1:20 pm**	10:20 am
☽ ⚹ ⚵	**5:31 pm**	2:31 pm
☽ □ ⚴	**6:16 pm**	3:16 pm
☽ ⚹ ⚳	**7:16 pm**	4:16 pm
⚴ ⚻ ♆	**8:18 pm**	5:18 pm
☽ □ ♆		9:36 pm
☽ △ ♀		9:57 pm

22 SUNDAY

☽ □ ♆	**12:36 am**	
☽ △ ♀	**12:57 am**	
☽ ⚺ ♇	**11:05 am**	8:05 am
☽ ⚹ ⚷	**2:01 pm**	11:01 am
☽ △ ♄	**4:04 pm**	1:04 pm
☽ ⚹ ♃	**4:53 pm**	1:53 pm
☽ △ ⚶	**9:54 pm**	6:54 pm

23 MONDAY

☽ □ ☉	**6:12 am**	3:12 am
☽ □ ☿	**7:31 am**	4:31 am
☽ □ ♅	**1:40 pm**	10:40 am
☉ ☌ ☿	**4:50 pm**	1:50 pm
☽ □ ♂	**7:51 pm**	4:51 pm
☽ ⚺ ⚵	**9:11 pm**	6:11 pm
☽ △ ⚴		9:19 pm
☽ □ ⚳		9:50 pm

24 TUESDAY

☽ △ ⚴	**12:19 am**	
☽ □ ⚳	**12:50 am**	
☽ ⚹ ♆	**4:09 am**	1:09 am
☽ ⚻ ♀	**8:28 am**	5:28 am
☽ ☌ ♇	**2:20 pm**	11:20 am
☽ ⚺ ⚷	**5:02 pm**	2:02 pm
☽ ⚻ ♄	**7:33 pm**	4:33 pm
☽ □ ♃	**8:42 pm**	5:42 pm
♂ △ ⚵	**11:21 pm**	8:21 pm
☽ □ ⚶		9:06 pm

25 WEDNESDAY

☽ □ ⚶	**12:06 am**	
☽ △ ☿	**7:13 am**	4:13 am
☽ △ ☉	**12:24 pm**	9:24 am
☽ ⚹ ♅	**3:53 pm**	12:53 pm
☽ ☌ ⚵	**11:09 pm**	8:09 pm
☽ △ ♂		9:19 pm

26 THURSDAY

☽ △ ♂	**12:19 am**	
☽ ⚻ ⚴	**4:22 am**	1:22 am
☽ △ ⚳	**4:29 am**	1:29 am
☽ ⚺ ♆	**6:00 am**	3:00 am
☽ ☍ ♀	**1:59 pm**	10:59 am
☽ ⚺ ♇	**4:01 pm**	1:01 pm
☽ ☌ ⚷	**6:32 pm**	3:32 pm
⚳ ⚺ ⚴	**7:04 pm**	4:04 pm
☽ ☍ ♄	**9:30 pm**	6:30 pm
☽ △ ♃	**10:58 pm**	7:58 pm
☽ ⚹ ⚶		9:53 pm

27 FRIDAY

☽ ⚹ ⚶	**12:53 am**	
☽ ⚻ ☿	**6:04 am**	3:04 am
☉ ☍ ♅	**2:41 pm**	11:41 am
☽ ⚺ ♅	**5:01 pm**	2:01 pm
☽ ⚻ ☉	**5:11 pm**	2:11 pm
♀ ⚻ ♇	**6:58 pm**	3:58 pm
♆ ☍ ⚴	**8:53 pm**	5:53 pm
☽ ⚺ ⚵		9:15 pm
♆ ⚻ ⚳		11:26 pm

28 SATURDAY

☽ ⚺ ⚵	**12:15 am**	
♆ ⚻ ⚳	**2:26 am**	
☽ ⚻ ♂	**3:46 am**	12:46 am
☽ ☌ ♆	**7:06 am**	4:06 am
☽ ⚻ ⚳	**7:16 am**	4:16 am
☽ ☍ ⚴	**7:32 am**	4:32 am
☽ ⚹ ♇	**5:13 pm**	2:13 pm
☽ ⚻ ♀	**6:54 pm**	3:54 pm
☽ ⚺ ⚷	**7:38 pm**	4:38 pm
☽ ⚻ ♄	**11:07 pm**	8:07 pm
☽ ⚻ ♃		9:57 pm
☽ ⚺ ⚶		10:26 pm

29 SUNDAY

☽ ⚻ ♃	**12:57 am**	
☽ ⚺ ⚶	**1:26 am**	
♀ ☍ ⚷	**4:56 am**	1:56 am
☽ ☍ ☿	**5:23 am**	2:23 am
♃ ☍ ⚶	**5:28 pm**	2:28 pm
☽ ☌ ♅	**6:28 pm**	3:28 pm
☽ ☍ ☉	**10:22 pm**	7:22 pm
☽ ⚹ ⚵		10:57 pm

30 MONDAY

☽ ⚹ ⚵	**1:57 am**	
☽ ☍ ♂	**8:00 am**	5:00 am
☽ ⚺ ♆	**9:01 am**	6:01 am
☽ ☍ ⚳	**10:57 am**	7:57 am
☽ ⚻ ⚴	**11:37 am**	8:37 am
☽ □ ♇	**7:36 pm**	4:36 pm
☽ ⚹ ⚷	**10:01 pm**	7:01 pm
☽ △ ♀		10:25 pm
☽ △ ♄		11:09 pm

31 TUESDAY

☽ △ ♀	**1:25 am**	
☽ △ ♄	**2:09 am**	
☽ ☌ ⚶	**3:23 am**	12:23 am
☽ ☍ ♃	**4:28 am**	1:28 am
♂ ⚻ ♆	**5:47 am**	2:47 am
☽ ⚻ ☿	**6:51 am**	3:51 am
♀ ☌ ♄	**12:08 pm**	9:08 am
☽ ⚺ ♅	**9:57 pm**	6:57 pm
♀ △ ⚶	**10:59 pm**	7:59 pm
☉ △ ⚵		11:39 pm

Eastern time in bold type
Pacific time in medium type

AUGUST 2004

☽ Last Aspect day	EST / hr:mn / PST		asp	☽ Ingress sign day	EST / hr:mn / PST	
1	**4:51 pm**	1:51 pm	△♀	♓ 1		9:34 pm
1	**4:51 pm**	1:51 pm	△♀	♓ 2	**12:34 am**	
3	**10:58 pm**	7:58 pm	□♀	♈ 4	**3:59 am**	12:59 am
6	**9:59 am**	6:59 am	⚹♀	♉ 6	**11:26 am**	8:26 am
8	**8:46 pm**	5:46 pm	□♂	♊ 8	**10:33 pm**	7:33 pm
10	**3:59 pm**	12:59 pm	□♃	♋ 11	**11:20 am**	8:20 am
13	**6:17 am**	3:17 am	☌♄	♌ 13	**11:30 pm**	8:30 pm
15	**9:24 pm**	6:24 pm	☌☉	♍ 16	**9:49 am**	6:49 am
18	**3:15 am**	12:15 am	☌♃	♎ 18	**6:09 pm**	3:09 pm
20	**9:39 pm**	6:39 pm	⚹☉	♏ 20		9:37 pm
20	**9:39 pm**	6:39 pm	⚹☉	♏ 21	**12:37 am**	
22	**4:53 pm**	1:53 pm	⚹♃	♐ 23	**5:08 am**	2:08 am
25	**7:13 am**	4:13 am	△☿	♑ 25	**7:46 am**	4:46 am
26	**10:58 pm**	7:58 pm	△♃	♒ 27	**9:08 am**	6:08 am
29	**5:23 am**	2:23 am	☍☿	♓ 29	**10:33 am**	7:33 am
31	**4:28 am**	1:28 am	☍♃	♈ 31	**1:46 pm**	10:46 am

☽ Phases & Eclipses phase	day	EST / hr:mn / PST	
4th Quarter	7	**6:01 pm**	3:01 pm
New Moon	15	**9:24 pm**	6:24 pm
2nd Quarter	23	**6:12 am**	3:12 am
Full Moon	29	**10:22 pm**	7:22 pm

Planet Ingress	day	EST / hr:mn / PST	
♀ ♌	4	**11:51 am**	8:51 am
♀ ♋	7	**7:02 am**	4:02 am
♂ ♍	10	**6:14 am**	3:14 am
☉ ♍	22	**2:53 pm**	11:53 am
☿ ♌	24	**9:33 pm**	6:33 pm

Planetary Motion	day	EST / hr:mn / PST	
☿ ℞	9	**8:32 pm**	5:32 pm
♇ D	30	**3:38 pm**	12:38 pm

DATE		SID.TIME	SUN	MOON	NODE	MERCURY	VENUS	MARS	JUPITER	SATURN	URANUS	NEPTUNE	PLUTO	CERES	PALLAS	JUNO	VESTA	CHIRON
1	Su	20:39:45	09 ♌ 05 03	12 ♒ 31	06 ♉ ℞ 23	05 ♍ 31	24 ♊ 38	24 ♌ 02	18 ♍ 34	19 ♋ 49	05 ♓ ℞ 50	14 ♒ ℞ 08	19 ♐ ℞ 46	01 ♍ 00	27 ♋ 52	12 ♑ ℞ 16	28 ♓ ℞ 19	22 ♑ ℞ 19
2	M	20:43:42	10 02 26	27 14	06 13	06 10	25 26	24 40	18 45	19 57	05 48	14 06	19 45	01 27	28 27	12 05	28 17	22 15
3	T	20:47:38	10 59 50	11 ♓ 35	06 03	06 45	26 14	25 18	18 57	20 04	05 46	14 05	19 45	01 54	29 02	11 54	28 15	22 12
4	W	20:51:35	11 57 16	25 29	05 56	07 16	27 04	25 56	19 08	20 12	05 44	14 03	19 44	02 21	29 37	11 43	28 12	22 09
5	Th	20:55:32	12 54 42	08 ♈ 54	05 52	07 43	27 54	26 34	19 19	20 19	05 42	14 01	19 43	02 48	00 ♌ 12	11 33	28 08	22 06
6	F	20:59:28	13 52 09	21 53	05 50	08 05	28 45	27 12	19 31	20 26	05 39	14 00	19 42	03 15	00 47	11 23	28 05	22 02
7	Sa	21:03:25	14 49 38	04 ♉ 27	05 49	08 23	29 36	27 50	19 43	20 34	05 37	13 58	19 41	03 42	01 22	11 14	28 00	21 59
8	Su	21:07:21	15 47 08	16 42	05 49	08 36	00 ♋ 28	28 28	19 54	20 41	05 35	13 57	19 41	04 09	01 57	11 04	27 55	21 56
9	M	21:11:18	16 44 40	28 44	05 49	08 44	01 21	29 06	20 06	20 48	05 33	13 55	19 40	04 37	02 32	10 55	27 50	21 53
10	T	21:15:14	17 42 13	10 ♊ 37	05 47	08 ℞ 46	02 14	29 44	20 18	20 56	05 31	13 53	19 39	05 04	03 06	10 47	27 44	21 50
11	W	21:19:11	18 39 47	22 26	05 42	08 44	03 08	00 ♍ 22	20 30	21 03	05 28	13 52	19 39	05 31	03 41	10 39	27 38	21 47
12	Th	21:23:07	19 37 23	04 ♋ 17	05 36	08 36	04 03	01 00	20 42	21 10	05 26	13 50	19 38	05 58	04 16	10 31	27 31	21 44
13	F	21:27:04	20 35 00	16 12	05 26	08 22	04 57	01 38	20 54	21 17	05 24	13 48	19 38	06 26	04 51	10 23	27 24	21 41
14	Sa	21:31:01	21 32 38	28 14	05 15	08 04	05 53	02 16	21 06	21 24	05 21	13 47	19 37	06 53	05 25	10 16	27 16	21 38
15	Su	21:34:57	22 30 18	10 ♌ 26	05 02	07 39	06 49	02 54	21 18	21 32	05 19	13 45	19 37	07 20	06 00	10 09	27 08	21 35
16	M	21:38:54	23 27 59	22 48	04 49	07 09	07 45	03 32	21 30	21 39	05 17	13 44	19 36	07 48	06 34	10 02	27 00	21 32
17	T	21:42:50	24 25 41	05 ♍ 21	04 38	06 35	08 42	04 10	21 42	21 46	05 15	13 42	19 36	08 15	07 09	09 56	26 51	21 30
18	W	21:46:47	25 23 24	18 05	04 28	05 55	09 40	04 48	21 54	21 53	05 12	13 40	19 35	08 42	07 43	09 51	26 41	21 27
19	Th	21:50:43	26 21 09	01 ♎ 00	04 22	05 12	10 37	05 26	22 06	21 59	05 10	13 39	19 35	09 10	08 17	09 45	26 32	21 24
20	F	21:54:40	27 18 55	14 07	04 17	04 24	11 36	06 04	22 19	22 06	05 07	13 37	19 34	09 37	08 52	09 40	26 22	21 22
21	Sa	21:58:36	28 16 42	27 25	04 D 16	03 34	12 34	06 42	22 31	22 13	05 05	13 36	19 34	10 05	09 26	09 36	26 11	21 19
22	Su	22:02:33	29 14 30	10 ♏ 57	04 16	02 42	13 33	07 21	22 43	22 20	05 03	13 34	19 34	10 32	10 00	09 31	26 00	21 17
23	M	22:06:30	00 ♍ 12 19	24 42	04 ℞ 16	01 49	14 33	07 59	22 56	22 27	05 00	13 33	19 34	11 00	10 34	09 27	25 49	21 14
24	T	22:10:26	01 10 10	08 ♐ 42	04 16	00 56	15 33	08 37	23 08	22 33	04 58	13 31	19 33	11 27	11 08	09 24	25 37	21 12
25	W	22:14:23	02 08 02	22 56	04 14	00 03	16 33	09 15	23 21	22 40	04 56	13 29	19 33	11 55	11 42	09 21	25 25	21 09
26	Th	22:18:19	03 05 55	07 ♑ 23	04 10	29 ♌ 13	17 33	09 53	23 33	22 47	04 53	13 28	19 33	12 22	12 16	09 18	25 13	21 07
27	F	22:22:16	04 03 49	21 59	04 04	28 26	18 34	10 31	23 46	22 53	04 51	13 26	19 33	12 50	12 50	09 16	25 00	21 05
28	Sa	22:26:12	05 01 44	06 ♒ 38	03 56	27 44	19 35	11 10	23 58	23 00	04 48	13 25	19 33	13 17	13 24	09 14	24 47	21 03
29	Su	22:30:09	05 59 41	21 14	03 47	27 06	20 37	11 48	24 11	23 06	04 46	13 23	19 33	13 45	13 57	09 12	24 34	21 01
30	M	22:34:05	06 57 39	05 ♓ 39	03 38	26 35	21 39	12 26	24 23	23 12	04 44	13 22	19 D 33	14 12	14 31	09 11	24 21	20 59
31	T	22:38:02	07 55 39	19 46	03 31	26 11	22 41	13 04	24 36	23 19	04 41	13 21	19 33	14 40	15 05	09 10	24 07	20 57

EPHEMERIS CALCULATED FOR 12 MIDNIGHT GREENWICH MEAN TIME. ALL OTHER DATA AND FACING ASPECTARIAN PAGE IN **EASTERN TIME (BOLD)** AND PACIFIC TIME (REGULAR).

SEPTEMBER 2004

1 WEDNESDAY

☉ △ ⚵	**2:39 am**	
☽ □ ⚵	**6:01 am**	3:01 am
☽ ⚻ ☉	**6:17 am**	3:17 am
☽ ⚹ ♆	**1:28 pm**	10:28 am
☽ ⚻ ♂	**3:08 pm**	12:08 pm
☽ ⚻ ⚳	**5:31 pm**	2:31 pm
☽ △ ♀	**6:39 pm**	3:39 pm
☽ △ ♇	**12:50 am**	9:50 pm

2 THURSDAY

♀ ⚹ ♃	**3:15 am**	12:15 am
☽ □ ⚷	**3:17 am**	12:17 am
♄ △ ⚶	**4:59 am**	1:59 am
☽ ⚺ ⚶	**8:11 am**	5:11 am
☽ □ ♄	**8:16 am**	5:16 am
☽ ⚻ ♃	**11:13 am**	8:13 am
☽ □ ♀	**11:46 am**	8:46 am
☽ △ ☿	**12:17 pm**	9:17 am
☿ ⚺ ♀	**6:15 pm**	3:15 pm

3 FRIDAY

☽ ⚹ ♅	**4:52 am**	1:52 am
☽ △ ⚵	**1:41 pm**	10:41 am
☽ △ ☉	**6:37 pm**	3:37 pm
☽ □ ♆	**9:31 pm**	6:31 pm
☽ △ ♂		11:28 pm

4 SATURDAY

☽ △ ♂	**2:28 am**	
☽ △ ⚳	**4:09 am**	1:09 am
☽ □ ♀	**5:51 am**	2:51 am
☽ ⚻ ♇	**9:47 am**	6:47 am
☽ △ ⚷	**12:15 pm**	9:15 am
☽ ⚹ ⚶	**4:28 pm**	1:28 pm
☽ ⚹ ♄	**6:10 pm**	3:10 pm
☽ △ ♃	**9:50 pm**	6:50 pm
☽ □ ☿	**10:54 pm**	7:54 pm
☽ ⚹ ♀		11:56 pm

5 SUNDAY

☽ ⚹ ♀	**2:56 am**	
☉ ⚻ ♆	**7:03 am**	4:03 am
☽ □ ♅	**3:18 pm**	12:18 pm
☽ ⚻ ⚵		9:51 pm

6 MONDAY

☽ ⚻ ⚵	**12:51 am**	
☽ △ ♆	**8:50 am**	5:50 am
☽ □ ☉	**11:10 am**	8:10 am
☽ □ ♂	**5:29 pm**	2:29 pm
☽ □ ⚳	**6:14 pm**	3:14 pm
☽ ⚹ ♀	**8:31 pm**	5:31 pm
☽ ☍ ♇	**9:42 pm**	6:42 pm
☽ ⚻ ⚷	**12:05 am**	9:05 pm

7 TUESDAY

☽ □ ⚶	**3:20 am**	12:20 am
☽ ⚺ ♄	**6:49 am**	3:49 am
☽ □ ♃	**11:11 am**	8:11 am
☽ ⚹ ☿	**2:08 pm**	11:08 am
☽ ⚺ ♀	**9:17 pm**	6:17 pm
♇ △ ♀	**10:13 pm**	7:13 pm

8 WEDNESDAY

☽ △ ♅	**3:40 am**	12:40 am
☽ ☍ ⚵	**1:41 pm**	10:41 am
♂ ☌ ⚳	**5:28 pm**	2:28 pm
☽ ⚻ ♆	**9:23 pm**	6:23 pm

9 THURSDAY

☽ ⚹ ☉	**5:12 am**	2:12 am
☽ ⚹ ⚳	**9:17 am**	6:17 am
☽ ⚹ ♂	**9:32 am**	6:32 am
☽ ⚻ ♇	**10:19 am**	7:19 am
☽ ⚺ ♀	**12:02 pm**	9:02 am
☽ ☍ ⚷	**12:33 pm**	9:33 am
☽ △ ⚶	**2:37 pm**	11:37 am
☽ ☌ ♄	**7:47 pm**	4:47 pm
⚷ ⚻ ♀	**10:59 pm**	7:59 pm
♂ □ ♇		9:06 pm
☽ ⚹ ♃		9:41 pm

10 FRIDAY

♂ □ ♇	**12:06 am**	
☽ ⚹ ♃	**12:41 am**	
☽ ⚺ ☿	**7:26 am**	4:26 am
♇ □ ⚳	**12:12 pm**	9:12 am
☽ ☌ ♀	**3:22 pm**	12:22 pm
☽ ⚻ ♅	**3:31 pm**	12:31 pm
♀ ⚻ ♅	**4:52 pm**	1:52 pm
☽ ⚻ ⚵		10:41 pm

11 SATURDAY

☽ ⚻ ⚵	**1:41 am**	
☿ ⚻ ⚶	**3:38 am**	12:38 am
☽ ☍ ♆	**8:47 am**	5:47 am
♂ △ ⚷	**4:09 pm**	1:09 pm
☉ □ ♇	**8:23 pm**	5:23 pm
☽ △ ♇	**9:22 pm**	6:22 pm
☽ ⚺ ☉	**9:27 pm**	6:27 pm
☽ ⚺ ⚳	**10:37 pm**	7:37 pm
☽ ⚻ ⚷	**11:24 pm**	8:24 pm
☽ ⚺ ♂	**11:48 pm**	8:48 pm
☽ ⚻ ⚶		9:18 pm
☽ ☌ ♀		10:41 pm

12 SUNDAY

☽ ⚻ ⚶	**12:18 am**	
☽ ☌ ♀	**1:41 am**	
☽ ⚺ ♄	**6:53 am**	3:53 am
♂ ☍ ⚶	**6:56 am**	3:56 am
☽ ⚺ ♃	**12:09 pm**	9:09 am
⚷ △ ⚳	**6:44 pm**	3:44 pm
☉ △ ⚷	**9:56 pm**	6:56 pm
☽ ☌ ☿	**11:49 pm**	8:49 pm
☉ ☌ ⚳		9:54 pm
☽ ☍ ♅		10:09 pm
☉ ☍ ⚶		11:58 pm

13 MONDAY

☉ ☌ ⚳	**12:54 am**	
☽ ☍ ♅	**1:09 am**	
☉ ☍ ⚶	**2:58 am**	
⚳ ☍ ⚶	**4:26 am**	1:26 am
☽ ⚺ ♀	**6:36 am**	3:36 am
☽ △ ⚵	**11:21 am**	8:21 am
☿ ☍ ♅	**11:54 am**	8:54 am
☽ ⚻ ♆	**5:44 pm**	2:44 pm
⚷ ⚹ ⚶	**11:52 pm**	8:52 pm

14 TUESDAY

☽ □ ♇	**5:53 am**	2:53 am
☽ ☍ ⚶	**7:34 am**	4:34 am
☽ △ ⚷	**7:43 am**	4:43 am
☽ ☌ ⚳	**9:07 am**	6:07 am
☽ ☌ ☉	**10:29 am**	7:29 am
☽ ☌ ♂	**11:05 am**	8:05 am
☽ ⚺ ♀	**12:25 pm**	9:25 am
☽ ⚹ ♄	**3:20 pm**	12:20 pm
☽ ☌ ♃	**8:55 pm**	5:55 pm

15 WEDNESDAY

☽ ⚻ ♅	**8:17 am**	5:17 am
☉ ☌ ♂	**8:55 am**	5:55 am
☽ ⚺ ☿	**2:00 pm**	11:00 am
♀ ⚻ ⚵	**5:40 pm**	2:40 pm
☽ □ ⚵	**6:33 pm**	3:33 pm
☽ ⚹ ♀	**6:38 pm**	3:38 pm
☽ △ ♆		9:17 pm

16 THURSDAY

☽ △ ♆	**12:17 am**	
☽ ⚹ ♇	**12:06 pm**	9:06 am
☽ ⚻ ⚶	**12:42 pm**	9:42 am
☽ □ ⚷	**1:46 pm**	10:46 am
☽ ⚺ ⚳	**5:05 pm**	2:05 pm
☉ ⚺ ♀	**5:58 pm**	2:58 pm
☽ ⚺ ♂	**7:45 pm**	4:45 pm
☽ ⚹ ♀	**8:35 pm**	5:35 pm
☽ ⚺ ☉	**8:41 pm**	5:41 pm
☽ □ ♄	**9:31 pm**	6:31 pm

17 FRIDAY

☽ ⚺ ♃	**3:27 am**	12:27 am
☿ △ ⚵	**5:40 am**	2:40 am
☉ ⚹ ♄	**9:32 am**	6:32 am
☽ △ ♅	**1:26 pm**	10:26 am
♇ □ ⚶	**8:01 pm**	5:01 pm
☽ ⚹ ⚵	**11:54 pm**	8:54 pm
♄ ⚺ ♀		9:40 pm
☽ ⚹ ☿		11:17 pm

18 SATURDAY

♄ ⚺ ♀	**12:40 am**	
☽ ⚹ ☿	**2:17 am**	
☽ □ ♀	**4:16 am**	1:16 am
☽ □ ♆	**5:03 am**	2:03 am
♀ ☍ ♆	**1:50 pm**	10:50 am
♂ ⚹ ♄	**2:32 pm**	11:32 am
☽ △ ⚶	**4:16 pm**	1:16 pm
☽ ⚺ ♇	**4:39 pm**	1:39 pm
☽ ⚹ ⚷	**6:12 pm**	3:12 pm
☽ ⚹ ⚳	**11:16 pm**	8:16 pm
☿ ⚻ ♆		9:15 pm
☽ △ ♄		11:07 pm
☽ ⚹ ♂		11:37 pm
☽ □ ♀		11:59 pm

19 SUNDAY

☿ ⚻ ♆	**12:15 am**	
☽ △ ♄	**2:07 am**	
☽ ⚹ ♂	**2:37 am**	
☽ □ ♀	**2:59 am**	
☽ ⚹ ☉	**4:55 am**	1:55 am
☽ ⚹ ♃	**8:24 am**	5:24 am
☽ □ ♅	**5:14 pm**	2:14 pm
☿ ⚺ ♀	**7:05 pm**	4:05 pm

20 MONDAY

☽ ⚺ ⚵	**4:00 am**	1:00 am
☽ ⚹ ♆	**8:35 am**	5:35 am
☽ △ ♀	**12:20 pm**	9:20 am
☽ □ ☿	**1:14 pm**	10:14 am
☽ □ ⚶	**6:47 pm**	3:47 pm
☽ ☌ ♇	**8:04 pm**	5:04 pm
☽ ⚺ ⚷	**9:32 pm**	6:32 pm
♂ ⚺ ♀	**11:13 pm**	8:13 pm

21 TUESDAY

☽ □ ⚳	**4:16 am**	1:16 am
☽ ⚻ ♄	**5:39 am**	2:39 am
☽ △ ♀	**8:12 am**	5:12 am
☽ □ ♂	**8:16 am**	5:16 am
☽ □ ☉	**11:54 am**	8:54 am
☽ □ ♃	**12:19 pm**	9:19 am
☉ ☌ ♃	**7:47 pm**	4:47 pm
☽ ⚹ ♅	**8:06 pm**	5:06 pm

22 WEDNESDAY

☿ ☍ ⚶	**4:21 am**	1:21 am
☽ ☌ ⚵	**7:17 am**	4:17 am
☽ ⚺ ♆	**11:20 am**	8:20 am
☿ □ ♇	**7:04 pm**	4:04 pm
☽ ⚻ ♀	**7:27 pm**	4:27 pm
☽ ⚹ ⚶	**8:39 pm**	5:39 pm
☽ ⚺ ♇	**10:48 pm**	7:48 pm
☽ △ ☿	**11:21 pm**	8:21 pm
☽ ☌ ⚷		9:11 pm

23 THURSDAY

☽ ☌ ⚷	**12:11 am**	
☿ △ ⚷	**5:52 am**	2:52 am
♄ ⚹ ⚳	**7:36 am**	4:36 am
♀ ⚻ ⚶	**8:15 am**	5:15 am
☽ ☍ ♄	**8:33 am**	5:33 am
☽ △ ⚳	**8:34 am**	5:34 am
☽ ⚻ ♀	**12:45 pm**	9:45 am
☽ △ ♂	**1:16 pm**	10:16 am
☽ △ ♃	**3:41 pm**	12:41 pm
☽ △ ☉	**6:12 pm**	3:12 pm
☽ ⚺ ♅	**10:31 pm**	7:31 pm

24 FRIDAY

☽ ⚺ ⚵	**10:16 am**	7:16 am
☽ ☌ ♆	**1:49 pm**	10:49 am
♀ △ ♇	**2:07 pm**	11:07 am
☽ ⚺ ⚶	**10:26 pm**	7:26 pm
☽ ⚹ ♇		10:27 pm
☽ ☍ ♀		11:25 pm
☽ ⚺ ⚷		11:46 pm

25 SATURDAY

☽ ⚹ ♇	**1:27 am**	
☽ ☍ ♀	**2:25 am**	
☽ ⚺ ⚷	**2:46 am**	
♀ ⚻ ⚷	**6:51 am**	3:51 am
☽ ⚻ ☿	**9:28 am**	6:28 am
☽ ⚻ ♄	**11:30 am**	8:30 am
☽ ⚻ ⚳	**12:57 pm**	9:57 am
☽ ☍ ♀	**5:26 pm**	2:26 pm
☽ ⚻ ♂	**6:25 pm**	3:25 pm
☽ ⚻ ♃	**7:14 pm**	4:14 pm
☽ ⚻ ☉		9:48 pm
☽ ☌ ♅		10:16 pm
☿ ⚹ ♄		10:38 pm

26 SUNDAY

☽ ⚻ ☉	**12:48 am**	
☽ ☌ ♅	**1:16 am**	
☿ ⚹ ♄	**1:38 am**	
☉ ⚻ ♅	**7:10 am**	4:10 am
☽ ⚹ ⚵	**1:52 pm**	10:52 am
☽ ⚺ ♆	**4:55 pm**	1:55 pm
☿ ☌ ⚳	**8:05 pm**	5:05 pm
♂ ☌ ♃	**8:17 pm**	5:17 pm
☽ ☌ ⚶		9:59 pm

27 MONDAY

☽ ☌ ⚶	**12:59 am**	
☽ □ ♇	**4:57 am**	1:57 am
☽ ⚹ ⚷	**6:16 am**	3:16 am
☽ ⚻ ♀	**10:34 am**	7:34 am
☽ △ ♄	**3:32 pm**	12:32 pm
☽ ☍ ⚳	**6:35 pm**	3:35 pm
☽ ☍ ☿	**9:12 pm**	6:12 pm
☽ ⚻ ♀	**11:29 pm**	8:29 pm
☽ ☍ ♃		9:06 pm
☽ ☍ ♂		10:02 pm

28 TUESDAY

☽ ☍ ♃	**12:06 am**	
☽ ☍ ♂	**1:02 am**	
☽ ⚺ ♅	**5:24 am**	2:24 am
☽ ☍ ☉	**9:09 am**	6:09 am
☽ □ ⚵	**7:16 pm**	4:16 pm
☿ ⚺ ♀	**8:04 pm**	5:04 pm
☿ ☌ ♃	**9:21 pm**	6:21 pm
☽ ⚹ ♆	**9:48 pm**	6:48 pm
♃ ⚺ ♀		11:50 pm

29 WEDNESDAY

♃ ⚺ ♀	**2:50 am**	
☽ ⚺ ⚶	**5:28 am**	2:28 am
☽ △ ♇	**10:31 am**	7:31 am
☽ □ ⚷	**11:51 am**	8:51 am
☿ ☌ ♂	**3:21 pm**	12:21 pm
☽ △ ♀	**9:33 pm**	6:33 pm
☽ □ ♄	**9:53 pm**	6:53 pm
♀ ⚺ ♄		10:28 pm
☽ ⚻ ⚳		11:47 pm

30 THURSDAY

♀ ⚺ ♄	**1:28 am**	
☽ ⚻ ⚳	**2:47 am**	
☽ ⚻ ♃	**7:33 am**	4:33 am
☽ △ ♀	**8:15 am**	5:15 am
☿ ⚻ ♅	**9:22 am**	6:22 am
☽ ⚻ ♂	**10:30 am**	7:30 am
☽ ⚹ ♅	**12:04 pm**	9:04 am
☽ ⚻ ☿	**12:32 pm**	9:32 am
☽ ⚻ ☉	**8:47 pm**	5:47 pm

Eastern time in bold type
Pacific time in medium type

SEPTEMBER 2004

☽ Last Aspect day	EST / hr:mn	PST	asp	☽ Ingress sign day	EST / hr:mn	PST
2	**12:17 pm**	9:17 am	△☿	♉ 2	**8:16 pm**	5:16 am
4		11:56 pm	⚹♀	♊ 5	**6:24 am**	3:24 am
5	**2:56 am**		⚹♀	♊ 5	**6:24 am**	3:24 am
7	**2:08 pm**	11:08 am	⚹☿	♋ 7	**6:50 pm**	3:50 pm
9		9:41 pm	⚹♃	♌ 10	**7:06 am**	4:06 am
10	**12:41 am**		⚹♃	♌ 10	**7:06 am**	4:06 am
11	**9:22 pm**	6:22 pm	△♇	♍ 12	**5:16 pm**	2:16 pm
14	**8:55 pm**	5:55 pm	☌♃	♎ 14		9:54 pm
14	**8:55 pm**	5:55 pm	☌♃	♎ 15	**12:54 am**	
16	**9:31 pm**	6:31 pm	□♄	♏ 17	**6:25 am**	3:25 am

☽ Last Aspect day	EST / hr:mn	PST	asp	☽ Ingress sign day	EST / hr:mn	PST
19	**8:24 am**	5:24 am	⚹♃	♐ 19	**10:30 am**	7:30 am
21	**12:19 pm**	9:19 am	□♃	♑ 21	**1:35 pm**	10:35 am
23	**3:41 pm**	12:41 pm	△♃	♒ 23	**4:10 pm**	1:10 pm
24		11:25 pm	☍♀	♓ 25	**6:55 pm**	3:55 pm
25	**2:25 am**		☍♀	♓ 25	**6:55 pm**	3:55 pm
27	**9:12 pm**	6:12 pm	☍☿	♈ 27	**10:57 pm**	7:57 pm
29	**9:53 pm**	6:53 pm	□♄	♉ 30	**5:24 pm**	2:24 pm

☽ Phases & Eclipses phase	day	EST / hr:mn	PST
4th Quarter	6	**11:10 am**	8:10 am
New Moon	14	**10:29 am**	7:29 am
2nd Quarter	21	**11:54 am**	8:54 am
Full Moon	28	**9:09 am**	6:09 am

Planet Ingress	day	EST / hr:mn	PST
♀ ♌	6	**6:16 pm**	3:16 pm
☿ ♍	10	**3:38 am**	12:38 am
☉ ♎	22	**12:30 pm**	9:30 am
♃ ♎	24	**11:23 pm**	8:23 pm
♂ ♎	26	**5:15 am**	2:15 am
♀ ♍	27	**9:33 am**	6:33 am
☿ ♎	28	**10:13 am**	7:13 am

Planetary Motion	day	EST / hr:mn	PST
⚵ D	1	**11:45 am**	8:45 am
☿ D	2	**9:09 am**	6:09 am
⚷ D	26	**1:20 pm**	10:20 am

DATE		SID.TIME	SUN	MOON	NODE	MERCURY	VENUS	MARS	JUPITER	SATURN	URANUS	NEPTUNE	PLUTO	CERES	PALLAS	JUNO	VESTA	CHIRON
1	W	22:41:59	08 ♍ 53 41	03 ♈ 32	03 ♉ ℞ 25	25 ♌ ℞ 54	23 ♋ 43	13 ♍ 43	24 ♍ 49	23 ♋ 25	04 ♓ ℞ 39	13 ♒ ℞ 19	19 ♐ 33	15 ♍ 07	15 ♌ 38	09 ♑ 10	23 ♓ ℞ 53	20 ♑ ℞ 55
2	Th	22:45:55	09 51 44	16 54	03 21	25 D 45	24 46	14 21	25 01	23 31	04 36	13 18	19 33	15 35	16 12	09 10	23 39	20 53
3	F	22:49:52	10 49 49	29 52	03 D 20	25 45	25 49	14 59	25 14	23 37	04 34	13 16	19 33	16 03	16 45	09 10	23 25	20 51
4	Sa	22:53:48	11 47 56	12 ♉ 27	03 20	25 53	26 53	15 38	25 27	23 43	04 32	13 15	19 33	16 30	17 18	09 11	23 10	20 49
5	Su	22:57:45	12 46 05	24 45	03 21	26 10	27 56	16 16	25 40	23 49	04 29	13 14	19 33	16 58	17 51	09 12	22 55	20 48
6	M	23:01:41	13 44 16	06 ♊ 48	03 ℞ 23	26 36	29 00	16 54	25 53	23 55	04 27	13 12	19 33	17 25	18 25	09 13	22 40	20 46
7	T	23:05:38	14 42 30	18 43	03 23	27 10	00 ♌ 05	17 33	26 05	24 01	04 25	13 11	19 33	17 53	18 58	09 15	22 25	20 45
8	W	23:09:34	15 40 45	00 ♋ 34	03 21	27 52	01 09	18 11	26 18	24 07	04 22	13 10	19 34	18 21	19 31	09 17	22 10	20 43
9	Th	23:13:31	16 39 02	12 27	03 18	28 42	02 14	18 49	26 31	24 13	04 20	13 08	19 34	18 48	20 04	09 20	21 55	20 42
10	F	23:17:28	17 37 21	24 25	03 13	29 40	03 19	19 28	26 44	24 19	04 18	13 07	19 34	19 16	20 36	09 23	21 40	20 41
11	Sa	23:21:24	18 35 42	06 ♌ 33	03 06	00 ♍ 45	04 24	20 06	26 57	24 24	04 15	13 06	19 35	19 44	21 09	09 26	21 25	20 40
12	Su	23:25:21	19 34 05	18 53	02 59	01 57	05 30	20 45	27 10	24 30	04 13	13 04	19 35	20 11	21 42	09 30	21 09	20 38
13	M	23:29:17	20 32 31	01 ♍ 26	02 51	03 15	06 35	21 23	27 23	24 35	04 11	13 03	19 35	20 39	22 15	09 34	20 54	20 37
14	T	23:33:14	21 30 58	14 15	02 44	04 38	07 41	22 02	27 36	24 41	04 08	13 02	19 36	21 06	22 47	09 38	20 39	20 36
15	W	23:37:10	22 29 26	27 19	02 38	06 06	08 47	22 40	27 48	24 46	04 06	13 01	19 36	21 34	23 20	09 43	20 23	20 35
16	Th	23:41:07	23 27 57	10 ♎ 36	02 34	07 39	09 54	23 19	28 01	24 51	04 04	13 00	19 37	22 02	23 52	09 48	20 08	20 35
17	F	23:45:03	24 26 30	24 05	02 D 32	09 16	11 00	23 57	28 14	24 57	04 02	12 59	19 37	22 29	24 24	09 53	19 53	20 34
18	Sa	23:49:00	25 25 04	07 ♏ 45	02 32	10 55	12 07	24 36	28 27	25 02	04 00	12 57	19 38	22 57	24 56	09 59	19 38	20 33
19	Su	23:52:56	26 23 40	21 35	02 33	12 38	13 14	25 14	28 40	25 07	03 57	12 56	19 39	23 25	25 29	10 05	19 23	20 32
20	M	23:56:53	27 22 18	05 ♐ 33	02 34	14 22	14 21	25 53	28 53	25 12	03 55	12 55	19 39	23 52	26 01	10 11	19 08	20 32
21	T	0:00:50	28 20 58	19 37	02 ℞ 35	16 09	15 28	26 32	29 06	25 17	03 53	12 54	19 40	24 20	26 33	10 18	18 54	20 31
22	W	0:04:46	29 19 39	03 ♑ 48	02 36	17 57	16 36	27 10	29 19	25 21	03 51	12 53	19 41	24 48	27 04	10 25	18 39	20 31
23	Th	0:08:43	00 ♎ 18 22	18 02	02 34	19 46	17 43	27 49	29 32	25 26	03 49	12 52	19 41	25 15	27 36	10 32	18 25	20 31
24	F	0:12:39	01 17 06	02 ♒ 17	02 32	21 35	18 51	28 28	29 45	25 31	03 47	12 51	19 42	25 43	28 08	10 40	18 11	20 30
25	Sa	0:16:36	02 15 52	16 30	02 28	23 25	19 59	29 06	29 58	25 35	03 45	12 50	19 43	26 10	28 39	10 48	17 58	20 30
26	Su	0:20:32	03 14 40	00 ♓ 38	02 24	25 15	21 08	29 45	00 ♎ 11	25 40	03 43	12 49	19 44	26 38	29 11	10 57	17 44	20 D 30
27	M	0:24:29	04 13 30	14 36	02 19	27 05	22 16	00 ♎ 24	00 24	25 44	03 41	12 49	19 45	27 05	29 42	11 05	17 31	20 30
28	T	0:28:26	05 12 21	28 20	02 16	28 55	23 25	01 03	00 37	25 49	03 39	12 48	19 45	27 33	00 ♍ 14	11 14	17 18	20 30
29	W	0:32:22	06 11 15	11 ♈ 47	02 13	00 ♎ 45	24 33	01 41	00 50	25 53	03 37	12 47	19 46	28 01	00 45	11 23	17 05	20 30
30	Th	0:36:19	07 10 10	24 56	02 D 12	02 34	25 42	02 20	01 03	25 57	03 35	12 46	19 47	28 28	01 16	11 33	16 53	20 31

EPHEMERIS CALCULATED FOR 12 MIDNIGHT GREENWICH MEAN TIME. ALL OTHER DATA AND FACING ASPECTARIAN PAGE IN **EASTERN TIME (BOLD)** AND PACIFIC TIME (REGULAR).

OCTOBER 2004

1 FRIDAY
☽△⚵ **3:35 am** 12:35 am
☽□♆ **5:28 am** 2:28 am
☽⚹⚶ **12:45 pm** 9:45 am
♂⚻♅ **4:21 pm** 1:21 pm
☽⚻♇ **7:04 pm** 4:04 pm
☽△⚷ **8:25 pm** 5:25 pm

2 SATURDAY
☽⚹♄ **7:18 am** 4:18 am
☽□♀ **12:34 pm** 9:34 am
☽△⚳ **2:24 pm** 11:24 am
☽△♃ **6:13 pm** 3:13 pm
☽□☿ **8:28 pm** 5:28 pm
☽□♅ **9:48 pm** 6:48 pm
☽△♂ **11:32 pm** 8:32 pm

3 SUNDAY
☽△☿ **8:29 am** 5:29 am
☽△☉ **12:17 pm** 9:17 am
☽⚻⚵ **3:05 pm** 12:05 pm
☽△♆ **4:08 pm** 1:08 pm
♀⚺⚳ **7:22 pm** 4:22 pm
☽□⚶ **10:54 pm** 7:54 pm
♅☍☿ 11:26 pm

4 MONDAY
♅☍☿ **2:26 am**
☽☍♇ **6:28 am** 3:28 am
☽⚻⚷ **7:49 am** 4:49 am
☽⚺♄ **7:22 pm** 4:22 pm

5 TUESDAY
☽□⚳ **4:47 am** 1:47 am
☉□⚵ **5:48 am** 2:48 am
☽⚹♀ **6:59 am** 3:59 am
☽□♃ **7:24 am** 4:24 am
☽△♅ **9:50 am** 6:50 am
☿□⚵ **10:03 am** 7:03 am
☉△♆ **10:59 am** 7:59 am
☽⚹♀ **11:19 am** 8:19 am
♀⚺♃ **12:14 pm** 9:14 am
☿△♆ **12:30 pm** 9:30 am
☉☌☿ **2:29 pm** 11:29 am
☽□♂ **3:14 pm** 12:14 pm

6 WEDNESDAY
☽☍⚵ **4:32 am** 1:32 am
☽⚻♆ **4:35 am** 1:35 am
☽□☉ **6:12 am** 3:12 am
☽□☿ **7:22 am** 4:22 am
♆⚺⚵ **7:36 am** 4:36 am
☽△⚶ **10:36 am** 7:36 am
♀☍♅ **11:23 am** 8:23 am
☽⚻♇ **7:09 pm** 4:09 pm
☽☍⚷ **8:28 pm** 5:28 pm

7 THURSDAY
☿⚻⚶ **3:56 am** 12:56 am
☽☌♄ **8:13 am** 5:13 am
☽⚹⚳ **7:37 pm** 4:37 pm
☽⚹♃ **8:55 pm** 5:55 pm
☽⚻♅ **10:04 pm** 7:04 pm
☽⚺♀ 10:52 pm
☽⚺☿ 11:18 pm

8 FRIDAY
☽⚺♀ **1:52 am**
☽⚺☿ **2:18 am**
☉⚻⚶ **4:36 am** 1:36 am
☽⚹♂ **6:55 am** 3:55 am
♀☌☿ **9:27 am** 6:27 am
☽☍♆ **4:29 pm** 1:29 pm
☽⚻⚵ **5:27 pm** 2:27 pm
☽⚻⚶ **9:37 pm** 6:37 pm
☽⚹☉ **11:20 pm** 8:20 pm

9 SATURDAY
☽⚹☿ **4:58 am** 1:58 am
☽△♇ **6:42 am** 3:42 am
☽⚻⚷ **7:57 am** 4:57 am
☿⚹♇ **5:49 pm** 2:49 pm
☽⚺♄ **7:25 pm** 4:25 pm
☿□⚷ 11:59 pm

10 SUNDAY
☿□⚷ **2:59 am**
♃⚻♅ **7:07 am** 4:07 am
☽⚺⚳ **8:14 am** 5:14 am
☽☍♅ **8:15 am** 5:15 am
☽⚺♃ **8:17 am** 5:17 am
♅⚻⚳ **8:47 am** 5:47 am
♃☌⚳ **10:26 am** 7:26 am
☽☌♀ **2:47 pm** 11:47 am
☽☌♀ **5:52 pm** 2:52 pm
☽⚺♂ **7:53 pm** 4:53 pm
☽⚻♆ 10:49 pm

11 MONDAY
☽⚻♆ **1:49 am**
☽△⚵ **3:43 am** 12:43 am
☽☍⚶ **6:07 am** 3:07 am
☽⚺☉ **1:01 pm** 10:01 am
☽□♇ **3:24 pm** 12:24 pm
☽△⚷ **4:34 pm** 1:34 pm
☽⚺☿ **10:00 pm** 7:00 pm

12 TUESDAY
☽⚹♄ **3:32 am** 12:32 am
☽⚻♅ **3:20 pm** 12:20 pm
☽☌♃ **4:21 pm** 1:21 pm
♀⚺♂ **4:26 pm** 1:26 pm
☽☌⚳ **5:21 pm** 2:21 pm
☉⚹♇ **9:10 pm** 6:10 pm
☽⚺♀ **11:42 pm** 8:42 pm

13 WEDNESDAY
☽☌♂ **5:10 am** 2:10 am
☽⚺♀ **5:43 am** 2:43 am
☽△♆ **8:01 am** 5:01 am
☽□⚵ **10:43 am** 7:43 am
☽⚻⚶ **11:39 am** 8:39 am
☉□⚷ **12:48 pm** 9:48 am
☿□♄ **7:14 pm** 4:14 pm
☽⚹♇ **9:00 pm** 6:00 pm
☽□⚷ **10:06 pm** 7:06 pm
☽☌☉ **10:48 pm** 7:48 pm

14 THURSDAY
♀⚻♆ **8:07 am** 5:07 am
☽□♄ **8:38 am** 5:38 am
☽☌☿ **10:22 am** 7:22 am
☽△♅ **7:38 pm** 4:38 pm
☽⚺♃ **9:29 pm** 6:29 pm
☽⚺⚳ **11:24 pm** 8:24 pm
⚵⚹⚶ 10:08 pm

15 FRIDAY
⚵⚹⚶ **1:08 am**
☽⚹♀ **5:37 am** 2:37 am
☽⚺♂ **11:30 am** 8:30 am
☽□♆ **11:42 am** 8:42 am
☽⚹♀ **2:14 pm** 11:14 am
☽△⚶ **2:51 pm** 11:51 am
☽⚹⚵ **3:10 pm** 12:10 pm
♂△♆ **4:02 pm** 1:02 pm
♀☍⚶ **9:05 pm** 6:05 pm
☽⚺♇ 9:21 pm
☽⚹⚷ 10:25 pm

16 SATURDAY
☽⚺♇ **12:21 am**
☽⚹⚷ **1:25 am**
♀△⚵ **3:59 am** 12:59 am
☽⚺☉ **5:50 am** 2:50 am
☽△♄ **11:43 am** 8:43 am
☽⚺☿ **7:46 pm** 4:46 pm
☽□♅ **10:14 pm** 7:14 pm
☽⚹♃ 9:52 pm

17 SUNDAY
☽⚹♃ **12:52 am**
☽⚹⚳ **3:39 am** 12:39 am
☽□♀ **9:52 am** 6:52 am
☽⚹♆ **2:04 pm** 11:04 am
☽⚹♂ **4:17 pm** 1:17 pm
☽□⚶ **4:53 pm** 1:53 pm
☿△♅ **5:30 pm** 2:30 pm
☽⚺⚵ **6:21 pm** 3:21 pm
☽□♀ **9:07 pm** 6:07 pm
☽☌♇ 11:40 pm

18 MONDAY
☽☌♇ **2:40 am**
☽⚺⚷ **3:44 am** 12:44 am
♂⚻⚶ **4:08 am** 1:08 am
☽⚹☉ **11:46 am** 8:46 am
☽⚻♄ **2:01 pm** 11:01 am
☿⚺♃ **11:37 pm** 8:37 pm
☽⚹♅ 9:18 pm

19 TUESDAY
☽⚹♅ **12:18 am**
☽□♃ **3:45 am** 12:45 am
☽⚹☿ **4:12 am** 1:12 am
☽□⚳ **7:26 am** 4:26 am
☽△♀ **1:48 pm** 10:48 am
☽⚺♆ **4:15 pm** 1:15 pm
☽⚹⚶ **6:51 pm** 3:51 pm
☽□♂ **8:54 pm** 5:54 pm
☉□♄ **9:25 pm** 6:25 pm
☽☌⚵ **9:27 pm** 6:27 pm

20 WEDNESDAY
☽△♀ **3:57 am** 12:57 am
☽⚺♇ **5:04 am** 2:04 am
☽☌⚷ **6:09 am** 3:09 am
♂□⚵ **3:51 pm** 12:51 pm
☽☍♄ **4:35 pm** 1:35 pm
♀□♇ **5:28 pm** 2:28 pm
☽□☉ **5:59 pm** 2:59 pm
☿⚺⚳ **8:02 pm** 5:02 pm
☽⚺♅ 11:50 pm

21 THURSDAY
☽⚺♅ **2:50 am**
♀△⚷ **6:44 am** 3:44 am
☽△♃ **7:10 am** 4:10 am
☽△⚳ **11:51 am** 8:51 am
☽□☿ **1:16 pm** 10:16 am
☽⚻♀ **6:27 pm** 3:27 pm
☽☌♆ **7:09 pm** 4:09 pm
☽⚺⚶ **9:36 pm** 6:36 pm
☽⚺⚵ 10:24 pm
☽△♂ 11:25 pm

22 FRIDAY
☽⚺⚵ **1:24 am**
☽△♂ **2:25 am**
☽⚹♇ **8:20 am** 5:20 am
☽⚺⚷ **9:28 am** 6:28 am
☽⚻♀ **11:56 am** 8:56 am
♆⚻♀ **2:56 pm** 11:56 am
☽⚻♄ **8:10 pm** 5:10 pm
☽△☉ 10:29 pm

23 SATURDAY
☽△☉ **1:29 am**
☽☌♅ **6:30 am** 3:30 am
☽⚻♃ **11:50 am** 8:50 am
☽⚻⚳ **5:37 pm** 2:37 pm
☿□♆ **6:20 pm** 3:20 pm
☽⚺♆ **11:21 pm** 8:21 pm
☽△☿ 9:00 pm
☽☍♀ 9:31 pm
☽☌⚶ 10:43 pm

24 SUNDAY
☽△☿ **12:00 am**
☽☍♀ **12:31 am**
☽☌⚶ **1:43 am**
☿⚹♀ **6:32 am** 3:32 am
☽⚹⚵ **6:50 am** 3:50 am
☽⚻♂ **9:31 am** 6:31 am
☽□♇ **1:04 pm** 10:04 am
☽⚹⚷ **2:16 pm** 11:16 am
☿△⚶ **3:02 pm** 12:02 pm
☽☍♀ **9:51 pm** 6:51 pm
☽△♄ 10:17 pm

25 MONDAY
☽△♄ **1:17 am**
♀☍⚶ **9:21 am** 6:21 am
☽⚻☉ **11:00 am** 8:00 am
☽⚺♅ **11:49 am** 8:49 am
☽☍♃ **6:14 pm** 3:14 pm
☉△♅ **9:49 pm** 6:49 pm
☽☍⚳ 10:18 pm

26 TUESDAY
☽☍⚳ **1:18 am**
☽⚹♆ **5:20 am** 2:20 am
☽⚺⚶ **7:43 am** 4:43 am
☽⚻♀ **8:35 am** 5:35 am
♀⚹♄ **12:49 pm** 9:49 am
☽⚻☿ **1:10 pm** 10:10 am
☽□⚵ **2:15 pm** 11:15 am
☽☍♂ **6:48 pm** 3:48 pm
☽△♇ **7:42 pm** 4:42 pm
☽□⚷ **8:59 pm** 5:59 pm
☿⚹⚵ 9:16 pm

27 WEDNESDAY
☿⚹⚵ **12:16 am**
☽□♄ **8:24 am** 5:24 am
☽⚻♀ **10:24 am** 7:24 am
♂⚹♇ **1:17 pm** 10:17 am
☽⚹♅ **7:12 pm** 4:12 pm
☽☍☉ **11:07 pm** 8:07 pm
☽⚻♃ 11:51 pm

28 THURSDAY
☽⚻♃ **2:51 am**
☽⚻⚳ **11:23 am** 8:23 am
☽□♆ **1:32 pm** 10:32 am
☽⚹⚶ **3:58 pm** 12:58 pm
♂□⚷ **4:14 pm** 1:14 pm
☽△♀ **7:04 pm** 4:04 pm
☿⚺♇ **10:24 pm** 7:24 pm
☽△⚵ 9:06 pm

29 FRIDAY
☽△⚵ **12:06 am**
☽⚻♇ **4:38 am** 1:38 am
☽☍☿ **5:28 am** 2:28 am
☽△⚷ **6:01 am** 3:01 am
☽⚻♂ **6:44 am** 3:44 am
☿⚹⚷ **10:08 am** 7:08 am
☽⚹♄ **5:50 pm** 2:50 pm
☿⚺♂ **11:27 pm** 8:27 pm
☽△♀ 11:05 pm

30 SATURDAY
☽△♀ **2:05 am**
☽□♅ **4:57 am** 1:57 am
☉⚺♃ **9:30 am** 6:30 am
☽△♃ **1:57 pm** 10:57 am
☽⚻☉ **2:16 pm** 11:16 am
♆△⚳ 9:04 pm
☽△♆ 9:05 pm
☽△⚳ 9:05 pm
☽□⚶ 11:40 pm

31 SUNDAY
♆△⚳ **12:04 am**
☽△♆ **12:05 am**
☽△⚳ **12:05 am**
☽□⚶ **1:40 am**
♀⚻♅ **5:44 am** 2:44 am
☽□♀ **7:09 am** 4:09 am
☽⚻⚵ **11:28 am** 8:28 am
☽☍♇ **2:52 pm** 11:52 am
☽⚻⚷ **4:22 pm** 1:22 pm
☽△♂ **8:21 pm** 5:21 pm
☽⚻☿ **11:56 pm** 8:56 pm

Eastern time in bold type
Pacific time in medium type

OCTOBER 2004

☽ Last Aspect			☽ Ingress		
day	EST / hr:mn / PST	asp	sign day	EST / hr:mn / PST	
2	**12:34 pm** 9:34 am	□ ♀	♊ 2	**2:55 pm** 11:55 am	
4	**6:28 am** 3:28 am	☍ ♇	♋ 4	11:54 pm	
4	**6:28 am** 3:28 am	☍ ♇	♋ 5	**2:54 am**	
7	**8:13 am** 5:13 am	☌ ♄	♌ 7	**3:23 pm** 12:23 pm	
9	**6:42 am** 3:42 am	△ ♇	♍ 9	11:00 pm	
9	**6:42 am** 3:42 am	△ ♇	♍ 10	**2:00 am**	
12	**3:32 am** 12:32 am	⚹ ♄	♎ 12	**9:32 am** 6:32 am	
14	**10:22 am** 7:22 am	☌ ☿	♏ 14	**2:10 pm** 11:10 am	
16	**11:43 am** 8:43 am	△ ♄	♐ 16	**4:58 pm** 1:58 pm	

☽ Last Aspect			☽ Ingress	
day	EST / hr:mn / PST	asp	sign day	EST / hr:mn / PST
18	**11:46 am** 8:46 am	⚹ ☉	♑ 18	**7:07 pm** 4:07 pm
20	**5:59 pm** 2:59 pm	□ ☉	≈ 20	**9:38 pm** 6:38 pm
22	**8:20 am** 5:20 am	⚹ ♇	♓ 22	10:13 pm
22	**8:20 am** 5:20 am	⚹ ♇	♓ 23	**1:13 am**
24	10:17 pm	△ ♄	♈ 25	**6:24 am** 3:24 am
25	**1:17 am**	△ ♄	♈ 25	**6:24 am** 3:24 am
27	**8:24 am** 5:24 am	□ ♄	♉ 27	**1:37 pm** 10:37 am
29	**5:50 pm** 2:50 pm	⚹ ♄	♊ 29	**11:11 pm** 8:11 pm
31	**8:21 pm** 5:21 pm	△ ♂	♋ 11/1	**9:53 am** 6:53 am

☽ Phases & Eclipses		
phase	day	EST / hr:mn / PST
4th Quarter	6	**6:12 am** 3:12 am
New Moon	13	**10:48 pm** 7:48 pm
(eclipse)	13	21° ♎ 06'
2nd Quarter	20	**5:59 pm** 2:59 pm
Full Moon	27	**11:07 pm** 8:07 pm
(eclipse)	27	5° ♉ 02'

Planet Ingress		
	day	EST / hr:mn / PST
⚳ ♎	3	**4:06 am** 1:06 am
♀ ♍	3	**1:20 pm** 10:20 am
☿ ♏	15	**6:57 pm** 3:57 pm
☉ ♏	22	**9:49 pm** 6:49 pm
♀ ♎	28	**8:39 pm** 5:39 pm

Planetary Motion		
	day	EST / hr:mn / PST
♆ D	24	**7:56 am** 4:56 am
⚶ D	27	10:50 pm
⚶ D	28	**1:50 am**

DATE		SID. TIME	SUN	MOON	NODE	MERCURY	VENUS	MARS	JUPITER	SATURN	URANUS	NEPTUNE	PLUTO	CERES	PALLAS	JUNO	VESTA	CHIRON
1	F	0:40:15	08 ♎ 09 08	07 ♉ 46	02 ♉ 12	04 ♎ 22	26 ♌ 51	02 ♎ 59	01 ♎ 16	26 ♋ 01	03 ♓ ℞ 33	12 ≈ ℞ 45	19 ♐ 48	28 ♍ 56	01 ♍ 47	11 ♑ 43	16 ♓ ℞ 41	20 ♑ 31
2	Sa	0:44:12	09 08 08	20 19	02 13	06 10	28 00	03 38	01 29	26 05	03 32	12 45	19 49	29 23	02 18	11 53	16 29	20 31
3	Su	0:48:08	10 07 10	02 ♊ 35	02 14	07 57	29 10	04 17	01 42	26 09	03 30	12 44	19 50	29 51	02 49	12 03	16 18	20 32
4	M	0:52:00	11 06 14	14 39	02 16	09 44	00 ♍ 19	04 56	01 55	26 13	03 28	12 43	19 51	00 ♎ 18	03 19	12 14	16 07	20 32
5	T	0:56:01	12 05 21	26 35	02 17	11 30	01 29	05 34	02 08	26 16	03 26	12 43	19 53	00 46	03 50	12 25	15 57	20 33
6	W	0:59:58	13 04 30	08 ♋ 27	02 ℞ 18	13 15	02 39	06 13	02 20	26 20	03 25	12 42	19 54	01 13	04 21	12 36	15 47	20 33
7	Th	1:03:54	14 03 41	20 20	02 18	14 59	03 49	06 52	02 33	26 23	03 23	12 41	19 55	01 41	04 51	12 48	15 37	20 34
8	F	1:07:51	15 02 55	02 ♌ 19	02 17	16 43	04 59	07 31	02 46	26 27	03 21	12 41	19 56	02 08	05 21	13 00	15 27	20 35
9	Sa	1:11:48	16 02 10	14 28	02 15	18 26	06 09	08 10	02 59	26 30	03 20	12 40	19 57	02 36	05 51	13 12	15 18	20 36
10	Su	1:15:44	17 01 29	26 51	02 13	20 08	07 19	08 49	03 12	26 33	03 18	12 40	19 59	03 03	06 22	13 24	15 10	20 37
11	M	1:19:41	18 00 49	09 ♍ 32	02 11	21 49	08 30	09 28	03 24	26 36	03 17	12 39	20 00	03 30	06 52	13 37	15 02	20 38
12	T	1:23:37	19 00 11	22 32	02 09	23 29	09 41	10 08	03 37	26 39	03 15	12 39	20 01	03 58	07 21	13 49	14 54	20 39
13	W	1:27:34	19 59 36	05 ♎ 51	02 08	25 09	00 51	10 47	03 50	26 42	03 14	12 39	20 02	04 25	07 51	14 02	14 47	20 40
14	Th	1:31:30	20 59 03	19 29	02 D 07	26 48	12 02	11 26	04 03	26 45	03 13	12 38	20 04	04 52	08 21	14 16	14 40	20 42
15	F	1:35:27	21 58 32	03 ♏ 24	02 07	28 27	13 13	12 05	04 15	26 48	03 11	12 38	20 05	05 20	08 50	14 29	14 34	20 43
16	Sa	1:39:23	22 58 02	17 32	02 07	00 ♏ 04	14 24	12 44	04 28	26 50	03 10	12 38	20 07	05 47	09 20	14 43	14 28	20 44
17	Su	1:43:20	23 57 35	01 ♐ 49	02 08	01 41	15 36	13 23	04 41	26 53	03 09	12 37	20 08	06 14	09 49	14 57	14 22	20 46
18	M	1:47:17	24 57 10	16 10	02 08	03 18	16 47	14 03	04 53	26 55	03 07	12 37	20 09	06 41	10 18	15 12	14 17	20 47
19	T	1:51:13	25 56 46	00 ♑ 32	02 09	04 53	17 58	14 42	05 06	26 58	03 06	12 37	20 11	07 09	10 47	15 26	14 13	20 49
20	W	1:55:10	26 56 25	14 50	02 ℞ 09	06 28	19 10	15 21	05 18	27 00	03 05	12 37	20 12	07 36	11 16	15 41	14 09	20 51
21	Th	1:59:06	27 56 05	29 03	02 09	08 03	20 21	16 00	05 31	27 02	03 04	12 37	20 14	08 03	11 45	15 56	14 05	20 53
22	F	2:03:03	28 55 46	13 ≈ 06	02 09	09 37	21 33	16 40	05 43	27 04	03 03	12 37	20 16	08 30	12 14	16 11	14 02	20 55
23	Sa	2:06:59	29 55 29	27 00	02 09	11 10	22 45	17 19	05 56	27 06	03 02	12 36	20 17	08 57	12 42	16 27	14 00	20 57
24	Su	2:10:56	00 ♏ 55 14	10 ♓ 43	02 09	12 43	23 57	17 58	06 08	27 07	03 01	12 D 36	20 19	09 24	13 11	16 43	13 57	20 59
25	M	2:14:52	01 55 01	24 13	02 D 09	14 15	25 09	18 38	06 20	27 09	03 00	12 36	20 20	09 51	13 39	16 59	13 56	21 01
26	T	2:18:49	02 54 49	07 ♈ 30	02 09	15 47	26 21	19 17	06 33	27 11	02 59	12 36	20 22	10 18	14 07	17 15	13 54	21 03
27	W	2:22:46	03 54 39	20 33	02 ℞ 09	17 18	27 33	19 57	06 45	27 12	02 59	12 37	20 24	10 45	14 35	17 31	13 54	21 05
28	Th	2:26:42	04 54 31	03 ♉ 23	02 09	18 48	28 46	20 36	06 57	27 13	02 58	12 37	20 25	11 12	15 03	17 48	13 D 53	21 07
29	F	2:30:39	05 54 25	15 59	02 09	20 18	29 58	21 16	07 09	27 15	02 57	12 37	20 27	11 39	15 31	18 04	13 53	21 10
30	Sa	2:34:35	06 54 21	28 22	02 08	21 48	01 ♎ 11	21 55	07 21	27 16	02 56	12 37	20 29	12 06	15 59	18 21	13 54	21 12
31	Su	2:38:32	07 54 19	10 ♊ 34	02 08	23 17	02 23	22 35	07 33	27 17	02 56	12 37	20 31	12 33	16 26	18 38	13 55	21 15

EPHEMERIS CALCULATED FOR 12 MIDNIGHT GREENWICH MEAN TIME. ALL OTHER DATA AND FACING ASPECTARIAN PAGE IN **EASTERN TIME (BOLD)** AND PACIFIC TIME (REGULAR).

NOVEMBER 2004

1 MONDAY

☽ ⚺ ♄ **4:27 am** 1:27 am
☽ △ ♅ **3:46 pm** 12:46 pm
☽ □ ♀ **7:39 pm** 4:39 pm
☽ □ ♃ 11:04 pm

2 TUESDAY

☽ □ ♃ **2:04 am**
☽ △ ☉ **6:54 am** 3:54 am
☽ ⚻ ♆ **11:25 am** 8:25 am
☿ △ ♄ **1:01 pm** 10:01 am
☽ □ ⚳ **1:45 pm** 10:45 am
☽ △ ⚶ **2:11 pm** 11:11 am
☽ ⚹ ⚴ **10:00 pm** 7:00 pm
☽ ☍ ⚵ 10:31 pm
⚳ ⚻ ⚶ 11:51 pm

3 WEDNESDAY

☽ ☍ ⚵ **1:31 am**
⚳ ⚻ ⚶ **2:51 am**
☽ ⚻ ♇ **3:34 am** 12:34 am
☽ ☍ ⚷ **5:09 am** 2:09 am
☽ □ ♂ **12:31 pm** 9:31 am
☽ ☌ ♄ **5:08 pm** 2:08 pm
☽ △ ☿ **9:00 pm** 6:00 pm

4 THURSDAY

☽ ⚻ ♅ **4:21 am** 1:21 am
☉ □ ♆ **12:34 pm** 9:34 am
☽ ⚹ ♀ **3:07 pm** 12:07 pm
☽ ⚹ ♃ **3:38 pm** 12:38 pm
♀ ☌ ♃ **9:11 pm** 6:11 pm
☽ ☍ ♆ **11:52 pm** 8:52 pm
☽ □ ☉ 9:53 pm
☽ ⚻ ⚶ 11:49 pm

5 FRIDAY

☽ □ ☉ **12:53 am**
☽ ⚻ ⚶ **2:49 am**
☽ ⚹ ⚳ **4:26 am** 1:26 am
☽ ⚺ ⚴ **12:31 pm** 9:31 am
☽ ⚻ ⚵ **3:11 pm** 12:11 pm
☽ △ ♇ **3:49 pm** 12:49 pm
☽ ⚻ ⚷ **5:26 pm** 2:26 pm
☉ △ ⚶ 10:35 pm

6 SATURDAY

☉ △ ⚶ **1:35 am**
☽ ⚹ ♂ **3:45 am** 12:45 am
☽ ⚺ ♄ **4:50 am** 1:50 am
☿ □ ♅ **10:18 am** 7:18 am
☽ ☍ ♅ **3:34 pm** 12:34 pm
☽ □ ☿ **4:15 pm** 1:15 pm
♇ ⚺ ⚵ **7:08 pm** 4:08 pm
♂ □ ♄ 9:03 pm

7 SUNDAY

♂ □ ♄ **12:03 am**
☽ ⚺ ♃ **3:18 am** 12:18 am
☽ ⚺ ♀ **8:10 am** 5:10 am
☽ ⚻ ♆ **10:15 am** 7:15 am
☽ ☍ ⚶ **1:20 pm** 10:20 am
☽ ⚹ ☉ **4:10 pm** 1:10 pm
☽ ⚺ ⚳ **4:37 pm** 1:37 pm
☽ ☌ ⚴ 9:13 pm
☽ □ ♇ 10:26 pm
☽ △ ⚵ 11:06 pm
☉ ⚺ ⚳ 11:23 pm

8 MONDAY

☽ ☌ ⚴ **12:13 am**
☽ □ ♇ **1:26 am**
☽ △ ⚵ **2:06 am**
☉ ⚺ ⚳ **2:23 am**
☽ △ ⚷ **3:02 am** 12:02 am
♀ △ ♆ **5:58 am** 2:58 am
☽ ⚹ ♄ **1:32 pm** 10:32 am
☽ ⚺ ♂ **3:32 pm** 12:32 pm
☽ ⚻ ♅ **11:35 pm** 8:35 pm

9 TUESDAY

☽ ⚹ ☿ **6:44 am** 3:44 am
☽ ☌ ♃ **11:22 am** 8:22 am
♇ □ ⚴ **2:43 pm** 11:43 am
☽ △ ♆ **5:05 pm** 2:05 pm
♀ ⚻ ⚶ **5:27 pm** 2:27 pm
☽ ⚻ ⚶ **8:16 pm** 5:16 pm
☽ ☌ ♀ **8:32 pm** 5:32 pm
⚷ ☌ ⚵ 9:03 pm
☽ ☌ ⚳ 9:49 pm
☽ ⚺ ☉ 11:52 pm

10 WEDNESDAY

⚷ ☌ ⚵ **12:03 am**
☽ ☌ ⚳ **12:49 am**
☽ ⚺ ☉ **2:52 am**
☽ ⚹ ♇ **7:21 am** 4:21 am
☽ ⚺ ⚴ **7:51 am** 4:51 am
☽ □ ⚷ **8:56 am** 5:56 am
☽ □ ⚵ **9:07 am** 6:07 am
☽ □ ♄ **6:32 pm** 3:32 pm
☽ ☌ ♂ **11:02 pm** 8:02 pm

11 THURSDAY

☽ △ ♅ **3:58 am** 12:58 am
☿ ⚹ ♃ **11:31 am** 8:31 am
☽ ⚺ ♃ **3:44 pm** 12:44 pm
☽ ⚺ ☿ **4:06 pm** 1:06 pm
☽ □ ♆ **8:28 pm** 5:28 pm
⚷ △ ⚴ **11:43 pm** 8:43 pm
☽ △ ⚶ **11:47 pm** 8:47 pm

12 FRIDAY

☽ ⚺ ♀ **4:24 am** 1:24 am
☽ ⚺ ⚳ **5:19 am** 2:19 am
☽ ☌ ☉ **9:27 am** 6:27 am
☽ ⚺ ♇ **10:03 am** 7:03 am
☽ ⚹ ⚷ **11:38 am** 8:38 am
☽ ⚹ ⚴ **11:56 am** 8:56 am
☽ ⚹ ⚵ **12:44 pm** 9:44 am
☉ ⚺ ♇ **6:24 pm** 3:24 pm
☽ △ ♄ **8:34 pm** 5:34 pm
♀ ☌ ⚳ **8:46 pm** 5:46 pm

13 SATURDAY

☽ ⚺ ♂ **3:15 am** 12:15 am
☽ □ ♅ **5:37 am** 2:37 am
☿ ⚹ ♆ **4:19 pm** 1:19 pm
☽ ⚹ ♃ **5:37 pm** 2:37 pm
☉ ⚹ ⚷ **6:40 pm** 3:40 pm
☽ ⚹ ♆ **9:37 pm** 6:37 pm
☽ ☌ ☿ **10:06 pm** 7:06 pm
☽ □ ⚶ 10:11 pm

14 SUNDAY

☽ □ ⚶ **1:11 am**
☽ ⚹ ⚳ **7:41 am** 4:41 am
☽ ⚹ ♀ **9:43 am** 6:43 am
☽ ☌ ♇ **10:58 am** 7:58 am
☽ ⚺ ⚷ **12:35 pm** 9:35 am
☽ ⚺ ☉ **1:49 pm** 10:49 am
☽ □ ⚴ **2:08 pm** 11:08 am
☽ ⚺ ⚵ **2:36 pm** 11:36 am
☽ ⚻ ♄ **9:11 pm** 6:11 pm
☉ ⚹ ⚴ **9:39 pm** 6:39 pm
♀ ⚹ ♇ 10:11 pm

15 MONDAY

♀ ⚹ ♇ **1:11 am**
☽ ⚹ ♂ **6:08 am** 3:08 am
☽ ⚹ ♅ **6:13 am** 3:13 am
☉ ⚹ ⚵ **6:38 am** 3:38 am
♂ △ ♅ **7:58 am** 4:58 am
☿ □ ⚶ **1:54 pm** 10:54 am
☽ □ ♃ **6:49 pm** 3:49 pm
♀ □ ⚷ **9:59 pm** 6:59 pm
☽ ⚺ ♆ **10:16 pm** 7:16 pm
☽ ⚹ ⚶ 11:15 pm

16 TUESDAY

☽ ⚹ ⚶ **2:15 am**
☽ ⚺ ☿ **3:15 am** 12:15 am
☽ □ ⚳ **9:54 am** 6:54 am
☽ ⚺ ♇ **11:51 am** 8:51 am
☽ ☌ ⚷ **1:35 pm** 10:35 am
☽ □ ♀ **2:57 pm** 11:57 am
☽ △ ⚴ **4:25 pm** 1:25 pm
☽ ☌ ⚵ **4:35 pm** 1:35 pm
☽ ⚹ ☉ **6:17 pm** 3:17 pm
☽ ☍ ♄ **10:07 pm** 7:07 pm

17 WEDNESDAY

☽ ⚺ ♅ **7:27 am** 4:27 am
☽ □ ♂ **9:45 am** 6:45 am
♀ ⚺ ⚴ **4:04 pm** 1:04 pm
♀ □ ⚵ **4:57 pm** 1:57 pm
☽ △ ♃ **9:06 pm** 6:06 pm
☽ ☌ ♆ 9:04 pm

18 THURSDAY

☽ ☌ ♆ **12:04 am**
⚴ △ ⚵ **3:22 am** 12:22 am
☽ ⚺ ⚶ **4:40 am** 1:40 am
☽ ⚹ ☿ **9:47 am** 6:47 am
☽ △ ⚳ **1:44 pm** 10:44 am
☽ ⚹ ♇ **2:18 pm** 11:18 am
☽ ⚺ ⚷ **4:12 pm** 1:12 pm
☽ ⚺ ⚵ **8:22 pm** 5:22 pm
☽ ⚻ ⚴ **8:27 pm** 5:27 pm
☽ △ ♀ **10:18 pm** 7:18 pm
☉ △ ♄ 9:33 pm
☽ ⚻ ♄ 9:49 pm
☽ □ ☉ 9:50 pm

19 FRIDAY

☉ △ ♄ **12:33 am**
☽ ⚻ ♄ **12:49 am**
☽ □ ☉ **12:50 am**
♇ ⚹ ⚳ **9:31 am** 6:31 am
☽ ☌ ♅ **10:41 am** 7:41 am
☽ △ ♂ **3:42 pm** 12:42 pm
☽ ⚻ ♃ 10:41 pm
♀ □ ♄ 11:12 pm

20 SATURDAY

☽ ⚻ ♃ **1:41 am**
♀ □ ♄ **2:12 am**
☽ ⚺ ♆ **4:10 am** 1:10 am
☽ ☌ ⚶ **9:32 am** 6:32 am
☽ □ ☿ **6:57 pm** 3:57 pm
☽ □ ♇ **7:12 pm** 4:12 pm
☽ ⚻ ⚳ **8:14 pm** 5:14 pm
☽ ⚹ ⚷ **9:19 pm** 6:19 pm
☿ ☌ ♇ **10:24 pm** 7:24 pm
☽ ⚹ ⚵ 11:53 pm

21 SUNDAY

☽ ⚹ ⚵ **2:53 am**
☽ ☍ ⚴ **3:13 am** 12:13 am
☽ △ ♄ **6:02 am** 3:02 am
☽ ⚻ ♀ **8:58 am** 5:58 am
☽ △ ☉ **10:35 am** 7:35 am
☽ ⚺ ♅ **4:32 pm** 1:32 pm
☽ ⚻ ♂ 9:42 pm
☿ ⚹ ⚳ 9:58 pm

22 MONDAY

☽ ⚻ ♂ **12:42 am**
☿ ⚹ ⚳ **12:58 am**
☿ ⚺ ⚷ **5:24 am** 2:24 am
☽ ☍ ♃ **9:00 am** 6:00 am
☽ ⚹ ♆ **10:55 am** 7:55 am
⚷ □ ⚳ **11:34 am** 8:34 am
☽ ⚺ ⚶ **5:11 pm** 2:11 pm
☽ △ ♇ 11:44 pm

23 TUESDAY

☽ △ ♇ **2:44 am**
☽ □ ⚷ **5:04 am** 2:04 am
☽ ☍ ⚳ **5:35 am** 2:35 am
☽ △ ☿ **6:43 am** 3:43 am
☽ □ ⚵ **12:11 pm** 9:11 am
☽ ⚻ ⚴ **12:46 pm** 9:46 am
☽ □ ♄ **1:47 pm** 10:47 am
☽ ☍ ♀ **11:03 pm** 8:03 pm
☽ ⚻ ☉ **11:32 pm** 8:32 pm
☽ ⚹ ♅ 9:52 pm

24 WEDNESDAY

☽ ⚹ ♅ **12:52 am**
☽ ☍ ♂ **12:33 pm** 9:33 am
☉ □ ♅ **4:19 pm** 1:19 pm
♀ △ ♅ **5:46 pm** 2:46 pm
☽ ⚻ ♃ **6:45 pm** 3:45 pm
♄ ⚹ ⚴ **7:28 pm** 4:28 pm
☽ □ ♆ **8:01 pm** 5:01 pm
☉ ⚺ ♀ 9:12 pm

25 THURSDAY

☉ ⚺ ♀ **12:12 am**
☽ ⚹ ⚶ **3:18 am** 12:18 am
☽ ⚻ ♇ **12:31 pm** 9:31 am
☽ △ ⚷ **3:04 pm** 12:04 pm
♄ ☍ ⚵ **4:23 pm** 1:23 pm
☽ ⚻ ⚳ **5:22 pm** 2:22 pm
☽ ⚻ ☿ **8:09 pm** 5:09 pm
☽ ⚹ ♄ **11:37 pm** 8:37 pm
☽ △ ⚵ **11:51 pm** 8:51 pm
☽ △ ⚴ 9:37 pm

26 FRIDAY

☽ △ ⚴ **12:37 am**
☽ □ ♅ **11:16 am** 8:16 am
☽ ☍ ☉ **3:07 pm** 12:07 pm
☽ ⚻ ♀ **3:56 pm** 12:56 pm
☽ ⚻ ♂ 11:42 pm

27 SATURDAY

☽ ⚻ ♂ **2:42 am**
☽ △ ♃ **6:28 am** 3:28 am
☽ △ ♆ **7:01 am** 4:01 am
☽ □ ⚶ **3:22 pm** 12:22 pm
☽ ☍ ♇ 9:02 pm
☽ ⚻ ⚷ 11:50 pm

28 SUNDAY

☽ ☍ ♇ **12:02 am**
☽ ⚻ ⚷ **2:50 am**
☽ △ ⚳ **7:00 am** 4:00 am
☽ ☍ ☿ **10:04 am** 7:04 am
☽ ⚺ ♄ **11:04 am** 8:04 am
☽ ⚻ ⚵ **1:21 pm** 10:21 am
☽ □ ⚴ **2:13 pm** 11:13 am
☽ △ ♅ **11:13 pm** 8:13 pm

29 MONDAY

♃ △ ♆ **3:26 am** 12:26 am
☽ ⚻ ☉ **8:40 am** 5:40 am
☽ △ ♀ **10:53 am** 7:53 am
☽ △ ♂ **6:29 pm** 3:29 pm
☽ ⚻ ♆ **7:22 pm** 4:22 pm
☽ □ ♃ **7:34 pm** 4:34 pm

30 TUESDAY

☽ △ ⚶ **4:49 am** 1:49 am
♂ □ ♆ **10:25 am** 7:25 am
☽ ⚻ ♇ **12:44 pm** 9:44 am
☽ ☍ ⚷ **3:44 pm** 12:44 pm
♂ ⚺ ♃ **7:05 pm** 4:05 pm
☽ □ ⚳ **9:48 pm** 6:48 pm
☽ ⚻ ☿ **11:10 pm** 8:10 pm
☽ ☌ ♄ **11:28 pm** 8:28 pm

Eastern time in bold type
Pacific time in medium type

NOVEMBER 2004

☽ Last Aspect day	EST / hr:mn / PST		asp	☽ Ingress sign	day	EST / hr:mn / PST	
10/31	**8:21 pm**	5:21 pm	△♂	♋	1	**9:53 am**	6:53 am
3	**9:00 pm**	6:00 pm	△☿	♌	3	**10:32 pm**	7:32 pm
6	**3:45 am**	12:45 am	⚹♂	♍	6	**10:00 am**	7:00 am
8	**1:32 pm**	10:32 am	⚹♄	♎	8	**6:23 pm**	3:23 pm
10	**11:02 pm**	8:02 pm	☌♂	♏	10	**11:05 pm**	8:05 pm
12	**8:34 pm**	5:34 pm	△♄	♐	12		9:56 pm
12	**8:34 pm**	5:34 pm	△♄	♐	13	**12:56 am**	
14	**10:58 am**	7:58 am	☌♇	♑	14		10:33 pm
14	**10:58 am**	7:58 am	☌♇	♑	15	**1:33 am**	
16	**10:07 pm**	7:07 pm	☍♄	♒	16		11:39 pm
16	**10:07 pm**	7:07 pm	☍♄	♒	17	**2:39 am**	
18		9:50 pm	□☉	♓	19	**5:38 am**	2:38 am
19	**12:50 am**		□☉	♓	19	**5:38 am**	2:38 am
21	**10:35 am**	7:35 am	△☉	♈	21	**11:11 am**	8:11 am
23	**1:47 pm**	10:47 am	□♄	♉	23	**7:16 pm**	4:16 pm
25	**11:37 pm**	8:37 pm	⚹♄	♊	26	**5:25 am**	2:25 am
28	**10:04 am**	7:04 am	☍☿	♋	28	**5:10 pm**	2:10 pm
30	**11:28 pm**	8:28 pm	☌♄	♌	12/1	**5:50 am**	2:50 am

☽ Phases & Eclipses phase	day	EST / hr:mn / PST	
4th Quarter	4		9:53 pm
4th Quarter	5	**12:53 am**	
New Moon	12	**9:27 am**	6:27 am
2nd Quarter	18		9:50 pm
2nd Quarter	19	**12:50 am**	
Full Moon	26	**3:07 pm**	12:07 pm

Planet Ingress		day	EST / hr:mn / PST	
☿	♐	4	**9:40 am**	6:40 am
♂	♏	10		9:11 pm
♂	♏	11	**12:11 am**	
☉	♐	21	**6:22 pm**	3:22 pm
♀	♏	22	**8:31 am**	5:31 am

Planetary Motion		day	EST / hr:mn / PST	
♄	℞	7		10:54 pm
♄	℞	8	**1:54 am**	
♅	D	11	**2:12 pm**	11:12 am
☿	℞	30	**7:17 am**	4:17 am

DATE		SID.TIME	SUN	MOON	NODE	MERCURY	VENUS	MARS	JUPITER	SATURN	URANUS	NEPTUNE	PLUTO	CERES	PALLAS	JUNO	VESTA	CHIRON
1	M	2:42:28	08 ♏ 54 19	22 ♊ 36	02 ♉ ℞ 07	24 ♏ 45	03 ♎ 36	23 ♎ 14	07 ♎ 45	27 ♋ 18	02 ♓ ℞ 55	12 ♒ 37	20 ♐ 33	12 ♎ 59	16 ♍ 54	18 ♑ 56	13 ♓ 56	21 ♑ 17
2	T	2:46:25	09 54 21	04 ♋ 31	02 06	26 13	04 49	23 54	07 57	27 18	02 55	12 38	20 34	13 26	17 21	19 13	13 58	21 20
3	W	2:50:21	10 54 25	16 23	02 05	27 41	06 01	24 33	08 09	27 19	02 54	12 38	20 36	13 53	17 48	19 31	14 01	21 23
4	Th	2:54:18	11 54 32	28 15	02 04	29 07	07 14	25 13	08 21	27 20	02 54	12 38	20 38	14 19	18 15	19 49	14 03	21 25
5	F	2:58:15	12 54 40	10 ♌ 12	02 D 04	00 ♐ 33	08 27	25 53	08 33	27 20	02 54	12 39	20 40	14 46	18 42	20 07	14 07	21 28
6	Sa	3:02:11	13 54 50	22 19	02 04	01 59	09 40	26 32	08 45	27 20	02 53	12 39	20 42	15 13	19 09	20 25	14 10	21 31
7	Su	3:06:08	14 55 03	04 ♍ 40	02 04	03 24	10 54	27 12	08 56	27 21	02 53	12 40	20 44	15 39	19 35	20 44	14 14	21 34
8	M	3:10:04	15 55 17	17 19	02 06	04 48	12 07	27 52	09 08	27 21	02 53	12 40	20 46	16 06	20 02	21 02	14 19	21 37
9	T	3:14:01	16 55 33	00 ♎ 20	02 07	06 11	13 20	28 32	09 19	27 ℞ 21	02 53	12 40	20 48	16 32	20 28	21 21	14 24	21 40
10	W	3:17:57	17 55 52	13 46	02 08	07 33	14 33	29 12	09 31	27 20	02 52	12 41	20 50	16 58	20 54	21 40	14 29	21 43
11	Th	3:21:54	18 56 12	27 36	02 ℞ 09	08 55	15 47	29 51	09 42	27 20	02 D 52	12 42	20 52	17 25	21 20	21 59	14 35	21 47
12	F	3:25:50	19 56 34	11 ♏ 50	02 08	10 15	17 00	00 ♏ 31	09 54	27 20	02 52	12 42	20 54	17 51	21 45	22 19	14 41	21 50
13	Sa	3:29:47	20 56 58	26 22	02 07	11 34	18 14	01 11	10 05	27 19	02 52	12 43	20 56	18 17	22 11	22 38	14 47	21 53
14	Su	3:33:44	21 57 24	11 ♐ 07	02 05	12 52	19 27	01 51	10 16	27 19	02 52	12 44	20 58	18 44	22 36	22 58	14 54	21 57
15	M	3:37:40	22 57 51	25 57	02 02	14 09	20 41	02 31	10 27	27 18	02 53	12 44	21 00	19 10	23 02	23 18	15 02	22 00
16	T	3:41:37	23 58 19	10 ♑ 45	02 00	15 23	21 55	03 11	10 38	27 17	02 53	12 45	21 02	19 36	23 27	23 37	15 09	22 04
17	W	3:45:33	24 58 49	25 23	01 57	16 36	23 09	03 51	10 49	27 16	02 53	12 46	21 04	20 02	23 52	23 58	15 17	22 07
18	Th	3:49:30	25 59 21	09 ♒ 47	01 55	17 47	24 22	04 31	11 00	27 15	02 53	12 47	21 06	20 28	24 16	24 18	15 26	22 11
19	F	3:53:26	26 59 53	23 52	01 D 54	18 55	25 36	05 11	11 11	27 14	02 54	12 47	21 08	20 54	24 41	24 38	15 34	22 14
20	Sa	3:57:23	28 00 26	07 ♓ 38	01 54	20 01	26 50	05 51	11 22	27 13	02 54	12 48	21 10	21 19	25 05	24 59	15 44	22 18
21	Su	4:01:19	29 01 01	21 05	01 55	21 04	28 04	06 31	11 32	27 12	02 55	12 49	21 12	21 45	25 30	25 20	15 53	22 22
22	M	4:05:16	00 ♐ 01 37	04 ♈ 16	01 57	22 03	29 18	07 12	11 43	27 10	02 55	12 50	21 14	22 11	25 54	25 41	16 03	22 26
23	T	4:09:13	01 02 14	17 10	01 59	22 58	00 ♏ 32	07 52	11 54	27 08	02 56	12 51	21 16	22 36	26 17	26 02	16 13	22 30
24	W	4:13:09	02 02 52	29 52	02 ℞ 00	23 49	01 46	08 32	12 04	27 07	02 56	12 52	21 19	23 02	26 41	26 23	16 24	22 34
25	Th	4:17:06	03 03 32	12 ♉ 22	01 59	24 35	03 01	09 12	12 14	27 05	02 57	12 53	21 21	23 28	27 05	26 44	16 35	22 38
26	F	4:21:02	04 04 12	24 42	01 57	25 15	04 15	09 52	12 24	27 03	02 58	12 54	21 23	23 53	27 28	27 06	16 46	22 42
27	Sa	4:24:59	05 04 55	06 ♊ 53	01 53	25 49	05 29	10 33	12 35	27 01	02 58	12 55	21 25	24 18	27 51	27 27	16 57	22 46
28	Su	4:28:55	06 05 38	18 57	01 48	26 15	06 43	11 13	12 45	26 59	02 59	12 56	21 27	24 44	28 14	27 49	17 09	22 50
29	M	4:32:52	07 06 23	00 ♋ 54	01 41	26 34	07 58	11 53	12 55	26 57	03 00	12 58	21 30	25 09	28 36	28 11	17 21	22 54
30	T	4:36:49	08 07 09	12 48	01 34	26 ℞ 43	09 12	12 34	13 04	26 54	03 01	12 59	21 32	25 34	28 59	28 33	17 34	22 58

EPHEMERIS CALCULATED FOR 12 MIDNIGHT GREENWICH MEAN TIME. ALL OTHER DATA AND FACING ASPECTARIAN PAGE IN **STANDARD TIME (BOLD)** AND PACIFIC TIME (REGULAR).

DECEMBER 2004

1 WEDNESDAY

☽ ☍ ⚵	**3:55 am**	12:55 am
☽ ⚹ ⚴	**4:49 am**	1:49 am
☽ ⚻ ♅	**11:59 am**	8:59 am
☿ ⚹ ⚳		9:18 pm

2 THURSDAY

☿ ⚹ ⚳	**12:18 am**	
☽ △ ☉	**3:00 am**	12:00 am
☽ □ ♀	**6:38 am**	3:38 am
☽ ☍ ♆	**8:08 am**	5:08 am
☽ ⚹ ♃	**9:03 am**	6:03 am
☽ □ ♂	**10:47 am**	7:47 am
♄ □ ⚳	**5:14 pm**	2:14 pm
☽ ⚻ ⚶	**6:31 pm**	3:31 pm
♀ □ ♆	**9:22 pm**	6:22 pm
☽ △ ♇		10:25 pm

3 FRIDAY

☽ △ ♇	**1:25 am**	
☽ ⚻ ⚷	**4:33 am**	1:33 am
♀ ⚺ ♃	**9:01 am**	6:01 am
☽ △ ☿	**9:52 am**	6:52 am
☽ ⚺ ♄	**11:34 am**	8:34 am
☽ ⚹ ⚳	**12:17 pm**	9:17 am
☽ ⚻ ⚵	**6:02 pm**	3:02 pm
☽ ⚺ ⚴	**6:52 pm**	3:52 pm
☽ ☍ ♅		9:05 pm

4 SATURDAY

☽ ☍ ♅	**12:05 am**	
☉ ⚹ ♆	**4:32 pm**	1:32 pm
☽ ⚻ ♆	**7:37 pm**	4:37 pm
☽ □ ☉	**7:53 pm**	4:53 pm
☽ ⚺ ♃	**9:09 pm**	6:09 pm
☽ ⚹ ♀		9:39 pm
☽ ⚹ ♂		10:27 pm

5 SUNDAY

☽ ⚹ ♀	**12:39 am**	
☽ ⚹ ♂	**1:27 am**	
☽ ☍ ⚶	**6:34 am**	3:34 am
☽ □ ♇	**12:13 pm**	9:13 am
☉ ⚹ ♃	**1:57 pm**	10:57 am
☽ △ ⚷	**3:22 pm**	12:22 pm
☽ □ ☿	**4:45 pm**	1:45 pm
♀ ☌ ♂	**5:13 pm**	2:13 pm
☽ ⚹ ♄	**9:28 pm**	6:28 pm
☽ ⚺ ⚳		9:18 pm

6 MONDAY

☽ ⚺ ⚳	**12:18 am**	
☽ △ ⚵	**5:33 am**	2:33 am
☽ ☌ ⚴	**6:13 am**	3:13 am
☿ ⚺ ⚷	**8:37 am**	5:37 am
☽ ⚻ ♅	**9:36 am**	6:36 am

7 TUESDAY

☽ △ ♆	**3:55 am**	12:55 am
☽ ☌ ♃	**5:54 am**	2:54 am
☽ ⚹ ☉	**8:42 am**	5:42 am
☽ ⚺ ♂	**12:14 pm**	9:14 am
☽ ⚺ ♀	**2:13 pm**	11:13 am
☽ ⚻ ⚶	**3:02 pm**	12:02 pm
☿ ☌ ♇	**6:03 pm**	3:03 pm
☽ ⚹ ☿	**7:19 pm**	4:19 pm
☽ ⚹ ♇	**7:26 pm**	4:26 pm
☽ □ ⚷	**10:31 pm**	7:31 pm
♀ △ ⚶		10:03 pm

8 WEDNESDAY

♀ △ ⚶	**1:03 am**	
☽ □ ♄	**3:41 am**	12:41 am
☽ ☌ ⚳	**8:09 am**	5:09 am
☽ □ ⚵	**12:54 pm**	9:54 am
☽ ⚺ ⚴	**1:22 pm**	10:22 am
☽ △ ♅	**3:13 pm**	12:13 pm
☿ ⚺ ♀	**7:49 pm**	4:49 pm

9 THURSDAY

☿ □ ⚶	**7:24 am**	4:24 am
☽ □ ♆	**8:12 am**	5:12 am
☽ ⚺ ♃	**10:30 am**	7:30 am
☽ ⚺ ☉	**4:29 pm**	1:29 pm
☿ ⚺ ♂	**4:31 pm**	1:31 pm
☽ ⚺ ☿	**6:08 pm**	3:08 pm
☽ ☌ ♂	**6:22 pm**	3:22 pm
☽ △ ⚶	**7:22 pm**	4:22 pm
☽ ☌ ♀	**10:31 pm**	7:31 pm
☽ ⚺ ♇	**10:41 pm**	7:41 pm
♀ ⚺ ♇		9:27 pm
☽ ⚹ ⚷		10:41 pm

10 FRIDAY

♀ ⚺ ♇	**12:27 am**	
☽ ⚹ ⚷	**1:41 am**	
☉ ☌ ☿	**3:21 am**	12:21 am
☽ △ ♄	**6:03 am**	3:03 am
☽ ⚺ ⚳	**11:51 am**	8:51 am
☽ ⚹ ⚵	**4:14 pm**	1:14 pm
☽ ⚹ ⚴	**4:28 pm**	1:28 pm
☽ □ ♅	**5:08 pm**	2:08 pm

11 SATURDAY

♂ △ ⚶	**3:52 am**	12:52 am
☽ ⚹ ♆	**9:11 am**	6:11 am
☽ ⚹ ♃	**11:45 am**	8:45 am
♀ ⚹ ⚷	**1:59 pm**	10:59 am
☽ ☌ ☿	**2:32 pm**	11:32 am
☽ ☌ ☉	**8:29 pm**	5:29 pm
☽ □ ⚶	**8:35 pm**	5:35 pm
☽ ⚺ ♂	**9:04 pm**	6:04 pm
☉ □ ⚶	**10:31 pm**	7:31 pm
☽ ☌ ♇	**11:03 pm**	8:03 pm
♅ ⚻ ⚴		9:58 pm
☽ ⚺ ⚷		11:04 pm

12 SUNDAY

♅ ⚻ ⚴	**12:58 am**	
☽ ⚺ ⚷	**2:04 am**	
☽ ⚺ ♀	**3:05 am**	12:05 am
♅ ⚺ ⚵	**4:54 am**	1:54 am
☽ ⚻ ♄	**5:51 am**	2:51 am
☽ ⚹ ⚳	**12:56 pm**	9:56 am
☽ ⚹ ♅	**4:52 pm**	1:52 pm
☽ ⚺ ⚵	**5:09 pm**	2:09 pm
☽ □ ⚴	**5:11 pm**	2:11 pm
☿ ⚹ ♃	**7:46 pm**	4:46 pm
☉ ⚺ ♂	**9:29 pm**	6:29 pm
⚴ △ ⚵	**9:44 pm**	6:44 pm

13 MONDAY

☽ ⚺ ♆	**8:38 am**	5:38 am
☽ ⚺ ☿	**10:17 am**	7:17 am
♀ △ ♄	**11:26 am**	8:26 am
☽ □ ♃	**11:33 am**	8:33 am
☉ ☌ ♇	**12:04 pm**	9:04 am
♂ ⚺ ♇	**7:45 pm**	4:45 pm
☽ ⚹ ⚶	**8:46 pm**	5:46 pm
☽ ⚺ ♇	**10:30 pm**	7:30 pm
☽ ⚹ ♂	**10:38 pm**	7:38 pm
☽ ⚺ ☉	**11:14 pm**	8:14 pm
☽ ☌ ⚷		10:41 pm

14 TUESDAY

☽ ☌ ⚷	**1:41 am**	
☽ ☍ ♄	**5:03 am**	2:03 am
☽ ⚹ ♀	**6:43 am**	3:43 am
☿ ⚹ ♆	**8:45 am**	5:45 am
☽ □ ⚳	**1:43 pm**	10:43 am
☽ ⚺ ♅	**4:31 pm**	1:31 pm
☽ △ ⚴	**5:48 pm**	2:48 pm
☽ ☌ ⚵	**6:02 pm**	3:02 pm

15 WEDNESDAY

☽ ⚹ ☿	**7:17 am**	4:17 am
☽ ☌ ♆	**8:45 am**	5:45 am
☽ △ ♃	**12:08 pm**	9:08 am
☉ ⚺ ⚷	**2:30 pm**	11:30 am
☽ ⚺ ⚶	**10:14 pm**	7:14 pm
☽ ⚹ ♇	**11:13 pm**	8:13 pm
☽ □ ♂		10:38 pm
☽ ⚺ ⚷		11:42 pm

16 THURSDAY

☽ □ ♂	**1:38 am**	
☽ ⚺ ⚷	**2:42 am**	
☽ ⚹ ☉	**3:33 am**	12:33 am
☽ ⚻ ♄	**5:45 am**	2:45 am
☽ □ ♀	**12:25 pm**	9:25 am
☽ △ ⚳	**4:31 pm**	1:31 pm
☽ ☌ ♅	**6:09 pm**	3:09 pm
☽ ⚻ ⚴	**8:31 pm**	5:31 pm
☽ ⚺ ⚵	**9:06 pm**	6:06 pm

17 FRIDAY

♂ ⚹ ⚷	**3:05 am**	12:05 am
☽ □ ☿	**7:24 am**	4:24 am
☉ ⚻ ♄	**8:50 am**	5:50 am
☽ ⚺ ♆	**11:24 am**	8:24 am
☽ ⚻ ♃	**3:24 pm**	12:24 pm
☽ ☌ ⚶		11:48 pm
☽ □ ♇		11:54 pm

18 SATURDAY

☽ ☌ ⚶	**2:48 am**	
☽ □ ♇	**2:54 am**	
☽ ⚹ ⚷	**6:48 am**	3:48 am
☽ △ ♂	**8:06 am**	5:06 am
♇ □ ⚶	**8:09 am**	5:09 am
☽ △ ♄	**9:30 am**	6:30 am
☽ □ ☉	**11:40 am**	8:40 am
☽ △ ♀	**10:22 pm**	7:22 pm
☽ ⚻ ⚳	**10:54 pm**	7:54 pm
☽ ⚺ ♅	**11:09 pm**	8:09 pm
☽ ☍ ⚴		11:48 pm

19 SUNDAY

☽ ☍ ⚴	**2:48 am**	
☽ ⚹ ⚵	**3:53 am**	12:53 am
♀ ⚺ ⚳	**6:15 am**	3:15 am
♀ □ ♅	**6:53 am**	3:53 am
♅ △ ⚳	**8:25 am**	5:25 am
♂ △ ♄	**9:10 am**	6:10 am
☽ △ ☿	**12:03 pm**	9:03 am
☽ ⚹ ♆	**5:37 pm**	2:37 pm
☽ ☍ ♃	**10:18 pm**	7:18 pm

20 MONDAY

☽ △ ♇	**10:12 am**	7:12 am
☽ ⚺ ⚶	**11:14 am**	8:14 am
☽ □ ⚷	**2:32 pm**	11:32 am
☽ □ ♄	**4:45 pm**	1:45 pm
☽ ⚻ ♂	**6:45 pm**	3:45 pm
☽ △ ☉		9:16 pm

21 TUESDAY

☽ △ ☉	**12:16 am**	
☽ ⚹ ♅	**7:40 am**	4:40 am
☽ ☍ ⚳	**9:03 am**	6:03 am
♀ ⚹ ⚴	**9:50 am**	6:50 am
☽ ⚻ ⚴	**12:44 pm**	9:44 am
☽ ⚻ ♀	**12:59 pm**	9:59 am
☽ □ ⚵	**2:26 pm**	11:26 am
☽ ⚻ ☿	**9:35 pm**	6:35 pm

22 WEDNESDAY

☽ □ ♆	**3:06 am**	12:06 am
☽ ⚻ ♃	**8:27 am**	5:27 am
♀ ⚹ ⚵	**9:48 am**	6:48 am
☽ ⚻ ♇	**8:29 pm**	5:29 pm
☽ ⚹ ⚶	**10:51 pm**	7:51 pm
☽ △ ⚷		10:14 pm
☽ ⚹ ♄		11:47 pm

23 THURSDAY

☽ △ ⚷	**1:14 am**	
☽ ⚹ ♄	**2:47 am**	
☽ ☍ ♂	**8:41 am**	5:41 am
☽ ⚻ ☉	**4:19 pm**	1:19 pm
☽ □ ♅	**6:44 pm**	3:44 pm
☽ ⚻ ⚳	**9:55 pm**	6:55 pm
☽ △ ⚴		10:10 pm

24 FRIDAY

☽ △ ⚴	**1:10 am**	
☽ △ ⚵	**3:38 am**	12:38 am
☽ ☍ ♀	**6:54 am**	3:54 am
☽ ☍ ☿	**11:10 am**	8:10 am
☽ △ ♆	**2:42 pm**	11:42 am
☽ △ ♃	**8:37 pm**	5:37 pm
☉ ⚹ ♅	**9:50 pm**	6:50 pm

25 SATURDAY

☽ ☍ ♇	**8:30 am**	5:30 am
☽ □ ⚶	**12:19 pm**	9:19 am
☽ ⚻ ⚷	**1:35 pm**	10:35 am
☽ ⚺ ♄	**2:22 pm**	11:22 am
☽ ⚻ ♂		9:24 pm

26 SUNDAY

☽ ⚻ ♂	**12:24 am**	
☽ △ ♅	**7:06 am**	4:06 am
☽ ☍ ☉	**10:06 am**	7:06 am
☽ △ ⚳	**12:08 pm**	9:08 am
☽ □ ⚴	**2:49 pm**	11:49 am
☽ ⚻ ⚵	**6:07 pm**	3:07 pm
☿ ⚹ ♆		9:35 pm
☽ ⚻ ♀		11:20 pm

27 MONDAY

☽ ⚻ ♀	**2:20 am**	
☽ ⚻ ♆	**3:17 am**	12:17 am
☽ ⚻ ☿	**3:28 am**	12:28 am
☽ □ ♃	**9:39 am**	6:39 am
♀ ⚹ ♆	**11:32 am**	8:32 am
☽ ⚻ ♇	**9:14 pm**	6:14 pm
☉ ⚹ ⚳	**10:11 pm**	7:11 pm
♄ ☍ ⚷		9:32 pm
☽ △ ⚶		11:33 pm
☽ ☌ ♄		11:34 pm
☽ ☍ ⚷		11:35 pm
♄ △ ⚶		11:52 pm

28 TUESDAY

♄ ☍ ⚷	**12:32 am**	
☽ △ ⚶	**2:33 am**	
☽ ☌ ♄	**2:34 am**	
☽ ☍ ⚷	**2:35 am**	
♄ △ ⚶	**2:52 am**	
⚷ ⚹ ⚶	**4:29 am**	1:29 am
☿ ☌ ♀	**1:23 pm**	10:23 am
☽ △ ♂	**4:43 pm**	1:43 pm
☽ ⚻ ♅	**7:54 pm**	4:54 pm
☽ □ ⚳		11:42 pm

29 WEDNESDAY

☽ □ ⚳	**2:42 am**	
☽ ⚻ ☉	**4:24 am**	1:24 am
☽ ⚹ ⚴	**4:44 am**	1:44 am
☽ ☍ ⚵	**8:57 am**	5:57 am
☉ □ ⚴	**9:18 am**	6:18 am
☽ ☍ ♆	**4:02 pm**	1:02 pm
☽ △ ☿	**9:14 pm**	6:14 pm
☽ △ ♀	**10:01 pm**	7:01 pm
☽ ⚹ ♃	**10:44 pm**	7:44 pm

30 THURSDAY

♀ ⚹ ♃	**5:19 am**	2:19 am
☽ △ ♇	**9:54 am**	6:54 am
☽ ⚺ ♄	**2:37 pm**	11:37 am
☽ ⚻ ⚷	**3:28 pm**	12:28 pm
☿ ⚹ ♃	**4:07 pm**	1:07 pm
☽ ⚻ ⚶	**4:40 pm**	1:40 pm
♂ □ ♅		11:49 pm

31 FRIDAY

♂ □ ♅	**2:49 am**	
☽ ☍ ♅	**8:18 am**	5:18 am
☽ □ ♂	**8:37 am**	5:37 am
☽ ⚹ ⚳	**4:39 pm**	1:39 pm
☽ ⚺ ⚴	**5:58 pm**	2:58 pm
☽ △ ☉	**9:57 pm**	6:57 pm
☽ ⚻ ⚵	**11:04 pm**	8:04 pm

Eastern time in bold type
Pacific time in medium type

DECEMBER 2004

☽ Last Aspect day	EST / hr:mn / PST	asp	☽ Ingress sign day	EST / hr:mn / PST
11/30	**11:28 pm** 8:28 pm	☌ ♄	♌ 1	**5:50 am** 2:50 am
3	**9:52 am** 6:52 am	△ ☿	♍ 3	**6:00 pm** 3:00 pm
5	**9:28 pm** 6:28 pm	⚹ ♄	♎ 6	**3:46 am** 12:46 am
8	**3:41 am** 12:41 am	□ ♄	♏ 8	**9:43 am** 6:43 am
10	**6:03 am** 3:03 am	△ ♄	♐ 10	**11:54 am** 8:54 am
11	**11:03 pm** 8:03 pm	☌ ♇	♑ 12	**11:42 am** 8:42 am
14	**6:43 am** 3:43 am	⚹ ♀	♒ 14	**11:10 am** 8:10 am
16	**3:33 am** 12:33 am	⚹ ☉	♓ 16	**12:24 pm** 9:24 am
18	**11:40 am** 8:40 am	□ ☉	♈ 18	**4:52 pm** 1:52 pm
20	9:16 pm	△ ☉	♉ 20	9:52 pm
21	**12:16 am**	△ ☉	♉ 21	**12:52 am**
23	**8:41 am** 5:41 am	☍ ♂	♊ 23	**11:32 am** 8:32 am
25	**8:30 am** 5:30 am	☍ ♇	♋ 25	**11:38 pm** 8:38 pm
27	11:34 pm	☌ ♄	♌ 28	**12:14 pm** 9:14 am
28	**2:34 am**	☌ ♄	♌ 28	**12:14 pm** 9:14 am
30	**9:54 am** 6:54 am	△ ♇	♍ 30	9:33 pm
30	**9:54 am** 6:54 am	△ ♇	♍ 31	**12:33 am**

☽ Phases & Eclipses phase	day	EST / hr:mn / PST
4th Quarter	4	**7:53 pm** 4:53 pm
New Moon	11	**8:29 pm** 5:29 pm
2nd Quarter	18	**11:40 am** 8:40 am
Full Moon	26	**10:06 am** 7:06 am

Planet Ingress	day	EST / hr:mn / PST
♀ ♎	2	**1:36 pm** 10:36 am
⚵ ♒	3	**4:47 pm** 1:47 pm
⚳ ♏	10	**1:51 pm** 10:51 am
♀ ♐	16	**12:10 pm** 9:10 am
☉ ♑	21	**7:42 am** 4:42 am
♂ ♐	25	**11:04 am** 8:04 am

Planetary Motion	day	EST / hr:mn / PST
☿ D	19	10:28 pm
☿ D	20	**1:28 am**

DATE		SID.TIME	SUN	MOON	NODE	MERCURY	VENUS	MARS	JUPITER	SATURN	URANUS	NEPTUNE	PLUTO	CERES	PALLAS	JUNO	VESTA	CHIRON
1	W	4:40:45	09 ♐ 07 57	24 ♋ 39	01 ♉ ℞ 27	26 ♐ ℞ 43	10 ♏ 26	13 ♏ 14	13 ♎ 14	26 ♋ ℞ 52	03 ♓ 02	13 ♒ 00	21 ♐ 34	25 ♎ 59	29 ♍ 21	28 ♑ 55	17 ♓ 46	23 ♑ 03
2	Th	4:44:42	10 08 46	06 ♌ 31	01 21	26 33	11 41	13 54	13 24	26 50	03 03	13 01	21 36	26 24	29 43	29 17	17 59	23 07
3	F	4:48:38	11 09 36	18 27	01 17	26 12	12 55	14 35	13 33	26 47	03 04	13 03	21 38	26 49	00 ♎ 05	29 40	18 13	23 11
4	Sa	4:52:35	12 10 27	00 ♍ 30	01 14	25 40	14 10	15 15	13 43	26 44	03 05	13 04	21 41	27 14	00 27	00 ♒ 02	18 26	23 16
5	Su	4:56:31	13 11 20	12 46	01 D 13	24 57	15 24	15 56	13 52	26 41	03 06	13 05	21 43	27 39	00 48	00 25	18 40	23 20
6	M	5:00:28	14 12 14	25 20	01 14	24 02	16 39	16 37	14 01	26 39	03 07	13 07	21 45	28 03	01 09	00 47	18 54	23 25
7	T	5:04:24	15 13 10	08 ♎ 14	01 15	22 59	17 54	17 17	14 10	26 36	03 09	13 08	21 47	28 28	01 30	01 10	19 09	23 29
8	W	5:08:21	16 14 07	21 35	01 ℞ 16	21 47	19 08	17 58	14 19	26 32	03 10	13 09	21 50	28 52	01 51	01 33	19 23	23 34
9	Th	5:12:18	17 15 05	05 ♏ 24	01 17	20 28	20 23	18 38	14 28	26 29	03 11	13 11	21 52	29 17	02 11	01 56	19 38	23 38
10	F	5:16:14	18 16 04	19 41	01 15	19 06	21 38	19 19	14 37	26 26	03 13	13 12	21 54	29 41	02 31	02 20	19 54	23 43
11	Sa	5:20:11	19 17 04	04 ♐ 23	01 11	17 43	22 52	20 00	14 46	26 23	03 14	13 14	21 56	00 ♏ 05	02 51	02 43	20 09	23 48
12	Su	5:24:07	20 18 05	19 26	01 06	16 22	24 07	20 40	14 54	26 19	03 16	13 15	21 59	00 29	03 11	03 06	20 25	23 53
13	M	5:28:04	21 19 08	04 ♑ 38	00 58	15 05	25 22	21 21	15 03	26 16	03 17	13 17	22 01	00 53	03 31	03 30	20 41	23 57
14	T	5:32:00	22 20 10	19 51	00 50	13 56	26 37	22 02	15 11	26 12	03 19	13 18	22 03	01 17	03 50	03 54	20 57	24 02
15	W	5:35:57	23 21 14	04 ♒ 53	00 42	12 54	27 52	22 43	15 19	26 08	03 20	13 20	22 05	01 41	04 09	04 18	21 13	24 07
16	Th	5:39:53	24 22 18	19 35	00 35	12 03	29 06	23 24	15 27	26 05	03 22	13 22	22 08	02 05	04 27	04 41	21 30	24 12
17	F	5:43:50	25 23 22	03 ♓ 53	00 31	11 23	00 ♐ 21	24 05	15 35	26 01	03 24	13 23	22 10	02 28	04 46	05 05	21 47	24 17
18	Sa	5:47:47	26 24 26	17 45	00 D 29	10 54	01 36	24 45	15 43	25 57	03 25	13 25	22 12	02 52	05 04	05 30	22 04	24 22
19	Su	5:51:43	27 25 31	01 ♈ 11	00 28	10 35	02 51	25 26	15 51	25 53	03 27	13 27	22 15	03 15	05 22	05 54	22 21	24 27
20	M	5:55:40	28 26 36	14 13	00 29	10 D 27	04 06	26 07	15 58	25 49	03 29	13 28	22 17	03 39	05 39	06 18	22 39	24 31
21	T	5:59:36	29 27 41	26 56	00 ℞ 30	10 30	05 21	26 48	16 05	25 45	03 31	13 30	22 19	04 02	05 57	06 42	22 57	24 36
22	W	6:03:33	00 ♑ 28 47	09 ♉ 23	00 30	10 41	06 36	27 29	16 13	25 41	03 33	13 32	22 21	04 25	06 14	07 07	23 15	24 41
23	Th	6:07:29	01 29 53	21 39	00 27	11 01	07 51	28 10	16 20	25 36	03 35	13 34	22 24	04 48	06 30	07 32	23 33	24 47
24	F	6:11:26	02 30 59	03 ♊ 45	00 22	11 29	09 06	28 51	16 27	25 32	03 37	13 36	22 26	05 11	06 47	07 56	23 51	24 52
25	Sa	6:15:22	03 32 06	15 46	00 14	12 03	10 21	29 32	16 34	25 28	03 39	13 37	22 28	05 33	07 03	08 21	24 10	24 57
26	Su	6:19:19	04 33 12	27 42	00 04	12 44	11 36	00 ♐ 14	16 40	25 23	03 41	13 39	22 30	05 56	07 19	08 46	24 28	25 02
27	M	6:23:16	05 34 19	09 ♋ 36	29 ♈ 51	13 30	12 51	00 55	16 47	25 19	03 43	13 41	22 32	06 18	07 34	09 11	24 47	25 07
28	T	6:27:12	06 35 27	21 28	29 38	14 21	14 06	01 36	16 53	25 14	03 46	13 43	22 35	06 41	07 49	09 36	25 07	25 12
29	W	6:31:09	07 36 34	03 ♌ 21	29 25	15 17	15 21	02 17	16 59	25 10	03 48	13 45	22 37	07 03	08 04	10 01	25 26	25 17
30	Th	6:35:05	08 37 42	15 15	29 12	16 16	16 36	02 58	17 06	25 05	03 50	13 47	22 39	07 25	08 19	10 26	25 45	25 22
31	F	6:39:02	09 38 50	27 13	29 03	17 18	17 51	03 40	17 11	25 01	03 52	13 49	22 41	07 47	08 33	10 52	26 05	25 28

EPHEMERIS CALCULATED FOR 12 MIDNIGHT GREENWICH MEAN TIME. ALL OTHER DATA AND FACING ASPECTARIAN PAGE IN **EASTERN TIME (BOLD)** AND PACIFIC TIME (REGULAR).

JANUARY 2005

1 SATURDAY
☽ ⚻ ♆ **4:00 am** 1:00 am
☽ ⚺ ♃ **10:50 am** 7:50 am
☽ □ ☿ **2:42 pm** 11:42 am
☽ □ ♀ **4:26 pm** 1:26 pm
☉ ⚺ ⚵ **7:56 pm** 4:56 pm
☽ □ ♇ **9:23 pm** 6:23 pm
☽ ✶ ♄ 10:23 pm
☽ △ ⚷ 11:59 pm

2 SUNDAY
☽ ✶ ♄ **1:23 am**
☽ △ ⚷ **2:59 am**
☽ ☍ ⚴ **5:21 am** 2:21 am
☽ ⚻ ♅ **6:56 pm** 3:56 pm
☽ ✶ ♂ **10:25 pm** 7:25 pm

3 MONDAY
☽ ⚺ ⚳ **4:25 am** 1:25 am
☽ ☌ ♀ **5:00 am** 2:00 am
☽ △ ⚵ **10:49 am** 7:49 am
☽ □ ☉ **12:46 pm** 9:46 am
☽ △ ♆ **1:39 pm** 10:39 am
♀ ☌ ♇ **6:33 pm** 3:33 pm
☽ ☌ ♃ **8:23 pm** 5:23 pm
☉ ⚺ ♆ 9:26 pm

4 TUESDAY
☉ ⚺ ♆ **12:26 am**
☽ ✶ ☿ **5:22 am** 2:22 am
☽ ✶ ♇ **6:04 am** 3:04 am
☽ ✶ ♀ **7:15 am** 4:15 am
☽ □ ♄ **9:20 am** 6:20 am
☽ □ ⚷ **11:33 am** 8:33 am
☿ ☌ ♇ **12:58 pm** 9:58 am
☽ ⚻ ⚴ **2:52 pm** 11:52 am
☽ △ ♅ 11:16 pm

5 WEDNESDAY
☽ △ ♅ **2:16 am**
♀ ⚻ ♄ **4:06 am** 1:06 am
⚳ ⚺ ♀ **6:56 am** 3:56 am
☽ ⚺ ♂ **8:17 am** 5:17 am
☽ ⚺ ♀ **12:19 pm** 9:19 am
☽ ☌ ⚳ **12:22 pm** 9:22 am
☽ □ ⚵ **6:37 pm** 3:37 pm
☽ □ ♆ **7:39 pm** 4:39 pm
☿ ⚻ ♄ **8:30 pm** 5:30 pm

Eastern time in bold type
Pacific time in medium type

☽ ✶ ☉ **10:57 pm** 7:57 pm
☽ ⚺ ♃ 11:05 pm

6 THURSDAY
☽ ⚺ ♃ **2:05 am**
♀ ⚺ ⚷ **7:55 am** 4:55 am
☽ ⚺ ♇ **10:53 am** 7:53 am
☽ △ ♄ **1:29 pm** 10:29 am
☽ ⚺ ☿ **3:17 pm** 12:17 pm
☽ ✶ ⚷ **4:10 pm** 1:10 pm
☽ ⚺ ♀ **4:54 pm** 1:54 pm
☽ △ ⚴ **8:11 pm** 5:11 pm
☿ ⚺ ⚷ 10:29 pm

7 FRIDAY
☿ ⚺ ⚷ **1:29 am**
☽ □ ♅ **5:39 am** 2:39 am
♆ ☌ ⚵ **6:47 am** 3:47 am
☽ ☌ ♂ **1:36 pm** 10:36 am
☽ ✶ ♀ **3:31 pm** 12:31 pm
☽ ⚺ ⚳ **4:07 pm** 1:07 pm
☉ □ ♃ **9:12 pm** 6:12 pm
☽ ✶ ♆ **9:48 pm** 6:48 pm
☽ ✶ ⚵ **10:13 pm** 7:13 pm

8 SATURDAY
☽ ✶ ♃ **3:58 am** 12:58 am
☽ ⚺ ☉ **4:25 am** 1:25 am
☽ ☌ ♇ **12:05 pm** 9:05 am
☽ ⚻ ♄ **2:10 pm** 11:10 am
☽ ⚺ ⚷ **5:14 pm** 2:14 pm
♀ □ ⚴ **7:50 pm** 4:50 pm
☽ ☌ ☿ **8:49 pm** 5:49 pm
☽ □ ⚴ **9:54 pm** 6:54 pm
☽ ☌ ♀ **10:02 pm** 7:02 pm

9 SUNDAY
☽ ✶ ♅ **5:54 am** 2:54 am
☿ □ ⚴ **12:47 pm** 9:47 am
☽ ⚺ ♂ **3:37 pm** 12:37 pm
☽ □ ♀ **3:46 pm** 12:46 pm
☽ ✶ ⚳ **4:52 pm** 1:52 pm
♂ ✶ ♀ **7:59 pm** 4:59 pm
☽ ⚺ ♆ **9:23 pm** 6:23 pm
☽ ⚺ ⚵ **11:03 pm** 8:03 pm

10 MONDAY
☽ □ ♃ **3:28 am** 12:28 am
☽ ☌ ☉ **7:03 am** 4:03 am
☽ ⚺ ♇ **11:17 am** 8:17 am

☽ ☍ ♄ **12:58 pm** 9:58 am
☽ ☌ ⚷ **4:31 pm** 1:31 pm
☽ ✶ ⚴ **9:58 pm** 6:58 pm
☽ ⚺ ☿ 9:23 pm
☽ ⚺ ♀ 10:09 pm

11 TUESDAY
☽ ⚺ ☿ **12:23 am**
☽ ⚺ ♀ **1:09 am**
☽ ⚺ ♅ **4:56 am** 1:56 am
☽ △ ♀ **3:14 pm** 12:14 pm
☽ ✶ ♂ **4:49 pm** 1:49 pm
☽ □ ⚳ **4:54 pm** 1:54 pm
♂ ⚺ ⚳ **8:24 pm** 5:24 pm
☽ ☌ ♆ **8:30 pm** 5:30 pm
☽ ☌ ⚵ **11:30 pm** 8:30 pm
☽ △ ♃ 11:49 pm

12 WEDNESDAY
☽ △ ♃ **2:49 am**
☽ ⚺ ☉ **9:43 am** 6:43 am
☽ ✶ ♇ **10:44 am** 7:44 am
☽ ⚻ ♄ **12:06 pm** 9:06 am
☽ ⚺ ⚷ **4:19 pm** 1:19 pm
☽ ⚺ ⚴ **10:52 pm** 7:52 pm
♀ ✶ ♅ 9:59 pm
☉ ⚺ ♇ 10:01 pm

13 THURSDAY
♀ ✶ ♅ **12:59 am**
☉ ⚺ ♇ **1:01 am**
☿ ✶ ♅ **3:33 am** 12:33 am
☽ ☌ ♅ **5:07 am** 2:07 am
☽ ✶ ☿ **5:17 am** 2:17 am
☽ ✶ ♀ **5:29 am** 2:29 am
☽ ⚻ ♀ **4:19 pm** 1:19 pm
☉ ☍ ♄ **6:06 pm** 3:06 pm
☽ △ ⚳ **6:42 pm** 3:42 pm
☽ □ ♂ **7:56 pm** 4:56 pm
☽ ⚺ ♆ **9:30 pm** 6:30 pm
☿ ☌ ♀ **9:35 pm** 6:35 pm
☽ ⚺ ⚵ 11:08 pm

14 FRIDAY
☽ ⚺ ⚵ **2:08 am**
☽ ⚻ ♃ **4:17 am** 1:17 am
☽ □ ♇ **12:39 pm** 9:39 am
☽ △ ♄ **1:42 pm** 10:42 am
☽ ✶ ☉ **3:22 pm** 12:22 pm
☽ ✶ ⚷ **6:50 pm** 3:50 pm
☽ ☌ ⚴ 11:57 pm

15 SATURDAY
☽ ☌ ⚴ **2:57 am**
♂ ✶ ♆ **5:39 am** 2:39 am
☽ ⚺ ♅ **8:28 am** 5:28 am
☽ □ ♀ **1:56 pm** 10:56 am
☽ □ ☿ **2:34 pm** 11:34 am
☽ ☍ ♀ **8:56 pm** 5:56 pm
☽ ⚻ ⚳ 9:16 pm
☽ ✶ ♆ 11:08 pm

16 SUNDAY
☽ ⚻ ⚳ **12:16 am**
☽ ✶ ♆ **2:08 am**
☽ △ ♂ **3:12 am** 12:12 am
☽ ✶ ⚵ **8:51 am** 5:51 am
☽ ☍ ♃ **9:33 am** 6:33 am
☽ △ ♇ **6:30 pm** 3:30 pm
☉ ☌ ⚷ **6:42 pm** 3:42 pm
☽ □ ♄ **7:09 pm** 4:09 pm
☽ □ ⚷ 10:26 pm
☽ □ ☉ 10:57 pm

17 MONDAY
☽ □ ⚷ **1:26 am**
☽ □ ☉ **1:57 am**
♃ △ ⚵ **7:57 am** 4:57 am
☽ ⚺ ⚴ **11:27 am** 8:27 am
☽ ✶ ♅ **3:57 pm** 12:57 pm

18 TUESDAY
☽ △ ♀ **3:51 am** 12:51 am
☿ □ ♀ **5:12 am** 2:12 am
☽ ⚻ ♀ **5:40 am** 2:40 am
☽ △ ☿ **5:44 am** 2:44 am
☽ ☍ ⚳ **10:11 am** 7:11 am
☽ □ ♆ **10:51 am** 7:51 am
☽ ⚻ ♂ **3:14 pm** 12:14 pm
☽ ⚻ ♃ **6:49 pm** 3:49 pm
☽ □ ⚵ **8:00 pm** 5:00 pm
♀ □ ♀ **11:32 pm** 8:32 pm

19 WEDNESDAY
☽ ⚻ ♇ **4:15 am** 1:15 am
☽ ✶ ♄ **4:24 am** 1:24 am
☽ △ ⚷ **11:51 am** 8:51 am
♆ □ ⚳ **3:46 pm** 12:46 pm
☽ △ ☉ **5:19 pm** 2:19 pm
♄ ⚻ ♇ **8:37 pm** 5:37 pm
☽ ✶ ⚴ **11:50 pm** 8:50 pm
☿ ⚺ ♆ 10:11 pm
☽ □ ♅ 11:56 pm

20 THURSDAY
☿ ⚺ ♆ **1:11 am**
☽ □ ♅ **2:56 am**
☿ ✶ ⚳ **3:20 am** 12:20 am
☽ △ ♀ **5:30 pm** 2:30 pm
☽ ⚻ ♀ **10:01 pm** 7:01 pm
☽ △ ♆ **10:32 pm** 7:32 pm
☽ ⚻ ⚳ **11:15 pm** 8:15 pm
☽ ⚻ ☿ 10:32 pm
♀ ⚺ ♆ 11:59 pm

21 FRIDAY
☽ ⚻ ☿ **1:32 am**
♀ ⚺ ♆ **2:59 am**
☽ ☍ ♂ **6:35 am** 3:35 am
☽ △ ♃ **6:46 am** 3:46 am
♂ ✶ ♃ **9:54 am** 6:54 am
☽ △ ⚵ **10:08 am** 7:08 am
♀ ✶ ⚳ **1:03 pm** 10:03 am
☽ ⚺ ♄ **4:01 pm** 1:01 pm
☽ ☍ ♇ **4:26 pm** 1:26 pm
☽ ⚻ ⚷ 9:30 pm

22 SATURDAY
☽ ⚻ ⚷ **12:30 am**
☽ ⚻ ☉ **11:16 am** 8:16 am
☽ □ ⚴ **2:14 pm** 11:14 am
☽ △ ♅ **3:38 pm** 12:38 pm
☿ □ ♃ **7:24 pm** 4:24 pm

23 SUNDAY
☽ □ ♀ **6:32 am** 3:32 am
☽ ⚻ ♆ **11:21 am** 8:21 am
☽ △ ⚳ **1:28 pm** 10:28 am
☽ ☍ ♀ **5:49 pm** 2:49 pm
☽ □ ♃ **7:36 pm** 4:36 pm
☿ ⚺ ♂ **10:08 pm** 7:08 pm
☽ ⚻ ♂ **11:03 pm** 8:03 pm
☽ ☍ ☿ **11:07 pm** 8:07 pm
☽ ⚻ ⚵ 10:12 pm

24 MONDAY
☽ ⚻ ⚵ **1:12 am**
☽ ☌ ♄ **4:17 am** 1:17 am
☽ ⚻ ♇ **5:16 am** 2:16 am
♀ □ ♃ **11:09 am** 8:09 am
☽ ☍ ⚷ **1:37 pm** 10:37 am
♅ ⚺ ⚴ **4:15 pm** 1:15 pm
☉ ⚺ ♅ **4:38 pm** 1:38 pm
☉ ✶ ⚴ **4:50 pm** 1:50 pm
☿ ⚺ ⚵ **8:51 pm** 5:51 pm

25 TUESDAY
☽ ⚻ ♅ **4:29 am** 1:29 am
☽ △ ⚴ **4:51 am** 1:51 am
☽ ☍ ☉ **5:32 am** 2:32 am
☿ ☍ ♄ **1:04 pm** 10:04 am
☽ ✶ ♀ **7:21 pm** 4:21 pm
☿ ⚺ ♇ **11:00 pm** 8:00 pm
☽ ☍ ♆ **11:59 pm** 8:59 pm

26 WEDNESDAY
☽ □ ⚳ **3:24 am** 12:24 am
☽ ✶ ♃ **8:05 am** 5:05 am
☽ ⚻ ♀ **1:12 pm** 10:12 am
☽ △ ♂ **3:05 pm** 12:05 pm
☽ ☍ ⚵ **3:51 pm** 12:51 pm
☽ ⚺ ♄ **4:08 pm** 1:08 pm
☽ △ ♇ **5:39 pm** 2:39 pm
☽ ⚻ ☿ **8:23 pm** 5:23 pm
♄ ⚻ ⚵ **10:28 pm** 7:28 pm
☽ ⚻ ⚷ 11:11 pm

27 THURSDAY
☽ ⚻ ⚷ **2:11 am**
♂ ⚻ ♄ **7:24 am** 4:24 am
♀ ☍ ♄ **3:52 pm** 12:52 pm
☽ ☍ ♅ **4:38 pm** 1:38 pm
☽ ⚻ ⚴ **6:42 pm** 3:42 pm
☽ ⚻ ☉ **10:53 pm** 7:53 pm
♂ ✶ ⚵ 11:52 pm

28 FRIDAY
♂ ✶ ⚵ **2:52 am**
♀ ⚺ ⚵ **3:33 am** 12:33 am
♀ ⚺ ♂ **3:51 am** 12:51 am
☽ ⚺ ♀ **7:11 am** 4:11 am
♀ ⚺ ♇ **8:45 am** 5:45 am
☽ ⚻ ♆ **11:42 am** 8:42 am
♂ ☌ ♇ **12:47 pm** 9:47 am
☽ ✶ ⚳ **4:16 pm** 1:16 pm
♇ ✶ ⚵ **6:26 pm** 3:26 pm
☿ ☌ ⚷ **6:54 pm** 3:54 pm
☽ ⚺ ♃ **7:31 pm** 4:31 pm
☽ ✶ ♄ 11:57 pm

29 SATURDAY
☽ ✶ ♄ **2:57 am**
☽ □ ♇ **4:56 am** 1:56 am
☽ ⚻ ⚵ **5:18 am** 2:18 am
☽ □ ♂ **5:52 am** 2:52 am
☽ △ ♀ **7:09 am** 4:09 am

☽ △ ⚷ **1:31 pm** 10:31 am
☽ △ ☿ **4:07 pm** 1:07 pm

30 SUNDAY
☽ ⚻ ♅ **3:24 am** 12:24 am
☽ ☍ ⚴ **7:02 am** 4:02 am
☽ △ ☉ **2:18 pm** 11:18 am
☽ ☌ ♀ **5:20 pm** 2:20 pm
☽ △ ♆ **9:45 pm** 6:45 pm

31 MONDAY
☽ ⚺ ⚳ **3:14 am** 12:14 am
☽ ☌ ♃ **5:08 am** 2:08 am
☽ □ ♄ **11:53 am** 8:53 am
☽ ✶ ♇ **2:14 pm** 11:14 am
☽ △ ⚵ **4:35 pm** 1:35 pm
☽ ✶ ♂ **6:18 pm** 3:18 pm
☽ □ ♀ **10:21 pm** 7:21 pm
☽ □ ⚷ **10:43 pm** 7:43 pm
♀ ☌ ⚷ 11:19 pm

JANUARY 2005

☽ Last Aspect day	EST / hr:mn / PST	asp	☽ Ingress sign day	EST / hr:mn / PST
1	10:23 pm	✶ ♄	♎ 2	**11:19 am** 8:19 am
2	**1:23 am**	✶ ♄	♎ 2	**11:19 am** 8:19 am
4	**9:20 am** 6:20 am	□ ♄	♏ 4	**7:00 pm** 4:00 pm
6	**1:29 pm** 10:29 am	△ ♄	♐ 6	**10:44 pm** 7:44 pm
8	**10:02 pm** 7:02 pm	☌ ♀	♑ 8	**11:11 pm** 8:11 pm
10	**12:58 pm** 9:58 am	☍ ♄	♒ 10	**10:07 pm** 7:07 pm
12	**10:44 am** 7:44 am	✶ ♇	♓ 12	**9:50 pm** 6:50 pm
14	**3:22 pm** 12:22 pm	✶ ☉	♈ 14	9:27 pm
14	**3:22 pm** 12:22 pm	✶ ☉	♈ 15	**12:27 am**
16	10:57 pm	□ ☉	♉ 17	**7:06 am** 4:06 am
17	**1:57 am**	□ ☉	♉ 17	**7:06 am** 4:06 am
19	**5:19 pm** 2:19 pm	△ ☉	♊ 19	**5:24 pm** 2:24 pm
21	**4:26 pm** 1:26 pm	☍ ♇	♋ 22	**5:42 am** 2:42 am
24	**4:17 am** 1:17 am	☌ ♄	♌ 24	**6:21 pm** 3:21 pm
26	**5:39 pm** 2:39 pm	△ ♇	♍ 27	**6:24 am** 3:24 am
29	**4:07 pm** 1:07 pm	△ ☿	♎ 29	**5:13 pm** 2:13 pm
31	**10:21 pm** 7:21 pm	□ ♀	♏ 31	10:51 pm
31	**10:21 pm** 7:21 pm	□ ♀	♏ 2/1	**1:51 am**

☽ Phases & Eclipses phase	day	EST / hr:mn / PST
4th Quarter	3	**12:46 pm** 9:46 am
New Moon	10	**7:03 am** 4:03 am
2nd Quarter	16	10:57 pm
2nd Quarter	17	**1:57 am**
Full Moon	25	**5:32 am** 2:32 am

Planet Ingress	day	EST / hr:mn / PST
♀ ♑	9	**11:56 am** 8:56 am
☿ ♑	9	**11:09 pm** 8:09 pm
⚵ ♈	11	**4:36 am** 1:36 am
☉ ♒	19	**6:22 pm** 3:22 pm
☿ ♒	29	9:37 pm
☿ ♒	30	**12:37 am**

Planetary Motion

day **EST** / hr:mn / PST

DATE		SID.TIME	SUN	MOON	NODE	MERCURY	VENUS	MARS	JUPITER	SATURN	URANUS	NEPTUNE	PLUTO	CERES	PALLAS	JUNO	VESTA	CHIRON
1	Sa	6:42:58	10 ♑ 39 59	09 ♍ 18	28 ♈ R 55	18 ♐ 24	19 ♐ 06	04 ♐ 21	17 ♎ 17	24 ♋ R 56	03 ♓ 55	13 ♒ 51	22 ♐ 43	08 ♏ 09	08 ♎ 47	11 ♒ 17	26 ♓ 25	25 ♑ 33
2	Su	6:46:55	11 41 07	21 32	28 51	19 32	20 21	05 02	17 23	24 51	03 57	13 53	22 46	08 30	09 00	11 43	26 45	25 38
3	M	6:50:51	12 42 16	04 ♎ 01	28 D 49	20 43	21 36	05 44	17 28	24 46	04 00	13 55	22 48	08 52	09 14	12 08	27 05	25 43
4	T	6:54:48	13 43 25	16 49	28 R 49	21 56	22 51	06 25	17 34	24 42	04 02	13 57	22 50	09 13	09 26	12 34	27 25	25 49
5	W	6:58:45	14 44 35	00 ♏ 00	28 49	23 10	24 06	07 07	17 39	24 37	04 04	13 59	22 52	09 34	09 39	12 59	27 46	25 54
6	Th	7:02:41	15 45 45	13 38	28 48	24 27	25 22	07 48	17 44	24 32	04 07	14 01	22 54	09 55	09 51	13 25	28 06	25 59
7	F	7:06:38	16 46 55	27 45	28 46	25 45	26 37	08 29	17 49	24 27	04 10	14 03	22 56	10 16	10 03	13 51	28 27	26 04
8	Sa	7:10:34	17 48 05	12 ♐ 21	28 40	27 04	27 52	09 11	17 53	24 22	04 12	14 05	22 58	10 37	10 14	14 17	28 48	26 10
9	Su	7:14:31	18 49 16	27 21	28 32	28 24	29 07	09 53	17 58	24 17	04 15	14 07	23 01	10 58	10 25	14 43	29 09	26 15
10	M	7:18:27	19 50 26	12 ♑ 38	28 22	29 46	00 ♑ 22	10 34	18 02	24 12	04 17	14 09	23 03	11 18	10 35	15 09	29 30	26 20
11	T	7:22:24	20 51 36	28 01	28 10	01 ♑ 08	01 37	11 16	18 06	24 07	04 20	14 11	23 05	11 39	10 46	15 36	29 51	26 26
12	W	7:26:21	21 52 45	13 ♒ 17	27 58	02 32	02 52	11 57	18 10	24 02	04 23	14 14	23 07	11 59	10 55	16 02	00 ♈ 13	26 31
13	Th	7:30:17	22 53 55	28 15	27 48	03 56	04 08	12 39	18 14	23 58	04 26	14 16	23 09	12 19	11 05	16 28	00 35	26 36
14	F	7:34:14	23 55 03	12 ♓ 49	27 41	05 22	05 23	13 21	18 18	23 53	04 28	14 18	23 11	12 38	11 14	16 55	00 56	26 42
15	Sa	7:38:10	24 56 11	26 53	27 37	06 48	06 38	14 02	18 21	23 48	04 31	14 20	23 13	12 58	11 22	17 21	01 18	26 47
16	Su	7:42:07	25 57 18	10 ♈ 27	27 35	08 14	07 53	14 44	18 24	23 43	04 34	14 22	23 15	13 17	11 30	17 48	01 40	26 52
17	M	7:46:03	26 58 24	23 33	27 34	09 42	09 08	15 26	18 27	23 38	04 37	14 24	23 17	13 37	11 38	18 15	02 02	26 58
18	T	7:50:00	27 59 29	06 ♉ 15	27 34	11 10	10 23	16 08	18 30	23 33	04 40	14 27	23 19	13 56	11 45	18 41	02 24	27 03
19	W	7:53:56	29 00 34	18 39	27 33	12 39	11 39	16 50	18 33	23 28	04 43	14 29	23 21	14 15	11 52	19 08	02 47	27 08
20	Th	7:57:53	00 ♒ 01 38	00 ♊ 48	27 30	14 08	12 54	17 31	18 36	23 23	04 46	14 31	23 23	14 33	11 58	19 35	03 09	27 14
21	F	8:01:50	01 02 41	12 48	27 24	15 39	14 09	18 13	18 38	23 18	04 49	14 33	23 24	14 52	12 04	20 02	03 32	27 19
22	Sa	8:05:46	02 03 43	24 42	27 16	17 09	15 24	18 55	18 40	23 13	04 52	14 35	23 26	15 10	12 09	20 29	03 55	27 24
23	Su	8:09:43	03 04 44	06 ♋ 34	27 04	18 41	16 39	19 37	18 42	23 08	04 55	14 38	23 28	15 28	12 14	20 56	04 17	27 30
24	M	8:13:39	04 05 45	18 26	26 50	20 13	17 54	20 19	18 44	23 04	04 58	14 40	23 30	15 46	12 18	21 23	04 40	27 35
25	T	8:17:36	05 06 45	00 ♌ 19	26 35	21 45	19 10	21 01	18 46	22 59	05 01	14 42	23 32	16 04	12 22	21 50	05 03	27 40
26	W	8:21:32	06 07 43	12 16	26 20	23 18	20 25	21 43	18 47	22 54	05 04	14 44	23 34	16 21	12 26	22 17	05 26	27 46
27	Th	8:25:29	07 08 41	24 16	26 07	24 52	21 40	22 25	18 48	22 49	05 07	14 47	23 35	16 38	12 29	22 45	05 50	27 51
28	F	8:29:25	08 09 38	06 ♍ 22	25 56	26 27	22 55	23 07	18 49	22 45	05 10	14 49	23 37	16 55	12 31	23 12	06 13	27 56
29	Sa	8:33:22	09 10 34	18 34	25 47	28 02	24 10	23 49	18 50	22 40	05 14	14 51	23 39	17 12	12 33	23 39	06 36	28 01
30	Su	8:37:19	10 11 30	00 ♎ 56	25 42	29 38	25 25	24 31	18 51	22 35	05 17	14 54	23 41	17 29	12 35	24 07	07 00	28 07
31	M	8:41:15	11 12 25	13 29	25 D 40	01 ♒ 14	26 41	25 14	18 51	22 31	05 20	14 56	23 42	17 45	12 36	24 34	07 23	28 12

EPHEMERIS CALCULATED FOR 12 MIDNIGHT GREENWICH MEAN TIME. ALL OTHER DATA AND FACING ASPECTARIAN PAGE IN **EASTERN TIME (BOLD)** AND PACIFIC TIME (REGULAR).

FEBRUARY 2005

1 TUESDAY

♀ ☌ ⚷	**2:19 am**	
☉ △ ♀	**4:08 am**	1:08 am
☽ □ ☿	**8:48 am**	5:48 am
☽ △ ♅	**11:47 am**	8:47 am
☽ ⚻ ⚶	**4:43 pm**	1:43 pm
☽ ⚺ ♀		9:45 pm
☽ □ ☉		11:27 pm

2 WEDNESDAY

☽ ⚺ ♀	**12:45 am**	
☽ □ ☉	**2:27 am**	
☽ □ ♆	**5:04 am**	2:04 am
☿ ⚺ ♅	**9:31 am**	6:31 am
☽ ☌ ⚳	**11:11 am**	8:11 am
☽ ⚺ ♃	**11:54 am**	8:54 am
☽ △ ♄	**5:56 pm**	2:56 pm
☽ ⚺ ♇	**8:34 pm**	5:34 pm
☽ □ ⚵		9:32 pm

3 THURSDAY

☽ □ ⚵	**12:32 am**	
☽ ⚺ ♂	**3:10 am**	12:10 am
☽ ⚹ ⚷	**4:45 am**	1:45 am
☽ ⚹ ♀	**9:23 am**	6:23 am
☉ ☌ ♆	**2:28 pm**	11:28 am
☽ □ ♅	**4:52 pm**	1:52 pm
☽ ⚹ ☿	**8:53 pm**	5:53 pm
☽ △ ⚶	**10:48 pm**	7:48 pm
♃ ⚺ ⚳	**11:38 pm**	8:38 pm

4 FRIDAY

☽ ⚹ ♀	**4:45 am**	1:45 am
☽ ⚹ ♆	**8:59 am**	5:59 am
☽ ⚹ ☉	**10:21 am**	7:21 am
♂ ⚺ ⚷	**2:19 pm**	11:19 am
☽ ⚹ ♃	**3:14 pm**	12:14 pm
☽ ⚺ ⚳	**3:31 pm**	12:31 pm
☿ ⚹ ⚶	**5:43 pm**	2:43 pm
☽ ⚻ ♄	**8:40 pm**	5:40 pm
☽ ☌ ♇	**11:28 pm**	8:28 pm

5 SATURDAY

☽ ⚹ ⚵	**4:46 am**	1:46 am
☽ ⚺ ⚷	**7:22 am**	4:22 am
☽ ☌ ♂	**8:07 am**	5:07 am
☽ ⚺ ♀	**4:05 pm**	1:05 pm
☽ ⚹ ♅	**6:42 pm**	3:42 pm
☽ □ ⚶		10:30 pm

6 SUNDAY

☽ □ ⚶	**1:30 am**	
☽ ⚺ ☿	**4:33 am**	1:33 am
☽ □ ♀	**5:40 am**	2:40 am
☽ ⚺ ♆	**9:57 am**	6:57 am
☿ △ ♀	**2:15 pm**	11:15 am
☽ ⚺ ☉	**2:38 pm**	11:38 am
☽ □ ♃	**3:45 pm**	12:45 pm
☽ ⚹ ⚳	**4:52 pm**	1:52 pm
☽ ☍ ♄	**8:47 pm**	5:47 pm
☽ ⚺ ♇	**11:47 pm**	8:47 pm
♀ ⚺ ♅		9:28 pm

7 MONDAY

♀ ⚺ ♅	**12:28 am**	
☽ ⚺ ⚵	**6:20 am**	3:20 am
☉ △ ♃	**7:03 am**	4:03 am
☽ ☌ ⚷	**7:37 am**	4:37 am
☽ ⚺ ♂	**10:24 am**	7:24 am
☽ ⚺ ♅	**6:33 pm**	3:33 pm
☽ ☌ ♀	**8:06 pm**	5:06 pm
☽ ⚹ ⚶		11:20 pm

8 TUESDAY

☽ ⚹ ⚶	**2:20 am**	
☽ △ ♀	**5:00 am**	2:00 am
☿ ☌ ♆	**5:10 am**	2:10 am
☽ ☌ ♆	**9:32 am**	6:32 am
☉ □ ⚳	**9:37 am**	6:37 am
☽ ☌ ☿	**10:04 am**	7:04 am
☽ △ ♃	**3:07 pm**	12:07 pm
☽ □ ⚳	**5:03 pm**	2:03 pm
☽ ☌ ☉	**5:28 pm**	2:28 pm
☽ ⚻ ♄	**8:00 pm**	5:00 pm
☽ ⚹ ♇	**11:19 pm**	8:19 pm

9 WEDNESDAY

☽ ☌ ⚵	**7:22 am**	4:22 am
☽ ⚺ ⚷	**7:24 am**	4:24 am
⚷ ⚺ ⚵	**8:44 am**	5:44 am
☽ ⚹ ♂	**12:20 pm**	9:20 am
☽ ☌ ♅	**6:27 pm**	3:27 pm
☽ ⚺ ♀		9:17 pm

10 THURSDAY

☽ ⚺ ♀	**12:17 am**	
☽ ⚺ ⚶	**3:40 am**	12:40 am
☽ ⚻ ♀	**4:49 am**	1:49 am
☉ ⚻ ♄	**5:11 am**	2:11 am
☿ △ ♃	**5:43 am**	2:43 am
☽ ⚺ ♆	**9:52 am**	6:52 am
☽ ⚻ ♃	**3:29 pm**	12:29 pm
☽ ⚺ ☿	**4:51 pm**	1:51 pm
☽ △ ⚳	**6:22 pm**	3:22 pm
☽ △ ♄	**8:27 pm**	5:27 pm
☽ ⚺ ☉	**9:41 pm**	6:41 pm
☽ □ ♇		9:14 pm

11 FRIDAY

☽ □ ♇	**12:14 am**	
☿ □ ⚳	**7:01 am**	4:01 am
☽ ⚹ ⚷	**8:58 am**	5:58 am
☽ ⚺ ⚵	**10:20 am**	7:20 am
♀ ☍ ⚶	**2:03 pm**	11:03 am
☽ □ ♂	**4:32 pm**	1:32 pm
☽ ⚺ ♅	**8:37 pm**	5:37 pm
☿ ⚻ ♄	**9:34 pm**	6:34 pm
♀ △ ♀		11:17 pm

12 SATURDAY

♀ △ ♀	**2:17 am**	
☽ ☍ ♀	**7:09 am**	4:09 am
☽ ⚹ ♀	**7:41 am**	4:41 am
☽ ☌ ⚶	**7:48 am**	4:48 am
♀ ⚹ ⚶	**9:38 am**	6:38 am
☉ ⚹ ♇	**10:31 am**	7:31 am
☽ ⚹ ♆	**1:02 pm**	10:02 am
☽ ☍ ♃	**6:49 pm**	3:49 pm
☽ ⚻ ⚳	**10:54 pm**	7:54 pm
☽ □ ♄		9:03 pm

13 SUNDAY

☽ □ ♄	**12:03 am**	
☽ ⚹ ☿	**4:16 am**	1:16 am
☽ △ ♇	**4:27 am**	1:27 am
☿ ⚹ ♇	**5:38 am**	2:38 am
☽ ⚹ ☉	**5:53 am**	2:53 am
☽ □ ⚷	**2:08 pm**	11:08 am
☽ ⚹ ⚵	**5:15 pm**	2:15 pm
☽ △ ♂		10:04 pm
☽ ⚹ ♅		11:37 pm

14 MONDAY

☽ △ ♂	**1:04 am**	
☽ ⚹ ♅	**2:37 am**	
☉ ☌ ☿	**5:50 am**	2:50 am
☽ ⚻ ♀	**1:18 pm**	10:18 am
☽ ⚺ ⚶	**4:18 pm**	1:18 pm
♀ ☌ ♆	**7:47 pm**	4:47 pm
☽ □ ♆	**8:17 pm**	5:17 pm
☽ □ ♀	**8:20 pm**	5:20 pm
☽ ⚻ ♃		11:10 pm

15 TUESDAY

☽ ⚻ ♃	**2:10 am**	
♂ ⚹ ♅	**7:31 am**	4:31 am
☽ ☍ ⚳	**7:41 am**	4:41 am
☽ ⚹ ♄	**7:42 am**	4:42 am
♄ △ ⚳	**7:56 am**	4:56 am
☽ ⚻ ♇	**12:47 pm**	9:47 am
☽ □ ☉	**7:16 pm**	4:16 pm
☽ □ ☿	**10:07 pm**	7:07 pm
☽ △ ⚷	**11:26 pm**	8:26 pm

16 WEDNESDAY

☽ □ ⚵	**4:41 am**	1:41 am
☿ ⚺ ⚷	**7:20 am**	4:20 am
☽ □ ♅	**12:38 pm**	9:38 am
☽ ⚻ ♂	**2:18 pm**	11:18 am
☽ △ ♀	**11:03 pm**	8:03 pm

17 THURSDAY

☽ ⚹ ⚶	**4:55 am**	1:55 am
♀ △ ♃	**5:10 am**	2:10 am
☽ △ ♆	**7:12 am**	4:12 am
☽ △ ♃	**12:59 pm**	9:59 am
☽ △ ♀	**1:56 pm**	10:56 am
☽ ⚺ ♄	**6:42 pm**	3:42 pm
☽ ⚻ ⚳	**7:58 pm**	4:58 pm
☽ ☍ ♇		9:23 pm
☉ ⚺ ⚷		11:05 pm

18 FRIDAY

☽ ☍ ♇	**12:23 am**	
☉ ⚺ ⚷	**2:05 am**	
☿ ☌ ⚵	**6:51 am**	3:51 am
☽ ⚻ ⚷	**11:44 am**	8:44 am
☽ △ ☉	**12:33 pm**	9:33 am
☽ △ ⚵	**7:14 pm**	4:14 pm
☽ △ ☿	**8:56 pm**	5:56 pm
☽ △ ♅		10:11 pm

19 SATURDAY

☽ △ ♅	**1:11 am**	
☽ ☍ ♂	**6:27 am**	3:27 am
♀ ⚻ ♄	**9:45 am**	6:45 am
☽ □ ♀	**10:45 am**	7:45 am
☽ □ ⚶	**7:41 pm**	4:41 pm
☽ ⚻ ♆	**7:59 pm**	4:59 pm
☿ ☌ ♅		9:44 pm
☽ □ ♃		10:21 pm

20 SUNDAY

☿ ☌ ♅	**12:44 am**	
☽ □ ♃	**1:21 am**	
♆ ⚹ ⚶	**4:44 am**	1:44 am
☽ ☌ ♄	**7:06 am**	4:06 am
♀ □ ⚳	**8:28 am**	5:28 am
☽ △ ⚳	**9:37 am**	6:37 am
☽ ⚻ ♀	**9:44 am**	6:44 am
☽ ⚻ ♇	**1:11 pm**	10:11 am
☽ ☍ ⚷		9:50 pm

21 MONDAY

☽ ☍ ⚷	**12:50 am**	
☽ ⚻ ☉	**6:51 am**	3:51 am
☽ ⚻ ⚵	**10:25 am**	7:25 am
☽ ⚻ ♅	**2:05 pm**	11:05 am
♂ □ ♀	**4:58 pm**	1:58 pm
♀ ⚹ ♇	**7:00 pm**	4:00 pm
☽ ⚻ ☿	**8:48 pm**	5:48 pm
☽ ⚹ ♀	**10:24 pm**	7:24 pm
☽ ⚻ ♂	**10:50 pm**	7:50 pm

22 TUESDAY

☿ ⚻ ♀	**6:13 am**	3:13 am
☽ ☍ ♆	**8:33 am**	5:33 am
☽ △ ⚶	**10:15 am**	7:15 am
☽ ⚹ ♃	**1:21 pm**	10:21 am
☿ ⚹ ♂	**4:24 pm**	1:24 pm
☽ ⚺ ♄	**7:03 pm**	4:03 pm
☽ □ ⚳	**10:37 pm**	7:37 pm
☽ △ ♇		10:21 pm

23 WEDNESDAY

☽ △ ♇	**1:21 am**	
☽ ☍ ♀	**4:47 am**	1:47 am
☽ ⚻ ⚷	**1:02 pm**	10:02 am
☽ ☍ ☉	**11:54 pm**	8:54 pm
☽ ☍ ⚵		9:27 pm
☽ ☍ ♅		10:53 pm

24 THURSDAY

☽ ☍ ⚵	**12:27 am**	
☽ ☍ ♅	**1:53 am**	
☽ ⚺ ♀	**8:48 am**	5:48 am
☉ ☌ ⚵	**12:08 pm**	9:08 am
☽ △ ♂	**1:46 pm**	10:46 am
☽ ☍ ☿	**6:50 pm**	3:50 pm
☽ ⚻ ♆	**7:46 pm**	4:46 pm
☽ ⚻ ⚶	**11:19 pm**	8:19 pm
☽ ⚺ ♃	**11:57 pm**	8:57 pm
☿ ⚺ ♆		10:00 pm
☉ ☌ ♅		10:33 pm

25 FRIDAY

☿ ⚺ ♆	**1:00 am**	
☉ ☌ ♅	**1:33 am**	
☽ ⚹ ♄	**5:35 am**	2:35 am
☽ ⚹ ⚳	**10:01 am**	7:01 am
☽ □ ♇	**12:00 pm**	9:00 am
♃ ☍ ⚶	**3:01 pm**	12:01 pm
♅ ☌ ⚵	**6:13 pm**	3:13 pm
☽ ⚻ ♀	**9:45 pm**	6:45 pm
☽ △ ⚷	**11:38 pm**	8:38 pm

26 SATURDAY

☿ ⚻ ♃	**3:28 am**	12:28 am
☿ ⚺ ⚶	**7:45 am**	4:45 am
☽ ⚻ ♅	**12:00 pm**	9:00 am
☽ ⚻ ⚵	**12:37 pm**	9:37 am
☽ ⚻ ☉	**2:48 pm**	11:48 am
☽ ☌ ♀	**5:29 pm**	2:29 pm
♀ ⚺ ⚷	**5:44 pm**	2:44 pm
☽ □ ♂		11:39 pm

27 SUNDAY

☽ □ ♂	**2:39 am**	
☽ △ ♆	**5:12 am**	2:12 am
☽ ☌ ♃	**8:46 am**	5:46 am
☽ ☍ ⚶	**10:27 am**	7:27 am
☽ ⚻ ☿	**1:56 pm**	10:56 am
☽ □ ♄	**2:22 pm**	11:22 am
☿ △ ♄	**4:51 pm**	1:51 pm
☉ ⚻ ♀	**6:56 pm**	3:56 pm
☽ ⚺ ⚳	**7:28 pm**	4:28 pm
☽ ⚹ ♇	**8:49 pm**	5:49 pm

28 MONDAY

☽ □ ⚷	**8:17 am**	5:17 am
☽ △ ♀	**12:08 pm**	9:08 am
☽ △ ♅	**8:08 pm**	5:08 pm
☽ △ ⚵	**10:37 pm**	7:37 pm
☽ ⚺ ♀		9:13 pm
♂ ⚺ ♆		11:22 pm

Eastern time in bold type
Pacific time in medium type

FEBRUARY 2005

☽ Last Aspect				☽ Ingress			
day	EST	hr:mn / PST	asp	sign	day	EST	hr:mn / PST
1/31	**10:21 pm**	7:21 pm	□ ♀	♏	1/31		10:51 pm
1/31	**10:21 pm**	7:21 pm	□ ♀	♏	1	**1:51 am**	
2	**5:56 pm**	2:56 pm	△ ♄	♐	3	**7:21 am**	4:21 am
5	**8:07 am**	5:07 am	☌ ♂	♑	5	**9:32 am**	6:32 am
6	**8:47 pm**	5:47 pm	☍ ♄	♒	7	**9:26 am**	6:26 am
8	**11:19 pm**	8:19 pm	⚹ ♇	♓	9	**8:59 am**	5:59 am
10		9:14 pm	□ ♇	♈	11	**10:21 am**	7:21 am
11	**12:14 am**		□ ♇	♈	11	**10:21 am**	7:21 am
13	**5:53 am**	2:53 am	⚹ ☉	♉	13	**3:18 pm**	12:18 pm
15	**10:07 pm**	7:07 pm	□ ☿	♊	15		9:18 pm
15	**10:07 pm**	7:07 pm	□ ☿	♊	16	**12:18 am**	
17		9:23 pm	☍ ♇	♋	18	**12:13 pm**	9:13 am
18	**12:23 am**		☍ ♇	♋	18	**12:13 pm**	9:13 am
20	**7:06 am**	4:06 am	☌ ♄	♌	20		9:54 pm
20	**7:06 am**	4:06 am	☌ ♄	♌	21	**12:54 am**	
23	**4:47 am**	1:47 am	☍ ♀	♍	23	**12:44 pm**	9:44 am
25	**12:00 pm**	9:00 am	□ ♇	♎	25	**10:59 pm**	7:59 pm
27	**8:49 pm**	5:49 pm	⚹ ♇	♏	28	**7:21 am**	4:21 am

☽ Phases & Eclipses			
phase	day	EST	hr:mn / PST
4th Quarter	1		11:27 pm
4th Quarter	2	**2:27 am**	
New Moon	8	**5:28 pm**	2:28 pm
2nd Quarter	15	**7:16 pm**	4:16 pm
Full Moon	23	**11:54 pm**	8:54 pm

Planet Ingress				
		day	EST	hr:mn / PST
♀	♒	2	**10:42 am**	7:42 am
♂	♑	6	**1:32 pm**	10:32 am
⚵	♓	11	**11:07 am**	8:07 am
☿	♓	16	**12:46 pm**	9:46 am
☉	♓	18	**8:32 am**	5:32 am
⚷	♒	21	**12:39 pm**	9:39 am
♀	♓	26	**10:07 am**	7:07 am

Planetary Motion				
		day	EST	hr:mn / PST
⚴	℞	1	**5:27 am**	2:27 am
♃	℞	1	**9:26 pm**	6:26 pm

DATE		SID.TIME	SUN	MOON	NODE	MERCURY	VENUS	MARS	JUPITER	SATURN	URANUS	NEPTUNE	PLUTO	CERES	PALLAS	JUNO	VESTA	CHIRON
1	T	8:45:12	12 ♒ 13 18	26 ♎ 17	25 ♈ 39	02 ♒ 51	27 ♑ 56	25 ♐ 56	18 ♎ 52	22 ♋℞ 26	05 ♓ 23	14 ♒ 58	23 ♐ 44	18 ♏ 01	12 ♎℞ 36	25 ♒ 02	07 ♈ 47	28 ♑ 17
2	W	8:49:08	13 14 12	09 ♏ 24	25 ℞ 39	04 29	29 11	26 38	18 ℞ 52	22 22	05 26	15 00	23 46	18 17	12 36	25 30	08 11	28 22
3	Th	8:53:05	14 15 04	22 54	25 39	06 07	00 ♒ 26	27 20	18 52	22 17	05 30	15 03	23 47	18 33	12 36	25 57	08 35	28 27
4	F	8:57:01	15 15 56	06 ♐ 48	25 37	07 47	01 41	28 03	18 51	22 13	05 33	15 05	23 49	18 48	12 35	26 25	08 59	28 33
5	Sa	9:00:58	16 16 47	21 08	25 33	09 27	02 56	28 45	18 51	22 09	05 36	15 07	23 50	19 04	12 33	26 53	09 23	28 38
6	Su	9:04:54	17 17 37	05 ♑ 51	25 26	11 08	04 11	29 27	18 50	22 05	05 40	15 09	23 52	19 19	12 31	27 21	09 47	28 43
7	M	9:08:51	18 18 26	20 52	25 17	12 49	05 27	00 ♑ 10	18 49	22 00	05 43	15 12	23 53	19 33	12 28	27 49	10 11	28 48
8	T	9:12:48	19 19 14	06 ♒ 04	25 07	14 31	06 42	00 52	18 48	21 56	05 46	15 14	23 55	19 48	12 25	28 17	10 35	28 53
9	W	9:16:44	20 20 01	21 14	24 57	16 15	07 57	01 34	18 47	21 52	05 50	15 16	23 56	20 02	12 21	28 45	11 00	28 58
10	Th	9:20:41	21 20 46	06 ♓ 13	24 48	17 58	09 12	02 17	18 46	21 48	05 53	15 19	23 58	20 16	12 17	29 13	11 24	29 03
11	F	9:24:37	22 21 30	20 52	24 41	19 43	10 27	02 59	18 44	21 44	05 56	15 21	23 59	20 29	12 12	29 41	11 48	29 08
12	Sa	9:28:34	23 22 13	05 ♈ 04	24 37	21 29	11 42	03 42	18 42	21 40	06 00	15 23	24 01	20 43	12 07	00 ♓ 09	12 13	29 13
13	Su	9:32:30	24 22 54	18 47	24 D 35	23 15	12 57	04 24	18 40	21 37	06 03	15 25	24 02	20 56	12 01	00 38	12 38	29 18
14	M	9:36:27	25 23 33	02 ♉ 01	24 35	25 02	14 12	05 07	18 38	21 33	06 07	15 28	24 03	21 08	11 54	01 06	13 02	29 23
15	T	9:40:23	26 24 10	14 50	24 36	26 50	15 27	05 50	18 36	21 29	06 10	15 30	24 05	21 21	11 47	01 34	13 27	29 28
16	W	9:44:20	27 24 46	27 17	24 ℞ 36	28 39	16 43	06 32	18 33	21 26	06 13	15 32	24 06	21 33	11 40	02 02	13 52	29 33
17	Th	9:48:17	28 25 20	09 ♊ 28	24 36	00 ♓ 29	17 58	07 15	18 31	21 22	06 17	15 34	24 07	21 45	11 32	02 31	14 17	29 38
18	F	9:52:13	29 25 53	21 28	24 33	02 19	19 13	07 57	18 28	21 19	06 20	15 37	24 08	21 57	11 23	02 59	14 42	29 42
19	Sa	9:56:10	00 ♓ 26 23	03 ♋ 21	24 28	04 10	20 28	08 40	18 25	21 16	06 24	15 39	24 09	22 08	11 14	03 28	15 07	29 47
20	Su	10:00:06	01 26 52	15 12	24 20	06 01	21 43	09 23	18 21	21 13	06 27	15 41	24 11	22 19	11 04	03 56	15 32	29 52
21	M	10:04:03	02 27 19	27 04	24 11	07 53	22 58	10 05	18 18	21 10	06 31	15 43	24 12	22 30	10 54	04 25	15 57	29 57
22	T	10:07:59	03 27 45	09 ♌ 00	24 01	09 46	24 13	10 48	18 14	21 07	06 34	15 45	24 13	22 40	10 44	04 54	16 22	00 ♒ 01
23	W	10:11:56	04 28 08	21 02	23 51	11 39	25 28	11 31	18 11	21 04	06 37	15 48	24 14	22 50	10 32	05 22	16 47	00 06
24	Th	10:15:52	05 28 30	03 ♍ 11	23 42	13 31	26 43	12 14	18 07	21 01	06 41	15 50	24 15	23 00	10 21	05 51	17 13	00 10
25	F	10:19:49	06 28 50	15 29	23 35	15 24	27 58	12 57	18 03	20 58	06 44	15 52	24 16	23 09	10 09	06 20	17 38	00 15
26	Sa	10:23:46	07 29 08	27 55	23 29	17 17	29 13	13 39	17 58	20 55	06 48	15 54	24 17	23 18	09 56	06 49	18 03	00 20
27	Su	10:27:42	08 29 25	10 ♎ 32	23 26	19 09	00 ♓ 28	14 22	17 54	20 53	06 51	15 56	24 18	23 27	09 43	07 17	18 29	00 24
28	M	10:31:39	09 29 40	23 20	23 D 25	21 01	01 43	15 05	17 49	20 50	06 55	15 58	24 19	23 35	09 29	07 46	18 54	00 28

EPHEMERIS CALCULATED FOR 12 MIDNIGHT GREENWICH MEAN TIME. ALL OTHER DATA AND FACING ASPECTARIAN PAGE IN **EASTERN TIME (BOLD)** AND PACIFIC TIME (REGULAR).

MARCH 2005

1 TUESDAY
☽ ⚺ ⚴ **12:13 am**
♂ ⚺ ♆ **2:22 am**
☽ △ ☉ **3:11 am** 12:11 am
☿ △ ⚳ **7:21 am** 4:21 am
☽ □ ♆ **12:35 pm** 9:35 am
☽ ⚹ ♂ **1:08 pm** 10:08 am
☿ □ ♇ **2:39 pm** 11:39 am
☽ ⚺ ♃ **3:32 pm** 12:32 pm
☽ ⚻ ⚶ **7:16 pm** 4:16 pm
☽ △ ♄ **9:04 pm** 6:04 pm
☽ ☌ ⚳ 11:39 pm

2 WEDNESDAY
☽ ☌ ⚳ **2:39 am**
☽ ⚺ ♇ **3:28 am** 12:28 am
⚴ ⚻ ⚵ **4:17 am** 1:17 am
☽ △ ☿ **5:25 am** 2:25 am
☽ ⚹ ⚷ **2:41 pm** 11:41 am
☽ □ ♀ **11:29 pm** 8:29 pm
☽ □ ♅ 10:57 pm

3 THURSDAY
☽ □ ♅ **1:57 am**
☽ ⚹ ⚴ **4:41 am** 1:41 am
♂ □ ♃ **5:14 am** 2:14 am
☽ □ ⚵ **6:01 am** 3:01 am
☽ □ ☉ **12:36 pm** 9:36 am
☽ ⚹ ♆ **5:33 pm** 2:33 pm
☽ ⚹ ♃ **7:55 pm** 4:55 pm
☽ ⚺ ♂ **8:48 pm** 5:48 pm
♄ □ ⚶ **11:41 pm** 8:41 pm
☽ ⚻ ♄ 10:24 pm
☽ △ ⚶ 10:27 pm

4 FRIDAY
☽ ⚻ ♄ **1:24 am**
☽ △ ⚶ **1:27 am**
♀ ☌ ♅ **3:44 am** 12:44 am
☽ ⚺ ⚳ **7:17 am** 4:17 am
☽ ☌ ♇ **7:41 am** 4:41 am
☽ □ ☿ **4:45 pm** 1:45 pm
☽ ⚺ ⚷ **6:36 pm** 3:36 pm
♀ ⚻ ⚴ **11:47 pm** 8:47 pm

5 SATURDAY
☽ ⚹ ♅ **5:18 am** 2:18 am
☽ □ ⚴ **6:48 am** 3:48 am
☽ ⚹ ♀ **7:37 am** 4:37 am
☿ ⚹ ⚷ **9:17 am** 6:17 am
☽ ⚹ ⚵ **10:46 am** 7:46 am
☽ ⚹ ☉ **7:04 pm** 4:04 pm
☽ ⚺ ♆ **8:10 pm** 5:10 pm
☽ □ ♃ **10:00 pm** 7:00 pm
☽ ☌ ♂ 10:46 pm

6 SUNDAY
☽ ☌ ♂ **1:46 am**
☽ ☍ ♄ **3:28 am** 12:28 am
☽ □ ⚶ **5:09 am** 2:09 am
☽ ⚹ ⚳ **9:36 am** 6:36 am
☽ ⚺ ♇ **9:40 am** 6:40 am
☉ ⚺ ♆ **11:40 am** 8:40 am
♇ ⚺ ⚳ **7:43 pm** 4:43 pm
☽ ☌ ⚷ **8:25 pm** 5:25 pm
☽ ⚹ ☿ 9:27 pm

7 MONDAY
☽ ⚹ ☿ **12:27 am**
☽ ⚺ ♅ **6:46 am** 3:46 am
☽ △ ⚴ **7:09 am** 4:09 am
☉ ⚻ ♃ **10:19 am** 7:19 am
♂ ☍ ♄ **11:15 am** 8:15 am
☽ ⚺ ♀ **1:22 pm** 10:22 am
☽ ⚺ ⚵ **1:35 pm** 10:35 am
♀ ☌ ⚵ **5:17 pm** 2:17 pm
☽ ☌ ♆ **9:14 pm** 6:14 pm
☽ △ ♃ **10:36 pm** 7:36 pm
☽ ⚺ ☉ **11:35 pm** 8:35 pm
♅ ⚻ ⚴ 9:07 pm

8 TUESDAY
♅ ⚻ ⚴ **12:07 am**
☽ ⚻ ♄ **4:13 am** 1:13 am
☽ ⚺ ♂ **5:07 am** 2:07 am
☽ ⚹ ⚶ **7:26 am** 4:26 am
☽ ⚹ ♇ **10:28 am** 7:28 am
☽ □ ⚳ **10:41 am** 7:41 am
☽ ⚺ ⚷ **9:21 pm** 6:21 pm

9 WEDNESDAY
☽ ⚺ ☿ **6:27 am** 3:27 am
☽ ⚻ ⚴ **6:59 am** 3:59 am
☽ ☌ ♅ **7:42 am** 4:42 am
☿ ☍ ⚴ **11:25 am** 8:25 am
☽ ☌ ⚵ **4:04 pm** 1:04 pm
☽ ☌ ♀ **6:44 pm** 3:44 pm
☿ ⚺ ♅ **9:12 pm** 6:12 pm
☽ ⚺ ♆ **10:16 pm** 7:16 pm
☽ ⚻ ♃ **11:13 pm** 8:13 pm

10 THURSDAY
☽ ☌ ☉ **4:10 am** 1:10 am
☽ △ ♄ **5:13 am** 2:13 am
☽ ⚹ ♂ **8:47 am** 5:47 am
☽ ⚺ ⚶ **10:05 am** 7:05 am
☽ □ ♇ **11:44 am** 8:44 am
☽ △ ⚳ **12:11 pm** 9:11 am
☉ △ ♄ **6:54 pm** 3:54 pm
☽ ⚹ ⚷ **11:10 pm** 8:10 pm

11 FRIDAY
☽ ☍ ⚴ **7:55 am** 4:55 am
☽ ⚺ ♅ **9:53 am** 6:53 am
♀ ⚺ ♆ **12:54 pm** 9:54 am
☽ ☌ ☿ **1:07 pm** 10:07 am
♀ ⚻ ♃ **7:18 pm** 4:18 pm
☽ ⚺ ⚵ **8:17 pm** 5:17 pm
☽ ⚹ ♆ 10:04 pm
☽ ☍ ♃ 10:35 pm
☽ ⚺ ♀ 11:15 pm

12 SATURDAY
☽ ⚹ ♆ **1:04 am**
☽ ☍ ♃ **1:35 am**
☽ ⚺ ♀ **2:15 am**
☽ □ ♄ **8:13 am** 5:13 am
☽ ⚺ ☉ **11:13 am** 8:13 am
☽ □ ♂ **2:55 pm** 11:55 am
☽ ☌ ⚶ **3:08 pm** 12:08 pm
☽ △ ♇ **3:13 pm** 12:13 pm
☽ ⚻ ⚳ **3:54 pm** 12:54 pm
♇ △ ⚶ **5:44 pm** 2:44 pm
♂ ⚺ ♇ **8:34 pm** 5:34 pm
♂ □ ⚶ 9:46 pm

13 SUNDAY
♂ □ ⚶ **12:46 am**
☽ □ ⚷ **3:35 am** 12:35 am
♂ ⚹ ⚳ **10:54 am** 7:54 am
☽ ⚻ ⚴ **11:30 am** 8:30 am
☽ ⚹ ♅ **3:00 pm** 12:00 pm
⚳ ⚻ ⚶ **6:29 pm** 3:29 pm
☽ ⚺ ☿ **10:23 pm** 7:23 pm
♃ △ ♆ 11:46 pm

14 MONDAY
♃ △ ♆ **2:46 am**
☽ ⚹ ⚵ **4:00 am** 1:00 am
☽ ⚻ ♃ **7:06 am** 4:06 am
☽ □ ♆ **7:09 am** 4:09 am
☽ ⚹ ♀ **2:06 pm** 11:06 am
☽ ⚹ ♄ **2:36 pm** 11:36 am
☉ □ ♇ **6:16 pm** 3:16 pm
♀ △ ♄ **7:11 pm** 4:11 pm
☽ ⚻ ♇ **10:12 pm** 7:12 pm
☽ ⚹ ☉ **10:32 pm** 7:32 pm
☽ ☍ ⚳ **11:08 pm** 8:08 pm
☽ ⚺ ⚶ 9:02 pm
☽ △ ♂ 10:10 pm

15 TUESDAY
☽ ⚺ ⚶ **12:02 am**
☽ △ ♂ **1:10 am**
☉ △ ⚳ **6:18 am** 3:18 am
☽ △ ⚷ **11:41 am** 8:41 am
☽ △ ⚴ **6:29 pm** 3:29 pm
☽ □ ♅ **11:52 pm** 8:52 pm

16 WEDNESDAY
☉ ⚺ ⚶ **7:08 am** 4:08 am
☽ ⚹ ☿ **10:36 am** 7:36 am
☽ □ ⚵ **3:50 pm** 12:50 pm
☽ △ ♃ **4:12 pm** 1:12 pm
☽ △ ♆ **4:56 pm** 1:56 pm
♃ ⚻ ⚵ **11:12 pm** 8:12 pm
☽ ⚺ ♄ 9:36 pm

17 THURSDAY
☽ ⚺ ♄ **12:36 am**
☽ □ ♀ **6:49 am** 3:49 am
☽ ☍ ♇ **8:43 am** 5:43 am
☽ ⚻ ⚳ **9:49 am** 6:49 am
☽ ⚹ ⚶ **12:48 pm** 9:48 am
☽ □ ☉ **2:19 pm** 11:19 am
☽ ⚻ ♂ **3:33 pm** 12:33 pm
♆ ⚺ ⚵ **8:32 pm** 5:32 pm
☽ ⚻ ⚷ **11:07 pm** 8:07 pm
♀ □ ♇ 10:14 pm

18 FRIDAY
♀ □ ♇ **1:14 am**
☽ □ ⚴ **4:23 am** 1:23 am
☽ △ ♅ **11:45 am** 8:45 am
♀ △ ⚳ **12:19 pm** 9:19 am
☽ □ ☿ 9:03 pm

19 SATURDAY
☽ □ ☿ **12:03 am**
☽ □ ♃ **3:45 am** 12:45 am
☽ ⚻ ♆ **5:14 am** 2:14 am
☽ △ ⚵ **6:33 am** 3:33 am
☽ ☌ ♄ **12:53 pm** 9:53 am
☉ ⚹ ♂ **5:01 pm** 2:01 pm
☽ ⚻ ♇ **9:11 pm** 6:11 pm
☽ △ ⚳ **10:22 pm** 7:22 pm
☽ △ ♀ 11:18 pm

20 SUNDAY
☽ △ ♀ **2:18 am**
☽ □ ⚶ **3:37 am** 12:37 am
☽ ☍ ♂ **7:59 am** 4:59 am
☽ △ ☉ **8:21 am** 5:21 am
☽ ☍ ⚷ **11:59 am** 8:59 am
☽ ⚹ ⚴ **3:24 pm** 12:24 pm
♀ ⚺ ⚶ **8:46 pm** 5:46 pm
☽ ⚻ ♅ 9:37 pm

21 MONDAY
☽ ⚻ ♅ **12:37 am**
☽ △ ☿ **12:15 pm** 9:15 am
☽ ⚹ ♃ **3:36 pm** 12:36 pm
☽ ☍ ♆ **5:48 pm** 2:48 pm
☽ ⚻ ⚵ **9:33 pm** 6:33 pm
☽ ⚺ ♄ 10:11 pm

22 TUESDAY
☽ ⚺ ♄ **1:11 am**
☉ ⚹ ⚷ **6:16 am** 3:16 am
☽ △ ♇ **9:20 am** 6:20 am
☽ □ ⚳ **10:29 am** 7:29 am
☽ △ ⚶ **5:51 pm** 2:51 pm
☽ ⚻ ♀ **9:10 pm** 6:10 pm
☽ ⚻ ♂ **11:38 pm** 8:38 pm
☽ ⚻ ⚷ 9:03 pm
☽ ⚻ ☉ 10:32 pm
☽ ⚺ ⚴ 10:34 pm
☉ ☍ ⚴ 10:58 pm

23 WEDNESDAY
☽ ⚻ ⚷ **12:03 am**
☽ ⚻ ☉ **1:32 am**
☽ ⚺ ⚴ **1:34 am**
☉ ☍ ⚴ **1:58 am**
♂ ☌ ⚷ **7:07 am** 4:07 am
☽ ☍ ♅ **12:17 pm** 9:17 am
☽ ⚻ ☿ **9:35 pm** 6:35 pm
♂ △ ⚴ **11:01 pm** 8:01 pm
☽ ⚺ ♃ 10:56 pm
♀ ⚹ ⚷ 11:37 pm

24 THURSDAY
☽ ⚺ ♃ **1:56 am**
♀ ⚹ ⚷ **2:37 am**
☽ ⚻ ♆ **4:46 am** 1:46 am
♀ ☍ ⚴ **8:35 am** 5:35 am
☽ ☍ ⚵ **10:39 am** 7:39 am
☽ ⚹ ♄ **11:45 am** 8:45 am
☽ □ ♇ **7:36 pm** 4:36 pm
☽ ⚹ ⚳ **8:37 pm** 5:37 pm

25 FRIDAY
♀ ⚹ ♂ **3:41 am** 12:41 am
⚷ △ ⚴ **3:49 am** 12:49 am
☽ ⚻ ⚶ **5:50 am** 2:50 am
☽ ☌ ⚴ **9:47 am** 6:47 am
☽ △ ⚷ **9:57 am** 6:57 am
☽ △ ♂ **12:47 pm** 9:47 am
☽ ☍ ♀ **1:12 pm** 10:12 am
♄ △ ⚵ **2:45 pm** 11:45 am
☽ ☍ ☉ **3:58 pm** 12:58 pm
☽ ⚻ ♅ **9:42 pm** 6:42 pm

26 SATURDAY
☽ ☍ ☿ **3:50 am** 12:50 am
☽ ☌ ♃ **10:00 am** 7:00 am
☽ △ ♆ **1:23 pm** 10:23 am
☽ □ ♄ **8:00 pm** 5:00 pm
☽ ⚻ ⚵ **9:08 pm** 6:08 pm

27 SUNDAY
☽ ⚹ ♇ **3:30 am** 12:30 am
☽ ⚺ ⚳ **4:20 am** 1:20 am
☽ ☍ ⚶ **3:13 pm** 12:13 pm
☽ ⚺ ⚴ **3:50 pm** 12:50 pm
☽ □ ⚷ **5:30 pm** 2:30 pm
☽ □ ♂ **11:11 pm** 8:11 pm
☽ ⚻ ♀ 11:05 pm
⚴ ⚻ ⚶ 11:20 pm

28 MONDAY
☽ ⚻ ♀ **2:05 am**
⚴ ⚻ ⚶ **2:20 am**
☽ ⚻ ☉ **3:29 am** 12:29 am
☽ △ ♅ **4:47 am** 1:47 am
☽ ⚻ ☿ **7:33 am** 4:33 am
☽ ⚺ ♃ **3:55 pm** 12:55 pm
☽ □ ♆ **7:48 pm** 4:48 pm
☉ ⚺ ♅ **10:02 pm** 7:02 pm
☽ △ ♄ 11:06 pm

29 TUESDAY
☽ △ ♄ **2:06 am**
☽ △ ⚵ **5:12 am** 2:12 am
♀ ⚺ ♅ **8:23 am** 5:23 am
☽ ⚺ ♇ **9:18 am** 6:18 am
☽ ☌ ⚳ **9:55 am** 6:55 am
☉ ☌ ☿ **11:11 am** 8:11 am
☿ ☌ ♀ **3:29 pm** 12:29 pm
☽ ⚹ ⚴ **8:03 pm** 5:03 pm
☽ ⚻ ⚶ **10:24 pm** 7:24 pm
☽ ⚹ ⚷ **11:01 pm** 8:01 pm
☿ ⚺ ♅ 9:55 pm

30 WEDNESDAY
☿ ⚺ ♅ **12:55 am**
☽ ⚹ ♂ **7:16 am** 4:16 am
☽ △ ☿ **9:24 am** 6:24 am
☽ □ ♅ **9:57 am** 6:57 am
☽ △ ♀ **12:22 pm** 9:22 am
☽ △ ☉ **12:34 pm** 9:34 am
⚷ □ ⚶ **7:53 pm** 4:53 pm
☽ ⚹ ♃ **8:04 pm** 5:04 pm
☉ ☌ ♀ **10:30 pm** 7:30 pm
☽ ⚹ ♆ 9:24 pm

31 THURSDAY
☽ ⚹ ♆ **12:24 am**
☿ ⚹ ♂ **3:06 am** 12:06 am
☽ ⚻ ♄ **6:29 am** 3:29 am
☽ □ ⚵ **11:22 am** 8:22 am
☽ ☌ ♇ **1:24 pm** 10:24 am
☽ ⚺ ⚳ **1:47 pm** 10:47 am
☽ □ ⚴ **10:47 pm** 7:47 pm
☽ ⚺ ⚷ 11:56 pm

Eastern time in bold type
Pacific time in medium type

MARCH 2005

☽ Last Aspect day	EST / hr:mn / PST	asp	☽ Ingress sign day	EST / hr:mn / PST
2	**5:25 am** 2:25 am	△ ☿	♐ 2	**1:29 pm** 10:29 am
4	**4:45 pm** 1:45 pm	□ ☿	♑ 4	**5:12 pm** 2:12 pm
6	**3:28 am** 12:28 am	☍ ♄	♒ 6	**6:49 pm** 3:49 pm
8	**10:28 am** 7:28 am	⚹ ♇	♓ 8	**7:32 pm** 4:32 pm
10	**11:44 am** 8:44 am	□ ♇	♈ 10	**9:03 pm** 6:03 pm
12	**3:13 pm** 12:13 pm	△ ♇	♉ 12	10:05 pm
12	**3:13 pm** 12:13 pm	△ ♇	♉ 13	**1:05 am**
14	10:10 pm	△ ♂	♊ 15	**8:44 am** 5:44 am
15	**1:10 am**	△ ♂	♊ 15	**8:44 am** 5:44 am
17	**2:19 pm** 11:19 am	□ ☉	♋ 17	**7:44 pm** 4:44 pm
20	**7:59 am** 4:59 am	☍ ♂	♌ 20	**8:17 am** 5:17 am
22	**9:20 am** 6:20 am	△ ♇	♍ 22	**8:10 pm** 5:10 pm
24	**7:36 pm** 4:36 pm	□ ♇	♎ 25	**6:00 am** 3:00 am
27	**3:30 am** 12:30 am	⚹ ♇	♏ 27	**1:29 pm** 10:29 am
28	11:06 pm	△ ♄	♐ 29	**6:56 pm** 3:56 pm
29	**2:06 am**	△ ♄	♐ 29	**6:56 pm** 3:56 pm
31	**1:24 pm** 10:24 am	☌ ♇	♑ 31	**10:48 pm** 7:48 pm

☽ Phases & Eclipses phase	day	EST / hr:mn / PST
4th Quarter	3	**12:36 pm** 9:36 am
New Moon	10	**4:10 am** 1:10 am
2nd Quarter	17	**2:19 pm** 11:19 am
Full Moon	25	**3:58 pm** 12:58 pm

Planet Ingress	day	EST / hr:mn / PST
☿ ♈	4	**8:34 pm** 5:34 pm
☉ ♈	20	**7:33 am** 4:33 am
♂ ♒	20	**1:02 pm** 10:02 am
♀ ♈	22	**11:25 am** 8:25 am
⚶ ♉	25	**10:38 am** 7:38 am
⚴ ♍	31	**9:55 pm** 6:55 pm

Planetary Motion	day	EST / hr:mn / PST
☿ R	19	**7:13 pm** 4:13 pm
⚳ R	21	**4:29 am** 1:29 am
♄ D	21	**9:54 pm** 6:54 pm
♇ R	26	**9:29 pm** 6:29 pm

DATE		SID.TIME	SUN	MOON	NODE	MERCURY	VENUS	MARS	JUPITER	SATURN	URANUS	NEPTUNE	PLUTO	CERES	PALLAS	JUNO	VESTA	CHIRON
1	T	10:35:35	10 ♓ 29 54	06 ♏ 21	23 ♈ 26	22 ♓ 51	02 ♓ 58	15 ♑ 48	17 ♎ R 44	20 ♋ R 48	06 ♓ 58	16 ♒ 01	24 ♐ 20	23 ♏ 43	09 ♎ R 16	08 ♓ 15	19 ♈ 20	00 ♒ 33
2	W	10:39:32	11 30 06	19 36	23 27	24 40	04 13	16 31	17 40	20 46	07 02	16 03	24 20	23 51	09 01	08 44	19 45	00 37
3	Th	10:43:28	12 30 17	03 ♐ 08	23 R 29	26 27	05 28	17 14	17 34	20 44	07 05	16 05	24 21	23 58	08 46	09 13	20 11	00 42
4	F	10:47:25	13 30 26	16 57	23 29	28 12	06 42	17 57	17 29	20 42	07 08	16 07	24 22	24 05	08 31	09 42	20 36	00 46
5	Sa	10:51:21	14 30 34	01 ♑ 04	23 28	29 53	07 57	18 40	17 24	20 40	07 12	16 09	24 23	24 12	08 15	10 11	21 02	00 50
6	Su	10:55:18	15 30 40	15 29	23 25	01 ♈ 32	09 12	19 23	17 18	20 38	07 15	16 11	24 23	24 18	07 59	10 40	21 28	00 54
7	M	10:59:15	16 30 45	00 ♒ 07	23 20	03 07	10 27	20 06	17 13	20 36	07 19	16 13	24 24	24 24	07 43	11 10	21 54	00 58
8	T	11:03:11	17 30 48	14 53	23 15	04 37	11 42	20 49	17 07	20 35	07 22	16 15	24 25	24 30	07 26	11 39	22 19	01 02
9	W	11:07:08	18 30 49	29 40	23 10	06 02	12 57	21 32	17 01	20 33	07 26	16 17	24 25	24 35	07 09	12 08	22 45	01 07
10	Th	11:11:04	19 30 49	14 ♓ 21	23 05	07 22	14 12	22 15	16 55	20 32	07 29	16 19	24 26	24 39	06 52	12 37	23 11	01 11
11	F	11:15:01	20 30 46	28 47	23 01	08 36	15 27	22 58	16 49	20 31	07 32	16 21	24 27	24 44	06 35	13 07	23 37	01 14
12	Sa	11:18:57	21 30 42	12 ♈ 53	22 D 59	09 43	16 41	23 42	16 43	20 29	07 36	16 23	24 27	24 48	06 17	13 36	24 03	01 18
13	Su	11:22:54	22 30 35	26 35	22 59	10 44	17 56	24 25	16 36	20 28	07 39	16 25	24 28	24 51	05 59	14 05	24 29	01 22
14	M	11:26:50	23 30 26	09 ♉ 53	23 00	11 37	19 11	25 08	16 30	20 27	07 42	16 27	24 28	24 54	05 40	14 35	24 55	01 26
15	T	11:30:47	24 30 16	22 47	23 02	12 22	20 26	25 51	16 23	20 26	07 46	16 29	24 28	24 57	05 22	15 04	25 21	01 30
16	W	11:34:44	25 30 03	05 ♊ 20	23 03	12 59	21 41	26 34	16 16	20 26	07 49	16 31	24 29	25 00	05 03	15 34	25 47	01 33
17	Th	11:38:40	26 29 48	17 35	23 R 04	13 29	22 55	27 18	16 09	20 25	07 52	16 32	24 29	25 02	04 45	16 03	26 13	01 37
18	F	11:42:37	27 29 30	29 38	23 05	13 49	24 10	28 01	16 02	20 25	07 56	16 34	24 30	25 03	04 26	16 33	26 39	01 41
19	Sa	11:46:33	28 29 11	11 ♋ 33	23 04	14 02	25 25	28 44	15 55	20 24	07 59	16 36	24 30	25 04	04 07	17 02	27 05	01 44
20	Su	11:50:30	29 28 49	23 25	23 02	14 R 06	26 40	29 27	15 48	20 24	08 02	16 38	24 30	25 05	03 48	17 32	27 32	01 48
21	M	11:54:26	00 ♈ 28 25	05 ♌ 19	22 59	14 02	27 54	00 ♒ 11	15 41	20 24	08 06	16 40	24 30	25 R 05	03 29	18 01	27 58	01 51
22	T	11:58:23	01 27 58	17 17	22 56	13 50	29 09	00 54	15 34	20 D 24	08 09	16 41	24 30	25 05	03 09	18 31	28 24	01 54
23	W	12:02:19	02 27 30	29 24	22 52	13 31	00 ♈ 24	01 37	15 27	20 24	08 12	16 43	24 31	25 05	02 50	19 01	28 50	01 58
24	Th	12:06:16	03 26 59	11 ♍ 42	22 49	13 05	01 38	02 21	15 19	20 24	08 15	16 45	24 31	25 04	02 31	19 30	29 17	02 01
25	F	12:10:13	04 26 26	24 12	22 47	12 33	02 53	03 04	15 12	20 24	08 18	16 47	24 31	25 03	02 12	20 00	29 43	02 04
26	Sa	12:14:09	05 25 51	06 ♎ 55	22 45	11 55	04 07	03 48	15 04	20 24	08 22	16 48	24 31	25 01	01 53	20 30	00 ♉ 09	02 07
27	Su	12:18:06	06 25 14	19 52	22 D 45	11 12	05 22	04 31	14 57	20 25	08 25	16 50	24 R 31	24 59	01 34	20 59	00 35	02 10
28	M	12:22:02	07 24 34	03 ♏ 03	22 45	10 26	06 37	05 14	14 49	20 26	08 28	16 52	24 31	24 57	01 16	21 29	01 02	02 13
29	T	12:25:59	08 23 54	16 26	22 46	09 38	07 51	05 58	14 42	20 26	08 31	16 53	24 31	24 54	00 57	21 59	01 28	02 16
30	W	12:29:55	09 23 11	00 ♐ 02	22 47	08 47	09 06	06 41	14 34	20 27	08 34	16 55	24 31	24 50	00 39	22 29	01 55	02 19
31	Th	12:33:52	10 22 26	13 49	22 48	07 57	10 20	07 25	14 26	20 28	08 37	16 56	24 31	24 47	00 20	22 59	02 21	02 22

EPHEMERIS CALCULATED FOR 12 MIDNIGHT GREENWICH MEAN TIME. ALL OTHER DATA AND FACING ASPECTARIAN PAGE IN **EASTERN TIME (BOLD)** AND PACIFIC TIME (REGULAR).

APRIL 2005

1 FRIDAY

☽ ⚺ ⚷	**2:56 am**	
☽ △ ⚶	**3:50 am**	12:50 am
☽ □ ☿	**10:01 am**	7:01 am
☽ ⚺ ♂	**1:36 pm**	10:36 am
☽ ⚹ ♅	**1:37 pm**	10:37 am
♂ ⚺ ♅	**1:58 pm**	10:58 am
☽ □ ☉	**7:50 pm**	4:50 pm
☽ □ ♀	**8:44 pm**	5:44 pm
☽ □ ♃	**10:51 pm**	7:51 pm

2 SATURDAY

☽ ⚺ ♆	**3:38 am**	12:38 am
☽ ☍ ♄	**9:34 am**	6:34 am
☽ ⚹ ⚵	**4:08 pm**	1:08 pm
☽ ⚺ ♇	**4:17 pm**	1:17 pm
☽ ⚹ ⚳	**4:23 pm**	1:23 pm
♀ ☍ ♃	**6:52 pm**	3:52 pm
♇ □ ⚵	**8:17 pm**	5:17 pm
⚳ △ ⚵	**10:06 pm**	7:06 pm
☽ △ ♀		9:29 pm

3 SUNDAY

☽ △ ♀	**12:29 am**	
☽ ☌ ⚷	**6:44 am**	3:44 am
☽ □ ⚶	**9:05 am**	6:05 am
♇ ⚺ ⚳	**9:59 am**	6:59 am
☽ ⚹ ☿	**10:59 am**	7:59 am
☉ ☍ ♃	**11:30 am**	8:30 am
☽ ⚺ ♅	**5:17 pm**	2:17 pm
☽ ☌ ♂	**7:47 pm**	4:47 pm
☽ △ ♃		10:48 pm
☽ ⚹ ☉		11:59 pm

4 MONDAY

☽ △ ♃	**1:48 am**	
☽ ⚹ ☉	**2:59 am**	
☽ ⚹ ♀	**4:55 am**	1:55 am
☽ ☌ ♆	**7:04 am**	4:04 am
☿ ⚺ ⚶	**10:23 am**	7:23 am
☽ ⚻ ♄	**12:57 pm**	9:57 am
☽ □ ⚳	**7:19 pm**	4:19 pm
☽ ⚹ ♇	**7:32 pm**	4:32 pm
☽ ⚺ ⚵	**9:13 pm**	6:13 pm
☽ ⚻ ♀		11:44 pm

5 TUESDAY

☽ ⚻ ♀	**2:44 am**	
♀ ⚹ ♆	**6:11 am**	3:11 am
☽ ⚺ ⚷	**9:07 am**	6:07 am
☽ ⚺ ☿	**11:02 am**	8:02 am
☽ ⚹ ⚶	**12:55 pm**	9:55 am
☽ ☌ ♅	**7:44 pm**	4:44 pm
☽ ⚺ ♂		9:46 pm

6 WEDNESDAY

☽ ⚺ ♂	**12:46 am**	
☽ ⚻ ♃	**3:40 am**	12:40 am
☽ ⚺ ☉	**9:04 am**	6:04 am
☽ ⚺ ♆	**9:31 am**	6:31 am
☽ ⚺ ♀	**12:06 pm**	9:06 am
☽ △ ♄	**3:29 pm**	12:29 pm
☉ ⚹ ♆	**3:49 pm**	12:49 pm
☽ △ ⚳	**9:29 pm**	6:29 pm
☽ □ ♇	**10:03 pm**	7:03 pm
☽ ☌ ⚵		10:39 pm

7 THURSDAY

☽ ☌ ⚵	**1:39 am**	
☽ ☍ ♀	**4:26 am**	1:26 am
☽ ⚹ ⚷	**12:04 pm**	9:04 am
☽ ☌ ☿	**12:07 pm**	9:07 am
☿ ⚹ ⚷	**1:33 pm**	10:33 am
☽ ⚺ ⚶	**5:29 pm**	2:29 pm
☽ ⚺ ♅	**10:59 pm**	7:59 pm
♂ △ ♃		10:31 pm

8 FRIDAY

♂ △ ♃	**1:31 am**	
♀ □ ♄	**3:45 am**	12:45 am
☽ ☍ ♃	**6:30 am**	3:30 am
☽ ⚹ ♂	**6:49 am**	3:49 am
☽ ⚹ ♆	**1:07 pm**	10:07 am
☽ ☌ ☉	**4:32 pm**	1:32 pm
☽ □ ♄	**7:19 pm**	4:19 pm
☽ ☌ ♀	**8:50 pm**	5:50 pm
☽ ⚻ ⚳		9:59 pm
☽ △ ♇		11:00 pm

9 SATURDAY

☽ ⚻ ⚳	**12:59 am**	
☽ △ ♇	**2:00 am**	
♀ ☍ ⚵	**5:49 am**	2:49 am
☽ ⚻ ♀	**7:40 am**	4:40 am
☽ ⚺ ⚵	**7:46 am**	4:46 am
☽ ⚺ ☿	**3:27 pm**	12:27 pm
☽ □ ⚷	**4:47 pm**	1:47 pm
☽ ☌ ⚶		9:07 pm

10 SUNDAY

☽ ☌ ⚶	**12:07 am**	
☽ ⚹ ♅	**4:15 am**	1:15 am
☉ □ ♄	**8:36 am**	5:36 am
☽ ⚻ ♃	**11:27 am**	8:27 am
♀ ⚻ ⚳	**2:20 pm**	11:20 am
☽ □ ♂	**3:27 pm**	12:27 pm
☽ □ ♆	**7:01 pm**	4:01 pm
☽ ⚹ ♄		10:37 pm
☽ ⚺ ☉		11:58 pm

11 MONDAY

☽ ⚹ ♄	**1:37 am**	
☽ ⚺ ☉	**2:58 am**	
♀ △ ♇	**5:05 am**	2:05 am
☽ ☍ ⚳	**6:53 am**	3:53 am
☽ ⚻ ♇	**8:29 am**	5:29 am
☽ ⚺ ♀	**8:51 am**	5:51 am
☽ △ ♀	**1:27 pm**	10:27 am
☽ ⚹ ⚵	**4:52 pm**	1:52 pm
☽ ⚹ ☿	**10:13 pm**	7:13 pm
☽ △ ⚷		9:18 pm

12 TUESDAY

☽ △ ⚷	**12:18 am**	
☽ ⚺ ⚶	**9:57 am**	6:57 am
☽ □ ♅	**12:29 pm**	9:29 am
☽ △ ♃	**7:20 pm**	4:20 pm
☉ ⚻ ⚳		9:24 pm
♀ ⚻ ♀		10:36 pm

13 WEDNESDAY

☉ ⚻ ⚳	**12:24 am**	
♀ ⚻ ♀	**1:36 am**	
☽ △ ♂	**3:39 am**	12:39 am
☽ △ ♆	**3:58 am**	12:58 am
♂ ☌ ♆	**9:11 am**	6:11 am
☽ ⚺ ♄	**11:02 am**	8:02 am
☽ ⚻ ⚳	**3:44 pm**	12:44 pm
☽ ⚹ ☉	**5:17 pm**	2:17 pm
☽ ☍ ♇	**6:03 pm**	3:03 pm
☽ □ ♀	**10:14 pm**	7:14 pm
☽ ⚹ ♀		10:01 pm
☉ △ ♇		11:51 pm

14 THURSDAY

☽ ⚹ ♀	**1:01 am**	
☉ △ ♇	**2:51 am**	
☽ □ ⚵	**5:26 am**	2:26 am
☽ □ ☿	**8:56 am**	5:56 am
☽ ⚻ ⚷	**10:51 am**	7:51 am
☽ ⚹ ⚶	**11:03 pm**	8:03 pm
☽ △ ♅	**11:40 pm**	8:40 pm

15 FRIDAY

☽ □ ♃	**5:58 am**	2:58 am
☽ ⚻ ♆	**3:38 pm**	12:38 pm
♅ ⚹ ⚶	**5:32 pm**	2:32 pm
☽ ⚻ ♂	**7:04 pm**	4:04 pm
☉ ⚻ ♀	**8:39 pm**	5:39 pm
☽ ☌ ♄	**11:02 pm**	8:02 pm
☽ △ ⚳		11:52 pm

16 SATURDAY

☽ △ ⚳	**2:52 am**	
☽ ⚻ ♇	**5:59 am**	2:59 am
☽ ⚹ ♀	**9:15 am**	6:15 am
☽ □ ☉	**10:37 am**	7:37 am
☽ □ ♀	**8:09 pm**	5:09 pm
☽ △ ⚵	**8:20 pm**	5:20 pm
☽ △ ☿	**10:46 pm**	7:46 pm
♀ ⚺ ⚵	**10:54 pm**	7:54 pm
☽ ☍ ⚷	**11:20 pm**	8:20 pm

17 SUNDAY

☽ ⚻ ♅	**12:22 pm**	9:22 am
☽ □ ⚶	**1:51 pm**	10:51 am
☿ ⚹ ⚷	**3:42 pm**	12:42 pm
☽ ⚹ ♃	**5:51 pm**	2:51 pm

18 MONDAY

♀ □ ⚷	**3:17 am**	12:17 am
☽ ☍ ♆	**4:12 am**	1:12 am
☿ ⚺ ♀	**10:06 am**	7:06 am
☽ ☍ ♂	**11:26 am**	8:26 am
☽ ⚺ ♄	**11:43 am**	8:43 am
☽ □ ⚳	**2:25 pm**	11:25 am
♂ ⚻ ♄	**4:23 pm**	1:23 pm
☽ △ ♇	**6:17 pm**	3:17 pm
☽ ⚺ ♀	**8:36 pm**	5:36 pm

19 TUESDAY

☽ △ ☉	**4:13 am**	1:13 am
☽ ⚻ ⚵	**11:02 am**	8:02 am
☽ ⚻ ⚷	**11:29 am**	8:29 am
☽ ⚻ ☿	**1:19 pm**	10:19 am
☽ △ ♀	**3:03 pm**	12:03 pm
⚷ ⚹ ⚵	**10:36 pm**	7:36 pm
☽ ☍ ♅		9:14 pm

20 WEDNESDAY

☽ ☍ ♅	**12:14 am**	
♂ □ ⚳	**3:28 am**	12:28 am
☽ △ ⚶	**3:42 am**	12:42 am
☽ ⚺ ♃	**4:46 am**	1:46 am
☽ ⚻ ♆	**3:23 pm**	12:23 pm
☽ ⚹ ♄	**10:45 pm**	7:45 pm
☽ ⚹ ⚳		9:15 pm
☽ ⚻ ♂		10:51 pm

21 THURSDAY

☽ ⚹ ⚳	**12:15 am**	
☽ ⚻ ♂	**1:51 am**	
♃ ⚻ ⚶	**3:39 am**	12:39 am
☽ □ ♇	**4:45 am**	1:45 am
☽ ☌ ♀	**6:12 am**	3:12 am
☽ ⚻ ☉	**7:05 pm**	4:05 pm
☽ △ ⚷	**9:18 pm**	6:18 pm
☽ ☍ ⚵	**11:07 pm**	8:07 pm
☽ ☍ ☿		11:04 pm

22 FRIDAY

☽ ☍ ☿	**2:04 am**	
☽ ⚻ ♀	**6:40 am**	3:40 am
☽ ⚻ ♅	**9:28 am**	6:28 am
☽ ☌ ♃	**1:06 pm**	10:06 am
☽ ⚻ ⚶	**2:34 pm**	11:34 am
☽ △ ♆	**11:43 pm**	8:43 pm
☉ □ ⚷		9:45 pm

23 SATURDAY

☉ □ ⚷	**12:45 am**	
♂ ⚹ ♇	**3:10 am**	12:10 am
☽ □ ♄	**6:51 am**	3:51 am
☽ ⚺ ⚳	**7:14 am**	4:14 am
☽ ⚹ ♇	**12:14 pm**	9:14 am
☽ △ ♂	**12:46 pm**	9:46 am
♀ ⚹ ♅	**12:52 pm**	9:52 am
☽ ⚺ ♀	**1:00 pm**	10:00 am
♂ ⚻ ♀	**4:32 pm**	1:32 pm

24 SUNDAY

♄ △ ⚳	**3:09 am**	12:09 am
☽ □ ⚷	**4:02 am**	1:02 am
☽ ☍ ☉	**6:06 am**	3:06 am
☽ ⚻ ⚵	**7:48 am**	4:48 am
☽ ⚻ ☿	**11:55 am**	8:55 am
☽ △ ♅	**3:39 pm**	12:39 pm
☽ ☍ ♀	**6:14 pm**	3:14 pm
☽ ⚺ ♃	**6:31 pm**	3:31 pm
♀ ⚻ ♃	**9:08 pm**	6:08 pm
☽ ☍ ⚶	**10:09 pm**	7:09 pm

25 MONDAY

☽ □ ♆	**5:06 am**	2:06 am
☽ ☌ ⚳	**11:28 am**	8:28 am
☽ △ ♄	**12:05 pm**	9:05 am
☽ ⚺ ♇	**4:57 pm**	1:57 pm
☽ ⚹ ♀	**5:13 pm**	2:13 pm
☽ □ ♂	**8:24 pm**	5:24 pm

26 TUESDAY

☉ ⚺ ⚵	**5:27 am**	2:27 am
☽ ⚹ ⚷	**8:13 am**	5:13 am
☽ △ ⚵	**1:43 pm**	10:43 am
☽ ⚻ ☉	**2:01 pm**	11:01 am
☽ △ ☿	**7:26 pm**	4:26 pm
☽ □ ♅	**7:30 pm**	4:30 pm
☿ ⚺ ♅	**8:29 pm**	5:29 pm
☽ ⚹ ♃	**9:44 pm**	6:44 pm
☽ ⚻ ♀		11:46 pm

27 WEDNESDAY

☽ ⚻ ♀	**2:46 am**	
☽ ⚻ ⚶	**3:18 am**	12:18 am
♇ □ ♀	**3:27 am**	12:27 am
☽ ⚹ ♆	**8:26 am**	5:26 am
♀ ☌ ⚶	**11:56 am**	8:56 am
☽ ⚺ ⚳	**1:51 pm**	10:51 am
☽ ⚻ ♄	**3:24 pm**	12:24 pm
☽ □ ♀	**7:46 pm**	4:46 pm
☽ ☌ ♇	**7:53 pm**	4:53 pm
☿ ☍ ♃		9:37 pm
☽ ⚹ ♂		11:02 pm

28 THURSDAY

☿ ☍ ♃	**12:37 am**	
☽ ⚹ ♂	**2:02 am**	
☽ ⚺ ⚷	**10:57 am**	7:57 am
☽ □ ⚵	**6:10 pm**	3:10 pm
☽ △ ☉	**8:18 pm**	5:18 pm
☽ ⚹ ♅	**10:09 pm**	7:09 pm
☽ □ ♃	**11:52 pm**	8:52 pm
☽ □ ☿		10:56 pm

29 FRIDAY

☽ □ ☿	**1:56 am**	
☽ △ ⚶	**7:21 am**	4:21 am
☽ △ ♀	**9:59 am**	6:59 am
☽ ⚺ ♆	**10:53 am**	7:53 am
☽ ⚹ ⚳	**3:29 pm**	12:29 pm
☽ ☍ ♄	**6:00 pm**	3:00 pm
♀ □ ♆	**8:33 pm**	5:33 pm
☽ △ ♀	**9:45 pm**	6:45 pm
☽ ⚺ ♇	**10:11 pm**	7:11 pm
☉ ⚹ ♅		9:35 pm

30 SATURDAY

☉ ⚹ ♅	**12:35 am**	
☽ ⚺ ♂	**7:05 am**	4:05 am
☽ ☌ ⚷	**1:22 pm**	10:22 am
☉ ⚻ ♃	**8:25 pm**	5:25 pm
☽ ⚹ ⚵	**10:26 pm**	7:26 pm
☽ ⚺ ♅		9:42 pm
☽ △ ♃		10:57 pm
☽ □ ☉		11:24 pm

Eastern time in bold type
Pacific time in medium type

APRIL 2005

☽ Last Aspect day	EST	PST	asp	☽ Ingress sign	day	EST	PST
2	**9:34 am**	6:34 am	☍ ♄	♒	2		10:31 pm
2	**9:34 am**	6:34 am	☍ ♄	♒	3	**1:31 am**	
4	**7:32 pm**	4:32 pm	⚹ ♇	♓	5	**4:45 am**	1:45 am
6	**10:03 pm**	7:03 pm	□ ♇	♈	7	**7:28 am**	4:28 am
8		11:00 pm	△ ♇	♉	9	**11:50 am**	8:50 am
9	**2:00 am**		△ ♇	♉	9	**11:50 am**	8:50 am
10		10:37 pm	⚹ ♄	♊	11	**6:55 pm**	3:55 pm
11	**1:37 am**		⚹ ♄	♊	11	**6:55 pm**	3:55 pm
13		10:01 pm	⚹ ♀	♋	14	**5:03 am**	2:03 am
14	**1:01 am**		⚹ ♀	♋	14	**5:03 am**	2:03 am
16	**10:37 am**	7:37 am	□ ☉	♌	16	**5:17 pm**	2:17 pm
19	**4:13 am**	1:13 am	△ ☉	♍	19	**5:27 am**	2:27 am
21	**4:45 am**	1:45 am	□ ♇	♎	21	**3:27 pm**	12:27 pm
23	**12:46 pm**	9:46 am	△ ♂	♏	23	**10:25 pm**	7:25 pm
25	**8:24 pm**	5:24 pm	□ ♂	♐	25		11:46 pm
25	**8:24 pm**	5:24 pm	□ ♂	♐	26	**2:46 am**	
27		11:02 pm	⚹ ♂	♑	28	**5:33 am**	2:33 am
28	**2:02 am**		⚹ ♂	♑	28	**5:33 am**	2:33 am
29	**6:00 pm**	3:00 pm	☍ ♄	♒	30	**7:54 am**	4:54 am

☽ Phases & Eclipses phase	day	EST	PST
4th Quarter	1	**7:50 pm**	4:50 pm
New Moon	8	**4:32 pm**	1:32 pm
☌	8	19° ♈ 06'	
2nd Quarter	16	**10:37 am**	7:37 am
Full Moon	24	**6:06 am**	3:06 am
☍	24	4° ♏ 20'	
4th Quarter	30		11:24 pm
4th Quarter	5/1	**2:24 am**	

Planet Ingress		day	EST	PST
⚵	♈	13	**8:29 pm**	5:29 pm
♀	♉	15	**4:37 pm**	1:37 pm
☉	♉	19	**7:37 pm**	4:37 pm
♂	♓	30	**10:58 pm**	7:58 pm

Planetary Motion		day	EST	PST
☿	D	12	**3:45 am**	12:45 am

DATE		SID.TIME	SUN	MOON	NODE	MERCURY	VENUS	MARS	JUPITER	SATURN	URANUS	NEPTUNE	PLUTO	CERES	PALLAS	JUNO	VESTA	CHIRON
1	F	12:37:48	11 ♈ 21 40	27 ♐ 47	22 ♈ 48	07 ♈ ℞ 06	11 ♈ 35	08 ♒ 08	14 ♎ ℞ 19	20 ♋ 29	08 ♓ 40	16 ♒ 58	24 ♐ ℞ 31	24 ♏ ℞ 43	00 ♎ ℞ 02	23 ♓ 29	02 ♉ 47	02 ♒ 25
2	Sa	12:41:45	12 20 52	11 ♑ 53	22 ℞ 49	06 17	12 49	08 52	14 11	20 30	08 43	16 59	24 30	24 38	29 ♍ 44	23 59	03 14	02 27
3	Su	12:45:42	13 20 02	26 07	22 49	05 31	14 04	09 35	14 03	20 31	08 46	17 01	24 30	24 33	29 27	24 29	03 40	02 30
4	M	12:49:38	14 19 11	10 ♒ 26	22 48	04 47	15 18	10 19	13 56	20 33	08 49	17 02	24 30	24 28	29 09	24 58	04 07	02 32
5	T	12:53:35	15 18 18	24 46	22 47	04 07	16 33	11 02	13 48	20 34	08 52	17 04	24 30	24 22	28 52	25 28	04 33	02 35
6	W	12:57:31	16 17 23	09 ♓ 05	22 46	03 32	17 47	11 46	13 40	20 36	08 55	17 05	24 29	24 16	28 36	25 59	05 00	02 37
7	Th	13:01:28	17 16 26	23 17	22 46	03 01	19 01	12 29	13 32	20 38	08 58	17 06	24 29	24 09	28 19	26 29	05 26	02 40
8	F	13:05:24	18 15 27	07 ♈ 18	22 45	02 35	20 16	13 13	13 25	20 39	09 01	17 08	24 29	24 02	28 03	26 59	05 53	02 42
9	Sa	13:09:21	19 14 26	21 04	22 D 45	02 14	21 30	13 56	13 17	20 41	09 04	17 09	24 28	23 55	27 47	27 29	06 19	02 44
10	Su	13:13:17	20 13 23	04 ♉ 33	22 45	01 59	22 45	14 40	13 09	20 43	09 06	17 10	24 28	23 48	27 32	27 59	06 46	02 46
11	M	13:17:14	21 12 18	17 44	22 45	01 49	23 59	15 24	13 02	20 45	09 09	17 12	24 27	23 40	27 17	28 29	07 12	02 48
12	T	13:21:10	22 11 11	00 ♊ 35	22 ℞ 45	01 D 45	25 13	16 07	12 54	20 48	09 12	17 13	24 27	23 31	27 02	28 59	07 39	02 50
13	W	13:25:07	23 10 02	13 08	22 45	01 46	26 28	16 51	12 47	20 50	09 15	17 14	24 26	23 22	26 48	29 29	08 05	02 52
14	Th	13:29:04	24 08 51	25 25	22 45	01 52	27 42	17 34	12 39	20 52	09 17	17 15	24 26	23 13	26 34	29 59	08 32	02 54
15	F	13:33:00	25 07 37	07 ♋ 30	22 45	02 03	28 56	18 18	12 32	20 55	09 20	17 16	24 25	23 04	26 21	00 ♈ 30	08 59	02 56
16	Sa	13:36:57	26 06 21	19 27	22 D 45	02 19	00 ♉ 10	19 01	12 24	20 57	09 23	17 17	24 25	22 54	26 08	01 00	09 25	02 58
17	Su	13:40:53	27 05 03	01 ♌ 21	22 45	02 40	01 25	19 45	12 17	21 00	09 25	17 18	24 24	22 44	25 56	01 30	09 52	02 59
18	M	13:44:50	28 03 43	13 15	22 45	03 06	02 39	20 28	12 10	21 03	09 28	17 19	24 23	22 34	25 44	02 00	10 18	03 01
19	T	13:48:46	29 02 20	25 14	22 46	03 35	03 53	21 12	12 03	21 06	09 30	17 21	24 23	22 23	25 32	02 31	10 45	03 03
20	W	13:52:43	00 ♉ 00 56	07 ♍ 23	22 46	04 09	05 07	21 56	11 56	21 09	09 33	17 21	24 22	22 13	25 21	03 01	11 11	03 04
21	Th	13:56:39	00 59 29	19 46	22 47	04 47	06 21	22 39	11 49	21 12	09 35	17 22	24 21	22 01	25 11	03 31	11 38	03 05
22	F	14:00:36	01 58 00	02 ♎ 25	22 48	05 29	07 36	23 23	11 42	21 15	09 38	17 23	24 20	21 50	25 01	04 01	12 05	03 07
23	Sa	14:04:33	02 56 29	15 23	22 ℞ 48	06 14	08 50	24 06	11 35	21 19	09 40	17 24	24 20	21 38	24 51	04 32	12 31	03 08
24	Su	14:08:29	03 54 56	28 39	22 48	07 03	10 04	24 50	11 28	21 22	09 42	17 25	24 19	21 27	24 42	05 02	12 58	03 09
25	M	14:12:26	04 53 21	12 ♏ 13	22 48	07 55	11 18	25 33	11 22	21 25	09 45	17 26	24 18	21 15	24 34	05 32	13 24	03 10
26	T	14:16:22	05 51 44	26 04	22 47	08 50	12 32	26 17	11 15	21 29	09 47	17 27	24 17	21 02	24 26	06 03	13 51	03 11
27	W	14:20:19	06 50 06	10 ♐ 07	22 45	09 48	13 46	27 00	11 09	21 33	09 49	17 28	24 16	20 50	24 18	06 33	14 17	03 12
28	Th	14:24:15	07 48 26	24 19	22 43	10 49	15 00	27 44	11 02	21 37	09 51	17 28	24 15	20 37	24 11	07 04	14 44	03 13
29	F	14:28:12	08 46 45	08 ♑ 37	22 41	11 53	16 14	28 28	10 56	21 40	09 54	17 29	24 14	20 24	24 04	07 34	15 11	03 14
30	Sa	14:32:08	09 45 02	22 55	22 40	13 00	17 28	29 11	10 50	21 44	09 56	17 30	24 13	20 11	23 58	08 04	15 37	03 14

EPHEMERIS CALCULATED FOR 12 MIDNIGHT GREENWICH MEAN TIME. ALL OTHER DATA AND FACING ASPECTARIAN PAGE IN **EASTERN TIME (BOLD)** AND PACIFIC TIME (REGULAR).

MAY 2005

1 SUNDAY

☽ ⚺ ♅	**12:42 am**	
☽ △ ♃	**1:57 am**	
☽ □ ☉	**2:24 am**	
☽ ⚹ ☿	**8:50 am**	5:50 am
☽ □ ⚶	**11:29 am**	8:29 am
☽ ☌ ♆	**1:27 pm**	10:27 am
♀ ☍ ⚳	**5:04 pm**	2:04 pm
☽ □ ⚳	**5:18 pm**	2:18 pm
☽ □ ♀	**5:20 pm**	2:20 pm
☽ ⚻ ♄	**8:52 pm**	5:52 pm
☽ ⚻ ⚴		9:06 pm
☽ ⚹ ♇		9:47 pm

2 MONDAY

☽ ⚻ ⚴	**12:06 am**	
☽ ⚹ ♇	**12:47 am**	
☽ ☌ ♂	**12:40 pm**	9:40 am
☽ ⚺ ⚷	**4:18 pm**	1:18 pm

3 TUESDAY

☽ ⚺ ⚵	**3:26 am**	12:26 am
☽ ☌ ♅	**3:56 am**	12:56 am
☽ ⚻ ♃	**4:45 am**	1:45 am
☿ ⚺ ⚶	**6:38 am**	3:38 am
☽ ⚹ ☉	**9:23 am**	6:23 am
♀ ⚹ ♄	**12:11 pm**	9:11 am
☿ ⚹ ♆	**1:55 pm**	10:55 am
☽ ⚹ ⚶	**4:31 pm**	1:31 pm
☽ ⚺ ♆	**4:52 pm**	1:52 pm
☽ ⚺ ☿	**5:10 pm**	2:10 pm
♅ ⚺ ⚵	**6:03 pm**	3:03 pm
☽ △ ⚳	**7:57 pm**	4:57 pm
☽ △ ♄		9:41 pm
☽ ⚹ ♀		10:50 pm

4 WEDNESDAY

☽ △ ♄	**12:41 am**	
☽ ⚹ ♀	**1:50 am**	
☽ ☍ ⚴	**3:28 am**	12:28 am
♆ □ ⚶	**3:58 am**	12:58 am
☽ □ ♇	**4:22 am**	1:22 am
♃ ☍ ⚵	**10:12 am**	7:12 am
☿ ⚻ ⚳	**6:39 pm**	3:39 pm
♀ △ ⚴	**7:12 pm**	4:12 pm
☽ ⚺ ♂	**7:30 pm**	4:30 pm
☽ ⚹ ⚷	**8:21 pm**	5:21 pm

Eastern time in bold type
Pacific time in medium type

5 THURSDAY

♀ ⚻ ♇	**5:40 am**	2:40 am
☽ ⚺ ♅	**8:24 am**	5:24 am
☽ ☍ ♃	**8:47 am**	5:47 am
☽ ☌ ⚵	**9:49 am**	6:49 am
♂ ⚺ ⚷	**11:40 am**	8:40 am
☽ ⚺ ☉	**5:57 pm**	2:57 pm
☽ ⚹ ♆	**9:38 pm**	6:38 pm
☽ ⚺ ⚶	**11:01 pm**	8:01 pm
☽ ⚻ ⚳	**11:54 pm**	8:54 pm

6 FRIDAY

☽ ☌ ☿	**3:45 am**	12:45 am
☽ □ ♄	**5:57 am**	2:57 am
☽ ⚻ ⚴	**8:18 am**	5:18 am
☽ △ ♇	**9:22 am**	6:22 am
☽ ⚺ ♀	**12:14 pm**	9:14 am
⚳ ☍ ⚶	**5:04 pm**	2:04 pm
☿ □ ♄		10:55 pm
☽ □ ⚷		10:59 pm

7 SATURDAY

☿ □ ♄	**1:55 am**	
☽ □ ⚷	**1:59 am**	
♃ ⚻ ♅	**3:36 am**	12:36 am
☽ ⚹ ♂	**4:12 am**	1:12 am
☽ ⚻ ♃	**2:30 pm**	11:30 am
☽ ⚹ ♅	**2:35 pm**	11:35 am
☽ ⚺ ⚵	**6:06 pm**	3:06 pm
☉ □ ♆	**9:26 pm**	6:26 pm
☿ ⚻ ⚴	**9:52 pm**	6:52 pm

8 SUNDAY

☽ □ ♆	**4:13 am**	1:13 am
☽ ☌ ☉	**4:45 am**	1:45 am
☽ ☍ ⚳	**5:36 am**	2:36 am
☽ ☌ ⚶	**7:34 am**	4:34 am
☿ △ ♇	**8:01 am**	5:01 am
☽ ⚹ ♄	**1:10 pm**	10:10 am
☉ ☍ ⚳	**2:08 pm**	11:08 am
☽ △ ⚴	**3:08 pm**	12:08 pm
☽ ⚻ ♇	**4:18 pm**	1:18 pm
☽ ⚺ ☿	**5:24 pm**	2:24 pm
☽ ☌ ♀		10:15 pm

9 MONDAY

☽ ☌ ♀	**1:15 am**	
☽ △ ⚷	**9:42 am**	6:42 am
☽ □ ♂	**3:24 pm**	12:24 pm
☽ △ ♃	**10:23 pm**	7:23 pm
☽ □ ♅	**10:58 pm**	7:58 pm

10 TUESDAY

☽ ⚹ ⚵	**4:54 am**	1:54 am
☽ △ ♆	**1:05 pm**	10:05 am
☽ ⚻ ⚳	**1:30 pm**	10:30 am
☽ ⚺ ☉	**6:27 pm**	3:27 pm
☽ ⚺ ⚶	**6:40 pm**	3:40 pm
☽ ⚺ ♄	**10:47 pm**	7:47 pm
☉ ☌ ⚶	**11:27 pm**	8:27 pm
☽ □ ⚴		9:23 pm
☽ ☍ ♇		10:35 pm

11 WEDNESDAY

☽ □ ⚴	**12:23 am**	
☽ ☍ ♇	**1:35 am**	
☽ ⚹ ☿	**10:58 am**	7:58 am
♆ □ ⚳	**11:49 am**	8:49 am
☽ ⚺ ♀	**5:30 pm**	2:30 pm
☽ ⚻ ⚷	**7:49 pm**	4:49 pm

12 THURSDAY

☽ △ ♂	**5:28 am**	2:28 am
☽ □ ♃	**8:41 am**	5:41 am
☽ △ ♅	**9:46 am**	6:46 am
♀ △ ⚷	**4:16 pm**	1:16 pm
☽ □ ⚵	**6:25 pm**	3:25 pm
☽ △ ⚳	**11:38 pm**	8:38 pm
☽ ⚻ ♆		9:18 pm

13 FRIDAY

☽ ⚻ ♆	**12:18 am**	
☉ ⚹ ♄	**6:29 am**	3:29 am
☽ ⚹ ⚶	**8:20 am**	5:20 am
☽ ☌ ♄	**10:43 am**	7:43 am
☽ ⚹ ☉	**11:04 am**	8:04 am
☽ ⚹ ⚴	**11:58 am**	8:58 am
☽ ⚻ ♇	**1:06 pm**	10:06 am
☉ △ ⚴	**10:25 pm**	7:25 pm

14 SATURDAY

☿ □ ⚷	**5:24 am**	2:24 am
♂ ⚻ ♃	**6:55 am**	3:55 am
☽ ☍ ⚷	**7:54 am**	4:54 am
☽ □ ☿	**8:18 am**	5:18 am
☉ ⚻ ♇	**11:41 am**	8:41 am
☽ ⚹ ♀	**12:29 pm**	9:29 am
☽ ⚹ ♃	**8:42 pm**	5:42 pm
☽ ⚻ ♂	**9:40 pm**	6:40 pm
☽ ⚻ ♅	**10:16 pm**	7:16 pm

15 SUNDAY

♂ ☌ ♅	**7:53 am**	4:53 am
☽ △ ⚵	**9:36 am**	6:36 am
☽ □ ⚳	**11:03 am**	8:03 am
☽ ☍ ♆	**12:51 pm**	9:51 am
☽ □ ⚶	**11:13 pm**	8:13 pm
☽ ⚺ ♄	**11:44 pm**	8:44 pm
☽ ⚺ ⚴		9:38 pm
☽ △ ♇		10:32 pm

16 MONDAY

☽ ⚺ ⚴	**12:38 am**	
☽ △ ♇	**1:32 am**	
☽ □ ☉	**4:57 am**	1:57 am
⚳ ⚻ ⚵	**9:50 am**	6:50 am
♄ ⚹ ⚶	**4:10 pm**	1:10 pm
☽ ⚻ ⚷	**8:16 pm**	5:16 pm

17 TUESDAY

☽ △ ☿	**6:43 am**	3:43 am
☽ □ ♀	**7:39 am**	4:39 am
☽ ⚺ ♃	**8:35 am**	5:35 am
☽ ☍ ♅	**10:31 am**	7:31 am
☽ ☍ ♂	**1:36 pm**	10:36 am
♀ △ ♃	**4:34 pm**	1:34 pm
⚴ △ ⚶	**5:01 pm**	2:01 pm
☿ ⚻ ♃	**7:04 pm**	4:04 pm
☽ ⚹ ⚳	**9:48 pm**	6:48 pm
☽ ⚻ ⚵		9:01 pm
☽ ⚻ ♆		9:35 pm
☿ ⚺ ♀		9:47 pm

18 WEDNESDAY

☽ ⚻ ⚵	**12:01 am**	
☽ ⚻ ♆	**12:35 am**	
☿ ⚺ ♀	**12:47 am**	
☿ ⚹ ♅	**8:47 am**	5:47 am
♇ ⚻ ⚶	**11:09 am**	8:09 am
☽ ⚹ ♄	**11:29 am**	8:29 am
☽ ☌ ⚴	**12:08 pm**	9:08 am
♀ □ ♅	**12:36 pm**	9:36 am
☽ □ ♇	**12:42 pm**	9:42 am
☽ △ ⚶	**12:45 pm**	9:45 am
♆ ⚹ ⚵	**1:48 pm**	10:48 am
☽ △ ☉	**9:00 pm**	6:00 pm

19 THURSDAY

☽ △ ⚷	**6:37 am**	3:37 am
☽ ☌ ♃	**6:06 pm**	3:06 pm
☽ ⚻ ♅	**8:16 pm**	5:16 pm
☽ △ ♀	**11:32 pm**	8:32 pm
☽ ⚻ ☿		11:04 pm
☽ ⚻ ♂		11:27 pm

20 FRIDAY

☽ ⚻ ☿	**2:04 am**	
☽ ⚻ ♂	**2:27 am**	
☽ ⚺ ⚳	**5:54 am**	2:54 am
☿ ⚹ ♂	**6:02 am**	3:02 am
☽ △ ♆	**9:24 am**	6:24 am
☽ ☍ ⚵	**11:10 am**	8:10 am
☽ □ ♄	**8:02 pm**	5:02 pm
☽ ⚺ ⚴	**8:29 pm**	5:29 pm
☽ ⚹ ♇	**8:40 pm**	5:40 pm
☽ ⚻ ⚶	**10:44 pm**	7:44 pm
☿ ☍ ⚳		11:16 pm

21 SATURDAY

☿ ☍ ⚳	**2:16 am**	
☽ ⚻ ☉	**8:49 am**	5:49 am
☽ □ ⚷	**1:29 pm**	10:29 am
♇ □ ⚴	**11:44 pm**	8:44 pm
☽ ⚺ ♃		9:05 pm
☽ △ ♅		11:22 pm

22 SUNDAY

☽ ⚺ ♃	**12:05 am**	
☽ △ ♅	**2:22 am**	
♂ △ ⚳	**4:03 am**	1:03 am
☿ □ ♆	**4:20 am**	1:20 am
♀ ⚻ ⚳	**10:15 am**	7:15 am
☽ ☌ ⚳	**10:32 am**	7:32 am
☽ ⚻ ⚴	**10:34 am**	7:34 am
☽ △ ♂	**10:59 am**	7:59 am
☽ □ ♆	**2:35 pm**	11:35 am
☽ ☍ ☿	**4:14 pm**	1:14 pm
☽ ⚻ ⚵	**6:14 pm**	3:14 pm
♀ □ ♂	**9:21 pm**	6:21 pm
☽ △ ♄		9:54 pm
☽ ⚺ ♇		10:03 pm
☽ ⚹ ⚴		10:14 pm

23 MONDAY

☽ △ ♄	**12:54 am**	
☽ ⚺ ♇	**1:03 am**	
☽ ⚹ ⚴	**1:14 am**	
☽ ☍ ⚶	**4:46 am**	1:46 am
☿ ⚺ ⚵	**10:46 am**	7:46 am
☽ ☍ ☉	**4:18 pm**	1:18 pm
☽ ⚹ ⚷	**4:56 pm**	1:56 pm
♄ ⚻ ♇	**6:47 pm**	3:47 pm
☉ △ ⚷		10:28 pm
☽ ⚹ ♃		11:54 pm

24 TUESDAY

☉ △ ⚷	**1:28 am**	
☽ ⚹ ♃	**2:54 am**	
☽ □ ♅	**5:16 am**	2:16 am
♀ △ ♆	**8:11 am**	5:11 am
☽ ⚺ ⚳	**12:20 pm**	9:20 am
☽ □ ♂	**4:02 pm**	1:02 pm
☽ ⚹ ♆	**4:52 pm**	1:52 pm
☽ ☍ ♀	**5:40 pm**	2:40 pm
☽ △ ⚵	**10:11 pm**	7:11 pm
☽ ⚻ ☿		11:23 pm
☽ ☌ ♇		11:52 pm

25 WEDNESDAY

☽ ⚻ ☿	**2:23 am**	
☽ ☌ ♇	**2:52 am**	
☽ ⚻ ♄	**3:08 am**	12:08 am
☽ □ ⚴	**3:25 am**	12:25 am
☿ ⚻ ♇	**5:50 am**	2:50 am
☿ ⚹ ♄	**8:02 am**	5:02 am
☽ ⚻ ⚶	**8:03 am**	5:03 am
♂ ⚺ ♆	**9:00 am**	6:00 am
☿ △ ⚴	**10:10 am**	7:10 am
☽ ⚺ ⚷	**6:16 pm**	3:16 pm
☽ ⚻ ☉	**9:10 pm**	6:10 pm

26 THURSDAY

☽ □ ♃	**3:59 am**	12:59 am
☽ ⚹ ♅	**6:28 am**	3:28 am
☽ ⚹ ⚳	**12:46 pm**	9:46 am
☽ ⚺ ♆	**5:51 pm**	2:51 pm
☽ ⚹ ♂	**7:32 pm**	4:32 pm
☽ ⚻ ♀	**11:07 pm**	8:07 pm
☽ □ ⚵		9:55 pm

27 FRIDAY

☽ □ ⚵	**12:55 am**	
☽ ⚺ ♇	**3:44 am**	12:44 am
☿ ☌ ⚶	**4:07 am**	1:07 am
☽ ☍ ♄	**4:25 am**	1:25 am
☽ △ ⚴	**4:43 am**	1:43 am
☽ △ ⚶	**10:31 am**	7:31 am
☽ △ ☿	**11:22 am**	8:22 am
☽ ☌ ⚷	**7:13 pm**	4:13 pm
☽ △ ☉		10:41 pm

28 SATURDAY

☽ △ ☉	**1:41 am**	
☽ △ ♃	**5:02 am**	2:02 am
☽ ⚺ ♅	**7:43 am**	4:43 am
♀ ⚹ ⚵	**10:49 am**	7:49 am
☽ □ ⚳	**1:28 pm**	10:28 am
☽ ☌ ♆	**7:15 pm**	4:15 pm
☽ ⚺ ♂	**11:35 pm**	8:35 pm

29 SUNDAY

☽ ⚹ ⚵	**4:20 am**	1:20 am
☽ △ ♀	**5:18 am**	2:18 am
☽ ⚹ ♇	**5:19 am**	2:19 am
♀ ☍ ♇	**5:31 am**	2:31 am
☽ ⚻ ♄	**6:28 am**	3:28 am
☽ ⚻ ⚴	**6:48 am**	3:48 am
☽ □ ⚶	**1:59 pm**	10:59 am
☿ △ ⚷	**4:48 pm**	1:48 pm
♀ ⚺ ♄	**8:03 pm**	5:03 pm
☽ ⚺ ⚷	**9:18 pm**	6:18 pm
☽ □ ☿	**10:07 pm**	7:07 pm
♀ □ ⚴		9:37 pm

30 MONDAY

♀ □ ⚴	**12:37 am**	
☉ △ ♃	**3:23 am**	12:23 am
♇ △ ⚵	**6:33 am**	3:33 am
☽ ⚻ ♃	**7:29 am**	4:29 am
☽ □ ☉	**7:47 am**	4:47 am
☽ ☌ ♅	**10:23 am**	7:23 am
☽ △ ⚳	**3:43 pm**	12:43 pm
☽ ⚺ ♆	**10:19 pm**	7:19 pm

31 TUESDAY

☽ ☌ ♂	**5:38 am**	2:38 am
☽ □ ♇	**8:44 am**	5:44 am
☽ ⚺ ⚵	**9:48 am**	6:48 am
☽ △ ♄	**10:25 am**	7:25 am
☽ ☍ ⚴	**10:52 am**	7:52 am
☽ □ ♀	**1:53 pm**	10:53 am
☽ ⚹ ⚶	**7:35 pm**	4:35 pm
☉ □ ♅	**9:58 pm**	6:58 pm
☽ ⚹ ⚷		10:24 pm

MAY 2005

☽ Last Aspect				☽ Ingress			
day	EST / hr:mn / PST		asp	sign	day	EST / hr:mn / PST	
1		9:47 pm	⚹ ♇	♓	2	**10:43 am**	7:43 am
2	**12:47 am**		⚹ ♇	♓	2	**10:43 am**	7:43 am
4	**4:22 am**	1:22 am	□ ♇	♈	4	**2:36 pm**	11:36 am
6	**9:22 am**	6:22 am	△ ♇	♉	6	**8:01 pm**	5:01 pm
8		10:15 pm	☌ ♀	♊	9	**3:29 am**	12:29 am
9	**1:15 am**		☌ ♀	♊	9	**3:29 am**	12:29 am
11	**10:58 am**	7:58 am	⚹ ☿	♋	11	**1:20 pm**	10:20 am
13	**11:04 am**	8:04 am	⚹ ☉	♌	13		10:17 pm
13	**11:04 am**	8:04 am	⚹ ☉	♌	14	**1:17 am**	
16	**4:57 am**	1:57 am	□ ☉	♍	16	**1:46 pm**	10:46 am
18	**9:00 pm**	6:00 pm	△ ☉	♎	18		9:30 pm
18	**9:00 pm**	6:00 pm	△ ☉	♎	19	**12:30 am**	
20	**8:40 pm**	5:40 pm	⚹ ♇	♏	21	**7:49 am**	4:49 am
22		9:54 pm	△ ♄	♐	23	**11:38 am**	8:38 am
23	**12:54 am**		△ ♄	♐	23	**11:38 am**	8:38 am
24		11:52 pm	☌ ♇	♑	25	**1:11 pm**	10:11 am
25	**2:52 am**		☌ ♇	♑	25	**1:11 pm**	10:11 am
27	**11:22 am**	8:22 am	△ ☿	♒	27	**2:10 pm**	11:10 am
29	**5:19 am**	2:19 am	⚹ ♇	♓	29	**4:09 pm**	1:09 pm
31	**1:53 pm**	10:53 am	□ ♀	♈	31	**8:07 pm**	5:07 pm

☽ Phases & Eclipses			
phase	day	EST / hr:mn / PST	
4th Quarter	4/30		11:24 pm
4th Quarter	1	**2:24 am**	
New Moon	8	**4:45 am**	1:45 am
2nd Quarter	16	**4:57 am**	1:57 am
Full Moon	23	**4:18 pm**	1:18 pm
4th Quarter	30	**7:47 am**	4:47 am

Planet Ingress				
		day	EST / hr:mn / PST	
♀	♊	9		9:14 pm
♀	♊	10	**12:14 am**	
☿	♉	12	**5:13 am**	2:13 am
☉	♊	20	**6:47 pm**	3:47 pm
☿	♊	28	**6:44 am**	3:44 am

Planetary Motion				
		day	EST / hr:mn / PST	
⚷	℞	8	**9:47 pm**	6:47 pm
⚳	D	11	**9:45 pm**	6:45 pm
♆	℞	19	**7:36 pm**	4:36 pm

DATE		SID.TIME	SUN	MOON	NODE	MERCURY	VENUS	MARS	JUPITER	SATURN	URANUS	NEPTUNE	PLUTO	CERES	PALLAS	JUNO	VESTA	CHIRON
1	Su	14:36:05	10 ♉ 43 17	07 ♒ 11	22 ♈ 39	14 ♈ 09	18 ♉ 42	29 ♒ 55	10 ♎ ℞ 44	21 ♋ 48	09 ♓ 58	17 ♒ 30	24 ♐ ℞ 12	19 ♏ ℞ 58	23 ♍ ℞ 53	08 ♈ 35	16 ♉ 04	03 ♒ 15
2	M	14:40:02	11 41 31	21 22	22 40	15 21	19 56	00 ♓ 38	10 39	21 53	10 00	17 31	24 11	19 45	23 47	09 05	16 30	03 16
3	T	14:43:58	12 39 44	05 ♓ 25	22 40	16 35	21 10	01 22	10 33	21 57	10 02	17 31	24 10	19 32	23 43	09 36	16 57	03 16
4	W	14:47:55	13 37 54	19 20	22 42	17 51	22 24	02 05	10 27	22 01	10 04	17 32	24 09	19 19	23 39	10 06	17 23	03 16
5	Th	14:51:51	14 36 04	03 ♈ 05	22 43	19 10	23 38	02 49	10 22	22 05	10 06	17 33	24 08	19 05	23 35	10 37	17 50	03 17
6	F	14:55:48	15 34 12	16 38	22 ℞ 44	20 31	24 52	03 32	10 17	22 10	10 08	17 33	24 07	18 52	23 32	11 07	18 16	03 17
7	Sa	14:59:44	16 32 18	29 59	22 44	21 55	26 05	04 15	10 12	22 14	10 10	17 33	24 06	18 38	23 29	11 38	18 43	03 17
8	Su	15:03:41	17 30 23	13 ♉ 07	22 43	23 20	27 19	04 59	10 07	22 19	10 11	17 34	24 04	18 25	23 27	12 08	19 09	03 17
9	M	15:07:37	18 28 27	26 02	22 40	24 48	28 33	05 42	10 02	22 24	10 13	17 34	24 03	18 11	23 25	12 39	19 36	03 ℞ 17
10	T	15:11:34	19 26 29	08 ♊ 42	22 36	26 18	29 47	06 26	09 57	22 29	10 15	17 35	24 02	17 57	23 24	13 09	20 03	03 17
11	W	15:15:31	20 24 29	21 08	22 32	27 49	01 ♊ 01	07 09	09 53	22 34	10 16	17 35	24 01	17 44	23 23	13 40	20 29	03 17
12	Th	15:19:27	21 22 27	03 ♋ 23	22 27	29 23	02 15	07 52	09 48	22 38	10 18	17 35	24 00	17 30	23 D 23	14 10	20 55	03 17
13	F	15:23:24	22 20 24	15 26	22 23	00 ♉ 59	03 28	08 36	09 44	22 43	10 20	17 35	23 58	17 17	23 23	14 41	21 22	03 17
14	Sa	15:27:20	23 18 19	27 23	22 19	02 37	04 42	09 19	09 40	22 49	10 21	17 36	23 57	17 04	23 24	15 11	21 48	03 16
15	Su	15:31:17	24 16 12	09 ♌ 16	22 16	04 17	05 56	10 02	09 36	22 54	10 23	17 36	23 56	16 51	23 25	15 42	22 15	03 16
16	M	15:35:13	25 14 03	21 09	22 D 15	06 00	07 10	10 45	09 33	22 59	10 24	17 36	23 54	16 38	23 27	16 12	22 41	03 16
17	T	15:39:10	26 11 53	03 ♍ 07	22 15	07 44	08 23	11 28	09 29	23 04	10 26	17 36	23 53	16 25	23 29	16 43	23 08	03 15
18	W	15:43:06	27 09 41	15 16	22 16	09 30	09 37	12 12	09 26	23 10	10 27	17 36	23 52	16 12	23 31	17 14	23 34	03 14
19	Th	15:47:03	28 07 27	27 39	22 18	11 19	10 51	12 55	09 23	23 15	10 28	17 ℞ 36	23 50	15 59	23 34	17 44	24 01	03 14
20	F	15:51:00	29 05 12	10 ♎ 21	22 ℞ 19	13 09	12 04	13 38	09 20	23 21	10 30	17 36	23 49	15 47	23 37	18 15	24 27	03 13
21	Sa	15:54:56	00 ♊ 02 55	23 25	22 20	15 01	13 18	14 21	09 17	23 26	10 31	17 36	23 47	15 34	23 41	18 45	24 53	03 12
22	Su	15:58:53	01 00 36	06 ♏ 54	22 19	16 56	14 31	15 04	09 14	23 32	10 32	17 36	23 46	15 22	23 45	19 16	25 20	03 11
23	M	16:02:49	01 58 16	20 46	22 16	18 52	15 45	15 47	09 12	23 38	10 33	17 36	23 45	15 10	23 50	19 46	25 46	03 10
24	T	16:06:46	02 55 55	05 ♐ 00	22 12	20 51	16 59	16 30	09 10	23 44	10 34	17 36	23 43	14 59	23 55	20 17	26 12	03 09
25	W	16:10:42	03 53 33	19 30	22 06	22 51	18 12	17 13	09 07	23 49	10 35	17 36	23 42	14 47	24 00	20 47	26 38	03 08
26	Th	16:14:39	04 51 09	04 ♑ 11	22 00	24 54	19 26	17 55	09 05	23 55	10 36	17 36	23 40	14 36	24 06	21 18	27 05	03 07
27	F	16:18:36	05 48 45	18 54	21 54	26 58	20 39	18 38	09 04	24 01	10 37	17 35	23 39	14 25	24 12	21 49	27 31	03 06
28	Sa	16:22:32	06 46 19	03 ♒ 33	21 49	29 03	21 53	19 21	09 02	24 07	10 38	17 35	23 37	14 14	24 18	22 19	27 57	03 04
29	Su	16:26:29	07 43 53	18 02	21 45	01 ♊ 11	23 06	20 04	09 01	24 14	10 39	17 35	23 36	14 04	24 25	22 50	28 23	03 03
30	M	16:30:25	08 41 26	02 ♓ 16	21 D 44	03 19	24 20	20 46	08 59	24 20	10 40	17 35	23 34	13 54	24 32	23 20	28 50	03 02
31	T	16:34:22	09 38 57	16 14	21 44	05 29	25 33	21 29	08 58	24 26	10 40	17 34	23 33	13 44	24 40	23 51	29 16	03 00

EPHEMERIS CALCULATED FOR 12 MIDNIGHT GREENWICH MEAN TIME. ALL OTHER DATA AND FACING ASPECTARIAN PAGE IN **EASTERN TIME (BOLD)** AND PACIFIC TIME (REGULAR).

JUNE 2005

1 WEDNESDAY

☽⚹⚷	**1:24 am**	
♄□⚵	**6:45 am**	3:45 am
☿△♃	**10:11 am**	7:11 am
☽☍♃	**12:04 pm**	9:04 am
☽⚹☿	**12:26 pm**	9:26 am
☽⚺♅	**3:12 pm**	12:12 pm
☽⚹☉	**4:31 pm**	1:31 pm
☽⚻⚳	**8:06 pm**	5:06 pm
⚴⚻⚵		9:29 pm

2 THURSDAY

⚴⚻⚵	**12:29 am**	
☽⚹♆	**3:35 am**	12:35 am
☿□♅	**5:18 am**	2:18 am
☽⚺♂	**2:18 pm**	11:18 am
☽△♇	**2:21 pm**	11:21 am
♂□♇	**3:27 pm**	12:27 pm
☽□♄	**4:39 pm**	1:39 pm
☽⚻⚴	**5:15 pm**	2:15 pm
☽☌⚵	**5:44 pm**	2:44 pm
☽⚹♀		10:24 pm

3 FRIDAY

☽⚹♀	**1:24 am**	
☽⚺⚶	**3:38 am**	12:38 am
☉☌☿	**5:12 am**	2:12 am
☽□⚷	**7:41 am**	4:41 am
☿⚻⚳	**8:32 am**	5:32 am
☉⚻⚳	**12:20 pm**	9:20 am
☽⚻♃	**6:53 pm**	3:53 pm
☽⚹♅	**10:12 pm**	7:12 pm
☽☍⚳		11:38 pm

4 SATURDAY

☽☍⚳	**2:38 am**	
☽⚺☉	**3:58 am**	12:58 am
☽⚺☿	**6:38 am**	3:38 am
☽□♆	**10:59 am**	7:59 am
♀⚺⚶	**1:07 pm**	10:07 am
♂△♄	**5:42 pm**	2:42 pm
☽⚻♇	**10:05 pm**	7:05 pm
☽⚹♄		10:03 pm
☽⚹♂		10:25 pm
☽△⚴		10:53 pm

Eastern time in bold type
Pacific time in medium type

5 SUNDAY

☽⚹♄	**1:03 am**	
☽⚹♂	**1:25 am**	
☽△⚴	**1:53 am**	
☽⚺⚵	**4:03 am**	1:03 am
☿△♆	**7:48 am**	4:48 am
♂☍⚴	**11:49 am**	8:49 am
☽☌⚶	**1:58 pm**	10:58 am
☽⚺♀	**3:42 pm**	12:42 pm
☽△⚷	**4:00 pm**	1:00 pm
♀⚻⚷	**6:50 pm**	3:50 pm

6 MONDAY

☽△♃	**3:43 am**	12:43 am
☽□♅	**7:12 am**	4:12 am
☽⚻⚳	**11:09 am**	8:09 am
☽☌☉	**5:55 pm**	2:55 pm
☽△♆	**8:20 pm**	5:20 pm

7 TUESDAY

☽☌☿	**4:15 am**	1:15 am
☽☍♇	**7:43 am**	4:43 am
☽⚺♄	**11:27 am**	8:27 am
☽□⚴	**12:34 pm**	9:34 am
☽□♂	**2:50 pm**	11:50 am
☽⚹⚵	**4:32 pm**	1:32 pm
⚷△⚶	**9:03 pm**	6:03 pm
☿☍♇	**11:43 pm**	8:43 pm
☉△♆		9:52 pm
☽⚻⚷		11:12 pm
☽⚺⚶		11:25 pm

8 WEDNESDAY

☉△♆	**12:52 am**	
☽⚻⚷	**2:12 am**	
☽⚺⚶	**2:25 am**	
☽☌♀	**8:34 am**	5:34 am
☽□♃	**2:29 pm**	11:29 am
☽△♅	**6:03 pm**	3:03 pm
☽△⚳	**9:32 pm**	6:32 pm
☿⚺♄	**10:59 pm**	7:59 pm

9 THURSDAY

☿□⚴	**7:02 am**	4:02 am
☽⚻♆	**7:31 am**	4:31 am
☽⚺☉	**10:12 am**	7:12 am
☽⚻♇	**7:08 pm**	4:08 pm
☽☌♄	**11:40 pm**	8:40 pm
☽⚹⚴		10:09 pm

10 FRIDAY

☽⚹⚴	**1:09 am**	
☽⚺☿	**4:44 am**	1:44 am
☽△♂	**6:18 am**	3:18 am
☽□⚵	**6:58 am**	3:58 am
☽☍⚷	**2:02 pm**	11:02 am
☽⚹⚶	**4:42 pm**	1:42 pm
☿□♂	**5:18 pm**	2:18 pm
♀□♃	**7:38 pm**	4:38 pm
☿⚹⚵	**8:48 pm**	5:48 pm
☽⚹♃		11:49 pm

11 SATURDAY

☽⚹♃	**2:49 am**	
☽⚺♀	**3:38 am**	12:38 am
☽⚻♅	**6:25 am**	3:25 am
☽□⚳	**9:25 am**	6:25 am
☽☍♆	**8:00 pm**	5:00 pm
♂⚺⚵	**10:30 pm**	7:30 pm

12 SUNDAY

☽⚹☉	**4:06 am**	1:06 am
♀△♅	**6:41 am**	3:41 am
☽△♇	**7:40 am**	4:40 am
☿⚻⚷	**9:16 am**	6:16 am
☽⚺♄	**12:56 pm**	9:56 am
☽⚺⚴	**2:50 pm**	11:50 am
☽△⚵	**10:23 pm**	7:23 pm
☽⚻♂	**10:47 pm**	7:47 pm
☽⚻⚷		11:33 pm

13 MONDAY

☽⚻⚷	**2:33 am**	
☽⚹☿	**6:10 am**	3:10 am
☽□⚶	**7:40 am**	4:40 am
♀△⚳	**8:23 am**	5:23 am
☽⚺♃	**3:33 pm**	12:33 pm
☿⚺⚶	**5:06 pm**	2:06 pm
☽☍♅	**7:00 pm**	4:00 pm
☽⚹⚳	**9:31 pm**	6:31 pm
☽⚹♀	**11:06 pm**	8:06 pm
☉☍♇	**11:15 pm**	8:15 pm

14 TUESDAY

☽⚻♆	**8:17 am**	5:17 am
☽□♇	**7:36 pm**	4:36 pm
☽□☉	**9:22 pm**	6:22 pm
☽⚹♄		10:24 pm

15 WEDNESDAY

☽⚹♄	**1:24 am**	
☽☌⚴	**3:41 am**	12:41 am
♂⚹⚷	**12:03 pm**	9:03 am
☽⚻⚵	**12:30 pm**	9:30 am
☽△⚷	**1:46 pm**	10:46 am
☽☍♂	**1:53 pm**	10:53 am
☿□♃	**3:42 pm**	12:42 pm
☽△⚶	**8:58 pm**	5:58 pm
☽☌♃		11:31 pm

16 THURSDAY

☽☌♃	**2:31 am**	
☽□☿	**4:26 am**	1:26 am
☽⚻♅	**5:40 am**	2:40 am
☽⚺⚳	**7:44 am**	4:44 am
☿△♅	**12:36 pm**	9:36 am
☽□♀	**3:45 pm**	12:45 pm
⚷□⚵	**5:18 pm**	2:18 pm
☽△♆	**6:11 pm**	3:11 pm
☿△⚳		10:50 pm

17 FRIDAY

☿△⚳	**1:50 am**	
☽⚹♇	**4:46 am**	1:46 am
☉⚺♄	**7:47 am**	4:47 am
☽□♄	**10:50 am**	7:50 am
☽△☉	**11:02 am**	8:02 am
☽⚺⚴	**1:23 pm**	10:23 am
♀⚻♆	**5:04 pm**	2:04 pm
☽□⚷	**9:41 pm**	6:41 pm
☽☍⚵	**10:53 pm**	7:53 pm
☽⚻♂		10:00 pm

18 SATURDAY

☽⚻♂	**1:00 am**	
☽⚻⚶	**6:23 am**	3:23 am
☽⚺♃	**9:51 am**	6:51 am
☽△♅	**12:37 pm**	9:37 am
☽☌⚳	**2:19 pm**	11:19 am
☽△☿	**8:10 pm**	5:10 pm
☽□♆		9:11 pm

19 SUNDAY

☽□♆	**12:11 am**	
☽△♀	**3:12 am**	12:12 am
☉□⚴	**4:28 am**	1:28 am
☽⚺♇	**9:56 am**	6:56 am
☽△♄	**4:06 pm**	1:06 pm
☽⚹⚴	**6:52 pm**	3:52 pm
☽⚻☉	**7:40 pm**	4:40 pm
☽⚹⚷		10:34 pm
☿⚻♆		11:58 pm

20 MONDAY

☽⚹⚷	**1:34 am**	
☿⚻♆	**2:58 am**	
☽⚻⚵	**4:45 am**	1:45 am
☽△♂	**7:25 am**	4:25 am
☽☍⚶	**11:23 am**	8:23 am
☽⚹♃	**1:13 pm**	10:13 am
☽□♅	**3:38 pm**	12:38 pm
☽⚺⚳	**5:05 pm**	2:05 pm
☽⚹♆		11:25 pm

21 TUESDAY

☽⚹♆	**2:25 am**	
☽⚻☿	**5:35 am**	2:35 am
☽⚻♀	**9:48 am**	6:48 am
☽☌♇	**11:34 am**	8:34 am
☽⚻♄	**5:54 pm**	2:54 pm
☽□⚴	**8:55 pm**	5:55 pm
☽☍☉		9:14 pm
☽⚺⚷		11:22 pm

22 WEDNESDAY

☽☍☉	**12:14 am**	
☽⚺⚷	**2:22 am**	
♀⚻♇	**6:55 am**	3:55 am
☽△⚵	**7:14 am**	4:14 am
☽□♂	**10:25 am**	7:25 am
☽⚻⚶	**1:20 pm**	10:20 am
☽□♃	**1:50 pm**	10:50 am
☽⚹♅	**4:00 pm**	1:00 pm
☽⚹⚳	**5:20 pm**	2:20 pm
☽⚺♆		11:26 pm

23 THURSDAY

☽⚺♆	**2:26 am**	
☉⚻⚷	**8:17 am**	5:17 am
♃△⚶	**9:41 am**	6:41 am
☿⚻♇	**9:55 am**	6:55 am
☽⚺♇	**11:22 am**	8:22 am
☽☍☿	**11:32 am**	8:32 am
☽☍♀	**1:54 pm**	10:54 am
☽☍♄	**6:04 pm**	3:04 pm
☽△⚴	**9:27 pm**	6:27 pm
☽☌⚷		10:56 pm

24 FRIDAY

☽☌⚷	**1:56 am**	
☽⚻☉	**3:11 am**	12:11 am
☽□⚵	**8:37 am**	5:37 am
☽⚹♂	**12:24 pm**	9:24 am
☽△♃	**1:45 pm**	10:45 am
☽△⚶	**2:28 pm**	11:28 am
☽⚺♅	**3:44 pm**	12:44 pm
☽□⚳	**5:03 pm**	2:03 pm
☽☌♆		11:17 pm

25 SATURDAY

☽☌♆	**2:17 am**	
☽⚹♇	**11:23 am**	8:23 am
☽⚻☿	**5:28 pm**	2:28 pm
☽⚻♀	**6:26 pm**	3:26 pm
☽⚻♄	**6:46 pm**	3:46 pm
♂☍♃	**9:03 pm**	6:03 pm
☽⚻⚴	**10:41 pm**	7:41 pm
♀☌♄	**10:59 pm**	7:59 pm
☽⚺⚷		11:20 pm

26 SUNDAY

☽⚺⚷	**2:20 am**	
☿☌♄	**6:58 am**	3:58 am
☽△☉	**7:14 am**	4:14 am
♅□⚶	**10:26 am**	7:26 am
☽⚹⚵	**11:12 am**	8:12 am
☽⚻♃	**3:01 pm**	12:01 pm
☽⚺♂	**3:49 pm**	12:49 pm
☽☌♅	**4:51 pm**	1:51 pm
☽□⚶	**5:03 pm**	2:03 pm
☽△⚳	**6:14 pm**	3:14 pm

27 MONDAY

☽⚺♆	**3:52 am**	12:52 am
☽□♇	**1:26 pm**	10:26 am
♂⚺♅	**1:29 pm**	10:29 am
☿☌♀	**2:39 pm**	11:39 am
☽△♄	**9:47 pm**	6:47 pm
☽△♀		10:51 pm
☽△☿		11:04 pm
☽☍⚴		11:27 pm

28 TUESDAY

☽△♀	**1:51 am**	
☽△☿	**2:04 am**	
☽☍⚴	**2:27 am**	
☽⚹⚷	**5:09 am**	2:09 am
☿⚹⚴	**6:21 am**	3:21 am
⚳⚻⚶	**9:59 am**	6:59 am
♀⚹⚴	**10:15 am**	7:15 am
☽□☉	**2:23 pm**	11:23 am
☽⚺⚵	**4:44 pm**	1:44 pm
☽☍♃	**7:02 pm**	4:02 pm
♂⚻⚳	**8:03 pm**	5:03 pm
☽⚺♅	**8:42 pm**	5:42 pm
☽⚻⚳	**10:15 pm**	7:15 pm
☽☌♂	**10:21 pm**	7:21 pm
☽⚹⚶	**10:38 pm**	7:38 pm

29 WEDNESDAY

☿☍⚷	**6:59 am**	3:59 am
☽⚹♆	**8:21 am**	5:21 am
♂⚹⚶	**12:40 pm**	9:40 am
♀☍⚷	**1:51 pm**	10:51 am
☽△♇	**6:29 pm**	3:29 pm

30 THURSDAY

☽□♄	**3:57 am**	12:57 am
☽⚻⚴	**9:30 am**	6:30 am
☽□⚷	**11:02 am**	8:02 am
☽□♀	**1:19 pm**	10:19 am
☽□☿	**2:28 pm**	11:28 am
☽⚹☉		10:24 pm
☽☌⚵		10:42 pm
☽⚻♃		11:12 pm

JUNE 2005

☽ Last Aspect day	EST / hr:mn / PST	asp	☽ Ingress sign day	EST / hr:mn / PST
2	10:24 pm	⚹♀	♉ 2	11:20 pm
3	**1:24 am**	⚹♀	♉ 3	**2:20 am**
4	10:25 pm	⚹♂	♊ 5	**10:36 am** 7:36 am
5	**1:25 am**	⚹♂	♊ 5	**10:36 am** 7:36 am
7	**2:50 pm** 11:50 am	□♂	♋ 7	**8:46 pm** 5:46 pm
10	**6:18 am** 3:18 am	△♂	♌ 10	**8:39 am** 5:39 am
12	**7:40 am** 4:40 am	△♇	♍ 12	**9:22 pm** 6:22 pm
14	10:24 pm	⚹♄	♎ 15	**8:59 pm** 5:59 pm
15	**1:24 am**	⚹♄	♎ 15	**8:59 pm** 5:59 pm
17	**11:02 am** 8:02 am	△☉	♏ 17	**5:23 pm** 2:23 pm
19	**4:06 pm** 1:06 pm	△♄	♐ 19	**9:45 pm** 6:45 pm
21	**11:34 am** 8:34 am	☌♇	♑ 21	**10:52 pm** 7:52 pm
23	**6:04 pm** 3:04 pm	☍♄	♒ 23	**10:36 pm** 7:36 pm
25	**11:23 am** 8:23 am	⚹♇	♓ 25	**11:03 pm** 8:03 pm
27	10:51 pm	△♀	♈ 27	10:51 pm
28	**1:51 am**	△♀	♈ 28	**1:51 am**
30	**3:57 am** 12:57 am	□♄	♉ 30	**7:45 am** 4:45 am

☽ Phases & Eclipses phase	day	EST / hr:mn / PST
New Moon	6	**5:55 pm** 2:55 pm
2nd Quarter	14	**9:22 pm** 6:22 pm
Full Moon	21	9:14 pm
Full Moon	22	**12:14 am**
4th Quarter	28	**2:23 pm** 11:23 am

Planet Ingress	day	EST / hr:mn / PST
⚶ ♊	1	**12:31 pm** 9:31 am
♀ ♋	3	**11:18 am** 8:18 am
☿ ♋	11	**3:03 am** 12:03 am
♂ ♈	11	**10:30 pm** 7:30 pm
⚵ ♉	11	**10:30 pm** 7:30 pm
☉ ♋	20	11:46 pm
☉ ♋	21	**2:46 am**
⚴ ♎	26	**7:04 pm** 4:04 pm
☿ ♌	27	9:01 pm
☿ ♌	28	**12:01 am**

Planet Ingress	day	EST / hr:mn / PST
♀ ♌	27	10:53 pm
♀ ♌	28	**1:53 am**

Planetary Motion	day	EST / hr:mn / PST
♃ D	5	**3:20 am** 12:20 am
♅ ℞	14	**6:38 pm** 3:38 pm
⚷ D	26	**8:27 am** 5:27 am

DATE		SID.TIME	SUN	MOON	NODE	MERCURY	VENUS	MARS	JUPITER	SATURN	URANUS	NEPTUNE	PLUTO	CERES	PALLAS	JUNO	VESTA	CHIRON
1	W	16:38:18	10 ♊ 36 28	29 ♓ 56	21 ♈ 44	07 ♊ 40	26 ♊ 46	22 ♓ 12	08 ♎ ℞ 58	24 ♋ 32	10 ♓ 41	17 ♒ ℞ 34	23 ♐ ℞ 31	13 ♍ ℞ 35	24 ♍ 48	24 ♈ 21	29 ♉ 42	02 ♒ ℞ 59
2	Th	16:42:15	11 33 59	13 ♈ 22	21 ℞ 45	09 51	28 00	22 54	08 57	24 39	10 42	17 34	23 30	13 25	24 56	24 52	00 ♊ 08	02 57
3	F	16:46:11	12 31 28	26 33	21 46	12 03	29 13	23 37	08 56	24 45	10 42	17 33	23 28	13 16	25 05	25 22	00 34	02 55
4	Sa	16:50:08	13 28 57	09 ♉ 32	21 44	14 15	00 ♋ 27	24 19	08 56	24 51	10 43	17 33	23 27	13 08	25 14	25 53	01 00	02 53
5	Su	16:54:05	14 26 25	22 19	21 40	16 27	01 40	25 01	08 D 56	24 58	10 43	17 32	23 25	13 00	25 23	26 23	01 26	02 52
6	M	16:58:01	15 23 52	04 ♊ 55	21 34	18 39	02 53	25 44	08 56	25 04	10 44	17 32	23 24	12 52	25 32	26 54	01 52	02 50
7	T	17:01:58	16 21 18	17 21	21 26	20 50	04 07	26 26	08 56	25 11	10 44	17 31	23 22	12 44	25 42	27 24	02 19	02 48
8	W	17:05:54	17 18 44	29 37	21 16	23 00	05 20	27 08	08 56	25 18	10 45	17 30	23 20	12 37	25 53	27 55	02 45	02 46
9	Th	17:09:51	18 16 08	11 ♋ 44	21 05	25 09	06 33	27 50	08 57	25 24	10 45	17 30	23 19	12 30	26 03	28 25	03 10	02 44
10	F	17:13:47	19 13 32	23 43	20 55	27 17	07 47	28 32	08 58	25 31	10 45	17 29	23 17	12 24	26 14	28 56	03 36	02 42
11	Sa	17:17:44	20 10 55	05 ♌ 37	20 46	29 23	09 00	29 14	08 59	25 38	10 45	17 29	23 16	12 18	26 25	29 26	04 02	02 39
12	Su	17:21:40	21 08 16	17 28	20 39	01 ♋ 28	10 13	29 56	09 00	25 45	10 46	17 28	23 14	12 12	26 37	29 57	04 28	02 37
13	M	17:25:37	22 05 37	29 19	20 34	03 31	11 26	00 ♈ 37	09 01	25 52	10 46	17 27	23 13	12 07	26 48	00 ♉ 27	04 54	02 35
14	T	17:29:34	23 02 57	11 ♍ 16	20 31	05 31	12 40	01 19	09 03	25 59	10 ℞ 46	17 26	23 11	12 02	27 01	00 58	05 20	02 32
15	W	17:33:30	24 00 16	23 22	20 D 31	07 30	13 53	02 01	09 04	26 05	10 46	17 26	23 09	11 57	27 13	01 28	05 46	02 30
16	Th	17:37:27	24 57 34	05 ♎ 42	20 31	09 27	15 06	02 42	09 06	26 12	10 46	17 25	23 08	11 53	27 25	01 58	06 11	02 28
17	F	17:41:23	25 54 51	18 22	20 ℞ 31	11 21	16 19	03 24	09 08	26 20	10 46	17 24	23 06	11 49	27 38	02 29	06 37	02 25
18	Sa	17:45:20	26 52 07	01 ♏ 26	20 31	13 13	17 32	04 05	09 10	26 27	10 46	17 23	23 05	11 46	27 51	02 59	07 03	02 23
19	Su	17:49:16	27 49 22	14 58	20 29	15 03	18 45	04 46	09 13	26 34	10 45	17 22	23 03	11 43	28 05	03 29	07 29	02 20
20	M	17:53:13	28 46 37	28 58	20 24	16 50	19 58	05 27	09 15	26 41	10 45	17 21	23 01	11 40	28 18	04 00	07 54	02 17
21	T	17:57:09	29 43 52	13 ♐ 24	20 17	18 35	21 11	06 08	09 18	26 48	10 45	17 20	23 00	11 38	28 32	04 30	08 20	02 15
22	W	18:01:06	00 ♋ 41 05	28 13	20 08	20 18	22 24	06 49	09 21	26 55	10 45	17 19	22 58	11 36	28 46	05 00	08 45	02 12
23	Th	18:05:03	01 38 19	13 ♑ 15	19 58	21 59	23 37	07 30	09 24	27 02	10 44	17 18	22 57	11 34	29 01	05 31	09 11	02 09
24	F	18:08:59	02 35 32	28 22	19 48	23 37	24 50	08 11	09 27	27 10	10 44	17 17	22 55	11 33	29 15	06 01	09 36	02 06
25	Sa	18:12:56	03 32 45	13 ♒ 23	19 40	25 13	26 03	08 52	09 30	27 17	10 43	17 16	22 54	11 33	29 30	06 31	10 02	02 03
26	Su	18:16:52	04 29 57	28 09	19 33	26 46	27 16	09 32	09 34	27 24	10 43	17 15	22 52	11 D 32	29 45	07 01	10 27	02 00
27	M	18:20:49	05 27 10	12 ♓ 35	19 29	28 17	28 29	10 13	09 37	27 32	10 42	17 14	22 51	11 32	00 ♎ 01	07 31	10 53	01 57
28	T	18:24:45	06 24 22	26 38	19 D 28	29 45	29 42	10 53	09 41	27 39	10 42	17 13	22 49	11 33	00 16	08 01	11 18	01 55
29	W	18:28:42	07 21 35	10 ♈ 18	19 ℞ 28	01 ♌ 12	00 ♌ 55	11 33	09 45	27 47	10 41	17 12	22 48	11 33	00 32	08 31	11 43	01 51
30	Th	18:32:38	08 18 48	23 36	19 28	02 35	02 08	12 13	09 49	27 54	10 41	17 11	22 46	11 34	00 48	09 01	12 09	01 48

EPHEMERIS CALCULATED FOR 12 MIDNIGHT GREENWICH MEAN TIME. ALL OTHER DATA AND FACING ASPECTARIAN PAGE IN **EASTERN TIME (BOLD)** AND PACIFIC TIME (REGULAR).

JULY 2005

1 FRIDAY

☽✶☉	**1:24 am**	
☽☌⚴	**1:42 am**	
☽⊼♃	**2:12 am**	
☽✶♅	**3:36 am**	12:36 am
☽☍⚳	**5:23 am**	2:23 am
☽⊻⚵	**7:34 am**	4:34 am
☽⊻♂	**8:27 am**	5:27 am
☉✶⚴	**9:38 am**	6:38 am
☉□♃	**1:10 pm**	10:10 am
☽□♆	**3:51 pm**	12:51 pm
♃⊼⚴	**4:57 pm**	1:57 pm
☽⊼♇		11:26 pm

2 SATURDAY

☽⊼♇	**2:26 am**	
☉△♅	**6:40 am**	3:40 am
☽✶♄	**1:02 pm**	10:02 am
☽△♀	**7:32 pm**	4:32 pm
☽△⚷	**7:37 pm**	4:37 pm
⚷△♀	**10:44 pm**	7:44 pm
♅✶⚴		10:16 pm

3 SUNDAY

♅✶⚴	**1:16 am**	
☽✶♀	**4:25 am**	1:25 am
☽✶☿	**6:02 am**	3:02 am
☉△⚳	**8:54 am**	5:54 am
☽△♃	**12:00 pm**	9:00 am
☽□♅	**1:01 pm**	10:01 am
☽⊻⚴	**1:32 pm**	10:32 am
☽⊼⚳	**3:07 pm**	12:07 pm
☽⊻☉	**3:37 pm**	12:37 pm
☽☌⚵	**7:15 pm**	4:15 pm
☽✶♂	**9:24 pm**	6:24 pm
☽△♆		10:40 pm

4 MONDAY

☽△♆	**1:40 am**	
☽☍♇	**12:36 pm**	9:36 am
☽⊻♄		9:15 pm

5 TUESDAY

☽⊻♄	**12:15 am**	
☽⊼⚷	**6:08 am**	3:08 am
☽□♀	**7:43 am**	4:43 am
⚳☍⚴	**8:45 am**	5:45 am
☽⊻♀	**10:03 pm**	7:03 pm
☽⊻☿	**11:26 pm**	8:26 pm
☽□♃	**11:38 pm**	8:38 pm
☽△♅		9:11 pm
☿✶♃		10:52 pm
☽△⚳		11:40 pm

6 WEDNESDAY

☽△♅	**12:11 am**	
☿✶♃	**1:52 am**	
☽△⚳	**2:40 am**	
☽✶⚴	**3:21 am**	12:21 am
☿⊼♅	**7:43 am**	4:43 am
☽☌☉	**8:02 am**	5:02 am
☽⊻⚵	**8:47 am**	5:47 am
☽□♂	**12:17 pm**	9:17 am
☽⊼♆	**1:06 pm**	10:06 am
♀✶♃	**2:52 pm**	11:52 am
♀⊼♅	**7:03 pm**	4:03 pm
☉⊻⚵	**11:57 pm**	8:57 pm
☽⊼♇		9:15 pm
♂✶♆		11:59 pm

7 THURSDAY

☽⊼♇	**12:15 am**	
♂✶♆	**2:59 am**	
☽☌♄	**12:54 pm**	9:54 am
☿□⚳	**2:13 pm**	11:13 am
☽☍⚷	**5:59 pm**	2:59 pm
☽✶♀	**9:21 pm**	6:21 pm
♀□⚳	**10:11 pm**	7:11 pm

8 FRIDAY

☽✶♃	**12:29 pm**	9:29 am
☽⊼♅	**12:30 pm**	9:30 am
♃⊼♅	**2:21 pm**	11:21 am
☽□⚳	**3:27 pm**	12:27 pm
☽☌♀	**5:18 pm**	2:18 pm
☽☌☿	**5:36 pm**	2:36 pm
☽□⚴	**6:27 pm**	3:27 pm
☉⊼♆	**10:17 pm**	7:17 pm
☽✶⚵	**11:30 pm**	8:30 pm
☽☍♆		10:34 pm
☽⊻☉		10:51 pm

9 SATURDAY

☽☍♆	**1:34 am**	
☽⊻☉	**1:51 am**	
☽△♂	**4:21 am**	1:21 am
☿☌♀	**5:43 am**	2:43 am
♀□⚴	**11:25 am**	8:25 am
☽△♇	**12:49 pm**	9:49 am
☿□⚴	**3:09 pm**	12:09 pm
☽⊻♄		11:20 pm

10 SUNDAY

☽⊻♄	**2:20 am**	
☽⊼⚷	**6:29 am**	3:29 am
☽⊻♀	**11:42 am**	8:42 am
☽☍♅		10:10 pm
☽⊻♃		10:45 pm

11 MONDAY

☽☍♅	**1:10 am**	
☽⊻♃	**1:45 am**	
☽✶⚳	**4:37 am**	1:37 am
♆△⚵	**7:26 am**	4:26 am
☽△⚴	**9:47 am**	6:47 am
☽⊻☿	**11:14 am**	8:14 am
☽⊻♀	**12:53 pm**	9:53 am
☽⊼♆	**2:06 pm**	11:06 am
☽□⚵	**2:21 pm**	11:21 am
☽✶☉	**7:46 pm**	4:46 pm
☽⊼♂	**8:25 pm**	5:25 pm
♀☍♆		9:46 pm
☽□♇		10:12 pm

12 TUESDAY

♀☍♆	**12:46 am**	
☽□♇	**1:12 am**	
♀✶⚵	**10:14 am**	7:14 am
☽✶♄	**3:12 pm**	12:12 pm
☽△⚷	**6:20 pm**	3:20 pm
☉□♂	**7:00 pm**	4:00 pm
☽☌♀		10:14 pm

13 WEDNESDAY

☽☌♀	**1:14 am**	
☿☍♆	**7:12 am**	4:12 am
☽⊼♅	**12:37 pm**	9:37 am
☽☌♃	**1:46 pm**	10:46 am
☽⊻⚳	**4:29 pm**	1:29 pm
☽⊼⚴	**11:26 pm**	8:26 pm
☽△♆		10:01 pm
☽✶☿		11:05 pm

14 THURSDAY

☽△♆	**1:01 am**	
☽✶☿	**2:05 am**	
☽△⚵	**3:23 am**	12:23 am
☽✶♀	**6:16 am**	3:16 am
☽☍♂	**10:15 am**	7:15 am
☽□☉	**11:20 am**	8:20 am
☽✶♇	**11:36 am**	8:36 am
☉⊼♇	**2:55 pm**	11:55 am
☽□♄		10:32 pm

15 FRIDAY

☽□♄	**1:32 am**	
☽□⚷	**3:39 am**	12:39 am
☽⊻♀	**11:47 am**	8:47 am
♂△♇	**12:37 pm**	9:37 am
♆□⚴	**2:13 pm**	11:13 am
☽△♅	**8:56 pm**	5:56 pm
☽⊻♃	**10:34 pm**	7:34 pm
☽☌⚳		10:06 pm

16 SATURDAY

☽☌⚳	**1:06 am**	
☽□♆	**8:29 am**	5:29 am
☽☍⚴	**9:12 am**	6:12 am
☽□☿	**12:03 pm**	9:03 am
☽⊼⚵	**12:30 pm**	9:30 am
♀△♇	**1:13 pm**	10:13 am
☽⊻♇	**6:19 pm**	3:19 pm
☽□♀	**6:49 pm**	3:49 pm
☽⊼♂	**7:47 pm**	4:47 pm
☽△☉	**10:15 pm**	7:15 pm

17 SUNDAY

☽△♄	**7:48 am**	4:48 am
☽✶⚷	**9:01 am**	6:01 am
♀△♂	**4:27 pm**	1:27 pm
☽✶♀	**5:59 pm**	2:59 pm
☽□♅		10:09 pm

18 MONDAY

☽□♅	**1:09 am**	
☽✶♃	**3:09 am**	12:09 am
☽⊻⚳	**5:32 am**	2:32 am
☽✶♆	**11:50 am**	8:50 am
☽⊼⚴	**2:22 pm**	11:22 am
☽△☿	**4:45 pm**	1:45 pm
☽☍⚵	**5:07 pm**	2:07 pm
☽☌♇	**8:59 pm**	5:59 pm
☽△♂		9:39 pm
☽△♀		11:03 pm

19 TUESDAY

☽△♂	**12:39 am**	
☽△♀	**2:03 am**	
☽⊼☉	**4:12 am**	1:12 am
☽⊼♄	**10:04 am**	7:04 am
☽⊻⚷	**10:36 am**	7:36 am
☽□♀	**8:17 pm**	5:17 pm
☽✶♅		10:53 pm

20 WEDNESDAY

☽✶♅	**1:53 am**	
☽□♃	**4:15 am**	1:15 am
☽✶⚳	**6:32 am**	3:32 am
☽⊻♆	**12:02 pm**	9:02 am
☽△⚴	**4:08 pm**	1:08 pm
☽⊼☿	**5:39 pm**	2:39 pm
☽⊼⚵	**6:29 pm**	3:29 pm
☽⊻♇	**8:49 pm**	5:49 pm
☽□♂		11:24 pm

21 THURSDAY

☽□♂	**2:24 am**	
♄☍⚷	**4:09 am**	1:09 am
☽⊼♀	**5:50 am**	2:50 am
☽☍☉	**7:00 am**	4:00 am
☽☌⚷	**9:52 am**	6:52 am
☽☍♄	**9:56 am**	6:56 am
☽△♀	**8:33 pm**	5:33 pm
☽⊻♅		9:57 pm

22 FRIDAY

☽⊻♅	**12:57 am**	
☽△♃	**3:45 am**	12:45 am
☽□⚳	**6:05 am**	3:05 am
☽☌♆	**11:03 am**	8:03 am
☽□⚴	**4:46 pm**	1:46 pm
☽☍☿	**5:03 pm**	2:03 pm
☽△⚵	**6:52 pm**	3:52 pm
☽✶♇	**7:52 pm**	4:52 pm
☿□⚴		11:04 pm
☉☍⚷		11:30 pm

23 SATURDAY

☿□⚴	**2:04 am**	
☉☍⚷	**2:30 am**	
☽✶♂	**3:33 am**	12:33 am
♀⊼⚷	**6:59 am**	3:59 am
☽⊻⚷	**8:59 am**	5:59 am
☽☍♀	**9:10 am**	6:10 am
☽⊼☉	**9:27 am**	6:27 am
☽⊼♄	**9:39 am**	6:39 am
☉☌♄	**1:00 pm**	10:00 am
♀⊻♄	**3:49 pm**	12:49 pm
☽⊼♀	**9:12 pm**	6:12 pm
☽☌♅		9:35 pm
☉⊻♀		10:12 pm

24 SUNDAY

☽☌♅	**12:35 am**	
☉⊻♀	**1:12 am**	
☽⊼♃	**3:59 am**	12:59 am
☽△⚳	**6:29 am**	3:29 am
♇☍⚵	**7:19 am**	4:19 am
☽⊻♆	**11:04 am**	8:04 am
☽⊼☿	**5:13 pm**	2:13 pm
☽✶⚴	**6:47 pm**	3:47 pm
☽□♇	**8:19 pm**	5:19 pm
☽□⚵	**8:43 pm**	5:43 pm

25 MONDAY

☽⊻♂	**6:37 am**	3:37 am
☽✶⚷	**10:01 am**	7:01 am
☽△♄	**11:22 am**	8:22 am
☽△☉	**2:16 pm**	11:16 am
☽⊼♀	**2:59 pm**	11:59 am
☽☍♀		9:26 pm
☽⊻♅		11:41 pm

26 TUESDAY

☽☍♀	**12:26 am**	
☽⊻♅	**2:41 am**	
☽☍♃	**6:54 am**	3:54 am
☽⊼⚳	**9:41 am**	6:41 am
☽✶♆	**1:54 pm**	10:54 am
♇⊼⚴	**3:35 pm**	12:35 pm
☽△☿	**7:43 pm**	4:43 pm
☽△♇	**11:50 pm**	8:50 pm
☽⊻⚴		9:09 pm
☽✶⚵		10:54 pm

27 WEDNESDAY

☽⊻⚴	**12:09 am**	
☽✶⚵	**1:54 am**	
☽☌♂	**1:23 pm**	10:23 am
☽□⚷	**2:22 pm**	11:22 am
☽□♄	**4:34 pm**	1:34 pm
☽□☉	**11:19 pm**	8:19 pm
☽△♀		10:16 pm

28 THURSDAY

☽△♀	**1:16 am**	
☽⊼♀	**7:31 am**	4:31 am
☽✶♅	**8:21 am**	5:21 am
♂□⚷	**9:37 am**	6:37 am
☽⊼♃	**1:33 pm**	10:33 am
☽☍⚳	**4:42 pm**	1:42 pm
☽□♆	**8:21 pm**	5:21 pm
☽□☿		9:59 pm

29 FRIDAY

☽□☿	**12:59 am**	
☽⊼♇	**7:00 am**	4:00 am
☽☌⚴	**9:34 am**	6:34 am
☽⊻⚵	**11:04 am**	8:04 am
♅⊼♀	**12:03 pm**	9:03 am
☽△⚷	**10:16 pm**	7:16 pm
☽⊻♂		9:13 pm
☽✶♄		10:27 pm

30 SATURDAY

☽⊻♂	**12:13 am**	
☽✶♄	**1:27 am**	
☽✶☉	**12:45 pm**	9:45 am
☽□♀	**4:11 pm**	1:11 pm
☽□♅	**5:22 pm**	2:22 pm
☽△♀	**6:18 pm**	3:18 pm
☽△♃	**11:39 pm**	8:39 pm

31 SUNDAY

☽⊼⚳	**3:09 am**	12:09 am
♀☍♅	**4:08 am**	1:08 am
☽△♆	**6:00 am**	3:00 am
☽✶☿	**8:23 am**	5:23 am
♂□♄	**9:59 am**	6:59 am
☽☍♇	**5:10 pm**	2:10 pm
♀⊻♀	**10:09 pm**	7:09 pm
☽⊻⚴	**10:18 pm**	7:18 pm
☽☌⚵	**11:28 pm**	8:28 pm

Eastern time in bold type
Pacific time in medium type

JULY 2005

☽ Last Aspect			☽ Ingress		
day	EST / hr:mn / PST	asp	sign day	EST / hr:mn / PST	
2	**1:02 pm** 10:02 am	⚹ ♄	♊ 2	**4:26 pm** 1:26 pm	
4	**12:36 pm** 9:36 am	☍ ♇	♋ 5	**3:07 am** 12:07 am	
7	**12:54 pm** 9:54 am	☌ ♄	♌ 7	**3:11 pm** 12:11 pm	
9	**12:49 pm** 9:49 am	△ ♇	♍ 10	**3:57 am** 12:57 am	
12	**3:12 pm** 12:12 pm	⚹ ♄	♎ 12	**4:09 pm** 1:09 pm	
14	10:32 pm	□ ♄	♏ 14	10:51 pm	
15	**1:32 am**	□ ♄	♏ 15	**1:51 am**	
16	**10:15 pm** 7:15 pm	△ ☉	♐ 17	**7:35 am** 4:35 am	
18	11:03 pm	△ ♀	♑ 19	**9:26 am** 6:26 am	
19	**2:03 am**	△ ♀	♑ 19	**9:26 am** 6:26 am	
21	**7:00 am** 4:00 am	☍ ☉	♒ 21	**8:55 am** 5:55 am	
23	**3:33 am** 12:33 am	⚹ ♂	♓ 23	**8:12 am** 5:12 am	
24	**8:19 pm** 5:19 pm	□ ♇	♈ 25	**9:23 am** 6:23 am	
27	**1:23 pm** 10:23 am	☌ ♂	♉ 27	**1:54 pm** 10:54 am	
28	9:59 pm	□ ☿	♊ 29	**10:02 pm** 7:02 pm	
29	**12:59 am**	□ ☿	♊ 29	**10:02 pm** 7:02 pm	
31	**5:10 pm** 2:10 pm	☍ ♇	♋ 8/1	**8:52 am** 5:52 am	

☽ Phases & Eclipses		
phase	day	EST / hr:mn / PST
New Moon	6	**8:02 am** 5:02 am
2nd Quarter	14	**11:20 am** 8:20 am
Full Moon	21	**7:00 am** 4:00 am
4th Quarter	27	**11:19 pm** 8:19 pm

Planet Ingress		
	day	EST / hr:mn / PST
♄ ♌	16	**8:30 am** 5:30 am
☉ ♌	22	**1:41 pm** 10:41 am
♀ ♍	22	**9:01 pm** 6:01 pm
♂ ♉	27	10:12 pm
♂ ♉	28	**1:12 am**
⚷ ♑	31	**11:39 pm** 8:39 pm

Planetary Motion		
	day	EST / hr:mn / PST
☿ ℞	22	**10:59 pm** 7:59 pm

DATE		SID.TIME	SUN	MOON	NODE	MERCURY	VENUS	MARS	JUPITER	SATURN	URANUS	NEPTUNE	PLUTO	CERES	PALLAS	JUNO	VESTA	CHIRON
1	F	18:36:35	09 ♋ 16 00	06 ♉ 36	19 ♈ ℞ 27	03 ♌ 56	03 ♌ 21	12 ♈ 53	09 ♎ 54	28 ♋ 02	10 ♓ ℞ 40	17 ♒ ℞ 10	22 ♐ ℞ 45	11 ♏ 36	01 ♎ 04	09 ♉ 31	12 ♊ 34	01 ♒ ℞ 45
2	Sa	18:40:32	10 13 13	19 20	19 24	05 15	04 34	13 33	09 58	28 09	10 39	17 08	22 43	11 38	01 20	10 01	12 59	01 42
3	Su	18:44:28	11 10 27	01 ♊ 51	19 18	06 31	05 46	14 13	10 03	28 17	10 38	17 07	22 42	11 40	01 37	10 31	13 24	01 39
4	M	18:48:25	12 07 40	14 12	19 10	07 44	06 59	14 52	10 08	28 24	10 37	17 06	22 40	11 42	01 54	11 01	13 50	01 36
5	T	18:52:21	13 04 53	26 24	18 59	08 55	08 12	15 32	10 13	28 32	10 36	17 05	22 39	11 45	02 10	11 31	14 15	01 33
6	W	18:56:18	14 02 07	08 ♋ 29	18 46	10 03	09 25	16 11	10 18	28 39	10 35	17 03	22 37	11 49	02 28	12 01	14 40	01 29
7	Th	19:00:14	14 59 21	20 29	18 32	11 08	10 37	16 50	10 23	28 47	10 34	17 02	22 36	11 52	02 45	12 31	15 05	01 26
8	F	19:04:11	15 56 34	02 ♌ 23	18 19	12 10	11 50	17 29	10 28	28 55	10 33	17 01	22 34	11 56	03 02	13 01	15 30	01 23
9	Sa	19:08:08	16 53 48	14 14	18 06	13 09	13 03	18 08	10 34	29 02	10 32	16 59	22 33	12 01	03 20	13 30	15 55	01 19
10	Su	19:12:04	17 51 01	26 05	17 56	14 05	14 15	18 47	10 40	29 10	10 31	16 58	22 32	12 05	03 38	14 00	16 19	01 16
11	M	19:16:01	18 48 15	07 ♍ 56	17 49	14 58	15 28	19 25	10 45	29 17	10 30	16 57	22 30	12 10	03 56	14 30	16 44	01 13
12	T	19:19:57	19 45 29	19 52	17 44	15 47	16 41	20 04	10 51	29 25	10 29	16 55	22 29	12 16	04 14	14 59	17 09	01 09
13	W	19:23:54	20 42 42	01 ♎ 57	17 42	16 33	17 53	20 42	10 58	29 33	10 28	16 54	22 27	12 21	04 33	15 29	17 34	01 06
14	Th	19:27:50	21 39 56	14 15	17 42	17 15	19 06	21 20	11 04	29 41	10 26	16 52	22 26	12 27	04 51	15 58	17 58	01 03
15	F	19:31:47	22 37 09	26 52	17 42	17 54	20 18	21 58	11 10	29 48	10 25	16 51	22 25	12 34	05 10	16 28	18 23	00 59
16	Sa	19:35:43	23 34 23	09 ♏ 52	17 41	18 28	21 31	22 35	11 17	29 56	10 24	16 50	22 23	12 40	05 29	16 57	18 47	00 56
17	Su	19:39:40	24 31 37	23 20	17 39	18 59	22 43	23 13	11 23	00 ♌ 04	10 22	16 48	22 22	12 47	05 48	17 26	19 12	00 52
18	M	19:43:37	25 28 50	07 ♐ 17	17 34	19 25	23 55	23 50	11 30	00 11	10 21	16 47	22 21	12 55	06 07	17 55	19 36	00 49
19	T	19:47:33	26 26 05	21 43	17 27	19 47	25 08	24 27	11 37	00 19	10 19	16 45	22 20	13 02	06 26	18 25	20 01	00 45
20	W	19:51:30	27 23 19	06 ♑ 36	17 18	20 04	26 20	25 04	11 44	00 27	10 18	16 44	22 18	13 10	06 46	18 54	20 25	00 42
21	Th	19:55:26	28 20 34	21 46	17 07	20 17	27 32	25 41	11 51	00 35	10 16	16 42	22 17	13 18	07 05	19 23	20 49	00 38
22	F	19:59:23	29 17 49	07 ♒ 05	16 57	20 25	28 45	26 18	11 59	00 42	10 15	16 41	22 16	13 27	07 25	19 52	21 14	00 35
23	Sa	20:03:19	00 ♌ 15 05	22 20	16 48	20 ℞ 28	29 57	26 54	12 06	00 50	10 13	16 39	22 15	13 35	07 45	20 21	21 38	00 32
24	Su	20:07:16	01 12 22	07 ♓ 21	16 41	20 26	01 ♍ 09	27 30	12 14	00 58	10 11	16 37	22 14	13 45	08 05	20 50	22 02	00 28
25	M	20:11:12	02 09 39	22 01	16 37	20 19	02 21	28 06	12 21	01 06	10 10	16 36	22 13	13 54	08 25	21 19	22 26	00 25
26	T	20:15:09	03 06 57	06 ♈ 14	16 D 35	20 08	03 33	28 42	12 29	01 13	10 08	16 34	22 12	14 03	08 46	21 47	22 50	00 21
27	W	20:19:06	04 04 16	20 01	16 35	19 51	04 46	29 17	12 37	01 21	10 06	16 33	22 10	14 13	09 06	22 16	23 14	00 18
28	Th	20:23:02	05 01 36	03 ♉ 21	16 ℞ 35	19 29	05 58	29 52	12 45	01 29	10 04	16 31	22 09	14 23	09 27	22 45	23 38	00 14
29	F	20:26:59	05 58 57	16 18	16 35	19 03	07 10	00 ♉ 27	12 53	01 37	10 02	16 30	22 08	14 34	09 47	23 13	24 02	00 11
30	Sa	20:30:55	06 56 19	28 56	16 33	18 32	08 22	01 02	13 02	01 44	10 01	16 28	22 07	14 45	10 08	23 41	24 25	00 07
31	Su	20:34:52	07 53 43	11 ♊ 20	16 28	17 58	09 34	01 37	13 10	01 52	09 59	16 26	22 06	14 55	10 29	24 10	24 49	00 04

EPHEMERIS CALCULATED FOR 12 MIDNIGHT GREENWICH MEAN TIME. ALL OTHER DATA AND FACING ASPECTARIAN PAGE IN **EASTERN TIME (BOLD)** AND PACIFIC TIME (REGULAR).

AUGUST 2005

1 MONDAY
☽ ⚻ ⚷ **8:50 am** 5:50 am
☽ ⚺ ♄ **1:02 pm** 10:02 am
☽ ⚹ ♂ **2:04 pm** 11:04 am
☉ ⚻ ♅ **10:31 pm** 7:31 pm

2 TUESDAY
☽ △ ♅ **4:40 am** 1:40 am
☿ ☍ ♆ **4:52 am** 1:52 am
☽ ⚺ ☉ **5:13 am** 2:13 am
☽ □ ♀ **7:35 am** 4:35 am
☽ ⚹ ♀ **10:13 am** 7:13 am
☽ □ ♃ **11:59 am** 8:59 am
☽ △ ⚳ **3:50 pm** 12:50 pm
☽ ⚺ ☿ **4:56 pm** 1:56 pm
☽ ⚻ ♆ **5:39 pm** 2:39 pm

3 WEDNESDAY
☽ ⚻ ♇ **5:07 am** 2:07 am
♀ ⚺ ♃ **6:10 am** 3:10 am
☿ □ ⚳ **6:31 am** 3:31 am
☽ ⚹ ⚵ **12:53 pm** 9:53 am
☽ ⚺ ⚶ **1:38 pm** 10:38 am
☽ ☍ ⚷ **8:50 pm** 5:50 pm
☽ ☌ ♄ 11:03 pm

4 THURSDAY
☽ ☌ ♄ **2:03 am**
☉ ⚹ ♀ **3:00 am** 12:00 am
☽ □ ♂ **5:25 am** 2:25 am
☿ ⚺ ♀ **5:50 am** 2:50 am
☽ ⚻ ♅ **5:02 pm** 2:02 pm
☽ ⚹ ♀ **10:02 pm** 7:02 pm
☽ ☌ ☉ **11:05 pm** 8:05 pm
☽ ⚹ ♃ 10:21 pm
☽ ☌ ☿ 10:54 pm

5 FRIDAY
☽ ⚹ ♃ **1:21 am**
☽ ☌ ☿ **1:54 am**
♀ ⚹ ⚳ **4:30 am** 1:30 am
☽ □ ⚳ **5:31 am** 2:31 am
☽ ⚺ ♀ **5:36 am** 2:36 am
☽ ☍ ♆ **6:09 am** 3:09 am
☿ ⚹ ♃ **8:40 am** 5:40 am
♀ ⚻ ♆ **10:50 am** 7:50 am
☽ △ ♇ **5:45 pm** 2:45 pm
☉ ☌ ☿ **7:36 pm** 4:36 pm

Eastern time in bold type
Pacific time in medium type

6 SATURDAY
☽ □ ⚵ **4:05 am** 1:05 am
☽ ⚹ ⚶ **4:25 am** 1:25 am
☉ ⚹ ♃ **8:08 am** 5:08 am
☽ ⚻ ⚷ **9:17 am** 6:17 am
♆ □ ⚳ **1:16 pm** 10:16 am
☽ ⚺ ♄ **3:26 pm** 12:26 pm
☿ ⚹ ♀ **5:11 pm** 2:11 pm
☽ △ ♂ **9:05 pm** 6:05 pm

7 SUNDAY
☽ ☍ ♅ **5:33 am** 2:33 am
☽ ⚺ ☿ **10:54 am** 7:54 am
☽ ⚺ ♀ **12:36 pm** 9:36 am
☽ ⚺ ♃ **2:47 pm** 11:47 am
☽ ⚺ ☉ **5:02 pm** 2:02 pm
☽ ⚻ ♆ **6:37 pm** 3:37 pm
☽ ⚹ ⚳ **7:13 pm** 4:13 pm
☽ ☌ ♀ 9:56 pm

8 MONDAY
☽ ☌ ♀ **12:56 am**
☽ □ ♇ **6:10 am** 3:10 am
⚵ ⚺ ⚶ **8:33 am** 5:33 am
☉ ☍ ♆ **12:11 pm** 9:11 am
☽ □ ⚶ **6:45 pm** 3:45 pm
☽ △ ⚵ **6:49 pm** 3:49 pm
☽ △ ⚷ **9:16 pm** 6:16 pm

9 TUESDAY
☉ □ ⚳ **3:35 am** 12:35 am
☽ ⚹ ♄ **4:13 am** 1:13 am
☽ ⚻ ♂ **11:51 am** 8:51 am
☽ ⚻ ♅ **5:12 pm** 2:12 pm
☽ ⚹ ☿ **7:28 pm** 4:28 pm
☽ ☌ ♀ 11:04 pm

10 WEDNESDAY
☽ ☌ ♀ **2:04 am**
☽ ☌ ♃ **3:08 am** 12:08 am
♀ □ ♇ **4:54 am** 1:54 am
☽ △ ♆ **5:56 am** 2:56 am
☽ ⚺ ⚳ **7:44 am** 4:44 am
☽ ⚹ ☉ **9:33 am** 6:33 am
☽ ⚹ ♇ **5:10 pm** 2:10 pm
☽ ⚺ ♀ **6:29 pm** 3:29 pm

11 THURSDAY
⚷ △ ⚵ **5:28 am** 2:28 am
☽ △ ⚶ **7:09 am** 4:09 am
☽ □ ⚷ **7:30 am** 4:30 am
☽ ⚻ ⚵ **7:35 am** 4:35 am
☽ □ ♄ **2:58 pm** 11:58 am
⚷ ⚻ ⚶ **5:16 pm** 2:16 pm
☽ ☍ ♂ 9:06 pm
☽ △ ♅ 11:34 pm
☽ □ ☿ 11:39 pm

12 FRIDAY
☽ ☍ ♂ **12:06 am**
☽ △ ♅ **2:34 am**
☽ □ ☿ **2:39 am**
☿ ⚻ ♅ **5:43 am** 2:43 am
☽ ⚺ ♀ **12:48 pm** 9:48 am
☽ ⚺ ♃ **12:50 pm** 9:50 am
☽ □ ♆ **2:40 pm** 11:40 am
♃ ☌ ♀ **3:25 pm** 12:25 pm
☽ ☌ ⚳ **5:29 pm** 2:29 pm
☽ □ ☉ **10:38 pm** 7:38 pm
☽ ⚺ ♇ 10:19 pm

13 SATURDAY
☽ ⚺ ♇ **1:19 am**
☽ ⚹ ♀ **8:06 am** 5:06 am
☽ ⚹ ⚷ **2:34 pm** 11:34 am
☿ □ ♂ **3:41 pm** 12:41 pm
☽ ⚻ ⚶ **4:03 pm** 1:03 pm
☽ ☍ ⚵ **4:46 pm** 1:46 pm
☽ △ ♄ **10:16 pm** 7:16 pm

14 SUNDAY
☽ △ ☿ **7:28 am** 4:28 am
☽ ⚻ ♂ **8:20 am** 5:20 am
☽ □ ♅ **8:25 am** 5:25 am
♂ ⚹ ♅ **10:45 am** 7:45 am
☉ △ ♇ **11:03 am** 8:03 am
☽ ⚹ ♃ **6:46 pm** 3:46 pm
☽ ⚹ ♀ **7:33 pm** 4:33 pm
☽ ⚹ ♆ **7:43 pm** 4:43 pm
☽ ⚺ ⚳ **11:22 pm** 8:22 pm
♆ △ ♀ 10:22 pm

15 MONDAY
♆ △ ♀ **1:22 am**
☽ ☌ ♇ **5:42 am** 2:42 am
☽ △ ☉ **7:03 am** 4:03 am
☽ □ ♀ **4:43 pm** 1:43 pm
☽ ⚺ ⚷ **5:53 pm** 2:53 pm
☽ ☍ ⚶ **8:49 pm** 5:49 pm
☽ ⚻ ⚵ **9:45 pm** 6:45 pm
☽ ⚻ ♄ 10:42 pm

16 TUESDAY
☽ ⚻ ♄ **1:42 am**
♀ △ ⚷ **6:26 am** 3:26 am
☽ ⚻ ☿ **9:36 am** 6:36 am
☽ ⚹ ♅ **10:37 am** 7:37 am
☽ △ ♂ **12:24 pm** 9:24 am
☽ □ ♃ **9:02 pm** 6:02 pm
☽ ⚺ ♆ **9:17 pm** 6:17 pm
☽ □ ♀ **10:30 pm** 7:30 pm
☽ ⚹ ⚳ 10:38 pm

17 WEDNESDAY
☽ ⚹ ⚳ **1:38 am**
☽ ⚺ ♇ **6:45 am** 3:45 am
☽ ⚻ ☉ **11:25 am** 8:25 am
♃ △ ♆ **3:36 pm** 12:36 pm
☽ ☌ ⚷ **6:13 pm** 3:13 pm
☽ △ ♀ **9:23 pm** 6:23 pm
☽ ⚻ ⚶ **10:23 pm** 7:23 pm
☽ △ ⚵ **11:31 pm** 8:31 pm
☽ ☍ ♄ 11:15 pm

18 THURSDAY
☽ ☍ ♄ **2:15 am**
☽ ☍ ☿ **10:01 am** 7:01 am
☽ ⚺ ♅ **10:20 am** 7:20 am
☽ □ ♂ **1:44 pm** 10:44 am
♀ □ ⚶ **3:31 pm** 12:31 pm
☽ ☌ ♆ **8:44 pm** 5:44 pm
☽ △ ♃ **9:06 pm** 6:06 pm
☽ △ ♀ **11:13 pm** 8:13 pm
☿ ⚻ ♅ **11:21 pm** 8:21 pm
☽ □ ⚳ 10:51 pm

19 FRIDAY
☽ □ ⚳ **1:51 am**
☽ ⚹ ♇ **6:05 am** 3:05 am
☽ ☍ ☉ **1:53 pm** 10:53 am
♀ △ ⚵ **3:12 pm** 12:12 pm
☽ ⚺ ⚷ **5:18 pm** 2:18 pm
☽ △ ⚶ **10:47 pm** 7:47 pm
☽ □ ⚵ 9:08 pm
☽ ⚻ ♀ 9:36 pm
☽ ⚻ ♄ 10:52 pm

20 SATURDAY
☽ □ ⚵ **12:08 am**
☽ ⚻ ♀ **12:36 am**
☽ ⚻ ♄ **1:52 am**
☽ ☌ ♅ **9:30 am** 6:30 am
☽ ⚻ ☿ **10:40 am** 7:40 am
☽ ⚹ ♂ **2:34 pm** 11:34 am
♀ ⚹ ♄ **6:27 pm** 3:27 pm
☽ ⚺ ♆ **8:06 pm** 5:06 pm
☽ ⚻ ♃ **9:08 pm** 6:08 pm
☽ ⚻ ♀ **11:59 pm** 8:59 pm
☽ △ ⚳ 11:16 pm

21 SUNDAY
☽ △ ⚳ **2:16 am**
☽ □ ♇ **5:45 am** 2:45 am
☽ ⚻ ☉ **5:12 pm** 2:12 pm
☽ ⚹ ⚷ **5:14 pm** 2:14 pm
☉ ⚻ ⚷ **5:40 pm** 2:40 pm
☽ □ ⚶ 9:20 pm
☽ ⚹ ⚵ 10:59 pm
☽ △ ♄ 11:44 pm

22 MONDAY
☽ □ ⚶ **12:20 am**
☽ ⚹ ⚵ **1:59 am**
☽ △ ♄ **2:44 am**
☽ ☍ ♀ **5:19 am** 2:19 am
☽ ⚺ ♅ **10:13 am** 7:13 am
☽ △ ☿ **2:01 pm** 11:01 am
☽ ⚺ ♂ **5:18 pm** 2:18 pm
☽ ⚹ ♆ **9:26 pm** 6:26 pm
☽ ☍ ♃ **11:15 pm** 8:15 pm

23 TUESDAY
☽ ☍ ♀ **3:04 am** 12:04 am
☽ ⚻ ⚳ **5:03 am** 2:03 am
☽ △ ♇ **7:46 am** 4:46 am
♄ ⚹ ⚵ **1:06 pm** 10:06 am
☽ □ ⚷ **7:53 pm** 4:53 pm
☽ △ ☉ **11:53 pm** 8:53 pm

24 WEDNESDAY
☽ ⚹ ⚶ **5:04 am** 2:04 am
☽ □ ♄ **6:42 am** 3:42 am
☽ ⚺ ⚵ **7:06 am** 4:06 am
☽ ⚻ ♀ **2:00 pm** 11:00 am
☽ ⚹ ♅ **2:07 pm** 11:07 am
♀ ⚻ ♅ **3:10 pm** 12:10 pm
☽ □ ☿ **10:24 pm** 7:24 pm
☽ ☌ ♂ **11:41 pm** 8:41 pm
☽ □ ♆ 11:14 pm

25 THURSDAY
☽ □ ♆ **2:14 am**
☽ ⚻ ♃ **5:01 am** 2:01 am
☽ ⚻ ♀ **10:02 am** 7:02 am
☽ ☍ ⚳ **11:40 am** 8:40 am
☽ ⚻ ♇ **1:26 pm** 10:26 am
☿ □ ♂ **9:30 pm** 6:30 pm
☽ △ ⚷ 11:17 pm

26 FRIDAY
☽ △ ⚷ **2:17 am**
☽ □ ☉ **11:18 am** 8:18 am
☽ ⚺ ⚶ **1:57 pm** 10:57 am
☽ ⚹ ♄ **2:37 pm** 11:37 am
☿ ☍ ♆ **4:25 pm** 1:25 pm
☽ ☌ ⚵ **4:26 pm** 1:26 pm
☽ □ ♅ **9:50 pm** 6:50 pm

27 SATURDAY
☽ △ ♀ **3:45 am** 12:45 am
☽ ⚺ ♂ **10:13 am** 7:13 am
☽ △ ♆ **10:49 am** 7:49 am
☽ ⚹ ☿ **1:03 pm** 10:03 am
☽ △ ♃ **2:46 pm** 11:46 am
☽ △ ♀ **9:08 pm** 6:08 pm
☽ ⚻ ⚳ **10:17 pm** 7:17 pm
☽ ☍ ♇ **10:49 pm** 7:49 pm
♄ ⚺ ⚶ 10:07 pm

28 SUNDAY
♄ ⚺ ⚶ **1:07 am**
♂ □ ♆ **3:30 am** 12:30 am
☿ ⚹ ♃ **6:28 am** 3:28 am
☉ ⚺ ♄ **12:06 pm** 9:06 am
☽ ⚻ ⚷ **12:12 pm** 9:12 am
☉ ⚹ ⚶ **4:16 pm** 1:16 pm
♇ ⚺ ⚳ **8:55 pm** 5:55 pm
☽ ⚺ ♄ 10:55 pm
☽ ☌ ⚶ 11:25 pm
☽ ⚹ ☉ 11:59 pm

29 MONDAY
☽ ⚺ ♄ **1:55 am**
☽ ☌ ⚶ **2:25 am**
☽ ⚹ ☉ **2:59 am**
☽ ⚺ ⚵ **5:20 am** 2:20 am
☽ △ ♅ **8:40 am** 5:40 am
☽ □ ♀ **9:29 am** 6:29 am
☽ ⚻ ♆ **10:14 pm** 7:14 pm
☽ ⚹ ♂ **11:47 pm** 8:47 pm
♇ ⚹ ♀ 9:55 pm

30 TUESDAY
♇ ⚹ ♀ **12:55 am**
☽ □ ♃ **3:22 am** 12:22 am
♀ △ ♆ **4:50 am** 1:50 am
☽ ⚺ ☿ **9:03 am** 6:03 am
☽ ⚻ ♇ **10:42 am** 7:42 am
☽ □ ♀ **11:03 am** 8:03 am
☽ △ ⚳ **11:39 am** 8:39 am
☿ △ ♇ **9:25 pm** 6:25 pm
☽ ☍ ⚷ 9:14 pm

31 WEDNESDAY
☽ ☍ ⚷ **12:14 am**
☉ □ ⚵ **3:35 am** 12:35 am
☿ ⚹ ♀ **4:05 am** 1:05 am
♀ ⚻ ♂ **7:00 am** 4:00 am
☿ □ ⚳ **7:49 am** 4:49 am
☽ ☌ ♄ **3:00 pm** 12:00 pm
☽ ⚺ ⚶ **4:44 pm** 1:44 pm
☽ ⚹ ⚵ **8:00 pm** 5:00 pm
☽ ⚺ ☉ **8:51 pm** 5:51 pm
☽ ⚻ ♅ **9:02 pm** 6:02 pm
☉ ☍ ♅ **11:03 pm** 8:03 pm

AUGUST 2005

☽ Last Aspect day	EST	hr:mn / PST	asp	☽ Ingress sign	day	EST	hr:mn / PST
7/31	**5:10 pm**	2:10 pm	☍ ♇	♋	1	**8:52 am**	5:52 am
2	**11:59 am**	8:59 am	□ ♃	♌	3	**9:10 pm**	6:10 pm
5	**5:45 pm**	2:45 pm	△ ♇	♍	6	**9:54 am**	6:54 am
8	**6:10 am**	3:10 am	□ ♇	♎	8	**10:08 pm**	7:08 pm
10	**5:10 pm**	2:10 pm	⚹ ♇	♏	11	**8:35 am**	5:35 am
13	**8:06 am**	5:06 am	⚹ ♀	♐	13	**3:47 pm**	12:47 pm
15	**4:43 pm**	1:43 pm	□ ♀	♑	15	**7:13 pm**	4:13 pm
16	**9:02 pm**	6:02 pm	□ ♃	♒	17	**7:39 pm**	4:39 pm
19	**1:53 pm**	10:53 am	☍ ☉	♓	19	**6:52 pm**	3:52 pm
21	**5:45 am**	2:45 am	□ ♇	♈	21	**7:01 pm**	4:01 pm
23	**7:46 am**	4:46 am	△ ♇	♉	23	**9:58 pm**	6:58 pm
24		11:14 pm	□ ♆	♊	26	**4:43 am**	1:43 am
25	**2:14 am**		□ ♆	♊	26	**4:43 am**	1:43 am
27	**10:49 pm**	7:49 pm	☍ ♇	♋	28	**2:57 pm**	11:57 am
30	**3:22 am**	12:22 am	□ ♃	♌	31	**3:14 am**	12:14 am

☽ Phases & Eclipses phase	day	EST	hr:mn / PST
New Moon	4	**11:05 pm**	8:05 pm
2nd Quarter	12	**10:38 pm**	7:38 pm
Full Moon	19	**1:53 pm**	10:53 am
4th Quarter	26	**11:18 am**	8:18 am

Planet Ingress		day	EST	hr:mn / PST
⚵	♊	12	**11:26 am**	8:26 am
⚶	♋	13	**6:45 am**	3:45 am
♀	♎	16	**11:05 pm**	8:05 pm
☉	♍	22	**8:45 pm**	5:45 pm

Planetary Motion		day	EST	hr:mn / PST
☿	D	15	**11:49 pm**	8:49 pm

DATE		SID.TIME	SUN	MOON	NODE	MERCURY	VENUS	MARS	JUPITER	SATURN	URANUS	NEPTUNE	PLUTO	CERES	PALLAS	JUNO	VESTA	CHIRON
1	M	20:38:48	08 ♌ 51 07	23 ♊ 31	16 ♈℞ 21	17 ♌℞ 20	10 ♍ 46	02 ♉ 11	13 ♎ 19	02 ♌ 00	09 ♓℞ 57	16 ♒℞ 25	22 ♐℞ 05	15 ♏ 07	10 ♎ 50	24 ♉ 38	25 ♊ 13	00 ♒℞ 01
2	T	20:42:45	09 48 32	05 ♋ 34	16 12	16 38	11 57	02 45	13 27	02 08	09 55	16 23	22 05	15 18	11 11	25 06	25 36	29 ♑ 57
3	W	20:46:41	10 45 59	17 32	16 01	15 55	13 09	03 19	13 36	02 15	09 53	16 21	22 04	15 30	11 33	25 34	26 00	29 54
4	Th	20:50:38	11 43 26	29 26	15 49	15 09	14 21	03 52	13 45	02 23	09 51	16 20	22 03	15 42	11 54	26 02	26 23	29 50
5	F	20:54:35	12 40 55	11 ♌ 17	15 37	14 23	15 33	04 25	13 54	02 31	09 49	16 18	22 02	15 54	12 15	26 30	26 46	29 47
6	Sa	20:58:31	13 38 24	23 08	15 26	13 37	16 45	04 58	14 03	02 38	09 47	16 17	22 01	16 06	12 37	26 58	27 09	29 44
7	Su	21:02:28	14 35 54	05 ♍ 00	15 18	12 51	17 56	05 31	14 12	02 46	09 45	16 15	22 00	16 19	12 59	27 26	27 33	29 40
8	M	21:06:24	15 33 25	16 55	15 11	12 07	19 08	06 03	14 21	02 54	09 43	16 13	21 59	16 32	13 21	27 53	27 56	29 37
9	T	21:10:21	16 30 57	28 55	15 08	11 25	20 20	06 35	14 31	03 01	09 40	16 12	21 59	16 45	13 43	28 21	28 19	29 34
10	W	21:14:17	17 28 30	11 ♎ 04	15 D 06	10 47	21 31	07 06	14 40	03 09	09 38	16 10	21 58	16 58	14 05	28 48	28 42	29 31
11	Th	21:18:14	18 26 04	23 25	15 06	10 13	22 43	07 38	14 50	03 16	09 36	16 08	21 57	17 12	14 27	29 15	29 04	29 27
12	F	21:22:10	19 23 39	06 ♏ 03	15 07	09 43	23 54	08 09	14 59	03 24	09 34	16 07	21 57	17 26	14 49	29 43	29 27	29 24
13	Sa	21:26:07	20 21 15	19 01	15 ℞ 08	09 19	25 06	08 39	15 09	03 32	09 32	16 05	21 56	17 40	15 11	00 ♊ 10	29 50	29 21
14	Su	21:30:04	21 18 51	02 ♐ 23	15 07	09 01	26 17	09 10	15 19	03 39	09 29	16 04	21 55	17 54	15 34	00 37	00 ♋ 12	29 18
15	M	21:34:00	22 16 29	16 12	15 05	08 50	27 28	09 40	15 29	03 47	09 27	16 02	21 55	18 08	15 56	01 03	00 35	29 15
16	T	21:37:57	23 14 08	00 ♑ 29	15 01	08 D 45	28 40	10 09	15 39	03 54	09 25	16 00	21 54	18 23	16 19	01 30	00 57	29 12
17	W	21:41:53	24 11 47	15 11	14 54	08 48	29 51	10 38	15 49	04 02	09 23	15 59	21 54	18 38	16 42	01 56	01 20	29 09
18	Th	21:45:50	25 09 28	00 ♒ 14	14 47	08 57	01 ♎ 02	11 07	15 59	04 09	09 20	15 57	21 53	18 52	17 05	02 23	01 42	29 06
19	F	21:49:46	26 07 10	15 28	14 40	09 15	02 13	11 36	16 10	04 16	09 18	15 55	21 53	19 08	17 28	02 49	02 04	29 03
20	Sa	21:53:43	27 04 53	00 ♓ 43	14 34	09 39	03 24	12 04	16 20	04 24	09 16	15 54	21 52	19 23	17 51	03 15	02 26	29 00
21	Su	21:57:39	28 02 37	15 49	14 29	10 12	04 35	12 31	16 30	04 31	09 13	15 52	21 52	19 39	18 14	03 41	02 48	28 57
22	M	22:01:36	29 00 23	00 ♈ 36	14 D 26	10 51	05 46	12 59	16 41	04 38	09 11	15 51	21 52	19 54	18 37	04 07	03 10	28 54
23	T	22:05:33	29 58 11	14 58	14 25	11 38	06 57	13 26	16 51	04 46	09 09	15 49	21 51	20 10	19 00	04 33	03 32	28 52
24	W	22:09:29	00 ♍ 56 00	28 53	14 26	12 32	08 08	13 52	17 02	04 53	09 06	15 48	21 51	20 26	19 23	04 58	03 53	28 49
25	Th	22:13:26	01 53 51	12 ♉ 20	14 27	13 33	09 19	14 18	17 13	05 00	09 04	15 46	21 51	20 42	19 47	05 24	04 15	28 46
26	F	22:17:22	02 51 43	25 22	14 ℞ 29	14 41	10 29	14 44	17 24	05 07	09 02	15 44	21 50	20 59	20 10	05 49	04 36	28 44
27	Sa	22:21:19	03 49 38	08 ♊ 02	14 29	15 54	11 40	15 09	17 35	05 15	08 59	15 43	21 50	21 15	20 34	06 14	04 57	28 41
28	Su	22:25:15	04 47 34	20 24	14 27	17 14	12 51	15 33	17 46	05 22	08 57	15 41	21 50	21 32	20 57	06 39	05 19	28 39
29	M	22:29:12	05 45 33	02 ♋ 32	14 24	18 39	14 01	15 57	17 57	05 29	08 54	15 40	21 50	21 49	21 21	07 03	05 40	28 36
30	T	22:33:08	06 43 33	14 32	14 20	20 09	15 12	16 21	18 08	05 36	08 52	15 38	21 50	22 06	21 45	07 28	06 01	28 34
31	W	22:37:05	07 41 35	26 25	14 14	21 44	16 22	16 44	18 19	05 43	08 50	15 37	21 50	22 23	22 09	07 52	06 22	28 31

EPHEMERIS CALCULATED FOR 12 MIDNIGHT GREENWICH MEAN TIME. ALL OTHER DATA AND FACING ASPECTARIAN PAGE IN **EASTERN TIME (BOLD)** AND PACIFIC TIME (REGULAR).

SEPTEMBER 2005

1 THURSDAY
☽ ☍ ♆ **10:47 am** 7:47 am
☽ □ ♂ **2:28 pm** 11:28 am
☽ ⚹ ♀ **4:50 pm** 1:50 pm
☽ ⚹ ♃ **5:03 pm** 2:03 pm
♀ ☌ ♃ **7:30 pm** 4:30 pm
☽ △ ♇ **11:26 pm** 8:26 pm
♅ □ ⚵ 9:11 pm
☽ ⚹ ⚴ 10:53 pm
☽ □ ⚳ 10:54 pm

2 FRIDAY
♅ □ ⚵ **12:11 am**
☽ ⚹ ⚴ **1:53 am**
☽ □ ⚳ **1:54 am**
⚳ ⚺ ⚴ **3:01 am** 12:01 am
☽ ☌ ☿ **7:44 am** 4:44 am
☽ ⚻ ⚷ **12:45 pm** 9:45 am

3 SATURDAY
☽ ⚺ ♄ **4:13 am** 1:13 am
☽ ⚹ ⚶ **7:08 am** 4:08 am
☽ ☍ ♅ **9:24 am** 6:24 am
☽ □ ⚵ **10:39 am** 7:39 am
☽ ☌ ☉ **2:45 pm** 11:45 am
☿ ⚻ ⚷ **4:36 pm** 1:36 pm
☽ ⚻ ♆ **11:05 pm** 8:05 pm

4 SUNDAY
☽ △ ♂ **4:40 am** 1:40 am
☽ ⚺ ♃ **6:21 am** 3:21 am
☽ ⚺ ♀ **11:39 am** 8:39 am
☽ □ ♇ **11:40 am** 8:40 am
♀ ⚹ ♇ **11:46 am** 8:46 am
☽ ⚹ ⚳ **3:36 pm** 12:36 pm
☽ ⚺ ⚴ **4:09 pm** 1:09 pm
☽ △ ⚷ 9:34 pm

5 MONDAY
☽ △ ⚷ **12:34 am**
☽ ⚺ ☿ **6:23 am** 3:23 am
☽ ⚹ ♄ **4:26 pm** 1:26 pm
☽ □ ⚶ **8:24 pm** 5:24 pm
☽ ⚻ ♅ **8:45 pm** 5:45 pm
☽ △ ⚵ 9:06 pm

6 TUESDAY
☽ △ ⚵ **12:06 am**
☽ ⚺ ☉ **7:15 am** 4:15 am
♅ △ ⚶ **7:50 am** 4:50 am
☽ △ ♆ **10:09 am** 7:09 am
☽ ⚻ ♂ **5:18 pm** 2:18 pm
♀ ⚺ ⚳ **5:30 pm** 2:30 pm
☽ ☌ ♃ **6:17 pm** 3:17 pm
☽ ⚹ ♇ **10:30 pm** 7:30 pm

7 WEDNESDAY
☽ ⚺ ⚳ **3:46 am** 12:46 am
☽ ☌ ♀ **4:33 am** 1:33 am
☽ ☌ ⚴ **4:48 am** 1:48 am
♀ ☌ ⚴ **8:30 am** 5:30 am
☽ □ ⚷ **10:50 am** 7:50 am
☉ ⚻ ♆ **7:26 pm** 4:26 pm
☿ ⚺ ♄ 11:40 pm
☽ □ ♄ 11:48 pm
☽ ⚹ ☿ 11:49 pm

8 THURSDAY
☿ ⚺ ♄ **2:40 am**
☽ □ ♄ **2:48 am**
☽ ⚹ ☿ **2:49 am**
☽ △ ♅ **6:16 am** 3:16 am
☽ △ ⚶ **7:39 am** 4:39 am
☽ ⚻ ⚵ **11:25 am** 8:25 am
☽ □ ♆ **7:12 pm** 4:12 pm
☽ ⚹ ☉ **9:11 pm** 6:11 pm
☿ ☍ ♅ 10:22 pm

9 FRIDAY
☿ ☍ ♅ **1:22 am**
☽ ☍ ♂ **3:31 am** 12:31 am
☽ ⚺ ♃ **3:57 am** 12:57 am
☽ ⚺ ♇ **7:07 am** 4:07 am
☽ ☌ ⚳ **1:30 pm** 10:30 am
☽ ⚺ ⚴ **2:56 pm** 11:56 am
☿ ⚹ ⚶ **4:35 pm** 1:35 pm
☽ ⚺ ♀ **6:22 pm** 3:22 pm
☽ ⚹ ⚷ **6:44 pm** 3:44 pm
♀ □ ⚷ **10:33 pm** 7:33 pm

10 SATURDAY
☽ △ ♄ **10:30 am** 7:30 am
☽ □ ♅ **1:10 pm** 10:10 am
☽ ⚻ ⚶ **4:00 pm** 1:00 pm
☽ □ ☿ **7:14 pm** 4:14 pm
☽ ☍ ⚵ **7:45 pm** 4:45 pm
☿ □ ⚵ **11:36 pm** 8:36 pm
☽ ⚹ ♆ 10:30 pm

11 SUNDAY
☽ ⚹ ♆ **1:30 am**
☽ □ ☉ **7:37 am** 4:37 am
☽ ⚻ ♂ **10:33 am** 7:33 am
☽ ⚹ ♃ **10:38 am** 7:38 am
☽ ☌ ♇ **12:52 pm** 9:52 am
☽ ⚺ ⚳ **8:07 pm** 5:07 pm
☽ ⚹ ⚴ **9:50 pm** 6:50 pm
☽ ⚺ ⚷ **11:43 pm** 8:43 pm

12 MONDAY
☽ ⚹ ♀ **4:16 am** 1:16 am
♂ ⚻ ♃ **5:30 am** 2:30 am
☽ ⚻ ♄ **3:06 pm** 12:06 pm
☿ ⚻ ♆ **3:17 pm** 12:17 pm
☽ ⚹ ♅ **5:05 pm** 2:05 pm
☽ ☍ ⚶ **9:06 pm** 6:06 pm
☽ ⚻ ⚵ 9:46 pm

13 TUESDAY
☽ ⚻ ⚵ **12:46 am**
☽ ⚺ ♆ **4:48 am** 1:48 am
☽ △ ☿ **6:53 am** 3:53 am
☉ ⚺ ♃ **12:41 pm** 9:41 am
☽ □ ♃ **2:15 pm** 11:15 am
☽ △ ☉ **2:20 pm** 11:20 am
☽ △ ♂ **2:22 pm** 11:22 am
☉ △ ♂ **2:49 pm** 11:49 am
☽ ⚺ ♇ **3:40 pm** 12:40 pm
☽ ⚹ ⚳ **11:40 pm** 8:40 pm
☽ □ ⚴ 10:38 pm
☽ ☌ ⚷ 10:52 pm

14 WEDNESDAY
☽ □ ⚴ **1:38 am**
☽ ☌ ⚷ **1:52 am**
⚷ □ ⚴ **9:47 am** 6:47 am
☉ □ ♇ **10:21 am** 7:21 am
☽ □ ♀ **10:34 am** 7:34 am
☽ ☍ ♄ **5:00 pm** 2:00 pm
☽ ⚺ ♅ **6:26 pm** 3:26 pm
☽ ⚻ ⚶ **11:29 pm** 8:29 pm

15 THURSDAY
☽ △ ⚵ **3:08 am** 12:08 am
☽ ☌ ♆ **5:46 am** 2:46 am
☽ ⚻ ☿ **2:56 pm** 11:56 am
☽ △ ♃ **3:39 pm** 12:39 pm
☽ □ ♂ **3:51 pm** 12:51 pm
☽ ⚹ ♇ **4:23 pm** 1:23 pm
☽ ⚻ ☉ **6:28 pm** 3:28 pm
☿ ⚺ ♃ **9:12 pm** 6:12 pm
☿ △ ♂ **11:05 pm** 8:05 pm
☽ □ ⚳ 10:13 pm
☽ ⚺ ⚷ 11:14 pm
☿ □ ♇ 11:32 pm

16 FRIDAY
☽ □ ⚳ **1:13 am**
☽ ⚺ ⚷ **2:14 am**
☿ □ ♇ **2:32 am**
☽ △ ⚴ **3:27 am** 12:27 am
☽ △ ♀ **2:52 pm** 11:52 am
☽ ⚻ ♄ **5:31 pm** 2:31 pm
☽ ☌ ♅ **6:29 pm** 3:29 pm
☽ △ ⚶ 9:37 pm

17 SATURDAY
☽ △ ⚶ **12:37 am**
☽ □ ⚵ **4:22 am** 1:22 am
☽ ⚺ ♆ **5:49 am** 2:49 am
♂ ⚻ ♇ **7:20 am** 4:20 am
☽ ⚻ ♃ **4:27 pm** 1:27 pm
☽ □ ♇ **4:33 pm** 1:33 pm
☽ ⚹ ♂ **4:40 pm** 1:40 pm
⚷ ⚹ ⚳ **9:13 pm** 6:13 pm
☽ ☍ ☿ **9:58 pm** 6:58 pm
☽ ☍ ☉ **10:01 pm** 7:01 pm
☉ ☌ ☿ **10:38 pm** 7:38 pm
♃ ⚹ ♇ **11:57 pm** 8:57 pm
☽ ⚹ ⚷ 11:25 pm
☽ △ ⚳ 11:33 pm

18 SUNDAY
☽ ⚹ ⚷ **2:25 am**
☽ △ ⚳ **2:33 am**
♀ □ ♄ **4:34 am** 1:34 am
☽ ⚻ ⚴ **5:07 am** 2:07 am
♀ △ ♅ **12:31 pm** 9:31 am
☽ △ ♄ **6:27 pm** 3:27 pm
☽ ⚺ ♅ **6:58 pm** 3:58 pm
☽ ⚻ ♀ **7:32 pm** 4:32 pm
☽ □ ⚶ 11:29 pm

19 MONDAY
☽ □ ⚶ **2:29 am**
☽ ⚹ ⚵ **6:27 am** 3:27 am
☽ ⚹ ♆ **6:44 am** 3:44 am
☿ △ ⚷ **9:31 am** 6:31 am
☽ △ ♇ **6:01 pm** 3:01 pm
☿ ⚹ ⚳ **6:03 pm** 3:03 pm
♆ △ ⚵ **6:27 pm** 3:27 pm
☽ ☍ ♃ **6:36 pm** 3:36 pm
☽ ⚺ ♂ **6:44 pm** 3:44 pm

20 TUESDAY
☽ ⚻ ☉ **3:24 am** 12:24 am
☽ □ ⚷ **4:15 am** 1:15 am
☽ ⚻ ⚳ **5:40 am** 2:40 am
☽ ⚻ ☿ **7:04 am** 4:04 am
☽ ☍ ⚴ **8:42 am** 5:42 am
☉ △ ⚷ **3:32 pm** 12:32 pm
☽ □ ♄ **9:37 pm** 6:37 pm
☽ ⚹ ♅ **9:40 pm** 6:40 pm
☿ ⚺ ⚴ **11:05 pm** 8:05 pm
♄ ⚻ ♅ 10:49 pm

21 WEDNESDAY
♄ ⚻ ♅ **1:49 am**
☽ ☍ ♀ **3:04 am** 12:04 am
☽ ⚹ ⚶ **6:56 am** 3:56 am
☽ □ ♆ **10:15 am** 7:15 am
♂ ⚻ ♃ **11:06 am** 8:06 am
☽ ⚺ ⚵ **11:16 am** 8:16 am
☽ ⚻ ♇ **10:24 pm** 7:24 pm
☽ ☌ ♂ **11:45 pm** 8:45 pm
☽ ⚻ ♃ **11:49 pm** 8:49 pm

22 THURSDAY
☉ ⚹ ⚳ **3:39 am** 12:39 am
☽ △ ⚷ **9:15 am** 6:15 am
☽ ☍ ⚳ **12:14 pm** 9:14 am
☽ △ ☉ **12:41 pm** 9:41 am
☽ ⚻ ⚴ **3:52 pm** 12:52 pm
☽ △ ☿ **8:50 pm** 5:50 pm

23 FRIDAY
☽ □ ♅ **3:50 am** 12:50 am
☽ ⚹ ♄ **4:21 am** 1:21 am
☽ ⚻ ♀ **3:12 pm** 12:12 pm
☽ ⚺ ⚶ **3:13 pm** 12:13 pm
♀ △ ⚶ **3:29 pm** 12:29 pm
☽ △ ♆ **5:24 pm** 2:24 pm
☽ ☌ ⚵ **7:58 pm** 4:58 pm

24 SATURDAY
☽ ☍ ♇ **6:32 am** 3:32 am
☽ ⚺ ♂ **8:30 am** 5:30 am
☽ △ ♃ **8:57 am** 5:57 am
♀ □ ♆ **3:15 pm** 12:15 pm
☽ ⚻ ⚷ **6:00 pm** 3:00 pm
☽ ⚻ ⚳ **10:51 pm** 7:51 pm
☿ ⚻ ♅ **11:27 pm** 8:27 pm
☽ □ ☉ 11:41 pm

25 SUNDAY
☽ □ ☉ **2:41 am**
☽ △ ⚴ **3:08 am** 12:08 am
☿ ⚹ ♄ **6:59 am** 3:59 am
☉ ⚺ ⚴ **12:24 pm** 9:24 am
☽ △ ♅ **1:37 pm** 10:37 am
☽ ⚺ ♄ **2:48 pm** 11:48 am
☽ □ ☿ **4:02 pm** 1:02 pm

26 MONDAY
☽ ☌ ⚶ **3:13 am** 12:13 am
☽ ⚻ ♆ **4:00 am** 1:00 am
☽ △ ♀ **7:55 am** 4:55 am
☽ ⚺ ⚵ **8:15 am** 5:15 am
♀ ⚻ ⚵ **12:41 pm** 9:41 am
☽ ⚻ ♇ **5:53 pm** 2:53 pm
☽ ⚹ ♂ **8:19 pm** 5:19 pm
☽ □ ♃ **9:24 pm** 6:24 pm

27 TUESDAY
☽ ☍ ⚷ **5:41 am** 2:41 am
♆ ⚻ ⚶ **11:49 am** 8:49 am
☽ △ ⚳ **12:32 pm** 9:32 am
☽ □ ⚴ **5:23 pm** 2:23 pm
☽ ⚹ ☉ **8:06 pm** 5:06 pm
☽ ⚻ ♅ 10:44 pm

28 WEDNESDAY
☽ ⚻ ♅ **1:44 am**
☽ ☌ ♄ **3:35 am** 12:35 am
☽ ⚹ ☿ **2:28 pm** 11:28 am
☽ ☍ ♆ **4:29 pm** 1:29 pm
☽ ⚺ ⚶ **5:12 pm** 2:12 pm
☽ ⚹ ⚵ **10:20 pm** 7:20 pm
☽ □ ♀ 11:55 pm

29 THURSDAY
☽ □ ♀ **2:55 am**
☿ △ ♆ **4:38 am** 1:38 am
☽ △ ♇ **6:38 am** 3:38 am
☽ □ ♂ **9:17 am** 6:17 am
☽ ⚹ ♃ **11:12 am** 8:12 am
☿ □ ⚶ **1:03 pm** 10:03 am
☽ ⚻ ⚷ **6:21 pm** 3:21 pm

30 FRIDAY
☽ □ ⚳ **3:02 am** 12:02 am
☽ ⚹ ⚴ **8:16 am** 5:16 am
☉ ⚻ ♅ **2:04 pm** 11:04 am
☽ ⚺ ☉ **2:09 pm** 11:09 am
☽ ☍ ♅ **2:09 pm** 11:09 am
☽ ⚺ ♄ **4:35 pm** 1:35 pm
♀ ⚺ ♇ **6:25 pm** 3:25 pm

Eastern time in bold type
Pacific time in medium type

SEPTEMBER 2005

☽ Last Aspect day	EST	hr:mn / PST	asp	☽ Ingress sign	day	EST	hr:mn / PST
2	**7:44 am**	4:44 am	☌ ☿	♍	2	**3:56 pm**	12:56 pm
4	**11:40 am**	8:40 am	□ ♇	♎	5	**3:52 am**	12:52 am
7	**4:33 am**	1:33 am	☌ ♀	♏	7	**2:10 pm**	11:10 am
9	**3:31 am**	12:31 am	☍ ♂	♐	9	**10:03 pm**	7:03 pm
11	**12:52 pm**	9:52 am	☌ ♇	♑	11		11:56 pm
11	**12:52 pm**	9:52 am	☌ ♇	♑	12	**2:56 am**	
13	**2:22 pm**	11:22 am	△ ♂	♒	14	**5:02 am**	2:02 am
15	**4:23 pm**	1:23 pm	⚹ ♇	♓	16	**5:24 am**	2:24 am
17	**10:01 pm**	7:01 pm	☍ ☉	♈	18	**5:43 am**	2:43 am
19	**6:36 pm**	3:36 pm	☍ ♃	♉	20	**7:47 am**	4:47 am

☽ Last Aspect day	EST	hr:mn / PST	asp	☽ Ingress sign	day	EST	hr:mn / PST
22	**12:41 pm**	9:41 am	△ ☉	♊	22	**1:07 pm**	10:07 am
24	**8:57 am**	5:57 am	△ ♃	♋	24	**10:10 pm**	7:10 pm
26	**9:24 pm**	6:24 pm	□ ♃	♌	27	**10:03 am**	7:03 am
29	**11:12 am**	8:12 am	⚹ ♃	♍	29	**10:44 pm**	7:44 pm

☽ Phases & Eclipses phase	day	EST	hr:mn / PST
New Moon	3	**2:45 pm**	11:45 am
2nd Quarter	11	**7:37 am**	4:37 am
Full Moon	17	**10:01 pm**	7:01 pm
4th Quarter	24		11:41 pm
4th Quarter	25	**2:41 am**	

Planet Ingress		day	EST	hr:mn / PST
☿	♍	4	**1:52 pm**	10:52 am
♀	♏	11	**12:14 pm**	9:14 am
⚵	♏	18		11:10 pm
⚵	♏	19	**2:10 am**	
☿	♎	20	**12:40 pm**	9:40 am
☉	♎	22	**6:23 pm**	3:23 pm
⚳	♐	23	**10:19 pm**	7:19 pm

Planetary Motion		day	EST	hr:mn / PST
♇	D	2	**6:52 am**	3:52 am

DATE		SID.TIME	SUN	MOON	NODE	MERCURY	VENUS	MARS	JUPITER	SATURN	URANUS	NEPTUNE	PLUTO	CERES	PALLAS	JUNO	VESTA	CHIRON
1	Th	22:41:02	08 ♍ 39 38	08 ♌ 17	14 ♈ R 07	23 ♌ 23	17 ♎ 33	17 ♉ 07	18 ♎ 30	05 ♌ 50	08 ♓ R 47	15 ♒ R 35	21 ♐ R 50	22 ♏ 41	22 ♎ 33	08 ♊ 16	06 ♋ 42	28 ♑ R 29
2	F	22:44:58	09 37 43	20 08	14 01	25 05	18 43	17 29	18 42	05 57	08 45	15 34	21 D 49	22 58	22 56	08 40	07 03	28 27
3	Sa	22:48:55	10 35 50	02 ♍ 01	13 55	26 50	19 53	17 50	18 53	06 04	08 43	15 32	21 49	23 16	23 21	09 04	07 24	28 25
4	Su	22:52:51	11 33 59	13 58	13 51	28 38	21 03	18 11	19 05	06 10	08 40	15 31	21 50	23 34	23 45	09 28	07 44	28 22
5	M	22:56:48	12 32 09	26 02	13 48	00 ♍ 28	22 14	18 32	19 16	06 17	08 38	15 30	21 50	23 52	24 09	09 51	08 04	28 20
6	T	23:00:44	13 30 21	08 ♎ 12	13 D 46	02 20	23 24	18 51	19 28	06 24	08 35	15 28	21 50	24 10	24 33	10 14	08 24	28 18
7	W	23:04:41	14 28 35	20 32	13 46	04 13	24 34	19 11	19 40	06 31	08 33	15 27	21 50	24 28	24 57	10 37	08 44	28 16
8	Th	23:08:37	15 26 50	03 ♏ 04	13 47	06 07	25 44	19 29	19 51	06 37	08 31	15 25	21 50	24 47	25 22	11 00	09 04	28 14
9	F	23:12:34	16 25 07	15 50	13 49	08 02	26 53	19 47	20 03	06 44	08 28	15 24	21 50	25 05	25 46	11 22	09 24	28 13
10	Sa	23:16:31	17 23 26	28 52	13 51	09 57	28 03	20 05	20 15	06 50	08 26	15 23	21 50	25 24	26 11	11 44	09 43	28 11
11	Su	23:20:27	18 21 46	12 ♐ 14	13 R 51	11 52	29 13	20 21	20 27	06 57	08 23	15 21	21 51	25 43	26 35	12 06	10 03	28 09
12	M	23:24:24	19 20 07	25 58	13 51	13 47	00 ♏ 23	20 37	20 39	07 03	08 21	15 20	21 51	26 02	27 00	12 28	10 22	28 07
13	T	23:28:20	20 18 31	10 ♑ 03	13 50	15 42	01 32	20 53	20 51	07 10	08 19	15 19	21 51	26 21	27 25	12 49	10 41	28 06
14	W	23:32:17	21 16 55	24 29	13 48	17 36	02 41	21 07	21 03	07 16	08 16	15 18	21 52	26 40	27 49	13 10	11 00	28 04
15	Th	23:36:13	22 15 22	09 ♒ 13	13 46	19 29	03 51	21 21	21 15	07 22	08 14	15 16	21 52	26 59	28 14	13 31	11 19	28 03
16	F	23:40:10	23 13 49	24 08	13 43	21 22	05 00	21 35	21 27	07 29	08 12	15 15	21 52	27 19	28 39	13 52	11 38	28 01
17	Sa	23:44:06	24 12 19	09 ♓ 07	13 40	23 14	06 09	21 47	21 39	07 35	08 10	15 14	21 53	27 38	29 04	14 12	11 56	28 00
18	Su	23:48:03	25 10 50	24 01	13 39	25 05	07 18	21 59	21 51	07 41	08 07	15 13	21 53	27 58	29 29	14 33	12 15	27 59
19	M	23:52:00	26 09 23	08 ♈ 43	13 D 38	26 55	08 27	22 10	22 04	07 47	08 05	15 12	21 54	28 18	29 54	14 52	12 33	27 58
20	T	23:55:56	27 07 59	23 05	13 38	28 45	09 36	22 21	22 16	07 53	08 03	15 11	21 54	28 37	00 ♏ 19	15 12	12 51	27 57
21	W	23:59:53	28 06 36	07 ♉ 03	13 39	00 ♎ 33	10 45	22 31	22 28	07 59	08 01	15 09	21 55	28 57	00 44	15 31	13 09	27 55
22	Th	0:03:49	29 05 15	20 36	13 40	02 20	11 54	22 39	22 41	08 05	07 58	15 08	21 56	29 18	01 09	15 50	13 26	27 55
23	F	0:07:46	00 ♎ 03 57	03 ♊ 44	13 41	04 07	13 02	22 48	22 53	08 10	07 56	15 07	21 56	29 38	01 34	16 09	13 44	27 54
24	Sa	0:11:42	01 02 41	16 28	13 42	05 52	14 11	22 55	23 06	08 16	07 54	15 06	21 57	29 58	01 59	16 27	14 01	27 53
25	Su	0:15:39	02 01 27	28 53	13 R 43	07 37	15 19	23 01	23 18	08 22	07 52	15 05	21 58	00 ♐ 18	02 24	16 45	14 18	27 52
26	M	0:19:35	03 00 16	11 ♋ 03	13 42	09 20	16 27	23 07	23 31	08 27	07 50	15 04	21 58	00 39	02 50	17 03	14 35	27 51
27	T	0:23:32	03 59 07	23 02	13 42	11 03	17 35	23 12	23 43	08 33	07 48	15 03	21 59	01 00	03 15	17 20	14 52	27 51
28	W	0:27:29	04 57 59	04 ♌ 55	13 41	12 45	18 44	23 16	23 56	08 38	07 46	15 03	22 00	01 20	03 40	17 37	15 08	27 50
29	Th	0:31:25	05 56 55	16 46	13 40	14 25	19 51	23 19	24 09	08 44	07 44	15 02	22 01	01 41	04 06	17 54	15 25	27 50
30	F	0:35:22	06 55 52	28 39	13 39	16 05	20 59	23 21	24 21	08 49	07 42	15 01	22 02	02 02	04 31	18 10	15 41	27 49

EPHEMERIS CALCULATED FOR 12 MIDNIGHT GREENWICH MEAN TIME. ALL OTHER DATA AND FACING ASPECTARIAN PAGE IN **EASTERN TIME (BOLD)** AND PACIFIC TIME (REGULAR).

OCTOBER 2005

1 SATURDAY

☽ ⚻ ♆	**4:46 am**	1:46 am
☽ ⚹ ⚶	**6:54 am**	3:54 am
☿ △ ⚵	**8:02 am**	5:02 am
☽ □ ⚵	**11:56 am**	8:56 am
☽ ⚺ ☿	**12:26 pm**	9:26 am
☽ □ ♇	**6:47 pm**	3:47 pm
☽ ⚹ ♀	**9:14 pm**	6:14 pm
☽ △ ♂	**9:22 pm**	6:22 pm
☉ ⚹ ♄	**10:23 pm**	7:23 pm
♀ ☍ ♂	**10:45 pm**	7:45 pm
☽ ⚺ ♃		9:13 pm

2 SUNDAY

☽ ⚺ ♃	**12:13 am**	
☽ △ ⚷	**6:06 am**	3:06 am
☽ ⚹ ⚳	**4:20 pm**	1:20 pm
☽ ⚺ ⚴	**9:46 pm**	6:46 pm
☽ ⚻ ♅		10:12 pm

3 MONDAY

☽ ⚻ ♅	**1:12 am**	
☽ ⚹ ♄	**4:07 am**	1:07 am
☽ ☌ ☉	**6:28 am**	3:28 am
☿ ⚹ ♇	**12:20 pm**	9:20 am
♀ ⚺ ♃	**12:37 pm**	9:37 am
☽ △ ♆	**3:26 pm**	12:26 pm
☽ □ ⚶	**6:47 pm**	3:47 pm
☽ △ ⚵	**11:35 pm**	8:35 pm

4 TUESDAY

☽ ⚹ ♇	**5:05 am**	2:05 am
☿ ⚻ ♂	**6:55 am**	3:55 am
☽ ⚻ ♂	**7:25 am**	4:25 am
☽ ☌ ☿	**7:29 am**	4:29 am
☽ ☌ ♃	**11:15 am**	8:15 am
☽ ⚺ ♀	**1:02 pm**	10:02 am
☽ □ ⚷	**3:54 pm**	12:54 pm

5 WEDNESDAY

☽ ⚺ ⚳	**3:24 am**	12:24 am
☽ ☌ ⚴	**8:58 am**	5:58 am
☽ △ ♅	**10:09 am**	7:09 am
☽ □ ♄	**1:28 pm**	10:28 am
☿ ☌ ♃	**5:39 pm**	2:39 pm
☽ ⚺ ☉	**8:03 pm**	5:03 pm
♀ ⚹ ⚷	**9:39 pm**	6:39 pm
☽ □ ♆	**11:55 pm**	8:55 pm

Eastern time in bold type
Pacific time in medium type

6 THURSDAY

☽ △ ⚶	**4:18 am**	1:18 am
☽ ⚻ ⚵	**8:49 am**	5:49 am
☽ ⚺ ♇	**1:09 pm**	10:09 am
☽ ☍ ♂	**3:05 pm**	12:05 pm
♅ △ ⚴	**6:18 pm**	3:18 pm
☽ ⚺ ♃	**7:56 pm**	4:56 pm
☽ ⚺ ☿	**10:59 pm**	7:59 pm
☽ ⚹ ⚷	**11:29 pm**	8:29 pm
☽ ☌ ♀		10:51 pm

7 FRIDAY

☽ ☌ ♀	**1:51 am**	
☿ □ ⚷	**3:12 am**	12:12 am
☽ ☌ ⚳	**12:03 pm**	9:03 am
☽ □ ♅	**4:53 pm**	1:53 pm
☽ ⚺ ⚴	**5:41 pm**	2:41 pm
☽ △ ♄	**8:31 pm**	5:31 pm
☉ △ ♆	**10:28 pm**	7:28 pm

8 SATURDAY

☽ ⚹ ♆	**6:12 am**	3:12 am
☽ ⚹ ☉	**6:48 am**	3:48 am
☽ ⚻ ⚶	**11:25 am**	8:25 am
☽ ☍ ⚵	**3:40 pm**	12:40 pm
☽ ☌ ♇	**7:02 pm**	4:02 pm
☽ ⚻ ♂	**8:28 pm**	5:28 pm
☽ ⚹ ♃		11:20 pm

9 SUNDAY

☽ ⚹ ♃	**2:20 am**	
☽ ⚺ ⚷	**4:55 am**	1:55 am
☽ ⚹ ☿	**11:10 am**	8:10 am
☽ ⚺ ♀	**11:51 am**	8:51 am
☽ ⚺ ⚳	**6:24 pm**	3:24 pm
☽ ⚹ ♅	**9:32 pm**	6:32 pm
☽ ⚹ ⚴		9:05 pm
☽ ⚻ ♄		10:25 pm

10 MONDAY

☽ ⚹ ⚴	**12:05 am**	
☽ ⚻ ♄	**1:25 am**	
☿ ⚺ ♀	**8:10 am**	5:10 am
☽ ⚺ ♆	**10:26 am**	7:26 am
☽ □ ☉	**3:01 pm**	12:01 pm
☽ ☍ ⚶	**4:22 pm**	1:22 pm
☽ ⚻ ⚵	**8:21 pm**	5:21 pm
☽ ⚺ ♇	**10:56 pm**	7:56 pm
☽ △ ♂	**11:48 pm**	8:48 pm

11 TUESDAY

☽ □ ♃	**6:42 am**	3:42 am
☽ ☌ ⚷	**8:25 am**	5:25 am
☉ □ ⚶	**3:36 pm**	12:36 pm
☽ ⚹ ♀	**7:24 pm**	4:24 pm
☽ □ ☿	**8:31 pm**	5:31 pm
☽ ⚹ ⚳	**10:47 pm**	7:47 pm
☽ ⚺ ♅		9:24 pm

12 WEDNESDAY

☽ ⚺ ♅	**12:24 am**	
♄ □ ⚴	**3:34 am**	12:34 am
☽ ☍ ♄	**4:32 am**	1:32 am
☽ □ ⚴	**4:33 am**	1:33 am
☽ ☌ ♆	**1:00 pm**	10:00 am
☽ ⚻ ⚶	**7:36 pm**	4:36 pm
☽ △ ☉	**9:12 pm**	6:12 pm
☽ △ ⚵	**11:20 pm**	8:20 pm
☿ ⚺ ⚳		9:46 pm
☽ ⚹ ♇		10:17 pm
☽ □ ♂		10:32 pm

13 THURSDAY

☿ ⚺ ⚳	**12:46 am**	
☽ ⚹ ♇	**1:17 am**	
☽ □ ♂	**1:32 am**	
☿ △ ♅	**9:20 am**	6:20 am
☽ △ ♃	**9:34 am**	6:34 am
☽ ⚺ ⚷	**10:31 am**	7:31 am
♂ ⚻ ♇	**8:22 pm**	5:22 pm
☽ □ ♀		10:20 pm
☽ □ ⚳		10:54 pm
☽ ☌ ♅		11:06 pm

14 FRIDAY

☽ □ ♀	**1:20 am**	
☽ □ ⚳	**1:54 am**	
☽ ☌ ♅	**2:06 am**	
☽ △ ☿	**4:02 am**	1:02 am
☽ ⚻ ♄	**6:30 am**	3:30 am
☽ △ ⚴	**7:48 am**	4:48 am
♅ □ ⚳	**9:33 am**	6:33 am
☉ △ ⚵	**10:19 am**	7:19 am
♀ □ ♅	**11:17 am**	8:17 am
♀ ☌ ⚳	**12:13 pm**	9:13 am
☽ ⚺ ♆	**2:37 pm**	11:37 am
☽ △ ⚶	**9:55 pm**	6:55 pm
☽ □ ⚵		10:29 pm
☽ ⚻ ☉		11:25 pm
☽ ⚹ ♂		11:29 pm
☽ □ ♇		11:55 pm

15 SATURDAY

☽ □ ⚵	**1:29 am**	
☽ ⚻ ☉	**2:25 am**	
☽ ⚹ ♂	**2:29 am**	
☽ □ ♇	**2:55 am**	
☉ ⚻ ♂	**3:25 am**	12:25 am
☿ □ ♄	**5:44 am**	2:44 am
☉ ⚹ ♇	**10:05 am**	7:05 am
☽ ⚻ ♃	**11:53 am**	8:53 am
☽ ⚹ ⚷	**12:07 pm**	9:07 am

16 SUNDAY

☽ ⚺ ♅	**3:40 am**	12:40 am
☽ △ ⚳	**4:51 am**	1:51 am
♃ □ ⚷	**4:56 am**	1:56 am
☽ △ ♀	**7:03 am**	4:03 am
☿ ☌ ⚴	**8:17 am**	5:17 am
☽ △ ♄	**8:25 am**	5:25 am
☽ ⚻ ⚴	**11:04 am**	8:04 am
☽ ⚻ ☿	**11:17 am**	8:17 am
☽ ⚹ ♆	**4:24 pm**	1:24 pm
♂ ⚺ ⚵	**7:09 pm**	4:09 pm
☽ □ ⚶		9:36 pm
♀ △ ♄		11:24 pm

17 MONDAY

☽ □ ⚶	**12:36 am**	
♀ △ ♄	**2:24 am**	
☽ ⚺ ♂	**3:49 am**	12:49 am
☽ ⚹ ⚵	**4:03 am**	1:03 am
☽ △ ♇	**5:04 am**	2:04 am
☽ ☍ ☉	**8:14 am**	5:14 am
☽ □ ⚷	**2:29 pm**	11:29 am
☽ ☍ ♃	**2:58 pm**	11:58 am

18 TUESDAY

☽ ⚹ ♅	**6:25 am**	3:25 am
☽ ⚻ ⚳	**9:08 am**	6:08 am
☽ □ ♄	**11:41 am**	8:41 am
☽ ⚻ ♀	**2:21 pm**	11:21 am
☿ □ ♆	**2:40 pm**	11:40 am
☽ ☍ ⚴	**3:51 pm**	12:51 pm
☽ □ ♆	**7:45 pm**	4:45 pm
☽ ☍ ☿	**8:20 pm**	5:20 pm

19 WEDNESDAY

☽ ⚹ ⚶	**5:06 am**	2:06 am
☽ ☌ ♂	**6:50 am**	3:50 am
☽ ⚺ ⚵	**8:28 am**	5:28 am
☽ ⚻ ♇	**9:08 am**	6:08 am
☽ ⚻ ☉	**4:32 pm**	1:32 pm
☽ △ ⚷	**7:01 pm**	4:01 pm
☽ ⚻ ♃	**8:20 pm**	5:20 pm
♀ ⚺ ⚴	**9:45 pm**	6:45 pm

20 THURSDAY

☽ □ ♅	**11:43 am**	8:43 am
☽ ☍ ⚳	**4:16 pm**	1:16 pm
☽ ⚹ ♄	**5:38 pm**	2:38 pm
☽ ⚻ ⚴	**11:42 pm**	8:42 pm
☽ ☍ ♀		10:06 pm
☽ △ ♆		10:57 pm
☉ □ ⚷		11:31 pm

21 FRIDAY

☽ ☍ ♀	**1:06 am**	
☽ △ ♆	**1:57 am**	
☉ □ ⚷	**2:31 am**	
☽ ⚻ ☿	**9:10 am**	6:10 am
♀ ⚹ ♆	**11:19 am**	8:19 am
♂ ⚹ ⚶	**11:34 am**	8:34 am
☽ ⚺ ♂	**12:39 pm**	9:39 am
☽ ⚺ ⚶	**12:42 pm**	9:42 am
☽ ☌ ⚵	**4:00 pm**	1:00 pm
☽ ☍ ♇	**4:18 pm**	1:18 pm
☽ ⚻ ⚷		11:48 pm

22 SATURDAY

☽ ⚻ ⚷	**2:48 am**	
☽ △ ☉	**4:52 am**	1:52 am
☽ △ ♃	**5:07 am**	2:07 am
☉ ☌ ♃	**8:54 am**	5:54 am
☿ ☍ ♂	**12:55 pm**	9:55 am
☽ △ ♅	**8:23 pm**	5:23 pm
☿ △ ⚶	**10:41 pm**	7:41 pm
♄ △ ⚳	**11:27 pm**	8:27 pm

23 SUNDAY

☽ ⚺ ♄	**3:02 am**	12:02 am
☽ ⚻ ⚳	**3:08 am**	12:08 am
☽ △ ⚴	**11:20 am**	8:20 am
☽ ⚻ ♆	**11:34 am**	8:34 am
☽ ⚻ ♀	**4:12 pm**	1:12 pm
♆ □ ⚴	**5:51 pm**	2:51 pm
☽ ⚹ ♂	**9:32 pm**	6:32 pm
☽ ☌ ⚶	**11:46 pm**	8:46 pm
♇ ☍ ⚵		11:08 pm
☽ △ ☿		11:29 pm
☽ ⚻ ♇		11:51 pm
☽ ⚺ ⚵		11:51 pm

24 MONDAY

♇ ☍ ⚵	**2:08 am**	
☽ △ ☿	**2:29 am**	
☽ ⚻ ♇	**2:51 am**	
☽ ⚺ ⚵	**2:51 am**	
☿ ⚺ ♇	**5:51 am**	2:51 am
☿ ⚻ ⚵	**6:01 am**	3:01 am
☽ ☍ ⚷	**1:52 pm**	10:52 am
☽ □ ♃	**5:16 pm**	2:16 pm
☽ □ ☉	**9:17 pm**	6:17 pm

25 TUESDAY

☽ ⚻ ♅	**7:59 am**	4:59 am
☽ ☌ ♄	**3:13 pm**	12:13 pm
♀ ⚻ ♂	**4:59 pm**	1:59 pm
☽ △ ⚳	**5:02 pm**	2:02 pm
☽ ☍ ♆	**11:44 pm**	8:44 pm
☽ □ ⚴		10:47 pm

26 WEDNESDAY

☽ □ ⚴	**1:47 am**	
☽ □ ♂	**8:25 am**	5:25 am
☽ △ ♀	**10:21 am**	7:21 am
☽ ⚺ ⚶	**1:01 pm**	10:01 am
☽ △ ♇	**3:29 pm**	12:29 pm
☽ ⚹ ⚵	**3:43 pm**	12:43 pm
☽ □ ☿	**10:23 pm**	7:23 pm
☽ ⚻ ⚷		11:38 pm

27 THURSDAY

☽ ⚻ ⚷	**2:38 am**	
☽ ⚹ ♃	**7:04 am**	4:04 am
☽ ⚹ ☉	**3:30 pm**	12:30 pm
☽ ☍ ♅	**8:34 pm**	5:34 pm
♀ ⚻ ⚶	**9:07 pm**	6:07 pm

28 FRIDAY

☽ ⚺ ♄	**4:04 am**	1:04 am
☽ □ ⚳	**7:37 am**	4:37 am
☽ ⚻ ♆	**12:15 pm**	9:15 am
☿ ⚹ ⚷	**3:46 pm**	12:46 pm
☽ ⚹ ⚴	**4:33 pm**	1:33 pm
☽ △ ♂	**7:11 pm**	4:11 pm
♀ ☌ ♇	**10:15 pm**	7:15 pm
♀ ☍ ⚵		10:58 pm
☽ ⚹ ⚶		11:00 pm

29 SATURDAY

♀ ☍ ⚵	**1:58 am**	
☽ ⚹ ⚶	**2:00 am**	
☽ □ ♇	**3:50 am**	12:50 am
☽ □ ⚵	**4:08 am**	1:08 am
☽ □ ♀	**4:20 am**	1:20 am
☽ △ ⚷	**2:40 pm**	11:40 am
☽ ⚹ ☿	**5:06 pm**	2:06 pm
☽ ⚺ ♃	**7:54 pm**	4:54 pm

30 SUNDAY

☉ △ ♅	**2:07 am**	12:07 am
☽ ⚻ ♅	**6:47 am**	3:47 am
☽ ⚺ ☉	**7:12 am**	4:12 am
♂ ☍ ⚴	**9:32 am**	6:32 am
☽ ⚹ ♄	**2:16 pm**	11:16 am
☽ ⚹ ⚳	**7:19 pm**	4:19 pm
☽ △ ♆	**9:53 pm**	6:53 pm
☽ ⚻ ♂		11:58 pm

31 MONDAY

☽ ⚻ ♂	**2:58 am**	
☿ ⚺ ♃	**3:43 am**	12:43 am
☽ ⚺ ⚴	**4:05 am**	1:05 am
☽ □ ⚶	**11:36 am**	8:36 am
☽ ⚹ ♇	**12:53 pm**	9:53 am
☽ △ ⚵	**1:09 pm**	10:09 am
☽ ⚹ ♀	**6:17 pm**	3:17 pm
☽ □ ⚷	**11:13 pm**	8:13 pm

OCTOBER 2005

☽ Last Aspect day	EST / hr:mn / PST		asp	☽ Ingress sign day	EST / hr:mn / PST	
1	**9:22 pm**	6:22 pm	△♂	♎ 2	**10:24 am**	7:24 am
4	**11:15 am**	8:15 am	☌♃	♏ 4	**8:03 pm**	5:03 pm
6		10:51 pm	☌♀	♐ 7	**3:28 am**	12:28 am
7	**1:51 am**		☌♀	♐ 7	**3:28 am**	12:28 am
8		11:20 pm	⚹♃	♑ 9	**8:43 am**	5:43 am
9	**2:20 am**		⚹♃	♑ 9	**8:43 am**	5:43 am
11	**6:42 am**	3:42 am	□♃	♒ 11	**12:05 pm**	9:05 am
13	**9:34 am**	6:34 am	△♃	♓ 13	**2:05 pm**	11:05 am
14		11:55 pm	□♇	♈ 15	**3:39 pm**	12:39 pm
15	**2:55 am**		□♇	♈ 15	**3:39 pm**	12:39 pm
17	**2:58 pm**	11:58 am	☍♃	♉ 17	**6:04 pm**	3:04 pm
19	**6:50 am**	3:50 am	☌♂	♊ 19	**10:44 pm**	7:44 pm
22	**5:07 am**	2:07 am	△♃	♋ 22	**6:41 am**	3:41 am
24	**5:16 pm**	2:16 pm	□♃	♌ 24	**5:48 pm**	2:48 pm
26	**10:23 pm**	7:23 pm	□☿	♍ 27	**6:28 am**	3:28 am
29	**5:06 pm**	2:06 pm	⚹☿	♎ 29	**6:15 pm**	3:15 pm
31	**6:17 pm**	3:17 pm	⚹♀	♏ 31		11:29 pm
31	**6:17 pm**	3:17 pm	⚹♀	♏ 11/1	**2:29 am**	

☽ Phases & Eclipses phase	day	EST / hr:mn / PST	
New Moon	3	**6:28 am**	3:28 am
●	3	10° ♎ 19'	
2nd Quarter	10	**3:01 pm**	12:01 pm
Full Moon	17	**8:14 am**	5:14 am
●	17	24° ♈ 13'	
4th Quarter	24	**9:17 pm**	6:17 pm

Planet Ingress	day	EST / hr:mn / PST	
♀ ♐	7	**9:00 pm**	6:00 pm
☿ ♏	8	**1:15 pm**	10:15 am
☉ ♏	23	**3:42 am**	12:42 am
♃ ♏	25	**10:52 pm**	7:52 pm
☿ ♐	30	**4:02 am**	1:02 am

Planetary Motion	day	EST / hr:mn / PST	
♂ ℞	1	**6:04 pm**	3:04 pm
⚷ D	4		10:32 pm
⚷ D	5	**1:32 am**	
♆ D	26	**7:24 pm**	4:24 pm

DATE		SID.TIME	SUN	MOON	NODE	MERCURY	VENUS	MARS	JUPITER	SATURN	URANUS	NEPTUNE	PLUTO	CERES	PALLAS	JUNO	VESTA	CHIRON
1	Sa	0:39:18	07♎54 51	10 ♍ 36	13 ♈℞ 38	17 ♎ 44	22 ♏ 07	23 ♉℞ 22	24 ♎ 34	08 ♌ 54	07 ♓℞ 40	15 ♒℞ 00	22 ♐ 03	02 ♐ 23	04 ♏ 57	18 ♊ 26	15 ♋ 57	27 ♑℞ 49
2	Su	0:43:15	08 53 53	22 41	13 37	19 22	23 15	23 22	24 47	08 59	07 38	14 59	22 04	02 44	05 22	18 41	16 13	27 49
3	M	0:47:11	09 52 57	04 ♎ 55	13 D 37	20 59	24 22	23 22	25 00	09 04	07 36	14 58	22 04	03 05	05 48	18 56	16 28	27 48
4	T	0:51:08	10 52 02	17 21	13 37	22 36	25 29	23 20	25 13	09 09	07 34	14 58	22 05	03 26	06 13	19 11	16 43	27 48
5	W	0:55:04	11 51 10	29 58	13 37	24 11	26 37	23 18	25 25	09 14	07 32	14 57	22 06	03 48	06 39	19 25	16 59	27 D 48
6	Th	0:59:01	12 50 20	12 ♏ 49	13 ℞ 37	25 46	27 44	23 15	25 38	09 19	07 30	14 56	22 08	04 09	07 05	19 39	17 13	27 48
7	F	1:02:57	13 49 32	25 53	13 37	27 20	28 50	23 11	25 51	09 24	07 29	14 56	22 09	04 31	07 30	19 52	17 28	27 48
8	Sa	1:06:54	14 48 45	09 ♐ 11	13 37	28 53	29 57	23 06	26 04	09 28	07 27	14 55	22 10	04 52	07 56	20 05	17 42	27 48
9	Su	1:10:51	15 48 01	22 44	13 37	00 ♏ 26	01 ♐ 04	23 00	26 17	09 33	07 25	14 54	22 11	05 14	08 22	20 18	17 57	27 49
10	M	1:14:47	16 47 18	06 ♑ 30	13 D 37	01 58	02 10	22 53	26 30	09 38	07 23	14 54	22 12	05 36	08 48	20 30	18 10	27 49
11	T	1:18:44	17 46 37	20 30	13 37	03 29	03 17	22 45	26 43	09 42	07 22	14 53	22 13	05 58	09 14	20 42	18 24	27 49
12	W	1:22:40	18 45 58	04 ♒ 42	13 37	04 59	04 23	22 37	26 56	09 46	07 20	14 53	22 14	06 20	09 39	20 53	18 38	27 50
13	Th	1:26:37	19 45 20	19 05	13 37	06 28	05 29	22 27	27 09	09 51	07 19	14 52	22 16	06 42	10 05	21 04	18 51	27 50
14	F	1:30:33	20 44 44	03 ♓ 35	13 38	07 57	06 34	22 17	27 22	09 55	07 17	14 52	22 17	07 04	10 31	21 14	19 04	27 51
15	Sa	1:34:30	21 44 10	18 07	13 39	09 25	07 40	22 06	27 35	09 59	07 15	14 51	22 18	07 26	10 57	21 24	19 16	27 52
16	Su	1:38:26	22 43 38	02 ♈ 37	13 ℞ 39	10 52	08 45	21 54	27 48	10 03	07 14	14 51	22 20	07 48	11 23	21 33	19 28	27 52
17	M	1:42:23	23 43 07	16 59	13 39	12 18	09 50	21 42	28 01	10 07	07 13	14 51	22 21	08 10	11 49	21 42	19 41	27 53
18	T	1:46:20	24 42 39	01 ♉ 08	13 39	13 44	10 55	21 28	28 14	10 10	07 11	14 50	22 22	08 33	12 15	21 51	19 52	27 54
19	W	1:50:16	25 42 13	14 59	13 38	15 09	12 00	21 14	28 27	10 14	07 10	14 50	22 24	08 55	12 41	21 59	20 04	27 55
20	Th	1:54:13	26 41 49	28 29	13 36	16 33	13 04	20 59	28 40	10 18	07 09	14 50	22 25	09 17	13 07	22 06	20 15	27 56
21	F	1:58:09	27 41 27	11 ♊ 38	13 34	17 56	14 09	20 43	28 53	10 21	07 07	14 50	22 27	09 40	13 33	22 13	20 26	27 57
22	Sa	2:02:06	28 41 07	24 25	13 32	19 18	15 13	20 27	29 06	10 25	07 06	14 49	22 28	10 02	13 59	22 19	20 37	27 59
23	Su	2:06:02	29 40 49	06 ♋ 53	13 31	20 39	16 16	20 10	29 19	10 28	07 05	14 49	22 30	10 25	14 25	22 25	20 47	28 00
24	M	2:09:59	00♏40 34	19 05	13 29	21 59	17 20	19 53	29 32	10 31	07 04	14 49	22 31	10 48	14 52	22 30	20 57	28 01
25	T	2:13:56	01 40 21	01 ♌ 05	13 D 29	23 18	18 23	19 35	29 45	10 34	07 03	14 49	22 33	11 11	15 18	22 35	21 07	28 03
26	W	2:17:52	02 40 10	12 59	13 29	24 36	19 26	19 16	29 58	10 37	07 02	14 D 49	22 34	11 33	15 44	22 39	21 16	28 04
27	Th	2:21:49	03 40 02	24 49	13 30	25 53	20 29	18 57	00 ♏ 12	10 40	07 01	14 49	22 36	11 56	16 10	22 43	21 25	28 06
28	F	2:25:45	04 39 55	06 ♍ 43	13 32	27 08	21 31	18 37	00 25	10 43	07 00	14 49	22 38	12 19	16 36	22 46	21 34	28 07
29	Sa	2:29:42	05 39 51	18 43	13 34	28 21	22 34	18 17	00 38	10 46	06 59	14 49	22 39	12 42	17 02	22 48	21 42	28 09
30	Su	2:33:38	06 39 48	00 ♎ 54	13 35	29 33	23 35	17 57	00 51	10 48	06 58	14 49	22 41	13 05	17 29	22 50	21 50	28 11
31	M	2:37:35	07 39 48	13 19	13 ℞ 36	00 ♐ 43	24 37	17 36	01 04	10 51	06 57	14 49	22 43	13 28	17 55	22 52	21 58	28 12

EPHEMERIS CALCULATED FOR 12 MIDNIGHT GREENWICH MEAN TIME. ALL OTHER DATA AND FACING ASPECTARIAN PAGE IN **EASTERN TIME (BOLD)** AND PACIFIC TIME (REGULAR).

NOVEMBER 2005

1 TUESDAY
☽ ☌ ♃ **5:01 am** 2:01 am
☽ ⚺ ☿ **6:57 am** 3:57 am
☽ △ ♅ **3:17 pm** 12:17 pm
☽ ☌ ☉ **8:25 pm** 5:25 pm
☽ □ ♄ **10:37 pm** 7:37 pm

2 WEDNESDAY
☽ ⚺ ⚳ **4:56 am** 1:56 am
☽ □ ♆ **5:42 am** 2:42 am
☽ ☍ ♂ **9:05 am** 6:05 am
☽ ☌ ♀ **1:28 pm** 10:28 am
☽ △ ⚴ **7:13 pm** 4:13 pm
☽ ⚺ ♇ **8:05 pm** 5:05 pm
☽ ⚻ ⚵ **8:13 pm** 5:13 pm
☉ □ ♄ 11:21 pm

3 THURSDAY
☉ □ ♄ **2:21 am**
☽ ⚺ ♀ **5:33 am** 2:33 am
☽ ✶ ⚷ **5:56 am** 2:56 am
♆ ✶ ⚳ **7:27 am** 4:27 am
♀ ⚺ ⚷ **10:56 am** 7:56 am
☽ ⚺ ♃ **12:14 pm** 9:14 am
☽ ☌ ☿ **5:42 pm** 2:42 pm
☽ □ ♅ **9:07 pm** 6:07 pm

4 FRIDAY
☽ △ ♄ **4:19 am** 1:19 am
☽ ⚺ ☉ **6:18 am** 3:18 am
♇ ☍ ⚵ **9:27 am** 6:27 am
☽ ✶ ♆ **11:01 am** 8:01 am
☽ ☌ ⚳ **11:48 am** 8:48 am
☽ ⚻ ♂ **12:55 pm** 9:55 am
☽ ⚺ ♀ **8:13 pm** 5:13 pm
☽ ⚻ ⚴ 9:24 pm
☽ ☍ ⚵ 9:54 pm
☽ ☌ ♇ 9:58 pm

5 SATURDAY
☽ ⚻ ⚴ **12:24 am**
☽ ☍ ⚵ **12:54 am**
☽ ☌ ♇ **12:58 am**
♂ ⚻ ⚳ **8:49 am** 5:49 am
☽ ⚺ ⚷ **10:31 am** 7:31 am
☽ ☌ ♀ **2:03 pm** 11:03 am
☽ ✶ ♃ **5:19 pm** 2:19 pm
☿ □ ♅ **7:19 pm** 4:19 pm

Eastern time in bold type
Pacific time in medium type

☽ ✶ ♅ 10:06 pm
☽ ⚺ ☿ 10:29 pm

6 SUNDAY
☽ ✶ ♅ **1:06 am**
☽ ⚺ ☿ **1:29 am**
☽ ⚻ ♄ **8:17 am** 5:17 am
☽ ✶ ☉ **2:05 pm** 11:05 am
☽ ⚺ ♆ **2:44 pm** 11:44 am
☽ △ ♂ **3:18 pm** 12:18 pm
☽ ⚺ ⚳ **4:57 pm** 1:57 pm
☉ □ ♆ **11:11 pm** 8:11 pm
☽ ✶ ♀ 10:22 pm
☉ ☍ ♂ 11:57 pm

7 MONDAY
☽ ✶ ♀ **1:22 am**
☉ ☍ ♂ **2:57 am**
☽ ☍ ⚴ **4:09 am** 1:09 am
☽ ⚻ ⚵ **4:10 am** 1:10 am
☽ ⚺ ♇ **4:30 am** 1:30 am
⚵ ⚺ ⚴ **5:59 am** 2:59 am
♂ □ ♆ **1:26 pm** 10:26 am
☽ ☌ ⚷ **1:56 pm** 10:56 am
☽ ⚺ ♀ **9:05 pm** 6:05 pm
☽ □ ♃ **9:17 pm** 6:17 pm
♀ ✶ ♃ 9:46 pm

8 TUESDAY
♀ ✶ ♃ **12:46 am**
☽ ⚺ ♅ **4:10 am** 1:10 am
☽ ✶ ☿ **7:30 am** 4:30 am
☽ ☍ ♄ **11:24 am** 8:24 am
☽ □ ♂ **5:02 pm** 2:02 pm
☽ ☌ ♆ **5:44 pm** 2:44 pm
☽ □ ☉ **8:57 pm** 5:57 pm
☽ ✶ ⚳ **9:22 pm** 6:22 pm

9 WEDNESDAY
☽ □ ♀ **5:54 am** 2:54 am
☉ ⚺ ⚳ **6:13 am** 3:13 am
☽ △ ⚵ **6:51 am** 3:51 am
☽ ⚻ ⚴ **7:19 am** 4:19 am
☽ ✶ ♇ **7:31 am** 4:31 am
☽ ⚺ ⚷ **4:57 pm** 1:57 pm
☽ △ ♃ 9:56 pm

10 THURSDAY
☽ △ ♃ **12:56 am**
☽ ✶ ♀ **3:40 am** 12:40 am
☽ ☌ ♅ **7:00 am** 4:00 am
♀ ⚻ ⚵ **7:56 am** 4:56 am
☽ □ ☿ **12:29 pm** 9:29 am
☽ ⚻ ♄ **2:21 pm** 11:21 am
☽ ✶ ♂ **6:41 pm** 3:41 pm
☽ ⚺ ♆ **8:38 pm** 5:38 pm
☽ □ ⚳ 10:42 pm

11 FRIDAY
☽ □ ⚳ **1:42 am**
☽ △ ☉ **3:44 am** 12:44 am
☽ □ ⚵ **9:29 am** 6:29 am
♀ △ ⚴ **10:11 am** 7:11 am
☽ △ ♀ **10:27 am** 7:27 am
☽ △ ⚴ **10:27 am** 7:27 am
☽ □ ♇ **10:33 am** 7:33 am
♇ ⚺ ♀ **1:38 pm** 10:38 am
☽ ✶ ⚷ **8:05 pm** 5:05 pm

12 SATURDAY
☽ ⚻ ♃ **4:46 am** 1:46 am
♀ ✶ ♅ **5:28 am** 2:28 am
☽ ⚺ ♅ **10:05 am** 7:05 am
☽ □ ♀ **10:25 am** 7:25 am
☽ △ ☿ **4:52 pm** 1:52 pm
☽ △ ♄ **5:36 pm** 2:36 pm
☽ ⚺ ♂ **8:43 pm** 5:43 pm
☽ ✶ ♆ **11:55 pm** 8:55 pm

13 SUNDAY
☽ △ ⚳ **6:31 am** 3:31 am
☽ ⚻ ☉ **11:05 am** 8:05 am
☽ ✶ ⚵ **12:33 pm** 9:33 am
☽ □ ⚴ **2:04 pm** 11:04 am
☽ △ ♇ **2:07 pm** 11:07 am
☽ ⚻ ♀ **3:35 pm** 12:35 pm
☽ □ ⚷ **11:53 pm** 8:53 pm

14 MONDAY
☉ ⚻ ⚵ **5:22 am** 2:22 am
☽ ☍ ♃ **9:23 am** 6:23 am
☽ ✶ ♅ **2:00 pm** 11:00 am
☽ △ ♀ **6:06 pm** 3:06 pm
☽ ⚻ ☿ **9:05 pm** 6:05 pm
☽ □ ♄ **9:45 pm** 6:45 pm
☽ ☌ ♂ **11:43 pm** 8:43 pm

15 TUESDAY
☽ □ ♆ **4:13 am** 1:13 am
☉ △ ⚴ **5:22 am** 2:22 am
☉ ⚺ ♇ **6:17 am** 3:17 am
☽ ⚻ ⚳ **12:34 pm** 9:34 am
☽ ⚺ ⚵ **4:45 pm** 1:45 pm
☽ ✶ ⚴ **6:53 pm** 3:53 pm
☽ ⚻ ♇ **6:58 pm** 3:58 pm
☽ ☍ ☉ **7:58 pm** 4:58 pm
☽ ☍ ♀ **10:08 pm** 7:08 pm

16 WEDNESDAY
☽ △ ⚷ **5:07 am** 2:07 am
☿ ⚺ ♀ **6:08 am** 3:08 am
☽ ⚻ ♃ **3:39 pm** 12:39 pm
☽ □ ♅ **7:35 pm** 4:35 pm
☽ ☍ ☿ 10:43 pm
♀ ⚻ ♄ 11:06 pm

17 THURSDAY
☽ ☍ ☿ **1:43 am**
♀ ⚻ ♄ **2:06 am**
☽ ✶ ♄ **3:44 am** 12:44 am
☽ ⚻ ♀ **3:51 am** 12:51 am
☽ ⚺ ♂ **4:31 am** 1:31 am
☽ △ ♆ **10:29 am** 7:29 am
♀ △ ♂ **11:23 am** 8:23 am
☽ ☍ ⚳ **8:55 pm** 5:55 pm
☉ ☌ ♀ **9:21 pm** 6:21 pm
☽ ☌ ⚵ **10:59 pm** 7:59 pm
☽ ⚺ ⚴ 10:52 pm
☽ ☍ ♇ 11:02 pm

18 FRIDAY
☽ ⚺ ⚴ **1:52 am**
☽ ☍ ♇ **2:02 am**
☽ ⚻ ♀ **7:10 am** 4:10 am
☽ ⚻ ☉ **7:39 am** 4:39 am
☽ ⚻ ⚷ **12:46 pm** 9:46 am
♂ □ ♄ **3:28 pm** 12:28 pm
☽ △ ♃ 9:36 pm

19 SATURDAY
☽ △ ♃ **12:36 am**
☽ △ ♅ **3:48 am** 12:48 am
☽ ⚻ ☿ **7:15 am** 4:15 am
☽ ✶ ♂ **11:56 am** 8:56 am
☽ ⚺ ♄ **12:24 pm** 9:24 am
☽ ☍ ♀ **4:48 pm** 1:48 pm
☽ ⚻ ♆ **7:33 pm** 4:33 pm
⚳ ☍ ⚵ **9:40 pm** 6:40 pm

20 SUNDAY
☽ ⚺ ⚵ **7:55 am** 4:55 am
☽ ⚻ ⚳ **8:24 am** 5:24 am
☽ ☌ ⚴ **11:39 am** 8:39 am
☽ ⚻ ♇ **12:01 pm** 9:01 am
☽ △ ♀ **7:26 pm** 4:26 pm
☽ △ ☉ **11:03 pm** 8:03 pm
☽ ☍ ⚷ **11:23 pm** 8:23 pm
☿ □ ♅ 10:17 pm

21 MONDAY
☿ □ ♅ **1:17 am**
☉ ✶ ⚷ **3:18 am** 12:18 am
♀ ⚺ ♆ **9:17 am** 6:17 am
☽ □ ♃ **12:34 pm** 9:34 am
☽ △ ☿ **1:39 pm** 10:39 am
☽ ⚻ ♅ **2:53 pm** 11:53 am
☽ □ ♂ **10:06 pm** 7:06 pm
☿ ⚺ ♃ **10:33 pm** 7:33 pm
☽ ☌ ♄ **11:50 pm** 8:50 pm

22 TUESDAY
☽ ☍ ♆ **7:19 am** 4:19 am
☽ ⚻ ♀ **8:57 am** 5:57 am
☽ ✶ ⚵ **7:10 pm** 4:10 pm
☽ △ ⚳ **10:38 pm** 7:38 pm
☽ ⚺ ⚴ **11:46 pm** 8:46 pm
☽ △ ♇ 9:25 pm

23 WEDNESDAY
☽ △ ♇ **12:25 am**
☽ □ ♀ **10:10 am** 7:10 am
☽ ⚻ ⚷ **12:10 pm** 9:10 am
☽ □ ☉ **5:11 pm** 2:11 pm
☽ □ ☿ **8:21 pm** 5:21 pm
☽ ✶ ♃ 11:21 pm

24 THURSDAY
☽ ✶ ♃ **2:21 am**
☽ ☍ ♅ **3:37 am** 12:37 am
⚳ ⚻ ⚴ **5:22 am** 2:22 am
☽ △ ♂ **9:44 am** 6:44 am
☉ ☌ ☿ **10:43 am** 7:43 am
☽ ⚺ ♄ **12:35 pm** 9:35 am
☽ ⚻ ♆ **8:09 pm** 5:09 pm
☽ △ ♀ 11:06 pm

25 FRIDAY
☽ △ ♀ **2:06 am**
☽ □ ⚵ **6:53 am** 3:53 am
♇ ☌ ⚳ **8:24 am** 5:24 am
☽ ✶ ⚴ **12:08 pm** 9:08 am
☽ □ ♇ **1:10 pm** 10:10 am
☽ □ ⚳ **1:19 pm** 10:19 am
⚷ ✶ ♀ **11:58 pm** 8:58 pm
☽ △ ⚷ 9:46 pm
☽ ✶ ♀ 9:47 pm
☽ ✶ ☿ 11:26 pm

26 SATURDAY
☽ △ ⚷ **12:46 am**
☽ ✶ ♀ **12:47 am**
☽ ✶ ☿ **2:26 am**
☽ ✶ ☉ **10:48 am** 7:48 am
☿ ☌ ♀ **1:43 pm** 10:43 am
☽ ⚺ ♃ **3:15 pm** 12:15 pm
☽ ⚻ ♅ **3:30 pm** 12:30 pm
☿ ✶ ⚷ **5:43 pm** 2:43 pm
☽ ⚻ ♂ **8:24 pm** 5:24 pm
☽ ✶ ♄ 9:02 pm

27 SUNDAY
☽ ✶ ♄ **12:02 am**
♃ △ ♅ **6:56 am** 3:56 am
☽ △ ♆ **7:23 am** 4:23 am
♀ ⚻ ⚵ **2:08 pm** 11:08 am
☽ △ ⚵ **4:36 pm** 1:36 pm
☽ □ ♀ **4:48 pm** 1:48 pm
☽ □ ⚴ **10:13 pm** 7:13 pm
☽ ✶ ♇ **11:38 pm** 8:38 pm
☽ ✶ ⚳ 10:30 pm

28 MONDAY
☽ ✶ ⚳ **1:30 am**
☽ ⚺ ☿ **7:10 am** 4:10 am
☽ □ ⚷ **10:41 am** 7:41 am
☽ ⚺ ♀ **12:27 pm** 9:27 am
☉ □ ♅ **8:17 pm** 5:17 pm
☽ △ ♅ 9:18 pm
☽ ⚺ ☉ 9:38 pm
☽ ☌ ♃ 9:56 pm

29 TUESDAY
☽ △ ♅ **12:18 am**
☽ ⚺ ☉ **12:38 am**
☽ ☌ ♃ **12:56 am**
☽ ☍ ♂ **4:10 am** 1:10 am
☉ ⚺ ♃ **5:12 am** 2:12 am
☽ □ ♄ **8:13 am** 5:13 am
☽ □ ♆ **3:13 pm** 12:13 pm
☽ ⚻ ⚵ **10:55 pm** 7:55 pm

30 WEDNESDAY
☽ ✶ ♀ **3:06 am** 12:06 am
☽ △ ⚴ **4:44 am** 1:44 am
☽ ⚺ ♇ **6:31 am** 3:31 am
☽ ⚺ ⚳ **9:47 am** 6:47 am
☽ ☌ ☿ **10:16 am** 7:16 am
☿ ⚺ ⚳ **4:34 pm** 1:34 pm
☽ ✶ ⚷ **4:58 pm** 1:58 pm
☉ ⚻ ♂ **5:23 pm** 2:23 pm
☽ ☌ ♀ **8:09 pm** 5:09 pm

NOVEMBER 2005

☽ Last Aspect day	EST / hr:mn / PST		asp	☽ Ingress sign day	EST / hr:mn / PST	
10/31	**6:17 pm**	3:17 pm	⚹♀	♏ 10/31		11:29 pm
10/31	**6:17 pm**	3:17 pm	⚹♀	♏ 1	**2:29 am**	
2	**9:05 am**	6:05 am	☍♂	♐ 3	**8:55 am**	5:55 am
4		9:58 pm	☌♇	♑ 5	**1:17 pm**	10:17 am
5	**12:58 am**		☌♇	♑ 5	**1:17 pm**	10:17 am
6	**3:18 pm**	12:18 pm	△♂	♒ 7	**4:31 pm**	1:31 pm
9	**7:31 am**	4:31 am	⚹♇	♓ 9	**7:22 pm**	4:22 pm
11	**10:33 am**	7:33 am	□♇	♈ 11	**10:22 pm**	7:22 pm
13	**2:07 pm**	11:07 am	△♇	♉ 13		11:02 pm
13	**2:07 pm**	11:07 am	△♇	♉ 14	**2:02 am**	
15	**7:58 pm**	4:58 pm	☍☉	♊ 16	**7:10 am**	4:10 am

☽ Last Aspect day	EST / hr:mn / PST		asp	☽ Ingress sign day	EST / hr:mn / PST	
17		11:02 pm	☍♇	♋ 18	**2:42 pm**	11:42 pm
18	**2:02 am**		☍♇	♋ 18	**2:42 pm**	11:42 pm
20	**11:03 pm**	8:03 pm	△☉	♌ 20		10:10 pm
20	**11:03 pm**	8:03 pm	△☉	♌ 21	**1:10 am**	
22		9:25 pm	△♇	♍ 23	**1:41 pm**	10:41 am
23	**12:25 am**		△♇	♍ 23	**1:41 pm**	10:41 am
25	**1:10 pm**	10:10 am	□♇	♎ 25		10:58 pm
25	**1:10 pm**	10:10 am	□♇	♎ 26	**1:58 am**	
27	**11:38 pm**	8:38 pm	⚹♇	♏ 28	**11:33 am**	8:33 am
30	**10:16 am**	7:16 am	☌☿	♐ 30	**5:32 pm**	2:32 pm

☽ Phases & Eclipses phase	day	EST / hr:mn / PST	
New Moon	1	**8:25 pm**	5:25 pm
2nd Quarter	8	**8:57 pm**	5:57 pm
Full Moon	15	**7:58 pm**	4:58 pm
4th Quarter	23	**5:11 pm**	2:11 pm

Planet Ingress	day	EST / hr:mn / PST	
♀ ♑	5	**3:10 am**	12:10 am
☉ ♐	21		9:15 pm
☉ ♐	22	**12:15 am**	
☿ ♏	26	**6:53 am**	3:53 am
♀ ♐	27	**9:32 am**	6:32 am

Planetary Motion	day	EST / hr:mn / PST	
⚵ R	1	**4:45 pm**	1:45 pm
☿ R	13		9:42 pm
☿ R	14	**12:42 am**	
♅ D	15	**7:07 pm**	4:07 pm
⚶ R	18	**6:41 pm**	3:41 pm
♄ R	22	**4:01 am**	1:01 am

DATE		SID. TIME	SUN	MOON	NODE	MERCURY	VENUS	MARS	JUPITER	SATURN	URANUS	NEPTUNE	PLUTO	CERES	PALLAS	JUNO	VESTA	CHIRON
1	T	2:41:31	08 ♏ 39 50	25 ♎ 59	13 ♈ R 35	01 ♐ 52	25 ♐ 38	17 ♉ R 15	01 ♏ 17	10 ♌ 53	06 ♓ R 56	14 ♒ 49	22 ♐ 44	13 ♐ 51	18 ♏ 21	22 ♊ R 53	22 ♋ 05	28 ♑ 14
2	W	2:45:28	09 39 54	08 ♏ 57	13 33	02 57	26 39	16 54	01 30	10 56	06 56	14 50	22 46	14 15	18 47	22 53	22 12	28 16
3	Th	2:49:24	10 39 59	22 12	13 30	04 01	27 40	16 33	01 43	10 58	06 55	14 50	22 48	14 38	19 14	22 53	22 19	28 18
4	F	2:53:21	11 40 07	05 ♐ 42	13 26	05 01	28 40	16 12	01 56	11 00	06 54	14 50	22 50	15 01	19 40	22 52	22 25	28 20
5	Sa	2:57:18	12 40 16	19 26	13 21	05 59	29 40	15 50	02 09	11 02	06 54	14 50	22 51	15 25	20 06	22 50	22 31	28 23
6	Su	3:01:14	13 40 27	03 ♑ 20	13 17	06 52	00 ♑ 39	15 29	02 22	11 04	06 53	14 51	22 53	15 48	20 32	22 48	22 37	28 25
7	M	3:05:11	14 40 40	17 21	13 13	07 42	01 38	15 08	02 35	11 05	06 53	14 51	22 55	16 11	20 59	22 45	22 42	28 27
8	T	3:09:07	15 40 54	01 ♒ 28	13 11	08 28	02 37	14 46	02 48	11 07	06 52	14 51	22 57	16 35	21 25	22 42	22 47	28 30
9	W	3:13:04	16 41 09	15 37	13 D 10	09 08	03 35	14 26	03 01	11 09	06 52	14 52	22 59	16 58	21 51	22 39	22 51	28 32
10	Th	3:17:00	17 41 26	29 47	13 10	09 44	04 33	14 05	03 13	11 10	06 51	14 52	23 01	17 22	22 18	22 34	22 55	28 34
11	F	3:20:57	18 41 44	13 ♓ 55	13 12	10 13	05 30	13 44	03 26	11 11	06 51	14 53	23 03	17 45	22 44	22 29	22 58	28 37
12	Sa	3:24:53	19 42 03	28 01	13 13	10 35	06 26	13 24	03 39	11 13	06 51	14 53	23 05	18 09	23 10	22 24	23 02	28 40
13	Su	3:28:50	20 42 24	12 ♈ 03	13 R 14	10 49	07 22	13 04	03 52	11 14	06 51	14 54	23 07	18 33	23 36	22 18	23 04	28 42
14	M	3:32:47	21 42 47	25 57	13 13	10 R 56	08 18	12 45	04 05	11 15	06 51	14 55	23 09	18 56	24 03	22 12	23 07	28 45
15	T	3:36:43	22 43 11	09 ♉ 42	13 10	10 54	09 13	12 26	04 17	11 16	06 51	14 55	23 11	19 20	24 29	22 05	23 09	28 48
16	W	3:40:40	23 43 36	23 14	13 06	10 42	10 08	12 08	04 30	11 16	06 D 51	14 56	23 13	19 44	24 55	21 57	23 10	28 51
17	Th	3:44:36	24 44 04	06 ♊ 31	12 59	10 20	11 01	11 50	04 43	11 17	06 51	14 57	23 15	20 08	25 22	21 50	23 11	28 54
18	F	3:48:33	25 44 32	19 32	12 52	09 47	11 55	11 32	04 56	11 18	06 51	14 57	23 17	20 32	25 48	21 41	23 R 12	28 57
19	Sa	3:52:29	26 45 03	02 ♋ 15	12 44	09 04	12 47	11 16	05 08	11 18	06 51	14 58	23 19	20 55	26 14	21 32	23 12	29 00
20	Su	3:56:26	27 45 35	14 42	12 36	08 11	13 39	10 59	05 21	11 18	06 51	14 59	23 21	21 19	26 40	21 23	23 12	29 03
21	M	4:00:23	28 46 09	26 54	12 30	07 09	14 30	10 44	05 33	11 19	06 51	15 00	23 23	21 43	27 07	21 13	23 11	29 06
22	T	4:04:19	29 46 45	08 ♌ 54	12 25	05 59	15 21	10 29	05 46	11 R 19	06 51	15 01	23 25	22 07	27 33	21 03	23 10	29 09
23	W	4:08:16	00 ♐ 47 22	20 47	12 D 23	04 42	16 10	10 15	05 58	11 19	06 52	15 01	23 27	22 31	27 59	20 52	23 08	29 12
24	Th	4:12:12	01 48 01	02 ♍ 37	12 22	03 21	16 59	10 01	06 11	11 19	06 52	15 02	23 29	22 55	28 25	20 41	23 06	29 16
25	F	4:16:09	02 48 41	14 29	12 23	01 59	17 47	09 49	06 23	11 18	06 53	15 03	23 31	23 19	28 52	20 30	23 04	29 19
26	Sa	4:20:05	03 49 23	26 29	12 24	00 39	18 34	09 37	06 36	11 18	06 53	15 04	23 33	23 43	29 18	20 18	23 01	29 23
27	Su	4:24:02	04 50 07	08 ♎ 42	12 R 25	29 ♏ 22	19 20	09 25	06 48	11 17	06 54	15 05	23 36	24 07	29 44	20 06	22 58	29 26
28	M	4:27:58	05 50 52	21 11	12 24	28 12	20 06	09 15	07 00	11 17	06 54	15 06	23 38	24 31	00 ♐ 10	19 54	22 54	29 30
29	T	4:31:55	06 51 39	04 ♏ 02	12 22	27 10	20 50	09 05	07 12	11 16	06 55	15 07	23 40	24 55	00 37	19 41	22 50	29 33
30	W	4:35:52	07 52 27	17 15	12 17	26 18	21 33	08 57	07 24	11 15	06 56	15 09	23 42	25 20	01 03	19 29	22 45	29 37

EPHEMERIS CALCULATED FOR 12 MIDNIGHT GREENWICH MEAN TIME. ALL OTHER DATA AND FACING ASPECTARIAN PAGE IN **EASTERN TIME (BOLD)** AND PACIFIC TIME (REGULAR).

DECEMBER 2005

1 THURSDAY
☽□♅ 5:35 am 2:35 am
☽⚺♃ 6:54 am 3:54 am
♀☍⚶ 7:21 am 4:21 am
☽⚻♂ 8:40 am 5:40 am
☽☌☉ 10:01 am 7:01 am
☽△♄ 12:56 pm 9:56 am
☽⚹♆ 7:41 pm 4:41 pm
☽☍⚵ 11:07 pm

2 FRIDAY
☽☍⚵ 2:07 am
☽⚻⚶ 8:07 am 5:07 am
☽⚺♀ 9:32 am 6:32 am
☽☌♇ 10:17 am 7:17 am
☽⚺☿ 12:09 pm 9:09 am
☽☌⚳ 2:46 pm 11:46 am
☽⚺⚷ 8:22 pm 5:22 pm
☽⚺♀ 9:49 pm
☉△♄ 10:41 pm
♀⚺♇ 11:44 pm

3 SATURDAY
☽⚺♀ 12:49 am
☉△♄ 1:41 am
♀⚺♇ 2:44 am
☽⚹♅ 8:21 am 5:21 am
☽⚹♃ 10:17 am 7:17 am
☽△♂ 10:56 am 7:56 am
☽⚻♄ 3:22 pm 12:22 pm
☽⚺☉ 4:25 pm 1:25 pm
☽⚺♆ 10:05 pm 7:05 pm

4 SUNDAY
☽⚻⚵ 3:31 am 12:31 am
☽☍⚶ 9:48 am 6:48 am
☽⚺♇ 12:26 pm 9:26 am
☽☌♀ 1:54 pm 10:54 am
☽⚹☿ 1:56 pm 10:56 am
☿⚹♀ 3:06 pm 12:06 pm
☽⚺⚳ 6:10 pm 3:10 pm
♂☍♃ 7:44 pm 4:44 pm
☽☌⚷ 10:30 pm 7:30 pm

5 MONDAY
☽⚹♀ 4:14 am 1:14 am
☽⚺♅ 10:15 am 7:15 am
☽□♂ 12:31 pm 9:31 am
☽□♃ 12:49 pm 9:49 am
☽☍♄ 5:07 pm 2:07 pm
☽⚹☉ 10:03 pm 7:03 pm
☽☌♆ 9:01 pm

6 TUESDAY
☽☌♆ 12:01 am
☽△⚵ 4:38 am 1:38 am
☽⚻⚶ 11:20 am 8:20 am
☽⚹♇ 2:33 pm 11:33 am
☽□☿ 4:58 pm 1:58 pm
☽⚺♀ 6:05 pm 3:05 pm
☽⚹⚳ 9:42 pm 6:42 pm
☽⚺⚷ 9:52 pm
☉⚹♆ 11:30 pm

7 WEDNESDAY
☽⚺⚷ 12:52 am
☉⚹♆ 2:30 am
☽□♀ 8:03 am 5:03 am
☽☌♅ 12:40 pm 9:40 am
☽⚹♂ 2:45 pm 11:45 am
☽△♃ 3:56 pm 12:56 pm
☽⚻♄ 7:32 pm 4:32 pm
☽⚺♆ 11:45 pm

8 THURSDAY
☽⚺♆ 2:45 am
☽□☉ 4:36 am 1:36 am
☽□⚵ 6:35 am 3:35 am
☽△⚶ 1:46 pm 10:46 am
☽□♇ 5:43 pm 2:43 pm
☽△☿ 10:17 pm 7:17 pm
☽⚹♀ 11:16 pm 8:16 pm
☽□⚳ 11:27 pm

9 FRIDAY
☽□⚳ 2:27 am
☉☍⚵ 3:09 am 12:09 am
☽⚹⚷ 4:25 am 1:25 am
☽△♀ 1:13 pm 10:13 am
☽⚺♅ 4:21 pm 1:21 pm
☽⚺♂ 6:22 pm 3:22 pm
☽⚻♃ 8:23 pm 5:23 pm
☽△♄ 11:13 pm 8:13 pm

10 SATURDAY
☽⚹♆ 6:52 am 3:52 am
☽⚹⚵ 9:50 am 6:50 am
☽△☉ 12:52 pm 9:52 am
☿⚹♀ 5:00 pm 2:00 pm
☽□⚶ 5:30 pm 2:30 pm
☽△♇ 10:18 pm 7:18 pm

11 SUNDAY
☽□♀ 5:50 am 2:50 am
☽⚻☿ 6:17 am 3:17 am
☽△⚳ 8:46 am 5:46 am
☽□⚷ 9:26 am 6:26 am
☽⚻♀ 7:58 pm 4:58 pm
☽⚹♅ 9:31 pm 6:31 pm
☽☌♂ 11:32 pm 8:32 pm
☽☍♃ 11:21 pm

12 MONDAY
☽☍♃ 2:21 am
☽□♄ 4:21 am 1:21 am
⚷⚺⚳ 11:34 am 8:34 am
☽□♆ 12:26 pm 9:26 am
☽⚺⚵ 2:29 pm 11:29 am
☉⚻⚶ 6:42 pm 3:42 pm
☽⚹⚶ 10:37 pm 7:37 pm
☽⚻☉ 11:00 pm 8:00 pm

13 TUESDAY
☿⚹⚷ 3:50 am 12:50 am
☽⚻♇ 4:22 am 1:22 am
☿⚺⚳ 12:01 pm 9:01 am
☽△♀ 1:46 pm 10:46 am
☽△⚷ 3:59 pm 12:59 pm
☽⚻⚳ 4:44 pm 1:44 pm
☽☍☿ 5:00 pm 2:00 pm
♅□♀ 10:36 pm 7:36 pm

14 WEDNESDAY
☽□♅ 4:14 am 1:14 am
☽☍♀ 4:24 am 1:24 am
☽⚺♂ 6:24 am 3:24 am
☽⚻♃ 9:56 am 6:56 am
☽⚹♄ 11:01 am 8:01 am
☽△♆ 7:39 pm 4:39 pm
☽☌⚵ 8:43 pm 5:43 pm

15 THURSDAY
☽⚺⚶ 5:16 am 2:16 am
☽☍☉ 11:16 am 8:16 am
☽☍♇ 12:11 pm 9:11 am
☉☌♇ 11:12 pm 8:12 pm
☽⚻♀ 11:20 pm 8:20 pm
☽⚻⚷ 9:22 pm
☽☍⚳ 11:41 pm

16 FRIDAY
☽⚻⚷ 12:22 am
☽☍⚳ 2:41 am
☽⚻☿ 6:48 am 3:48 am
☽△♅ 12:52 pm 9:52 am
☽⚻♀ 2:58 pm 11:58 am
☽⚹♂ 3:20 pm 12:20 pm
☽△♃ 7:33 pm 4:33 pm
☽⚺♄ 7:38 pm 4:38 pm
♃□♄ 9:16 pm

17 SATURDAY
♃□♄ 12:16 am
♂⚻♀ 4:27 am 1:27 am
♆△⚵ 4:39 am 1:39 am
☽⚻♆ 4:55 am 1:55 am
☽⚺⚵ 4:55 am 1:55 am
☽☌⚶ 1:54 pm 10:54 am
☽⚻♇ 10:12 pm 7:12 pm
☽⚻☉ 11:19 pm

18 SUNDAY
☽⚻☉ 2:19 am
☽☍♀ 10:56 am 7:56 am
☽☍⚷ 11:03 am 8:03 am
☽⚻⚳ 3:09 pm 12:09 pm
☿□♅ 8:14 pm 5:14 pm
♀☌⚷ 10:26 pm 7:26 pm
☽⚻♅ 11:51 pm 8:51 pm
☽△☿ 9:17 pm
☽□♂ 11:46 pm

19 MONDAY
☽△☿ 12:17 am
☽□♂ 2:46 am
☽△♀ 4:04 am 1:04 am
☽☌♄ 6:31 am 3:31 am
☽□♃ 7:34 am 4:34 am
☽⚹⚵ 3:21 pm 12:21 pm
☽☍♆ 4:31 pm 1:31 pm
☽⚺⚶ 9:37 pm
☿⚻♂ 9:56 pm

20 TUESDAY
☽⚺⚶ 12:37 am
☿⚻♂ 12:56 am
☽△♇ 10:25 am 7:25 am
☽△☉ 8:09 pm 5:09 pm
☽⚻⚷ 11:50 pm 8:50 pm
☽⚻♀ 9:13 pm
☿☌♀ 9:45 pm

21 WEDNESDAY
☽⚻♀ 12:13 am
☿☌♀ 12:45 am
☽△⚳ 5:47 am 2:47 am
☿△♄ 6:27 am 3:27 am
☽☍♅ 12:39 pm 9:39 am
☽△♂ 4:09 pm 1:09 pm
♄△♀ 5:36 pm 2:36 pm
☽⚺♄ 7:01 pm 4:01 pm
☽□♀ 7:05 pm 4:05 pm
☽□☿ 8:44 pm 5:44 pm
☽⚹♃ 9:17 pm 6:17 pm
☿⚺♃ 11:04 pm

22 THURSDAY
☿⚺♃ 2:04 am
☽□⚵ 3:14 am 12:14 am
☽⚻♆ 5:32 am 2:32 am
☽⚹⚶ 12:24 pm 9:24 am
☉⚺⚷ 6:06 pm 3:06 pm
☉⚺♀ 11:27 pm 8:27 pm
☽□♇ 11:30 pm 8:30 pm

23 FRIDAY
☽△⚷ 12:59 pm 9:59 am
☽△♀ 1:21 pm 10:21 am
☽□☉ 2:36 pm 11:36 am
☽□⚳ 8:34 pm 5:34 pm
☿☍⚵ 10:13 pm 7:13 pm
☽⚻♅ 10:19 pm

24 SATURDAY
☽⚻♅ 1:19 am
☽⚻♂ 5:21 am 2:21 am
☽⚹♄ 7:05 am 4:05 am
☽⚹♀ 9:36 am 6:36 am
☽⚺♃ 10:25 am 7:25 am
☽△⚵ 2:25 pm 11:25 am
☽⚹☿ 4:47 pm 1:47 pm
☽△♆ 5:39 pm 2:39 pm
☽□⚶ 11:00 pm 8:00 pm
☿⚹♆ 9:25 pm

25 SUNDAY
☿⚹♆ 12:25 am
☽⚹♇ 10:53 am 7:53 am
♀☌⚷ 1:51 pm 10:51 am
☽□♀ 11:42 pm 8:42 pm
☽□⚷ 11:49 pm 8:49 pm
♃⚺♀ 10:10 pm

26 MONDAY
♃⚺♀ 1:10 am
☽⚹☉ 6:03 am 3:03 am
☽⚹⚳ 8:29 am 5:29 am
☽△♅ 11:11 am 8:11 am
☿⚻⚶ 3:18 pm 12:18 pm
☽☍♂ 3:39 pm 12:39 pm
☽□♄ 4:12 pm 1:12 pm
☽☌♃ 8:19 pm 5:19 pm
☽⚺♀ 8:42 pm 5:42 pm
☽⚻⚵ 10:35 pm 7:35 pm
☽□♆ 11:26 pm

27 TUESDAY
☽□♆ 2:26 am
☽△⚶ 6:15 am 3:15 am
☽⚺☿ 8:23 am 5:23 am
☽⚺♇ 6:27 pm 3:27 pm
♂□♄ 7:12 pm 4:12 pm

28 WEDNESDAY
☽⚹♀ 5:42 am 2:42 am
☽⚹⚷ 6:35 am 3:35 am
☉☌⚳ 7:29 am 4:29 am
☽⚺⚳ 3:55 pm 12:55 pm
♀☍⚵ 4:09 pm 1:09 pm
☽⚺☉ 4:19 pm 1:19 pm
☽□♅ 4:56 pm 1:56 pm
☽△♄ 9:14 pm 6:14 pm
☽⚻♂ 9:44 pm 6:44 pm
☉⚹♅ 10:07 pm
☽⚺♃ 10:55 pm
☽☍⚵ 11:49 pm

29 THURSDAY
☉⚹♅ 1:07 am
☽⚺♃ 1:55 am
☽☍⚵ 2:49 am
☽☌♀ 3:16 am 12:16 am
☽⚹♆ 7:04 am 4:04 am
☽⚻⚶ 9:36 am 6:36 am
☽☌☿ 6:25 pm 3:25 pm
☽☌♇ 10:01 pm 7:01 pm

30 FRIDAY
♅⚹⚳ 6:24 am 3:24 am
☽⚺♀ 7:43 am 4:43 am
☽⚺⚷ 9:33 am 6:33 am
☽⚹♅ 7:11 pm 4:11 pm
☽☌⚳ 7:30 pm 4:30 pm
♃⚻⚵ 9:12 pm 6:12 pm
☽☌☉ 10:12 pm 7:12 pm
☽⚻♄ 10:55 pm 7:55 pm
☽△♂ 9:24 pm

31 SATURDAY
☽△♂ 12:24 am
☽⚻⚵ 4:01 am 1:01 am
☽⚹♃ 4:09 am 1:09 am
☿☌♇ 6:18 am 3:18 am
☽⚺♀ 6:19 am 3:19 am
☉⚻♄ 7:58 am 4:58 am
☽⚺♆ 8:37 am 5:37 am
☽☍⚶ 10:06 am 7:06 am
☽⚺♇ 11:02 pm 8:02 pm
☽⚺☿ 9:50 pm

Eastern time in bold type
Pacific time in medium type

DECEMBER 2005

☽ Last Aspect day	EST / hr:mn / PST		asp	☽ Ingress sign	day	EST / hr:mn / PST	
2	**10:17 am**	7:17 am	☌ ♇	♑	2	**8:42 pm**	5:42 pm
4	**1:56 pm**	10:56 am	✶ ☿	♒	4	**10:36 pm**	7:36 pm
6	**4:58 pm**	1:58 pm	□ ☿	♓	6		9:44 pm
6	**4:58 pm**	1:58 pm	□ ☿	♓	7	**12:44 am**	
8	**11:16 pm**	8:16 pm	✶ ♀	♈	9	**4:02 am**	1:02 am
11	**5:50 am**	2:50 am	□ ♀	♉	11	**8:46 am**	5:46 am
13	**1:46 pm**	10:46 am	△ ♀	♊	13	**2:59 pm**	11:59 am
15	**12:11 pm**	9:11 am	☍ ♇	♋	15	**11:01 pm**	8:01 pm
16	**7:33 pm**	4:33 pm	△ ♃	♌	18	**9:18 am**	6:18 am
20	**8:09 pm**	5:09 pm	△ ☉	♍	20	**9:39 pm**	6:39 pm
22	**11:30 pm**	8:30 pm	□ ♇	♎	23	**10:26 am**	7:26 am
25	**10:53 am**	7:53 am	✶ ♇	♏	25	**9:04 pm**	6:04 pm
26		11:26 pm	□ ♆	♐	28	**3:43 am**	12:43 am
27	**2:26 am**		□ ♆	♐	28	**3:43 am**	12:43 am
29	**10:01 pm**	7:01 pm	☌ ♇	♑	30	**6:35 am**	3:35 am
31	**4:09 am**	1:09 am	✶ ♃	♒	1/1	**7:14 am**	4:14 am

☽ Phases & Eclipses phase	day	EST / hr:mn / PST	
New Moon	1	**10:01 am**	7:01 am
2nd Quarter	8	**4:36 am**	1:36 am
Full Moon	15	**11:16 am**	8:16 am
4th Quarter	23	**2:36 pm**	11:36 am
New Moon	30	**10:12 pm**	7:12 pm

Planet Ingress		day	EST / hr:mn / PST	
⚷	♒	5	**8:10 pm**	5:10 pm
⚳	♑	11	**8:41 am**	5:41 am
☿	♐	12	**4:19 pm**	1:19 pm
♀	♒	15	**10:57 am**	7:57 am
☉	♑	21	**1:35 pm**	10:35 am

Planetary Motion		day	EST / hr:mn / PST	
☿	D	3	**9:22 pm**	6:22 pm
♂	D	9	**11:03 pm**	8:03 pm
♀	R	24	**4:36 am**	1:36 am

DATE		SID.TIME	SUN	MOON	NODE	MERCURY	VENUS	MARS	JUPITER	SATURN	URANUS	NEPTUNE	PLUTO	CERES	PALLAS	JUNO	VESTA	CHIRON
1	Th	4:39:48	08 ♐ 53 17	00 ♐ 50	12 ♈ R 10	25 ♏ R 38	22 ♑ 16	08 ♉ R 49	07 ♏ 37	11 ♌ R 14	06 ♓ 56	15 ♒ 10	23 ♐ 44	25 ♐ 44	01 ♐ 29	19 ♊ R 15	22 ♋ R 40	29 ♑ 41
2	F	4:43:45	09 54 08	14 47	12 01	25 08	22 57	08 41	07 49	11 13	06 57	15 11	23 46	26 08	01 55	19 02	22 34	29 44
3	Sa	4:47:41	10 55 00	28 59	11 51	24 51	23 37	08 35	08 01	11 12	06 58	15 12	23 49	26 32	02 21	18 49	22 28	29 48
4	Su	4:51:38	11 55 53	13 ♑ 22	11 41	24 D 44	24 16	08 30	08 13	11 11	06 59	15 13	23 51	26 56	02 47	18 35	22 22	29 52
5	M	4:55:34	12 56 47	27 50	11 32	24 48	24 53	08 25	08 25	11 10	07 00	15 15	23 53	27 21	03 13	18 21	22 15	29 56
6	T	4:59:31	13 57 42	12 ♒ 16	11 26	25 02	25 29	08 21	08 36	11 08	07 01	15 16	23 55	27 45	03 39	18 08	22 07	00 ♒ 00
7	W	5:03:27	14 58 37	26 36	11 22	25 25	26 04	08 18	08 48	11 07	07 02	15 17	23 58	28 09	04 05	17 54	21 59	00 04
8	Th	5:0724	15 59 33	10 ♓ 46	11 D 21	25 57	26 38	08 16	09 00	11 05	07 03	15 19	24 00	28 33	04 31	17 40	21 51	00 08
9	F	5:11:21	17 00 30	24 47	11 21	26 35	27 10	08 15	09 11	11 03	07 04	15 20	24 02	28 58	04 57	17 26	21 42	00 12
10	Sa	5:15:17	18 01 27	08 ♈ 36	11 R 21	27 20	27 40	08 D 14	09 23	11 01	07 05	15 21	24 04	29 22	05 23	17 12	21 33	00 16
11	Su	5:19:14	19 02 25	22 15	11 21	28 11	28 09	08 14	09 35	10 59	07 07	15 23	24 06	29 46	05 49	16 58	21 24	00 20
12	M	5:23:10	20 03 24	05 ♉ 44	11 18	29 07	28 36	08 15	09 46	10 57	07 08	15 24	24 09	00 ♑ 10	06 15	16 44	21 14	00 24
13	T	5:27:07	21 04 23	19 03	11 13	00 ♐ 07	29 01	08 17	09 57	10 55	07 09	15 26	24 11	00 35	06 41	16 31	21 03	00 29
14	W	5:31:03	22 05 23	02 ♊ 11	11 05	01 11	29 25	08 20	10 09	10 53	07 11	15 27	24 13	00 59	07 07	16 17	20 53	00 33
15	Th	5:35:00	23 06 24	15 08	10 54	02 18	29 47	08 23	10 20	10 50	07 12	15 29	24 15	01 23	07 33	16 04	20 42	00 37
16	F	5:38:56	24 07 25	27 53	10 41	03 29	00 ♒ 06	08 27	10 31	10 48	07 13	15 30	24 18	01 48	07 58	15 51	20 30	00 41
17	Sa	5:42:53	25 08 27	10 ♋ 25	10 27	04 42	00 24	08 32	10 42	10 45	07 15	15 32	24 20	02 12	08 24	15 38	20 18	00 46
18	Su	5:46:50	26 09 30	22 45	10 14	05 57	00 40	08 38	10 53	10 42	07 17	15 34	24 22	02 36	08 50	15 25	20 06	00 50
19	M	5:50:46	27 10 33	04 ♌ 53	10 02	07 14	00 54	08 44	11 04	10 40	07 18	15 35	24 24	03 01	09 16	15 13	19 54	00 55
20	T	5:54:43	28 11 37	16 51	09 53	08 33	01 05	08 51	11 15	10 37	07 20	15 37	24 27	03 25	09 41	15 00	19 41	00 59
21	W	5:58:39	29 12 42	28 42	09 47	09 54	01 14	08 59	11 26	10 34	07 22	15 39	24 29	03 49	10 07	14 48	19 28	01 04
22	Th	6:02:36	00 ♑ 13 48	10 ♍ 30	09 43	11 15	01 21	09 07	11 36	10 31	07 23	15 40	24 31	04 14	10 32	14 37	19 14	01 08
23	F	6:06:32	01 14 54	22 20	09 D 41	12 38	01 26	09 16	11 47	10 28	07 25	15 42	24 33	04 38	10 58	14 26	19 01	01 13
24	Sa	6:10:29	02 16 01	04 ♎ 17	09 R 41	14 02	01 R 28	09 26	11 57	10 24	07 27	15 44	24 36	05 02	11 23	14 15	18 47	01 17
25	Su	6:14:25	03 17 08	16 27	09 41	15 27	01 28	09 36	12 08	10 21	07 29	15 46	24 38	05 27	11 49	14 04	18 32	01 22
26	M	6:18:22	04 18 17	28 55	09 40	16 52	01 25	09 47	12 18	10 18	07 31	15 47	24 40	05 51	12 14	13 54	18 18	01 27
27	T	6:22:19	05 19 26	11 ♏ 46	09 37	18 19	01 20	09 58	12 28	10 14	07 33	15 49	24 42	06 15	12 40	13 44	18 03	01 31
28	W	6:26:15	06 20 35	25 03	09 31	19 46	01 12	10 10	12 39	10 10	07 35	15 51	24 45	06 40	13 05	13 35	17 48	01 36
29	Th	6:30:12	07 21 45	08 ♐ 49	09 22	21 13	01 02	10 23	12 49	10 07	07 37	15 53	24 47	07 04	13 30	13 26	17 33	01 41
30	F	6:34:08	08 22 55	23 00	09 11	22 42	00 49	10 36	12 59	10 03	07 39	15 55	24 49	07 28	13 55	13 18	17 18	01 46
31	Sa	6:38:05	09 24 06	07 ♑ 35	08 59	24 10	00 34	10 50	13 08	09 59	07 41	15 57	24 51	07 53	14 21	13 10	17 02	01 50

EPHEMERIS CALCULATED FOR 12 MIDNIGHT GREENWICH MEAN TIME. ALL OTHER DATA AND FACING ASPECTARIAN PAGE IN **EASTERN TIME (BOLD)** AND PACIFIC TIME (REGULAR).

Notes

Notes

Notes